African Traditional
Religion in South Africa

Recent Titles in
Bibliographies and Indexes in Religious Studies

African Traditional Religion in South Africa

An Annotated Bibliography

David Chidester,
Chirevo Kwenda, Robert Petty,
Judy Tobler, and Darrel Wratten

Bibliographies and Indexes in Religious Studies, Number 42

Greenwood Press
Westport, Connecticut • London

Library of Congress Cataloging-in-Publication Data

African traditional religion in South Africa : an annotated
  bibliography / David Chidester . . . [et al.].
     p.   cm.—(Bibliographies and indexes in religious studies,
  ISSN 0742–6836 ; no. 42)
   Includes bibliographical references and index.
   ISBN 0–313–30474–2 (alk. paper)
   1. South Africa—Religion—Bibliography. 2. Blacks—South Africa—
Religion—Bibliography. I. Chidester, David. II. Series.
Z7834.S6A47   1997
[BL2470.S6]
016.299′698—dc21   97–6414

British Library Cataloguing in Publication Data is available.

Library of Congress Catalog Card Number: 97–6414
ISBN: 0–313–30474–2
ISSN: 0742–6836

First published in 1997

Greenwood Press, 88 Post Road West, Westport, CT 06881
An imprint of Greenwood Publishing Group, Inc.

Printed in the United States of America

The paper used in this book complies with the
Permanent Paper Standard issued by the National
Information Standards Organization (Z39.48–1984).

10 9 8 7 6 5 4 3 2 1

Contents

Preface

The singing filled the air. The drumming kept the rhythm. In a loud and clear voice, the ritual elder invoked the ancestors. The people—men in long robes, women with painted faces—indicated their assent by exclaiming, "Camagu," to the beat of the drum. "Camagu," they agreed. "We are present. Let the ancestors be present."

We could have been at a rural homestead. We could have been in an urban township. Instead, we were at the University of Cape Town for a conference on African traditional religion. On 19 August 1995, academics, community leaders, and practitioners of traditional religion gathered for a one-day conference sponsored by the Institute for Comparative Religion in Southern Africa (ICRSA). At the very least, this event confirmed the continuing vitality of traditional religion in a changing South African society.

This book, a product of an ICRSA research project, is a guide to literature on African traditional religion in South Africa. It collects and describes books, articles, and theses that have addressed the indigenous religious heritage of the region. It organizes and annotates selected texts—the general overviews and detailed case studies; the accounts of religious beliefs, practices, and experiences; the analyses of historical tradition and social change—that have been produced in this field of study. We are convinced that a review of these resources can support and stimulate further inquiry into African traditional religion.

Above all, we hope that this book will be useful. Of course, readers find their own ways to use books. However, since this book does not tell a single story, some "instructions for use" might be helpful. Accordingly, we offer three suggestions that might appeal to readers who are interested in exploring the field of African traditional religion in South Africa that is profiled here.

First, introductory essays to each chapter provide brief outlines of topics that have been investigated and that bear further investigation. After reviewing general overviews of African traditional religion in South Africa, the chapters proceed through literature on Khoisan, Xhosa, Zulu, Sotho-Tswana, Swazi, Tsonga, and Venda religion. We have adopted these linguistic designations without presuming that they represent uniform or separate ethnic identities. As the introductory essays suggest, considerable common ground can be found across these language groups when we consider the indigenous religious heritage of South Africa.

Second, the index provides a map for tracking specific topics. Arranged alphabetically by subject, the index refers readers to entries on such topics as ancestors, beer, divination, sacrifice, and witch detection. This approach to reading might be of greatest interest to students and researchers who want to focus on some particular aspect of African traditional religion. As a guide to relevant literature, the index can be a useful tool for assembling a database for research.

Third, since the entire book might be read as a library of works on African traditional religion in South Africa, we invite readers to take a random walk through the collection. We could invoke a "postmodern" justification for this approach. The library we have assembled refuses the imposition of any "master narrative." It is fragmentary and episodic. Like any library, it allows readers to wander through the stacks and pull any item off the shelves. In the process of writing this book, we have found that taking random walks through the collection has become our favorite method of reading. Every time we wander through these texts, we learn something new. We find that new patterns emerge, but we also find that new questions arise that inspire further reading.

As the first of a series of volumes on South African religions, this collection on African traditional religion has been organized according to two simple principles of selection: The literature that is annotated must deal with South Africa and it must deal with religion. Although these principles appear straightforward, they do involve some complications that require brief mention.

Although South Africa is a geographical region, it is also a political construction, a nation among nations. Arguably, South Africa did not exist, at least not with any international legitimacy, until the first democratic elections were held in April 1994. In the post-apartheid era, an emergent South African nationalism will require revisiting the historical geography of the region. New perspectives on history and territory will be discovered. While we cannot undertake that task of rediscovery here, we have allowed considerable geographical latitude in determining what counts as being inside South Africa. Some boundaries have been blurred, but a general sense of place and region has been maintained. As a result, the literature reviewed can be regarded as representative of African traditional religion in South Africa.

The question of what counts as religion also raises special problems. In general terms, religion might be defined as a dimension of human belief, practice, and experience that engages the superhuman or the sacred. A vast body of literature on defining religion might be invoked to support this general definition. However, we have decided to allow wider latitude for what counts as relevant to religion by including samples of some literature—on precapitalist social formations, for example—that are crucial for understanding the character of precolonial African religion. Although much more could have been included, we have tried to indicate some of the ways in which religion is necessarily related to historical and social contexts.

In determining what to include in a collection of literature on African traditional religion, we have had to make a decision about the place of theology. Although significant theological innovations have appeared in South Africa, often in conversation with the resources of indigenous religious heritage, we have opted not to review very many explicitly theological works in this volume on African traditional religion. Christian theology has had a troubled history with indigenous religion. Theologians have often denied its legitimacy as a religion; and they have frequently regarded its persistence, especially in the continuing vitality of religious relations with ancestors, as a Christian pastoral problem. More recently, Christian reevaluations of African traditional resources have appeared in African theology, Black theology, and the work of independent churches. Although they engage African resources, these theological initiatives obviously reflect specifically Christian concerns. Bibliographies that provide access to this theological literature are available elsewhere. In this volume, however, we have concentrated on works that have undertaken the description and analysis of African traditional religion as a religion in its own right. Rather than theological discourse, we are interested in literature that raises questions of theory and method for the study of the indigenous religious heritage of South Africa.

Just as we do not adopt a theological position on African traditional religion, we also do not endorse all of the literature contained in this annotated bibliography. Much of it is dated; much of it is based on colonialist, racialist, or covertly theological prejudices that have no place in the academic study of religion. However, even the outdated and the outrageous are instructive, if not about African traditional religion, then about the kinds of academic representations that have obstructed recognition and understanding of the indigenous religious heritage of South Africa.

For readers interested in a history of colonial representations (or misrepresentations) of African religion we offer David Chidester, *Savage Systems: Colonialism and Comparative Religion in Southern Africa* (Charlottesville: University Press of Virginia, 1996). Since detailed accounts of the reports on African religion by travelers, missionaries, and colonial agents are provided in that volume, we have annotated only a small selection here. Nevertheless, colonial assumptions persist in much of the literature we have collected and annotated. In the interests of gaining a broader and deeper understanding, we must critically confront a long legacy of misunderstanding. In the end, this annotated bibliography can be read as a history of both the misunderstanding and the understanding of African traditional religion in South Africa.

Over five years in the making, this book has truly been a cooperative venture undertaken by the ICRSA Comparative Religion Project research team. Although the authors have assumed primary responsibility for research and writing, they have been supported by a host of talented researchers that has included Graeme Cowley, Ayesha Dollie, Gad Kaplan, Anne-Marie Leatt, Chris Lund, Henry Mann, Sibusiso Masondo, Michael Mbokazi, Clinton Minnaar, Sa'diyya Shaikh, and Elise Theunissen. All have learned something about the joys of writing an abstract. We thank them all. In another wing of ICRSA, the authors have been in close conversation with the practical, applied research of the Religion Education Project, which has been developing and testing new ways to teach and learn about religious diversity in the public schools. That project team—Jean Goldblatt, Nokuzola Mndende, A. Rashied Omar, Isabel Apawo Phiri, and Janet Stonier—has assisted this book by keeping us in touch with the realities of teaching and learning about African traditional religion in South Africa.

Although the creation of this book has been a collective effort, primary responsibility for the various sections was assumed by different authors. Chirevo Kwenda wrote the introduction on African Traditional Religion that appears in Chapter One. David Chidester wrote the narratives that introduce each subsequent chapter. Robert Petty assumed primary responsibility for Chapter Three; Judy Tobler for Chapters Two, Four, Five, and Seven; and Darrel Wratten for Chapters Six, Eight, and Nine, as well as for the editorial task of pulling the entire project together and bringing it to completion.

This book would not exist without the moral support or financial sponsorship of the Board of Directors, the Centre for Science Development, and the University Research Committee of the University of Cape Town. We have greatly appreciated the tangible signs of their trust. However, we must also observe that the opinions expressed and conclusions arrived at in this book are those of the authors and are not necessarily to be attributed to any of these agencies. We absolve anyone and everyone from sharing the burden of our opinions or conclusions. But we are thankful for the financial support that has made it possible to arrive at them.

African Traditional
Religion in South Africa

1   African Traditional Religion

One thing that will strike the reader of this guide, or of any such reference work on Africa, is the enormous volume of the material. While this may be a reflection of the vastness and diversity—geographic, cultural, linguistic, and historical—of the continent, it also relates to the prolific efforts of researchers. However, one must question whether this scholarly productivity occurs in spite of the place of traditional religion as a "residual category" in the taxonomy of religious studies or because of it (see Shaw, 1990: 339-53). Either way, the volume of material cannot escape even a casual observer's notice.

What might not so readily appear to the reader is the fact that the material constitutes part of an academic representation or what Mudimbe refers to as an academic "invention of Africa" (1988). In these terms, the material confronts the reader as evidence, not only in the academic sense of that which confirms, but in the forensic sense of litigation. The material is at once illuminating information and damaging interpretation. The possibility of this dual perspective is reflected in Todorov's observation that "Columbus discovered America but not the Americans" (1987: 49). In our case, we should like to know if these representations by which Africa was invented help or hinder a meaningful encounter with the Africans, an encounter in which all are subjects and accept one another as such. This is an important question for the study of African religion as part of the humanities and social sciences. Unfortunately, the preponderance of testimony hands down a negative verdict. Hence the plethora of refutations and remonstrations by African and other apologists who, motivated variously by nationalist or theological interests, set about setting the record straight and giving Africa and Africans a more acceptable image. As Okot p'Bitek stresses, the smelling out of error in Western scholarship and exorcising it is a primary task of the African intellectual, especially the scholar of religious studies (1970: 7).

However, articulate Africans, the elite, did not escape the indignity of paying homage to the shrine-keepers of Western discourse. Even as they articulated their protest they continued to be beholden not only to how Westerners think, in the sense of what makes them tick, but to what Westerners think, in terms of what is normative (Towa, 1971). Their response to the short shrift Africa received in Western discourse was predicated on a wish to prove something to the West, namely, that Africa was at least as good as Europe. Rosalind Shaw suggests that this is how an "authorized version" of African traditional religion came into being: African intellectuals wishing to correct the Western Christian representations of African culture and religion ended up reinforcing that interloping tradition (1990: 339-53). Apart from the obvious frustrations it engenders in critical Africans, this *cul de sac* reminds one of the power of these representations. Yet invention, be it of tradition, identity, or image, far from being in and of itself a negative thing, is the process by which people negotiate their way through history. The negative element only rears its head when invention degenerates into a servile act put on for the benefit of foreign opinion.

In the light of this servitude to the West, any definition of African traditional religion of necessity has to have a negative dimension. African traditional religion (of the academic type) is what African elites concoct when, suffering from an acute sense of insecurity induced by Western images of Africa, they invent something they hope will receive the nod of approval from the West. On the other hand, the popular version of African traditional religion is what Africans (including some elites, though mostly the masses) do with no regard for what Westerners, or anyone else, may or may not think about it. It is what Africans do when they are just being Africans. Now this does not mean that such a practice is completely untouched by alien influences, be they religious (such as Christianity or Islam) or secular (such as modernity); what it means is that in full cognizance of their historical context Africans do what they do for their own reasons rather than to impress someone else. In other words, while talking to the West is unavoidable—for the elite—and talking back to the West may be progressive, it is only through turning away from and not talking to the West that the possibility of considering African traditional religion in its own right translates into a reality. Consider the example of Kenyatta's *Facing Mount Kenya*. Note that this "facing" is a metaphor for orientation in space and time as well as for motivation. To face Mount Kenya means to think and do African without any concern for non-African opinion. The first significance of this act of indifference lies in facing towards an African center. Implied in the act is a facing away from other centers of meaning and power. Now this is not to suggest that these other centers are denied either existence or power within their sphere of influence; it is to stress, however, that Africans recognize a space and a moment in which every other center can only register as subordinate to an African center. It is in this space that the core of African identity inheres. There should be no confusion, however, between practice and discourse. What is lack of awareness (of the West) or sheer indifference at the level of practice must necessarily become not emulation of the West but defiance at the level of formal discourse. This is not to fail to appreciate the scientific and technological advances of the West but to renounce the West's attitude to the works of its hands (and heads) and on account of this its relation to the rest of the world. This is why there is something intriguing about the choice of Kenyatta to illustrate the correct posture for the African intellectual. For while in the preface to *Facing Mount Kenya* he entertains the romantic hope that the Gikuyu might, in spite of the colonial onslaught, continue to practice their traditional religion in undisturbed peace, facing Mount Kenya, he goes on in the rest of the monograph to face strange mountains (the Alps, presumably), as he falls prey to the urge to prove Africa's worth to the West. Thus, Kenyatta is very much a child of his times, a curious coin displaying on one side what it means to be moored around an unmistakably African center and, on the other, the difficulty, especially for elites, of resisting the enticements of Western approval. For this reason he is a perfect representative of the problem that lies at the heart of the study of African traditional religion today, namely, the problem of the Africanness of the religion.

The distinction between elites and masses is quite important. For the problem of being beholden to the West is an elitist problem. The masses could not care less what Europeans or Americans think about their religious practice or expression. Frederick B. Welbourn has an interesting view on this issue. While his account is clearly colored by his obviously Christian agenda, the point he makes is illuminating for our purpose:

> There comes all over East Africa a resurgence of tribalism and recourse once more to the diviners, with all the fear that it implies of ghosts and witches. Just when political independence is gained by the elite there comes a refusal on the part of the masses to accept the responsibilities of independence; a withdrawal to the imagined security of tribal life, an insistence once more on man's dependence on the irrational forces of nature. (Welbourn, 1963: xx-xxi)

A number of points call for special attention in this passage. First, why do these East Africans formulate a religious response to a political move? The theory that African cultures along with other non-European cultures are "religion-oriented" is certainly to be rejected (Jarvie, 1964; see Kwenda, 1993: 151-52). Africans do in many other instances respond politically to political situations. It may very well be that what Welbourn sees as a refusal to accept the responsibilities of independence, or "the responsibilities of living in a technological age" and the embracing of irrational forces of nature, is actually a turning away from a Western-style independence and Westernism generally. It is to face towards a distinctly African center, the clearest expression of which takes religious form. The reason it takes religious form may be that the character of that to which response is being made—a technocratic frame of mind and not technology *per se*—is perceived and experienced as religious (Hodgson, 1974).

Second, there is a clear disjunction between the African elite and the masses, and the dividing line is drawn at the parting of ways between African traditional religion and the religions of the Westernized elite. What is at stake here is the (often unconscious) elevation of "talking to the West" to the status of a methodological assumption in academic discourse generally and in the study of African traditional religion in particular. A distinction between a popular, practiced version of African traditional religion and an intellectual, theoretical invention seems the right place to start the search for an African center at which the West is something that is experienced only and not something that is thought. One of the ways in which the West is experienced without being thought is in terms of social change resulting from Western presence and Western ways. As an analytic category, change has been accorded an elevation approximating tyranny in the study of Africa generally and African traditional religion in particular. It therefore deserves special attention.

There is no doubt that in colonial and neo-colonial Africa, as elsewhere, a multiplicity of complex changes is taking place with breath-taking rapidity. It would be *naïveté* verging on criminal omission not to take this fact seriously in academic studies of African life. But this is not what is at issue here. What is of concern to us here is the illegitimate elevation of change to a determinant in the creation of the object of study. One often sees in studies of African traditional religion a peremptory mumbling about the religion as the writer rushes on to what is obviously regarded as the real substance, that is, change. In many cases the conclusion cannot be avoided that the study is really about change and that African traditional religion, or some other aspect of African life, is being used only as fodder for the researcher's canon. While there is nothing to suggest that this is an illegitimate procedure, such use of data cannot be a substitute for analysis of the tradition itself. In any case, where African traditional religion is concerned, the analysis of change becomes especially problematic when, as Jean and John Comaroff have pointed out, the process is viewed in terms of the ideologically charged category of conversion (Comaroff and Comaroff, 1991). Very often such analyses have ended up being little more than presentations about a "force" of change, usually a missionary faith. In this regard Ninian Smart's view that something changes in order to stay the same demands more than casual attention as it helps observers to avoid imposing arbitrary hierarchies on encounters between and among cultures or religious traditions (see Alexander, 1994: 17-35).

Heeding this counsel also ensures that there is no prejudging the purpose for which symbols are appropriated from other cultures or religious traditions, keeping in mind the Africans' search for an empowered and empowering identity in a world that denied space to be human as African. More sophisticated and complex theories and analytic categories than the unproblematized "conversion model" are necessary, for instance, to illuminate a situation where the symbols of one religion are appropriated for the sole purpose of resisting or opposing that very religion (Hackett, 1991). It is close to reckless to hastily see conversion as the inevitable outcome of encounters between religious or cultural traditions. Even Robin Horton, who saw African traditional thought as "closed," conceded that in many cases traditional Africans were so "accommodative" that in the encounter with scientific thought they retained their "thought pattern," rather than abandoning it, and still found ways of accommodating the new scientific knowledge (Horton, 1967; see Masolo, 1994). Thus conversion is often a well-meaning but misguided oversimplification of an extremely complex process of give-and-take, the outcome of which is no less ambiguous.

There are other insufficiently examined assumptions in relation to religious change. According to Ninian Smart, upon encountering a universal religion a non-universal religion must universalize or perish (Alexander, 1994: 17-35). Quite obviously, countless examples can be adduced to this effect. But it is the exceptions, however few and far between, that need to be specially accounted for. And Africa seems to specialize in providing awkward cases for this purpose. Take, for instance, the quotation from Welbourn cited above. There the movement for survival is not in the direction of the macrocosm but towards the smaller deities and spirits (Horton, 1971; see Fisher, 1973). To describe this movement merely as "irrational" does not tell us much, if anything at all. The least we can do is to problematize the category of universalism (thus deconstructing one of the Western norms of "good" religion) instead of tacitly, possibly subconsciously, celebrating its imagined normativity.

In a detailed study of conversion in Matabeleland, western Zimbabwe, Ngwabi Bhebe (1979) contests Horton's theory of religious change whereby people abandon their lesser spirits in favor of a high god as their microcosm gives way to a wider world (macrocosm). He finds continued preoccupation with details of the microcosm in the midst of intense interaction with a universal tradition and other elements of a macrocosm. Caution must be urged with regard to universalism as an analytic category, seeing how it is implicated in the Christian commitment to the search for a high god in African traditional religion (Kiernan, 1995).

The issue of the high god in Africa demonstrates the need to send much of the data contained in this volume to the cleaners before it is usable. If African traditional religion is considered as a tradition in its own right, there should be no problem in agreeing with Edwin W. Smith (1950) that African traditional religion has the idea of a supreme being. The problem arises when the word God, loaded as it is with cultural, ideological, and theological content, is introduced. The sad thing is that much of whatever these African deities might have meant in their ever-changing contexts was obscured in the abusive treatment they received in European theoretical debates. Returning to the question of universalism, it is evident that even its definition, whether in terms of trans-ethnic identity or a catch-all cosmology, is highly problematic. But above all, the requirement to "universalize or perish" sounds too much like the many ultimatums to which Africa has grown accustomed. They come in the idiom of modernization or in the rhetoric of development. The message is the same: Salvation lies in one or another form of universalization, which is shorthand for accepting subordination to the West. Only one among many garments that must be accompanied to the cleaners with special stain-removing instructions, this category must either be discarded or used with extreme caution in the study of African traditional religion.

As this work of sanitizing the received information and interpretations of African traditional religion proceeds, we note that the kinds of questions we ask in formulating research proposals and priorities, and the assumptions these reveal, are crucially important to the health of our subject. Many studies of African traditional religion set out to assess the impact of some agent or force of change on the traditional religion. While this academic practice looks quite innocent and proper, it hides certain assumptions that are not quite so neutral. Implied in this approach is a history of the conquest of African people, culture, and religion as passive objects upon which more proactive forces such as Christianity and modernity exert unrelenting pressure. Yet we know that despite their status as vanquished people, Africans have never accepted the passive role of pawns in the drama of history (Hexham, 1990). Instead, they have been extremely active in creative and imaginative ways in the ongoing process of the reconstruction of self and world (McAllister, 1980; Van Beek and Blakely, 1994). A more fruitful approach is one that methodologically acknowledges this vitality of African life, even in its decimated form, and accords it space as an actor on the stage of history by asking how African traditional religion dealt with the challenges and threats it encountered in the form of other religious traditions or secular ideologies and practices. In short, it makes a world of difference to ask not what was done to Africa but what Africa did. Similarly, it is one thing to treat African traditional religion as alive and well and quite another to treat it as if it were already dead or dying, and as if this death was "both necessary and inevitable" (Hackett, 1990: 135-48). In other words, the scholarship of those who hold a death-wish for African traditional religion will certainly be tainted, to say the least.

Related to the debate about supreme beings in Africa is the perennial debate as to the justification of positing a unified African traditional religion or separate and independent religions, which may or may not share a family resemblance. It will be noted that we have taken the former option, especially as we are very reliably informed by the southern African context. As the introductions to each chapter of this volume maintain, the similarities among the religious traditions of the various ethnic or language groups in South Africa outweigh the differences sufficiently to allow us to posit a traditional religion of South Africa.

Lastly, there is the politics of space. So contested has the discussion of religious traditions become in the world at large, and in Africa specifically, that the positioning of a chapter or section in a book has come to be governed by a politics of signification. Locating African traditional religion is an especially tricky business, given the long history of conflicted debates on one or another issue. Situating African traditional religion at the beginning of a book or series may draw charges of regarding it as an antiquarian piece, a dinosaur. On the other hand, placing it at the end might portray African traditional religion as an afterthought, a misfit that had to be tacked on to the real matter of the "world religions." Against this background, it seemed proper to us to open this multi-volume bibliography on South African religions with African traditional religion. After all, in Africa, age is not a negative quality, and to be given priority of place is not to be denigrated but to receive deference; it is to be acknowledged as custodian of the most advanced and most esoteric knowledge of the group (Baum, 1990).

Although African traditional religion has neither sacred text nor authoritative canon, its study is framed by a body of written material such as that which is presented in this volume. As part of the new cosmogony by which a new Africa is created, these materials are implicated in the African search for identity and well-being in a world in which religion is used to measure and distribute humanity. As such, it cannot afford the luxury of pretensions to methodological neutrality. Laundering scholarly linen, like soiling it, is not a neutral task. Commitments must be declared; apparently innocent analytic categories such as social change, universal tradition, impact, conversion, and many others must be subjected to critical examination. History has shown that while treating African traditional religion as a religion in its own right seems the normal thing to do, the reality on the ground is totally different. The scholar, and especially the teacher of African traditional religion, must register commitment to liberate the tradition from all kinds of bondage. This is all the more necessary in South Africa, where in the past religious hegemony has sought to dominate the political system, along with law, education, and the whole public arena, and where the present has not gone anywhere beyond good intentions.

References

Alexander, Kay (1994). "A View from California." In Peter Masefield and Donald Wiebe (eds.) *Aspects of Religion: Essays in Honour of Ninian Smart.* New York: Peter Lang Publishing. 17-35.

Baum, Robert M. (1990). "Graven Images: Scholarly Representations of African Religions." *Religion*, vol. 20: 355-60.

Bhebe, Ngwabi (1979). *Christianity and Traditional Religion in Western Zimbabwe 1859-1923*. London: Longman.

p'Bitek, Okot (1970). *African Religions in Western Scholarship*. Nairobi: East African Literature Bureau.

Comaroff, Jean, and John Comaroff (1991). *Of Revelation and Revolution: Christianity, Colonialism and Consciousness in South Africa*. Vol. 1. Chicago: University of Chicago Press.

Fisher, H. J. (1973). "Conversion Reconsidered: Some Historical Aspects of Religious Conversion in Black Africa." *Africa*, vol. 43, no. 1: 27-39.

Hackett, I. J. (1991). "Revitalization in African Traditional Religion." In Jacob K. Olupona (ed.) *African Traditional Religion in Contemporary Society*. New York: Paragon House. 135-48.

Hodgson, Marshall G. S. (1974). *The Venture of Islam: Conscience and History in a World Civilization*. Vol. 1. Chicago: University of Chicago Press.

Horton, Robin (1967). "African Traditional Religion and Western Science." *Africa*, vol. 37, no. 1: 50-71; no. 2: 155-87.

Horton, Robin (1971). "African Conversion." *Africa*, vol. 41, no. 2: 85-108.

Jarvie, Ian (1967). *The Revolution in Anthropology*. Orig. edn. 1964. London: Routledge & Kegan Paul.

Kenyatta, Jomo (1953). *Facing Mount Kenya: The Tribal Life of the Gikuyu*. Orig. edn. 1938. London: Secker & Warburg.

Kiernan, Jim (1995). "African Traditional Religions in South Africa." In Martin Prozesky and John de Gruchy (eds.) *Living Faiths in South Africa*. Cape Town and Johannesburg: David Philip. 15-27.

Kwenda, Chirevo V. (1993). *True Colors: A Critical Assessment of Victor Turner's Study of Ndembu Religion*. Ph. D. thesis, Syracuse University.

Kwenda, Chirevo V. (forthcoming). "African Traditional Religion and Human Rights." In Charles Villa-Vicencio and Ebrahim Moosa (eds.) *Religion and Human Rights*. Cape Town: David Philip.

Masolo, D. A. (1994). *African Philosophy in Search of Identity*. Bloomington and Indianapolis: Indiana University Press.

McAllister, P. A. (1979). *The Rituals of Labour Migration Among the Gcaleka.* M. A. thesis, Rhodes University.

McAllister, P. A. (1980). "Work, Homestead, and the Shades: The Ritual Interpretation of Labour Migration Among the Gcaleka." In Philip Mayer (ed.) *Black Villagers in an Industrial Society.* Cape Town: Oxford University Press. 205-46.

Mudimbe, V. Y. (1988). *The Invention of Africa: Gnosis, Philosophy and the Order of Knowledge.* Bloomington: Indiana University Press.

Shaw, Rosalind (1990). "The Invention of African Traditional Religion." *Religion*, vol. 20: 339-53.

Smith, Edwin W. (1950). *African Ideas of God.* London: Edinburgh House Press.

Todorov, Tzvetan (1987). *The Conquest of America: The Question of the Other.* Trans. Richard Howard. New York: Harper Torchbooks.

Towa, Marcien (1971). *Essai sur la problematique philosophique dans l'Afrique actuelle.* Yaoande: Editions CLE.

Van Beek, Walter E. A., and Thomas D. Blakely (1994). "Introduction." In Thomas D. Blakely, Walter E. A. van Beek, and Dennis L. Thomson (eds.) *Religion in Africa: Experience and Expression.* London: James Currey.

Welbourn, F. B. (1963). "The Importance of Ghosts." In Victor E. W. Hayward (ed.) *African Independent Church Movements.* London: Edinburgh House Press for the World Council of Churches, Commission on World Mission and Evangelism. 15-26.

2   General Overviews

In the midst of the South African War (1899-1902), the Royal Anthropological Institute and the Folklore Society in London submitted a formal appeal to the British Secretary of State for the Colonies calling for the establishment of a commission to study "native laws and customs" in South Africa. In part, this request was motivated by the political interests of imperial governance in the region. Political relations between Africans and Europeans would be improved in South Africa, they argued, if Europeans gained greater knowledge of "native customs and superstitions." Accordingly, the study of African traditional religion would form an important part of the work of this imperial commission (see Anthropological Institute and Folklore Society, 1903).

Although this commission was never established, the earliest researches on African religion displayed similar concerns with serving imperial or colonial interests in trying to understand people who were under European domination. The existence of indigenous religions in South Africa was long denied. Once discovered, however, African religions tended to be represented in terms that were suited to the interests of political containment and administrative control. In particular, two ways of representing African religion—the construction of an inventory and the abstraction of a mentality—became standard.

In the inventory, basic elements of African religion could be identified and organized into a system. As demonstrated by MacDonald (1889) and Theal (1910), for example, the inventory provided a convenient way to summarize, but also to contain, the resources of African religion. Revolving around "ancestor worship," the indigenous religion of South Africa could be represented as a distinctive type of religious system among the religions of the world. Throughout the twentieth century, the inventory of basic elements—belief in a supreme being, reverence for ancestors, rites of passage, and practices of divination, healing, rainmaking, and detection of witchcraft—remained the dominant style of representation in general overviews of African traditional religion. Such inventories can be found in the influential anthropological overviews provided by Eiselen and Schapera (1937) and by Hammond-Tooke (1974). But a similar way of representing African religion also appeared in early African accounts written in English such as those by Thoka (1927) and Molema (1963).

A second standard approach to representing African traditional religion appeared in the abstraction of an African "mentality." In this approach, traditional religious life did not merely constitute a distinctive system; it supposedly constituted a distinctive way of thinking. That "mentality" was characterized by absences—as non-rational and non-scientific—and it was stereotyped as a kind of thinking that was entirely absorbed in ignorance, fear, fraud, superstition, and magic. In the general overviews provided by Kidd (1904), Smith (1929), and H. P. Junod (1938), for example, the whole point of studying African traditional religion was to distill the "mentality" that allegedly animated it. Like the inventory, the representation of a mentality provided a convenient way to contain and control African traditional religion. This concern with studying African religion in order to identify a "mentality" intersected with the interests of government and capital. Praising H. P. Junod's research on the "Bantu mind" in 1938, for example, mining-industry spokesman William Gemmill recommended the volume because it explained "the races whose work makes European life in South Africa, as we know it, possible." Even in the 1980s, scholarship on African religion could continue to abstract a "mentality" to be used or converted by business or government.

Certain elements of the inventory have received special attention in general overviews of African religion. In particular, the question of God has preoccupied researchers. At the beginning of the nineteenth century the Protestant missionary J. T. van der Kemp found that Africans held no belief in God and practiced no worship of God. During the course of the century, however, Theophilus Hahn found the "unknown God" among the Khoikhoi, J. W. Colenso among the Zulu, Henry Callaway among the Xhosa, and D. F. Ellenberger among the Sotho-Tswana. By the beginning of the twentieth century, therefore, European commentators found that belief in a supreme being was a common feature of African religion throughout the region. However, some investigators might continue to wonder, like Callaway (1878), whether African beliefs in a supreme being contain "the echo of missionary teaching." Wrestling with theoretical problems in Europe, scholars in London might agree with E. Sidney Hartland (1901) that African supreme beings marked the beginning of a process of religious evolution, or they might agree with Andrew Lang (1901) that they were evidence of a long process of degeneration from an original monotheism. However, with few exceptions, such as Eiselen (1924), scholars during the twentieth century have agreed with Edwin W. Smith (1950) that the "idea of God" is an important aspect of indigenous religion in South Africa. As Gabriel Setiloane has argued more recently, the African "idea of God," which is invoked under many names—Thixo, Qamatha, uNkulunkulu, uMvelinqangi, Modimo, Raluvhimba—represents a conception of divinity more ancient and powerful than the God of the nineteenth-century Christian missions in South Africa.

While defining the nature of God in African religion has obviously concerned Christian missionaries and theologians, the role of ancestors has also been problematic. During the nineteenth-century, European commentators began to label the indigenous religion in South Africa as "ancestor worship" to distinguish it as a species of religion that was different than either the "God worship" of Christianity, Judaism, and Islam or the so-called "idol worship" of Asia. Under the designation, "ancestor worship," therefore, African religion was first recognized by Europeans as a religious tradition.

The question of whether or not "worship" is an appropriate term for the respect, veneration, and ritual attention shown to ancestors in African traditional religion has been vexed by two concerns—to avoid the imposition of a Christian category and to protect African traditional religion from the implication of being an "idolatrous" worship of the dead. As Hammond-Tooke (1978) has argued, however, "worship" might in fact be a useful cross-cultural term in the study of religion that could be properly defined and carefully applied to ancestral ritual. Nevertheless, most commentators have chosen to avoid the term. As a feature of African religion, ritual attention to ancestors has persisted under the impact of Christian conversion (see Kuckertz, 1981) and social change (see Pauw, 1974). However defined, religious relations with ancestors remain a significant resource within the indigenous religious heritage of South Africa.

Instead of constructing an inventory or abstracting a mentality, we might better represent African traditional religion as power relations that operate in three spheres—the homestead, the polity, and the disciplines of sacred specialists (see Chidester, 1992). Although more detail will be provided in the specific case studies that are annotated in subsequent chapters, the general overviews collected here can provide some hints of the religious power that is mobilized within these three social spheres.

First, the homestead is built up by means of ritual relations that are established among persons. Those relations are established among the living, but also among the living and ancestors. In this respect, ancestral ritual is anchored in the home. In building up the life of a homestead, ancestral ritual supports a gendered division of labor and spheres of authority (Guy, 1987); it reinforces kinship relations (Gluckman, 1937; Hammond-Tooke, 1985); and it sanctions those rites of passage that mediate the transitions of birth, initiation, marriage, and death (Krige, 1937; on marriage, see Burman and van der Werff, 1993; Kuper, 1982). If the sacred order of the home is transgressed, ancestors can chastise their descendants by bringing misfortune or suffering (Kiernan, 1982). However, the significance of ancestors in domestic religion resides in more than merely maintaining the order of the home. Ancestors represent a spiritual dimension of existence that engages human beings (Hammond-Tooke,

1986). As the sacred center of religious life, the home operates as the "umbilical cord" that connects people with that spiritual reality.

Second, the polity is another sphere of power relations that is invested with religious significance. Ancestral ritual also plays a role in this sphere, but it is directed toward reinforcing the political authority of kings, chiefs, or other traditional leaders. Through ritual praises, political leadership can be affirmed and public opinion can be mobilized (Apter, 1983). Some commentators have argued that the relation between religion and politics in precolonial African religion should be understood as an institution of "divine kingship" (Huffman, 1986; Pettersson, 1953). With a powerful ancestral lineage, the political leader can preside over rituals of fertility, rainmaking, and warfare that strengthen the people and the land.

Third, sacred specialists—diviners, healers, and other specialized practitioners—operate in a sphere of religious power that is independent of either the home or polity but is available to both. The practices of sacred specialists have been characterized (and often stigmatized) as magic (see W. Hoernlé, 1937); and they have been contrasted with Western medicine and psychotherapy (Hammond-Tooke, 1975). However, they are better understood as ritual techniques, which are often learned through special initiation, that can be used for diagnosis, healing, and the acquisition of knowledge. In many cases, that knowledge is practical insight into the cause of some affliction or misfortune, whether the cause is identified as ancestral displeasure, a violation of purity, or the evil effects of witchcraft.

The religious beliefs and practices of these three spheres—the home, the polity, and the disciplines of sacred specialists—will appear in much greater detail in subsequent chapters on Xhosa, Zulu, Sotho-Tswana, Swazi, Tsonga, and Venda religion. The general overviews of African traditional religion that follow provide only a preliminary orientation.

A1   Anthropological Institute and Folklore Society (1903). "A Plea for the Scientific Study of the Native Laws and Customs of South Africa." *Man*, vol. 3, no. 37: 70-74.

This journal contribution records a petition sent jointly by the Anthropological Institute of Great Britain and Ireland and Folklore Society in 1900 to the British Secretary of State for the Colonies, followed by further exchanges of correspondence. The initial memorial requests that an official commission be set up to inquire into the customs and institutions of the indigenous peoples (Zulu, Sotho-Tswana, and Khoisan) and their relations with European settlers in the Transvaal and Orange River Colonies of South Africa. Twelve points are advanced as a rationale for the scientific study of African laws and customs. Here, the Anthropological Institute and Folklore Society argue that difficulties between Africans and Europeans in the region result from European ignorance of "native customs and superstitions." Thus, reports from missionaries and travelers are fragmentary and indigenous customs are often misunderstood by Europeans. For instance, the issue of *lobola* is raised, suggesting that attempts by some colonial magistrates to reject the custom as immoral, and therefore to ignore it in legislative matters, is a mistake. It is argued that the custom is appropriate in the context of the culture of those societies. A brief note in support of the petition from E. Sidney Hartland follows, with a reply from the Office of the Secretary, Joseph Chamberlain, in September 1900 denying the request. A further petition from the presidents of the Anthropological Society and Folklore Society in 1902, accompanied by a list of names in support of the deputation, is presented. A final reply from the Secretary further justifies delaying the formation of such a commission.

A2   Apter, Andrew H. (1983). "In Praise of High Office: The Politics of Panegyric Among Three Southern-Bantu Tribes." *Anthropos*, vol. 78: 149-68.

Apter's paper aims to analyze praises of high office as speech acts that mediate between a chief and his people, as practiced among the Tswana, Zulu, and Xhosa peoples. The author focuses on the role of this oratory as a form of political action, rather than on its symbolic significance as a form of literary art. This comparative study of Tswana, Zulu, and Xhosa praises of high office extends and generalizes John Comaroff's "incumbency model" which was initially used to analyze the political oratory of one Tswana chiefdom, the Tshidi. Apter therefore modifies the model to represent a more abstract, analytical concept that assesses the twin functions of the message communicated by the praises, namely, the distribution of legitimate authority "outwards" to the community and the channeling of public opinion "inwards" to the incumbent. By means of this approach, supported by a rudimentary content-analysis of Tswana, Zulu, and Xhosa praise-texts, Apter is able to identify the social values and institutional mechanisms invoked by these praises for the purposes of mobilizing or dividing public support, showing where these aspects coincide or differ among the three societies. In sum, he explains how the specialist praise-singer exploits the differences between addresser and speaker, addressee and hearer, and office and incumbent, to communicate two basic messages: First, the praises communicate a message to the public on behalf of its chief, distributing his legitimate authority in order to maintain public support. Second, the praises communicate a message to the chief on behalf of the public, imparting an evaluation of his performance as measured against the conventional requirements of his office. Maps and explanatory diagrams accompany the text and references are appended.

A3   Blackburn, Douglas, and N. W. Thomas (1904). "Animal Superstitions Among the Zulus, Basutos, Griquas, and Magatese, and the Kafirs of Natal." *Man*, vol. 4, no 115: 181-83.

This brief article, written by Blackburn from accounts Thomas sent him from South Africa, first lists a variety of animals—birds, snakes, oxen, lions, iguanas, and anteaters—that are reported to be in some way lucky or sacred to different indigenous peoples in southern Africa. The ancient Zulu belief in "spirit snakes," for instance, is mentioned. More detailed discussion is then advanced on the status and activities of "witch doctors" or "wizards" (diviners). Focusing on experiences in Natal and Zululand, Thomas notes the distinction between doctors who administer medicines and those who practice witchcraft. The techniques of the herbalist, he asserts, are far superior to European treatment for afflictions such as snake-bites and dysentery. African surgery, by contrast, is viewed as crude and often fatal. Turning to divination techniques, the writer relates an anecdotal account of the "smelling out" of an alleged thief. Finally, belief in the evils of a "creature called Togolosh" is argued to be universal in the region.

A4   Bleek, W. H. I. (1869). "Author's Preface." *On the Origin of Language*. Trans. Thomas Davidson. New York: Schmidt. ix-xxix.

In the preface to his work *On the Origin of Language* Bleek ponders the development of humanity and the place of the individual within that history, proposing that "the endowment of speech is the cement that binds together all the parts of the gigantic organism of humanity." Extending his thought to the realm of religious ideas and the question of life after death, Bleek argues that long before the advent of Jewish and Christian eschatology, the ancient religion of "ancestor-worship" was entirely based on the premise of the individual spirit's survival after death. "Ancestor-worship," continues Bleek, still prevails among several nations, including the indigenous peoples of southern Africa. As an example, he focuses on relations between the ancestral spirits and the living in Zulu society, noting the role of dreams and serpents as media for the manifestation of spirits. Ancestor-worship denotes the beginning of ethical thought, where action and thought is viewed in relation to "an invisible object grasped merely by the imagination" and expressed through myths and fables. Bleek links human progress in scientific thought, ethics, and religion to the development of sex-denoting language and particular grammatical classes and constructions. Even the "Hottentots," described by Bleek as the lowest form of culture to employ such language, created myths and fables that apprehended relations between heavenly bodies and animals, which, he argues, led to their practice of "sidereal worship." This, says Bleek, marked an important transition phase in humanity's "ascent towards true scientific knowledge." Religious ideas of the African peoples, like those of popular theology, rely on the mythological and anthropomorphic conception of God as a being who must be appeased. Adhering to the evolutionist theory of religion of nineteenth-century comparative religion, Bleek concludes that the full spiritual development of humanity requires progress from this false theology to the clarity of the scientific method.

A5   Burman, Sandra, and Nicolette van der Werff (1993). "Rethinking Customary Law on Bridewealth." *Social Dynamics*, vol. 19, no. 2: 111-27.

Against the backdrop of the changing structure of families in South Africa and, more specifically, the problems facing divorced African women, Burman and Van der Werff focus on the issue of customary bridewealth payments (*lobola, lobolo, bahedi,* etc.) in South Africa. Current situations and contemporary views about bridewealth practices are outlined. So too are the results of a small survey conducted by Burman to assess reactions to a suggested scheme for establishing a bridewealth fund to provide maintenance payment for children of broken marriages. Interviews carried out among mainly Xhosa- and Zulu-speaking people indicated that the institution of bridewealth shows no signs of declining and the costs involved, in reality, tend to be rising sharply. Discontents concerning social, psychological, and economic effects of customary bridewealth are analyzed, followed by the respondents' attitudes towards insurance and responses to the suggested bridewealth fund. Varied replies, both positive and negative, include some objections to the combination of an African cultural heritage with the Westernized notion of insurance policies which might further damage African culture. The authors conclude by reaffirming the need for ex-husbands to remain responsible for their children, whether bridewealth customs are adapted or not. They advocate a nationwide survey to gauge reactions to a variety of possible schemes. Before African customary law was codified and immobilized by the colonizers, they argue, it was flexible and adaptable to changing needs. Therefore, in a post-apartheid South Africa, Africans should regain confidence that their customs will not be erased by outside powers, thus allowing the creation of new structures to address future needs, while preserving the spirit of their traditions. Notes and references are appended.

A6   Callaway, Henry (1874). *A Fragment on Comparative Religion*. Natal: For Private Circulation.

This pamphlet was written by Callaway after the printing of his major work, *The Religious System of the Amazulu*, as an introduction to and a rationale for the publication of that work. Fundamentally, Callaway calls for European acceptance of the comparative and historical study of religions. The reason stated for his study responds to those nineteenth-century scholars and missionaries, such as Robert Moffat, who defined the indigenous peoples of South Africa as atheists. If atheism means to be without any idea of divinity, Callaway argues, then Africans are not atheists. He then advances several advantages to his work, the first being that "it will tend to moderate our own self-assertion" and reveal the misapprehensions evident in the Christian Church in relation to the underlying truth of religion. Second, Callaway advocates that such a study will encourage sympathy for the spiritual struggles of indigenous South Africans and moderate European prejudice that rejects them as an inferior people without spiritual potential. And third, claims Callaway, "it will increase our reverence for God and man." He continues by affirming the Christian truth as the most advanced religion in the world, but nevertheless warns against a spiritual arrogance that ignores the rest of humanity. God's love, he continues, is universal and intended for everyone and it is this love that forms the core of the Gospel of Christ. The remainder of this fragment is devoted to an explanation of this tenet as a justification for the Christian mission in Africa: "When we go to the heathen, let us believe that God has gone before us." European Christians, he concludes, must accept that there are other peoples outside the Christian tradition who have thought about and approached God. He therefore advocates the study of "various religions of man in a different spirit" and the diligent study of the history of religion.

A7   Callaway, Henry (1878). "South African Folk-Lore." *Cape Monthly Magazine* (N. S.), vol. 16, no. 94: 109-10.

This brief note presents an extract from a letter sent by Callaway to the Academy in which he updates his progress in the collection of Zulu "Medical Magic" and "Kafir Tales." Mentioning fragments of great antiquity from Zulu tales, he finds, for the first time, records of the magical use of medicine and the concept of resurrection after cremation. Turning to other southern African peoples, Callaway discovers that tales of creation exist everywhere. Some Xhosa-speaking groups, he notes, refer to the name of Uqamata for the Creator, using the name in a way that implies a theological discourse. Informants, says Callaway, claim it was the tribal name for Utixo before Xhosa contact with the Khoisan, admitting that they were significantly influenced by that exchange. Callaway concludes by surmising that he does not know whether this idea of Uqamata is a fact of Xhosa religion or "the echo of missionary teaching."

A8   Chidester, David (1992). "African Religion." In *Religions of South Africa*. London and New York: Routledge. 1-34.

The first chapter of Chidester's book is devoted to a study of African religion in southern Africa, based on an analysis of myth, symbol, and ritual. Chidester emphasizes that the term "traditional" applied to African religion does not imply a "timeless and unchanging" religion, but one that continues to generate dynamic, changing, and creative ways of "being human in the world." After defining the central terms and tools of analysis to be used in relation to southern African linguistic, sociocultural, and religious systems, Chidester divides the chapter into the following sections: myth; ancestor ritual; symbolisms of evil; sacred specialists; rites of passage; and rites of power. In the context of myth, various names for a high god and creation myths are discussed, as well as beliefs in various kinds of spirits, noting the effects of contact with Christian and Muslim missionaries. Examples of ancestor rituals are then described and their significance analyzed in terms of their potential to provide an explanatory system for affliction; a symbolic system to reinforce the authority of homestead elders; and a spiritual dimension to dissolve death. Under "symbolisms of evil" Chidester seeks to explain witchcraft and sorcery beliefs and practices as they relate to interpersonal conflicts; moral sanctions to reinforce social norms; and gaining public support against a common enemy. Next, the specialized knowledge, practices, and significance of diviners and herbalists are discussed in some detail. Chidester notes the inevitable conflict that emerged with the dominant legal code of South Africa in relation to identification of criminals in society. Various rites of passage marking birth, initiation, marriage, and death are then detailed and analyzed, giving attention to the significance of gender in this area. Finally, rites of power are examined in the context of religious ideology and its connection with the politics of homesteads, chiefdoms, and kingdoms, concluding with the disruptive economic effects brought by a new colonial and capitalist order. A comprehensive and valuable list of references is appended.

A9   De Heusch, Luc (1987). "Southern Bantu Religions." In Mircea Eliade (ed.) *The Encyclopaedia of Religion*. New York: Macmillan. 13: 539-46.

In this contribution to the *Encyclopedia of Religion*, De Heusch elucidates the symbolic systems underlying religious belief and practice among the Bantu-speaking peoples of southern Africa. Drawing on the work of anthropologists J. D. and Eileen Krige among the Lovedu, the author examines southern African myth and ritual within the framework of the concepts "heat" and "coolness." This "thermodynamic conception of the individual and the universe," claims the author, deems "heat" to upset equilibrium and cause dysphoria, while "coolness" restores harmony. He therefore explains how various cooling treatments are applied in order to end severe drought, heal sickness, and ward off persons who emanate heat (for example: twins; infants; warriors; menstruating and pregnant women; and the dead). Thus, for instance, communication with the ancestors is only possible when people are sufficiently "cool"—that is, neither angry nor spiteful. De Heusch claims that the same "thermal code" characterizes all rites of passage. For example, the Tsonga present their newborn infants to the moon, a feminine "cooling" agent that counters the "heat" of the child. Furthermore, the author interprets the mythological systems of the southern Bantu peoples through the proposed schema of coolness and heat. Successively, the "python cult" (extant, he claims, among almost all southern Bantu societies), "sacred kingship," and the "ritual complex of circumcision" are all interpreted according to this explanatory system of associating heat with disharmony and coolness with equilibrium. The masculine "python cult," for example, is contrasted with the feminine "rainbow cult" of the Zulu of Natal and the complex symbolism of the Swazi *ncwala* ceremony (associated with sacred kingship). Various circumcision rites are further analyzed according to this theoretical framework.

A10   Duggan-Cronin, A. M. (1928-1936). *The Bantu Tribes of South Africa: Reproductions of Photographic Studies.* 4 vols. Cambridge: Deighton, Bell & Co.; Kimberley, South Africa: Alexander MacGregor Memorial Museum.

Duggan-Cronin's renowned photographic studies of Bantu-speaking peoples in South Africa are produced in four volumes, comprising several sections that cover Venda, Sotho-Tswana, Nguni, and Tsonga societies respectively. Each section contains a comprehensive and informative introductory article about the particular society, as well as descriptive notes for each photographic plate. The photographic collections are as follows: Volume One, The Bavenda, with an introduction by G. P. Lestrade. Volume Two, Section One, "The Soto-Chuana Tribes: the Bechuana," with an introduction by G. P. Lestrade; Section Two, "The Soto-Chuana Tribes: the Bapedi," with an introduction by Werner Eiselen; Section Three, "The Southern Basotho," with an introduction by G. P. Lestrade. Volume Three, Sections One and Two, "The Nguni: the Xhosa and Thembu," introduced by W. G. Bennie; Section Three, "The Zulu," introduced by D. Malcolm; Section Four, "The Swazi," introduced by H. Beemer; Section Five, "Baca, Hlubi, and Xesibe," introduced by W. D. Hammond-Tooke. Volume Four, Section One, "The Vathonga (Thonga-Shangaan)," introduced by H. P. Junod, who also introduces Section Two, "Vachogi of Portuguese East Africa."

A11   Eiselen, W. M. (1924). "Geloofsvorme van Donker Afrika (Belief Patterns of Black Africa)." *Tydskrif vir Wetenskap en Kuns*, vol. 3, no. 1: 84-98.

Eiselen, perhaps one of South Africa's most influential ethnologists, introduces this essay on belief patterns in Africa with the assertion that since monotheism is absent in African religion, "animism" is the only reliable departure point for analysis. Comparative examples are traced from Egyptian, Amerindian, Greek, West African, and Roman Catholic religious traditions, cosmologies, and mythologies. He concludes by noting that belief in Modimo or uNkulunkulu, the

Tswana and Zulu names for a high god, originated from the Hamitic traditions of North African Ethiopians: "Totdusver het ons in Afrika nog geen spore van monoteisme ontdek wat nie aan die end van 'n lang ewolusiereeks staan nie. Ons mag dus animisme kies as uitgangspunt vir dir volgende bespreking (Up until now we have not discovered any trace of monotheism in Africa which was not the result of a long evolutionary series. We must, therefore, choose animism as the starting point for this discussion)." The text is in Afrikaans.

A12 Eiselen, W. M., and Isaac Schapera (1937). "Religious Beliefs and Practices." In Isaac Schapera (ed.) *The Bantu-Speaking Tribes of South Africa: An Ethnographical Survey.* London: George Routledge & Sons. 247-70.

Following on Hoernlé's chapter on "magic" among indigenous South African societies, Eiselen and Schapera address African belief in "certain supernatural beings able to influence for good or for evil the destinies of the living." They argue that it is the spirits of the dead ancestors that play the central role in a complex system of ritual worship among Bantu-speaking peoples. First, the authors discuss African belief in survival after death; the hierarchical structure of the spirit world; and the influence the spirits continue to have over their remaining relatives. Spirits, they continue, will appear to the living, for example, to warn of danger, to demand a sacrifice, or to reproach the living for some wrong-doing. Revelation may occur to an individual through dreams or in the form of a snake, for instance, after which he or she is required to consult a diviner. Eiselen and Schapera define the diviner as mediator of communication between the living and the dead but highlight only their negative influence, without any analysis of their social and religious significance. "Worship" of the ancestors and important sacrificial rituals offered to them are discussed and comparisons of varying symbolic meanings among different societies are undertaken. This is followed by discussion of the implications of African belief in and various names for a supreme being who, they suggest, is generally associated with the sky. The authors find no link between African traditional religion and morality. Although the Bantu-speaking peoples, they admit, follow moral precepts with regard to good and evil that are in accord with biblical commandments, the filial piety demanded by their ancestor beliefs requires moral behavior only within the family and tribe, rather than moral behavior in general. Footnotes accompany the text.

A13 Frazer, James (1901). "South African Totemism." *Man*, vol. 1, no. 111: 135-36.

Frazer's contribution offers a brief extract from G. M. Theal's *Records of South-Eastern Africa* on the "totemic system" of the indigenous peoples of the region. Frazer suggests that Theal's work elucidates contemporary discussions on the origins of totemism. In the extract, Theal argues that a certain species of animal, such as the lion, crocodile, python, or buck, was sometimes regarded as the embodiment of an ancestor spirit and was thus held sacred by the society that had appropriated that particular animal. Although many of the peoples in the interior no longer held those ancient beliefs, says Theal, each still venerated the animal their ancestors believed might embody a spirit. The peoples of the coastal regions, he continues, all regarded the same species of snake as the embodiment of their ancestral "shades." Frazer concludes that Theal's account shows that the Bantu-speaking peoples of South Africa venerated totem animals as incarnations of the souls of dead ancestors which, he adds, supports the general theory of totemism advocated by G. A. Wilken and E. B. Tylor at the turn of the century.

A14   Garbutt, H. W. (1909). "Native Witchcraft and Superstition in South Africa." *Journal of the Royal Anthropological Institute*, vol. 39: 530-58.

Compiled by the Secretary for the Rhodesia Scientific Association, this paper draws on extensive bibliographic material, including extracts from the works of Henri-Alexandre Junod; Robert Moffat; Andrew Smith; Henry Callaway; George McCall Theal, and many Native Affairs commissioners. The paper is divided into the following sections: Witches; Witchdoctors—diviners of the cause of sickness; Witchdoctors—diviners of witches; Bone-throwers; Rain-doctors; Grave-doctors; Necromancers; Sacrificers; and Dancers to the Ancestors. While the paper deals mostly with Matabeleland, a comparison with practices in Basutoland and elsewhere are made. See also comparisons with France and Ireland.

A15   Gluckman, Max (1936). *The Realm of the Supernatural among the South-Eastern Bantu*. 2 vols. D.Phil. thesis. Oxford University.

Gluckman's comprehensive and important doctoral thesis investigates the ritual practices of the Xhosa- and Zulu-speaking peoples, referred to by the author as the Thonga, Zulu, and Transkei tribes. Based on his collection and evaluation of existing ethnographic studies of African indigenous peoples, Gluckman aims to collate and evaluate descriptions of ritual practices among the south-eastern Bantu-speaking peoples, such as those associated with the ancestral cult, magic, witchcraft, rites of passage, and vegetation ceremonies. In addition, the author also seeks to provide a sociological description of these ritual practices which focuses on the social significance of the participants' ritual behavior. The first two of a total of nine chapters delineates and defines the territories and culture of the societies under consideration. Chapter Three then explores ritual in the context of social and individual life, emphasizing rites of passage performed for birth, initiation, marriage, and death. While Chapter Four offers a detailed analysis of medicines used for healing practices, Chapter Five looks at rituals rooted in economic life, including first fruit ceremonies and the rites devoted to the female deity, Nomkubulwana. Ritual practices that form the foundation of national life, such as those connected with war, morality and the law, and the sacred character of the chief, form the focus of Chapter Six. Examining the realm of the supernatural, Gluckman then discusses witchcraft, sorcery, cosmogony, and creation to investigate the role of diviners, "witchdoctors," "magicians," and "exorcists." The final two chapters of the thesis are devoted to the construction of a taxonomy of ritual behavior (magic; ancestral cult; substantive ritual; factitive ritual) and a comparative study of ritual organization among the societies studied. Gluckman concludes that a number of common ritual themes are revealed—particularly magical and sacrificial ritual—but with varying levels of emphasis on the role of medicine, sacrifice, and special rites. A table of ritual practices under the headings of Thonga, Zulu, and Transkei is included in the final chapter; a bibliography and references are appended.

A16   Gluckman, Max (1937). "Mortuary Customs and the Belief in the Survival After Death among South-Eastern Bantu." *Bantu Studies*, vol. 11: 117-36.

In this article which draws from his doctoral thesis, Gluckman conducts a comparative analysis of the beliefs and ritual practices associated with death among a number of south-eastern Bantu-speaking peoples, including the Mpondo, Xhosa, Zulu, and Swazi. Frequent reference is also made to Junod's study of the Thonga in what was then Portuguese East Africa. Mystical beliefs about the cause of death, and beliefs about death itself are all incorporated in the various complex mortuary ceremonies. Within the context of kinship and affinal relationships, Gluckman therefore sets out to analyze how these elements affect the following aspects: the readjustment and reconstitution of social relationships; the disposal of the body; reaction to mystical causes and forces of death; the life of the ghost in the afterworld; and the nature of the links between that afterworld and this world. When relations between the living and the dead are socially contextualized within an ancestor cult, social attention to the journey of the spirit to and its existence in another realm appears to be largely excluded. Most emphasis therefore rests on the role of the ancestral spirits in the life of their kin and the mediation of ritual offered by the living to the ancestors. Gluckman concludes that social morphology affects mortuary customs and beliefs about immortality, in this case, in the form of an ancestral cult that maintains kinship groupings. Lineage is more socially significant, therefore, than is immortality as a compensation for death. However, it is stressed that in none of the societies is death conceived as part of the natural order. Death myths, argues Gluckman, reveal a desire for life and explicitly state that death was introduced to humanity as a result of negligence or evil. Footnotes accompany the text and a bibliography is appended.

A17   Gqoba, W. (1885). "The Native Tribes, Their Laws, Customs and Beliefs." *Christian Express*, vol. 15, no. 179: 93-94.

Presented to the Lovedale Literary Society in April 1885, Gqoba's paper comprises a brief history of the indigenous peoples of South Africa. He begins by tracing a detailed genealogy of the Xhosa-speaking chiefs and chiefdoms of precolonial south-eastern Africa, noting the theory that some came from the north of Africa and were influenced by Jewish ceremonies and customs. After briefly mentioning the variety of indigenous languages in South Africa, all of which, he suggests, contain many similarities, Gqoba turns to African laws and "superstitions." Indigenous systems of law, says the author, have been handed down by oral tradition, based on precedents set by chiefs in relation to issues such as marriage, inheritance, and criminal jurisprudence. Superstitious beliefs, sorcery, and witchcraft, however, have obstructed justice and humanity. Treaties between African chiefdoms and colonial authorities in "British Kaffraria" from 1840 to 1855 are outlined. Gqoba concludes by noting the changes effected by Governors Grey and Cathcart in the 1850s concerning "the administration of justice among the natives."

A18   Guy, Jeff (1987). "Analysing Pre-Capitalist Societies in Southern Africa." *Journal of Southern African Studies*, vol. 14, no. 1: 18-37.

Guy applies historical analysis to what he considers to be shortcomings in the largely ahistorical anthropological research on southern African pre-capitalist societies. He argues that the transfer of cattle between families operated as a form of labor transfer against the reproductive capacity of women but also suggests that bridewealth transactions cannot be seen as solely indicative of pre-capitalist societies. Rather, these societies were founded upon the dynamic social principle of continuous acquisition, creation, control, and appropriation of labor power. This, says Guy, generated two classes: the subordinate class comprising women and children who provided labor power and the dominant class of married men or homestead-heads who owned cattle and land. This profoundly exploitative class division within the homestead was articulated in class struggle, a struggle that was ritually expressed in the marriage ceremony and economically expressed in the resistance of wives to husbands and daughters to fathers. The author further analyzes the effects of the political authority of the chiefs on the homestead unit, as well as the implications of the separation of fertility and sexuality in relation to the reproduction of labor power. But in analyzing the process of change to capitalist production, Guy identifies the relationship between father and son to be of central significance. Control of production had formerly been passed on from father to son, a process that was increasingly disrupted by the involvement of young men in wage labor. Women, however, remained tied to agricultural and domestic production in the homestead, only to start moving to urban areas after the virtual collapse of rural production after the 1930s depression. This desertion of the homestead by sons, and then by wives and daughters, was indicative not only of the social disruption caused by capitalism but also of the demise of the dominant class in southern African societies. Footnotes accompany the text.

A19   Hall, Martin (1984). "The Burden of Tribalism: The Social Context of Southern African Iron Age Studies." *American Antiquity*, vol. 49, no. 3: 455-67.

The underlying argument of Hall's paper is that specific, detailed critiques of archaeological practice in differing sociopolitical environments are vital for developing an understanding of how the present shapes the past. Hall's point of departure is that the archaeological study of farming communities in southern Africa is a political activity, thus calling for a critical analysis of the role of social context in shaping problems and solutions in an apparently neutral, scholarly discipline. The history of Iron Age research south of the Zambesi, argues Hall, reveals the consistent influence of colonial ideologies on its earliest conceptions of an African cultural past as well as on contemporary archaeological methodologies. Concepts such as ethnicity, for instance, have acquired specific meanings in the political context of southern Africa. Hall charts the interrelationship between archaeology and colonial expansion, linking the development of archaeological constructs of "cultures" or "peoples" in African prehistory with colonial interpretations of African history and ethnography. In particular, ideological constructions of "tribalism" and ethnicity in both Zimbabwe and South Africa are examined. In southern African countries where white minorities hold power, or have done so until recently, notes the author, Iron Age research has moved towards ideas of ethnic diversity and emphasis on cultural changelessness over time, thus reinforcing the ideology of social evolutionism that pervades white interpretations of a black past. The prehistory of southern Africa told from a black nationalist point of view, concludes Hall, will certainly reject the emphasis on tribalism and ethnicity and its association with the colonial period. References are appended.

A20   Hall, Martin (1987). "Archaeology and Modes of Production in Pre-Colonial Africa." *Journal of Southern African Studies*, vol. 14, no. 1: 1-17.

Hall advances an historical-material analysis uncovering the dynamics of human behavior among the indigenous peoples of precolonial southern Africa. He draws on materialist theory that emphasizes relations of production in order to redirect attention to the totality of human behavior and avoid the reductionism inherent in migration and technological development theories. Using this materialist theoretical approach, Hall argues, reinforces the explanatory power of archaeological evidence pertaining to activities such as rock art, burial practice, and architecture. For example, it is suggested that the trance dance performed by San medicine men constituted a form of "symbolic labor" that represented general cooperation within the camp. Three modes of production relevant to precolonial southern African social structures are therefore defined and analyzed in this article: "The Primitive Communist Mode of Production"; "The Lineage Mode of Production"; and "The Tributary Mode of Production." The author emphasizes that his analysis is of a preliminary nature and aims to provide a basis for further research and theoretical refinement in this area of archaeological study. The article provides useful resources for readers in comparative religion interested in the prehistory of southern Africa. Footnotes accompany the text.

A21   Hammond-Tooke, W. D. (1974). "World-view I: A System of Beliefs"; "World-view II: A System of Action." In W. D. Hammond-Tooke (ed.) *The Bantu-Speaking Peoples of Southern Africa*. London: Routledge & Kegan Paul. 318-43; 344-63.

Hammond-Tooke's Chapters Ten and Eleven in *The Bantu-Speaking Peoples of Southern Africa* provide a broad introduction to prominent aspects of African traditional religion, with reference to, among others, Xhosa, Zulu, Sotho-Tswana, Tsonga, and Venda societies. The first of the two essays elucidates the system of belief that comprises the Bantu-speaking peoples' worldview, focusing on concepts concerning the nature of the supernatural. Thus, while beliefs in high gods and nature spirits are analyzed, the greater part of the chapter is devoted to a description of belief in ancestral spirits as the normative influence on African life. The importance of belief in witchcraft and sorcery as a means of accommodating the problem of evil is also stressed in this chapter. The second essay serves to examine these beliefs as they are actively expressed in everyday life, placing particular emphasis on ritual activity as the symbolic expression of such belief systems. In addition, the significance of divination, as an interpretation of misfortune and a prominent social vocation, is examined. The author concludes these systematic accounts of African traditional belief and ritual practice by exploring the consequences that such a worldview holds for the question of morality. Accordingly, Hammond-Tooke suggests that African morality can be wholly contained within the principles of harmonious cooperation and good neighborliness, with its unmistakable communal emphasis. Notes are appended to each chapter. These essays update, revise, and expand the general overviews found in Eiselen and Schapera (1937) and Hoernlé (1937).

A22   Hammond-Tooke, W. D. (1975). "African Worldview and its Relevance for Psychiatry." *Psychologia Africana*, vol. 16: 25-32.

In this article Hammond-Tooke looks at the diagnosis of psychotic states in African patients, bearing in mind cross-cultural clinical interpretations of what signifies normal or pathological behavior. He identifies the central problem as one of meaning in the context of religion or worldview, in other words, ideas concerning reality, the relationship between people and the natural world, and the causes of illness and misfortune. Ideas of causation, in particular, are fundamentally different in Western and African cultures. Focusing on the four main African language groups in South Africa, the author notes that all misfortune, illness, and death (except old age) are sent by supernatural beings—that is, either by the ancestral "shades" or by a witch or sorcerer. From a psychoanalytical point of view, argues Hammond-Tooke, witchcraft accusations represent a clear case of projection often evident in a close community. For the anthropologist they also indicate tensions and stresses in the community. Examining Zulu witchcraft beliefs as an example, the author assesses the psychological aspects of witchcraft accusations and confessions in the African worldview, emphasizing the role of diviners and the illness of *ukuthwasa* that characterizes the calling to become a diviner. Noting psychological differences between female and male diviners, Hammond-Tooke asserts that many symptoms that are defined as neurotic and even psychotic in terms of Western psychiatry may not be so defined in terms of the shared cultural constructs in an African worldview. References are appended.

A23   Hammond-Tooke, W. D. (1978). "Do the South Eastern Bantu Worship their Ancestors?" In J. Argyle and E. Preston-Whyte (eds.) *Social System and Tradition in Southern Africa*. Cape Town: Oxford University Press. 134-49.

Hammond-Tooke's point of departure in this paper is the trend in African ethnography to view the term "worship," used in connection with the so-called ancestor cult, as inappropriate. Although other terms, such as communion, propitiation, conciliation, libation, respect, and veneration have been used by other writers (for example, Kopytoff, West, and Mbiti), Hammond-Tooke argues that we might be rejecting an analytically useful term for the cross-cultural study of religion simply because we are importing Judaeo-Christian ideas of what worship should be. Taking into consideration Ninian Smart's criteria for worship, the paper focuses on the question of whether the south-eastern Bantu-speaking peoples, especially the Cape Nguni and Zulu, can be perceived as worshipping their ancestors. In this respect, Hammond-Tooke's study of ancestor ritual indicates that invocations and ritual acts constitute a formal distancing between the living and the ancestor spirits, thus fulfilling an essential aspect of worship where ritual functions as mediator between them. Objects of religious ritual are set apart and consecrated and, as such, have to be constructed for the purposes of the ritual. The act of focusing on the interaction between the living and the ancestors essentially sets apart the profane situation in order to create a sacred one, which is accomplished verbally through special invocations, and spatially through ritual killing in the cattle byre. Hammond-Tooke therefore strongly advocates that indigenous societies do worship their ancestors and that to avoid the use of the term "worship" would amount to cultural arrogance. Notes and references are appended.

A24   Hammond-Tooke, W. D. (1981a). "Ancestor Religion." In Heinz Kuckertz (ed.) *Ancestor Religion in Southern Africa*. Transkei: Lumko Missiological Institute. 22-33.

Defining religion as a shared social phenomenon that involves belief in beings or a Being "immeasurably superior to men" that addresses existential issues concerning life and death, Hammond-Tooke thus substantiates his use of the term "traditional ancestor religion" in reference to African traditional religion. In this sense, he situates ancestor veneration in the wider context of a worldview, emphasizing the cognitive aspects of religious belief and practice that in African religion includes ancestor veneration and belief in a sky-god. African ancestor religion, Hammond-Tooke argues, is not a cult of the dead, since cults of the dead do not typically include the concept of the dead's concern, active influence, or assistance in the affairs of the living. A significant section of the paper is therefore occupied with relating ancestor religion to the kinship system within which it operates. Focusing on the Nguni- and Sotho-speaking peoples, the writer's structural analysis shows how the shades and their kin-group reflect each other. In conclusion, Hammond-Tooke locates the position of traditional ancestor veneration within the paradigm of "World Religions," while also tracing its evolution in the midst of rapid urbanization and a changing religious climate marked by the intrusion of Christianity. Footnotes and references are appended.

A25   Hammond-Tooke, W. D. (1981b). *Patrolling the Herms: Social Structure, Cosmology and Pollution Concepts in Southern Africa*. Eighteenth Raymond Dart Lecture, 30th April, 1980. Johannesburg: Witwatersrand University Press.

In this paper Hammond-Tooke analyzes the importance of boundary-marking in traditional cosmological systems in southern Africa, noting the similar significance of "Herms" (sculptured pillars) as boundary-markers in ancient Greek and Roman religion. Clearly defined boundaries, argues the author, are essential for effective communication and the avoidance of chaos. It is religious systems, then, that provide cognitive ordering of the world and their rituals—especially those concerning pollution beliefs—and make statements about boundaries. Hammond-Tooke points out that many differences exist between the social structures of the various Bantu-speaking peoples of South Africa, arguably accompanied by similar differences between the cosmological and symbolic systems created by them. The paper focuses, however, on a comparative study of pollution beliefs and rituals among the Zulu-speaking Nguni and the North-Sotho Kgaga in order to determine the relationship (if any) between social substructure and cosmological superstructure. Drawing on Mary Douglas' insight that rituals concerning impurity reflect a society's feelings about its boundaries, Hammond-Tooke finds, paradoxically, that Zulu society, while "outward-looking," conducts "inward-looking" pollution rituals. By contrast, the more "inward-looking" Kgaga participate in "outward-looking" rituals. Furthermore, Kgaga pollution rituals seem to possess high public communication value compared with the minimal communication involved in Zulu pollution beliefs and practices. However, the author points out that Zulu society does focus on pollution beliefs to the same extent that the Kgaga do because Zulu boundaries between social categories are far more clearly defined. Nevertheless, he argues that the paradoxical problems involved in maintaining boundaries among both societies can never be permanently resolved. He concludes that pollution beliefs function as myths of impurity and danger to bring attention to the "sacred Herms" that mark boundaries between social categories. Pollution rituals provide a potent means for patrolling and reconsecrating those boundaries. The text is annotated and references are appended.

A26   Hammond-Tooke, W. D. (1985). "Who Worships Whom: Agnates and Ancestors Among the Nguni." *African Studies*, vol. 44, no. 1: 47-64.

Hammond-Tooke's article addresses the issue of ancestor religion in southern Africa, particularly the contentious debate concerning the term "worship." The paper aims to clarify the issue in the context of the Nguni, who, the writer argues, represent the most significant example of patrilineal emphasis among South African indigenous peoples. In this respect, Hammond-Tooke points to the importance of exploring the relationship between cosmological constructs on the one hand and social structures of kinship and descent on the other, particularly in relation to two problems: first, the exact nature of the influence of the agnatic principle on Nguni conceptualizations of their "objects of worship"; and second, the implications of ancestor ritual that often involves the intervention of ancestors who are not drawn from agnatic kin—for example, the specific, troubling ancestor in the core part of a Nguni ritual that may be perceived as a mother or affinal kinsman. Hammond-Tooke's detailed and cogent analysis draws on research conducted among the Cape Nguni, including Thembu, Mpondomise, Bhaca, and Xhosa groups in the Transkei, and refers to the work of scholars on the Natal Nguni, such as Berglund, Vilakazi, Ngubane, and Preston-Whyte. The writer concludes that the problem can be approached in two ways—either by questioning whether the so-called extra-descent group ancestors are in fact ancestral spirits in any acceptable sense of the term; or, to accept that at the level of the agnatic cluster the relationship between the cluster members and their dead is an explicitly bilateral one reflecting wider kinship interests than simply the agnatic. A comprehensive bibliography is appended.

A27   Hammond-Tooke, W. D. (1986). "The Aetiology of Spirit in Southern Africa." *African Studies*, vol. 45, no. 2: 157-70.

The expressed intention of this study is to conduct a general survey of the conception of spirit among indigenous peoples of southern Africa, although the author specifically seeks to identify the potential causal rationale behind such beliefs. Recognizing the irreducible importance of ancestral spirits in traditional religious worship, Hammond-Tooke suggests that the extensive influence wielded by the ancestors from beyond the grave merely reinforces and reflects the cherished kinship principles dominant in traditional social life. A significant section of this work is devoted to an analysis of witch beliefs and possession cults, diagnosing each as either metaphors for social expression or as important ingredients of indigenous psychological theory. The concluding section provides apt commentary on the alleged syncretism of southern African Christianity, especially that of Zulu Zionism. Hammond-Tooke attempts to provide a logic for the existence of such syncretism, suggesting that certain features of Pentecostal-type religious movements allowed smooth assimilation into the indigenous mindset. A bibliography is appended.

A28   Hammond-Tooke, W. D. (1989). *Rituals and Medicines: Indigenous Healing in South Africa.* Johannesburg: Ad. Donker.

This book by anthropologist Hammond-Tooke aims to explain, in a style accessible to the general public, black South Africans' approach to the problem of health—an approach that is inextricably interwoven with indigenous religious beliefs and practices. Including reference to the Nguni-, Sotho-, Tsonga-. and Venda-speaking peoples, the author addresses the causes of illness and healing techniques as an integral part of the South African indigenous or "traditional" worldview. He cautions, however, that not all present-day black South Africans necessarily adhere to every aspect of this complex system of symbols, codes, and structures. Hammond-Tooke's particular focus is the problem of developing a satisfactory accommodation between "first-world" Western medical systems in South Africa and traditional medicine. Furthermore, he emphasizes that the problem of health among black South Africans has emerged within the wider

framework of colonialism, industrialization, and the inequalities and deprivation of later apartheid rule, which have brought poverty, unemployment, and
proliferation of disease to black South African societies. Hammond-Tooke seeks
to communicate an understanding of the nature of indigenous thought and its
view of health as a pivotal part of a larger cosmology that includes notions of a
supreme being; ancestral spirits; witchcraft beliefs; and the more recent phenomena of "possession cults" and faith-healing. The role of the ancestors in
healing, and of witches and sorcerers in illness and misfortune, are analyzed in
some detail as well as the significance of notions of pollution. The techniques
and medicines of traditional healers and their therapeutic relationships with
patients are further analyzed. The book concludes with an evaluation of the possibilities for integration of traditional and Western medical systems. References,
bibliography, and index are appended.

A29   Hammond-Tooke, W. D. (1991). "Kinship Authority and Political
Authority in Precolonial South Africa." In A. D. Spiegel and P. A. McAllister
(eds.) *Tradition and Transition in Southern Africa: Festschrift for Philip and
Iona Mayer. African Studies*, vol. 50: 185-99.

Hammond-Tooke's paper contributes to the ongoing debate between anthropologists and historians of precolonial South African history. It offers an anthropological critique of what appears to be an inappropriate and oversimplified
historical model of how government worked in precolonial South Africa, one
that presupposes a transition from pre-state to state systems. Focusing on attempts to trace the development of Swazi and Zulu states, the author shows how
the theory that formal government (chiefdomship) and descent group autonomy
(clans) coexisted is untenable. He argues, in contrast, that state-type organization (chiefdom) was the typical form of government among the southern Bantu-
speaking people for "as far back as we can go." The Zulu and Swazi kingdoms
were simply sophisticated developments of already existent state-type organization, as were the rise of Sekwati's Pedi federation and Moshoeshoe's South Sotho Kingdom. Pointing to historians' reification of descent groups as structural
entities with power and authority, Hammond-Tooke suggests that clans are too
large with far too long and complex genealogies for such systemization. In ancestor ritual, for instance, where the "clan" dead are invoked, only the name of
the founder is known and called upon. Kinship authority, he argues, is always
negotiated and does not reside in the realm of formally constituted political
authority. Some of the interpretive problems involved, it is suggested, lie in the
definition of terms. The author cites the loose use of "clan" and "lineage" in the
literature and the tendency to conflate "clan" and "chiefdom." Also problematic
are the classifications Nguni, Sotho, etc., that have been imposed by anthropologists and administrators. Hammond-Tooke concludes by affirming that the
arbitration of kinship authority gives way to the legal sanctions of political

authority, which is unequivocally located in chiefdoms. It is the fully centralized and powerful chiefdoms, according to the author, that go back at least a thousand years before the eighteenth century and the rise of the Zulu and Swazi kingdoms. Notes and a bibliography are appended.

A30   Hartland, E. Sidney (1901). "Some Problems of Early Religion in the Light of South African Folklore." *Folk-Lore*, vol. 12: 15-40.

Presenting the annual presidential address to the Folk-Lore Socicty in 1900, Hartland focuses on the religion of indigenous peoples in South Africa. Particularly, he examines the academic search for the origins of religion. He begins by documenting Lang's evolutionary theory of religion, which claims that original belief in a supreme being was later obscured by primitive humanity's awe and fear of the unknown, out of which emerged animism and then polytheism. The author sets out to test this hypothesis in the light of missionary interpretations of religious systems in South Africa, most specifically Callaway's work on the Zulu; Moffat's on the "Bechuana" (Sotho-Tswana); and Junod's on the Baronga (Tsonga). All, says Hartland, represent confusing and contradictory ideas in relation to belief in a supreme being. Arguing that the Zulu are not a primitive people and are no longer "savages," Hartland continues with an analysis of the core of Zulu religion—the "deeply-rooted cult of the dead." Claiming that the "Bantu race" emerged from nomadic savagery based on totemism and mother-right, the writer presents his own hypothesis proposing that "ancestor worship" supplanted totemism. It was, says the author, entirely due to the development of a partriarchal system and reverence for the authority of the father, a reverence that extended beyond death. "When death has conferred mystery upon him," Hartland proposes, "the reverence for a father rises into worship." Ancestor worship among the Zulu, it is further explained, takes on a hierarchical system of *amatongo* (ancestors), where the dead homestead head is worshipped by the children of that house and the dead chief is worshipped as the focal point of a wider tribal religion. Therefore, Hartland concludes, ancestor worship supplanted totemism by the passing of mother-right to father-right among the Bantu-speaking peoples.

A31   Hartland, E. Sidney (1909). "Bantu and South Africa." In James Hastings (ed.) *Encyclopaedia of Religion and Ethics.* Edinburgh: T. and T. Clark. 2: 350-67.

Hartland's entry in this volume refers to the Bantu-speaking peoples of the wider southern African region, including those situated in South Africa. The article is divided into seven sections, the first of which addresses "Race and Geographical Distribution of the Bantu," with reference to central, south-eastern, northern, south-western, and western areas and groupings. The culture and organization of these societies is then discussed, including language, the social and political structure of chiefdoms, and cultural customs such as puberty rites, circumcision, and marriage. Under the heading of "Totemism," the third section links the origins of tribal names and symbols with totem animals, plants, or objects, although Hartland acknowledges that totemism was no longer prevalent in most Bantu-speaking societies. Section Four, headed "Worship of the Dead and Other Spirits; Burial Rites," focuses on African beliefs concerning life after death and the preservation of the sociopolitical hierarchy in the spirit realm. Ritual practices of "ancestor-worship" are discussed in terms of national and family contexts and the appearance of spirits in dreams and in the form of animals is noted. Royal burial rites for chiefs are particularly emphasized. Hartland continues in Section Five with the topic of "Idols," focusing on a discussion of "fetishes" in West Africa and indicating that only "ancestor-worship" occurs among the Bantu-speaking societies of South Africa. "Priests, Medicine-Men, Diviners, and Sorcerers" form the content of Section Six, including a list of no less than nine classes of such ritual specialists among the Venda. The important practices of diviners among the Zulu-speaking peoples and various types of doctors among Xhosa-speakers are also discussed. Finally, Hartland addresses the debate concerning African notions of and names for a supreme being and missionary appropriations of some of those names to communicate the Christian concept of God.

A32   Hoernlé, A. Winifred (1937). "Magic and Medicine." In Isaac Schapera (ed.) *The Bantu-Speaking Tribes of South Africa: An Ethnographical Survey.* London: George Routledge and Sons. 221-45.

In her study of indigenous medicine and practice of "magic" in South Africa, Hoernlé indicates that both Western science and African magic are attempts to control the natural and human environment in the interests of the practitioner and the community. In either context, she argues, knowledge is power and the magical practitioner is acting on beliefs that constitute his or her knowledge of the universe. The greater part of Hoernlé's study provides a detailed exploration of the various specialists (*inyanga*) among the Bantu-speaking peoples of South Africa, making the distinction between the herbalist and the diviner. Diseases treated and medicines used by herbalists are outlined. Hoernlé notes the specialist's wide knowledge of the healing properties of plants and animals. Particular attention is paid to the prominent position and vocation of diviners who specialize in diagnosis and sometimes in the "smelling out" of witches. The author comprehensively describes the ancestors' calling of the diviner through the sickness known as *ukuthwasa* and the process of initiation, including spirit possession and intensive ritual practices. This is followed by a comparative study of different methods of divination. The writer concludes with an analysis of witchcraft beliefs, the various manifestations of evil powers, and methods of eradicating them, taking care to note the distinctions made between the witch and the sorcerer in some societies. Footnotes accompany the text.

A33   Hoernlé, R. F. Alfred (1945). "Prolegomena to the Study of the Black Man's Mind." In R. F. A. Hoernlé, *Race and Reason*. Ed. I. D. MacCrone. Johannesburg: University of Witwatersrand Press. 43-54.

German philosopher and champion of political liberalism, R. F. A. Hoernlé, lived in South Africa from 1923 until his death in 1943 and became a leading figure in the South African Institute of Race Relations in the 1930s. His collection of essays, *Race and Reason*, is based mainly on a critique of theories and philosophies of race. "Prolegomena to the Study of the Black Man's Mind" examines contemporary white South African conceptions of the mentality of the Bantu-speaking peoples of South Africa, arguing that very few scientific studies of indigenous peoples had been done. Hoernlé adopts a social-anthropological approach, indicating that the human mind is shaped by social institutions, customs, folk traditions, and established beliefs. He aims to reveal prejudices and clarify misconceptions about Bantu-speaking societies, for example, those concerning the customs of polygyny and *lobola*. Given the "communistic" economy and role of the ancestors in the family and community, suggests the author, it is *lobola* that engenders the moral bond between man and woman and between their kin and the ancestral spirits. The author conducts an incisive critique of evolutionist theory and its classification of Bantu-speaking peoples as primitive, although he commends the benefits of white economic life, education, and Christianity for the material and spiritual progress of black South Africans. Defining African religion as "animism," Hoernlé depicts the conflict Africans confront in turning away from their own beliefs, culture, and social structure. Psychological and intelligence testing is also addressed, questioning the validity of applying such methods in African society. Although the author affirms the view that the Bantu-speaking peoples' mentality is "prescientific," he concludes by stressing that this is a social phenomenon and not due to an intellectual capacity that is profoundly different from that of whites.

A34   Huffman, Thomas N. (1986). "Archaeological Evidence and Conventional Explanations of Southern Bantu Settlement Patterns." *Africa*, vol. 56, no. 3: 280-98.

In this article Huffman considers Africanist interest in the contrast between settlement patterns among the dispersed homesteads of the Nguni and the large towns of the Tswana. He presents archaeological evidence that calls into question conventional explanations that are most often based on variations in social stratification, environmental conditions, or cultural patterns. First, the writer addresses social stratification, developing models of the differing political and settlement hierarchies among the Nguni and Tswana communities. The complexity of different chiefly ranks and court levels reached in some Bantu-speaking societies is noted. Second, Huffman turns to environmental conditions, reviewing the argument of some scholars that differences between the eastern seaboard and the highveld to the west shaped the sociopolitical organization of different societies. Third, Huffman looks at settlement organization as a reflection of a society's culture pattern or worldview, including attitudes towards politics, economic issues, and religion. In contrasting the patterns inherent in the cattle culture of southern African Bantu-speakers with those of Zimbabwe, features such as bridewealth, burial rituals, religious symbols, the ritualization of leadership, and "divine kingship" are discussed. In the final section, Huffman presents archaeological data to argue that specific historical events constituted the primary cause of settlement differentiation among Bantu-speaking societies, rather than the influences discussed above. However, particularly in the case of the distinctive Tswana settlement pattern, he argues that certain aspects of the environment, agriculture, population, wealth, and political power also played a part within the specific historical context. References are appended.

A35　Junod, H. P. (1938). *Bantu Heritage*. Johannesburg: Hortors.

Henri-Philippe Junod, son of the Swiss missionary and scholar, Henri Alexandre Junod, delivered a series of lectures on the Bantu-speaking peoples of South Africa in 1937 to the medical officers and compound managers of the Transvaal gold mines. This book comprises a transcript of those lectures. The author states as his aim the eradication of European perceptions of Africans as savages and the promotion of understanding, although his perceptions are inevitably colored by a European colonialist view of Africans. There are seven chapters in all, of which the first five cover the following range of topics: African Races and Tribes; Bantu Languages; Bantu Folklore; Music; Social and Tribal Organization and Law; and Etiquette. Chapters Six and Seven examine "The Bantu Mind," providing rich material both for the study of African religion and a critique of colonial perspectives. Claiming that African mentality is completely "unscientific," Junod first discusses totemism, arguing that it has mostly disappeared among southern African indigenous peoples, except among the Pedi and Venda. In addressing the topic of magic, indigenous medicine, and divination systems in Chapter Six, the author focuses on witchcraft beliefs and witch detection techniques at some length, reporting case studies of spirit possession by displaced ancestral spirits. In Chapter Seven, Junod specifically turns to the religion and spiritual world of Bantu-speaking peoples, explaining his understanding of the distinction between magic and religion. He describes "ancestor-worship" and the central role of the "ancestor-gods" and sacrifice, for instance, in the context of rites of passage and family relations. In conclusion, Junod discusses African conceptions of a supreme being, heaven, and notions concerning creation and the spiritual power of natural elements. The text includes photographs by A. M. Duggan-Cronin. An annotated bibliography and index are appended.

A36   Kidd, Dudley (1904). *The Essential Kafir*. London: Adam & Charles Black.

Although Kidd insists in his introduction that the term "Kafir" is used in its "broadest sense" to describe indigenous peoples of South Africa, his own racist assumptions and excessively patronizing tone emerge in the quest for the "Essential Kafir." The twelve chapters of text deal with religious beliefs, magic, traditional healers, rituals, war, arts, domestic and legal matters, and folklore among South African indigenous societies. Arguing that African belief is fundamentally the same throughout South Africa, Kidd discusses African attitudes towards death, myths concerning the origins of death, and concepts of ancestor spirits and their manifestations. Cosmogonic mythology is also addressed. The writer discusses notions of and names for a creator or god among the Zulu, Xhosa, and Sotho-Tswana peoples. Beliefs concerning nature and the elements are dealt with, including rainmaking and the power of thunder and lightning. The chapter on "magic" reviews indigenous beliefs and practices concerning sickness and witchcraft; the role of "witchdoctors"; and sorcerers' illicit use of magic. A further chapter is devoted to a discussion of the diviner and his or her relations with the ancestor spirits, divination techniques, healing, and trance states. All such beliefs and practices, according to Kidd, are founded on ignorance and fraud. Chapter Five deals extensively with customs and ritual practices associated with birth, puberty, marriage, and death. The largely anecdotal material reveals as much about colonial attitudes towards African people as it does about the societies that Kidd studied. Photographs appear throughout the text and a short piece on the Khoisan, their ideas concerning deities, and the hero Heitsi-Eibib is appended, followed by an annotated bibliography and index.

A37   Kidd, Dudley (1906). *Savage Childhood: A Study of Kafir Children*. London: Adam & Charles Black.

Kidd's dated study provides a record of his observations of African children from infancy to adolescence. The author describes birth and infancy; the development of self-consciousness; the inter-dentition period; the development of the faculties; play; work; stories; and parties. Kidd approaches what he terms the "child savage" as a representation of the absolute "zero of some anthropological and Centigrade scale," thus providing an excellent informer of adult and European thought and behavior. Appendices follow the main text, the first entitled "Idhlozi and Itongo: The Permanence of the Self." That chapter addresses African conceptions of survival after death. Beliefs and rituals associated with the ancestor spirits are briefly discussed, emphasizing a distinction between the terms used for the ancestral spirits, namely, *idhlozi* and *itongo*. Kidd explains that a split is believed to take place at death where, on the one hand, the individual facet of the personality becomes *idhlozi*. On the other hand, the corporate aspect of the personality, which is associated with the clan, becomes *itongo*, implying that the personality merges into the corporate spirits of the ancestors. The second appendix contains descriptions of birth customs, such as the use of the left hand, and discussions on the significance of play and the "danger of looking backwards." Photographs accompany the text and an index is appended.

A38   Kidd, Dudley (1908). *Kafir Socialism and the Dawn of Individualism: An Introduction to the Study of the Native Problem*. London: Adam and Charles Black.

Kidd's work is devoted to the solution of what is termed the "Native Problem" of early twentieth-century colonial South Africa. The author focuses on one aspect of this topic, which he defines as a conflict of perspectives between Western ideas of individualism and the "ingrained socialism" of the indigenous Africans in South Africa. To get to the root of the "problem," says Kidd, a study of African customs and thought is essential. Challenging European conceptions of the "savage," he points to "the most extraordinarily well-developed spirit of altruism and camaraderie, which is very rarely equalled amongst Western nations." The three chapters of Part One, "Kafir Socialism," include some discussion of topics concerning religious belief and practice. Clan systems are outlined. Kidd stresses the relations between the paramount chief and his subjects, which are symbolized in rituals such as the first-fruits ceremonies in Zulu-speaking societies. In dealing with the subject of "magic," Kidd argues that Africans do not regard magic as supernatural but as a reality of daily life in association with the forces of nature. The role of the diviner as the "bulwark of society" is discussed, as well as that of the sorcerer or witch as enemy of the community. African religion is described as "a blend of a decadent form of totemism, an elementary type of ancestor worship, and an all-pervading totemism." In addition, Kidd continues, conceptions of a supreme being in this "primitive" religion are vague. The author briefly describes ancestor rituals within the clan system and concludes the section by criticizing white interference in the politics of that system, which he believes can only accelerate its disintegration. Part Two, "The Dawn of Individualism," is devoted to solutions for the "problem." The education of the African people, he argues, is one such solution: Europeans may "be able wisely to help the Kafir to make the best of his new day."

A39   Kiernan, James P. (1982). "The Problem of Evil in the Context of Ancestral Intervention in the Affairs of the Living In Africa." *Man*, vol. 17: 287-301.

The immediate intention of Kiernan's study is to apply the ethical categories of good and evil to the context of ancestral intervention in African religion. The greater part of this article is therefore devoted to evaluating either the benevolence or malevolence of ancestral spirits. Kiernan defines such ancestors as primarily well-disposed to the living, yet realizes their capacity also for inflicting misfortune. This capacity, however, is softened by the distinguishing the malignant intention of witches from the apparent ill-intent of the ancestors which, it is believed, is actually educational and bears the individual's best interests at heart. Mention is further made of the ambivalence of the maternal ancestor as well as that of non-lineal ancestors. Kiernan's argument points to the insolubility of the problem of evil from the point of view of ancestral intervention; instead, the writer attempts to restructure the paradigm of ethical dichotomy. From this alternative perspective, Kiernan concludes his study by proposing a division of ancestors into two non-ethical categories: those who *constitute* by reinforcing the solidarity of the group and those who *allocate* by electing certain individuals of the group for special consideration.

A40   Kiernan, James P. (1995a). "African Traditional Religions in South Africa." In Martin Prozesky and John de Gruchy (eds.) *Living Faiths in South Africa*. Cape Town and Johannesburg: David Philip; New York: St. Martin's Press; London: Hurst & Company. 15-27.

Kiernan's essay addresses the indigenous religions of the South African region, including the religious beliefs and practices of the Khoikhoi, San, and Bantu-speaking peoples. The characteristics of these religious systems are described independently of the influences of white settlers and missionaries. After introducing the fundamental elements that define a religious system, Kiernan first discusses Khoisan religion, identifying the geographical regions and socioeconomic organization of the Khoi and the San peoples. Beliefs in various supernatural beings and their significance in terms of good and evil forces are addressed, as well as ways of maintaining the health and welfare of individuals and the community. Kiernan then turns to the history of the Bantu-speaking peoples, their settlements, social structures, and farming practices. The ancestors are emphasized as central to the religious beliefs and practices of the community, identified as spiritual agents of human origin. Religious remembrance of the ancestors, the author explains, supports the social order and wider political environment, where the ancestors spiritually influence the living and the living are able to fulfill their obligations to the dead. Ways of communicating with the ancestors, particularly through sacrificial ritual, are discussed. The issue of misfortune and affliction, especially in relation to witchcraft and sorcery, is analyzed and the role of herbalists and diviners in mediating religious responses and restoring normality is examined. Kiernan concludes by identifying beliefs in a supreme being or creator among Bantu-speaking societies, but asserts that "at the heart of Bantu-speakers' religion lies the cultivation of the ancestors, of the human spirit released from the constraints of time and place." Notes and a bibliography are appended.

A41   Kiernan, James P. (1995b). "The Impact of White Settlement on African Traditional Religions." In Martin Prozesky and John de Gruchy (eds.) *Living Faiths in South Africa*. Cape Town and Johannesburg: David Philip; New York: St. Martin's Press; London: Hurst and Company. 72-82.

In this essay Kiernan argues that internal transformations precipitated by demographic pressures and the external influences of white settlement and expansion have both been implicated in the destruction of indigenous South African societies and their religions. The author first charts the virtual disappearance of the Khoikhoi and the disintegration of their distinctive way of life. The San, whose mobility has supported their survival, however, retain a diversity of religious expression based on a source of spiritual power that is drawn on to counteract the harshness of their environment. San healing techniques remain central to their struggle against evil and their relationship with divinity. Turning to the internal social upheaval and southerly expansion of the Bantu-speaking peoples, culminating in a Zulu-dominated state and terminating with the arrival of white invaders, the author traces the effects of both these forces on Bantu-speakers' religion. Certain militarized ritual festivals, such as the Swazi *ncwala*, argues Kiernan, have been the result of the emergence of the nation-state. The impact of Christianity on African religion is also analyzed in some detail, particularly in terms of the continuing but modified roles of the ancestors and diviners in finding ways to cope with the socioeconomic disruption caused by white domination, migrant labor, and urbanization. Despite the influx of Christianity, the author argues, African religion has not been supplanted or entirely destroyed. Belief in sorcery and witchcraft has persisted as an explanation of misfortune, meaning that the healing practices of herbalists and diviners remain essential to African urban life. Kiernan concludes the essay by explaining other effects of contact with settler populations, most particularly the incidence of possession by sinister spirits known as *indiki* and *ufufunyane*, where again the healing treatment and spiritual protection provided by the diviner against these mystical causes of illness are constantly engaged. Despite African compromises with Christianity, the author therefore argues, African religion has "demonstrated its resilience in another way by adjusting and extending its spiritual repertoire to new developments and changing conditions." Notes and a bibliography are appended.

A42   Knappert, Jan (1977). *Bantu Myths and Other Tales*. Leiden: E. J. Brill.

Knappert's collection of annotated myths and folk tales of Bantu-speaking societies in South Africa, southern Mozambique, East Africa, and Zaire includes several Xhosa, Zulu, Sotho, and Tsonga tales. The collection comprises seven chapters, each preceded by a brief introduction, which document myths, legends, sagas, fables, proverb tales, epic tales, and true stories. Knappert introduces the volume by discussing the meaning of myth, asserting that myths usually contain narrative descriptions of the creative actions of gods and spirits and, as suggested by Eliade, often tell sacred histories that provide models for human behavior. The creation myths of most nations, Knappert suggests, trace an unbroken tradition linking the primeval act to the birth and life of the first ancestor of the tribe, clan, or dynasty. An important narrative theme is found throughout this collection regarding spiritual beings who remain unequivocally superior to human beings in the context of relations between the spirit and human worlds. Belief in the power and divinity of the elements, such as thunder, water, and the earth (usually represented as female), is likewise a recurrent theme. The final chapter presents four Zulu "true stories" told to the writer by Zulu informants, who the author defines as urbanized and educated. These stories express a strongly-held belief in spiritual beings who actively intervene in the lives of humans. Although Knappert acknowledges the contribution made by the missionaries in writing down indigenous African myths, he does however add that by bringing the Christian gospel with them, they were also responsible for trivializing the social and cultural significance of African myths by turning them into fairy tales. An index is appended.

A43   Krige, Eileen Jensen (1937). "Individual Development." In Isaac Schapera (ed.) *The Bantu-Speaking Tribes of South Africa: An Ethnological Survey*. London: George Routledge & Sons. 95-118.

Krige's chapter on the stages of individual development in Bantu-speaking societies of South Africa points to ritual practice as the foundation of life transitions. First, Krige notes that rites surrounding childbirth vary from society to society and, following Junod, argues that infancy is considered a marginal period of life that needs the constant protection of various rites and medicines until weaning at two or three years old. In describing the typical activities of childhood, Krige indicates that children frequently play a leading part in some basic rituals, for example, in medicinal rainmaking ceremonies among the Venda, Northern Sotho, and Eastern Tswana. The attainment of puberty and the education and initiation of young girls and boys are addressed at some length. The writer establishes the essential role of ritual and ceremonial in the socialization of the individual. Imitation and participation in rites educate the youth in the importance of and correct attitudes towards what is valuable to his or her society, such as cattle and crops. Various initiation schools and puberty rites (including circumcision) for boys and girls are analyzed in relation to different societies. Lastly, the writer reviews sexual education, pre-marital sexual relations, and marriage, highlighting some of the similarities and differences among various Bantu-speaking peoples. Krige gives particular attention to clarifying European misconceptions of *lobola* (the handing over of cattle in marriage) practiced in these societies. After describing the intricacies and delicacy of marriage negotiations between the two families, Krige concludes by emphasizing that once married the individual is recognized as a full member of the community, "with all the privileges and duties that entails." The chapter is annotated throughout.

A44   Kuckertz, Heinz, ed. (1981a). *Ancestor Religion in Southern Africa*. Transkei: Lumko Missiological Institute.

Kuckertz's edited collection comprises seven papers presented at the Lumko Missiological Institute's 1981 seminar on ancestor religion in southern Africa (see the essays by W. D. Hammond-Tooke, "Ancestor Religion," and by H. Kuckertz, "Ancestor Religion in African Theology," that are annotated in this chapter; and see the essays by C. M. Lamla, "The Dead," and by C.W. Manona, "The Resurgence of the Ancestor Cult," in Chapter Four and the essay by J. A. Nxumalo, "Zulu Christians and Ancestor Cults," in Chapter Five). In his introduction, "Social Anthropology and the Theme of Ancestor Religion," Kuckertz seeks to acquaint Christian theologians and pastors with the social anthropological view of ancestor religion as one aspect of African traditional religion. He therefore begins by briefly outlining modern social anthropological methods in the study of African societies, beginning with the work of Evans-Pritchard, and then proceeds to contextualize the presented papers in terms of various aspects of ancestor religion that have been identified in social anthropological research. First, Kuckertz addresses ancestor religion in the context of social anthropologists' quest for an ideal pattern. Indicating that ancestor religion implies a belief system that provides the ideal pattern of a political order, Kuckertz discusses the ritual ascription of social status according to that ideal pattern, as well as the assumption, by some scholars, that ancestor belief constitutes a psychological projection. Second, Kuckertz discusses ancestor religion in terms of how the ritual actor communicates his or her vision, referring to the debate surrounding whether ancestors are worshipped or venerated. Lastly, ancestor religion is approached in relation to the process of change in African societies, including the impact of Christianity on reinterpretations of ancestor beliefs. References in this introduction refer to the bibliography appended to the main text.

A45   Kuckertz, Heinz (1981b). "Ancestor Religion in African Theology: A Review." In Heinz Kuckertz (ed.) *Ancestor Religion in Southern Africa*. Transkei: Lumko Missiological Institute. 79-91.

This concluding paper of the Lumko Institute's seminar on ancestor religion in southern Africa reviews the papers presented in relation to other major conferences and publications devoted to the theme of the ancestors. Appreciating the seminar's acceptance of the long-held African point of view that "we live with our ancestors," Kuckertz seeks to assess the present state of theological discussion on ancestor religion. To that end, he reviews the relevant literature of both African and non-African writers (including the contributions of Placide Tempels and Bengt Sundkler), as well as the papers presented at the seminar. Kuckertz particularly refers to Nxumalo's "pastoral approach" that aims to take adequate cognizance of ancestor religious beliefs and practices in the "Christianization" of an African theology. In conclusion, the writer asserts that African theology does in fact exist and that African theologians seek to address how Africans make sense of their existence and their world in the light of the Gospel. Ancestor religion, however, is an essential part of African spiritual life and consequently represents a "testing ground for an emerging African theology." Kuckertz asks "where to go from here" in terms of African theological and liturgical direction and expression. References are appended.

A46   Kuper, Adam (1982). *Wives for Cattle: Bridewealth and Marriage in Southern Africa*. London: Routledge & Kegan Paul.

Kuper's important anthropological study of southern Bantu-speaking societies is based on the following central theme: "Bridewealth," or "the exchange of cattle for wives," exists in diverse organizational, ideological, and ritual forms and pervades the social and cultural life of southern Africa. As an institution it has adapted to radical socioeconomic change and survived the intrusions of Christian missions in the region. Kuper thus adopts a method of structural and regional comparison of related cultures, providing a framework for analysis of cultural practices. The groupings studied are based on linguistic classifications adopted for academic study, namely, the Nguni (Cape Nguni; Zulu; Swazi; Transvaal Ndebele), Sotho-Tswana, Venda, and Tsonga. The book is divided into three parts, the first of which addresses southern Bantu-speaking peoples' ideas concerning men, women, fertility, and cattle that underpin various bridewealth systems, as well as identifying the regulations and transference of rights involved in the exchange of women and cattle. The chapters of Part Two analyze the forging of alliances through bridewealth as part of traditional African political systems, critiquing the myths of clan and lineage that pervade the literature on precolonial southern Africa. Case studies are presented to elucidate adaptive transformations in marriage practice. Parallel ideological transformations and local variants in wedding ceremonies and the layout of homesteads are addressed in Part Three. Here the author indicates the ritualization of social relations and status differentiation. The complex ritual involved in wedding ceremonials—the preliminaries, the main ceremony, and the aftermath—form a consistent theme of this analysis. The importance and symbolic meanings of sacrificial offerings to the ancestors is stressed. A discussion of "kinship categories and preferential marriage" is appended, followed by chapter notes, references, and an index.

A47   Kuper, Adam (1987). "Cannibals, Beasts and Twins." *South Africa and the Anthropologist*. London: Routledge & Kegan Paul. 167-96.

The twelfth chapter of Kuper's *South Africa and the Anthropologist* focuses attention on reports of cannibalism from Lesotho by nineteenth-century French evangelist missionaries such as Eugène Casalis and Thomas Arbousset. Turning to the skepticism of other missionaries, such as Henry Callaway, and later anthropologists who perceived cannibal stories as myth rather than history, Kuper approaches these tales as an entry point into the folklore and cosmological vision of southern Bantu-speaking peoples. Most southern Bantu languages, says Kuper, use a common root word for both cannibals and ancestor spirits, implying that cannibalism is situated in the category of the supernatural. Legends often depict cannibals in direct contrast to benevolent ancestral spirits, as well as to human beings, oppositions that are expressed in many different ways. The author engages in a detailed analysis of the symbolic themes of four cannibal folktales that exemplify an opposition between disruptive, cannibalistic tricksters and benevolent mediators, portraying an array of characters that include wild animals, twins, trickster birds, heroes, and heroines. Callaway's collection of Zulu folktales, and Hammond-Tooke's interpretive analysis of its central themes, is included in the stories discussed. In conclusion, Kuper speculates on the extent to which the proposed cosmological model of the folktale can be transposed to other more elaborate cosmologies in other cultural domains of southern African indigenous societies, such as the composition of medicines, initiation rituals, and ceremonies associated with hunting. Although folktales are simple and intended for children, asserts Kuper, their structure can reveal "profound cultural premises." Notes, bibliography, and index are appended.

A48   Lang, Andrew (1901). "South African Religion." *Magic and Religion*. London: Longmans, Green and Co. 224-40.

In Chapter Twelve of his *Magic and Religion*, Lang looks at notions of a supreme being or creator in indigenous South African societies, where, he argues, the ancestors are afforded more religious reverence than the creator. Although the idea of a creator (Unkulunkulu) exists among the Zulu-speaking peoples, says Lang, he is regarded only as a "magnified non-natural man" and it is the ancestral spirits who are worshipped. Lang therefore theorizes that Zulu practice represents a degeneration of religion, where the idea of a supreme being regressed to one of a "first man," who was then neglected in favor of "serviceable ghosts." Lang addresses the theories of Hartland and Callaway, the former claiming that the Zulu had no idea of creation at all and the latter offering evidence that the Zulu regard Unkulunkulu as the Creator. Drawing on Callaway's interviews with Zulu informants reported in his text, *The Religious System of the Amazulu*, Lang affirms the possibility of this theory. He then outlines evidence of names for a creator and creation myths among other southern African societies, including the Khoisan, Xhosa, and Sotho-Tswana peoples, drawing from missionary writers such as Kolb, Hahn, Moffat, and Livingstone. However, Lang claims that most evidence points to an archaic rather than extant belief in a creator and thus to the degeneration of religion. Concluding with reference to the evolution of religious ideas towards "high religion"—whether a theory accepts or denies its existence among "low savages"—Lang draws on Frazer's *The Golden Bough* to affirm religion as "a thing evolved by mankind in accordance with their essential nature. The only question is as to the sequence of stages of evolution."

A49   Lestrade, G. P. (1935). "Bantu Praise-Poems." *The Critic*, vol. 4, no. 1: 1-10.

The "praise-poems" of the Bantu-speaking peoples of southern Africa, says Lestrade, constitute a literary genre that is not found in the literature of more "sophisticated" peoples. In this now dated paper the author analyzes the structure and function of praise-poems in the social systems of the Xhosa-, Zulu-, Venda-, and Sotho-Tswana-speaking peoples. Each people, Lestrade notes, has a clan-name, but also a praise-name that is associated with the culture and history of that particular clan. Every individual, as well as classes of animals and plants, also have at least one such praise-name according to right of birth or class. Persons who are of important status in the clan, such as a chief or warrior, have special praise-names that eulogize each one's specifically remarkable quality. Lestrade discusses the form of the praise-names consisting of a single, but often complex word, followed by a detailed analysis of the metrical structure of praise-poetry. He argues that praise-names are possibly associated with clan "totems" or ancestors, while the names of the originators of praise-poems are lost. In terms of function, clan praise-names are heard at most formal occasions, while individual praise-names and praise-verses are recited only at festivals and ceremonies where oratory plays a central part. Although this literature has mostly been orally transmitted, modern praise-poets often compose written forms. Praise-poems, concludes the author, are regarded by the southern Bantu-speaking peoples as their highest form of literary art. In the author's view, they offer a contribution to the "simpler" literature of the world, as the authentic inspiration and craftsmanship of a "primitive" people. Verses are included in the text.

A50   Lewis, I. M. (1970). "A Structural Approach to Witchcraft and Spirit-Possession." In Mary Douglas (ed.) *Witchcraft Confessions and Accusations.* London: Tavistock Publications. 293-310.

Lewis notes that while theories of witchcraft accusation have highlighted its context of social tension, a corresponding situation is also applicable to spirit possession. Case studies are included from different regions of the world, including Africa, Fiji, and India, with some reference to the Venda, Zulu, and Pondo peoples in southern Africa. Lewis draws particularly on the ethnographies of H. Stayt's *The BaVenda* (1931); H. A. Junod's *The Life of a South African Tribe* (1922); and, more recently, M. G. Whisson's (1964) and P. Worsely's (1957) analysis of witchcraft. This paper focuses on peripheral possession and how divination upholds social morality. To explain his term "peripheral possession," Lewis first notes that the spirits concerned in this phenomenon are themselves peripheral, as they have no direct moral responsibility in the community and are quite separate from other types of spirits. Second, it is indicated that these spirits often manifest by possessing marginalized types of persons in a particular society, such as women or "despised categories" of men. Connections between possession and witchcraft are analyzed in detail. The writer argues that possession by peripheral spirits can, paradoxically, be perceived as both the source of witchcraft and affliction on the one hand, and of anti-witchcraft divination and healing on the other. Some instances, however, show that peripheral spirits only play a part in witchcraft, while divination is inspired solely by those powers that uphold the society's moral code. Tables accompany the text and notes and a bibliography are appended.

A51   Macdonald, James (1889-1890). "Manners, Customs, Superstitions, and Religions of South African Tribes." *The Journal of the Anthropological Institute*, vol. 19: 264-96; vol. 20: 113-40.

In these essays, Macdonald draws on his experience as a missionary in South Africa from 1875 to 1887. The papers focus on the Xhosa-, Zulu-, and Sotho-speaking peoples, describing a sociopolitical system of "clans, tribes, sub-tribes, and families" headed by paramount chiefs, subordinate chiefs, and heads of households. Section One of the first paper addresses birth, naming, and descent, followed by male puberty rites and marriage customs. Macdonald continues with a discussion of issues around disease and death, most often believed to be caused by witchcraft if not the result of "natural decay." The healing techniques of medicine-men and the role of the diviner are described, including claims of torture and execution of accused "wizards." Funeral and mourning rites for a chief are highlighted, emphasizing the participation of the ancestor spirits in the daily lives of the people. Section Two moves on to an explanation of African jurisprudence concerning property and inheritance, followed by details of customs to do with fire; food; hunting and fishing; agriculture; and war. In the third section, Macdonald interweaves observations about military, religious, and common law institutions among Bantu-speaking peoples, discussing a diverse range of topics that include oaths and ordeals; salutations; arithmetic; measurement of time; games and dances; magic and divination; and rain and lightning doctors. The second paper continues with a brief outline of Zulu political history and military organization. Claiming that "it is difficult to exhaust the customs and small ceremonial usages of a savage people," Macdonald discusses, again, a wide variety of beliefs and practices among southern African peoples. These include: female initiation ceremonies and sexual customs; murder; the "doctrine of souls" and the world of the ancestral spirits; ritual sacrifices associated with the ancestors; sidereal myths and rituals; beliefs about the origin of death; luck and evil omens; rules of social hierarchy; manners; and family customs. As well as his personal observations and interpretations, Macdonald at times draws on the writings and methods of other missionaries and scholars such as C. Brownlee; J. G. Frazer; J. Sutton; and G. M. Theal.

A52   Marquard, Leopold, and T. G. Standing (1939). *The Southern Bantu.* London: Oxford University Press.

Marquard and Standing's dated work on the Bantu-speaking peoples of South Africa in the mid-twentieth century covers economic, political, and social institutions and the effects of European colonization and Christianity. Religious belief forms a recurrent theme of the book, interwoven as it is with all spheres of African life. However, in Chapter Four, "Bantu Magic and Religion," the authors specifically address African religious beliefs and ritual practices. Although there is some form of belief in a supreme being, the authors assert, belief in the ancestral spirits is the foundation of religion among these peoples. Marquard and Standing thus interpret ancestor beliefs and veneration from the denigrating point of view that they represent not only the religion of a "primitive" people, but constitute a debased form of higher religions that existed earlier among the Chinese, Japanese, and Ancient Greeks and Romans. Different types of spirits and sorcery are discussed, as well as the participation of the ancestors among the living and sacrifices performed to propitiate them. Magical rites conducted in relation to the sacred position of chiefs are mentioned and rain-making is particularly highlighted in the context of the harsh natural environment of African life. Sacred specialists—both herbalists and diviners—are emphasized, detailing their alliance with the ancestors in healing techniques and divination. Divination techniques are referred to as "tricks of the trade" and diviners as the "cleverest people" in the community, who consequently hold the most power. Superstition and fear of sorcery and magical beings, such as the *Thikoloshe*, figure widely in the life of Bantu-speaking societies, say the authors, often leading to cruel and callous customs. The chapter concludes with derogatory observations about women in Bantu-speaking societies and further assertions about presumed and stereotypical differences between black Africans and white Europeans. A short bibliography and an index are appended to the main text.

A53   Mbiti, John S. (1969). *African Religions and Philosophy*. London: Heinemann.

Mbiti aims to address the difficulties involved in studying African traditional religions and philosophy, given that these religions are based solely on oral tradition. It is argued that each of the many peoples of the African continent has its own religious system, indicating a plurality of religions. However, the central aim of the study is to identify and analyze a singular philosophy that might lie behind the religious beliefs and practices of those plural systems and the different issues that permeate African life. Mbiti further emphasizes that there is no formal distinction between the sacred and the secular in African traditional life and therefore suggests that religion is inextricably interwoven with the everyday life of the community and individual, even extending to the spiritual realm beyond physical death. Underlying all these factors, Mbiti notes, is the overarching importance of the life of community, signifying that every individual born into an African community, as an inseparable part of that corporate structure, is religious. Twenty chapters cover a wide range of topics, including concepts, beliefs, and ritual practice concerning ideas of God; ancestral spirits; kinship and the stages of life; sacred specialists; mystical powers, witchcraft, and sorcery; and ethics. These issues are discussed in relation to many indigenous African societies, including frequent reference to South African groupings, most particularly the Khoisan; Sotho-Tswana; Zulu; and Venda. A bibliography and indexes are appended.

A54   Mbiti, John S. (1970). *Concepts of God in Africa*. London: SPCK.

Mbiti's book presents a systematic study of African reflection about God in the context of African traditional religion and philosophy. African names for and concepts of God are addressed, as well as notions of God in relation to the realm of spiritual beings, human beings, animals, plants, natural objects, and other phenomena. Mbiti draws on literature pertaining to more than two hundred and seventy African peoples, including frequent reference to the indigenous peoples of South Africa, such as Khoikhoi; Pondo; Sotho-Tswana; Swazi; Tsonga; Venda; and Zulu societies. Mbiti's approach takes on a broad perspective and the book is divided into four comprehensive sections. Part One addresses "the nature of God," covering intrinsic, eternal, and moral attributes of God identified in African religion. Part Two is devoted to "the active attributes of God" in the context of creation, nurture, healing, governance, and protection against evil and affliction. "Anthropomorphic and natural attributes of God" form the basis of Part Three, where Mbiti looks at how concepts of God relate to particular social roles in human life; animals; plants; other spiritual beings; and both heavenly and earthly phenomena. Part Four, "God and Man," offers a detailed account of human activity in the framework of African religion, focusing on methods and expressions of worship, ritual practices, sacred specialists, ethics, and eschatological concepts. The following are appended to the main text: notes; bibliography; a list of African peoples, their countries, and names for God; an index of African peoples; and an index of subjects.

A55   McAllister, P. A. (1993). "Indigenous Beer in Southern Africa: Functions and Fluctuations." *African Studies*, vol. 52, no. 1: 71-88.

McAllister's paper is divided into two main parts, the first of which offers an outline of the historical and contemporary use of beer in the ritual and social life of the southern Bantu-speaking peoples. The history of beer-brewing in southern Africa, the author notes, is recorded from the time of the Portuguese travelers in the sixteenth century. Regional variations in methods of brewing beer among Nguni, Sotho-Tswana, Tsonga, and Venda are accounted for, as well as the consumption of beer for its nutritional value rather than for intoxication. But it is the ritual use of beer all over southern Africa as a major component of reconciliation and the maintenance of sociability and communal harmony that is emphasized. Beer drinks might be a part of social gatherings, harvest celebration, work parties, and economic activities, sometimes exclusive to kin and at other times, open to wider communal attendance. In any event, drinking is subject to formal rules of distribution and social hierarchy. The second part of the paper focuses on a case study of fluctuations in the availability and use of beer among Xhosa-speakers of the Cape from 1800 to 1950. McAllister identifies several causes for the fluctuating rates of brewing and consumption of beer during that time: fluctuations in grain production; government regulation; missionary influence; and Xhosa resistance to white domination through the medium of millenarian movements and informal associations of Xhosa farm workers in the Eastern Cape. In the Transkei, McAllister concludes, changing rates of the brewing and consumption of beer among Xhosa-speakers has long been subject to fluctuating economic, political, and religious pressures. Furthermore, he argues, beer is a "cultural resource" for coping with deprivation, giving expression to social change over which the people themselves have little control. Notes and references are appended.

A56   McVeigh, Malcolm J. (1974). *God in Africa: Conceptions of God in African Traditional Religion and Christianity*. Hartford, Vermont: Claude Stark.

In this volume, McVeigh, an American theologian and Christian missionary to Africa, presents an in-depth analysis of Edwin Smith's view of the relationship between Christian and African traditional conceptions of God. McVeigh's definition of African traditional religion, as an equivalent of other world religions, refers to religious beliefs and practices of sub-Saharan Africa before the arrival of Islam and Christianity. Although the book therefore addresses the traditional religion of the indigenous peoples of the continent in general, significant reference to the religious life of Bantu-speaking peoples of South Africa is included. Topics addressed include: the "personality" of God; monotheism; God's love for humanity; divine revelation; and worship in relation to the ancestors and a supreme being or God. Identifying the major weakness of Smith's approach to be his use of an evolutionary framework for the study of religion, McVeigh focuses on drawing out the great value of Smith's work for understanding African traditional religion, particularly in the following areas: the relationship between the seen and unseen worlds; the role of diviners and prophets; the significance of dreams and taboos; and the importance of belief in God. Photographs accompany the text and a glossary, bibliography, and chapter notes are appended to the text.

A57   Molema, S. M. (1920). *The Bantu Past and Present*. Edinburgh: W. Green & Sons; reprint. Cape Town: Struik, 1963.

Molema's text on the indigenous peoples of Africa frequently addresses those encountered in South Africa in the days of the Christian mission to that region. Chapter Thirteen, "Religious Beliefs," begins by defining the religion of the "Bantu" as "Spiritism or Animism" and "Heathenism or Paganism." Drawing on the definitions of religion of F. Max Müller, James Williams, and James Frazer, Molema concludes that the Bantu had a religion, although it was "primitive and unevolved." Referring to Xhosa, Zulu, and Sotho-Tswana indigenous African societies, among others, Molema offers his interpretations of the components of religious belief. Arguing that the ancestor spirits constituted their deity and shaped their destinies to greater or lesser degrees of malevolence, the author emphasizes "magic" as the very foundation of African religion. It is defined as the art or science of controlling natural and supernatural forces, performed by sacred specialists who are commonly known as magicians, witchdoctors, medicine men, rain doctors, or diviners. Defining their rituals as superstition that is characteristic of ignorance, Molema refers to practices such as doctoring armies, diagnosis and healing, the smelling out of witches, and other forms of divination. Xhosa prophecies and the Cattle Killing of 1857 are described in some detail, advanced by Molema as an example of the "curse of superstition." Comparisons with European witchcraft beliefs in the Middle Ages are developed. The Africans' hazy and vague idea of God, as Molema defines it, is argued to show a spark of "higher faith." Some discussion is also devoted to African cosmogonic myth, as well as philosophy and practices associated with life and death. A bibliography and chronological chart precede the main text. Constitutional documents, brief accounts of the Thembu and Pondo peoples, and an index are appended.

A58   Müller, Aegidius (1906-1907). "Wahrsagerei bei den Kaffern." *Anthropos*, vol. 1: 762-78; vol. 2: 43-58.

Müller begins by asserting that superstition governs every aspect of African life. Laws, customs, practices, and religion all fall under its sway. The religious system rests upon the reverence of ancestors (*amadhlosi*) and the functions of sacred specialists called *isangoma*. According to the author, the *isangoma* is the "priest" of the people and mediates between the living and the dead. Special care must be taken to distinguish between the *isangoma* and "magicians." The *isangoma* is viewed as the guardian of society and works for the collective good, as opposed to magicians or witches who operate from private imperatives. This position in the group lends the office great respect and the influence of the practitioner is almost unlimited. The responsibilities of the *isangoma* lie in the "smelling out" of criminals or evil magicians; the location of lost objects; and the discovery of the type and cause of illness. At this point the office of the *isangoma* may overlap with that of the *inyanga* (doctor), and usually entails a wide knowledge of medicinal plants. However, Müller reiterates that the major functions are the "smelling out" of sources of evil and mediating between the group and the ancestors. A large section of the paper deals with the qualifications, selection, and training of the *isangoma*. Asserting that the office requires a blend of imagination and fraud, the author says that candidates are recruited from the most intelligent members of the group. Both sexes may practice. Once a candidate is located (usually on the basis of an active dream life), he or she is apprenticed to an experienced practitioner. A personal narrative by a woman named Paula illustrates the nature of this apprenticeship. The chief methods of the *isangoma* are the casting of bones or sticks and these are described in detail. The prolonged questioning of the client is also described and illustrated with an actual instance of the practice. The paper concludes with brief remarks on the use of crystals and the praying mantis in the *isangoma's* activities. The text is in German.

A59   Ngubane, Harriet (1986). "The Predicament of the Sinister Healer: Some Observations on 'Ritual Murder' and the Professional Role of the *Inyanga*." In Murray Last and G. L. Chavanduka (eds.) *The Professionalization of African Medicine*. Manchester: Manchester University Press. 189-204.

Ngubane's essay addresses the conceptual difficulties involved in relating indigenous and Western systems of medicine in southern Africa, focusing on the role of the *inyanga* and the issue of ritual homicide. In indigenous systems, the *inyanga* prescribes treatments, while the special clairvoyant powers of the *isangoma* (diviner) focus on diagnosis of a patient's affliction. The *inyanga*, however, must be able to provide medicine that will act on social, natural, and supernatural causes of misfortunes, social ailments, and physical illnesses. Turning to the contentious issue of the apparent increase in ritual killings prescribed by *inyangas* in recent years, particularly in Swaziland, Ngubane compares Western and traditional African conceptual systems and the different circumstances in which intentional ending of human life is condoned in both systems. In the past, argues Ngubane, African traditional medicine did entertain the possibility of attempting to remedy ills by cutting flesh from a living person who is then killed, but it was an extremely rare prescription in the direst of circumstances. It was not, as the missionaries once thought, a manifestation of African "benighted savagery," so today's "*muti* murders" do not mark a return of old evil practices. Ngubane concludes by arguing that these homicides, which are generally demanded by the client rather than by the *inyanga*, have emerged from the breakdown of society and from social conditions that have convinced the ambitious that they need this resource of power. She also suggests that the benefits of integrating indigenous medicine into Western systems are limited—although not impossible—not because of practical difficulties, but rather because of conceptual differences. More might be gained if the two systems continue to run in parallel and Western-trained students are taught about the conceptual systematics of indigenous medicine. Then they will gain an understanding of why African patients show no sign of abandoning traditional medicine.

A60   Opland, Jeff (1971). "'Scop' and Imbongi—Anglo-Saxon and Bantu Oral Poets." *English Studies in Africa*, vol. 14: 161-78.

While the objective of Opland's paper is to investigate how the oral tradition of Bantu-speaking peoples in South Africa might illuminate that of the Anglo-Saxon, it includes useful insights into indigenous South African literary forms that are often linked to religious myth and ancestor beliefs. Opland discusses the interplay between Slavic, Anglo-Saxon, and Bantu oral traditions, arguing that studies of the Slavic can lead to a deeper understanding of the Bantu oral tradition, while the Bantu oral tradition can increase our appreciation of the Anglo-Saxon. After examining existing literary studies of Slavic and Anglo-Saxon oral traditions, Opland suggests that the southern Bantu-speaking peoples live in a society that is in many ways similar to that of the ancient Anglo-Saxons. Furthermore, the relationship between the Nguni languages, such as Swazi, Xhosa, and Zulu, is analogous to early Germanic languages. He therefore turns to Nguni praise-poetry and focuses on Zulu oral tradition to analyze the structure and function of clan names, individual praises, and praise poems. The role of the *imbongi* (praise singer), who composes and sings the praises of the chief and his ancestors on important occasions, is highlighted. With reference to Cope's studies, he indicates that the *imbongi* is a mediator between chief and subjects, and his performances include praise and criticism. The dynamic spontaneity of his compositions and recitations show that it is the *imbongi's* facility with words, not his good memory, that is most admired. Opland concludes with a comparative study of Bantu *izibongo* (praise poems) and Anglo-Saxon poetry, identifying where the role of the "scop" may have been similar to that of the *imbongi*. Footnotes accompany the text.

A61   Opland, Jeff (1980). "Southeastern Bantu Eulogy and Early Indo-European Poetry." *Research in African Literature*, vol. 2, no. 3: 295-307.

In this paper Opland explores what is popularly known as "praise poetry" among Xhosa- and Zulu-speaking peoples in South Africa so as to understand analogous phenomena in early Indo-European societies. *Izibongo*, the poetry of Nguni language groups, speaks not only of persons, living or dead, but also of clans, animals, and even inanimate objects. However, among Xhosa-speaking people, not all who utter poetry are *imbongi*. Always male, the *imbongi* produces poems about the chief or important visitors at ceremonial occasions. Focusing on the emotional character of the performance, Opland shows how an intimate bond exists between chief and poet, where the *imbongi* functions as "herald, historian, genealogist, and custodian of lore." Most important, in terms of Xhosa religion, is Opland's reminder that *izibongo* must be seen in a ritual context, since it plays a critical role in the veneration of the ancestors. Likewise, Henry Callaway's transcriptions of oral testimonies about the Zulu religion point to a similar religious function of *izibongo* in the veneration of the ancestors. Since the Zulu chief is a sacred ruler, says Opland, he is the living representative of the royal lineage. The *imbongi* therefore not only addresses the chief's person, but he also invokes the blessings of the chief's ancestors for the well-being of the people. Noting that early Indo-European poetry was eulogistic in form, like that of Xhosa- and Zulu-speaking peoples today, Opland concludes that study of Xhosa and Zulu praise poetry not only increases our understanding of African folklore, but also that of ancient Indo-European culture. Notes are appended.

A62   Parrinder, Geoffrey (1967). *African Mythology*. London: Paul Hamlyn.

Parrinder's illustrated volume describes the mythology of the indigenous peoples of Africa south of the Sahara. In his introduction Parrinder discusses Africa's ancient oral tradition, noting that myths and stories have only begun to be collected and written down in recent times. He argues that African art also provides a "sacred literature" that symbolizes humanity's stages of birth, life, and death. Since religion is an essential part of African myth, it forms the basis of many of the chapters. Topics covered include myths, beliefs, and rituals associated with the creator; God; the first human beings; the mystery of birth and origins of death; gods and spirits; divination; ancestors; and witches and monsters. The material presented in this book is drawn from many parts of Africa, including myths and rituals from the Swazi, Xhosa, Zulu, Venda, and Sotho-Tswana. A reading list, acknowledgments, and index are appended. A richly diverse collection of illustrations and photographs appear throughout the text.

A63   Partridge, A. C., ed. (1973). *Folklore of Southern Africa*. Cape Town: Purnell.

Partridge's anthology comprises myths and legends collected from the oral traditions of the Khoisan and Bantu-speaking peoples of southern Africa. The editor emphasizes that the folklore of the indigenous African peoples was not written down before Europeans came to southern Africa. The first to record African folklore were mostly Christian missionaries. Some of the most notable of the editor's sources, from the late nineteenth and early twentieth centuries, include W. H. I. Bleek; Frank Brownlee; C. L. Harries; and G. M. Theal. In his introduction, Partridge offers a brief definition of folklore and myth; an account of his sources; and an outline of the history and languages of the Khoisan and Bantu-speaking peoples. The volume is divided into two parts, the first of which presents "Eight Bushman and Hottentot Tales" comprising six sections, each with a brief introduction by the editor. Khoisan stories, myths, and prayers are included, some of which provide a valuable source of insight into Khoisan religious beliefs, for example, "The Origin of Death." The eight sections of the second part, "Bantu Tales," present a range of stories from Xhosa, Zulu, Venda, and Sotho-Tswana mythology. Illustrations are included in the text and notes follow each section. A brief bibliography is appended to the main text.

A64   Pauw, B. A. (1974). "Ancestor Beliefs and Rituals Among Urban Africans." *African Studies*, vol. 33, no. 2: 99-111.

Pauw's work draws extensively on Monica Wilson's research in the eastern Cape; Hellman's in Johannesburg; and, especially, Möller's work among

Xhosa-speakers in Soweto. He also reviews studies of ancestor rituals and ancestor veneration among Zulu-speakers in KwaMashu; Langa; Port Elizabeth; and Atteridgeville, near Pretoria. The article addresses two views concerning ancestor beliefs among black South Africans: First, that ancestor cults have not been adapted to urban conditions and have therefore grown weaker, while "magical" beliefs and rituals have persisted and been adapted to urban needs. And second, that both witchcraft and, more importantly, ancestor beliefs continue to provide alternative explanations for the misfortunes experienced in urban life. Pauw favors the second view, presenting his interpretive analysis under the following topics: the incidence of ancestor beliefs and rituals; the adaptation of ancestor beliefs; the form of ancestor rituals; and ancestor beliefs and rituals in relation to social structure. In conclusion, Pauw argues that ancestor veneration, as well as divination and healing, are resorted to in these urban areas. He claims that reliance on ancestors is not an "anachronistic survival" but a specific adaptation to processes of cultural change in the urban social structure. For example, the importance of kinship ties—the basis of ancestor rituals—has been maintained in the cities, but with greater attention being given to non-patrilineal kin. Particular emphasis on a matrifocal trend, Pauw indicates, is thus a uniquely urban phenomenon. Association through groups other than kin as a basis for ancestor veneration is also discussed, especially in the context of groups formed for explicitly religious purposes. Some urban African Christian believers, for example, assert that the ancestors and God work together, a phenomenon that Pauw defines as a form of religious "syncretism." References are appended.

A65   Pettersson, Olof (1953). *Chiefs and Gods: Religious and Social Elements in the South Eastern Bantu Kingship*. Lund: CWK Gleerup.

This publication of Pettersson's doctoral thesis problematizes the sacred character of chieftainship among the indigenous societies of south-eastern South Africa, analyzed from a social and religious perspective. First, the author documents the sociopolitical structure of the peoples studied, namely, the Nguni (Xhosa- and Zulu-speakers); Tsonga; Sotho-Tswana; and Venda-Shona, asserting that the chief has supreme power over his people as their leader in war and owner of the land. Pettersson then accounts for the religious background of those societies. Included is an examination of ancestor veneration and associated ritual practices. This is followed by an analysis of African concepts of a supreme being, creation myths, and beliefs in heavenly beings. Following nineteenth-century evolutionist theories of "primitive" religions, the author claims that the dividing line between magic and religion in African religious life is blurred. Central to his study is the relation between chieftainship and religion (and magic). He indicates that the chief's authority and sacred character are founded on the authority of the ancestors and the "national cult" of the dead chiefs. Furthermore, he notes that the chief fulfills the position of supreme protector of the special "magic medicine" used at national ceremonies. These ceremonies are described in detail (such as the first-fruits festivals and rites connected with warfare), as well as ceremonies for the installation of the chief. Burial and death rites for deceased chiefs are likewise analyzed. Pettersson notes that the graves of chiefs represent the sacred space of national ancestors, who, he argues, constitute national "gods." The living chief's authority thus rests on the people's belief in his status as the representative of deceased national ancestor "gods." Only at their commission, Pettersson concludes, does the chief reign over his subjects and act as the sacred intermediary between the past and the present. A list of abbreviations, a bibliography, and indexes are appended.

A66   Riesman, Paul (1986). "The Person and the Life Cycle in African Social Life and Thought." *African Studies Review*, vol. 29, no. 2: 71-138.

Riesman's general analysis of African conceptions of the person or African understandings of the self reviews psychoanalytical, social-anthropological, and phenomenological approaches. Occasional references are made to examples of indigenous societies in South Africa. Divided into several sections, the article first looks at the "African person and personality in psychoanalysis and other psychologies." Particular emphasis is placed on psychoanalytical studies of the self in Africa, as well as on the valuable contributions of psychological anthropology and gender studies. Reference is made to Wulf Sachs' psychoanalysis of an African diviner-healer in South Africa, which was published in *Black Hamlet* (1937), and the relation between psychological instability and social conditions of oppression. "Contributions of social anthropology" includes notes on ethnographical studies in British research and theoretical studies of the person and the life cycle in Africa. Symbolic and structural studies of ritual are discussed, including children's rituals of transition and initiation, healing, and death rites. Luc de Heusch's work on rites of passage among the Thonga is highlighted, especially in relation to the treatment of newborn infants. In a section entitled "Symbolic analysis of the person in relation to social structure, history and mode of livelihood" particular attention is given to Berglund's and Ngubane's work on the Zulu-speakers of South Africa, indicating that these writers value the people's own understanding of the world as much as they do social context. Lastly, the author reviews research that focuses on "Phenomenological perspectives and artistic expressions." The essay as a whole moves between social scientific explanations of people's behavior and the people's own understanding of themselves, their humanity, and their society. Riesman concludes that being a person is "essentially a process of making meaning" in which "others" are an integral part of that process. Extensive notes and references are appended.

A67   Ross, B. J. (1926). "The Religion of the Bantu and that of Early Israel." *The South African Outlook*, vol. 56, no. 662: 156-58.

In this brief article Ross identifies some of the common elements he finds in the
religions of ancient Israel and the Bantu-speaking peoples of Africa, especially
among Xhosa-speakers. Sacrificial ritual and the role played by ancestral spirits
in that context are particularly noted. Adhering to an evolutionist framework for
the study of religion, Ross argues that the moral and ethical development of a
religion depends on the philosophy and spirituality of the minority elite above
the clinging of the "ignorant masses" to the gross, material elements of religious
practice. Tracing this progress of ancient Israelite religion through the spiritual
power of the prophets and great religious thinkers, Ross points to a similar
process at work in the religion of Bantu-speakers. Where the masses adhere to
the ancestral spirits, the thinkers perceive those spirits as mediators between
humanity and a supreme spiritual being. For Ross, this element of monotheism
and its similarity to Christianity indicates the onward progress of African religion and the presence of "thinkers" within it. Since African thinkers have not
had the benefit of written tradition, concludes Ross, they show even greater
mental and moral quality. Ross' conclusion shows his sympathetic attitude to
African religion, which is nevertheless trapped in colonialist stereotypes of race:
"The supreme test of a people's mind is the religion they have produced. Tried
by this standard the Bantu are far in advance in mental and moral fibre of Ne-
groes and Orientals who surpass them far in arts and crafts."

A68   Schapera, Isaac, ed. (1934). *Western Civilization and the Natives of
South Africa: Studies in Culture Contact*. London: George Routledge & Sons.

This collection of essays contributed by several prominent early twentieth-
century ethnologists and anthropologists traces the impact of European colonization and administration on the "traditional" life of Bantu-speaking peoples in
South Africa. In this context, Schapera offers the work as a contribution towards
informing European administrative policy and the solution of the European notion of the "Native problem." The introductory chapter, by Schapera, describes
precolonial Bantu-speaking culture and social structure and includes a detailed
discussion of religion and "magic" covering annual ceremonies; ancestor beliefs
and ritual practices; notions of a supreme being; diviners; and witchcraft. Although at times profoundly patronizing in tone, Schapera's depiction of African
traditional religion and culture challenges the derogatory misconceptions of
early colonists and missionaries. W. M. Eiselen's chapter, on the other hand,
discusses the effects of Christianity on indigenous religion and lauds the efforts
of pioneering missionaries and the progress of Christian conversion over African "heathenism." Subsequent chapters address the effects of Western education
and culture on the communal life, language, and music of Bantu-speaking peo-

ples. The economic and social conditions of Africans in rural and urban areas are further discussed, as is the structure of contemporary European "Native administration." Alfred Hoernlé's chapter offers an incisive critique of European fears of "race-mixture"—a theme that has shaped many white attitudes towards black South Africans—while D. D. T. Jabavu's concluding chapter outlines the injustices that underpin the discontent that Africans experience under European rule. Photographs appear in the text and a bibliography, index, and map are appended.

A69   Schapera, Isaac, ed. (1937). *The Bantu-speaking Tribes of South Africa: An Ethnographical Survey.* London: George Routledge and Sons.

Schapera's collection of essays represents a watershed work in the context of South African ethnology in the first half of the twentieth century. A total of eighteen chapters cover diverse aspects of life among Bantu-speaking peoples, including their environment and history; domestic, social, and economic institutions; political and legal systems; religion and culture; arts and language; and the influences of European colonization and culture contact. A variety of prominent ethnologists and anthropologists contribute to the volume, including, among others, N. J. van Warmelo; W. M. Eiselen; W. Hoernlé; E. J. Krige; and M. Hunter. Chapters that are most relevant to the study of African traditional religion in South Africa are listed in this section under the relevant authors (see: Eiselen and Schapera; Hoernlé; Krige). In the last three chapters, covering "Cultural Changes in Tribal Life" (Schapera); "The Bantu on European-owned Farms" (Hunter); and "The Native in the Towns" (Hellman), processes of change developing in African religious life and ritual practice form one of the consistent themes of discussion. The influence of the Christian missions and the emergence of African independent churches are also addressed. Photographs appear throughout the volume. A bibliography, indexes, and map are appended.

A70   Schapera, Isaac, ed. (1941). *Select Bibliography of South African Native Life and Problems: Compiled for the Inter-University Committee for African Studies.* London: Oxford University Press (Humphrey Milford).

This useful bibliography of books and articles relating to the indigenous peoples of South Africa comprises five main sections: physical anthropology; archaeology; ethnography; modern status and conditions; linguistics. The section on ethnography includes sub-sections covering the following: General works and comparative studies; Bushmen; Hottentots; Bergdama; Bantu; Ambo; Herero; Shona; Venda and Lemba; Transvaal Sotho; Tswana; South Sotho; South Nguni; North Nguni; Swazi; Nguni offshoots; Tonga; Chopi. Works on religion and related topics appear in all these sections. *Modern Status and Conditions:*

Supplements I-III, 1939-1963 (New York: Kraus Reprint Co.) has since been compiled by librarianship students at the University of Cape Town and published as an update of that section in Schapera's bibliography.

A71   Setiloane, Gabriel M. (1986). *African Theology: An Introduction*. Johannesburg: Skotaville Press.

In this brief book Setiloane defines African theology by identifying and explaining its main features and claims. Initiating an innovative theological path, the author shows how African traditional religion and culture form the basis of an African understanding of Christianity in South Africa. First, Setiloane returns to sources of knowledge in African oral tradition and creation mythology. A discussion of fundamental African conceptions of community and "being a person" follows. In explaining the role of the ancestors, Setiloane explains that participation in the community does not end with death. Moving to the question of African ideas of God or a supreme being, the author focuses on a case study of the Sotho-Tswana understanding of God, including the misinterpretations of this understanding by early Christian missionaries such as Casalis and Moffat. Setiloane concludes with sections devoted to defining African theology and its claims as well as discussing how it relates to Black theology. Analyzing the effects of interaction among traditional African spirituality, the Christian missions, and Western theology, Setiloane bases his definition on the argument that "African Theology is an attempt to verbalise African reflection about Divinity (do theology) from the perspective of African grassroots background and culture." Notes and a list of names and attributes of divinity in Africa are appended.

A72   Simons, H. J. (1957). "Tribal Medicine: Diviners and Herbalists." *African Studies*, vol. 16, no. 2: 85-92.

In this now dated article Simons assesses the legal status and therapeutic value of indigenous African medicine practiced by herbalists and diviners in South Africa. Approaching his analysis from a Western perspective, Simons notes that although "tribal" medicine is permeated with "magic" and "superstition," both the state and modern medical practice show little respect for the indigenous practitioner's remedies—both "magical" and "empirical"—that bring psychological and physiological relief to many Africans. Associated ideas in indigenous societies are surveyed, such as divination, witchcraft, and sorcery, and parallel attitudes towards magic in medieval European societies are identified. Pointing to a worldview that combines myth and reality and comprises a belief that all forms of life and substance are charged with a supernatural force or are subject to the spirit world, Simons specifies his interpretation of contradictions between this metaphysical cosmology and modern materialistic science. Adhering to an approach that defines African religion as superstition, Simons argues that "superstitious" beliefs and practices are still prevalent in South Africa, although, he continues, this does not deter Africans from using European medical and hospital services. Simons concludes that if the precedent of European medical history is followed, "superstitious" beliefs are likely to decline as more Africans become trained in science and "rational thought." Footnotes accompany the text.

A73   Smith, Edwin W. (1929). *The Secret of the African: Lectures on African Religion*. London: United Society's Press.

This book presents Smith's lectures on African religion delivered at the Church Missionary Society in 1927 and 1928, and aims to describe African religion in a way that is free from Christian bias. In Chapter One, "The Basis of African Religion," Smith argues that Africans possess dogmas and creeds that underpin religious experience, including belief in a creator, a soul, the survival of personality after death, and the reality of communication with the spirits of the deceased. Chapter Two looks at the complementary alliance between magic and religion (for example, in rain-making ceremonies) that exists not only in African religion, but also in aspects of Christianity. Smith critically analyzes the connotations of using the word "magic" in relation to African religion, critiquing former anthropological interpretations, such as James Frazer's. He suggests that the word be discarded in favor of the term "dynamism." Chapter Three, "African Spiritism," proposes that African belief in the spirit world is not analogous to Christian belief in the immortality of the soul. Smith discusses, rather, African belief in the survival of the human personality after death, describing burial and death rites and veneration of the ancestors. The next three chapters include discussion of an awareness of God in South, Central, and West Africa. In relation to the religion of the Bantu-speaking peoples of South Africa, Smith critically analyzes the missionaries' imposed understandings of African notions of a "Supreme God" symbolized in the names Tixo (Xhosa); Unkulunkulu and uMvelinqangi (Zulu); and Modimo (Sotho-Tswana). He concludes that South African peoples are aware of a God, but have no personal name for him and rarely pray to him, since the ancestors are central to their religious belief and practice. Smith's concluding chapter, "The Strengths and Weaknesses of African Religion," measures the worth of African religion against three criteria, comprising emotional, rational, and practical value. Smith finds that Africans are undoubtedly religious but, even so, they dwell "in the twilight" of religion. In the end, therefore, he measures African religion against Christianity, asserting that acceptance of the Christian Gospel is the only hope for African religious faith to withstand the "shock of contact with the materialism of Western civilization."

A74   Smith, Edwin W. (1950). "The Idea of God Among South African Tribes." In Edwin W. Smith (ed.) *African Ideas of God.* London: Edinburgh House Press. 78-134.

In this chapter of Smith's *African Ideas of God,* the writer discusses the social organization and religion of the Khoisan and Bantu-speaking peoples of southern Africa. He begins by reviewing literature on the subject, ranging from early European missionaries, who posited that the indigenous peoples of South Africa had no religion at all, to anthropological studies of ancestor veneration. But Smith's focus is to ask whether "these peoples have any idea of a supreme God over and above their human ancestors and the impersonal powers of dynamism." First, the author explores the rich mythology of the San and the Khoikhoi, drawing on the work of Theophilus Hahn to discuss their dualistic notions of good and evil gods personified in the names //Gaunab, the evil god, and Tsui//goab, who, according to Hahn, was revered as the supreme being. The next section, on the Xhosa, examines ideas of a supreme being, recognizing that the name Tixo, of Khoisan origin, became the missionaries' Xhosa name for the Christian God. Turning to the Zulu and their cosmogonic mythology, Smith discusses permutations of African and European missionary interpretations of uNkulunkulu, uMvelinqangi, and other Zulu names for heavenly beings. Finding similar notions and names for deities and original ancestors among the Swazi, the author refers to Hilda Kuper's anthropological studies of Swazi religion and ritual. Similar analyses are also presented on the religious beliefs and ideas of God among the Tsonga; Sotho-Tswana; and Lovedu, Venda, and Shona. Reference is made to several prominent anthropological and missionary writers. Smith concludes by arguing that the supreme being is overshadowed by the "ancestral gods" in the indigenous religion of South Africa, suggesting that a history of war and social disruption led to loss of faith and "bred unbelief and ethical deterioration." Footnotes accompany the text.

A75   Speight, W. L. (1935). "Human Sacrifice in South Africa." *The Nongqai,* vol. 26, no. 2: 15; 164.

This brief article in the South African police journal examines the practice of "ritual murder" among indigenous African societies in South Africa. The writer argues that European rule failed to eradicate this practice, which, he claims, might be carried out for various purposes, such as to manufacture "*muti*" from body parts for use by indigenous doctors or to bring rain during severe drought. Examples of cases that had come before the South African court are detailed, including the "execution" of a minor chief who was accused of witchcraft and held responsible for the cessation of rain. The article is entirely descriptive, although marked by its graphic and hyperbolic description of gruesome bodily mutilation and violence.

A76   Theal, George McCall (1919). *Ethnography and the Condition of South Africa Before A.D. 1505*. London: George Allen and Unwin.

Theal's comprehensive study of ancient documents and contemporary archaeological research describes the inhabitants of the region south of the Zambesi and Kunene Rivers before Europeans arrived in South Africa. The author draws extensively on the writings of nineteenth- and early twentieth-century missionaries and comparative religionists, such as T. Hahn; W. H. I. Bleek; and G. W. Stow. The first six of a total of seventeen chapters deal with diverse aspects of Khoisan life. The author's topics include Khoisan wall-paintings and rock engravings; "superstition" and religion; ritual dance; marriage and initiation customs; and myth and folklore. Discussion of Khoisan religion draws on Hahn's reports of invocations to the moon and the role of the hero Tsui//goab, or Heitsi-Eibib, in Khoisan myth. The remaining chapters cover aspects pertaining to the Bantu-speaking peoples of southern Africa, beginning with a discussion of their origins, migrations, and settlement patterns. Particular reference is made to Greek, Arabic, and Persian literature, including the reports of the traveler, Aboul Hacan Ali el Masoudi of Baghdad. Chapters Ten, Eleven, Fourteen, and Fifteen are of particular interest for the study of African religion, covering religious beliefs and practices; "superstitions" and customs; and folklore. Theal discusses beliefs in ancestral spirits and associated ritual practices, emphasizing beliefs associated with death and the burial rites for chiefs. Concepts of a powerful being or original ancestor, such as Qamata (Xhosa) and Unkulunkulu (Zulu) are further examined, as well as the place of river spirits and sacred animals in African cosmology. Witchcraft beliefs; rainmaking; herbalism; circumcision ceremonies; and marriage customs are other topics that receive attention. Some examples of myth and folklore, with discussion of their significance, are also included.

A77   Thoka, Albert (1925). "Bantu Religious Ideas." In William Loftus Hare (ed.) *Religions of the Empire: A Conference on some Living Religions within the Empire*. London: Duckworth. 356-67.

Thoka's paper discusses the religious beliefs and ritual practices of the South African Bantu-speaking peoples in general, with particular emphasis on Pedi religion. First, the author documents religious notions of the supreme being and various names used for God, for example, Modimo, Utixo, and Unkulunkulu. According to Thoka's view of African belief, God possesses perfect knowledge that is communicated to human beings through natural phenomena and the laws of nature. Noting that religious life is not separated from any other sphere of human life in African society, he argues that every home is not only a social unit but also a religious institution. As far as the realm of the supreme being is concerned, says the author, it is vaguely conceived as being "above" and is also thought to reside in every element of nature. Turning to the realm of the departed spirits, Thoka emphasizes that spirits of deceased relations are believed to continue to exist as human spirits and to participate in the lives of their relatives. Communal life, therefore, is conducted with due consideration for fellow human beings and relatives in this world and also for those who are deceased. The significance of belief in evil spirits is also discussed. The remainder of the paper addresses the social organization of the Pedi. The writer claims that totemism is still widely prevalent among Bantu-speaking peoples, especially among the Pedi. Defining a totem as a natural object, such as an animal, that is adopted as a clan or family emblem, the author indicates that every Pedi family identifies itself with a particular totem. Thoka suggests that Pedi veneration of the totem symbolizes their belief in a God who pervades every creature within the universe. In conclusion, sacred totemic rites and oratory are briefly examined.

A78   Van Warmelo, N. J., ed. (1977). *Anthropology of Southern Africa in Periodicals to 1950: An Analysis and Index.* Johannesburg: Witwatersrand University Press.

Van Warmelo's massive bibliography of periodical articles dating from 1795 to 1950 provides the most comprehensive annotated bibliography of materials relating to the anthropology, linguistics, history, and religion of the Bantu-speaking peoples of southern Africa (South Africa, Botswana, Lesotho, and Swaziland). Part One, the largest of five sections, provides a concise analysis of each article, listed by year and author, under the following sub-headings: subjects; tribes and groups; persons; and place names. Part Two provides indices of all the articles, classified according to sections headed General; Nguni; Tsonga; Sotho; Venda; and Lemba. Information under each of these main headings is organized into the following sub-headings: Subjects; tribes and groups; persons; language; and literature. Part Three comprises an index of place names; Part Four lists bibliographies; and Part Five provides an author index. A map of the region is appended. The exhaustive compilation thus represents an invaluable resource for students of African traditional religion in South Africa.

A79   Werner, Alice, ed. (1933). *Myths and Legends of the Bantu.* London: George C. Harap.

This volume presents a collection of myths and legends of the Xhosa-, Zulu-, and Sotho-Tswana-speaking peoples of southern Africa. Werner's introductory chapter discusses Bantu languages, stressing the major role of W. H. I. Bleek's nineteenth-century study of indigenous South African languages. The essential themes of the stories and myths are also addressed, focusing on the religious beliefs and practices of Bantu-speaking societies. Arguing that many beliefs are held in common, the author identifies those associated with the spirit world and the influence of the dead or ancestral spirits. In discussing beliefs in a high god, the writer argues that prayers and ritual sacrifice are more often offered to the ancestors. Ideas concerning creation and the origins of humankind also form a major theme of African religious myth. In addition, many stories contain a cast of ogres, monsters, and a variety of animal figures. Chapters Two to Twenty cover a wide range of categories of myth, many of which are of special interest for the study of African traditional religion. For example: "Where Man came from and how Death came" (Chapter Two); "Legends of the High Gods" (Chapter Three); "Mortals who have Ascended to Heaven" (Chapter Five); "Heroes and Demi-gods" (Chapter Eight); "Doctors, Prophets and Witches" (Chapter Sixteen). Each chapter includes examples of myths and legends associated with the particular topic, with an introduction and commentary by the editor. Photographs accompany the text and a bibliography and index are appended.

A80   West, Martin (1976). *Abantu: An Introduction to the Black People of South Africa*. Cape Town and Johannesburg: Struik.

West's text, accompanied throughout by Jean Morris's photographs, offers a general introduction to the sociopolitical organization, economics, religion, and culture of black South African societies in the 1970s. Indicating that traditional southern African Bantu-speaking societies no longer exist as such, the author stresses that precolonial social history was far from static. The intrusion of the Dutch, British, and French in the subcontinent of Africa served only to intensify change and precipitate a meeting and interweaving of the new with the old. The text is divided into the following sections: the Xhosa; the Zulu; the Swazi; the Ndebele; the Venda; the Tsonga; the Tswana; the North Sotho; and the South Sotho. With regard to African religious life, West's introductory chapter proposes that religious beliefs among Bantu-speaking peoples show a high degree of uniformity. Briefly outlining myths, beliefs, and ritual practices, the author indicates that those surrounding the ancestors are of central significance in African traditional religion. The important position of ritual specialists, most specifically the diviners, is noted in relation to their power to combat evil influences and witchcraft, supported by the medicinal therapies of the herbalists. Each chapter includes attention to religious beliefs and rituals of the particular people, such as rites associated with life cycle transitions and ancestor veneration. The final section, "The Changing Society," focuses on the effects of Westernization and urbanization on black South African societies, with particular attention to the impact of Christianity and the emergence of a range of African independent churches. Suggestions for further reading and an index are appended.

A81   Whisson, M. G., and Martin West (1975). *Religion and Social Change in South Africa*. Cape Town: David Philip.

Whisson and West's book provides valuable resources for the study of indigenous religion in South Africa, as well as aspects of African Christianity. The essays have been compiled as a tribute to the work of social anthropologist Monica Wilson. Part One, the first of three main sections, deals with belief and ritual in African traditional religion. Entries and abstracts for the essays comprising this section can be found in the relevant chapters of this volume: W. D. Hammond-Tooke's "The Symbolic Structure of Cape Nguni Cosmology" ("Xhosa Religion"); A.-I. Berglund's "Heaven-herds: A Study in Zulu Symbolism" ("Zulu Religion"); Harriet Sibisi's "The Place of Spirit Possession in Zulu Cosmology" ("Zulu Religion"); and Peter Carstens' "Some Implications of Change in Khoikhoi Supernatural Beliefs" ("Khoisan Religion"). A list of the published works of Monica and Godfrey Wilson, a bibliography, and an index are appended to the main text.

A82   Willoughby, W. C. (1928a). *The Soul of the Bantu: A Sympathetic Study of the Magico-Religious Practices and Beliefs of the Bantu Tribes of Africa*. London: Student Christian Movement.

The aim of Willoughby's study is to encourage a clearer understanding of indigenous religion in Africa in order to enhance the effectiveness of the Christian mission. Although the interpretations of African traditional religion are marked by the author's Christian worldview, his approach is a relatively sympathetic one, given the context of the early twentieth-century Christian mission in Africa. The work focuses on the ideas, beliefs, and practices of the Bantu-speaking peoples, including those in South Africa, in relation to the ancestors. The first chapter, "Ancestor-Spirits," discusses beliefs and rituals associated with death, survival of death, and the spirit realm. The ancestor spirits, he suggests, remain interested in the life of their descendants and individual character and social status persists in that realm. Chapter Two, devoted to revelations communicated by the ancestor spirits, looks at how messages in dreams and calamitous events are regarded as calls from the spirit world. Revelations mediated through trance states, spirit possession, prophets, divination, and reincarnation are also addressed. Willoughby construes the African understanding of the ancestors to be "gods" and their relations with them as "worship." In Chapters Three and Four he examines "ancestor worship" in terms of the circumstances that cause African people to turn to the ancestors and in terms of the ways in which they perform their worship. He further investigates what constitutes sacred space and sacred symbols, as well as ritual practices. Finally, in Chapter Five, Willoughby uses his "insight into the soul of the worshipper" to evaluate meanings and ethics found in the Bantu-speaking peoples' religious life and attempts to assess to what extent they are prepared to receive the message of Christianity. Footnotes accompany the text and indexes and a bibliography are appended.

A83   Willoughby, W. C. (1928b). "Some Conclusions Concerning the Bantu Concept of Soul." *Africa*, vol. 1: 338-47.

Committed to an evolutionist theory of religion, Willoughby nevertheless critiques the biased approach to the study of the "Bantu mind" and the religion of the Bantu-speaking peoples by many early twentieth-century European writers. Aiming to redress some of the misconceptions about African religious belief, Willoughby examines their ritual practices in order to elucidate beliefs concerning the soul. He focuses on rituals associated with the newborn infant; sacrificial offerings to the ancestral spirits; and burial and mourning rites. The observance of correct mortuary rites at the deceased person's home, says the author, is deemed essential to the liberation of the soul, even if the corpse is absent. Willoughby details his interpretation of Bantu cosmology, arguing that the location of the spirit world is believed to be underground. Their eschatology, however, is vague, according to the author, but the social stratification and lineage of the living community seems to persist in the spirit world. Willoughby further suggests that no division appears to exist among the spirits according to moral character. The article is concluded with brief examples of African interpretations of dreams concerning the activities of the spirits.

A84   Willoughby, W. C. (1932). *Nature-Worship and Taboo: Further Studies in "The Soul of the Bantu."* Hartford, Connecticut: Hartford Seminary Press.

This volume serves as a sequel to *The Soul of the Bantu* and aims to assess whether the Bantu-speaking peoples "pay homage also to Nature-spirits." African conceptions of "taboo" are also extensively examined. Willoughby's material is based largely on the close relationship he developed with an African chief in South Africa and observations of the community's practices. The author also draws extensively on the prominent European missionaries and writers on Africa in the late nineteenth and early twentieth centuries. The first chapter, "Nature-Worship," begins by looking at African beliefs in spirits that live in water, such as the mischievous and malign *Tikoloshe* found in Xhosa myth. Sacred places are then detailed, including sacred stones and cairns; caves and hills; and fountains, trees, and groves. Willoughby suggests that every region and community has its own "earth-god," each with a different name that is usually associated with the fertility of the earth and crops. Conceptions of "sky-gods" and attitudes towards sidereal phenomena are also discussed, as well as "spirits of the wild," which are defined as those marginalized spirits of persons who died with wrongs that had not been redressed. The author concludes that although evidence of "animism" is more readily observable among Bantu-speaking societies, it is "ancestor-worship" that constitutes the foundation of their social institutions. The second chapter represents an exhaustive account of taboos, classified according to Willoughby's own categories, into taboos pertaining to food; menstruation; pregnancy and childbirth; death; supernatural phenomena; the elements; luck and ill-luck. A discussion of attitudes towards taboos, and penalties for breaking them, follows. In conclusion, the author assesses how taboos interrelate with morality, religion, and Christianity. Footnotes accompany the text and an index and bibliography are appended.

A85   Wilson, Monica (1971). *Religion and the Transformation of a Society: A Study of Social Change in Africa.* Cambridge: Cambridge University Press.

Although reflecting on the relation between religion and radical social change taking place in Africa as a whole, Wilson's text offers valuable material concerning traditional religion in indigenous societies in South Africa. Situating both religion and ideology in a conceptual framework in which there is always a system of beliefs, judgment on right and wrong, and rituals to express those beliefs and values, Wilson distinguishes the ultimate concerns of religion as those which include belief in some form of transcendental reality. Her cogent analysis of religion and society aims to explore functional relations in the two dimensions of space and time, in terms of small-scale, isolated societies that become drawn into large-scale social relations and interactions. Three chapters are devoted to documenting evidence of religious change in some small-scale societies in twentieth-century Africa. Chapter Two focuses on African traditional religion, including the "shades," medicines, witchcraft, and God, indicating evidence of this process of expansion in southern and eastern African societies. The author draws on data from the Nyakyusa of Tanzania and the Nguni (Mpondo, Xhosa, Zulu, and Swazi peoples) of South Africa, as well as comparative evidence from the Bemba, Ndembu, and Tonga of Zambia. In the same context, Chapters Three and Four look at ritual and symbolism and the systems of morality in these societies. The final two chapters draw conclusions concerning the implications of change in scale for religion in contemporary society, in terms of belief and organization, ritual and choice. The text is annotated and a bibliography is appended.

A86   Wilson, Monica (1978). "Ritual: Resilience and Obligation." In John Argyle and Eleanor Preston-Whyte (eds.) *Social Systems and Tradition in Southern Africa.* Cape Town: Oxford University Press. 150-64.

Wilson's article questions why certain rituals persist and why others do not, particularly the rituals associated with the birth of twins. As an image of duplicity, she suggests, the existence of twins has always struck an ambivalent note in traditional African societies. While, at times, associated with God, the sky, the sea, and the shades, twins are, in other instances, regarded as inhuman and bestial, evoking an almost mystical fear in the community. Hence, twins could be viewed as both a source of blessing and pollution, as both divinely numinous and revoltingly abnormal. The extreme fear instigated accordingly to the birth of twins contributed much to the widespread phenomenon of twin-killing. Wilson suggests that twins were looked upon as carriers of treacherous duplicity and as an unnatural compromise on individuality. Therefore, twin rituals were designed to blend such duplicity into a single identity. The concluding section of this article plots the gradual disappearance of twin rituals, suggesting two contributing causes: the shift to secular ceremonies at multiple birth and the extensive use of medicines in such rituals at the exclusion of communal participation.

A87   Wilson, Monica (1987). "Southern African Religions: An Overview." In Mircea Eliade (ed.) *Encyclopedia of Religion*. New York: Macmillan. 13: 530-39.

Wilson's introductory essay provides a broad outline of the concepts and common practices of the indigenous religious traditions in southern African. The author contends that a basic similarity exists among the religious systems of Bantu-speaking peoples in the region. Drawing on the renowned work of Gabriel Setiloane, Wilson argues that in southern Africa there exists an apprehension of God as a numinous being associated with "light, brightness and sheen." Prayer or direct offerings to God rarely occur, however, in southern African traditional religious practice. Rather, the "shades" (or ancestors) act as mediators between humanity and divinity, so that human needs are communicated to the divine. The shades, claims the author, are of two types: the dead senior kin (male and female) of each family; and the "founding heroes" who have political significance for the chiefdom and are honored in communal rituals. Wilson details several rituals, such as the celebration of "first fruits," outbreak of war, summer solstice, and rites of passage (birth, initiation, marriage, and death). Thereafter, she describes the role of the diviner who maintains a particularly close relationship with the shades, fostered by "cleansing and purging, observance of taboos (including sexual abstinence), fasting, isolation in the bush, offerings to the shades, and dancing to clapping or drums." The diviners, contends Wilson, deal mostly with domestic problems and the health of clients who come to consult them. The article concludes with a discussion of witchcraft beliefs, a personification, claims the author, of evil that is manifest in the dispositions of anger, hatred, jealousy, envy, lust, greed, and so on, and is recognized as a potential within all humans. The advent of colonialism and the concomitant hardships have, she argues, resulted in countless prophets calling for the people to reject the evils of witchcraft. A map of central and southern Africa is included in the text.

A88   Zahan, Dominique (1979). *The Religion, Spirituality and Thought of Traditional Africa*. Trans. Kate Ezra and Lawrence M. Martin. Chicago and London: University of Chicago Press.

Zahan's work represents a broad overview of traditional religious beliefs and practices throughout the continent of Africa. The author focuses on African spirituality, arguing that it forms a common denominator across the diversity of African ethnic groups. The terms "fetishism" and "animism" that were coined in past scholarship to describe African religion are criticized, as is the search for common elements of religion across a multiplicity of African cultures. Instead, Zahan points to the individual's position and feeling of belonging in the universe as the common foundation of African traditional religion. For Zahan, an African emphasis on the individual human being as the keystone of spiritual life and religious organization implies that "humanism is the basis for an individual and social ethic whose normal development culminates in mystical life." The ten chapters of Zahan's study address different aspects of African spirituality and religious life. Each chapter draws on research pertaining to a variety of African societies, including both Khoisan and Bantu-speaking language groupings. Topics covered include divinity; worship and sacrifice; life and death; initiation; diviners and healers; mysticism and spirituality. Chapter notes, a bibliography, and an index are appended.

3   Khoisan Religion

In their earliest reports, European observers insisted that the indigenous herders and hunters of the Cape lacked any religion at all. They continued to issue similar denials into the eighteenth century (see Raven-Hart, 1971; Schapera, 1933). The herders, who lived within an economic, social, and ritual order that was based on cattle, were designated as "Hottentots." Known by modern scholarship as Khoikhoi, meaning "humans of humans," these pastoralists were distinguished from hunters and gatherers who were referred to as "Bushmen."

Although many modern scholars have adopted the term "San" for the hunters and gatherers of southern Africa, this designation seems to have originated as a derogatory epithet or a class distinction applied to them by Khoikhoi. Efforts to distinguish between Khoikhoi and San—on the basis of language, ethnicity, region, or religion—have been controversial, resulting in what one scholar has called "Khoisanosis," the process of identifying different groupings of people under the generic label, Khoisan (Wilson, 1986).

In drawing up an inventory of Khoisan religion, scholars have identified certain key elements: a high god who is the creator and benefactor of human beings; a destructive lesser god who stands in opposition to the high god; a trickster figure who appears as Heitsi-Eibib, Cagn, or the Mantis; a Lord of Animals; and the importance of the moon (see, for example, Barnard, 1988; Schmidt, 1973). According to some commentators, these elements comprise a coherent system, an underlying religious structure that unifies Khoisan religion as a religious system in spite of observable regional diversity (Schapera, 1930; see Hoff, 1993). More recently, however, analysts have emphasized the fluidity and mutability of these religious resources. As Mathias Guenther has argued, we must regard Khoisan religion as "deeply and pervasively ambiguous and heterogeneous, as fluid and lacking in standardization" (1994: 267). Instead of constituting a coherent or consistent religious structure, these elements represent an anti-structure, an alternative world that appears in myth and ritual, but does not affect the pragmatic concerns or practical conduct of daily life (see Barnard, 1992; Guenther, 1979).

Isolating the religion of Cape herders from "Bushman" hunters and gathers, the German visitor, Peter Kolb, first represented the basic elements of Khoikhoi religion as a religious system. In 1719 Kolb identified the Khoikhoi supreme God, a lesser God who appeared in the moon, an evil deity, and the importance of the Mantis. However, he also reported that Khoikhoi ritual life revolved around a "Pissing Ceremony" that required a male elder to urinate on all participants in rituals of birth, initiation, marriage, or death (Kolb, 1731: I: 37, 90-111, 316-17). This ceremony inspired Kolb to contrast the Cape with Europe: "Strange! The different Notions different Nations entertain of the same Thing! The Force, the Witchcraft of Custom! To be piss'd upon in Europe is a Token of the highest Contempt: To be piss'd on in the Hottentot Countries is a Token of the highest Honour. Pissing is the Glory of all the Hottentot Ceremonies" (Kolb, 1731: 316). Clearly, Kolb used Khoikhoi religion as a sign of difference in order to represent the Cape as the reverse of Europe.

Almost two centuries later, the first book-length account of Khoikhoi religion was produced by the philologist and Cape librarian, Theophilus Hahn (1881). Under the influence of the founder of the modern science of comparative religion, F. Max Müller, who had developed a method for analyzing religion that was based on classifying languages and tracing the etymology of religious terms, Theophilus Hahn attempted a linguistic analysis of Khoikhoi religion. Like Max Müller, Hahn found that religious myth arose out of the process of personifying impersonal objects, especially the sun, moon, and stars. Accordingly, Hahn interpreted the supreme being of Khoikhoi religion—Tsui-//goab— as the central figure in a solar and lunar mythology. In Hahn's account, therefore, Khoikhoi religion could be traced back to an original worship of the sky.

In recent scholarship, analysts have rejected this notion that Khoikhoi religion is based on the worship of the moon or other celestial phenomena (Barnard, 1988). Rather, Khoikhoi religious resources are deployed in understanding the interplay of good, evil, and ambiguity in the world. The supreme god, Tsui-//goab, is a beneficent deity—wise, omnipresent, and powerful (Schmidt, 1975-76). Although the supreme god can sometimes cause misfortune to befall human beings, an evil god—//Gaunab—is generally held responsible for causing evil, war, sickness, and death. The trickster figure, Heitsi-Eibib, has come in for special attention. Stone cairns throughout the Cape, the so-called graves of Heitsi-Eibib, memorialized this roguish prankster of myth and legend (Hahn, 1878). At some moments, Heitsi-Eibib appeared as an ancestral or cultural hero (Bengston, 1975); in other contexts, however, he could assume the role of the creator of the world (Schmidt, 1986). In multiple roles, the trickster represented an ambiguity that was neither good nor evil. As Sigrid Schmidt has argued, the ambiguity of the trickster deity demonstrates the fluidity of Khoi-khoi religious resources. The trickster could assume the roles of the cultural hero, Heitsi-Eibib, the high god who created the world, and the Mantis—an "oracle animal"—to whom prayers could be addressed in times of crisis (Schmidt, 1973; see Lewis-Williams, 1980).

Little research has been done on specifically Khoikhoi ritual. However, the social anthropologist Winifred Hoernlé undertook pioneering fieldwork on ritual and social organization among the Nama. Her reports on Nama rites of passage (1918) and rainmaking ritual (1923), for example, provided accounts of ritual practices among a surviving Khoikhoi community (see also Vedder, 1928).

By the end of the eighteenth century, Khoikhoi political independence had been destroyed. The population had been drastically reduced by the effects of disease and genocidal warfare. For the most part, survivors had been incorporated as laborers in the colonial economy and converts at Christian mission stations. Subject to the forces of Christian conversion, inter-cultural contact, and social marginalization, little of the indigenous Khoikhoi religious heritage persisted. Nevertheless, some attempt has been made to analyze continuity and change in Khoikhoi religious beliefs among communities of Christians in Namaqualand (Carstens, 1975).

Like the Khoikhoi, the San or Bushmen were colonized, marginalized, and exterminated. However, small communities have survived in South Africa, Namibia, and Botswana. Conventionally, the San have been characterized as maintaining a subsistence economy based on hunting and gathering (Keenan, 1977). During the nineteenth century, European scholars assumed that the Bushmen were living fossils of the prehistory of the human race. Just as their techniques of hunting and gathering had supposedly persisted unchanged from the dawn of humanity, their religion also was imagined to have remained unchanged over the centuries. According to the historian George McCall Theal, for example, Europe's "own far remote ancestors must have had beliefs similar to those of the Bushmen" (Bleek, 1911: xxxviii). In recounting those religious beliefs, nineteenth-century scholars identified the importance of the powerful supernatural being, Cagn, an expectation of immortality that was demonstrated by ritual regard for the dead, and the performance of all-night dances under the moon. These elements of Bushman religion also appeared in standard accounts during the first half of the twentieth-century (see, for example, Dornan, 1925; Duggan-Cronin, 1942; Schapera, 1930: 160-201; Vedder, 1937).

Four developments, however, have substantially altered this simple depiction of San or Bushman religion. First, rich and complex oral traditions have been collected and analyzed. Beginning with the earliest collections assembled by W. H. I. Bleek, Dorothea Bleek, and Lucy Lloyd, scholars have recorded the myths, folklore, and other oral traditions that play a significant role in San worldviews (D. Bleek, 1923; D. Bleek, 1931-35; W. H. I. Bleek, 1864; Bleek and Orpen, 1874; Bleek and Lloyd, 1911; see Deacon, 1986). Although these collections recorded the stories of informants in the Cape, they develop mythic themes that also appear in San oral traditions that have been found throughout southern Africa (see Biesele, 1976; 1978; 1993; Guenther, 1989; Hewitt, 1986; Schmidt, 1982; 1989). For example, San myth distinguishes between a "primal time," in which animals were human, and the "new order" of the world that human beings currently inhabit. Myths and folklore return in imaginative ways to that "primal time" (Guenther, 1989). As myth marks out a sacred time before the beginning of the present world, it also identifies sacred places, the water-holes, the north facing slopes, and other features of the landscape that are im-bued with special religious power (Deacon, 1988). In these ways, myth represents more than merely a set of beliefs; it provides a sense of orientation in time and space that is necessary for living in a meaningful world.

Second, cultural variation in San or Bushman religion has become ap-parent through detailed study of the beliefs and practices of specific groups. Intensive fieldwork has produced reports on the religion of such regional groupings as the //Xegwi of the eastern Transvaal (Potgieter, 1955), the Nharo of western Botswana (Guenther, 1986), the !Xo of the Namibian Kalahari (Heinz, 1975), and the !Kung of northern Botswana and Namibia (Lee, 1979; Marshall, 1957; 1962; 1969; 1976; Shostak, 1981). Differences in religious be-liefs and practices, however, are not only found in different regions. As Mathias Guenther discovered, the character of Nharo religion changed when people moved from their own village to become farm laborers. In that new context, traditional religion, which had been fluid, fragmentary, and playful, even in-spiring amusement, seemed to become more serious, systematic, and formal on the farm (Guenther, 1979).

Third, recent research has focused on the importance of ritual. In par-ticular, the medicine dance or trance dance has emerged as the central ritual practice in San or Bushman religion. As analyzed by Lorna Marshall among the !Kung, this ritual awakens a supernatural potency—*n/um*—that can be chan-neled into the healing of sickness and the protection of the community (Marshall, 1969). Evidence of this spiritual power appears in the heat generated in the pit of the stomach and the altered states of consciousness that are achieved by going into a trance. Although sacred specialists—shamans, medi-cine men, or ritual experts—are particularly adept at inducing trance states, in principle anyone can undergo this experience. As Richard Lee found among the !Kung in the 1960s, nearly half of the men and women of the community were capable of performing the trance inducing ritual (Lee, 1968). Trance states, therefore, represent a relatively egalitarian means of access to transcendent "revelations of religious reality" (Dowson, 1988; see Jolly, 1986; Katz, 1976; 1982; Katz and Biesele, 1986; Lee, 1967; Lewis-Williams, 1988).

Finally, theoretical advances in the study of rock art have been made by reinterpreting the paintings and engravings in relation to San or Bushman re-ligion. Rock art has been subjected to many interpretations: It has been under-stood as a purely artistic expression (Willcox, 1963; 1984), as a visual history of "ancient culture heroes" (Dart, 1931), or, in religious terms, as a "primitive" magic for achieving success in hunting or a "primitive" totemism in which animals represent social allegiances (Pager, 1975; see Davis, 1985). The religious motivation of rock art has increasingly come to be recognized (see Vinnicombe, 1972b; 1975; 1976). The interpretive key, however, has emerged in the trance.

In developing this "trance hypothesis," J. D. Lewis-Williams proposed to use ethnographic evidence of San or Bushman religion for the analysis of rock art. Referring to nineteenth-century accounts, such as the testimony of Qing found in Bleek and Orpen (1874), as well as modern fieldwork, Lewis-Williams established the link between the rock art and the rituals for inducing trance and achieving spiritual potency that were practiced by shamans. In this linkage between art and religion, the rock art appeared as another medium for representing (or perhaps inducing) the altered states of consciousness that were achieved in San or Bushman ritual. From this perspective, the rock art reveals an elaborate symbolic vocabulary of metaphors—nasal bleeding, lines coming from the head, animal forms, underwater scenes, and entoptic phenomena—that evoke the experience of trance. In a series of publications, Lewis-Williams has developed this religious, ritual, or shamanic character of rock art. Not only "paintings of power," but also engravings have been shown to emerge from shamanic practice and employ the same metaphors and images of altered states of consciousness (Dowson, 1992). The "trance hypothesis" has been accepted and extended by other researchers (see Maggs and Sealy, 1983; Yates, Golson, and Hall, 1985; Yates and Manhire, 1991; Yates, Parkington, and Manhire, 1990). As a result, the study of rock art has been established as an "archaeology of thought" or an "archaeology of human understanding" that has profoundly extended our appreciation of Khoisan religion.

B1   Barnard, Alan (1988). "Structure and Fluidity in Khoisan Religious Ideas." *Journal of Religion in Africa*, vol. 8, no. 3: 216-36.

Barnard's structuralist interpretation of Khoisan religious practice focuses on problems in the translation of religious concepts and the understanding of religious conversion in regionally-based systems of Khoisan economy, politics, and kinship. His extracts from the work of ethnographer E. F. Potgieter (1955) provides an outline of common elements in Khoisan religion, among them the belief in a high god and lesser deity, the transmigration of the souls of the dead, and the importance of the moon. In a brief criticism of Potgieter's work, however, he rejects the idea that moon-worship was a constituent element of Khoisan belief. After a detailed discussion of the way certain linguistic factors affect concepts of deity, Barnard analyzes the fluidity of belief among the Nama and Damara concerning the creator god, Tsui-//goab, his adversary, //Gaunab, the ancestral hero, Heitsi-Eibib, and his antagonist, Gama-Gorib. The following section of the paper deals with the manner in which Khoisan mythology traveled across linguistic, cultural, and environmental boundaries. A comparison of relatively fluid Bushman religious ideas with more rigid Khoikhoi structures is then undertaken. The writer concludes by drawing on the work of Mathias Guenther and Robin Horton to examine the manner in which fluidity and structure affected religious conversion. A substantial bibliography is included.

B2   Barnard, Alan (1992). *Hunters and Herders of Southern Africa*. Cambridge: Cambridge University Press.

This book provides a comprehensive and detailed ethnographic study of the !Kung, !Xo, Nharo, Nama, Damara, and G/wi. A chapter is devoted to each, and at the conclusion of each chapter the name of the group's god is given, along with a few remarks about ritual practice. Chapter Fourteen, entitled "Aspects of Khoisan Religious Ideology," consolidates much of this information while providing an assessment of the ideology and "grammar" of Khoisan religion. In this regard, Barnard establishes common elements in Khoisan belief and practice: belief in a high god, a lesser deity, the transmigration of the souls of the dead, and the importance of the moon. Citing Potgieter's assertion that the //Xegwi worship the moon, and Schapera's statement that both the Bushmen and Khoikhoi worship the moon, the author dismisses the notion of lunar-worship as a fantasy of European ethnographers. Drawing on his experience among the Nharo, he discusses concepts of "God," giving close attention to etymological variety, ideological structure, and the use of number and gender in divine names. Specific divine entities are examined, among them the G/wi sky god, N!adiba, the !Xo creator god, Gu/e, and the Nama creator, Tsui-//goab. Also mentioned are the ancestor-hero, Heitsi-Eibib, and the evil god, //Gaunab. Barnard concludes with some remarks on the fluidity of Khoisan belief and cites Guenther's argument that Bushman religion, in particular, and religion in general, is characterized by disorderliness, idiosyncrasy, and a lack of functionality. While partially agreeing with these statements, Barnard counters that a structural uniformity emerges from Khoisan religion when viewed from the perspective of collectivity. He claims that fluidity does not deny structure, but rather functions as an indigenous or creative explanatory device.

B3   Bengston, Dale R. (1975). "Three African Religious Founders." *Journal of Religion in Africa*, vol. 7, no. 1: 1-26.

Bengston's paper challenges an anthropological category or "classification of deity" assigned to African traditional religion, namely, the "culture hero." He asserts that this classification obscures the existence of sacred beings who are founders of cults, secret societies, or sacred sites. Criticizing writers, such as Mbiti, who deny the existence of founders in African traditions, Bengston provides a summary of anthropological theory concerning culture heroes. He then presents a typological analysis of what he views as three founder figures in Khoisan religion: Nyikang of the Shilluk, Tsoede of the Gikuyu, and Heitsi-Eibib of the Nama. In another section he elaborates on the role of the founder, invoking Van der Leeuw's definition of that figure as "primarily a witness to revelation." Bengston examines the special relationship between founder and deity based upon the founder's role as bearer of revelation. He argues that this revelatory aspect makes the founder an "archetype" in the believer's eyes. Joseph Campbell's analysis of the archetypal hero is deployed to strengthen his argument. Thus, for Bengston, the liminal events of the founder's life become the model for the initiatory rites of the group.

B4   Biesele, Megan (1976). "Aspects of !Kung Folklore." In Richard B. Lee and Irven DeVore (eds.) *Kalahari Hunter-Gatherers: Studies of the !Kung San and their Neighbours*. Cambridge, Mass.: Harvard University Press. 302-24.

This essay provides a preliminary report of material gathered in the course of fieldwork between the years 1970 and 1972. Biesele begins by listing previous collections of San folktales (in the writings of Bleek, Orpen, Metzger, Thomas, and Marshall) and indicates that her work is an attempt to fill out the knowledge of San oral traditions. She emphasizes the variegated nature of this tradition, and describes how each area and group has its own characteristic cycle of stories. The author also relates how the oral tradition appears to be purely the domain of the older members of each group. The article is chiefly concerned with the cycle of tales dealing with a trickster god named Kauha, and two long examples of this genre are reproduced. The remainder of the paper is devoted to folktales describing the hare and the moon and the origin of death, and the tale of /'Tuma/'tuma, which explains the origin of the social division between hunter-gatherers and herder-farmers.

B5   Biesele, Megan (1978). "Religion and Folklore." In Phillip Tobias (ed.) *The Bushmen: San Hunters and Herders of Southern Africa*. Cape Town: Human & Rousseau. 162-72.

Biesele's chapter provides an overview of the religio-cultural beliefs and practices of the Khoisan. She discusses Bushman religion and folklore with reference to specific groups, specific locations, and historical times. The chapter is divided into three sections that in turn describe the beliefs of the Bushmen, trance inducing dance, and Bushman folklore. In the first section, the writer points to the fact that there is great variation among the cultural traditions of the various Bushman groups. More specifically Biesele discusses the various interpretations of the "Great God" and the "Lesser God," the religious role of the shaman, and the religious dimension of human life in terms of the natural elements. In the section on dance and trance, Biesele places emphasis on the central focus of religious life which is supplied for most traditional Bushman groups by the dance and its attendant trance medicine. She points to the fact that the curing dance facilitates contact between the human world and the divine, and is substantially the same for most Bushman groups. In terms of folklore, she illustrates the way in which different Bushman groups evolved different tales and folklore heroes, including the central figure of the Mantis. Finally, Biesele shows that besides the hero cycles Bushman folklore has an abundance of tales involving animals that explain the origins of the world.

B6   Biesele, Megan (1993). *Women Like Meat: The Folklore and Foraging Ideology of the Kalahari Ju/'hoan.* Johannesburg: Witwatersrand University Press; Bloomington: Indiana University Press.

This book centers around a group of oral traditions collected by the author in western Botswana during the years 1970 to 1972. In an early section dealing with the archaeology and ethnography of the Bushmen, Biesele states that the title originates in a remark recorded by anthropologist Lorna Marshall during her fieldwork. For Biesele, the phrase illustrates the balance between men and women in hunter-gatherer society in terms of physical needs and social responsibilities. The theme of the book is set forth as "the man/woman cognitive opposition in Ju/'hoan culture and its mediation in folklore." Chapter One discusses the adaptations made by the Bushmen in response to changing environmental conditions and asks which reality grounds an oral tradition: the present, or an ancient past tracing back through significant environmental and social fluctuations. Biesele answers this question by saying that contemporary tales consist of a combination of conservative elements from the deep past with aspects originating in recent events and pressures. She catalogues and comments on previous collections, among them those of Bleek and Lloyd, Metzger, Guerreiro, Thomas, Marshall, Guenther, and Lee. The folklore is characterized as being highly localized, yet having certain paradigmatic thematic connections. She relates the circumstances surrounding the narration of the tales, describes the Ju/'hoan use of metaphor, and briefly compares Bushman folklore with that of the Bantu and Khoikhoi. Chapter Two then discusses the relationship between folklore and foraging, and in Chapter Three Biesele analyzes oral systems of communication. Chapter Four then explores the role of tradition and creativity in folklore, while in Chapter Five, "Understanding Ju/'hoan Tales," the writer analyzes the metaphors related to trance dance, among them the binary oppositions related to

heat and cold, the boiling force of *n/um*, animals, and the metaphors of transformation. An overarching metaphorical link is suggested that connects the
creator deity, people, and animals. Chapter Six presents the tales themselves,
along with sections of analysis that elaborate on specific metaphors. The trickster figure Kha//'an figures prominently in these tales. However, a number of
tales also relate to myths of origins and initiation, and heroine figures. The book
concludes with a series of theoretical remarks on the study of folklore.

B7   Bleek, Dorothea (1923). *The Mantis and His Friends: Bushman Folklore*. London: Basil Blackwell.

This short volume contains a collection of folktales that were collected by Wilhelm Bleek and his sister-in-law Lucy C. Lloyd in the 1870s. Lloyd edited the
volume and provided a brief introduction in which she describes the nature of
the mythological Mantis. He appears as the central figure in a large number of
tales and possesses supernatural powers. At the same time, she suggests, he
"shows great foolishness" and is capable of being confounded and thwarted,
especially by his own children. He has a large family that includes the Porcupine, who is an adopted daughter, the Blue Crane who is his sister, and the
mother of his pet springbok who appears to be another sister. The authors relate
that in the tales all these animals were humans at one time, prior to the appearance of contemporary humans. The Mantis has creative powers, and the moon
and stars are due to his activity. Nevertheless, as Bleek points out, he never
seems to be worshipped as a deity. Following her discussion of the Mantis,
Bleek provides a short ethnographical discussion of the people who told the
tales. The huts that made up their homes, and their clothing, tools, and weapons
are briefly described. Bleek emphasizes the fact that contrary to the widespread
notion that the San were aimless nomads, they were in fact intensely territorial.
She asserts that this misunderstanding has been at the root of the problematical
relations between colonists and San. She adds that the folktales reflect a period
before the appearance of any intruders, thus disclosing the San way of life in its
pristine form. Some of the motifs included in the tales are the Mantis' creation
of the Eland, the Mantis and the Will-O'-Wisp, the Mantis and the Lion, and
tales involving the Blue Crane.

B8   Bleek, Dorothea (1928). *Naron: A Bushman Tribe of the Central Kalahari*. Cambridge: Cambridge University Press.

This short monograph embodies the result of fieldwork carried out by Bleek at
Sandfontein in 1921 and 1922. It describes nearly every facet of Naron culture
in separate and concise sections. Bleek begins with a section entitled "Mode of
Life" which deals with social organization and nomadic movement. She empha-

sizes the fact that although the groups or "hordes" are nomadic, they identify themselves with a particular territory which they abandon only under extreme duress. She continues her discussion with the diet and food gathering techniques of the group, their dress, ornaments, and general appearance. Weapons, which consist mainly of the bow and arrow and spear are described, and this is followed by a section on techniques of hunting and trapping. After several sections that deal with cultural matters, such as games, dancing, and singing, Bleek provides a brief treatment of Naron religious beliefs. She finds their knowledge of these matters to be vague but elicits the existence of a sky deity, who she equates with the Khoisan deity Heitsi-Eibib. Her informants also described a belief in "ghosts" or "spirits," which they call *//gauwasi*, although other informants equated this word with the sky god. Bleek attributes this transformation to contact with other groups. She points out that the word *//gauwa* is used among the !Kung to mean dream or spirit, as well as ghost. She also claims to find traces of moon worship within the group. A section on folklore provides a collection of folktales in the original and in translation. Among these are the motifs of the Moon, Hare, Ostrich, Lion, and Hyena. Bleek concludes the monograph with a grammatical sketch of the Naron language.

B9   Bleek, Dorothea, ed. (1931-1935). "Customs and Beliefs of the /Xam Bushman." *Bantu Studies*, vol. 5: 167-79; vol. 6: 47-63, 233-49, 321-42; vol. 7: 297-312, 375-92; and vol. 9: 1-47.

This series of articles comprises a set of folktales collected between the years 1870 and 1880 from informants living south of the Orange River by Wilhelm Bleek and Lucy C. Lloyd. The editor has grouped them according to motif and presents them just as they were dictated in parallel columns, with original on the left and literal translation on the right. The first group deals with relations between baboons and humans. Bleek states in her introductory notes that the dividing line between humans and the animal world was never very deep for the /Xam and thus many human characteristics are attributed to the baboon and other animals. As one tale relates: "My parents used to say to me that the baboons were once people at the time when we who are people were not here." This concept of former human status is also applied to various animals and natural phenomena. The remaining groups of tales deal with lions; the eland (which was of particular importance); omens; wind and clouds; the rain and rainmaking rites; and sorcerers. This last section provides rich material not only for the study of /Xam religion, but for the general study of shamanism. Bleek provides a few notes on specific problems but offers no extended commentary or analysis. The collection constitutes raw source material which provides a comprehensive view into the manner of life and belief systems of the /Xam. The inclusion of original versions makes it extremely useful for ethnologists and linguists interested in the study of Khoisan dialects.

B10   Bleek, W. H. I. (1864). *Reynard the Fox in South Africa: Or, Hottentot Fables and Tales.* London: Trübner & Co.

In 1861 Bleek wrote to various missionaries in South Africa requesting that they collect and send examples of "native literature." The volume is the result of that effort. In his preface, Bleek raises several linguistic questions. He relates how he noticed a similarity between the gender signifiers in the Khoikhoi language and those of Coptic. This led further to the conclusion that all the "sex-denoting" languages known in Africa, Asia, and Europe were members of the same family, and that the Khoikhoi language seemed to represent the most primitive type of the family. He then asserts that while the imagination of African peoples is rich in historic and legendary material, this material was never fully developed into tales of the kind represented in the volume. This assertion leads him to a theory concerning the origin of myth which states that all fables are based on the "personification of impersonal beings." The inherent grammatical mechanism of ascribing gender to inanimate objects makes this type of personification an almost inevitable development. Since the Bantu languages are not "sex-denoting" languages, black Africans were not inspired to produce tales and fables in the way that the Khoikhoi were. The preface thus represents a formative moment in the history of comparative linguistics. The "fables" themselves are divided according to motif: Jackal, tortoise, baboon, and lion fables; sun and moon fables; and household tales. Of particular value for the study of Khoisan religious belief is the section devoted to Heitsi-Eibib.

B11   Bleek, W. H. I., and J. M. Orpen (1874). "A Glimpse into the Mythology of the Maluti Bushmen." *Cape Monthly Magazine*, vol. 9, no. 49: 1-13.

This article consists of two parts: a field report by Orpen and a more specialized analysis by Bleek. Orpen was the Chief Magistrate of what was then called St. John's Territory and made his discoveries while carrying out the functions of that position. He begins by describing the Maluti mountains and the occasional outcroppings of sandstone that form cave-like structures. He says that Bushman paintings were frequently found in these areas and describes the trips during which he made copies of paintings he encountered. He detected in the paintings what he refers to as "mythological meaning" and sought an informant who could interpret them. This he finally found in the person of Qing, who served as a guide on a military expedition. Orpen presents the narratives provided by Qing, which revolve around a creator deity called Cagn, who had a wife named Coti and a son Cogaz. Included in this cycle of myths are stories concerning the origin of the eland, snake-men, baboons, and the death and reanimation of Cagn. Occasionally, Qing connects his myths with specific paintings. It is this evidence that is presented to Bleek for professional evaluation. In his appended response, therefore, Bleek equates the figure Cagn (or /Kaggen) with the Mantis, which plays a central role in tales previously collected. In general, Bleek finds the narratives collected by Orpen to be quite similar but not identical to those provided by his own informants. The feature that interests him most is the fact that Cagn appears to be chiefly a "beneficent" being, while the Mantis is a "trickster" deity capable of great mischief. He adds that the Mantis is never worshipped, while Cagn is the recipient of a prayer recited by Qing. Bleek then moves to an analysis of the paintings provided by Orpen and points out what he believes to be representations of rainmaking ceremonies and other shamanistic elements. Lithographic copies of these paintings are provided with the article.

B12   Bleek, W. H. I., and Lucy C. Lloyd (1911). *Specimens of Bushman Folklore*. London: George Allen & Co.

The material in this pioneering volume was gathered by Bleek and Lloyd in the early 1870s. It is presented with the original and translation on facing pages. An introduction by George McCall Theal provides a discussion of the origins and dispersion of the Bushmen and Khoikhoi and a brief history of their presence and demise in South Africa. He describes the way in which the Bushmen were marginalized by the various groups surrounding them, tracing their decline as ancestral hunting grounds and springs were appropriated by whites moving westward and black Africans migrating from the east. Belated efforts to save them from extinction are also documented. Theal then moves to a biographical account of Bleek's involvement. He tells how Bleek turned away from completion of his ground-breaking *Comparative Grammar of South African Languages* to study the language and folklore of the Khoisan. At this point not only was their language unknown, but there was no system of writing the various clicks and gutturals that characterize it. Theal recounts Bleek's discovery of Bushman prisoners at the Cape Breakwater prison who would become his informants and the source of the material presented in the volume. Lloyd, who edited the work, has divided the material into two large groups: "Mythology, Fables, Legends, and Poetry"; and "History (Natural and Personal)." The first group is especially useful for its overview of Bushman belief and custom. Here, myths can be found involving the Mantis, the origin of death, and the creation of heavenly objects. Theal concludes in his Introduction that the volume will also be of great interest from a purely philological and linguistic perspective.

B13   Carstens, Peter (1975). "Some Implications of Change in Khoikhoi Supernatural Beliefs." In Michael G. Whisson and Martin West (eds.) *Religion and Social Change in Southern Africa*. Cape Town: David Philip. 78-95.

Carstens sets out to analyze the basic features of Khoikhoi belief in the supernatural while emphasizing changes that have occurred due to colonial domination and Christian missionary activity. He begins with a discussion of the Khoikhoi High God Tsui-//goab. After first correcting the view that the Khoi- khoi worshipped the moon, he enumerates the attributes of this "celestial" deity as successively creator god and omnipresent, wise, and powerful being. This god is opposed by another male figure //Gaunab, who personified evil in the world and is likened to the Christian devil. He is the source of war, sickness, death, and sorcery. A third entity, Heitsi-Eibib, who appears to be a type of me- diating ancestral hero, is also introduced, followed by a brief discussion of magic and sorcery. After a schematic breakdown of various mythological char- acters, Carstens moves to an analysis of nominally Christian beliefs in terms of religion, magic, rites of passage, and beliefs relating to the supernatural powers of animals and monsters. Carstens compares belief systems in three separate communities within the Coloured Reserves of Namaqualand. Three important factors involved in variations in belief include differences in the structure of church governments, differences in systems of social stratification, and the na- ture and intensity of interaction with the outside world. He concludes by invok- ing Max Weber, stating that the study of symbolic forms will steer anthropologists towards a clearer view of social relationships within less privi- leged groups—relationships that are quite different from those prevalent in the ruling classes.

B14   Carstens, Peter (1982). "The Socio-Economic Context of Initiation Ceremonies Among Two Southern African Peoples." *Canadian Journal of Afri- can Studies*, vol. 16, no. 3: 505-22.

Carstens wants to arrive at an understanding of why female initiation rites per- sisted among the Nama in rural areas long after similar ceremonies for boys had disappeared. Similarly, he inquires why the opposite situation is found among rural Xhosa. He states that he is guided by clues embedded in Nama and Xhosa traditions, as well as by a consideration of the roles of contemporary South Afri- can economic and political systems. A brief ethnographic description of both societies, which contrasts the role and status of women, provides a background for the discussion. Carstens argues that semi-nomadic pastoral Nama women enjoyed a high status and controlled the milk supply. Xhosa women were placed in a more subordinate position in a patriarchal society devoted to cattle-raising and agriculture. Drawing on the work of Hoernlé and Schapera, the author con- cisely describes Nama female initiation ceremonies. These are contrasted with Xhosa male initiation rites predominating in the Keiskammahoek Rural Survey of 1952. Carstens then turns to a comparative analysis of the two systems. His starting point is drawn from Judith K. Brown's assertion that female initiation occurs in societies where the women do not leave the domestic unit after mar- riage, and in societies where women make substantial contributions to subsis- tence activities. Carstens asks whether these principles could not be applied to males as well. His subsequent comparisons seem to bear this out. The Nama women are seen to be central in subsistence activities, while Xhosa women are relegated to minor roles, and even denied credit for the functions they perform. The analysis is then pressed forward into the contemporary situation. Here, Carstens asserts that even under the changing conditions imposed by a European capitalist culture and economy the generalizations hold their validity.

B15   Carstens, Peter, G. Klinghardt, and Martin West, eds. (1987). *Trails in the Thirstland: The Anthropological Field Diaries of Winifred Hoernlé.* Cape Town: University of Cape Town, Centre for African Studies.

Carstens points out in his introduction that Hoernlé was the first trained social anthropologist to conduct fieldwork in South Africa, adding that she was the first trained woman social anthropologist in the world to do "respected" field-work. Hoernlé made three field expeditions, in 1912, 1913, and 1922-23, in an attempt to reconstruct the culture of the Nama. Field notes from her trip to the Khoikhoi of Little and Great Namaqualand, however, were lost in a fire at the University of Witwatersrand in 1931. It is for this reason that the personal diaries assume importance for students of Khoikhoi culture, since many of the observations that received development in the lost field notes can be found here. Carstens' introduction also provides a detailed biography that places these journeys within the context of a remarkable career. Maps and references are included.

B16   Dart, Raymond (1931). "Rock Engravings in Southern Africa and Some Clues to their Significance and Age." *South African Journal of Science*, vol. 28: 475-86.

Dart's paper examines a series of engravings found in various locations throughout southern Africa. He begins by noting that although symbolic markings on rocks are widespread in the area, knowledge concerning them is highly inadequate. He then gives a very detailed description of several sites, among them Solwezi, in Zimbabwe. He concludes that the carvings at this site were made approximately four thousand years ago. According to Dart, the artists were probably members of a religious elite who were engaged in the manufacture of quartz implements. Contemporary natives, he says, view the carvings with religious awe, and he is convinced that they had a symbolic and magical purpose. Descriptions of other sites are added: Lubudi, where carvings of concentric circles, triangles, and wave-like lines were found, and Chifumbazi, where another collection of discrete symbols of various shapes exists. Dart compares some of these symbols to carvings found in the French Pyrenees and at Borge, in Norway. An attempt at interpretation is then made. Using remarks made by a native informant, as well as accounts by independent witnesses, he links the engravings to the movements of "ancient culture heroes." These in turn are identified as Neolithic metal gatherers and the engraved symbols are viewed in part as landmarks made by them as they traveled along streams in search of minerals. Evidence of metal working in the area is adduced to support this interpretation. A brief attempt to link the engravings with Bushman rock art is made, followed by the general conclusion that the rock engravings reflect the geographical movements and creation myths of Neolithic culture heroes.

B17   Davis, Whitney (1985). "Present and Future Directions in the Study of Rock Art." *The South African Archaeological Bulletin*, vol. 40, no. 41: 5-10.

Davis' paper documents major influences and suggests important theoretical issues for the study of rock art. While citing the relative progress made in the preceding decade he expresses the belief that the study of rock art will move to the forefront of anthropological and art historical theory. The greatest project for the future, he says, is an "archaeology of thought," and cites as founding texts works such as Leroi-Gourhan's *Dawn of European Art*, Lévi-Strauss' *Way of the Masks*, and Lewis-Williams' *Believing and Seeing*. In a section on methods of study, he discusses the need for more comparative study; the considered use of scientific or technical inquiry; a "formal" analysis that will recover the original meaning of a work rather than objectify the observer's biases; and statistical methods that will reveal patterns that escape mere visual inspection. He also emphasizes the importance of understanding the social context of art production, of clarifying the aims of studying rock art (art "for its own sake" is no longer a valid motive), and dispensing with "mythologies of the origin of art." He sets forth the advantages and disadvantages of methodological approaches such as environmental archaeology, anthropological materialism, and anthropological structuralism. Of most interest for the historian of religion is his analysis of semiotic and iconological analysis, the attempt to "look through systems of symbols to the worlds they project, classify, and re-order." In the conclusion, Davis emphasizes the heuristic nature of his remarks, while stating that analytic progress is being obstructed by modern ideologies of artistic expression. He also calls for more openness to the results of workers in related fields and a more concentrated effort to understand visual representation.

B18   Deacon, Janette (1986). "My Place is the Bitterpits: The Home Territory of Bleek and Lloyd's /Xam San Informants." *African Studies*, vol. 45, no. 2: 135-55.

Deacon notes in this paper that Bleek's pioneering account of San belief and practice was obtained through information provided by a number of informants who were prisoners at the Cape's Breakwater Prison. Her paper is thus an attempt to connect the informants with their geographical homes by using a sketch map drawn by Bleek from information given by a man named //Kabbo. Deacon made three field trips to the northern Karoo in 1985 and 1986 in an effort to verify and describe the sites contained in the map. In her paper she lists the names of the informants with the dialects of each, while identifying the sites and her findings. Occasionally, she is able to link a specific site with a particular myth or tale from Bleek's collection. She concludes from this exercise that the "territory" of the /Xam was somewhat smaller than is usually assumed of San groups. She also found that although material implements differed between groups of so-called "Flat Bushmen" and "Grass Bushmen," there seemed to be a continuity of religious beliefs. She implies that this finding supports Lewis-Williams' hypothesis of a "pan-San cognitive system." She adds that Bleek also viewed the folklore of the two groups as largely similar, despite the differences in dialect.

B19   Deacon, Janette (1988). "The Power of Place in Understanding Southern San Rock Engravings." *World Archaeology*, vol. 20: 129-40.

Deacon mentions the ritual importance that Australian aborigines attribute to the landscape and states her intention to draw attention to the similar importance of landscape features among the /Xam. The source material for the paper is contained in the writings of Bleek and Lloyd (1911), whose ethnographic collections provide detailed sketches of several of their informants' residential locations. Deacon claims that it is clear from this material that the /Xam attached importance to some landmarks and incorporated them into their beliefs, rituals, and folklore. This is illustrated in two examples from the collection that show how certain engravings were associated with locations important for rainmaking. The examples suggest that particular places near waterholes or north-facing slopes were felt to be imbued with power, and that the engravings at these locations were intended to reinforce this power. Deacon argues that the engravings probably illustrate shamanic trance experiences, but emphasizes that even though the metaphors employed in the engravings changed through time, the location itself continued to exert an unbroken influence on the beliefs of the people.

B20   Dornan, Samuel S. (1925). *Pygmies and Bushmen of the Kalahari.* London: Seeley, Service & Co.

Dornan, a fellow of the Royal Anthropological Institute, and member of the American Geographical Society, was renowned for his work on "moon-law," or sidereal worship among the San. In this paper, he provides a comprehensive account of San religious beliefs. In a chapter entitled "Immortality and the Spirits," he describes "vague" San concepts concerning the afterlife and discusses their belief in a spirit called Thora, or Huwe (Tsui-//goab). He says that according to his informants, this "Great One" reigns over all things and sends rain and luck in hunting. He is opposed by an evil spirit, Gaua (//Gaunab), who is viewed as "the destroyer." The chapter also contains information on the concepts of the soul and attitudes concerning the sun and moon. A chapter entitled "Omens and Divination" reveals the critical role that divination played in the lives of these people, especially manifested in the use of "divining bones." According to Dornan, a throw of these bones preceded nearly every activity or decision. In a separate chapter entitled "Heavenly Bodies," Dornan examines the question of whether the San actually worshipped the sun and moon. He tends to agree with Bleek, who felt this was certainly the case, but still found evidence that would argue against it. It is clear, however, that the heavenly bodies were held in great awe and reverence. A chapter on folklore emphasizes the vast quantity of material and provides a number of examples of San myths and folktales. Dornan adds that none of the tales or legends throw light on the origins or early migrations of these people.

B21   Dowson, Thomas A. (1988). "Revelations of Religious Reality: The Individual in San Rock Art." *World Archaeology*, vol. 20: 116-28.

Recent research on rock art has concentrated on common, widely repeated metaphors and hallucinations experienced during trance. In this paper, Dowson focuses on the rare idiosyncratic depictions that have been largely ignored. He begins by discussing the causes of repetitive subject matter detected in the traditional modes of expressing trance experience. Essentially, these are verbal accounts and pictorial depictions. The author recounts how in the Kalahari, the San listen to their shamans' descriptions of trance experience, and hence the shamans tend to hallucinate the same, culturally suggested objects and experiences. It is suggested that rock art played a similar role and may have served to "standardize" hallucinations. In addition to these culturally determined elements, Dowson points to neurologically controlled visual and somatic hallucinations such as luminous zigzags and corporal elongations that constantly reappear in the art. Against this backdrop of conformist representation he introduces several depictions that do not adhere to these categories, but which he argues are amenable to exegesis, since the thought processes involved in their creation are informed by San cognitive systems. The first category analyzed is "death," particularly in relation to imagery associated with the form of the eland painted with extended hind legs and raised tail, believed to be indicative of the defecation position. After elucidating the San tradition of trance as death, and the various artistic methods of portraying this, Dowson argues that the rare images under scrutiny can be located within a larger tradition. The dying eland, no matter how the symptoms are depicted, is to be equated with the shaman in trance. The second category the writer analyzes is aquatic (underwater) symbolism, which he says is a more unusual metaphor for signifying the trance state. The final category considers depictions of eland with both male and female characteristics, images which are explained by the neurological combination of optical imagery and the unifying cultural function of the eland among the San. In the conclusion, Dowson argues that consideration of these individualistic images is important in order to understand how symbols entered the artists' vocabulary.

B22   Dowson, Thomas A. (1992). *Rock Engravings of Southern Africa*. Johannesburg: Witwatersrand University Press.

The rock paintings of southern Africa have received a great deal of attention, but most people remain ignorant of the existence of rock engravings. Dowson states that the book is intended to redress this situation. The introduction describes techniques used by the artists to construct the images and attempts by art historians to date the work. By examining the patination of the rocks, he notes, experts have concluded that several scraped and pecked engravings go back to two thousand years before the present (B.P.). Fine line engravings, by contrast, date from 10,000 years B.P. Early reactions to and inhumane treatment of the San is also recounted, and the valuable ethnographic work of the Bleek family is mentioned. The author says that explanations of rock art have been aided by ethnographic work among contemporary Bushmen of the Kalahari, in particular, in the work of Lorna Marshall, Megan Biesele, and Richard Katz. These writers, he suggests, have discovered that the trance dance of these people forms the center of their religion and cosmology. In this regard, ancient rock art has also proven to be centered around trance experience. The remainder of the book, which is dominated by color photographs and tracings of various engravings, elaborates upon the shamanistic nature of rock art. Depictions of the dance, hallucinated "rain" animals, and trance-induced geometric patterns are explained and illustrated. Depictions of deeper levels of trance, where the shaman merges with a certain animal "power," are also presented. The book contains over 170 illustrations and constitutes a significant source for the study of San art and religion.

B23   Duggan-Cronin, A. M. (1942). *The Bushman Tribes of Southern Africa*. Kimberly: MacGregor Memorial Museum.

Duggan-Cronin's large collection of full-page photographs depicts various groups of Bushmen in a wide variety of geographical locations. Each photograph is accompanied by the author's descriptive remarks. The photographs comprise individual portraits, small groups, dwellings, dances, and activities such as water-gathering and fire-starting. An introductory section discusses geographical distribution, mode of life, and linguistic relationships between groups. The author briefly discusses religious beliefs, asserting that most groups worship the moon, which is viewed as a symbol of life after death. He details their beliefs concerning spirits and mentions the large cycle of myths and tales involving the trickster figure of the Mantis. The northern San groups knew of a creator god named Huwe (Tsui-//goab), but the author points out that the nature and function of this figure varied significantly from group to group. He concludes the discussion with several remarks concerning sorcery and initiation rites.

B24   Elphick, Richard (1977). *Khoikhoi and the Founding of White South Africa*. Johannesburg: Ravan Press.

This book provides the first systematic account of the history of the Khoikhoi, who originally occupied large areas of southern Africa. In his introduction, Elphick deals with the thorny issue of terminology, dismissing the old term "Hottentot" and describing the pejorative use of the term in Europe. He explains that the indigenous people of the region called themselves Khoikhoi in the Namaqua dialect and Kwena in the Cape dialect. Elphick makes no claim to comprehensiveness, due to the extensive materials that must be examined, and therefore limits himself to a study of the Cape Khoikhoi, a group that is now extinct. His goal is to understand the factors that led to their disappearance. He states at the outset that there were factors operating within Khoikhoi society itself that contributed to their decline. Part One of the book is devoted to an attempt at reconstructing the nature of Khoikhoi social structures and modes of life prior to the arrival of white settlers. Elphick makes a special effort to unravel the problematic relations and connections between the Khoikhoi and the group he prefers to call "hunters," but which have been referred to in the past as Bushmen or San. He points to linguistic evidence and other cultural affinities to suggest a common origin for both groups, an opinion that he says anthropologists are coming to embrace more frequently. This relationship is further developed in Chapter Two. The second part of the book chronicles the troubled history of Khoikhoi contact with white settlers and comprises separate chapters devoted to the Khoikhoi of the peninsula, the Cochoqua in the north, and the Chainouqua. The third and fourth parts deal with the decline and ultimate collapse of Khoikhoi society. In these parts, the writer advances a detailed examination of the complex causes of this human catastrophe. Brief notes on the general lack of sustained missionary activity among Khoikhoi groups are provided. Although religious matters play a relatively small role in the book, it nevertheless presents essential background material for students of Khoisan religion.

B25   Gordon, Robert J. (1986). "Bushman Banditry in Twentieth-Century Namibia." In Donald Crummey (ed.) *Banditry, Rebellion and Social Protest in Africa.* London: James Currey. 173-189.

In an effort to preserve the genre of "resistance studies" or "populism," Gordon writes with the intent of combining "historical research with an awareness of social-organisational arrangements." He begins with an account of the earliest colonial contact with and perception of the Bushmen, and finds the etymology of the term itself in the Dutch word "Bossiesman," meaning highwayman or bandit. Thumbnail sketches of the emergence of "the Bushman Problem" and German and South African strategies for dealing with the issue are provided. This is followed by a case study concerning the "notorious" "Hans' gang." Gordon then discusses motives and causes for Bushman stock theft that have been put forth in the past. These range from a farmer's notion of "inherent lust for slaughter," to simple hunger, and revenge for mistreatment at the hands of whites. A section on "Patterns and Forms of Banditry" describes the cycles of drought that usually preceded intense periods of stock theft. An overview of adaptive strategies adopted by the San when confronted with white colonial expansion is also narrated. Gordon concludes that the underlying rationale behind banditry was "the desire to escape colonial domination." A concluding section discusses the role of Bushman soldiers and trackers in the South African Defence Force's war against the South West African Peoples' Organisation (SWAPO) in Namibia.

B26   Guenther, Mathias (1979). "Bushman Religion and the (Non)sense of Anthropological Theory of Religion." *Sociologus*, vol. 29, no. 2: 102-32.

Guenther's paper provides a socioeconomic survey of San settlements in the Ghanzi district of western Botswana. He distinguishes between "Farm Bushmen," who serve as agricultural laborers, and free or "Roaming Bushmen," who follow a more traditional hunter-gatherer way of life. Social problems found among the Farm Bushmen, such as poverty, disease, and intra-ethnic strife are underscored, and this situation is contrasted with the harmonious "affluence without abundance" enjoyed by traditional, "roaming" groups. The author sets out a "heuristic" description of the religion of the two discrete communities of Bushmen in terms of a dual distinction of ideal type, namely, "traditional" and "modern." The central figure in this description is //Gauwa, a complex and ambiguous entity. His relationship to another deity, N!eri, forms part of this ambiguity, since some informants identify him with the sky god N!adiba, while others say he is N!eri's servant. This ambiguity is resolved by the Farm Bushmen who view N!eri as the source of good, and //Gauwa as a satanic figure. Another aspect of this deity that Guenther emphasizes is his role as a "hero-trickster." Eschatological beliefs are also briefly touched upon. Three salient characteristics of traditional Bushman religion are arrived at: First, that it displays unsystematic attributes such as amorphousness, fragmentation, and fluidity. Second, that belief is isolated from practical concerns. And third, that supernatural agents do not elicit fear and awe, but rather amusement and enchantment. In contrast, modern Bushman religion appears more systematic and tends to explain features of concrete reality. Guenther follows this discussion of belief with some remarks on ritual and shows how the traditional trance dance has become more formalized among the Farm Bushmen, with the emergence of a specialized shaman figure who is paid for his services. The development is attributed to increased stress and disease experienced in agricultural environments. The second part of the paper consists of a methodological critique of the inadequacy of structural-functionalist readings, in the works of Durkheim, Radcliffe-Brown, Malinowski, and Lévi-Strauss. Indeed, in contrast to these anthropologists, Guenther asserts that Bushman religion is inherently "anti-structural." The analysis is then broadened when the writer asserts that all religion, due to its symbolic nature, is fragmented, irrational, and culturally idiosyncratic. It is suggested that in order to properly analyze the symbolic quality of religion, research into alternative styles of rationality should be undertaken. The writer names Horton, Beattie, Leach, Gellner, Winch, Wilson, and Turner as exemplary exponents of this approach.

B27   Guenther, Mathias (1980). "From Brutal Savages to Harmless People: Notes on the Changing Western Image of the Bushmen." *Paideuma*, vol. 26: 123-40.

In this paper Guenther analyzes why the San were perceived by Europeans to be brutal savages at one time and "harmless people" at another. In this regard, he describes how Thomas' book, *The Harmless People,* fixed a romanticized stereotype that was taken up by both anthropologists and lay inquirers alike, and shows how the stereotype glossed over certain "harmful" aspects present in Bushman society. He then carefully describes the development of negative stereotypes that were the product of written impressions made by early travelers and missionaries. Quotations from these writings are presented and an image emerges of a culturally, morally, and physically debased society. Of primary importance here for students of religion is the fact that at this time Bushman religion was either completely misunderstood, or else completely overlooked. Guenther points out that in 1811 the German traveler Henry Lichtenstein claimed to find no trace of religion among the San. After discussing the sources of this stereotype and the way it operated on the imaginations of Europeans, the author isolates elements of the stereotype of "brutal savages" that have some basis in fact by demonstrating how they originated as a defensive response in the context of the violent incursions made on Khoisan territories by European settlers.

B28   Guenther, Mathias (1986). *The Nharo Bushmen of Botswana: Tradition and Change*. Hamburg: Helmut Buske Verlag.

Guenther devotes two chapters of his book on the Nharo Bushmen to "Belief and Ritual" associated with religious practice. He says that this is necessary due to the increasing importance of religious matters within Nharo life. The chapter on belief begins with a statement on the complexity, vagueness, and inconsistency that characterizes Nharo religion. He sees the reasons for this in the fact that there are no ritual specialists or "religious formulators" who might systematize the diverse body of belief; because there is no formal religious education of Bushman children, and because the mobility of the people leads to isolation for substantial periods of time. He admits that his presentation will be somewhat artificially coherent, but that it will focus on central beliefs that enjoy an acceptable range of consensus. The chapter is then broken down into sections on "Supernatural Agents" and "Myth" and "Folklore." In the section dealing with supernatural agents and deities, Guenther discusses the sky god N!eri and the trickster god //Gauwa who sometimes takes on an adversarial role. N!eri appears to be a vague sort of high deity, while //Gauwa wanders over the earth assuming different guises. In the section on mythology the author remarks that common distinctions made by folklorists between different genres such as legend, myth, and folktale, are difficult to apply in this context due to the overlap that appears in the Nharo corpus of stories. Examples are then provided to illustrate motifs dealing with creation and the Bushman place in nature. The chapter devoted to ritual focuses on the trance dance which is used chiefly for healing purposes. Guenther provides a detailed description of every aspect of preparation and execution of the dance and comments on its effectiveness. The chapter concludes with brief discussions of puberty rites and death rituals.

B29   Guenther, Mathias (1988). "Animals in Bushman Thought, Myth and Art." In Tim Ingold, David Riches, and James Woodburn (eds.) *Hunters and Gatherers: Property, Power and Ideology*, vol. 2. Oxford: Saint Martin's Press. 192-202.

Noting that Bushman art and mythology abound with animals, Guenther sets out to explain this interest in terms of aesthetic, cognitive, and symbolic factors, as well as in terms of the ontological condition of animals in relation to man. The prominence of animals is illustrated by a "double" creation myth, suggests Guenther. In this regard, he cites a Nharo variant of the genesis myth which views the present order of existence as a reversal of primal time—a time when animals were human and humans were animals. The main characters of Bushman myths and tales comprise the animal beings of that primal time. They retain animal traits, yet also exhibit human characteristics: They are bipedal, tool and language-using social beings. Guenther concludes from this observation that animality was an intrinsic component of the ontological condition of the "first race," and thus the forebears of Bushman society and culture. He notes that these theriomorphic entities appear in Bushman rock art and refers to Lewis-Williams' theory that rock art paintings depict the transformation that trance dancers believe themselves to experience. In an attempt to understand the pre-eminent position of animals in Bushman imagination, Guenther immediately rejects the notion that it is the result of gastronomic or subsistence-related concerns. Rather, he suggests that the motive of Bushman painting was aesthetic, but quickly moves beyond this assertion to cite the work of Vinnicombe and Lewis-Williams to argue that religious and symbolic elements were also of significance. Particularly noteworthy, he asserts, were certain animals, such as the eland. An ontological element, which points to the way in which the Bushman viewed the animal both as the same as humankind and as something "other," is also developed. In the conclusion Guenther emphasizes the non-totemic nature of Bushman society and sees his study as representing a contrast to the work on similar societies conducted by Boas, Malinowski, Radcliffe-Brown, and Lévi-Strauss. Animals beguile humans, he says, because of an "other-same" ambiguity, and not necessarily as a result of the mediation of social structure.

B30   Guenther, Mathias (1989). *Bushman Folktales: Oral Traditions of the Nharo of Botswana and the /Xam of the Cape.* Stuttgart: Franz Steiner Verlag Wiesbaden.

In the second chapter of this book, which analyzes the content of collected tales, Guenther establishes the sources of his data. In attributing the narratives to the Nharo, he states that he is not unaware of the complex and heterogeneous nature of the Bushman population in the Ghanzi District of Botswana. Intermarriage, he says, takes place between all three of the Bushman linguistic groups, making a discrete ethnic label something of a chimera. He then gives an encapsulation of Bushman mythology, describing the dual nature of creation into "primal time" and a "new order." The primal time was inhabited by theriomorphic beings who were actually the first humans. The author then introduces the figure of the "trickster," who is the subject of a large proportion of the narratives. Here he describes the various transmutations that the trickster is said to undergo, ultimately emerging as the deity //Gauwa. Another sky deity, N!eri, reverses the first order of existence, bringing on the "new order." Thus, in the Bushman mind, the humans of today were animals in the primal time, and vice-versa. There follows a section on Khoisan religious traditions, in which Guenther provides an analysis of the striking similarity among myths of various Bushman groups. Drawing on the work of Schapera and Schmidt, Guenther then extends the scope of homogeneity to include Khoikhoi groups. He ultimately asserts the religious unity of all Khoisan peoples. In a concluding section on typology, Guenther nevertheless expresses the difficulty of classifying various narratives due to the overlap of function implicit in them. He distinguishes between "legends," which are set in a more or less contemporary time frame, and "stories," set in mythic times, which deal with the themes of creation, primal times, and the trickster. Since many of these stories have no element of the numinous, he prefers to call them not myths but narratives, tales, or stories. Guenther also rejects Wilhelm Bleek's use of folktale genres on the grounds that its classification of stories is arbitrary.

B31   Guenther, Mathias (1994). "The Relationship of Bushman Art to Ritual and Folklore." In Thomas A. Dowson and David Lewis-Williams (eds.) *Contested Images: Diversity in Southern African Rock Art Research*. Johannesburg: Witwatersrand University Press. 257-73.

Guenther states that his purpose is to explore textual and symbolic divergence among the three genres of Bushman expressive culture, and to examine the methodological implications raised by the lack of homogeneity within these domains. He first discusses the close connections between art and ritual, mentioning the trance elements in rock painting identified by Lewis-Williams. Examples of entoptic phenomena and motifs of animal transformation are included. Social density is also mentioned as a common element in ritual and art. Certain characteristics of Bushman mythology are then described. The writer concludes that aside from the shared shamanistic theme of transformation, the figures and events depicted in myth are situated in times and places different from those of art or ritual. An analysis of differences between these genres along the lines of gender symbolism is also developed. A section that focuses specifically on the function of animals in myth and art draws a similar conclusion, namely, that although animals play a central role in both genres, the roles are clearly of a different nature. This analysis leads into a section dealing with theory and method. Guenther first refers to postmodernist criticism of the prevalent "holocentric" epistemological stance of foraging studies. He stresses that a number of features inherent in hunter-gatherer social organization, such as flexibility, fluidity, and autonomy, challenge theoretical constructions based on conventional functionalist premises. Guenther then critiques several approaches that err due to their adherence to the holistic paradigm, such as the attempt to ascribe "narrative" meaning to the rock art by interpreting it through the inappropriate filter of Bushman myth. The trance paradigm of Lewis-Williams, even though recognized as being generally valid, is criticized for imposing a uniformity and coherence to one expressive genre that goes against the culture's ambiguous and heterogeneous cognitive grain. References are appended.

B32   Hahn, Theophilus (1878). "The Graves of Heitsi-Eibib." *Cape Monthly Magazine*, vol. 16: 259-65.

Hahn sets out to explain the Xhosa practice of adding stones to artificial heaps. He begins by asserting that the practice was taken over from the Khoikhoi, and launches into a lengthy discussion of the geological and meteorological changes that occurred in the Kalahari region and their supposed effects on incipient Khoikhoi culture. He takes exception to the statements made by some philologists who see a relationship between the Khoikhoi and the ancient Egyptians, but agrees that the Khoikhoi dialects possess "high and sublime qualities" that would indicate a potential for advanced civilization that was cut short. According to Hahn, the rise of the Sahara and Kalahari regions from the sea bed initiated harsh climatic changes that impeded further development of Khoikhoi culture. After dispensing with this background, Hahn briefly analyzes the figure of Heitsi-Eibib, who he identifies with Tsui-//goab, a benevolent being who provides plenty and security. Both are viewed as wonder-workers and dispensers of immortality. Both are said to have died and risen repeatedly, and it is this belief that has led to the appearances of the stone heaps or the "graves" of Heitsi-Eibib. Hahn tells of his own sighting of these "graves" and their locations, and cites the accounts of other travelers. He then hypothesizes a scenario to explain the adoption of this practice by certain Xhosa groups. Hahn concludes by locating the practice of creating stone heaps within a larger perspective by comparing the "graves" with similar objects in Tanganyika, China, and ancient Greece.

B33   Hahn, Theophilus (1881). *Tsuni-//Goam: The Supreme Being of the Khoi-Khoi*. London: Trübner & Co.

The first chapter in this work of comparative philology consists of an introductory survey of the history of the Khoikhoi which Hahn hopes will "lay a secure basis for the study of the Science of Religion as regards the Khoikhoi branch." The origin of the term "Hottentot" is traced to the first Dutch settlers' reaction to the language of these indigenous peoples (the word "hottentot" was considered consonant with a "quacking sound" evidently indicative of Khoikhoi speech). Hahn objects to the term not because it is derogatory, but because it is used with anthropological and linguistic imprecision. The relationship of the San to the Khoikhoi is set out and the connections between their languages is explored. Hahn concludes that Khoikhoi and San languages have a similar relationship to that between the Indo-European languages, English and Sanskrit. He uses various derivatives from the root "khoi" as a starting point for an ethnographical account of family relationships and manner of living. Following his examination of Khoi and San languages, Hahn turns to a review of numerals. He asserts that the San cannot count beyond two. The second chapter presents a large collection of extracts from early travelers' observations of the worship of various deities, as well as related myths collected by Hahn. Included in this survey are Heitsi-Eibib, Tsui-//goab, //Gaunab, //Khab, and their numerous variants. In Chapter Three, Hahn states that the mythologist must trace each myth back to its root, and so sets out to discover the fundamental etymologies of these divine names. In the course of this technical linguistic analysis, Hahn adduces analogues from the ancient Greeks, Romans, Israelites, and Eskimos.

B34   Hammond-Tooke, W. D. (1982). "Symbol or Icon? A Breakthrough in the Study of Southern African Rock Art." *South African Archaeological Bulletin*, vol. 37, no. 136: 72-74.

In this review of Lewis-Williams' work, *Believing and Seeing*, Hammond-Tooke provides a thumbnail history of scholarly approaches to rock art. He states that the enigmatic nature of the paintings previously thwarted attempts at interpretation, which in turn led to the adoption by some writers of the "*art pour l'art*" argument. This argument, he claims, is little more than an acknowledgment of ignorance. However, with the publication of *Believing and Seeing*, he suggests, Lewis-Williams initiated a breakthrough: The crucial step was taken to determine the ideas that triggered artistic effort. Hammond-Tooke compares Lewis-Williams' approach with earlier "scientific" attempts, although he acknowledges that previous research remained at the level of empirical analysis, resulting in a treatment of the paintings as if they were "icons," or realistic models of reality. Citing Popper's assertion that scientific explanation does not automatically emerge from empirical data, but involves a creative act of insight, he argues that a satisfactory scientific explanation must go beyond surface manifestation and seek connections at a deeper level. Beyond this generalization, however, it is suggested that the rock art does not lend itself completely to this type of "scientific" approach, but rather requires an approach that demands that the San worldview be seen as a system of symbols. Therefore, the search for meaning should employ an approach that is humanistic and hermeneutic rather than "scientific" in the strict sense. Lewis-Williams' breakthrough is seen as a result of his accepting the paintings not as replications of social life but as a system of symbols that must be explicated. The essence of his theory is that the depiction of symbols triggered deep responses in San mental life. After summarizing some of its findings, the author concludes that the future study of rock art cannot afford to ignore the insights of Lewis-Williams' book.

B35   Heinz, Hans-Joachim (1975). "Elements of !Ko Bushman Religious Beliefs." *Anthropos*, vol. 70: 2-41.

Quoting Biesele's remark that "it is almost impossible to discuss Bushmen religion and folklore without referring to specific groups," Heinz provides a "descriptive" portrayal of !Ko beliefs using data obtained from informants over a period of twelve years. The first section of the paper discusses "Supreme Powers," among them a creator god called Gu/e, and a second intermediate power named /oa who can represent either good or evil. Other sections deal with doctrines of the soul, lesser supernatural beings, cosmology, human relations with supreme powers, sacred animals, and foreign influences. In a lengthy summarizing section Heinz concludes that the !Ko Bushman is "very much a realist, pragmatist, and protoscientist." Emphasis is placed on the individual's relation to divine forces. Heinz asserts that "corporate formalized religious worship has small scope in this society." Religious traditions are taught during initiation ceremonies and are otherwise not a common topic of discussion. The writer ends with an unresolved question concerning the possible results of Bantu and Christian influence.

B36   Hewitt, Roger L. (1986). *Structure, Meaning and Ritual in the Narratives of the Southern San*. Hamburg: Helmut Buske Verlag.

Hewitt's work begins with a review of textual resources for the study of San or /Xam mythology, drawing particularly on the nineteenth-century collections of Wilhelm Bleek. The first chapter provides an ethnographical backdrop to the study, and recounts the destruction of /Xam society in the Calvinia and Prieska districts of the Eastern Cape Karoo. In this regard, the writer draws on the narratives of nineteenth-century travelers among the San, including valuable material found in the works of the travelers John Barrow and Henry Lichtenstein, among others, which represents an inventory of San social structure, kinship, marriage, hunting, trade, belief, and ritual. Of particular interest is Hewitt's chapter on the Khoisan narrators in Bleek's collection, which offers new material for the historian of religion in the attempt to recover a plurality of voices in the production of San mythology and religiosity. A comprehensive bibliography is appended.

B37   Hoernlé, A. Winifred (1918). "Certain Rites of Transition and the Conception of !Nau Among the Hottentots." *Harvard African Studies*, vol. 2: 65-82.

Based on field-notes taken in 1912 and 1913, the writer describes in this paper details of !Nau ritual as represented by her informants. She notes that although the society was in a state of decline at the time (as it rapidly assimilated European culture), the "*rites de passage*" of the !Nau were surprisingly unaltered, even among geographically isolated communities. The writer thus initially discusses characteristics common to all transition rites among the Khoikhoi. Preeminent among them, she suggests, were strategies indicative of the "classic models" of separation, preparation (rebirth), and reintroduction. The belief in a state called /nau is central to these rites and the author provides a section detailing some of its aspects. The initiate in his or her seclusion is said to be /nau, and may have contact only with those who have passed through the trials of life and cannot be harmed by this dangerous force. The fire in the secluded hut is also perceived to be /nau, as are the clothes and utensils of initiates. Both are sources of danger and objects of strict rules of taboo. With this background established the author begins her description of the rites themselves. Detailed descriptions of female puberty ceremonies are provided, essentially because the writer's informants performed a complete reenactment of these activities for her benefit. Hoernlé also devotes sections of the article to remarriage ceremonies, the treatment of disease, and the purification of survivors following death.

B38   Hoernlé, A. Winifred (1922). "A Hottentot Rain Ceremony." *Bantu Studies*, vol. 1: 3-4.

This brief note describes a rain ceremony reported to the writer by three different informants.

B39   Hoernlé, A. Winifred (1923). "The Expression of the Social Value of Water among the Nama of South-West Africa." *South African Journal of Science*, vol. 20: 514-26.

In her attempt to analyze the value and importance of water among the Nama, Hoernlé introduces Radcliffe-Brown's central concept of "social value," or the expression of the way in which something is "capable of affecting the social life." The author elucidates and develops this concept, suggesting that it forms the psychological basis for many customs. The paper thus describes a number of ceremonies and customs dealing with water that illustrate the "social value" of the commodity. Among the rituals reviewed are graveside ceremonies, rituals associated with the protection of persons against spirits and other evil agencies (including //Gaunab), healing activities, and female puberty ceremonies. Throughout, the author places emphasis on the way various ceremonies express the importance of maintaining proper social structures, relationships, and group cohesion.

B40   Hoernlé, A. Winifred (1924). "The Social Organisation of the Nama Hottentots of Southwest Africa." *American Anthropologist*, vol. 27: 1-24.

Hoernlé begins this paper with a geographical description of Great Namaqualand and a brief history of its Nama peoples. Following that history, an account of the emergence in the region of a group of immigrants, called "Orlams" by the Nama, is described. Thereafter, a breakdown of the indigenous peoples of Namaqualand into seven discrete groups is developed. The author proposes to label all of these groups "tribes," because in spite of their claim to a common ancestry, they have been separated and independent for a substantial length of time. Some of them are now extinct, she tells us, and the fabric of Nama culture as a whole has been "hopelessly destroyed" by inter-group pressures and conflict with German colonists in the region. The result is that the social organization she describes is almost entirely historical, having been gathered from old head-men of the tribes. The core of the paper is thus concerned with cataloging and analyzing various the patrilineal clans into which these tribes are divided. The author states that a particular sib could claim seniority, and the chieftainship of this sib would be hereditary. Her analysis consequently describes the processes by which large families fragmented to create new sibs and tribes. These divisive processes are examined along with the procedures required for naming new formations. Brief statements on modes of living are provided, and the paper concludes with a detailed section devoted to kinship systems, the specific dialectical names for family relations, and the proper conduct deemed necessary for inter-family relations.

B41   Hoff, Ansie (1993). "Die Traditionele Wereldbeskouing van die Khoekhoen." *South African Journal of Ethnology*, vol. 16, no. 1: 1-9.

In this paper Hoff distinguishes between three essential threads in the Khoikhoi worldview: First, the entire universe is permeated by an impersonal supernatural power which in turn creates mutual bonds among all entities; second, these entities do not pose a threat to human beings; and third, their influence contrasts with the negative forces of nature. The text is in Afrikaans.

B42   Hromnik, Cyril A. (1993). "The Bow of Shiva alias Heitsi-Eibib in the Rock Art of the Cape Quena." *Journal of Asian and African Studies*, vol. 28, no. 3/4: 245-53.

Hromnik's article raises the problem posed by the appearance of triple curved bows in southern African rock art. The crux of the problem lies in what Hromnik terms as the "indisputable" Asian origin of the curved bow and the fact that the indigenous peoples of southern Africa have used the simple bow in historical times. He traces the progress of what he calls a "pseudo-controversy" over the indigenous or non-indigenous origin of the curved bow in Africa. On the one side of that controversy, represented by Schrire and Deacon, authors have denied the existence of the bow, arguing that its appearance in early travel illustrations of the Quena is a careless overlay of European culture on African reality. By contrast, opponents from "rock art" studies have insisted that the bow clearly and repeatedly appears in San art. Claiming that the solution to this problem bears significance for the interpretation of early African history, however, Hromnik examines the drawings of Robert Gordon to argue that the curved bow was used by the Quena as late a 1781. He goes on to say that Leaky's distribution maps of the bow's use in Africa show that it filtered in through north-east Africa and that other linguistic evidence shows that the bow was non-indigenous. He lists certain !Kung and Qwena words for "bow" that have cognates in the Dravidic and Sanskrit languages of India, a fact that he says should not be surprising since Africa had contacts with India from the early first millennium B.C.E. Interpreting the crescent shapes on arrows in rock art as symbols of the Hindu deity Shiva, and equating Shiva with the Khoisan deity Heitsi-Eibib, he views ithyphallic figures in San rock art as illustrative of a form of Shiva worship. In setting forth this interpretation, he directs a sharp barb against Lewis-Williams' shamanic trance explanation of San "art," labeling it "highly fictitious."

B43   Jacobson, L. (1975). "The Gemsbok Creation Myth and Brandberg Rock Art." *South African Journal of Science*, vol. 71: 314.

The author responds in this brief note to Vinnicombe's essay on motivation in African rock art. He mentions Vinnicombe's claim that a gemsbok creation myth, analogous to that of the eland, is reflected in the paintings of the northern desert regions, and notes that her argument is based on the distribution figures of Rudner. The author's own work in the Brandberg area leads him to suspect the preponderance of small antelope in Rudner's sampling. Focusing on a descriptive remark in Rudner's report, he finds evidence that Rudner's small antelope category must also contain springbok, an animal that dominates his own list. He concludes that the springbok represents a significant theme in the rock art of the area, thus diminishing the importance of the gemsbok within any interpretational framework.

B44   Jolly, Peter (1986). "A First Generation Descendant of the Transkei San." *South African Archaeological Bulletin*, vol. 41, no. 143: 6-9.

Jolly states that at the time of writing there were no San living a traditional hunting and gathering way of life in the Transkei. However, his informant, an elderly woman from the Tsolo district of the Eastern Cape, was directly descended from an extinct group of hunter-gatherers. Drawing on her reports, the author provides an important analysis of San myth and ritual. The paper begins, however, with an historical overview. Notes from the reports of Gibson (1891), Callaway (1919), and Hammond-Tooke (1950) are included. Attention is then turned to the information provided by the San woman, which includes a description of an eland hunt. In the course of this description, the informant mentioned the fact that many rock paintings contained the blood of a freshly killed eland. Jolly says that the ethnography supports her remarks and refers to the work of How, who had an informant demonstrate the way in which the San painted. How reported that he had asked for the blood of a freshly slaughtered eland as an ingredient for the paint, and that his informant had prepared it in a ritualistic fashion that implied that the paint would possess magical power. Thereafter, the writer recounts aspects of his own informant's description of the capture of a river snake. In this regard, Jolly mentions Lewis-Williams' interpretation of the ritual as an example of a trance experience. The informant was also asked by Jolly to explain paintings depicting therianthropic figures. She offered two possible explanations: First, the paintings represented hunting disguises, or second, they depicted dancing healers. Jolly presents further ethnographic material that supports the second explanation, but concludes that it would be naive to believe that all therianthropes simply depicted masked dancers. He invokes Lewis-Williams' theory that the therianthropic figures served as painted metaphors for trance experience where the medicine specialist became "fused" with a particular animal. Jolly proposes that the meaning of the eland painting would alter if the reader acknowledged that "magical" substances from the ritually slaughtered animal were incorporated into the paint itself.

B45   Katz, Richard (1976). "Education for Transcendence." In Richard B. Lee and Irven DeVore (eds.) *Kalahari Hunter-Gatherers: Studies of the !Kung San and their Neighbours*. Cambridge, Mass.: Harvard University Press. 280-301.

All religions possess an element that searches intensely for contact with an ultimate level of being. Katz suggests that this element usually expresses itself in mystical approaches such as Zen Buddhism and Sufism, and that the central experience in this search is that of transcendence. He claims that by studying the !Kung, who have a "stone-age type existence," we can understand how the search for ultimate reality functions in a crucial stage of the human evolutionary sequence. After establishing this conceptual framework, the author moves to an examination of *!kia*-healing among the !Kung. Particularly, he emphasizes the educational process that prepares the novice for the experience of *!kia*. The context of the *!kia*-healing dance is described along with the roles played by various members of the community. According to Katz, the dance functions as the primary expression of religious and cosmological feeling. The experience of *!kia* itself is described as a heating of the supernatural force *n/um*, which then rises along the spine and explodes in the brain. It is viewed as a transcendent experience because it raises the person above the ordinary level of existence and bestows unusual powers. Finally, the training undergone by the candidate is set out. The role of the teacher in overcoming the apprentice's fear of the unknown, and the support and protection he provides once the threshold has been crossed, figures largely in this discussion. Katz concludes with general remarks on the possible functions of the experience of transcendence within modern society.

B46   Katz, Richard (1982). *Boiling Energy: Community Healing Among the Kalahari !Kung.* Cambridge, Mass.: Harvard University Press.

Katz states in his prologue that his professional research has been fueled by personal interest in healing, altered states of consciousness, and human potential. His book grows out of three months of fieldwork among the Dobe !Kung during 1968. An early chapter is devoted to a detailed description of the hunter-gatherer way of life: group movements, subsistence, dress, dwellings, and social relations. This chapter also contains a brief discussion of !Kung religion, stressing its all encompassing nature. Katz says that the Western distinction between "sacred" and "profane" has no meaning in this culture. Information on !Kung deities is neither codified nor consistent and difficult to elicit. Drawing on Marshall, Katz mentions a great god Gao Na, and a lesser, "trickster god," Kauha. These are attended by the spirits of the dead, the *//gauwasi.* It is these spirits who are believed to bring sickness and misfortune, and which must be addressed by the healers in trance. The next chapter describes the nature and circumstances of the trance dance, which takes place four times a month. Katz states that the dance is intended to activate the *n/um* or spiritual heat or energy of the healers. In turn, the release of *n/um* leads to an altered state called *!kia.* He reports his informants' descriptions of *n/um* as residing in the pit of the stomach, becoming vapor during the dance and rising in the spine to the base of the skull, at which point *!kia* occurs. These two terms are central and appear repeatedly in Katz's interviews with the healers. Chapter Six is especially devoted to the mythology surrounding *n/um,* as well as its experience and the effects and applications of different levels of *!kia.* Other chapters discuss the healer's apprenticeship, typical career, and female perspectives. Separate chapters are devoted to the lives and statements of several specific healers.

B47   Katz, Richard, and Megan Biesele (1986). "!Kung Healing: The Symbolism of Sex Roles and Culture Change." In Megan Biesele, Robert Gordon, and Richard Lee (eds.) *The Past and Future of !Kung Ethnography: Critical Reflections and Symbolic Perspectives. Essays in Honour of Lorna Marshall.* Quellen zür Khoisan-Forschung, vol. 4. Hamburg: Helmut Buske Verlag. 195-230.

This paper focuses on the interrelationship between altered-state healing and religious and ceremonial life, sex roles, and cultural change. It seeks to continue

a line of research influenced by the emerging studies on women and development anthropology. Three dances are described, namely, the Giraffe, Drum, and
Tree dances. In each dance, assert Katz and Biesele, different roles are assigned
to male and female healers. In describing the dances, the writers consequently
attempt to illustrate changing sex roles and other social features in !Kung society. The authors first describe the general context of !Kung dancing, which their
informants argued brought them into contact with the realm of Gao Na, the
high god, and the //gauwasi, the spirits of the dead. Following a detailed description of the Giraffe Dance, an account of the role of women in healing rites
is undertaken. Essentially, note the writers, women provided the rhythmic and
musical background for male healers who, in their dances, attempted to access a
supernatural potency called n/um. Once this n/um was "heated," note the writers, it "boiled" up the spine of a dancer and an altered state named !kia occurred. In the Drum Dance, a more modern development, the roles were
reversed as the women went into !kia while the men provided music and
rhythm. The Tree Dance, by contrast, was a solo performance before a passive
group of onlookers. After the dances are described, the authors summarize and
analyze their data. They emphasize that the Giraffe Dance is central to !Kung
religion and culture. The equal and complementary roles that both sexes play in
it are underscored. Comparisons are made concerning male and female approaches to the acquisition and use of n/um. The paper concludes with some
remarks on the future of egalitarianism in a society undergoing substantial
change.

B48   Keenan, Jeremy (1977). "The Concept of the Mode of Production in
Hunter-Gatherer Societies." *African Studies*, vol. 36, no. 1: 57-69.

Keenan's paper on modes of production in southern African Khoisan communities provides notes on the resurgence of Marxist theory in the analysis of
"primitive" societies, especially with regard the application of historical materialist concepts. In so doing, however, the writer primarily confines himself to a
critique of the "primitive communist" theorists Hindess and Hirst. Setting out
the salient features of this position, he is surprised that Hindess and Hirst chose
Lévi-Strauss' "comments" on the Nambikwara for their concrete examples, instead of relying on the work of Meillassoux. Keenan mentions several other
problems in their analysis before examining how the intervention of ideological
social relations at the economic level affects modes of production. Meillassoux
is then brought into the discussion, partly as a corrective, but partly to advance
Keenan's thesis that an examination of social and economic relationships
within groups like the Australian Aborigines and the Bushmen of the Kalahari
will aid research. The essay concludes illustrating the basic principles of this
historical-materialist analysis through a detailed discussion of kinship categories among the !Kung.

B49   Kolb, Peter (1731). *The Present State of the Cape of Good Hope.*
Trans. Guido Medley. London: W. Innys.

Peter Kolb was a German astronomer who lived at the Cape of Good Hope from
1705 to 1712. He remains of particular importance to historians of comparative
religion in this region for his remarkable comments on the religion of the
"Hottentots." Indeed, Chapter Eight of the *Present State* provides one of the
earliest accounts of Khoikhoi belief and ritual ever recorded. The book begins
by relating the author's difficulty in obtaining information concerning religious
beliefs from the Khoikhoi peoples. Kolb states that it was only when he moved
further away from the Cape that he found informants who were willing to provide details concerning their religion. He states that they believed in a supreme
being who was "the Creator of Heaven and Earth." However, this being, called
"Gounja Ticqvoa" (Tsui-//goab), was not the object of any ritual activity. Kolb
asserts that it was the moon that was worshipped by his informants, even though
they denied this. He describes in some detail the prolonged dancing that took
place at the time of the full moon. Further rituals associated with rites of passage and the so-called "pissing ceremony" are related. He then describes what
he believes to be the worship of the Mantis, and claims to have found evidence
of the veneration of "saints" and departed "men of renown." A final belief,
which Kolb thought he uncovered, was the "worship of an evil deity," called
Touqua (//Gaunab). The chapter closes with some remarks on the difficulty of
converting the Khoikhoi to Christianity, and several anecdotes to support this
claim are included.

B50   Layton, Robert, A. R. Willcox, and J. David Lewis-Williams (1987).
"Correspondence: The Cultural Context of Hunter-Gatherer Rock Art." *Man,*
vol. 22: 171-75.

In this exchange of responses to an earlier article by Layton, Willcox and
Lewis-Williams delineate two major methodological stances in the study of San
rock art. Since Layton's article rests on the theories of Lewis-Williams and
Vinnicombe, Willcox points his attack in this direction. He addresses the issue
of the statistical frequency of eland as an object of representation, a frequency
that Lewis-Williams viewed as an indication of the symbolic and religious significance that the animal held for the artists. Willcox believes that the explanation is far simpler—the eland was merely the artists' favorite "quarry." He gives
several pragmatic reasons for this assertion, among them the animal's tender
flesh and high fat content. Thus, he reasons, it is only natural that a hunter
would paint "pin-ups" of his favorite prey. He also argues that there may have
been purely aesthetic reasons for the high proportion of eland depictions. Lewis-
Williams responds by criticizing scholars who assert that the meaning of the art
is beyond recovery. His position is that the extensive body of San ethnography

records the rituals and beliefs that informed the art, and that Willcox is perpetuating an earlier period of uncertainty that has been laid to rest. Having dismissed Willcox, Lewis-Williams proceeds to present a succinct history of the San "rock art" debate, beginning with the initiation of "quantification studies" in the 1960s. Following those early efforts, a methodological divergence took place between those who felt that the meaning of the art could be derived from the paintings themselves and those, like the writer, who felt that San ethnography held the key. Lewis-Williams then describes the nature of this ethnography, referring principally to the Orpen and Bleek collections. He notes how a coherent body of belief and ritual was discovered that held wide temporal and spatial validity. The conclusion he arrives at is that San painting is shamanistic in character, and that the shamanistic nature of the art is independent of the species depicted.

B51   Lee, Richard B. (1967). "Trance Cure of the !Kung Bushman." *Natural History*, vol. 76, no. 9: 31-37.

This article discusses the trance dance of the !Kung, a dance considered by scholars to be a particular form of San "medicine." Lee describes the physical arrangement of the dance, particularly with reference to gendered spatial structures. He notes, for example, that women sit in a tight group, singing and clapping as the men encircle them. Lee emphasizes, however, that women would also dance if they chose. Next, the writer describes five phases of the dance and the resulting trance states these phases induce. The first phase is called "working up" (*chaxni chi*). During this preliminary period, singing and dancing begins in a casual and jovial atmosphere. In the second phase, dancers begin to enter trance as the supernatural force called *n/um* begins to "boil" and ascend the spine, finally exploding in the brain. Once this happens, the dancers enter a new phase, called "half-death," in which they lay rigid and trembling. Eventually, dancers emerge from the comatose state and begin active curing by placing their hands on the bodies of those present. The final phase is a return to normal consciousness. Lee points out that the trance state is produced by a combination of auto-suggestion, rhythmic dancing, intense concentration, and hyperventilation, emphasizing that drugs or external chemical means play no role in this performance. Once the dance and the circumstances leading up to its performance have been set out, Lee analyzes the chief symbols associated with the dance: boiling (*n/um*), fire (*da*), and sweat (*cho*). Additional powers experienced in trance, such as the ability to see ghosts, and distance and x-ray vision, are mentioned. The author then contrasts the trance dancer with shamans in other societies. He underscores the fact that the Bushman trance healers remain tightly integrated within the community, whereas Siberian and Pawnee shamans, for example, are isolated and often feared. The article concludes with some remarks on the general social benefits of the healing */kia* dance.

B52   Lee, Richard B. (1968). "The Sociology of !Kung Bushman Trance Performance." In R. Prince (ed.) *Trance and Possession States*. Montreal: R. M. Bucke Memorial Society. 35-54.

Based on fieldwork conducted among an isolated population of 430 Bushmen in the years 1963 and 1965, Lee points out in this article on trance dance that the !Kung are one of the last remaining hunter-gatherer societies, and that this form of existence was, until 10,000 years ago, a universal mode of human organization. The author begins his discussion of trance by describing the !Kung dances that usually initiated healing. Spatial arrangements, sex roles, and the scheduling of the dances receive a brief overview. The various phases of trance are then set out, among them the "working up," "entering trance," "half death," "active curing," and "return to normal state" phases. Next, the main symbols of trance dance are enumerated, including boiling (*n/um*), fire (*da*), and sweat (*cho*). Additionally, powers bestowed by trance dance are mentioned. For example, Lee notes that the trance performer often received a second sight that allowed for the perception of ghosts (*//gauwasi*) and the faculty of telescopic vision. The ability to change into animal form and to offer mystical protection for the group was also perceived to be a corollary of the trance state. In another section, Lee describes the process of recruitment and training for potential trance performers. He emphasizes that trance is not an elitist function since approximately half of the men and women interviewed were capable of performing. The paper concludes with an examination of how trance dance might be compared to similar altered states of consciousness, shamanism, and witchcraft.

B53   Lee, Richard B. (1979). *The Dobe !Kung*. Toronto: Holt, Rinehart & Winston.

In this book Lee draws on an expansive period of fieldwork to describe subsistence strategies and aspects of social organization among the Dobe !Kung. However, in Chapter Eight, "Coping with Life: Religion, Worldview and Healing," the writer specifically deals with religious matters. For example, he describes beliefs associated with the *//gauwasi*, the ghosts of the recently deceased who were believed to cause illness and misfortune. He also illustrates this belief with an anecdote about a villager who had been caught in a lion trap: A healer told Lee that the wounded leg would not kill the man. Rather, the ghost of a specific villager, whom he identified while in trance, was responsible for the ailing man's suffering. The narrative leads Lee into a brief outline of !Kung belief in a high god, Gao Na, and a lesser god, Kauna. The roles of each of these gods in creation and destruction are a matter of dispute among his informants, but they all agree that the main source of misfortune is the *//gauwasi*. Lee attempts, with limited success, to elicit the reasons for the malevolence of these entities, and then passes to the chief topic of the chapter, the force of *n/um* and its use in trance and healing. One of Lee's informants describes the physical sensations of the onset of *n/um*, the trance state of *!kia*, and the erratic behavior of the dancer who has gone into trance. Lee provides an analysis of the trance dance as the primary form of !Kung ritual life. He relates the difficulties of young !Kung men as they attempt to obtain this healing power and traces the more recent history and development of women healers and trance dancers

B54   Lee, Richard B. (1968). "What Hunters do for a Living, or, How to Make Out on Scarce Resources." In Richard B. Lee and Irven DeVore (eds.) *Man the Hunter*. Chicago: Aldine. 30-48.

Lee begins by addressing some anthropological assumptions prevalent in hunter-gatherer research. He questions the notion that hunter-gatherer societies were primarily dependent on the hunting of game, and whether this way of life was generally as precarious and arduous as inquirers have insisted. He accuses anthropologists of consistently underestimating the viability of even those "marginal isolates" of hunting peoples that have been available to ethnographers. The purpose of his paper is to analyze the food gathering activities of one such "marginal" people, namely the !Kung of the Kalahari. In so doing, he concludes that plant and marine sources are far more important than are game animals in the diet. Moreover, he suggests that with a few conspicuous exceptions, hunter-gatherer subsistence economies are based on reliable strategies that routinely rendered abundant supplies. The paper provides comparative studies of different hunter-gatherer societies, and encompasses ecological inquiry. It is appended with maps and tables of the various hunter-gatherer communities discussed.

B55   Lewis-Williams, J. David (1977). "Led by the Nose: Observations on the Supposed use of Southern San Rock Art in Rain-Making Rituals." *African Studies*, vol. 36, no. 2: 155-59.

In this short paper Lewis-Williams argues that two schools in rock art studies have emerged, one that views art as a form of sympathetic magic, the other that sees art as simply an expression of "primitive aesthetics." He criticizes the second school for believing that their theory is self-evident and requires no demonstration. He then proceeds to examine the theoretical position set forth by Vinnicombe and Pager, who assert that San art played a role in "magical" rain-making rituals. Lewis-Williams cites Vinnicombe's selective use of informants to remark that that writer misinterpreted the meaning of San engravings. He concludes that direct evidence for the use of art in rainmaking rituals is suspect and that further speculation in that direction is profitless in the absence of further data. Lewis-Williams concludes by arguing that it would be more productive to examine the meaning of the representations in the broader context of San belief.

B56   Lewis-Williams, J. David (1980a). "Remarks on Southern San Religion and Art." *Religion in Southern Africa*, vol. 1, no. 2: 19-32.

Lewis-Williams' purpose in this paper is to reexamine nineteenth-century ethnographic descriptions of San religion, commenting on the relationship between San belief, ritual, and rock art. In the first part of the paper, the writer mentions the fact that some early missionaries thought that the San had no religion at all, citing remarks to that effect attributed to the London Missionary Society agents Robert Moffat and Joseph Tindall. He then discusses the problematic nature of the supernatural San deity /Kaggen, whose name translates as Mantis. The scholarly controversy over this identification is traced. Here, Lewis-Williams attempts to resolve debate by emphasizing the kaleidoscopic nature of this figure, who could assume many forms, including that of the Mantis. The name itself might have resulted from the Mantis' importance as a hunting oracle. The author then turns to a discussion of San medicine and trance dancing. Other rituals, among them female puberty rites, are mentioned. The second section of the article then examines theories advanced to explain the meaning of rock art as "art for art's sake" (Willcox); as depiction of religious subjects and personages (Johnson, How, and Rudner); and as "sympathetic hunting magic" (Klingender). Vinnicombe's work is singled out for its perceptive use of the ethnography in pointing towards underlying religious aspects concerned with *n/um* (heat, or supernatural force), and *!kia*. Lewis-Williams states that the real connection between art and religion is to be found in the use of metaphor and symbol. The remainder of the article is devoted to developing this suggestion through an analysis of the integrative symbolic role performed by the metaphor of the eland.

B57   Lewis-Williams, J. David (1980b). "Ethnography and Iconography: Aspects of Southern San Thought and Art." *Man*, vol. 15: 467-82.

The Southern San have been extinct for nearly a century, and their painting remains enigmatic since there are no living practitioners. Lewis-Williams feels, however, that a valid source of interpretation can still be found in the nineteenth-century ethnographic collections of Orpen and Bleek. He notes that Orpen was directed to some paintings by an informant named Qing, who then rendered explanations regarding content and meaning. Later, Bleek showed copies of these paintings to an informant named Dia!kwain who in turn offered his own interpretation. The author states that these comments are valuable for two reasons: First, they point to conceptual links between extinct southern San groups and contemporary Kalahari !Kung; and second, they show that the paintings were not "playthings," but in fact artistic representations of religious beliefs. The apparent confusion between these two accounts has troubled some researchers. However, Lewis-Williams explains the distinction, arguing that concepts inherent in the art are encoded in certain key metaphors that neither the recorders nor subsequent writers have understood. The article is an attempt to correct these misapprehensions. Through a close comparison of two informants' remarks, therefore, Lewis-Williams unpacks the symbolism of underwater journeys, therianthropic figures, and depictions of eland. Elements of the trance dance, such as certain postures and nasal bleeding, are also developed. Corroborating evidence apparent in contemporary !Kung ritual is used to amplify the statements of several informants. In conclusion, the author says that there is overall unanimity between both narratives and that it is clear that the paintings depict the rituals of healers and their trance experiences. Thus, a connection between ethnography and iconography can be established to mutually illuminate both accounts.

B58   Lewis-Williams, J. David (1981a). *Believing and Seeing: Symbolic Meanings in Southern San Rock Paintings*. London: Academic Press.

Following an overview of several methodological considerations in the first half of this book, Lewis-Williams reaffirms his central thesis that the meaning of San rock art cannot be reduced to a system of signs serving primarily aesthetic considerations. Rather, in departing from earlier "linguistic models," advocated by, among others Lévi-Strauss and Leach, he adopts a simplified semiotic system, derived from the works of Peirce and Morris, to assert that San art is an expression of ritual and trance experience. In the second chapter, therefore, he reviews previous scholarship to attack scholars, among them Willcox, who insist that San paintings are merely iconic references of artistic expression. In the next chapter, following Turner's admonition that a system of signs must have "position," the author then provides a detailed analysis of the types of paintings found at several San sites. Chapter Three discusses ethnographical resources, especially those contained in the collections of Bleek, Lloyd, and Orpen. A full history of these works is provided. In Part Two of the book, the writer illustrates the symbolism of the eland in various liminal situations in San culture. One chapter deals with female puberty rituals, another with hunting initiation rituals, and a third with marriage rituals. The central chapter then describes the beliefs and rituals of healers and trance dancers that constitute the primary resources of San religion. Here, Lewis-Williams argues that the most important function of rock art was to represent various aspects of dance and the shamanic trances that resulted from hyper-ventilation and rhythmic movement. The final chapters deal with rain ceremonies and divination. Lewis-Williams concludes the book by returning to a discussion of his simplified semiotic model and its

theoretical implications for the analysis of San rock art. The work is richly illustrated.

B59   Lewis-Williams, J. David (1981b). "The Thin Red Line: Southern San
Notions and Rock Paintings of Supernatural Potency." *South African Archaeological Bulletin*, vol. 36: 5-13.

Lewis-Williams points out that several enigmatic features found in San rock art
have puzzled writers for many years. Among the most prominent, both of the art
and of interpretive inquiry, remains the meaning of the sinuous and bifurcating
"red line," often fringed with white dots, that frequently embellishes the art
form. Some earlier attempts at interpretation are cited, included among them
the works of Pager, Du Toit, Woodhouse, and Vinnicombe. The author says that
these explanations are correct in pointing to an abstract entity, but aside from
Vinnicombe, they lack force because they are not based on an examination of
Southern San ethnography. He also finds the work extant on Northern San rock
art relevant, since it has been shown that these San share similar cognitive systems with the Southern Kalahari San. The starting point of Lewis-Williams'
interpretation, therefore, is a Northern San informant's statement that the red
line was a "sorcerer's thing." The statement is followed by a brief enumeration
of different types of /Xam healers, such as curers, game medicine doctors, and
rain makers. The author states that they all performed their functions by entering into a trance state. Also, their activities were associated with notions of a
supernatural potency connected with the notion of *n/um*, or spiritual heat. After
establishing this background, Lewis-Williams provides a detailed examination
of four paintings that contain the so-called red line, describing the key metaphors of potency that he argues Southern San painters translated into graphic
symbols. In a concluding section, Lewis-Williams suggests that the line owed its
popularity and diffusion to the fact that it effectively signified the diverse experiences of trance in an abstract, graphical form.

B60   Lewis-Williams, J. David (1982). "The Economic and Social Context
of Southern San Rock Art." *Current Anthropology*, vol. 23, no. 4: 429-49.

Lewis-Williams begins this paper with a critique of innatist and functionalist
approaches to San rock art. He feels that the innatist position (as represented by
Burkitt, Willcox, Batiss, Veder, and Rudner) is ultimately tautological insofar
as it infers a mental state to explain the meaning of art. The functionalist interpretation (represented by Vinnicombe, Dutton, Leroi-Gourhan, and Willis) is
found to be conceptually inadequate. Lewis-Williams suggests that a more interesting theoretical perspective is one that focuses on production in San society
and the social relations and ideology with which it is connected. He asserts that

a knowledge of this infrastructure is the key to understanding ritual activity and ideology. Basing his argument on ethnographical material collected by Wilhelm and Dorothea Bleek, the author provides a detailed account of the social and economic circumstances of the /Xam. He then moves to a discussion of the "symbolic" work of the healer in the context of trance dance. Rock art, he argues, was produced by healers and undertaken to represent trance experiences. In an analysis of a painting from Glenavon, Lewis-Williams articulates the central metaphor of the "dying eland" and its economic associations. Out-of-body travel is discussed in terms of cementing social and economic relations. In a concluding section, the writer summarizes new theoretical perspectives by reiterating that San rock art was a symbolic and ideological activity that reflected social order and economic production. The article is followed by comments from various scholars.

B61   Lewis-Williams, J. David (1983a). "Introductory Essay: Science and Rock Art." In *New Approaches to Southern African Rock Art. South African Archaeological Society Goodwin Series*, vol. 4: 3-13.

Lewis-Williams states in his Introduction that the study of rock art is only beginning to be accorded a position among the "scientific" branches of African archaeology; to maintain its status, new forms of method and theory will have to be produced. In this regard, he asserts that empiricist paradigms that have dominated archaeology are inadequate for interpretation. He suggests that an attempt be made to look beneath empirical surfaces for more "explanatory connections," dismissing the widely held notion that the meaning of San art is irrecoverable. The possibility of interpretation, he argues, is thus premised on the need for a new examination of ethnographical records, particularly the collections of Bleek, Lloyd, and Orpen. Correlating this nineteenth-century material with Vinnicombe's more recent work, Lewis-Williams asserts that the continuities of belief and ritual found within their combined records can be usefully engaged in examining the meaning of rock "art." He then gives a brief history of empiricist geological paradigms that have dominated the field and describes prevalent emphases on stratigraphy and typology. In this context, Willcox is accused of avoiding interpretation because of confining his work to dating and distribution studies. Stressing the importance of a paradigm shift toward ethnographic research, Lewis-Williams quotes Lévi-Strauss to argue that connections between the paintings can help simplify the task of interpretation, and that these connections occur in the form of repeated metaphors. Only the interpreter who is well versed in the ethnographic material will be in a position to recognize the unity that these metaphors produce through diverse images. In an examination of well-known paintings from the Drakensberg, a specific "metaphorical link"—the death of the eland—is unpacked and a contrast delineated between empiricist perceptions and the search for metaphorical connections. This method is shown to reveal linking metaphors in the art that are associated with the trance state of San healers.

B62   Lewis-Williams, J. David (1983b). *The Rock Art of Southern Africa.* Cambridge: Cambridge University Press.

This book forms part of the "Imprint of Man" series—a collection of scholarly works dedicated to prehistoric art. In the first chapter, Lewis-Williams stresses the difficulty and necessity of abandoning Eurocentric preconceptions to penetrate what original viewers thought about rock art. The second chapter presents an ethnological sketch of the San, drawing on materials collected by Bleek and supplemented by modern ethnographic studies of the Northern !Kung. Subsistence strategies, methods of hunting, and social structures are briefly described. While discussing the role of religion in San societies, the author elaborates on the role of indigenous healers and describes their practice of entering trance in order to ameliorate suffering, direct hunting, or bring rain. He suggests that most art is associated with the trance experience and hallucination. Chapter Three attempts to date the art, provide a system of classification, and describe the characteristics of art in specific areas of San diffusion. The author states that the uniformity of the art in space and time points to a continuity that stretches from the ethnography of the contemporary !Kung, through the collections of Bleek, to timeless !Kung paintings. This continuity, he asserts, justifies the use of ethnography in the interpretation of rock art. Chapter Four deals with theoretical matters and examines some of the quantitative methods that are employed in the quest for scientific objectivity. In Chapter Five, Lewis-Williams seeks to unfold the metaphors of death and transformation that are commonly used to describe trance experiences. The following chapters build on this discussion of metaphor to engage in a detailed analysis of several paintings. The final section of the book contains color photographs of paintings, engravings, and maps.

B63   Lewis-Williams, J. David (1984a). "The Empiricist Impasse in Southern African Rock Art Studies." *South African Archaeological Bulletin*, vol. 39, no. 139: 58-66.

Lewis-Williams examines two opposing interpretive positions in the evaluation of San rock art: one that views the art as an essentially aesthetic depiction of historical and mythical events, another that views the art as primarily a symbolic expression of shamanic trance experience. Lewis-Williams asserts that the epistemological and methodological differences between these positions are so profound that debate has become difficult. The paper assumes the form of a critique of the work of Willcox, the leading proponent of the "*art pour l'art*" position. Lewis-Williams states at the outset that this position probably represents a "degenerating research programme, incapable of resuscitation." His argument focuses on theoretical issues, and begins with an attack on the empiricist orientation itself. He attempts to invalidate the three central methods of the approach by denying first that data can be collected objectively, second that classification of data can precede analysis, and third, that inductive argumentation produces reliable conclusions. Willcox's assertion that the "simplest" explanation is always preferable is dismissed and the question of what constitutes an explanatory hypothesis is raised. Drawing on the philosophy of science, Lewis-Williams argues that the simple hypothesis is to be preferred only when it can match up with five criteria: compatibility with well-supported theory; internal consistency; quantity of data explained; diversity of data explained; and heuristic potential. Throughout the paper, Willcox's general distaste for theory and his consequent "inability" to contribute to the theoretical advance of the field of research is emphasized and illustrated. The contentions presented in the paper are supported by Lewis-Williams' own interpretive work within the "shamanic" school and, consequently, reference is made to his analysis of several specific paintings.

B64   Lewis-Williams, J. David (1984b). "Ideological Continuities in Prehistoric Southern Africa: The Evidence of Rock Art." In Carmel Schrire (ed.) *Past and Present in Hunter Gatherer Studies*. New York: Academic Press. 225-52.

Lewis-Williams asserts that although archaeologists analyzed prehistoric subsistence strategies in Africa, little effort was made to recover the ideological presuppositions implicit in these strategies or in the seasonal mobility tactics that accompanied them. However, by drawing on ethnographic materials from nineteenth-century ethnographers, among them Bleek and Orpen, as well as from twentieth-century anthropologists, including Lee, Marshall, Silberbauer, and Tobias, Lewis-Williams argues that some of these ideological assumptions can be recovered through a careful assessment of San rock art. The author focuses specifically on ideologies that are implicit in paintings portraying ritual dance and trance states. He sees a conceptual unity in these paintings that extends across fairly wide geographical distances, a fact that escaped many interpreters because they failed to recognize the broad metaphorical character of what seemed to be localized objects. Establishing kinship as the overriding ideology of the San, Lewis-Williams thus proceeds to analyze rock art in functional terms. Basic features of San socioeconomic life that are uncovered in this inquiry include access to resources, regulation of labor, and social forms of resource distribution. The study is supported by close examination of several paintings, many of which are reproduced. An extensive bibliography is included.

B65   Lewis-Williams, J. David (1985). "Testing the Trance Explanation of Southern African Rock Art." *Bollettino del Centro Camuno di Studi Preistorici,* vol. 22: 47-62.

In this paper Lewis-Williams once again criticizes trends in rock art interpretation that fail to consult San ethnography, claiming that particularist aesthetic inductions that purport to be "theory-free" are actually governed by Eurocentric notions about art. A more fruitful line of inquiry, he asserts, focuses on ethnographic records to suggest that San rock art is essentially an expression of shamanic experience. He emphasizes that the distinction between the two methods goes beyond a matter of degree to embody fundamental divergences in theory and method. Drawing on the philosophy of science, Lewis-Williams argues that a hypothesis must be properly tested and proceeds to present a series of canons for judging assumptions about the meaning of rock art. Essentially, an explanation will be superior if it refers to specific San beliefs, rituals, and customs, rather than to vague Eurocentric conceptions about the meaning of art and the function of the artist. In order to illustrate his argument, the author turns to an examination of paintings that portray felines, and attempts to elucidate the underlying concepts that provided the context for these images. In the course of his examination, Lewis-Williams identifies elements that were ignored by previous interpreters, but which are known from ethnographical reports to imply shamanistic trance experience. Among these are signs of nasal bleeding, lines issuing from the heads of painted figures, therianthropic figures, and red lines on the faces of figures. Additional weaknesses in literal or *"art pour l'art"* interpretations are pointed out. The author states in his conclusion that San beliefs adequately explain the various depictions, and that the trance explanation not only elucidates more details, but also allows the paintings to be located within a larger San cognitive system.

B66   Lewis-Williams, J. David (1986a). "Cognitive and Optical Illusions in San Rock Art Research." *Current Anthropology,* vol. 27: 171-78.

Citing Inskeep's distinction between "learning about" and "learning from" San rock art, the author points out that many researchers have prematurely pursued a course of inquiry consistent with the latter. Consequently, they have "discovered" cultural artifacts in the paintings that find no parallel in the ethnographic record. He stresses the importance of realizing the true nature of the art before trying to extract ethnographic data from it, and suggests that the art is of such a type that a "narrative" or solely "aesthetic" line of analysis could prove entirely fruitless. Lewis-Williams claims that the art portrays not only objects and practices from the "real" world, but also metaphors, symbols, and hallucinations derived from the trance experiences of San shamans. Thus, the student of rock art who has long viewed it as a record of daily life, will have difficulty accepting the fact that San art is essentially symbolic and hallucinatory. The author illustrates this assertion in his analysis of several examples. The first depicts what was formerly interpreted as a line of men running along a bridge. Through closer examination of this feature and other smaller details in the painting, the "bridge" is seen to disappear, and a symbolic representation of shamanic potency emerges. Lewis-Williams extends this type of analysis through a consideration of other paintings. In the process, he exposes emergent hallucinatory elements, such as zigzag phosphemes, corporal elongation, and metaphorical creatures. At the end of the paper Lewis-Williams states that his aim is not only to suggest a more authentic form of interpretation, but also to warn against a naive use of rock art as a source for learning about San material culture.

B67   Lewis-Williams, J. David (1986b). "Paintings of Power: Ethnography and Rock Art in Southern Africa." In Megan Biesele, Robert Gordon, and Richard B. Lee (eds.) *The Past and Future of !Kung Ethnography: Critical Reflections and Symbolic Performances. Essays in Honour of Lorna Marshall.* Quellen zür Khoisan-Forschung, vol. 4. Hamburg: Helmut Buske Verlag. 231-73.

The Marshall family's ethnography of the contemporary Northern San of the Kalahari desert, when compared to the earlier ethnography of the extinct Southern San, suggests Lewis-Williams, is signal to a possible pan-San cognitive system. In fact, the writer believes that the key to interpreting Southern San rock art lies in the descriptions of ritual found in this ethnography, and that any attempt at explanation that ignores the ethnographic record is suspect. The particular focus of this paper, however, is directed at trance dance rituals. In the trance, notes Lewis-Williams, San healers enter a hallucinatory state in order to approach the spiritual world; having accomplished the "journey," they are empowered to repulse threatening spirits and remove sickness. The central argument of the paper is that rock art is principally associated with these transcendent experiences and supermundane powers. The author develops his argument by referring to Marshall's accounts of the !Kung trance dance and compares details of the ritual with depictions commonly found in San rock art. Scenes of women clapping, men dancing in bent postures, and the presence of objects used in the dance are correlated with the ethnographic record. Symptoms of deep trance described by Marshall, such as nasal bleeding and the "arms back" position, are located in the painting. In the second half of the paper, Lewis-Williams also draws on recent neurological research to explain other elements found in the art. He describes how during the first level of trance San participants "see" geometric forms, or "form constants," such as zigzags, chevrons, dots, grids, and vortexes. The author suggests that rock paintings containing similar images represent the actual hallucinatory experiences of the artist. Lewis-Williams concludes this paper with a discussion of !Kung meta-phors, such as "death" and "flight," that are used in the rock art to capture trance experiences.

B68　Lewis-Williams, J. David (1986c). "The Last Testament of the South-ern San." *South African Archaeological Bulletin*, vol. 41, no. 143: 10-11.

This brief paper forms an adjunct to Jolly's (1986) more detailed presentation of information obtained from first generation Transkei San residents. The writer begins, however, by noting difficulties inherent in the interpretation of San rock art. He recalls that since the Southern San were essentially extinct by the turn of the century, researchers resorted to the nineteenth-century ethnographic collec-tions of Orpen and Bleek. However, Jolly's subsequent work among the North-ern San of the Kalahari confirmed that a pan-San cognitive system was prevalent—a fact that was to prove crucial for the interpretation of San art. Thus, Lewis-Williams states that certain symbolic features found in San paint-ing, viewed as an expression of this pan-San system, reinforced his opinion that rock art was shamanistic in nature. Since this conclusion was reached without the direct assistance of Southern San informants, its validity was questioned, and for this reason, Jolly's interviews were important. However, the author urges caution in evaluating the reliability of Jolly's statements on the meaning of rock art, submitting them to careful scrutiny in the light of ethnographic rec-ords. He finds that Jolly's repeated insistence on the shamanistic nature of the art conforms with Bleek's earlier assessment. In this regard, the Lewis-William's anthropological inquiry effectively dismisses competing interpreta-tions—the traditional "aesthetic," the "historical narrative," and the "sympathetic magic" interpretations—that have been applied to the study of San rock art.

B69　Lewis-Williams, J. David (1987). "A Dream of Eland: An Unexplored Component of San Shamanism and Rock Art." *World Archaeology*, vol. 19: 165-77.

For many years, notes Lewis-Williams, San rock painting was assumed to be an essentially decorative art. Rejecting this assumption, he notes that this interpre-tive position has been superseded by one that sees the art as essentially sha-manistic in nature. From this perspective, individual paintings are interpreted in terms of symbolic potency, significant postures, entoptic phenomena, and meta-phors of trance experience. A "syntax" and "vocabulary" are consequently ac-cumulated to allow researchers to "read" increasingly complex painted "texts." In this article, Lewis-Williams contributes to the interpretive process by ad-dressing an aspect of shamanic experience frequently ignored: dreaming. The author quotes passages from the Bleek collection that reveal how the shaman was able, while sleeping, to guard the village, or to transform himself into an animal form for the purpose of undertaking extracorporeal journeys. This "dreaming" phenomenon is further developed in a more detailed examination of /Xam belief. In that examination, the distinctions between dream activity and trance experience is viewed as ill-defined—a definitional fuzziness described, following Mircea Eliade, as being indicative of shamanic societies. Following this analysis, the author moves to a consideration of two specific paintings. Both include the eland. The significance of that animal as a symbol of potency is thus elucidated. Certain postures and experiences, such as nasal bleeding and face markings, suggests Lewis-Williams, indicate that the eland actually portrays shamans in their dreaming state. Thus, figures labeled "trance-bucks" are singled out as hallucinatory representations of a shamanic experience, particularly the experience of being "fused with animal potency." Lewis-Williams concludes his analysis by noting that even if some facets of his argument appear conjectural, the essentially shamanistic character of San rock art remains unquestionable.

B70   Lewis-Williams, J. David (1988a). "People of the Eland: An Archaeo-Linguistic Crux." In Tim Ingold, David Riches, and James Woodburn (eds.) *Hunters and Gatherers: Property, Power and Ideology*, vol. 2. Oxford: Saint Martin's Press. 203-12.

Following Werner's (1908) observation, and citing Vinnicombe's (1976) more sophisticated analysis, Lewis-Williams asserts that the eland was considered by the San to be a sacred animal cognate with /Kaggen, or the Mantis. Indeed, Vinnicombe's informant, he notes, actually employed the evocative phrase "people of the eland" to describe San associations with the animal. The writer's purpose in this paper, therefore, is to examine the social and cognitive context of San rock art, first by deploying linguistic methods to ascertain the context of the phrase, and second by drawing on the ethnographic records contained in the Bleek collection of /Xam texts. In so doing, he determines that the phrase "people of the eland" was used to refer to the relationship between trance dance healers and the animal. Focusing on the concept of !kia, or "possession by heat," he traces a series of meanings ranging from "control" over the eland during hunting, to the possession of personal power derived from the animal. The link between practitioner and animal is further developed through an examination of several therianthropic paintings. One /Xam informant, he recalls, said that the figures represented medicine people who "own" the eland and can transform themselves into the form of that animal. The author concludes that realistic paintings of animals in rock art may in fact be representations of the trance experiences of healers in animal form. In this way the social and cognitive context of rock painting is seen to be that of shamanism.

B71   Lewis-Williams, J. David (1988b). "Preparation for Transformation: Some Remarks on the Role of Metaphors in San Shamanism." In Edgard Sienaert and Nigel Bell (eds.) *Catching Winged Words: Oral Tradition and Education*. Natal University Documentation and Research Centre. Durban: University of Natal Press. 34-45.

Shamanism dominates the San's understanding of the world. Indeed, according to the author, San cosmology is based on shamanistic states of consciousness and the culture-specific interpretations that are placed on these experiences. An essential component of interpretation, therefore, should be metaphor, and the paper provides a description how an identifiable set of metaphors function to provide a conceptual framework for San ritual, myth, and art. Lewis-Williams begins by briefly summarizing the role of the shaman before moving to a discussion of the preparations necessary to induce trance and endure the new set of experiential parameters that it imposes. Drawing on research into altered states of consciousness, Lewis-Williams lists the stages that subjects pass through as trance deepens. A description of various hallucinatory experiences is undertaken. Arguing that these experiences are determined by the human nervous system, he claims that direct correlations can be drawn between laboratory subjects and the San shaman. The San novice is culturally conditioned to expect certain hallucinations by listening to accounts of trance that employ metaphors such as "death," "flight," and the "underwater world." Lewis-Williams explains how these metaphors operate in rock art through an analysis of several paintings. He concludes that the prominence of these metaphors in art and oral recitation serve to prepare the apprentice for the overwhelming experiences they were to encounter.

B72   Lewis-Williams, J. David (1989). "Southern Africa's Place in the Archaeology of Human Understanding." *South African Journal of Science*, vol. 85: 47-52.

Criticizing archaeologists for emphasizing technology and economy at the expense of belief, ritual, and religion, Lewis-Williams attempts in this paper to reinforce the necessity of pursuing studies in cognitive archaeology, or the "archaeology of the mind." In this regard, he argues that by limiting inquiry to objects that can be excavated, and analyzing merely economies of production that manufactured these objects, researchers exclude what is essential to human experience. For the sake of illustration, he turns to a consideration of Upper Paleolithic art and the specific types of questions that a cognitive archaeologist might ask. Instead of inquiring about the painter's hunting methods or stone artifacts, therefore, he or she would ask why the painting was made, and whether it was associated in some way with an early religion. Seeking to delineate southern Africa's contribution to this enterprise, the author traces the parallel history of the study of Upper Paleolithic and San rock art. While European art has remained enigmatic, he suggests, San rock art has been successfully interpreted by reexamining ethnographic records and neuro-psychological evidence. Lewis-Williams says that material contained in the ethnographic collections of Bleek and Orpen, supported by modern studies of the Northern !Kung, make it clear that San art is informed by the shamanistic practice of trance and its resulting experiences and hallucinations. Thus, altered-state research can successfully contribute to explaining certain elements of San art, among them entoptic phenomena. Extrapolating from the results of similar research paradigms, the author proves successfully that since the human nervous system is invariable, scholars can ascertain the type of hallucination an Upper Paleolithic artist might have had if their art reflected an altered state of consciousness. A table is provided that shows hallucinatory elements shared by laboratory experience, San rock art, and western European cave art. Thus, progress in the study of San rock art can shed light on the cognitive archaeology of other societies.

B73   Lewis-Williams, J. David (1990). *Discovering Southern African Rock Art*. Cape Town: David Philip.

In an introductory chapter to this general survey of southern African San art, Lewis-Williams uses the metaphors of optical illusion to illustrate the ways in which significant advances have been made in so-called "cognitive archaeology." Just as a "rabbit" in an optical illusion can change into a "duck" at the blink of an eye, he suggests, so too can a radical new theory transform the ways in which subjects are viewed. The "transformation" he presents in this book assumes that Western ways of "seeing" rock art have been subverted by more "authentic" paradigms implicit to San cognitive sets. The book is structured around the three most significant ways of analyzing San art, while the introduction locates their historical origins. In these terms, Lewis-Williams suggests that while John Barrow initiated an "aesthetic" approach and James Alexander a "narrative" inquiry, both nineteenth-century travelers foreshadowed recent interpretive strategies encompassing "shamanistic" analysis. Following this introduction, separate chapters are devoted to each approach. Here the possibilities and limitations of the aesthetic and narrative approaches are developed prior to an assessment of more reliable shamanistic interpretations. Lewis-Williams shows how statements found in the ethnographic collections of Bleek and Orpen led him to develop this approach. Knowledge of San belief and its application to rock art is illustrated in an examination of thematic codes in several paintings. This is followed, in Chapter Six, by an examination of the correlatives between hallucinatory entoptic phenomena in San paintings and contemporary "altered state" research. The concluding chapters deal with more scholarly debates concerning the polyvalent quality of San art. The volume is illustrated.

B74   Lewis-Williams, J. David (1992). "Ethnographic Evidence Relating to Trancing and Shamans Among Northern Bushmen." *South African Archaeological Bulletin*, vol. 47: 56-60.

Lewis-Williams begins this paper by stating that discussions of southern African rock art have focused on San ritual specialists variously labeled as "medicine people," "sorcerers," "magicians," or "shamans." Two questions are then put forward: First, do the specialists enter an altered "trance" state, and second, can they legitimately be called "shamans"? In answer to the first question, Lewis-Williams examines the logic of Katz's (1982) reluctance to use the word "trance." He quotes twelve workers in the field who prefer its use, and so accepts the term himself. Having established the fact that the modern !Kung enter trance, the author reexamines nineteenth-century ethnographic materials, notably in the collections of Bleek and Orpen, for traces of any trance-like experiences among Southern /Xam informers. The meaning of several terms are examined, among them the equivalent of the !Kung term */kia*—a word that explicitly refers to the experience of trance. Lewis-Williams then addresses his second question—"the feasibility of the term shaman"—citing Mircea Eliade's definition of shamanism and applying it to the southern African situation. Other writers who employ the term in the context of San rock art studies are also quoted, among them Winkelman, Noll, Hewitt, and Guenther. In order to justify his use of the term, however, Lewis-Williams again examines ethnographic evidence. /Xam equivalents of the !Kung expression *n/um* are compared. Lewis-Williams concludes from the analysis that the term "shaman" is an appropriate one in the southern African context.

B75   Lewis-Williams, J. David, and Megan Biesele (1978). "Eland Hunting Rituals among Northern and Southern San Groups: Striking Similarities." *Africa*, vol. 48: 117-34.

In this paper, Lewis-Williams and Biesele compare hunting rituals and eland myths drawn from two San groups, the !Kung of the Kalahari and the extinct Cape /Xam. At the outset, the authors establish the legitimacy of comparing materials obtained from !Kung ethnography and /Xam rock painting. They note that although ecological and linguistic differences abound, these are insufficient to warrant major discrepancies. Indeed, by using the results of fieldwork among the !Kung, they show that despite these differences evidence exists for a pan-San cognitive system. The argument is developed in three stages. First, the physical and behavioral characteristics of the eland are described. Second, remarks on the relationship between San groups and the significance of the eland in San thought and art is clarified and illustrated by using material garnered from the Bleek collection, statements made by !Kung informants, and quantitative studies of rock paintings in the Drakensberg. And third, having established that the eland is widely regarded with some respect in both groups, San hunting rituals are described in detail. Attention is drawn to the "first-kill" rituals for young men. Lewis-Williams and Biesele argue that structural equivalencies between Northern and Southern San groups suggest the feasibility of positing a common conceptual framework. Indeed, the writers believe that it is legitimate to employ !Kung material in order to amplify limited /Xam records, and to use both to examine eland symbolism in Southern San myth, ritual, and art.

B76   Lewis-Williams, J. David, and Thomas A. Dowson (1988). "Signs of All Times: Entoptic Phenomena in Upper Paleolithic Art." *Current Anthropology*, vol. 29: 201-45.

Upper Paleolithic art has posed an intractable challenge to archaeologists. Indeed, assert Lewis-Williams and Dowson, with the failure of both ethnographic analogy and internal induction, scholars are increasingly pessimistic about ever arriving at the meaning of this artistic period. Drawing on research in southern African San rock art, however, attention has shifted away from aesthetic considerations to focus on shamanism and altered states of consciousness. In this light, the authors propose a model for the classification of Upper Paleolithic signs that avoids the present impasse. They utilize the results of neuro-psychological research to describe the geometrical visual forms that occur in experimental trance states and appear in San rock paintings. Arguing that these entoptic images are merely the product of the human nervous system, they assert that similar images and signs found in art forms can be explained by a trance hypothesis. This assertion is developed by identifying three stages of trance experience and specifying the type of entoptic encounter perceived in each. The manifestation of one type of entoptic sign, a set of nested catenary curves, is traced through the three stages of trance in San art. The writers suggest that the results compare with similar geometrical signs in European Upper Paleolithic art. These conclusions are supported by comparative tables that illustrate how entoptic forms appear in each art type. With this basic model established, the authors investigate how meaning was applied to these products of the nervous system through cultural expectations. The historical relationship between interpreted entoptics and the emergence of representational art is also considered.

B77   Lewis-Williams, J. David, and Thomas A. Dowson (1989). *Images of Power: Understanding Bushman Rock Art*. Johannesburg: Southern Book Publishers.

Lewis-Williams and Thomas Dowson provide readers with an extensively illustrated text that draws on nineteenth-century ethnographic materials and fieldwork sketches to analyze aspects of the meaning and function of San rock art.

Following a brief overview of several "aesthetic" interpretations in Part One, the authors evaluate the utility of deploying Eurocentric categories of inquiry. They conclude that an "ethnographic" line of analysis, based on a close examination of several South African archival resources (primarily the Bleek and Orpen collections) renders more fruitful results. That line of inquiry, they note, also reveals San art to be essentially religious, or shamanistic in nature. Once this interpretive framework is established, specific explanations are introduced in Part Two. Details of San shamanism are described and illustrations of individual paintings are appended. The trance experience and its metaphors (especially flight and death), as well as rainmaking rites and the significance of animals, all receive extended treatment. Part Three, entitled "Artistic Splendour," consists of a spectacular color portfolio of selected paintings and engravings that serves as excellent source material for study, as well as aesthetic appreciation. Thereafter, Part Four provides practical information for those who wish to view the paintings, either in the field or in museums.

B78   Lewis-Williams, J. David, and Thomas A. Dowson (1990). "Through the Veil: San Rock Paintings and the Rock Face." *South African Archaeological Bulletin*, vol. 45: 5-16.

In this article Lewis-Williams and Thomas Dowson briefly contrast two dominant schools of interpretation in rock art studies, namely the "aesthetic" and the "shamanic." While these schools are deemed to be widely divergent in scope and intention, the writers find one concept of universal interest: The rock face in both cases was considered to be a mere *tabula rasa* and carried no meaning of its own. Arguing that there is no form of media that is value free, however, the authors set out to question what role the rock performs in articulating intent. A number of paintings are analyzed. Primarily, assert the writers, variations in rock surface and color were frequently used by San artists, notably in cases where the rock face was adorned with "red lines" that emerged from or gravitated toward small grooves. These lines, they argue, were used in the representation of therianthropes. A short summary of the "shamanistic" school's orientation is then presented. Here, the writers assert that San art comprises numerous symbols of supernatural potency, among them symbols associated with shamanic and trance dance experiences. The authors add that the detail of the hallucinatory depictions, as well as the ethnographic evidence, suggests that the artists were themselves shamans and that they were depicting their own experiences. In the hope of obtaining a clearer understanding of the shamanistic experience implied by the paintings, the evidence of neuro-psychological research is introduced. Lewis-Williams and Dowson argue that hallucinations of all types were determined by the structure of the human nervous system, and so the experiences of Western experimental subjects can shed light on the painted images. Elements such as vortices, tunnels, and cones are brought into conjunction with claims that shamans traveled through the earth or water. Thus, the experience of surreal three-dimensionality and magnification of detail, they suggest, helps to explain how crevices and red lines were used to represent "tunnels" into and out of shamanic realms. The authors conclude that the walls of rock-shelters were in some senses "painted veils" suspended between this world and the world of the spirit. Consequently, the rock face formed a shamanistic context for all paintings.

B79   Maggs, T. M., and J. Sealy (1983). "Elephants in Boxes." In *New Approaches to South African Rock Art. South African Archaeological Society Goodwin Series*, vol. 4: 44-48.

After noting the frequency with which certain animals are portrayed in rock art, the authors reexamine the works of Vinnicombe (1967; 1972) and Lewis-Williams to analyze the meaning of the eland in Bushman spiritual life. They state that rock art recorders in the Western Cape reported relatively large numbers of elephant paintings in addition to eland paintings, suggesting that in this region elephants played a similar role to eland. Three lines of evidence are put forward to support this theory: the large numbers of depictions, the special contexts in which some examples occurred, and the presence of therianthropic figures with human bodies but elephant-like heads. A series of paintings are then described that include therianthropic figures, groups of elephants surrounded by concentric, zigzag, and denticulate lines, and abstract, boat-shaped objects with zigzag lines. The authors assert that these lines represent conventional abstractions that were intended to evoke a certain set of associations in the viewer. The therianthropic figures, which seem to show a link between man and elephant, are interpreted in the light of nineteenth-century San observations. Orpen reported that the San recalled that the figures represented medicine men who entered trances. Lewis-Williams' support of this interpretation is cited. Arguing that the lines in Western Cape paintings also relate to trance, the authors introduce the work of Siegel to describe the hallucinations of experimental subjects under the influence of psychotropic substances. These drug-induced visual patterns are viewed by the authors as examples of abstract linear designs indicative of rock art. Siegel also interviewed several Huichol Indians from Mexico who partook of peyote, and they too were found to experience similar hallucinations of concentric and zigzag patterns. The authors conclude that the hypothesis of trance-induced rock art explains the range of paintings described in the paper.

B80   Marshall, Lorna (1957). "N!ow." *Africa*, vol. 27: 232-40.

At the beginning of her paper on !Kung religion, Marshall describes in detail several beliefs associated with rain, cold, and the concept of "*n!ow*." Thereafter, she provides an account of !Kung belief and ritual concerned with seasonal change. She notes that, in the context of seasonal change, the !Kung believe in "good *n!ow*" and "bad *n!ow*." The good brings rain, the bad brings cold. The concept of *n!ow* is differentiated from the Khoikhoi term *!nau* (heat or fire) and the Khoikhoi rain ceremony called *guriab*. The author admits that her informants could give her no clear account of the concept of *n!ow*. It could not be seen and was known only by observing its effects on the weather. *N!ow* existed in all human beings, entering the human being in the womb, and was associated with hair and urine, which could be burned in ritual acts designed to control the weather. Various stories told by hunters who killed a *n!ow* animal are recounted. The author concludes by saying that she never saw *n!ow* being used by her informants to control weather patterns and adduces some possible reasons for this.

B81   Marshall, Lorna (1962). "!Kung Bushman Religious Beliefs." *Africa*, vol. 32, no. 3: 221-51.

Based on fieldwork carried out between 1952 and 1955, Marshall provides in this article a comprehensive treatment of !Kung religion. The first section, concerned with the names of gods, gives a short description of the great god, lesser gods, and their families. It then analyzes various names and epithets applied to the gods in an attempt to trace their sources. Certain forms of address and taboos concerning these names are also reported. In the next section, Marshall examines myths related to the nature of the great god Gao Na. On one hand, she notes, Gao Na was the subject of a cycle of myths presenting him as a culture hero and trickster figure. On the other, he was considered a great god and creator whose name was to be avoided in public speech. Marshall provides extensive examples of myths and narratives gathered from the !Kung that illustrate both aspects of the deity. The figure of the lesser god, //Gauwa, is then taken up and the several valences of his name are examined. Among some groups the name referred to the spirit of a dead person (*//gauwasi*); a child born to the gods; or the lesser god himself. Drawing on the reports of Schapera, Vedder, and Lebzelter, the author describes this deity as essentially a destroyer and agent of evil who occasionally acted in the interests of humans. The various activities and functions of this figure are outlined. This outline is followed by an analytical overview of the role of the *//gauwasi*, or spirits of the dead. The spirits, notes Marshall, are said to live in the sky with the great god and act as his servants, often involving themselves in the affairs of individual humans. They bring illness and figure prominently in the ceremonial healing dance that is described in the concluding section. Marshall notes that the dance has both ritual and social aspects, and describes the circumstances surrounding the dance, its execution, and the behavior of the medical practitioners in trance. The various phases of the dance are illustrated.

B82   Marshall, Lorna (1969). "The Medicine Dance of the !Kung Bushman." *Africa*, vol. 39, no. 4: 347-80.

Marshall's observations on !Kung trance or medicine dance were made during the course of five expeditions to the Kalahari region of southern Africa in the years 1951 to 1961. A map is included that shows the geographical distribution of eleven groups of !Kung. The article is divided into several sections. The first two sections are devoted to providing a general overview of !Kung religious beliefs about supernatural powers. The gods who hover in the background of !Kung life are introduced and their roles are delineated. Marshall asserts that these gods include Gao Na, the great god, //Gauwa, the lesser god, and the //gauwasi, or spirits of the dead. //Gauwa and the //gauwasi are thought to lurk in the shadows of the dance. It is the medicine specialist's role either to negotiate the removal of some sickness or to drive away evil so that the illness can be "drawn out" of the victim. Marshall then gives a detailed account of the supernatural force called n/um which medicine specialists awaken through dance and employ in healing activities. Subsequent sections deal with various practical aspects of the dance, including the size of the dance group, the dance circle, the fire, garments, and songs. The final sections describe the trance and its social ramifications. Marshall relates that most men develop the ability to go into trance so that the phenomenon is common and is accorded great value for its healing properties. The author details the various stages of the trance which the !Kung describe as a heating of the n/um located in the pit of the stomach, followed by its rise and expansion in the brain. This process is broken down into three main stages: a beginning and middle stage of violent action, and a final stage that results in unconsciousness. Marshall describes her observations of individuals in each phase of trance, emphasizing that it is naturally induced without the aid of narcotics. A concluding section discusses the general social benefits afforded by the !Kung medicine dance. The article is illustrated with photographs.

B83   Marshall, Lorna (1976). *The !Kung of Nyae Nyae*. Cambridge, Mass.: Harvard University Press.

This massively detailed study is the result of eight expeditions to the Kalahari desert conducted during the 1950s. Compiled from interviews and observations, it deals with settlement patterns, food-gathering techniques, kinship systems, and various aspects of social behavior. References to !Kung religious belief and practice are few and made only in passing. Nevertheless, the book provides valuable background material for the author's other writings which deal specifically with religious matters. The book is annotated and a bibliography is included.

B84 Pager, Harald (1975). *Stone Age Myth and Magic*. Graz: Akademische Druck.

Pager's book provides a comprehensive treatment of southern African rock painting. The writer first mentions the large number of existing sites, and suggests that information found in the paintings can to a certain extent serve as a substitute for deficient archaeological research. He then provides a general background to the subject that includes a discussion of materials used in the paint, a history of the Bushmen, and scholarly methods employed in documenting their art. While dealing with the question of the origins of San rock art, Pager introduces several theories used to analyze the paintings. The first of these is the "art for art's sake" theory that sees the art as a type of intellectual play, an activity engaged in merely for expressive and aesthetic purposes. Citing the benefits of a comparative approach, the author introduces several Australian rock paintings as parallels. Pager finds this first explanatory theory deficient, since in his view the paintings show signs of derivation from magico-religious belief. This assertion leads Pager to an examination of the art as a form of sympathetic hunting magic or fertility and rainmaking magic. In these terms, individual paintings are thought to serve as a basis for the analysis of San magic. Pager then moves to a consideration of possible religious elements. He mentions the findings of Silberbauer and Posselt, who thought the Bushmen too primitive to hold religious beliefs. Tylor's theory on the origins of primitive religion is introduced, and continuities between San religion and totemism are discussed and then dismissed. In a chapter entitled "Antelope Spirits," Pager uses quantification studies to show a significant presence of human figures with antelope heads. He concludes that these therianthropic creatures are mythical figures and in some instances may represent the transformed spirits of the dead. The mythological entity Cagn (/Kaggen), renowned for his metamorphizing ability, is discussed in this connection. The possibility of the antelope's status as a deity is raised, and a comparison between the antelope and the Khoi figure of the Mantis is developed. A subsequent chapter analyzes the phenomenon of superpositioning at some sites. Pager concludes that for the artists, the newer paintings derived power from the older ones. A final chapter examines several paintings as a record of Stone Age ceremonial. Pager concludes that although many aspects of San art remain unsolved, its general thrust is the visual expression of a religious system. Color photographs of paintings are included.

B85 Pager, Harald (1983). "The Ritual Hunt: Parallels between Ethnological and Archaeological Data." *South African Archaeological Bulletin*, vol. 38, no. 138: 80-87.

Pager cites Köhler's (1973) account of hunting rituals to describe aspects of Kxoé belief and religious practice in Namibia. While stating that the rituals associated with hunting were in decline in that region, he points to archaeological evidence to suggest that at one time such rituals were ubiquitous. The writer then refers to the works of researchers who have found underlying beliefs in temporally and spatially distant groups of San, among them the now extinct /Xam of the Cape and the extant !Kung of the Kalahari. Following this brief reference, he recapitulates Köhler's account of the ritual hunt of large game animals believed to be the livestock of a supreme, bisexual deity. He notes that after careful ritual preparation the designated hunter pursues the quarry, closely following prescribed methods. Once the kill is made, the hunter presides over a sacrificial rite at the camp. Pager examines the use of the quarry's severed head at the place of sacrifice. He reports that rock paintings illustrating these activities have been discovered in South Africa, Namibia, Lesotho, and Zimbabwe, and asserts that they can be interpreted in terms of Köhler's report. In support of this thesis, Pager refers to a painting found in the Barkely East District that depicts eleven men dancing in front of a severed antelope head. He notes Lewis-Williams' interpretation of this painting as the depiction of a shamanic trance dance, but finds no incongruity since in different areas this type of dance may have completed the hunting ritual. Pager makes mention of two further aspects of Kxoé ritual that appear in rock painting: painted stripes on the faces of the quarry and sacrificer, and the presence of potent objects, especially animal tails. The article contains copies of several paintings and a map of the sites discussed.

B86   Potgieter, E. F. (1955). *The Disappearing Bushmen of Lake Chrissie: A Preliminary Survey*. Pretoria: J. L. van Schaik.

This short but comprehensive work, the result of two months of sporadic fieldwork, focuses on aspects of religion and social organization amongst the Batwa Bushmen of the Eastern Transvaal. Notes on geographic distribution, social and economic life, and Batwa language are included. A three-page chapter briefly sets out aspects of Batwa religious beliefs which, the writer notes, center around a supreme being named /a'an. This god is viewed as the benevolent creator of all things and is assisted by a lesser deity named /a'an 'e la tleni (/a'an the small). Potgieter believes that certain attitudes toward the moon point to previous systematic worship. The Batwa, he says, believe that the moon is a source of good and that its waxing and waning influence the life of the individual. A Batwa legend on the origin of livestock is also included.

B87   Raven-Hart, R. (1971). *Cape of Good Hope, 1653-1702: The First Fifty Years of Dutch Colonization*. Cape Town: A. A. Balkema.

Raven-Hart's exhaustive collection of early travel and ethnographic records contains extracts from the writings of some of the most important travelers to the Cape of Good Hope in the first fifty years of Dutch occupation. While most observations outline aspects of demography, local geography, and botany, occasional remarks concerning the "spiritual" state of indigenous Khoikhoi and San are recorded. These comments are chiefly useful for understanding the origins of several tenacious misconceptions about Khoisan. The collection serves as an indispensable resource for reviewing early ethnographic studies in southern Africa.

B88   Schapera, Isaac (1930). *The Khoisan Peoples of South Africa*. London: George Routledge & Sons.

Schapera's comprehensive work is divided into four parts concerned with different aspects of Khoikhoi and San culture and language. Chapter Seven is devoted to religion and magic among the San, a large section of which deals with beliefs concerning death and methods of burial. Drawing on the work of W. H. I. and Dorothea Bleek, Schapera reproduces the mythology of the origin of death and accounts for the Nharo belief that those who die a good death go to a being called !khutse, while those who die a bad death go to Gaua. Schapera then moves to a consideration of astral worship, and states that this worship forms the central cult of the Cape Bushmen. Using material from the Bleek and Orpen collections he describes rites and beliefs associated with the moon and other heavenly bodies. Several invocations to the moon are quoted. The next section deals with supernatural beings, especially the figure of the Mantis, or /Kaggen, who occupies a central position among them. The author presents a selection of tales and lore from the Mantis cycle of myths, taken from a number of San groups. Utilizing the reports of Dornan and Vedder, Schapera also provides an account of minor deities. The chapter on Khoikhoi religion follows the same structure, with considerable space devoted to death, burial, and mourning. The graves of Heitsi-Eibib are mentioned in this context. According to Schapera, the Khoikhoi also worshipped the moon and he describes dances associated with the new and the full moon. In the section on deities, he reproduces reports about Tsui-//goab, Heitsi-Eibib, and //Gaunab.

B89   Schapera, Isaac ed. (1933). *The Early Cape Hottentots*. Cape Town: Van Riebeeck Society.

In this volume Schapera presents a collection of early ethnographic descriptions of the Khoikhoi found in the writings of, amongst others, Olfert Dapper (1668), Willem ten Rhyne (1686), and Johannes G. de Grevenbroek (1695). The texts are given in the original Dutch (or Latin) with English translation. In this sense, the book is valuable both as a source for some of the first descriptions of the Cape and its inhabitants and as an index of how long-standing preconceptions of Khoikhoi religion (or its absence) came into being. Dapper, for example, finds no trace of religion among the Khoikhoi, while Rhyne discovered a very vague notion of a supreme being and an intense moon cult. De Grevenbroek, on the other hand, found that the Khoi despised the moon and worshipped the sun as the source of all good things. Schapera's general introduction tries to place these kinds of remarks in context. Noting that the Khoikhoi were notorious for their reticence, he suggests that early writers used their imagination to construct an account of Khoikhoi religion. He gives a brief account of that religion based on later research, mentioning the conflict between the creator god Tsui-//goab and the malevolent deity //Gaunab. The cycle of myths associated with the ancestor or trickster god Heitsi-Eibib is also described.

B90   Schmidt, Sigrid (1973). "Die Mantis religiosa in den Glaubensvorstellungen der Khoesan-Völker." *Zeitschrift für Ethnologie*, vol. 98: 102-27.

Schmidt begins with a brief list of elements constituent of Khoisan belief: first, belief in a high god that is both creator, benefactor, or disease-sender; second, a destructive lower god opposed to that high god; third a trickster figure; and fourth, a lord of animals. The author's purpose in the article is to go beyond this essential framework to examine the role played by the Mantis in Khoisan religion, a task especially necessitated by the lack of agreement in published views of this figure. Different views are presented verbatim, among them the works of Herrmann (1961), Holm (1965), and Gusinde (1966), that have regarded the Mantis as a trickster, as a "dying and rising" god, or as the equivalent of /Kaggen, a deity identified with the high god. In order to cut through this confusion Schmidt embarks on an exhaustive analytical examination of the names given the Mantis by a wide variety of Khoisan groups, as reported by researchers such as Bleek, Gusinde, Marshall, and Vedder. Included in his analysis are the names /Kaggen (Cagn), //Gauwa, //Gaunab, Tsui-//goab, and Heitsi-Eibib. The author devotes special attention to the figure of /Kaggen, who is variously reported to be the trickster, the lord of animals, the high god, or all three. In the final section of the article the results of this extensive and intricate analysis are drawn together. Schmidt concludes that although the Mantis generally shared one of the names of the highest god, he was not necessarily to be identified with that entity. Rather, the Mantis was to be viewed as one among a number of "oracle animals" to whom prayers were addressed in times of crisis. Schmidt asserts that because the Bleeks were unaware of this dynamic, they mistakenly equated the Mantis with the trickster god /Kaggen. Thus, the trickster god is actually the manifestation of one aspect of the high god. The author stresses that in the absence of a comprehensive analysis of this god's multi-faceted nature, the belief system of the Khoisan cannot be properly understood. The text is in German.

B91   Schmidt, Sigrid (1975-1976). "Alte Götter der khoisan-sprechenden Völker im südlichen Afrika." *Journal of the South West Africa Scientific Society*, vol. 30: 59-74.

In this paper Schmidt emphasizes the contemporary lack of knowledge concerning Khoisan religion, and mentions the first reports that came from the Cape to assert that these people had no religion. The author suggests that this absence of religion was partially a result of Khoisan stratagems feigning ignorance when questioned on religious matters, a ploy attributed to early taboos. In addition, the first settlers were incapable of comprehending a belief system unaccompanied by the religious paraphernalia to which they were accustomed. The result, according to Schmidt, was that while the religion of the Khoisan flourished, nothing trustworthy was recorded; it was only in the nineteenth century, at a time when the Khoisan and their traditions were in decline, that the first serious studies were made. Since researchers in different areas often provided conflicting reports, the goal of this article, Schmidt asserts, is merely to introduce aspects of the cognitive system of the Khoisan. The discussion begins with an overview of the role of the creator god Tsui-//goab, who appears to be a sky god, or the lord of wind, rain, and thunder. He is opposed by //Gauwa, the destroyer and chief of the spirits of the dead (//gauwasi). After using reports from Hahn and Bleek to sketch the nature of these major deities, the author devotes a lengthy section of the paper to the portrayal of the trickster figure, who may appear under the name of /Kaggen or Heitsi-Eibib. This leads into a treatment of the "Lord of Beasts." Schmidt shows how /Kaggen is sometimes viewed as a deity of this kind. The author concludes by examining reports that confuse or combine these discrete entities. Schmidt attempts to disentangle the resulting incongruity by deriving etymologies of the deities' names, adducing cognate names from various geographically separated groups, and comparing shifts in belief with those that occurred among Xhosa groups. Schmidt concludes that it is an understanding of this possibility of combinations of deity that provides the key for understanding Khoisan religion. The text is in German.

B92   Schmidt, Sigrid (1979). "The Rain Bull of the South African Bushmen." *African Studies*, vol. 38, no. 2: 201-24.

Schmidt's article focuses on the meaning of a painting copied by the magistrate J. M. Orpen and explained to him by an informant as a snake—although, as the writer notes, the meaning of the image was later interpreted by Bleek to be a water cow. Schmidt refers to Vinnicombe's discussion of the painting and her suggestion that three animals, the snake, the (mythical) water cow, and the hippopotamus, were closely associated by Bushmen with rain. Schmidt adds to this discussion of the "rain bull." First, she underscores the information obtained from Bleek's informant that rainmaking required two actions: the leading of the rain bull around the country, and the ritual killing and eating of its flesh. Second, similar rainmaking rituals from various groups such as the Tswana, the Korana, and the Ambo are cited in order to establish the point that the Southern Bushmen's rain bull must be seen in the context of similar rituals among southern African cattle herders. A similar comparative approach is applied to the notion that the rain animal lives in the sky and descends as rain. The third section then examines southern African beliefs concerning the rain snake in great detail. The folktale motif of young women being carried off by the rain bull is illustrated and then explicated by reference to similar myths including Zeus' rape of Europa in the form of a bull. Concluding sections deal with the function of the rain animal in female initiation and speculate on the possible origin of this creature.

B93   Schmidt, Sigrid (1982). "Khoisan Folktales: Original Sources and Republications." *African Studies*, vol. 41, no. 2: 203-12.

Schmidt's paper provides readers with a cross-referenced guide to original and secondary materials on Khoisan mythology, thus enabling students to avoid repeated or relatively valueless material. Although not an exhaustive record of primary and secondary resources, the work remains a useful guide. In this regard, Schmidt states that one of her main concerns was to draw attention to secondary materials that lacked any acknowledgment of or reference to original works. Consequently, she references the works of Charles John Anderson, Dorothea Bleek, Wilhelm Bleek, Samuel S. Dornan, Johannes Theophilus Hahn, James A. Honey, Arthur Markowitz, George W. Stow, George McCall Theal, Heinrich Vedder, and Gideon Retief von Wielligh.

B94   Schmidt, Sigrid (1986a). "Tales and Beliefs about Eyes-on-His-Feet: The Interrelatedness of Khoisan Folklore." In Megan Biesele, Robert Gordon, and Richard Lee (ed.) *The Past and Future of !Kung Ethnography: Critical Reflections and Symbolic Perspectives. Essays in Honour of Lorna Marshall.* Quellen zür Khoisan-Forschung, vol. 4. Hamburg: Helmut Buske Verlag. 169-94.

Lorna Marshall introduced the tale of the Eyes-on-His-Feet to ethnologists but, on her own admission, failed to penetrate either the meaning of the myth or determine its origin. Schmidt quotes this admission at the start of the article and sets herself the task of supplementing Marshall's report and tracing relationships within Khoisan folklore through an examination of variants of the tale. She begins by assembling a large number of these variants drawn by ethnologists from groups such as the !Kung, Nharo, /Xam, Nama, and Dama. From this survey she discovers three branches of tradition among Khoisan peoples that produce three types of tale. After delineating these types, she analyzes regional patterns and then attempts to trace possible developments within the traditions. Schmidt concludes with a section that distinguishes between folk-belief and folk-tales and shows how the mythical creature of "Eyes-on-His-Feet" figures in both. Her final remarks stress the need to focus on interrelationships within the broad spectrum of Khoisan groups in order to attain a more adequate view of individual folk motifs.

B95   Schmidt, Sigrid (1986b). "Heiseb—Trickster und Gott der Nama und Dama in Südwestafrika/Namibia." In Rainer Vossen and Klauss Keuthmann (eds.) *Contemporary Studies on Khoisan*, vol. 2. Hamburg: Helmut Buske Verlag. 205-56.

In this paper Schmidt attempts to provide a clearer elucidation of the religion of the Nama and Dama of Namibia that is effected through a detailed examination of the figure of Heitsi-Eibib, the trickster god. The article is divided into eleven sections. The first discusses the various forms of the name Heitsi-Eibib (Heigeib, Haicekooip) and their possible meanings. The following section takes a tale published by Bleek as a starting point and proceeds to investigate the motif of Heitsi-Eibib's victory over the deity known as the "in the hole pusher." Section three deals with another narrative from Bleek's collection, the "Raisin Eater." His account leads to a delineation of the "roguish" character of the god. Section four discusses Heitsi-Eibib's role in the creation of the world, while sections five through seven account for his family and their relationship to the Jackal and the Chameleon. In section eight the writer discusses the graves of Heitsi-Eibib. Sections nine and ten attempt to evaluate the position of this god in the context of the religious perspectives of the Dama and Nama. The concluding section reconciles the two threads of tradition concerning this figure, namely, the trickster and the god. A bibliography is appended. The text is in German.

B96   Schmidt, Sigrid (1989). *Catalogue of the Khoisan Folktales of Southern Africa*. 2 vols. Hamburg: Helmut Buske Verlag.

This two-volume resource provides both bibliographic materials as well as a catalogue and brief summary of all known Khoisan tales. The first volume contains a bibliography of the resources, a survey of the tales, and several indices. The myths are divided into a number of categories, including "Heavenly Bodies," "Deities," the "Otherworld," the "Origin of Mankind," the "Origins of Death," and the "Trickster." The indices include an index of motifs as well as an alphabetical index. The second volume contains the catalogue of tales with summaries.

B97   Schmidt, Wilhelm (1929). "Zür Erforschung der alten Buschmann-Religion." *Africa*, vol. 2: 291-301.

Schmidt states that the complexity of pre-Bantu ethnography is manifested most clearly in research devoted to the nature of ancient Bushman religion. Reliable conclusions, he says, can only be obtained through a detailed inquiry into the religion of the Khoikhoi and the Berg Dama. The complexity is exemplified by the figure of //Gaunab. Schmidt relates that this deity is a malevolent being in Khoikhoi religion, but appears as the Supreme Being among the Berg Dama, and in some Bushman groups may be viewed as a hero, an ancestor, or a malevolent being. Reference is made to other researchers who have wrestled with the problem of this figure, including Hahn (1881), Vedder (1923), and Dornan (1925). The author argues that the inconsistencies surrounding the figure raise the following questions: First, did the //Gaunab of the Khoikhoi arise from the Supreme Being of the Bushmen, or from the figure of the ancestor, or both? And second, did the ancient religion of the Bushmen recognize a distinction between the Supreme Being and the ancestor hero in such a way that both had a separate existence? He concludes, on the basis of his own detailed research, that both a Supreme Being and an ancestor hero can be attributed to the Eastern and North-western Bushmen. However, the possibility remains that among the Eastern Bushmen there was some confusion between the two. The text is in German.

B98   Schrire, Carmel (1984). "Wild Surmises on Savage Thoughts." In Carmel Schrire (ed.) *Past and Present in Hunter Gatherer Studies*. New York: Academic Press. 1-26.

This chapter serves as the introduction to a book that explores how archaeology and prehistory provide for a better understanding of contemporary hunting and gathering societies. Schrire states that the book represents a major step away from the evolutionary perspective in hunter-gatherer studies, a perspective that rests on the tacit assumption that these groups have no history. She then proceeds to perform an extensive review of the historical roots of the field, beginning with the public exhibitions of hunter-gatherers in England which started in the sixteenth century. The most notorious of these, according to Schrire, was the "Hottentot Venus," who was transported to England from the Cape Colony in 1809. The belief in Anglo-Saxon supremacy, and related attitudes which were prevalent during this period and which shaped the progress of ethnography, are mentioned. After proceeding through the emergence of Darwin's theories and the attempts to apply them to the relationship between hunter-gatherer societies and European culture, the author arrives at a discussion of the 1966 Chicago symposium, "Man the Hunter." She reviews at length the literature that emerged from that event in order to facilitate a comparison with later ideas. In conclusion, the writer advocates greater understanding of archaeological principles and inferences; calls for a recognition that data on hunter-gatherers invariably describe societies dealing with foreign incursion, and suggests that the studies of these groups be moved into the wider field of international affairs.

B99   Shostak, Marjorie (1981). *Nisa: The Life and Words of a !Kung Woman*. Cambridge, Mass.: Harvard University Press.

Shostak, an Associate of the Peabody Museum of Archaeology and Ethnology at Harvard University, took part in an extended field-trip to the !Kung in Botswana that ended in March of 1971. This was at the close of a project initiated by anthropologists Irven DeVore and Richard Lee and designed to gain a comprehensive knowledge of a traditional hunter-gatherer group. The chief subject and informant of this book, a fifty year old !Kung woman, provided the author with a personal, detailed account of what life is like for a woman within !Kung society. In fact, the book is explicitly informed by Shostak's wish to "clarify some of the issues the [Women's] Movement has raised." It is divided into chapters dealing with topics such as "Family Life," "Life in the Bush," "Sexuality," "Marriage," "Motherhood," and "Women and Men." Shostak introduces each chapter with material gleaned from previous anthropological research and then presents her informant's verbatim elaborations on these topics. While the book as a whole provides a useful background resource for the study of San religion, Chapter Thirteen gives an account of trance healing from a personal, experiential perspective. In her introductory remarks to this chapter the author states that the "spiritual realm" infuses every aspect of !Kung life, and is viewed as the critical determinant in matters of life and death, illness and health, abundance and scarcity. A major god dominates and is accompanied by a group of lesser deities. It is the erratic behavior of these deities that causes disease and misfortune. The healing power of *n/um* is described, along with methods of developing or possessing this spiritual heat or power. The social aspects of the trance dance and the activities of accomplished healers are also dealt with. In addition to illuminating a central facet of !Kung religious life, the book makes a valuable contribution to the general field of shamanic studies.

B100   Solomon, Anne (1989). *Division of the Earth: Gender, Symbolism, and the Archaeology of the Southern San*. M.A. thesis, University of Cape Town.

The author notes that gender studies in several areas, particularly anthropology, have indicated that the masculine-feminine dichotomy is often used to structure cultural oppositions, and that the representation of this dichotomy in cultural productions is then implicated in the construction of gender. It is this reciprocal process that forms the focus of Solomon's archaeological research, with rock art as the principal archaeological "trace" to be analyzed. Working from a feminist position, she evaluates archaeological materials in the context of contemporary gender issues, scrutinizing archaeological "reconstructions" as legitimizations of an existing gender order. Theoretically influenced by feminism, hermeneutics, Marxism, post-structuralism, semiotics, and discourse theory, she examines aspects of language in San oral narratives in order to establish how masculinity and femininity have been conceptualized and differentiated by San peoples. Arguing that gendering is more fundamental to San cultural texts than has been previously recognized, Solomon employs a "fertility hypothesis" derived from ethnographies to explain various elements in southern African rock art. Features that are interpreted through this hypothesis include human images, the motif of the thin red line fringed with white dots, "elephants in boxes," therianthropic figures, and androgynous figures. Solomon then conducts a critique of what she labels the "biophysical determinism," implicit in current rock art studies, which explains the art from a context of trance states, altered consciousness, and neuro-physiological constitution. In opposition to this trend she claims that rain, rather than trance, forms the central element of San ritual and religious practice. The thesis concludes with an examination of the treatment (or its absence) of gender in the archaeological record.

B101   Solomon, Anne (1992). "Gender, Representation, and Power in San Ethnography and Rock Art." *Journal of Anthropological Archaeology*, vol. 11: 291-329.

In this paper, Solomon points out that the San have been characterized as an egalitarian society and claims that this theoretical framework of cooperation and complementarity may obscure a social dynamic more appropriately interpreted in terms of conflict and hierarchy. She argues that gender forms a significant category of meaning in San rock art, and although Lewis-Williams' shamanistic model has been very productive, this line of analysis fails to account for the gendering of imagery and prominence of sexual symbolism. A section on theoretical considerations locates the paper in a post-structuralist feminist context, and lodges the analysis firmly within a theoretical framework that views metaphor as a key element in the gendering of cultural texts. The subsequent section applies this focus on metaphor to San ethnographies in order to elicit cultural constructions of gender. Material from the Bleek collection is analyzed with particular emphasis on female initiation, female potency, and the relation of femininity to rain. After presenting the pervasive gendering imagery found in the texts (where feminine is associated with all things round, fat, short, and full) Solomon examines gendering and sexual symbolism with reference to specific rock paintings. In her conclusion the author emphasizes the importance of gendered interpretive models for an elucidation of the art. Though productive, she asserts, the shamanistic model sheds no light on paintings that have no relation to trance. Features of the art that have been interpreted as shamanistic can also be viewed the from perspective of gender ideology. Since gender is both an organizing principle and a product of change, studies of gender relations, she concludes, hold the potential for providing a more revealing historical explanation of the art.

B102   Solomon, Anne (1994). "Mythic Women: A Study in Variability in San Rock Art and Narrative." In Thomas A. Dowson and David Lewis-Williams (eds.) *Contested Images: Diversity in Southern African Rock Art Research.* Johannesburg: Witwatersrand University Press. 331-71.

Solomon states that San expressive systems display a preoccupation with sexual symbolism, and although several researchers (Lewis-Williams, Pager, Vinnicombe, and Woodhouse) have noted the prominence of this symbolism in the rock art, more research is required. Consequently, the writer focuses on the recurring motif of "mythic women" in order to examine some theoretical, methodological, and interpretive issues surrounding gender and sexual symbolism in San society and art. She mentions the ethnographic approach used by Vinnicombe and Lewis-Williams and points out that it cannot adequately deal with problems of historicity, diversity, and change. It is suggested that new directions might be found in post-structuralist theorizations of difference (in the works of Derrida and Cixous); insights on the mutuality of space and time (in the writings of Giddens); and critiques of intentionality (in the work of Davis). The female motif that Solomon analyzes is examined with reference to raised arms, obese bodies, parted legs, and genital emissions. Details that differentiate various examples are examined in terms of historicity, referential intent, and practical context. San ethnography is introduced, and myths of creation and origin are scrutinized in terms of constructions of the body. The author suggests in this context that San cosmology is based on the female body. The final part of the paper is devoted to an extended interpretive analysis, with reference to specific paintings that are illustrated in the text. Solomon concludes that her interpretation is an attempt to deconstruct the analytical boundaries present in previous studies.

B103   Stow, George W. (1905). *The Native Races of South Africa: A History of the Intrusion of the Hottentots and Bantu into the Hunting Grounds of the Bushmen, the Aborigines of the Country.* London: Swan Sonnenschein & Co.

In this wide-ranging work, illustrated with plates from Lucy Lloyd's photographic collection, the government ethnographer and archivist George William Stow provides readers of comparative religion in southern Africa with invaluable materials relating to Khoikhoi and San religious belief and practice. The materials—collected, the author recalls, in order that several accounts of

Khoikhoi and San life were not irrevocably lost under the pressures of capitalist expansion and colonial rule—are organized into twenty-six chapters. In the first two chapters, the author draws on the writings of F. Max Müller and Wilhelm Bleek to examine the antiquity of the Bushmen or "Abatwa." Brief notes on San mythology and language are included. Thereafter, notes on the "Habits," "Weapons and Implements," "Methods of Hunting and Fishing," "Social Customs," and "Burial Practices" of the San are enumerated. Chapters Eight through Ten provide a "scientific" taxonomy of San clans and political groupings. After this discussion of San political organization, Stow provides extensive historical notes on the "encroachment" of the Korana, Griqua, and Tswana into traditional Khoikhoi and San hunting grounds. Of particular note for historians of religion in the region, the work describes in detail rituals and beliefs associated with San marriage and trance dance. The book is annotated and an index is appended.

B104   Thackeray, J. F. (1983). "On Concepts Expressed in Southern African Rock Art." *Antiquity*, vol. 64: 139-44.

Thackeray's paper refers to the advances in rock art studies effected by Lewis-Williams and his work on art as trance. In particular, he mentions the ability to recognize therianthropic figures such as the "trance-buck" as representations of hallucinations experienced by shamans. However, he questions the designation of the art as a "San" achievement, suggesting that the antiquity of the art and the known interaction of various southern African groups compels a wider view of the art than the present "San-centric" direction of study. He asserts that some of the concepts, customs, and beliefs held by San hunter-gatherers are similar to those of modern Bantu-speaking peoples, and a study of the latter may prove relevant. Thackeray suggests that linguistic data may unlock conceptual associations not made explicit in ethnographic accounts and offers several examples of how the method would proceed. Focusing on several Bantu words that share a common form (*-hele*) he examines a set of associations attached to the rhebok, ladders, and nets that represent the trance experience and its painted depiction. He concludes by repeating that the evidence from Bantu-speaking peoples should be used in the interpretation of the art.

B105   Vedder, H. (1928). "The Nama." In Carl Hugo Linsingen Hahn, Louis Fourie, and H. Vedder (eds.) *The Native Tribes of South West Africa*. Cape Town: Cape Times. 107-52.

Vedder's chapter provides a comprehensive ethnographical account of Nama physical characteristics, distribution, history, and mode of living. In a brief section on religion, he describes the difficulties that early travelers experienced while trying to elicit and comprehend information concerning Nama religion. The author then describes the central figures in Nama mythology: //Gaunab, the evil spirit; Tsui-//goab, who Vedder argues was originally a hero figure later elevated to divine status; and Heitsi-Eibib, the trickster deity. Tsui-//goab is viewed as the god of rain and fertility, and Vedder reproduces a prayer addressed to him that was preserved by Hahn. Vedder mentions Heitsi-Eibib's ability to transform himself and pass through mountains when pursued. The tradition concerning his many deaths and resurrections is recounted, as well as the custom of building piles of stones, which are then called "graves" of Heitsi-Eibib. The importance of the moon is indicated and dances associated with it are mentioned. Vedder concludes this account by remarking that most contemporary Nama have converted to Christianity.

B106   Vedder, H. (1937). "Die Buschmanner Sudwestafrikas und ihre Weltanschauung." *South African Journal of Science*, vol. 34: 416-36.

Vedder begins by stating that his paper will deal mostly with material acquired among the !Kung, and claims that a distinction should be made between this group and what he terms the San Bushman. He develops this argument on linguistic and physical grounds, and adds that the San and the Khoikhoi are very closely related. According to Vedder, a single worldview dominates the cognitive set of all these groups, and this worldview can be broken down into four "leading" ideas. The first entails the concept of a primal time when the original Bushmen possessed a magical ability to transform themselves into any form they chose. Eventually this magical time passed away and the transformational powers waned so that the animal forms reified into permanent species. However, Bushmen always recall in their myths and tales that animals were at one time human beings. Vedder shows how this concept operates by referring to several myths and legends, and discusses the role of the supernatural figures /Kaggen, Heitsi-Eibib, //Gaunab, and Tsui-//goab within this context. The second leading idea adduced by Vedder is that the "*Urmenschen*," who were confined to animal and heavenly forms, still possess the magical ability to influence the life of humans. A number of beliefs concerning the magical properties of animals are then related, and the section concludes with some brief remarks on Bushman dances. The third major idea examined is that a few individuals, the medicine men, still possess all the power that was available in the primordial era. The activities of the shaman are then described, with special emphasis on techniques used in healing. The fourth idea concerns eschatological beliefs among the Bushmen. In this regard, Vedder mentions several myths that describe the origin of death. The notion of a Primal Father, who protects the group and to whom the soul flies after death, is also discussed. Vedder concludes the paper with a brief discussion of Bushman ethical precepts. The text is in German.

B107   Vinnicombe, Patricia (1972a). "Motivation in African Rock Art." *Antiquity*, vol. 46: 124-33.

This is a review of four books: Brentjes' *African Rock Art,* Cooke's *Rock Art of Southern Africa,* Lee and Woodhouse's *Art on the Rocks of Southern Africa,* and the Rudners' *The Hunter and His Art: A Survey of Rock Art in Southern Africa.* After giving some general descriptions and evaluations of the books, Vinnicombe focuses on the question of motivation in the art. The books are said to highlight the imprecise nature of present knowledge about the art, the lack of objectivity, and the dearth of any corpus of systematic material on which to base analytical study. It is for these reasons that the views on motivation expressed by the authors of these books are so contradictory. Lee and Woodhouse, Cooke, and the Rudners favor the "art for art's sake" interpretation, while Brentjes states that the majority of the paintings were forms of sympathetic magic. Vinnicombe discusses elements in the paintings that the authors adduce in support of their arguments. She then points to the frequent superpositioning of paintings and resultant lack of clarity as an argument against the "aesthetic" theory. Rather, these features might indicate ritual practice associated with repetitive and rigid convention. The results of quantitative analysis which show that human figures outnumber animals would argue against the sympathetic magic explanation. This type of analysis also demonstrates that there was a type of "selectivity" when choosing which animals or actions to depict. The author concludes that the increasing use of objective and quantitative methods will force future workers to move away from naive and particularist explanations and to concentrate on the structural thought reflected in the significance of the subject matter selected for portrayal.

B108   Vinnicombe, Patricia (1972b). "Myth, Motive, and Selection in Southern African Rock Art." *Africa*, vol. 42: 192-204.

The author claims that because the collection of data in the study of rock art is unsystematic and subjective, valid analysis is difficult. Two emerging explanations for the motivation of the art are mentioned. The "sympathetic magic" school views the paintings as attempts to control the movements of animals and secure kills. Because these activities are associated with the acquisition of food, the art is seen as essentially functional or utilitarian. The "art for art's sake" school holds that human beings have an instinctive desire for artistic expression, and that given enough leisure human beings will decorate their surroundings merely for aesthetic pleasure. Vinnicombe believes these views to be too simplistic and particularist, and adds that they fail to consider the complexity of human thought that exists even in so-called "primitive" societies. After a brief discussion of the function of myth and ritual that draws on the work of Douglas and Tambiah, the author says that her fieldwork in Lesotho and South Africa has led her to believe that religion was a prime motive in the production of the art. She challenges the "magical" interpretation by noting that quantitative studies of the art reveal a larger proportion of human figures than animal, and that the animals selected for depiction do not truly reflect the faunal population of the area or the diet of the hunters. Counts taken in several areas reveal a high proportion of eland, indicating that the artists selected this animal for particular emphasis. Discounting both economic and totemic explanations for this fact, Vinnicombe points to the recorded mythology of the southern Bushmen, which clearly reveals a ritual relationship between man, eland, and the creator deity. She finds further support for the religious significance of selectivity in the concepts of *n/um*, *n!ow* and *soxa* reported from the Kalahari Bushmen. Each of these religious concepts is related to a corresponding aspect of certain rock paintings. The author concludes by saying that the Stone Age artist selected items for portrayal that symbolized a religious interpretation of life.

B109   Vinnicombe, Patricia (1975). "The Ritual Significance of Eland (*Taurotragus oryx*) in the Rock Art of Southern Africa." In E. Anati (ed.) *Les Religions de la Prehistoire*. Capo di Ponte: Centre Camuno di Studi Preistorici. 379-400.

Vinnicombe draws attention to results of the quantitative analysis of rock art samples that show a high degree of selectivity in choice of subject matter. In her view, the critical fact is that the selection of animal subjects is not related to animal population nor to the daily diet of the hunters. She suggests that the choice of subject matter resulted from the philosophy of the artists, and that numerical emphasis on various animals may reflect a hierarchy of values that influenced social structure. The author's purpose in this paper is to examine certain values embodied by the eland, a species that figures prominently in the paintings. The eland is then described physically, and the methods of its portrayal are briefly set out. The animal was preponderant numerically, dominant in size of representation, and received particularly elaborate treatment. Vinnicombe suggests that the importance of the animal might reside in the fact that its group migrant behavior reflected the organization of the Bushmen. She then points to Bushman mythology which clearly depicts a relationship between human, eland, and the deity /Kaggen. Three examples of myths relating the creation of the eland by /Kaggen are reproduced verbatim and briefly analyzed by using some of Lévi-Strauss' concepts. Drawing on the work of Robertson-Smith and Hubert and Mauss, the author develops a theoretical model that analyzes sacrifice in terms of the victim, the sacrificial weapon, the "sacrifier," the sacrificer, the sacrificial meal, purification, and the place of sacrifice. She then discusses each of these ingredients of sacrifice with reference to the hunting rites of the Bushmen. Vinnicombe concludes that the hunting of eland possessed a sacrificial significance for the Bushmen, and that the motivation of the hunting rites involved concepts of public sanctity. Thus, Vinnicombe concludes that the eland served as a symbol through which natural phenomena, human life, and divine activity were interrelated.

B110   Vinnicombe, Patricia (1976). *People of the Eland: Rock Paintings of the Drakensberg Bushmen as a Reflection of their Life and Thought.* Pietermaritzburg: University of Natal Press.

This comprehensive volume provides an overview of the study of the Bushmen and southern African rock art. The first chapter presents a general geographical and ecological description of the Drakensberg area, and is followed by a history of the Bushmen that chronicles the effects of their encounter with European settlers. Two subsequent chapters discuss the history of the study of Bushmen and their art, and describe the methods of analyzing and dating the paintings. Against this background, Vinnicombe closely examines the paintings, focusing first on animal subjects. There are sections devoted to domestic animals, eland, antelope, predators, baboons, serpents and winged creatures. Drawing on the Bleek collection and on contemporary ethnography, the author shows how certain animals were significant in Bushmen mythology. The eland is of particular importance and Vinnicombe elaborates on the prominence of the animal in the paintings, underscoring the economic and religious significance that the animal held for the Bushmen. The serpent's role as a rainmaking creature is also mentioned. The chapter devoted to human subjects has sections on weapons and equipment, food gathering, and hunting. The last two sections on dances and sorcerers contain the most valuable material for the study of Bushman religion. Paintings depicting long lines of men dancing are explained in the context of the healing trance dance of the contemporary !Kung. By employing details from Lee's description of this dance, along with photographs taken by Marshall, Vinnicombe is able explain many of the rock art dancing scenes as a ritual activity involving trance. The section on hunting-sorcerers and rainmakers addresses the presence of therianthropic figures in the paintings, which are explained with reference to the medicine specialist's need to undergo transformation into a powerful animal in order to carry out ritual functions. The book concludes with some remarks on the significance of the rock artists' selection of particular subjects for depiction. Most of the discussion in the volume is supported by reference to specific paintings interspersed throughout the text

B111   Willcox, A. R. (1963). *The Rock Art of South Africa.* Johannesburg: Nelson Press.

Willcox traces the history of European knowledge of rock art, first reported to the Royal Academy of History at Lisbon in 1721. However, we are told that it was George William Stow's copies (1867-1878) that first aroused serious interest outside of Africa. Willcox then reviews the geomorphological considerations that influenced the production of the art, and supplies detailed maps of their distribution. Chapter Two deals with the origin, culture, and physical anthropology of the Bushmen who produced the art. The discussion, however, contains no mention of religion. Willcox explains that his only concern is with matters that bear directly on the interpretation of the art. His chapter on "Folklore" reproduces some material from the Bleek collection on the Mantis and the Rain Animal, but he sees nothing of a religious nature here. The remainder of the volume discusses the age and classification of various paintings. Willcox concludes the volume by arguing that the art is entirely aesthetic. Although the author excludes any consideration of religion, the volume is lavishly illustrated and constitutes an excellent source for a close study of the paintings themselves.

B112   Willcox, A. R. (1984). "Meanings and Motives in San Rock Art—The Views of W. D. Hammond-Tooke and J. David Lewis-Williams Considered." *South African Archaeological Bulletin*, vol. 39, no. 139: 53-57.

In this article Willcox criticizes Hammond-Tooke and Lewis-Williams in order to defend his own "*art pour l'art*" interpretation of San rock art. In that defense, he traces some of the psychological arguments for the emergence of art as a source of pleasure. The theories of Jean Piaget, Rudolph Arnheim, and Rhoda Kellog are considered in this regard. Willcox concludes that pleasure in the exercise of skill is a chief motivator of art. He asserts that this "pleasure principle" applies not only to children and "primitive" societies, but to chimpanzees as well. Desmond Morris' *Biology of Art* is cited in support. Willcox criticizes Lewis-Williams for ignoring this explanation and emphasizes that it is sufficient to account for the great bulk of rock art. However he does not rule out other "further" motives such as the recording of significant events and the illustration of myth. He also grants that some depictions might arise from trance "hallucinations" as Lewis-Williams has suggested. His main point of difference is in the proportion of the whole corpus of the art that he feels can be explained by this theory. He asserts that Lewis-Williams' position that trance metaphors are the "key" to understanding San rock art goes far beyond the evidence.

B113   Wilmsen, Edwin (1987). "Khoi and San Religion." In Mircea Eliade (ed.) *The Encyclopaedia of Religion*. New York: Macmillan Press. 8: 292-95.

In this brief article, in which Wilmsen focuses primarily on Khoi and San cosmological concepts, an historical overview of the use of the derogatory terms "Hottentot" and "Bushman" prefaces notes on foraging and pastoral subsistence economies in southern Africa. Drawing on data gathered from !Kung informants in Namibia and Botswana, the writer examines several dichotomies indicative of Khoi and San divinities. Thereafter, he corrects pervasive nineteenth-century European reports that portrayed the Khoi as moon-worshipers. In this regard, he asserts that for the Khoi the moon functioned as an "accurate timepiece" in signaling menstrual cycles, for example. The article concludes with a description and analysis of shamanic practices and ritual trance dances and healing rites. The writer argues that with the destruction of Khoisan communities in the twentieth century, trance dances performed for the purposes of healing increased in frequency and myths associated with the Khoikhoi and San divinities of wrath were increasingly emphasized and elaborated upon.

B114   Wilson, M. L. (1986). "Khoisanosis: The Question of Separate Identities for Khoi and San." In R. Singer and J. K. Lundy (eds.) *Variation, Culture, and Evolution in African Populations.* Johannesburg: Witwatersrand University Press. 13-25.

Wilson coins the term "Khoisanosis" to denote the process by which the Khoikhoi and the San came to be grouped under the generic term "Khoisan." His aim in the paper is to examine evidence from ethnography, archaeology, and physical anthropology in order to determine what possibilities exist for differentiating the two. He begins by examining the hypotheses of Stow, Westphal, Robertshaw, and Cooke concerning Khoikhoi origins, and finds that despite points of difference they share a common belief that the Khoikhoi migrated from a point of origin to the areas which they have inhabited in the historical period. A reading of the Khoikhoi archaeological record, however, seems to preclude migration from the north-east into the Cape. Wilson then moves to the field of morphology and tells how the term "Khoisan" was created by Schultze in 1928 because he could not find sufficient physical difference to separate the Khoikhoi and San. After surveying the existing morphological studies, Wilson states that they are hampered by inherited notions of what characterizes a "typical" Khoikhoi or San. Genetic studies, which indicate a high degree hybridization, are also inconclusive. At the end of the paper the author concludes that the fundamental differences between the Khoikhoi and San are cultural rather than biological, and it is precisely in cultural terms that they must be viewed as possessing separate identities.

B115   Yates, R., J. Golson and M. Hall (1985). "Trance Performance: The Rock Art of Boontjieskloof and Sevilla." *South African Archaeological Bulletin*, vol. 40: 70-80.

Referring to the work of Vinnicombe and Lewis-Williams, the authors point out that recent explanatory models are derived from paintings located in the south-eastern escarpment of South Africa. They feel it is necessary to take Lewis-Williams' "trance" hypotheses from the context of the Drakensberg and systematically test their value in the south-western Cape. In so doing, they would also be testing the notion of a "pan-San cognitive system" that was first put forth by Theal and restated by Lewis-Williams. Following some methodological remarks, a background is laid out that contrasts the "*art pour l'art*" school of interpretation as exemplified by Willcox and the trance school of Lewis-Williams. They observe that the trance hypothesis depends on the identification of key concepts and metaphors from San ethnography. The analysis begins with realistic or literal images such as dances, postures, and nasal bleeding, all of which are found in the art of the study area. The thin red lines linking figures, which Lewis-Williams interpreted as a symbol for supernatural potency, are also found. Therianthropes, which Lewis-Williams argued was the symbolic conflation of a medicine specialist and the power animal, are found to be rare, but several instances exist. Other paintings are analyzed to show the presence of other significant trance elements within depictions of dancing groups, elephants, and women. The authors conclude that despite some differences in representation and preservation, the same key concepts which are known from the ethnography of the southern San and the rock art of other areas are present in this art.

B116   Yates, R., and A. Manhire (1991). "Shamanism and Rock Paintings: Aspects of the Use of the Rock Art in the South-West Cape, South Africa." *South African Archaeological Bulletin*, vol. 46: 3-11.

The authors state that the work of Lewis-Williams has firmly established the characterization of rock art as "essentially shamanistic." The paper explores three observations within this context that are not directly related to symbolic exegesis: smearing of pigment; repainting of images; and smoothing of painted surfaces. These elements are seen as suggesting direct physical interaction with the paintings by San individuals living in the south-western Cape. Following a description of these activities through analysis of selected paintings, the authors assert that any explanation must come from within the ritual context of the paintings, and so the shamanistic element of the art is further developed. The notion of "strong things" is introduced, and a brief discussion leads to the conclusion that the paintings themselves were "strong things," that is, they possessed a potency that a shaman could tap through ritual interaction. This conclusion is supported by referring to a similar concept among the California Chumash. The authors cite ethnographic accounts of the production of the pigment used in the painting, which required the blood or fat of a freshly killed eland, the quintessential "power" animal. The authors argue that the rock art painting, as shamanistic power object, was "art as process." The activities that they describe illustrate how the shaman/artist could revise or enhance the potency of his or her creation. Referring to the hypothesis of Lewis-Williams and Dowson that the rock face forms an interface with the spirit world, the authors also suggest that the smearing of pigment could have been an attempt to neutralize a powerful image out of which malevolent forces might emerge.

B117   Yates, R., J. Parkington and A. Manhire (1990). *Pictures from the Past: A History of the Interpretation of Rock Paintings and Engravings of Southern Africa.* Pietermaritzburg: Centaur.

The book begins with two sections dealing with historiography that briefly examine the nature of oral and written historical sources, and show how history can be "manufactured" through a manipulation of these sources. An outline of the history of hunter-gatherers is then provided, and the ethnographic work of Bleek and Lloyd is mentioned. In Chapter Eight, the "art for art's sake" explanation, which views the rock art merely as an aesthetic exercise, is discussed and criticized. Two subsequent chapters show how ethnographic studies of contemporary San groups highlighted the context of trance healing dance. Vinnicombe is credited with being the first scholar to connect this contemporary phenomenon with some remarks found in the work of Bleek and Orpen, and then to apply this combined ethnographic evidence to depictions of dancing in the rock art. The authors review how Lewis-Williams built on Vinnicombe's foundational work to elaborate the shamanistic explanation. The writers analyze several paintings to illustrate how the hypothesis serves to identify hallucinatory elements in the art. Chapter Eleven discusses eland symbolism and its function in representing various levels of trance experience. The final chapters examine the shaman's role as rainmaker, and the possibility of encountering hostile medicine specialists while in trance. The discussions contained in the book are supported by numerous illustrations of rock paintings.

4   Xhosa Religion

During 1856 and 1857, most Xhosa-speaking homesteads in the eastern Cape destroyed their crops and sacrificed their cattle in the hope that these ritual acts would facilitate the return of their ancestors. Inspired by the prophecy of a young women, Nongqawuse, the participants in this millenarian movement that came to be known as the Xhosa Cattle Killing acted on their faith in the imminent return of the ancestors who would reclaim the land and its wealth from the European colonizers. When the prophecy failed, however, an estimated 40,000 died of starvation and another 40,000 were forced to engage themselves as wage laborers in the colonial economy. Marking the end of Xhosa political independence, the disastrous aftermath of the Cattle Killing stands as a major turning point in the history of Xhosa-speaking people in South Africa (for the best account of these events, see Peires; 1985, 1986, 1987, 1989, but also see Keller, 1978; Lewis, 1991; Ralston, 1976; Thorpe, 1984; Zarwan, 1976).

The Cattle Killing also marked a watershed in European representations of Xhosa religion. Before that event, every European report about the indigenous people of the eastern Cape asserted that they lacked any trace of religion. At the beginning of the nineteenth century, the Protestant missionary J. T. van der Kemp, the German traveler Henry Lichtenstein, and the colonial magistrate Ludwig Alberti all reported that the Xhosa had no religion. All European commentators who considered the question during the first half of the nineteenth century agreed with this assessment (see, for example, Alberti, 1968 (orig. edn. 1810); J. Brownlee, 1968 (orig. edn. 1827); Fleming, 1853; Kay, 1833; Morgan, 1833; and Van der Kemp, 1804). After the Cattle Killing, however, European observers became convinced that the Xhosa did have a religion that was based on a system of "ancestor worship."

In the first detailed account of that religious system, the colonial magistrate, and former missionary, Joseph Cox Warner, found in 1858 that Xhosa religion could be identified as necromancy, the worship of the dead. Warner provided a detailed inventory of Xhosa religion, describing beliefs in ancestors; the initiation of diviners; rituals for the detection of witches; healing and rainmaking practices; male and female initiation; funerals and mourning; and rituals of sacrifice for strengthening and protecting the homestead, the chiefdom, and the land (Warner, 1858). All of these elements, however, revolved around the worship of deceased ancestors. In this discovery of a Xhosa religious system based on ancestor worship, Joseph Cox Warner was followed by every other commentator for the rest of the nineteenth century (see, for example, C. Brownlee, 1916; 1955; Callaway, 1880a; 1880b; McLaren, 1918).

Well into the twentieth century, scholars continued to try to represent Xhosa religion by drawing up an inventory of its basic elements (see Malan, 1968; Olivier, 1981; Oosthuizen, 1971; and Raum and De Jager, 1972; but also see Bigalke, 1969; 1982). During the apartheid era, such an effort to produce an inventory of Xhosa religion as a separate, distinct, and self-contained religious system arguably served the interests of a policy of "separate development" that sought to divide Africans into different states on the basis of differences of language, ethnicity, and religion. In these terms, scholars could argue that the Xhosa had a distinctive religious system that distinguished them from other African political groupings in southern Africa.

However, the distinctive features of Xhosa religion have much in common with the religious resources that animate African traditional religion throughout the region. Rather than representing a separate and distinct religious system, Xhosa religion shares with other forms of African religion an interest in identifying and deploying resources of spiritual meaning and power.

Under the name of Qamatha, a supreme deity has featured in Xhosa religion. In conversation with the early nineteenth-century Christian mission, however, Xhosa-speaking people engaged in an ongoing controversy over the precise location of that supreme divine power. While the convert Ntsikana followed the missionaries in locating God in the heavens, the militant Xhosa prophet, Nxele, insisted that God resided beneath the earth as a spiritual power underground that reinforced Xhosa religious claims on the land (see Hodgson, 1982).

The ancestors, however, have evoked the strongest claims on the people and the land. Xhosa ancestors—the *amathongo*—are present in the homestead, the polity, and the disciplines of sacred specialists in Xhosa religion. As Heinz Kuckertz has shown, ancestors can operate in all the different spheres of religious life; they can represent, in different situations, the bonds of kinship, the jural authority of elders, the transcendence of death, and the superhuman dimension of reality that gives meaning and purpose to any human life (Kuckertz, 1983-84; 1990; for Christian interests in the persistence of ancestors in Xhosa religion, see Lamla, 1981; Manona, 1981). Even in fictional literature, the power of Xhosa ancestors has persisted (see Jordan, 1980).

In Xhosa religion, the home is a sacred place that is reinforced by the presence of ancestors. Through rituals of sacrifice, lines of communication with ancestral spirits are opened and maintained (Soga, 1931). However, the domestic space of the home is also reinforced as a sacred space by separating and protecting it from the wild space of the forest. In that wild, uncontrollable, and unpredictable region, evil forces lurk—wild animals, witch familiars, and monstrous creatures—that can be harnessed by antisocial agents to disrupt the secure order of the home. Accordingly, the sacred space of the home must be reinforced by ancestral ritual and by constant vigilance against any incursions by the uncontrollable forces of the wild (Hammond-Tooke, 1975).

The religious life of the home is intimately integrated with relations of kinship and clanship (Hammond-Tooke, 1963; Jonas, 1986). But it also depends upon performing the rites of passage that mark out any human life cycle from birth, through initiation into adulthood, through marriage, to death. In particular, the ritual initiation of males into adulthood has often been observed as a crucial feature of Xhosa religion. As A. N. N. Ngxamngxa has argued, Xhosa rites of initiation that mark the transition from boyhood to manhood perform both a psychological function by mediating entry into adulthood and a social function by reinforcing the solidarity of the community (Ngxamngxa, 1971). Other researchers who have investigated Xhosa rituals of male initiation have made similar findings (see F. Brownlee, 1927; 1928; Carstens, 1982; Gitywa, 1978; Hammond-Tooke, 1958; Mayer, 1971; Mayer and Mayer, 1970; 1990).

In the context of dramatic social change, however, Xhosa initiation ritual has been adapted in significant ways to accommodate the impact of Christianity, the social effects of urbanization, and the shifts in the distribution of wealth and political power that determine who "owns" the ritual of initiation (Mayer, 1980; Seegar, 1989). As a living feature of Xhosa domestic religion, however, male initiation is only one practice that has been modified by social transformations. Other aspects of traditional religion that are anchored in the home—gender relations, labor relations, and the oppositional relations established between domestic space and wild space—have also undergone significant changes during the twentieth century.

For example, the work of P. A. McAllister has highlighted the new tensions in Xhosa domestic religion that have been created by migrant labor. As a new "wild space," the white-controlled mines, factories, farms, and other foreign working environments have created new possibilities, but they have also posed new threats to the sacred order of the home. By adapting the resources of the traditional rites of passage that mark out stages of separation, liminal status, and reincorporation, Xhosa homesteads have been able to employ traditional religious ritual in creative ways to deal with the modern challenges of migrant labor (McAllister, 1980; see also McAllister, 1979; 1981; 1985; 1986a; 1986b; 1988; 1991; 1993).

Although Xhosa political independence was ostensibly destroyed in the middle of the nineteenth century, religious rituals that reinforce the spiritual integrity of the polity have persisted in different forms. Under the authority of chiefs, rituals for fertility, such as the first-fruits ceremony, and rituals for rainmaking have continued to be performed during the twentieth century (Hammond-Tooke, 1953; Thelejane, 1963). However, under the political conditions of apartheid, Xhosa political rituals sometimes assumed strange new forms. In 1987, for example, a Xhosa ritual for strengthening the army, the *ukunzabela* ceremony, was performed in the apartheid-created Republic of Ciskei. However, this ritual, which was administered by Christian clergy, employed the traditional incense, oil, and consecrated water to strengthen the Ciskei army against the similarly artificial Xhosa-speaking Republic of Transkei (De Beer, 1988). On the other side of that apartheid boundary, a traditional Xhosa funeral ritual for a king was performed as a strategic maneuver in an ongoing battle over legitimate religious and political authority in the Republic of Transkei (Dennie, 1992). By 1994, these states no longer existed. It remains to be seen how the traditional religious resources of Xhosa religion might be deployed to reinforce traditional leadership in a new South Africa.

Between homestead and polity, the disciplines of Xhosa sacred specialists have provided spiritual resources of knowledge, healing, and protection from the evil influences of antisocial forces. Clearly, the *igqira*, or diviner, plays a significant role in Xhosa religious life. Combining religion, psychology, and medicine, diviners (*amagqira*) have been called by God and the ancestors; they have undergone special training and ritualized initiation; and they have employed techniques of trance, divination, and the interpretation of dreams in their work as sacred specialists of Xhosa religion (Dovey and Mjingwana, 1985). In the process of being called to the profession, diviners have to undergo a process of initiatory sickness, known as *ithwasa*, in which they experience severe physical illness and psychological distress. This process is understood as both a personal crisis, which is often accompanied by disturbing dreams, visions, and hallucinations, and a spiritual calling from the ancestors (Hammond-Tooke, 1955; Mills, 1985; Mqotsi, 1957). Emerging from this crisis and calling, they are initiated into the wisdom and power of the spiritual arts of divination (De Jager and Gitywa, 1963). Like any rite of passage, the initiation of diviners passes through three stages: the disintegration of their old identity, a liminal status of transition, and their reintegration into a new religious role in the community (Schweitzer and Bührman, 1979; see Schweitzer, 1977). In that new role as a sacred specialist, they are empowered to assist people in healing, solving problems, preventing harm, and detecting the source of evil influences that might disrupt personal or social life.

In recent research, the traditional resources mobilized by Xhosa diviners have been placed in the context of modern social conditions. For example, in new urban settings, the process of *ithwasa* that is undergone by initiate diviners has been interpreted as a response to the social stress created by migrant labor, land shortage, and acute poverty (O'Connell, 1982). At the same time, the practices of Xhosa diviners have been compared to modern psychoanalysis, even in ways that make the *igqira* look like a psychotherapist (Bührman, 1977; 1978; 1979; 1984). In comparing the roles of *amagqira* in old rural environments and new urban contexts, Teboho Victor Soul has concluded that we have every reason to believe that the *amagqira* will continue to play a vital role in Xhosa personal, social, and religious life. As Soul observed: "If for centuries they have been identified with healing, the solution of problems, and the prevention of harm, it is highly unlikely now that their task will suddenly come to an end" (Soul, 1974: 96). We can only expect, therefore, that Xhosa sacred specialists will continue to play significant roles in the future.

C1   Alberti, Ludwig (1968). *Ludwig Alberti's Account of the Tribal Life and Customs of the Xhosa in 1807.* Trans. William Fehr. Cape Town: Balkema (orig. edn. 1810).

Alberti's book, written by a German colonial military officer serving in the Cape Colony in 1802, represents the first substantial ethnographic account of the Xhosa nation. The first part of the text, "Tribal Life and Customs," comprises twenty brief chapters, beginning with the physical geography of "Xhosaland" and the physiological attributes of the people, and further describing their customs in relation to food, physical powers, clothing, and medicines. "The physical and moral upbringing of children" is discussed in detail, including male and female initiation rites. A later chapter examines the status of women in Xhosa society, noting their powerful influence in domestic affairs, but their exclusion from the political domain. In a chapter devoted to "God, Religion and Superstition," Alberti states that the Xhosa people have no conception of God or any kind of "invisible Being" with power over humans. Their religion, or lack of religion, is underpinned by superstitious notions that attribute mysterious powers to objects and animals. Belief in "magic," both benevolent and malevolent, is alleged to be central to their worldview. According to Alberti, benevolent magic for the purposes of healing is usually conducted by female "magicians." The divination and denunciation of malevolent magic is described in some detail, as are the rites of rainmaking. The second part of the text, "The Xhosa and the Colonists," describes relations between the Xhosa and colonial agents, missionaries, and travelers in the eastern Cape. The book is valuable as a primary source for the study of Xhosa religion and culture in the context of colonial encounters with the indigenous peoples of South Africa. Illustrations appear throughout the text.

C2   Ayliff, John, and Joseph Whiteside (1912). *History of the Abambo, Generally Known as the Fingos*. Butterworth: Gazette.

Ayliff and Whiteside's work is an historical account of the Abambo people that begins with their settlement in the Buffalo River Valley below the Drakensberg in Natal in 1800. The account describes their defeat by the Zulu in approximately 1818, and their subsequent dispersal as the Fingo to the Transkei, where, according to the authors, they lived as servants to the Xhosa before being "liberated" by the British Government. Descriptions follow of the War of the Axe and Mlanjeni; Fingo tribal expansion; the Disarmament Act; and the Glen Grey Act. The authors write from a colonialist perspective, and accounts of religious beliefs and practices tend to be superficial. Lists of Fingo chiefdoms, genealogical trees, and names of chiefs and headmen are appended.

C3   Bennie, W. G. (1939). "Ciskei and Southern Transkei Tribes (Xhosa and Thembu)." In A. M. Duggan-Cronin, *The Bantu Tribes of South Africa: Reproductions of Photographic Studies*. vol. 3, no. 1. Cambridge: Cambridge University Press.

Bennie provides a now dated anthropological and historical account of the Xhosa and Thembu peoples, beginning with a broad description of Nguni societies, which are defined as including all the African people inhabiting the Eastern Cape, Transkei, Natal, Swaziland, and the Eastern Transvaal. The sections relating to the Xhosa and Thembu describe their origin, geographical location, known history until the time of writing, cultural and religious practices, and language. The discussion of religion includes circumcision rituals, traditional healers, ancestors, and cosmology. Bennie's work forms a preface to Duggan-Cronin's photographs.

C4   Bigalke, Erich Heinrich (1969). *The Religious System of the Ndlambe of East London District*. M.A. thesis, Rhodes University.

Bigalke's ethnographic study of Ndlambe society in the Eastern Cape Province is based on fieldwork conducted in Tshabo, East London, during 1967 and 1968. The author attended many ceremonial and ritual occasions, conducted extensive interviews, and collected comprehensive demographic data. The thesis focuses on the Xhosa ancestor cult and analysis of its interrelationship with social structure. Chapter One addresses the historical, demographic, and geographical setting of the Ndlambe in the Ciskei region, noting the effects of social change and the division between "Red" and "School" households. Chapters Two and Three consider the social structure of Tshabo villages, followed by analysis of Ndlambe lineage as an institution. Chapters Four to Six then focus on traditional religious beliefs associated with the supreme being and the ancestors; ceremonial and ritual; and the interpretations of misfortune in Ndlambe life. Bigalke concludes that the basic principles of Ndlambe social structure are mirrored in and expressed through ritual practice. A distinction is made between ceremonial and ritual, where ritual specifically depends on invocation of the ancestors in terms of various lineage contexts. Lineage and clan ancestors are regarded as the guardians of morality, while ritual pollution, witchcraft, and sorcery, which are associated with the incomplete assimilation of wives into their husbands' lineages, are believed to be the cause of misfortune. Of central significance in contemporary Ndlambe life, Bigalke concludes, is the further distinction between two groups of rituals, one for named (communicating) ancestors, the other for non-specific (clan) ancestors, which, respectively, serve to reinforce lineage and clan ideologies. Many other types of ritual, including some communal rites, traditional doctoring of the army, and first-fruit ceremonies, have long been discontinued. The following are appended: fieldwork methodology; maps and village diagrams; bibliography; and index.

C5   Bigalke, Erich Heinrich (1982). *An Ethnographical Study of the Ndlambe of South-Eastern Africa*. Ph.D. thesis, Queens University of Belfast.

Bigalke's doctoral thesis aims to redress the lack of research on South Africa's indigenous music in the context of the anthropology of music. Based on fieldwork conducted in 1978 and 1979 among the Xhosa-speaking Ndlambe of the Eastern Cape Province, Bigalke investigates why, in a strictly patrilineal society, music seems to be mostly the preserve of women. Furthermore, given the Ndlambe's strong lineage system, he explores why music-making is mainly a communal activity, rather than one confined to the descent group only. Since the author assumes that music and cultural life influence each other, the association of music-making with religious practice in Ndlambe life constitutes one of the main themes of his thesis. Chapter Three is devoted to an account of Ndlambe history and social structure, highlighting the ideological opposition between the "Red" and "School" people and the role of Christianity in that division. Bigalke's examination of music and dance is contextualized in several areas of Ndlambe society, including daily life; social occasions; feasts; ritual sacrifices; and diviners' *intomble* (seances). Central to communal life among the "Red" people is the performance of ritual sacrifices to lineage ancestors for healing and the diviner's role at some of those rituals. Other public occasions associated with religious ritual include feasts held after the seclusion of young men for initiation and circumcision and after the seclusion of young women for *intonjane* (fertility observance), as well as feasts for traditional weddings. Music, and frequently dance, form a part of all these communal ritual events. Among the "School" people, music is associated with religious practice conducted in the context of church services and funerals. Bigalke's extensive analysis of Ndlambe music underlines the fact that music forms a central component of Ndlambe cultural life as a whole and that it is closely associated with traditional religious practice in particular. Photographs, diagrams, and maps appear in the text and a bibliography is appended.

C6   Blohm, W. (1933). "Das Opfer und dessen Sinn bei den Xosa in Sudafrika." *Archiv für Anthropologie*, vol. 23: 150-53.

Blohm describes general customs surrounding sacrifice among the Xhosa. As a missionary, he draws on his own observations as well as statements made by informants. The short paper begins with a description of the circumstances leading up to a sacrifice. The head of a family usually decides if a sacrifice is necessary. A sacrifice is directed towards the family ancestors, and the family head is believed to obtain information from them in dreams concerning the time and type of animal to be sacrificed. If a sacrifice is to be offered for the benefit of the entire group, the chief performs the ceremony. Blohm states that the ancestors are not gods as such, nor is there a specific god to whom the sacrifices are made. He develops the theme of the Xhosa's life being determined by magical forces that must be propitiated or guarded against. An example is put forward in the form of the amulets that are worn as protection from dark forces. Sacrifice is seen to originate in the sense of helplessness felt in the face of such forces or in the spirit of thanksgiving connected with a positive event. The author says that a sacrifice will be offered at the birth of a child, a son's circumcision, or before the beginning of a large undertaking. Sacrifices will be offered in the case of illness, a death in the family, drought, crop failure, or famine. The paper concludes with a brief discussion of the sociological aspects of sacrifice. As a communal feast, sacrifice serves to bind members of the group together. It reaffirms the group's connection to the earth, since the Xhosa, suggests the author, seem to have no concept of a heaven or an encompassing cosmos. According to Blohm, there is no human sacrifice among the Xhosa. The text is in German.

C7   Brownlee, Charles (1906). "Laws Relative to Religion and Other Customs." In John Maclean (ed.) *A Compendium of Kafir Laws and Customs, Including Genealogical Tables of Kafir Chiefs and Various Tribal Census Returns*. Grahamstown: J. Slater (orig. edn. 1858). 23-26.

Charles Brownlee was a Gaika Commissioner for the colonial government in South Africa. In this paper, he briefly outlines his observations of Xhosa customary laws concerning ritual. These include the fines and other penalties accorded for infringement of periods of separation during circumcision rites, as well as customs associated with states of pollution recognized after a person dies, which vary in length of time according to social status. Other customs concerned with states of pollution, such as attitudes towards the dead body and to lightning, and infringements of ritual regulations, are further noted. Regulations applying to "grave watchers" are detailed and also the ways in which the evils of witchcraft are dealt with in Xhosa society. Brownlee concludes by mentioning that Xhosa doctors are not recompensed unless the patient is cured. These notes are descriptive and are colored by the writer's own nineteenth-century Western perspective of religion and the law.

C8   Brownlee, Charles (1916). *Reminiscences of Kaffir Life and History.* 2nd edn. Lovedale: Lovedale Press (orig. edn. 1896).

This volume of Charles Brownlee's memoirs, papers, and letters tells of his years as Gaika Commissioner for the colonial government in nineteenth-century South Africa. Some accounts and perceptions of Xhosa customs and religious beliefs and practices are included. For example, Mrs. Charles Brownlee contributes an essay on the "Cattle-Killing Delusion." The prophecies of Mhlakaza and Nongqawuse concerning the resurrection of the dead Xhosa heroes are documented. The Xhosa peoples' responses to the prophetic demands to exterminate their cattle and destroy their corn are interpreted from the Brownlees' view of the Xhosa as "an intensely superstitious people." Concern for the protection of the lives and property of British settlers, the decimation of the Xhosa people, and the conflicts between chiefs who supported the prophecies and those who opposed them are all recounted. In a later section entitled "Superstitions and Customs among the Native Races," Charles Brownlee relates cases of alleged witchcraft brought before him as judicial authority and his efforts to persuade people that there was no such thing as witchcraft. The charms used to "bewitch" victims are described, including the possibility that flesh from corpses was sometimes used. Other "superstitions" ascertained from conversations with the Xhosa about the ancestors are noted, and the involvement of spirits in the daily life of the living is examined. Another short piece by Mrs. Brownlee describes a Xhosa betrothal ceremony. The volume contains a variety of anecdotal accounts, biographical sketches of Xhosa leaders, and relations between the Xhosa and Christian missions. Photographs are included in the text.

C9   Brownlee, Charles (1955). "A Fragment of Xhosa Religious Beliefs." *African Studies*, vol. 14: 37-41.

Published alongside an introductory synopsis, with extensive footnotes, by C. M. Doke, Brownlee's manuscript, written at some point between 1870 and 1890, provides a late nineteenth-century view of Xhosa beliefs and practices. The author speculates on the origin of Xhosa names for a supreme being and on

Xhosa religion in general, drawing on what was surmised about Zulu religious belief. Questions are raised relating to supernatural powers attributed to chiefs and to the ancestors. Notes are included on praise-poems; the role of animals, particularly in relation to "witchcraft"; and rituals of sacrifice, healing, and burial. Brownlee concludes with a brief comparative statement, drawing a distinction between Zulu and Xhosa beliefs with regard to the ancestors as agents of spiritual power.

C10   Brownlee, Frank (1927). "The In-Tonjane Ceremony, as Observed in Fingoland." *Bantu Studies*, vol. 3: 401-03.

This brief article describes the *intonjane*, or female initiation rites, conducted by the Mfengu in 1927. The author explains the derivation of the term *intonjane*, pointing to its association with the first menstruation. He also describes the seclusion of the girl, her supervision, and the celebration at the termination of the seclusion, which includes music, dancing, slaughtering a beast, and beer drinking. The article is entirely descriptive.

C11   Brownlee, Frank (1928). "The Circumcision Ceremony in Fingoland." *Bantu Studies*, vol. 3, no. 2: 179-83.

This brief article offers a description of a circumcision ceremony observed in August 1927 at Bawa in the Butterworth District of the Transkei. Brownlee, the magistrate of the district, describes in detail the circumcision of two boys and the rituals associated with the event. He documents the *uMguyo* or collecting of the boys, the dancing, the feast, the *isutu* hut, the surgeon, the circumcision itself, and the period of seclusion that follows circumcision. In addition to the important process of initiation for the boys, the central role of the surgeon is also highlighted. Brownlee notes the purificatory practices involved, such as fasting, before the surgeon performs the circumcision, and the healing medicines used afterwards. The article, although informative, is largely descriptive.

C12   Brownlee, Frank (1944). "Burial Places of Chiefs." *African Affairs*, vol. 43, no. 170: 23-24.

Brownlee's brief descriptive note lists the burial places of several important chiefs: Thaba Bosigo; the burial place of the Sotho Chief Seeiso Griffith; a high point overlooking the Kei River where the Xhosa Chief Rharhabe was buried; and a river pool where the Pondo Chief Ngwanya was buried. A more detailed description of the burial of Mtsiwake, a minor chieftain of the Bhaca, whom the author knew personally, is also provided.

C13   Brownlee, John (1968). "Account of the Amakosae, or Southern Caffers." In George Thompson, *Travels and Adventures in Southern Africa*. Parts 2 and 3. Ed. Vernon S. Forbes. Cape Town: The Van Riebeeck Society (orig. edn. 1827).

Brownlee's essay, appended to Thompson's text, offers an account of the history and royal lineage of the Xhosa people in the early nineteenth century. The essay also includes sections describing Xhosa customs, including crimes and punishments; religion and "superstitions"; circumcision; marriage; and funeral rites. Brownlee attributes the Xhosa people with belief in a supreme being and the immortality of the soul, but with no notion of future rewards or punishments. Their beliefs concerning thunder, animals, and the ancestral spirits are defined as "superstitions." Male initiation and the rite of circumcision is described in some detail, as well as ceremonies associated with female puberty. Brownlee's accounts of the customs and rites associated with marriage and funerals are also informative. These are followed by brief sections discussing agriculture, language, and geography. The essay concludes with Brownlee's account of an interview with the Xhosa chief, Hinza, who, it appears, asked insightful questions about Christianity, most notably: "What influence has it had on the conduct of men?" Although Brownlee's essay is typical of nineteenth-century colonial perceptions of South African indigenous people, being both pejorative and patronizing, Forbes' footnotes indicate that Brownlee's account of Xhosa history, customs, and religious practices is more detailed and accurate than those that preceded it. The footnotes also offer valuable references to other primary material.

C14   Brownlee, William T. (1924-1926). "Witchcraft Among the Natives of South Africa: Suggested Historical Origin of Superstitions." *Journal of the African Society*, vol. 24: 306-13; vol. 25: 27-46.

In this article W. T. Brownlee, past Chief Magistrate of the Transkeian Territories, traces the origins of witchcraft in South Africa, which he defines as "the playing upon the superstitious credulity of the natives by those who profess to be initiated into certain supposed supernatural mysteries and powers." The first part of the paper is devoted to the author's interpretations of the Xhosa *igqira* or diviner (described as "witch-doctor" or "witch-finder"), a man or woman who "smells" out those who are guilty of sorcery. Brownlee then reviews the calling and "semi-religious" initiation process of the diviner and his or her methods of practice. Describing the fate of those who are found guilty of evil, Brownlee concludes that the "witch-doctor" enjoys great power and influence in the land. Part Two of the paper provides a profile of the "wizard" or "sorcerer" who, says Brownlee, is more often than not innocent of the charges leveled against him or her. Gruesome methods of killing those found guilty are described. The author provides two examples of persons known to him who were accused of sorcery. Spells, spirits, and supernatural agents are described as instances of hysteria and profound superstition. The remainder of the paper speculates on the origins of these "superstitions," proposing similarities between Xhosa witchcraft beliefs and those of ancient Israel as they are recorded in the Old Testament. Supporting his theory with reference to the history of gold-mining in the region of Zimbabwe, which was supposedly undertaken by the ancient Hebrews and Phoenicians, and assuming that the ancient Jews acquired their gold in South Africa, Brownlee asserts that the Xhosa people have, in the past, had direct connections with Jews. In conclusion, Brownlee draws out a comparison that links Xhosa practices not only to Jewish customs but also to those of the ancient Hebrews and Phoenicians.

C15   Bührman, M. Vera (1977). "Xhosa Diviners as Psychotherapists." *Psychotherapeia*, vol. 3, no. 4: 17-20.

In this brief article based on extensive research into the therapeutic techniques of Xhosa diviners, Bührman defines the diviner as "a carrier of Xhosa history, customs, and beliefs." As such, she typifies the diviner as uniquely suited to treat the psychic ills of his or her people, and argues that much of the diviner's approach is comparable to that of the Western psychotherapist. Noting the use of "milieu therapy," and the authority and empathy that creates a relationship of communion with the patient, the author describes other techniques employed to induce a receptive state of mind. Central to the therapeutic process in this psychotherapy is access to the unconscious through the interpretation of dreams and the wishes of the ancestors. Bührman describes the intensive training of a diviner, which begins with the experience of *ithwasa*, a condition she compares to schizophrenia, but classifies as a "creative illness." The writer emphasizes that the diviner, like the competent psychotherapist, has fully experienced the "road" to the unconscious. But Xhosa psychic healers, says Bührman, know this road and its significance for their people—whether the individual, the family, or the clan—in a way that their white counterparts never could. Therefore, Bührman points to the urgent need for further research on the methods of Xhosa diviners. She advocates the benefits of incorporating diviners and their therapeutic skills into the mental health services in South Africa. References are appended.

C16   Bührman, M. Vera (1978). "Tentative Views on Dream Therapy by Xhosa Diviners." *Journal of Analytical Psychology*, vol. 23: 105-21.

Bührman's article, based on fieldwork conducted among Xhosa-speaking people in South Africa, presents a study of attitudes towards dreams and an assessment of therapeutic techniques used by Xhosa diviners. Using the phenomenological approach of a participant observer, Bührman provides in this study a comparative analysis of a series of dreams as perceived from two widely different cultural viewpoints—the Xhosa diviner and the Western analytical psychologist. A condensed history of a Xhosa patient's dream series over a number of years is documented, followed by analyses and therapeutic interpretations by the diviner and the author. The interpretations were carried out independently, but the two therapists subsequently commented on each other's work. The author indicates that despite different modes of expression no essential contradictions were apparent in the two sets of analyses. Bührman notes that the diviner's approach integrates cultural rituals and beliefs with an immediacy of experience that is underpinned by a profound reverence and respect for the patient. The author's comparative analysis shows that although basic similarities in the two therapeutic approaches can be observed, the specific techniques used are nevertheless different. Arguing that Xhosa diviners work on a less verbal level than Western analytical psychologists—a level she calls "psycho-physiological"—Bührman points to the need for further research in this area. References are appended to the text.

C17   Bührman, M. Vera (1979). "Why are Certain Procedures of the Indigenous Healers Effective?" *Psychotherapeia*, vol. 5: 20-5.

Drawing on her research among Xhosa-speaking healers, Bührman's paper challenges Western medical attitudes towards indigenous therapies, arguing that they cannot be labeled "witchcraft" or "superstition." Bührman first explores factors that are operative in the Xhosa indigenous healing system, particularly psychic procedures employed in treating both physiological and psychological afflictions. The intensive training of the neophyte *igqira* (indigenous healer) is emphasized, indicating the respect and reverence held for unconscious material and for the role of the ancestors. These factors, the author argues, define the work of the *igqira* as more of a "calling" than a mere profession. Second, Bührman presents a comparative analysis of psychotherapy and indigenous healing, revealing that most of the components that constitute effective psychotherapy are found in traditional Xhosa therapeutic techniques. The building of trust that is essential in the psychotherapeutic relationship, as well as work with the unconscious through dreams that is central to depth psychology, are important examples of Western psychotherapeutic techniques that are also fundamental to indigenous systems of healing among the Xhosa. The author documents indigenous healing methods in some detail, concluding that the understanding of dreams and the use of myth, ritual, and sacred dance represent a profound spiritual dimension to the work which reaches "archaic layers" of a patient's being and stimulates "progress towards health and wholeness." References are appended.

C18   Bührman, M. Vera (1984). *Living in Two Worlds: Communication between a White Healer and her Black Counterparts*. Cape Town: Human & Rousseau.

Bührman's study reports on her work among Xhosa-speaking traditional healers (*amagqira*) in the Keiskammahoek area of the Ciskei. Bührman lived and worked with several healers, exchanging her own Western Jungian psychiatric and depth psychology orientation for the methods of traditional African healers. The text discusses concepts of depth psychology, Xhosa cosmology, categories of illness, and aspects of *ithwasa* treatment, that is, the preliminary state which can lead to initiation as an *igqira*. Healing techniques include purification procedures, interpretation of dreams, herbal and environmental treatment, teaching of divination, dance, and various ritual ceremonies. Chapters are devoted to detailed documentation of the central components of the indigenous healing system: the use of dreams; the ritual healing dance (*intlombe* and *xhentsa*); the river ceremonies; the sacrificial ritual, *isiko lentambo*; and the *godusa*, or "taking home" ceremony that constitutes the graduation and initiation ceremony for the student *igqira*. The author argues that Western medicine and psychology has much to learn from the "intuitive non-rational" belief systems of African cosmology, and the archetypes which underpin them, particularly in the context of the therapeutic relationship. A glossary of terms precedes the introductory chapter and color photographs accompany the text. References are appended.

C19   Callaway, Henry (1880a). "A Fragment Illustrative of Religious Ideas among the Kafirs." *Folk-Lore Journal*, vol. 2, no. 4: 56-60.

This brief "fragment," regarded by Callaway as a "native literary gem," comprises two Xhosa verses or songs, with commentary also in the Xhosa language. Both are translated into English by Callaway. The first song, it is said, was sung by the people of ancient times before the missionaries came. Although some people of the present now consider it a fiction, many hold it to be true. The second verse speaks of God, who was worshipped before the missionaries came and was known as "Kamata" or "Tiko." He is not the God of the English, the commentary notes, for there is only one God and one "man." Rather, "he is one man who came forth from one God." Notes are appended.

C20   Callaway, Henry (1880b). "On the Religious Sentiment Amongst the Tribes of South Africa." *Cape Monthly Magazine*, vol. 2: 87-102.

Callaway's paper represents a nineteenth-century colonial missionary's search for a God in Xhosa cosmology that would be comparable to the God of Christianity. Callaway proposes that the Xhosa-speaking people of South Africa are not atheistic, as believed by many missionaries of his time, but are in fact theists who experience "religious sentiment." First, the author refers to the work of Professor Blackie, which addresses the "religious instincts of the human race," in relation to Callaway's own concern as a Christian missionary for teaching a people "higher religious truths." Relying on information gained from "Gqika" informants, Callaway then investigates creation myth and names for God in Xhosa religion, finding that before the use of the name "Utikxo" for God—a name appropriated by the missionaries to teach the Xhosa-speaking people about the Christian God—they referred to "Ukqamata." The author speculates that this ancient name might represent the Xhosa-speaking peoples' own notion of a supreme being in whom resides ultimate power. Power, says Callaway, is the first attribute of God, a power to which the individual can appeal amidst the human experience of powerlessness. Further information related to past worship and sacrificial rites offered to "Ukqamata" confirms for Callaway his premise that although the word may originally have referred to the name of an ancestor, it has more recently been "stripped of its anthropomorphism" to become the name of God.

C21   Carstens, Peter (1982). "The Socio-Economic Context of Initiation Ceremonies Among Two Southern African Peoples." *Canadian Journal of African Studies*, vol. 16, no. 3: 505-22.

Carstens' extensively annotated article provides a comparative analysis of the initiation rituals of the Nama of the north-western Cape and the Xhosa of the eastern Cape at the turn of the nineteenth century. Continuities and divergences are documented within the context of rites of passage, with reference both to the past and to the current changing socioeconomic milieus in contemporary South Africa. Carstens focuses on how the Nama and Xhosa reacted differently to European conquest in terms of the transformational status of girls and boys represented in initiation rites. The article describes in some detail both Nama and Xhosa traditional initiation rituals, as well as the place of initiation in contemporary society. The writer's conclusions focus on the significance of gender roles, noting that, for example, Xhosa men were characterized as "managers of production units," taking the credit for their wives' work, while Nama women enjoyed greater freedom and even some control over the men in the domestic realm. Carstens further explains the disappearance of Nama boys' and Xhosa girls' initiation ceremonies, in terms of the changing socioeconomic roles of men and women, against the background of colonial domination and marginalized domestic situations in a capitalist economy. For example, the importance of Xhosa male initiation in the contemporary context of migratory labor is emphasized. Carstens suggests that initiation thus reinforces residential roots and contributes to a family's subsistence. Nama women, on the other hand, are seen as "manageresses" in the context of matrifocal households. Notes are appended.

C22   Casset, A. (1904). "Notes on Kafir Customs and Superstitions in the Transkei." *Zambezi Mission Record*, vol. 2: 334-37.

Casset discusses religious and cultural practices of the Xhosa-speaking people of the Transkei from the perspective of Europeans in South Africa at the turn of the century. Divided into three parts, the first, "Sacrifices in Honour of Departed Ancestors," addresses the practice of ritual animal sacrifice in propitiation of the ancestral spirits. Described in detail as a cruel and "horrible performance," Casset notes that this ritual is performed at the birth of a child, when a girl reaches puberty, and at the death of a headman. The offerings of grain and libations for the harvest and "beer-drinking season" are also mentioned. Part Two, "Witch-doctors and their Tricks," introduces Xhosa herbalists, diviners, and rain-doctors as those "who oppose the introduction of Christianity with all their strength" and prey on "the superstitious character of a nation of children." The practice of "smelling out" wrong-doers is discussed in some detail, as well as the abilities of discovery, healing, and rainmaking that make up the diviner's power. Finally, a section on "How the Witch-doctor Is Made" is devoted to the calling, training, and initiation of diviners, a process that, in the view of the author, requires "a great deal of cunning" on the part of the aspirant "witch-doctor." Although suffused with Christian missionary invective against Xhosa religious beliefs and practices, the article is of value in tracing the history of the comparative study of religion in South Africa.

C23   Crais, Clifton C. (1991). "Peires and the Past." *South African Historical Journal*, vol. 25: 236-40.

While paying tribute to Peires' monumental achievement in *The Dead Will Arise*, Crais expresses surprise at two glaring omissions: the issue of consciousness and the problem of history as representation. With reference to consciousness, Crais argues, it is important to explore the world of nineteenth-century Xhosa as they made and inhabited it. Unfortunately, argues Crais, Peires pays insufficient attention to this problem. Although he devotes space to the central beliefs of the Cattle Killing and tackles the creation myth about Uhlanga, Peires is unable to find access to the religious import of Nongqawuse's tragic prophecies. In other words, Crais suggests that the prophecies demand to be interpreted as religious texts, even by historians. The question of representation goes to the heart of history as a self-conscious enterprise. The historian owes it to himself or herself, and especially to the reader, to bare the ideological wellsprings of his or her scholarly praxis. The writing of history as an exercise of power can, unless limited by deliberate methodological, epistemological, and rhetorical devices, all too easily find itself wallowing in the mire of colonial and imperial orgies of power and excess. Crais regrets that Peires has unintentionally fallen victim to this pitfall, and he concludes by expressing the hope that in a day when radical historiography is in the grip of a malaise, history will focus on the "experience of consciousness."

C24   Crais, Clifton C. (1992). *The Making of the Colonial Order: White Supremacy and Black Resistance in the Eastern Cape, 1770-1865.* Johannesburg: Witwatersrand University Press.

Crais' book explores questions of culture and dominance in the construction of an unequal and racially divided society in the Eastern Cape of South Africa from the late eighteenth century. The author's analysis of this violent and complex history of colonial expansion, involving British and Dutch-speaking colonizers and mainly Xhosa-speaking Africans, grapples with the interweaving of socioeconomic issues with those of power, discourse, and identity. Divided into four main parts, Part One of the book addresses the interaction of economics, ideology, and the creation and re-creation of social boundaries that occurred in a context of "the frontier" as a site of intensive social interaction and construction. Chapter One particularly addresses the social structure of Xhosa settlements and their spiritual cosmology. It includes a discussion of the central importance of religious beliefs and ritual practices. Part Two focuses on early British rule at the Cape and the reactions of Dutch-speaking colonists to British power. Part Three looks more closely at the part played by European intellectual discursive constructions of the "character" of the African as "Other" in the creation of colonial society, and the forms of African resistance to British domination. Part Four, which is of special interest for the study of Xhosa religious belief and practice, analyzes how Xhosa-speakers perceived and frequently rejected the colonial world, a rejection that included appeals to millenarian prophecies and myths of cosmogenesis. Close attention is given to "myth and history as resistance," focusing on an analysis of the meaning of Nongqawuse's prophecies and the Xhosa Cattle-Killing movement. Crais argues that the Cattle Killing was neither an irrational response to extreme social disruption and deprivation, nor solely religiously inspired, but represented "a mode of controlling the future through a representation of the past in the present." Notes and a comprehensive bibliography of primary and secondary sources are appended.

C25   Davies, C. (1927). "Customs Governing Beer-Drinking among the Ama-Bomvana." *South African Journal of Science*, vol. 24: 521-24.

In this brief, descriptive paper, Davies explores the customs associated with the recognition of local groupings through ceremonial beer drinks among the Xhosa-speaking Bomvana of the Transkei, from the time of the Cattle Killing in 1857. Davies traces the government division of land into "locations" in the region, which coincided with original *isiduko*, which were further subdivided into *imihlaba*, each headed by a chief. In each *umhlaba* were several kraals, where a beer-name (*inkabi*) was used as a means of identification with a particular kraal. These beer-names were central to the Bomvana social structure, involving a complex system of belonging to an *umhlaba* and attaining ownership of a kraal and *inkabi*. The author goes on to discuss in some detail who is eligible to participate in a beer drink given by the headman of a kraal, which is attended by members of neighboring *imihlaba*, as well as the elaborate ritual performed. Davies particularly emphasizes the position of women in the social structure and their role at the beer drink. Beer is also brewed and distributed, however, at celebrations after initiations, where the heads of various *imihlaba* distribute the beer to their own people. The author concludes by outlining occasions when it is not possible to attend a beer drink, such as after the death of a member of the kraal. Xhosa key-words accompany the text.

C26   De Beer, N. J. (1988). Ukunzabela-seremonie herleef." *South African Journal of Ethnography*, vol. 11, no. 1: 15-20.

In this article, "*Ukunzabela* ceremony revives," De Beer describes a performance of the *ukunzabela* or war ceremony in Ciskei during February 1987. The writer draws on a review of the literature to interpret the historical precedents on which the recent ceremony was based. Two such traditions are detailed: the doctoring of an army before war and the decoration of heroes after war. The 1987 ceremony presents a significant symbol of the strained relations between Ciskei and Transkei since Ciskei's "independence" in 1981. De Beer describes how these relations culminated in an attack carried out by Transkeians on the house of the president of Ciskei. A successful counter-attack was celebrated as a victory for Ciskei. Therefore the *ukunzabela* ceremony was held to honor the heroes of that encounter. Led by ministers of the Ethiopian Church, the ceremony included the ritual treatment of the army personnel with incense, consecrated water, and oil to ensure the continuance of their loyalty and fearlessness in the future. Participants in the ceremony included members of the Ciskeian Executive Council and their wives, praise singers, a number of speakers, and choirs. De Beer concludes that this event signifies that the traditional cultural heritage of the Xhosa people of Ciskei, at the time of writing, still formed an integral part of Ciskeian society. Notes and references are appended. The text is in Afrikaans; with an abstract and summary in English.

C27   De Jager, E. J. (1963). "Notes on the Magical Charms of the Cape Nguni Tribes." *Fort Hare Papers*, vol. 2, no. 6: 193-302.

De Jager discusses Cape Nguni charms as part of a specific coherent magical lore, which is not always distinct from traditional medicine or healing methods.

The author defines witchcraft and sorcery and describes magical methods of harming people, after which the bulk of the text is given to a list of magical charms, including love charms, charms for the protection of children, charms worn by expectant and nursing mothers, and charms worn as protection against animals, diseases, and natural elements. The main purpose of the charms, De Jager concludes, is to counteract witchcraft through preventative and curative methods. Footnotes accompany the text.

C28   De Jager, E. J. (1971). "'Traditional' Xhosa Marriage in the Rural Areas of the Ciskei, South Africa." In E. J. De Jager (ed.) *Man: Anthropological Essays Presented to O. F. Raum.* Cape Town: Struik. 160-82.

De Jager provides a descriptive analysis of marriage beliefs and practices in the rural Ciskei, examining continuity and reconstitution of tradition due to cultural contact and socioeconomic change. The writer classifies different types of marriage found in the region, but focuses on traditional Xhosa marriage customs, which are still the most prevalent. De Jager goes on to describe the initial steps towards marriage and their symbolic significance, highlighting the negotiations between the parents of both families and the arrangements for *lobola* (dowry) cattle given by the boy's family to the parents of the girl. The betrothal ceremony is then discussed, stressing that it is entirely different from the Western concept of betrothal, particularly in relation to attitudes towards sexuality. The marriage ceremony itself is described in some detail, followed by an extensive analysis of the significance of *lobola*. The writer concludes that while young Xhosa people today enjoy more freedom of choice in marriage partners, marriage is still an arrangement between two kin-groups. *Lobola* still survives as an important component of this arrangement, although cash, in addition to cattle, is an increasingly important medium of payment. In terms of gender relations, De Jager points out the strains of economic instability and migrant labor on the married man's position as "pillar of the home." Because of these disruptive socioeconomic forces, a distinct matrifocal tendency can be identified in rural Ciskei, where the woman frequently participates in spheres of life that would formerly have been taboo. References are appended.

C29   De Jager, E. J., and V. Z. Gitywa (1963). "A Xhosa Umhlwayelelo Ceremony in the Ciskei." *African Studies*, vol. 22, no. 3: 109-16.

The authors describe the *Umhlwayelelo* (diviner initiation) ritual of the Xhosa-speaking people of the Ciskei, stressing its association with human illness and the presence of ancestor spirits. Drawing particularly on Monica Hunter's work, De Jager and Gitywa first address the common occurrence of illness and its treatment by an *igqira* (diviner) among men or women who are called to be diviners. A descriptive case study of a diviner's initiation follows. The authors note the experiential dimensions of the ritual, including trance states and the significance of coded dreams. The ritual preparation of beer and the festivities accompanying the ceremony are also detailed. In conclusion, the authors extrapolate several sociological functions of the ceremony, underscoring the factors of social integration and reciprocity. Briefly, examples of the function of the ritual are identified: The ritual provides a medium for a purely social gathering and festive occasion; it brings people together and counteracts the tendency of modernization to separate people and erode tradition; it shows that traditional beliefs, such as the role of the ancestor spirits, are still active in the community, strengthening ritual and social ties; it maintains a hierarchical structure of traditional authority; and finally the payment of the diviner and the help of neighbors imply that traditional economies still operate in Xhosa rural societies. The paper is annotated and photographs and diagrams accompany the text.

C30   Dennie, Garrey (1992). "One King, Two Burials: The Politics of Funerals in South Africa's Transkei." *Journal of Contemporary African Studies*, vol. 11, no. 2: 76-87.

Dennie's astute analysis of the burial of the deposed Paramount Chief of the Thembu in the Transkei, King Sabata Jonguhlanga Dalindyebo, illuminates the interaction between politics, culture, and religion. The author defines the king's body as a highly complex text that was suffused with meaning, a text authored by Dalindyebo himself and circumscribed by his sociocultural and political experiences in life. The first burial—"a tawdry affair," according to the author—served to highlight the bitter conflict between Dalindyebo and Matanzima. The exhumation, reburial, and subsequent political "resurrection of the king," when General Bantu Holomisa came to power, definitively exploited traditional Thembu cultural and religious practices. In an attempt to appropriate the meanings attached to Dalindyebo's corpse, Holomisa hoped to increase his own legitimacy by using the public event to separate himself from the politics of Matanzima and to align himself with the politics of Dalindyebo. Dennie's analysis indicates the appropriation of the dead body as part of a politics of burial that provided a vehicle for the often contradictory expressions of political interests, cultural understandings, and religious protestations. Dalindyebo's burials showed that religious notions of the sacrality of the dead body and the value of customary practices generated an incisive critique of the secular political order and, put together with political ideas, disrupted an unjust political system. Dennie argues that the blurring of lines dividing different social, ethnic, national, religious, and secular practices facilitated resistance to an old order and the articulation of the new. In this case, Dalindyebo's dead body was the medium for articulating such ideas. Notes and references are appended to the text.

C31   Dovey, Ken, and Ray Mjingwana (1985). "Psychology, Religion and Healing: The *'Amagqira'* in Traditional Xhosa Society." *Theoria*, vol. 64: 77-83.

Dovey and Mjingwana's empathetic analysis of traditional healers among the Xhosa moves beyond the pejorative label of "witchdoctors" attributed to healers by whites in South Africa and the Christian rejection of traditional healing as evil. These derogatory definitions, the authors argue, have been employed to discredit an alternative political ideology. Instead, Dovey and Mjingwana enter into dialogue with modern psychologies that have also rejected the notion of traditional healing as rooted in a "magical mindset." Drawing on interviews with traditional healers in the Eastern Cape and Transkei, the authors stress the religious nature of the healing profession, which is founded on a belief in God and in the ancestors as the communication link between the *igqira* (healer) and God. The paper offers an account of the healer's calling and training; techniques of trance and interpretation of dreams; and ritual divination. Despite the intrusion of modern, Western influences, the authors contend that Xhosa communities have successfully retained the integrity of their religious beliefs. This opinion is supported by the *igqira*, who fulfills the social functions of priest, medical practitioner, and psychologist. However, Dovey and Mjingwana note the defensive stance taken by traditional healers that can lead to stagnation of creativity, as well as the lack of credibility currently suffered by modern psychologists. They therefore advocate that the incorporation of traditional practices into modern therapy could both enhance the effectiveness of psychological practice and facilitate the survival of *amagqira* in a modernized setting. Brief notes are appended.

C32   Elliot, Aubrey (1970). *The Magic World of the Xhosa*. London; Johannesburg; Cape Town: Collins.

Elliot's anthropological study of rural Xhosa-speaking society covers the most significant aspects of the social, cultural, and religious life of the "Red Blankets" (Xhosa traditionalists). The author draws on his own experience of growing up in the Ciskei, as well as his extensive field research. The account is largely descriptive and often anecdotal, portraying a romanticized picture of the Xhosa way of life. Religious beliefs and practices associated with rites of passage are extensively addressed. For example, a chapter is devoted to birth, describing certain customs and ritual animal sacrifice that serve to protect both mother and child from illness and evil spirits. Another chapter documents the lengthy process of male initiation, explaining the complex ceremonies and symbolic meanings involved. Elliot also discusses Xhosa beliefs in "People of the River" who are said to live on the bed of the river and to be benevolent towards human beings. In addressing the beliefs and practices concerned with "magic" among the Xhosa, the author distinguishes between sorcery and witchcraft, emphasizing that both are associated only with evil. The role of the herbalist in treating and immunizing against evil is also noted. Detailed attention is given to the position of the diviner in Xhosa society, who is called and guided by ancestral spirits in the use of several different techniques of divination, as well as detection of witches. Lastly, the author discusses the fundamental role of the ancestors or *amathongo* in Xhosa religion, explaining the significance of death rites and sacrificial rituals performed to venerate the ancestors. Excellent color photographs appear throughout the text and a glossary of Xhosa words, a brief bibliography, and an index are appended.

C33   Fleming, Francis (1853). *Kaffraria and Its Inhabitants*. London: Smith Elder & Company.

Fleming's work comprises a broad mid-nineteenth century study of "Kaffraria," a region roughly corresponding with the later Transkei or the Eastern Cape. Beginning with an account of the establishment of "British Kaffraria" in the Cape Colony, the author proceeds to discuss the area's geography and zoology in detail. Xhosa history, tribal sub-divisions, language, customs, religious beliefs, and ritual practices are covered in Chapter Four. Describing the Xhosa as a "wandering and marauding race," Fleming detects their few remaining "indistinct traces of religion." In relation to Xhosa beliefs in both good and evil spirits, he stresses the "witchdoctor's" assumed role in providing protection against evil. The diviner's "smelling out" of witches, claims the author, is manipulated by the chiefs to reinforce their oppression of the ordinary people. The ingrained superstition of the Xhosa, he continues, keeps them blind to the diviner's impostures. Fleming also mentions the performance of propitiatory sacrifice before going to war for the purpose of invoking success, but no analysis of ancestor beliefs is offered. A map and illustrations accompany the text, followed by appendices that include a list of colonial governors, excerpts from other historical sources, and population statistics of colonies.

C34   Gitywa, Vincent Zanoxolo (1971). "Xhosa Cosmetic Practices." In E. J. de Jager (ed.) *Man: Anthropological Essays Presented to O. F. Raum*. Cape Town: Struik. 205-11.

Gitywa's essay first explains the biased accounts by nineteenth-century missionaries and travelers concerning Xhosa ceremonies and cosmetic practices. The main part of the essay then details past and present Xhosa cosmetic practices and their symbolic significance. The red ochre (*imbhola*) is mainly used by Xhosa women and it is the importance attached to this cosmetic that led to the name "Reds" being given to "traditionalist" Xhosa-speaking people. White ochre is mainly used for newly born babies and for mothers who have just given birth. Gitywa explains that the use of cosmetics is related to sex, age, and status and is often linked to particular stages of life and accompanying rituals. Explaining the cosmetic practices surrounding birth, initiation, and marriage, the author gives particular detail of those used during male initiation rites of passage, including the now discontinued practice of tattooing. The various medicinal and aesthetic uses of the cosmetic ochres are also described. The final section looks at how the effects of cultural change and European influence have modified the use of traditional cosmetics. Since the incursion of European "beauty" cosmetics into Xhosa culture, the use of indigenous cosmetics remains only for ceremonial ritual. A bibliography is appended.

C35   Gitywa, Vincent Zanoxolo (1978). *Male Initiation in the Ciskei: Formal Incorporation into Bantu Society.* D.Litt. thesis, University of Fort Hare.

In this doctoral thesis Gitywa aims not only to evaluate the initiation system of the Xhosa, but also to assess reasons for the "generation gap" between parents and youth. Noting that Xhosa culture is in a state of flux, the author recognizes the conflict of ideals that signifies shifting values and meanings with regard to traditions such as initiation. Gitywa draws on literary and oral sources, as well as anthropological theory in relation to "primitive" education. Extensive fieldwork in the Ciskei strongly supports the research project, including visits to fifty initiation lodges. Several aspects of initiation ritual are comprehensively described and analyzed, such as the reconstruction of traditional initiation; case histories of initiands; the personnel who officiate the rites; the paraphernalia associated with initiation rituals; and the changing meanings of initiation. Gitywa concludes that circumcision and initiation have shown both tenacity and plasticity under the impact of European cultural contact, but the educational value of the rite has, however, been greatly reduced. Deeply rooted in Xhosa culture and closely linked to ancestor veneration and marriage, initiation has persisted as a simple rite of passage into adulthood rather than as the socializing institution that used to produce men of warrior caliber and political status. Initiation today accommodates two worlds—the traditional and the modern—and fulfills a vital function in some aspects of the Xhosa-speaking world. But in other aspects, argues the author, it has become an anachronism. Photographs, maps, and a glossary accompany the text. A bibliography is appended.

C36   Gqoba, W. (1885). "The Native Tribes, Their Laws, Customs and Beliefs." *Christian Express*, vol. 15, no. 179: 93-94.

Presented to the Lovedale Literary Society in April 1885, Gqoba's paper comprises a brief history of the indigenous peoples of South Africa. He begins by tracing a detailed genealogy of the Xhosa-speaking chiefs and chiefdoms of precolonial south-east Africa, citing the diffusionist theory that some came from the north of Africa and were influenced by Jewish ceremonies and customs. After briefly mentioning the variety of indigenous languages in South Africa, all of which, he suggests, contain many similarities, Gqoba turns to African laws and "superstitions." Indigenous systems of law, says the author, have been handed down by oral tradition, based on precedents set by chiefs in relation to issues such as marriage, inheritance, and criminal jurisprudence. Superstitious beliefs, sorcery, and witchcraft, however, have obstructed justice and humanity. Treaties between African chiefdoms and colonial authorities in British Kaffraria from 1840 to 1855 are outlined, concluding with changes effected by Governors Grey and Cathcart in the 1850s concerning "the administration of justice among the natives."

C37   Guy, Jeff (1991). "A Landmark, Not a Breakthrough," *South African Historical Journal*, vol. 25: 227-43.

In this review article Jeff Guy revises his initially enthusiastic reception and high opinion of Jeff Peires' *The Dead Will Arise*. He questions Peires' historiographical, methodological, and epistemological practices and challenges his polemical treatment of such central figures in the drama as Governor Grey and Commissioner Maclean. The author under review might have benefited from a wealth of insights on the themes of religion, ritual, and sacrifice from other disciplines. For instance, Guy suggests that Peires would probably have come to understand the Cattle Killing and related events not so much as a rational response but as an intelligible act, following Raymond Firth's distinction in this regard. In any event, argues the reviewer, the term "Cattle Killing" betrays a preoccupation with only one aspect of this particular Xhosa response to foreign domination, cattle, and the male power they represented. Agriculture, which was the decisive factor in terms of Xhosa chances of survival, and the women who practiced it, could not have featured in an ungendered analysis which fails to think through power relations on the material and human levels. Only such an analysis can do justice to the data, hence the reviewer's call for new perspectives.

C38   Hammond-Tooke, W. D. (1953). "The Function of Annual First Fruit Ceremonies in Baca Social Structure." *African Studies*, vol. 12, no. 2: 75-87.

Noting that annual first-fruit ceremonies have been prominent in Nguni culture in the past, Hammond-Tooke indicates that they still exist as an important rite among the Swazi and Bhaca. The paper thus analyzes the first-fruit ceremonies (*ingcuba*) of the Bhaca in the Mount Frere district in South Africa. Instead of interpreting these ceremonies as simply a harvest festival or sacralization of crops, the writer argues that for the Bhaca, at least, they constitute a "magico-political" ritual closely associated with the maintenance of "tribal well-being" and a system of "army doctorings." Most of the paper is given to a discussion of the martial rituals that take place at the time of the ripening of crops. The full three-day ritual may only be performed by a reigning chief, and until it is completed, no male may partake of the crops. Hammond-Tooke describes the "stealing" of green maize, calabash, and sweet reed from neighboring fields, which are then cooked on the sacred fire; military marches past the chief; the washing of the army in the river with protective medicines; the killing of the sacred bull and eating its medicated flesh; and the doctoring of the army by the "tribal magician." In conclusion, Hammond-Tooke's analysis of the ritual symbolism indicates the central significance of the martial and protective functions of the festival, arguing that it serves to support social solidarity and the integrity of the community as a whole. Diagrams to elucidate the process of the ritual accompany the text and the article is annotated. In "Notes and News," *African Studies*, vol. 16, no. 4 (1957): 236, Hammond-Tooke offers an additional note to this article, indicating that further investigation of the *ingcuba* among the Bhaca, like the Zulu and Swazi, show that the festival includes criticism of the chief as part of the ritual procedure. The ceremony, he argues, is a typical "ritual of rebellion," as theorized by Max Gluckman, providing a type of catharsis and avenue for expression of rivalry and rebellion within a repetitive social structure.

C39   Hammond-Tooke, W. D. (1955). "The Initiation of a Baca Isangoma Diviner." *African Studies*, vol. 14: 16-22.

Hammond-Tooke's article focuses on a ceremony for the initiation of a diviner (*isangoma*) observed among the Bhaca of the Mount Frere district during field research conducted in East Griqualand in 1949. The author thus provides a case study that aims to redress the lack of empirical research on Nguni diviners. Hammond-Tooke notes that most Bhaca diviners are women and that a diviner has a special relationship with the ancestral spirits, having been "called" by them to the profession. First, the pre-initiatory experiences of the novice diviner are outlined, describing the onset of the *ithwasa* illness and her intensive training under a well-known diviner. Emphasizing communications from the spirits through the medium of dreams, the author also details other purificatory practices and social taboos observed, as well as the use of symbolic objects and ornaments, special clothing, cosmetics, and medicines. The initiation itself consists of *iintlombe* (seances), to enhance the initiate's relations with the ancestral spirits, and the ritual killing of a white goat and another beast (revealed to the novice in a dream). A final *intlombe* is held in the open air, marking the moment when the initiate dons her full regalia and is accorded full professional status as an *isangoma*. The novice is supported throughout the ceremony by the other diviners in attendance, after which celebrations take place in the diviners' hut. Footnotes accompany the text and an account of an *ithwasa* dream is appended.

C40   Hammond-Tooke, W. D. (1958). "The Attainment of Adult Status Among the Mount Frere Bhaca." *African Studies*, vol. 17: 16-20.

In Bhaca society, an Nguni people who settled in the Mount Frere district of East Griqualand, circumcision is no longer practiced and initiation rites only remain for girls. The transition from childhood to adulthood, says Hammond-Tooke, no longer holds the social recognition among the Bhaca as it still does among the Xhosa, Thembu, Mfengu, and Bomvana in the southern part of the Transkeian territories. However, it is noted that reported instances of circumcision among Bhaca boys can be attributed to the spread of Hlubi puberty rites to the Bhaca. In the context of increasing urbanization, the author suggests that periods spent away from home working in the gold or coal mines often take the place of formalized rites of passage. The dangers and hardships faced by the youth, Hammond-Tooke argues, provide a test of his attainment of manhood. The author then details the complex traditional puberty rites performed for girls when they first start to menstruate, including several days of seclusion and concluding with a celebratory feast. The ways the ceremony has been Christianized and modified are also mentioned. Bhaca initiation, says Hammond-Tooke, not only marks entry into womanhood, but also prepares the girl for adult membership of society and marriage. Notes accompany the text.

C41   Hammond-Tooke, W. D. (1960). "Some Bhaca Religious Categories." *African Studies*, vol. 19, no. 1: 1-13.

Hammond-Tooke's sociological study of religion notes that the Bhaca had been under the constant influence of Christianity since 1839. Although the majority of Bhaca were at least nominally Christians, belief and veneration of the ancestors still formed the basis of their religious practice. Intellectual expression of religious experience, says the author, was not highly developed in Bhaca religion, but vaguely defined beliefs were overtly expressed in religious ritual activity. Hammond-Tooke therefore addresses Bhaca religious life under three headings: dogma, ritual, and ethics. First, the "dogma" of the ancestral shades, the "shadowy substance" or "soul" that is believed to survive death of the body is discussed, focusing on the sociological importance of the ancestral spirits (*amathongo*) in Bhaca life. The *amathongo* are the "gods" of the Bhaca, argues Hammond-Tooke, since any notion of a creator is too overlaid by Christian doctrine to retain any element of original Bhaca religious meaning. Second, the author describes how Bhaca religious belief is articulated through ritual. Ritual sacrifices to propitiate the *amathongo* are documented, such as rites of passage, the initiation of a diviner, and rites connected with illness and thanksgiving. Finally, the ethical implications of Bhaca religion are assessed. Hammond-Tooke argues that moral rules are utilitarian in character, correlating closely with social relations and social structure, rather than embodying a philosophical ethics pertaining to good and evil. The author concludes that Bhaca religion provides a powerful sanction for social control, embedded in family and kinship solidarity, that is founded on the ancestral cult. Underlying all consideration of Bhaca religion is the ever-deepening cleavage in Bhaca society between Christians and adherents of indigenous religion, although, according to the author, synthesis, rather than complete displacement, seems to be emerging. Footnotes accompany the text.

C42   Hammond-Tooke, W. D. (1962). *Bhaca Society: A People of the Transkeian Uplands, South Africa*. Cape Town: Oxford University Press.

Based on extensive fieldwork among the Bhaca, an Nguni people in the Mount Frere district of the Transkeian Territories, Hammond-Tooke's study offers a contemporary ethnographic description of the territorial and kinship systems of that society. The Bhaca have a unique identity and their own dialect (although the latter has mostly given way to standard Xhosa) and, for the purposes of anthropological study, the author argues, they form a cultural and historical bridge between the North and South Nguni. The first two chapters place Bhaca society in space and time and describe the ecological environment that impinges on every aspect of the community's physical and psychic life. Chapter Three presents the central focus of the book, namely, Bhaca social structure and relations that are fundamentally organized according to kinship and neighborhood principles. Chapters Four to Six address stages of life and rites of passage, with particular attention to marriage and the complex ritual and social significance of the process. After discussing economic activities in Chapter Seven, the remaining chapters address the control mechanisms, both political and religious, that maintain the social order. Emphasizing ancestor veneration and ritual as the central features of Bhaca religion, Hammond-Tooke describes Bhaca cosmology and relations with the ancestors, highlighting the pivotal role of the *isangoma* (diviner) in those relations. Bhaca belief in "magic" is further discussed. Hammond-Tooke explains the distinction between the *inyanga* (herbalist) and *isangoma* in the socially-sanctioned work of healing and divination techniques. In contrast to these ritual activities, the negative and discordant aspects of "magic"—witchcraft and sorcery—are analyzed. Hammond-Tooke concludes that religion and magic join forces in Bhaca society to combat misfortune and death. Various explanatory notes and tables, a bibliography, and an index are appended.

C43   Hammond-Tooke, W. D. (1963). "Kinship, Locality, and Association: Hospitality Groups Among the Cape Nguni." *Ethnology*, vol. 2, no. 3: 302-19.

In this paper Hammond-Tooke describes and classifies the role of *isithebe*, that is, social segmentation into "hospitality groups," in Mpondomise social life. These "hospitality groups" primarily serve to facilitate the distribution of meat and beer at feasts, says the author, but they are also utilized in the indigenous local administration of communal labor and the raising of levies. Hammond-Tooke details the complex rules of etiquette surrounding the allocation of meat and beer (*ukulawula*) at certain types of feasts that are closely associated with ritual, including initiation; circumcision; marriage; the incorporation of a wife into her husband's lineage; the ceremonial return of a bride to her husband's home after the birth of her first child at her father's homestead; and killing "merely for meat." Most notably, *ukulawula* is never done at funerals, death rites, sacrifices to the ancestors, or thanksgiving for a birth, since these ceremonies are associated with death or limited to the immediate family group. A detailed analysis of the composition of *isithebe* is given. Hammond-Tooke notes that although the groups are most often based on agnatic lineage, they are not always limited to kin. Ranking and hereditary leadership as well as the splitting of an *isithebe* are explained in terms of social and political function. Communal work in a location, for instance, is frequently organized on an *isithebe* basis. A brief comparative study further addresses similarities and differences between Mpondomise *isithebe* systems and groupings in other Cape Nguni societies. Hammond-Tooke concludes that the central elements of beef and beer in *isithebe* groups reflects the social and economic value of those commodities in Mpondomise life and the ritual role of cattle in relation to the ancestral shades. Notes and bibliography are appended.

C44   Hammond-Tooke, W. D. (1969). "The Present State of Cape Nguni Ethnographic Studies." In *Ethnological and Linguistic Studies in Honour of N. J. van Warmelo*. Pretoria: Government Printer. 81-98.

Hammond-Tooke's essay constitutes a comprehensive survey of ethnographic literature pertaining to Cape Nguni societies. Most particularly, Hammond-Tooke sets out to identify the several areas where further research is required, notably in the study of ritual and religion. After reviewing works on the history, tribal classifications, and hierarchical social and kinship structures of the Cape Nguni, the writer asserts that more research should be conducted on the ritual position of chiefs and the number of esoteric rituals that are performed. For example, it has been found that the Bhaca are the only Cape Nguni society where the first-fruits festival still occurs. Initiation rituals for girls, however, still occur throughout the area, although male initiation is no longer performed among the Mpondo, Xesibe, and Bhaca. Religion among the Cape Nguni, says the writer, reflects social structure and is articulated through the beliefs and ritual practices of the ancestor cult. Noting the paucity of knowledge concerning the symbolism used in such rituals, Hammond-Tooke argues that this is as much a consequence of the Cape Nguni's apparent lack of awareness and interest in the meanings of their own ritual symbols, as it is a result of the inadequacy of anthropological study. More specifically, investigation of beliefs in the "people of the river" among the Xhosa is required, particularly in the light of debate surrounding whether they are, or are not, ancestral shades. Knowledge of Cape Nguni witchcraft and sorcery beliefs, especially in relation to social context, should likewise be extended. Affirming that much work still needs to be done, Hammond-Tooke contends that South African anthropologists have a responsibility to build on the foundations laid by Dr. van Warmelo. An exhaustive bibliography is appended.

C45   Hammond-Tooke, W. D. (1975). "The Symbolic Structure of Cape Nguni Cosmology." In M. G. Whisson and M. West (eds.) *Religion and Social Change in Southern Africa.* Cape Town: David Philip. 15-33.

Hammond-Tooke's study represents a significant reinterpretation of Cape Nguni religious data along cultural lines, rather than the predominant sociological approach. The author attempts to draw out the symbolism of prominent Nguni beliefs and relate them to the broader cosmological perspectives of the Nguni. The initial section of the work presents an informative anthology of superhuman intelligences subscribed to by the Cape Nguni royal family, including a discussion of concepts such as the supreme being, ancestral shades, witches, people of the river, and animal and animal-spirit categories. The concluding section provides an analysis of the symbolic code of such beliefs, splitting the Nguni cosmology into two poles representing the dichotomy of the domestic and the wild. In between these two spheres, diviners and the "People of the River" play ambiguous roles in mediating between the domestic order of the homestead and wild forces that threaten to disrupt it. A comprehensive diagram serves to elucidate the author's interpretation of these symbolic relations.

C46   Hewat, Matthew L. (1906). *Bantu Folk Lore: Medical and General.* Cape Town: Maskew Miller.

Hewat's work represents an attempt to capture "Bantu" medicinal and general folklore before it becomes "contaminated" by the advance of "civilization." The author begins with a brief discussion of the history of the Bantu-speaking peoples, followed by an account of his own observations as a medical doctor. Topics included are as follows: folklore; rituals; medical practices (the treatment of measles, typhoid, small pox, malaria, syphilis, leprosy, epilepsy, and insanity); religious beliefs; traditional healers; sacrifices; initiation rites; childbirth; and surgery. The book serves as a manual to inform health workers who were working among Xhosa-speaking communities at the time.

C47   Hodgson, Janet (1982). *The God of the Xhosa.* Cape Town: Oxford University Press.

Hodgson's reconstruction of Xhosa religious history makes a valuable contribution to the study of African traditional religion. Drawing frequently on John Cumpsty's theoretical model of religious change, the study traces the process of social and religious transformation that occurred among the Xhosa in the past. In examining Xhosa oral tradition, she finds that history and myth are inextricably interwoven, providing a framework for social and religious experience. Chapter Two looks at the early history of interaction between the Xhosa and Khoisan peoples, while Chapters Three and Four focus on both Xhosa and Khoisan cosmogonic and death myths. Hodgson argues that Xhosa religious thought and experience constitutes a monistic worldview that articulates a closed system of cause and effect. Divination is used to reveal the causes of misfortune, so that means can be found to restore harmony and integrity to the community. Chapters Five to Eight are devoted to analysis of the meaning and significance of a wide variety of god-names among the Xhosa-speaking peoples. Some of those names are found to belong to the wider Nguni tradition (Cape and North Nguni) in expressing two concepts of the supreme being: one relating to origin and the other to phenomena of the sky. The Xhosa designations Qamatha and Thixo, however, were "borrowed" from the Khoisan, Hodgson argues, during a process of cultural and religious diffusion, the former arguably much earlier than the latter. Changes in meaning of these two names are discussed in the context of Christian missionary intrusion and influence. Today, the author concludes, many Xhosa Christians accept Qamatha as the same as the Christian God, while the name Thixo is perceived as one that was imposed by early Christian missionaries. Notes follow each chapter and appendices provide extracts from missionary manuscripts and a list of "God-names." A bibliography and index are appended.

C48   Hunter, Monica (1936). *Reaction to Conquest: Effects of Contact with Europeans on the Pondo of South Africa.* London: Oxford University Press (2nd edn. 1961; 3rd abridged edn. Cape Town: David Philip, 1979).

Hunter's comprehensive social anthropological study of Pondo traditional societies offers extensive and invaluable material for the study of indigenous traditional religion in South Africa. The text is divided into three parts, based on the author's fieldwork in rural Pondoland; urban Pondo communities in East London; and European farms on which Xhosa-speaking people worked in the districts of Albany, Adelaide, and Bedford in the Cape Province. The work is contextualized in a period of rapid social change and Hunter's information on any social institution is therefore mainly gathered from conservative families and old people who discuss how institutions were modified. In Part One, Chapters Three and Four address concepts and practices surrounding birth, initiation, and marriage, including a discussion of ritual and the role of the ancestors. Chapters Five to Seven specifically examine religious beliefs and practices, including "the ancestor cult," "witchcraft and magic," and "doctors." Hunter analyzes the influence of the *amathongo* (ancestral spirits) on the life of the community, as well as how the living, in turn, influence and communicate with the ancestors through ritual (for example, through animal sacrifice and beer offerings). The author further notes that there is no evidence to suggest that the Pondo believed in a supreme being before the arrival of the Europeans. Witchcraft, sorcery, magical elements, and associated practices are defined and interpreted in terms of beliefs about the causes of disease and misfortune. In examining the role of doctors in the community, both herbalists and diviners are discussed with particular attention given to the initiation and functions of diviners. Chapter Eight is devoted to interpretations of the Christian mission in Pondoland. Further chapters reassess aspects of Pondo religion as they have been interpreted, maintained, and used in different social environments. A glossary of Xhosa terms, a bibliography, and an index are appended.

C49   Jonas, P. J. (1986). "Clanship as a Cognitive Orientation in Xhosa World-View." *South African Journal of Ethnology*, vol. 9, no. 2: 58-66.

In this anthropological study Jonas evaluates the presupposition that clanship is a fundamental cognitive orientation in Xhosa society. As such, he examines clanship in the context of basic categories of any worldview, categories that include the notion of a basic distinction between Self and Other; an idea of a relationship between the two; the classification of phenomena; views in relation to causality; and conceptions of space and time. First, the writer defines Xhosa clanship as patrilineal and exogamous, constituting dispersed units of people who claim a common ancestor and have a common clan name. Reciprocal use of kinship terms are maintained among its units of members, as well as appropriate behavior expected of kinship relations. However, these clans do not form organized groups in terms of economic, political, and religious activities. Jonas' analysis is based on data gathered from fieldwork conducted from 1974 to 1978 among the Ntinde and Qhayi, two Xhosa chiefdoms in the Ciskei. He argues that Xhosa clanship most significantly emphasizes thought categories that directly concern human relations. In other words, the Self, society as the domain of the Other, interpersonal relations, and classification of people are all important elements of the Xhosa worldview. Relations between human beings and nature and the supernatural are also essential to the Xhosa worldview, most particularly evident in their perceptions of causality, where misfortune is frequently ascribed to disturbed social relations and remedial actions focus on mediation to restore the integrity of these relations. References are appended to the text.

C50   Jordan, A. C. (1980). *Ingqumbo Yeminyanya: The Wrath of the Ancestors*. Lovedale: Lovedale Press.

Jordan's historical novel, translated into English from the original Xhosa, tells the story of a young Mpondomise prince who reluctantly leaves the University College of Fort Hare to go back to the land of his ancestors and take his place as the king of Mpondomise. However, his ideas prove to be too advanced for the people he has to lead, and his reign ends tragically and prematurely. Through fictional characters, the author offers insight into Xhosa religious practice, culture, political life, and the effect of Western influences on Xhosa life. In his introduction, Peteni contends that much of the richness of the original text is lost in the translation.

C51   Kay, Stephen (1833). *Travels and Researches in Caffraria*. London: John Mason.

This volume comprises Kay's writings on his return to England after touring the Christian missions of nineteenth-century southern Africa. Kay writes about the Xhosa-speaking peoples from his experiences of "daily intercourse with them under all the varied circumstances of savage life." While religious customs constitute a recurring theme throughout Kay's text, Chapter Eight is specifically devoted to religious and cultural practices. Ancient ceremonies of betrothal, marriage feasts, and animal sacrifice are discussed. Kay asserts that polygamy represents the greatest barrier to the Christian gospel. Burial and death rites are similarly addressed, noting that because the body is considered a source of pollution until the spirit has departed, sick people are sometimes dragged to the forest even before they are dead. Chiefs and their principal wives, however, are buried with appropriate rites in the cattle enclosure. Noting the frequent rejection and abandonment of widows, the author surmises "How great and manifold are the horrors of Paganism! And how great the contrast between its principles and those of Christianity!" Comparisons are ventured between Xhosa customs and Mosaic law, such as circumcision, language, rituals of purification associated with death and childbirth, and ceremonial sacrifice. Xhosa belief in a deity is mentioned, apparently associated with thunder and lightning. Although "wise men," "wizards" (herbalists), and rainmakers are mentioned, as well as the sacred nature of certain stone heaps, no understanding or analysis of Xhosa rituals and beliefs, or their relation to the ancestors, is presented.

C52   Keller, Bonnie B. (1978). "Millenarianism and Resistance: The Xhosa Cattle Killing." *Journal of Asian and African Studies*, vol. 13: 95-111.

Keller's sensitive analysis of the Xhosa Cattle-Killing movement in terms of millenarian forms of resistance to colonization argues that the Xhosa-speaking peoples' destruction of their economic resources represented one of the most extreme reactions to cultural contact and foreign conquest ever recorded. Drawing on the work of other scholars, particularly the work of T. O. Ranger, the first section of the paper looks at the theory of millenarian movements in general that defines them as alternatives to military resistance. In the second and third sections, a brief ethnographic summary of the societies that participated in the Cattle Killing is provided, as well as their history of wars, land theft, and political threats that provide a rationale for understanding the movement. Of particular significance, according to Keller, is the Xhosa-speaking peoples' belief in the efficacy of sacrifice, especially the sacrificial killing of their most valued possession, cattle. The final section is devoted to the Cattle Killing of 1856-57 itself, which took place as a result of the visions of a young girl, Nongqawuse, the niece of a renowned diviner, Mhlakaza, in Gcalekaland. Prophetic visions and millenarian dreams served to instruct the Xhosa to disavow witchcraft and appease the ancestors by killing their cattle, with the promise of replenishment in the coming millennium. Describing the extremes of suffering, starvation, and disease that followed, especially evident in the primary accounts of white observers, Keller concludes that ultimately neither armed resistance nor the religious solution of millenarian prophecy could stop the colonial subjugation of the Xhosa-speaking peoples. References are appended.

C53   Kopke, D. (1982). "Concepts of Time Among the Xhosa." *Fort Hare Papers*, vol. 7, no. 4: 229-38.

Although the traditional Xhosa world is often thought to have existed in a state of relative timelessness, notes Kopke, this paper attempts to systematize concepts of time in Xhosa society. While acknowledging that those concepts might be regarded as philosophical assumptions in the context of Xhosa cosmology, Kopke focuses on the functional features of the traditional Xhosa understanding of time. As a geographer, he also concentrates on the natural and celestial phenomena that are incorporated within the traditional Xhosa concept of time. The author therefore discusses celestial time at some length, showing how the Xhosa divide time into an almost fixed celestial time frame, and then into a more variable social time that is set within that framework of celestial phenomena. Specific times of the day, week, month, and year are described. Kopke explains how these are all divided into social times according to the tasks which have to be performed. The inclusion and influence of historical events is also discussed. In urban areas, the author notes, these "traditional times" have been largely superseded by the hours used in Western society. The complex and diverse names given to the seasons of the year are defined in the context of an "ecological clock" which the Xhosa relate to environmental conditions. Reference is further made to Xhosa customs that emphasize the future, particularly in relation to ideas about death, the ancestors, the spirit world, and the calling of the diviner. Without developing a detailed comparative analysis, Kopke argues that the dichotomy revealed in Xhosa concepts of time are also found in other parts of Africa. He concludes by advocating further research in other academic disciplines on aspects of time in Xhosa custom and folklore. References are appended.

C54   Kuckertz, Heinz (1983-1984). "Symbol and Authority in Mpondo Ancestor Religion. Parts 1 and 2." *African Studies*, vol. 42, no. 2: 113-33; vol. 43, no. 1: 1-17.

Kuckertz's dense paper, written in two parts, draws on fieldwork conducted during 1978 and 1979 in a small Mthwa chieftanship in Port St. John's, western Pondoland. The writer introduces Part One with an outline of Mthwa cosmology, including a discussion of the following features: various names for the supreme being; ancestors and ancestor-spirits, whose significance is universal in the daily life of Mthwa society; "spirits" who are thought to live in the deep forest or the river; familiars, who are extra-human beings that are believed to assume the appearance of people or animals; and finally, the neutral negative force of pollution that exists and acts without human agency. The last is only identifiable through circumstances of ritual pollution and social unacceptability, such as during the female cycle of the menses; conviction in a court case; during the time a person is preparing for an ancestral ritual; and lastly, the pollution that occurs at death, which affects the homestead members and agnatic relatives of the deceased. The structure of the ancestral feast is then analyzed in detail as a basis for understanding death and the role of the ancestors. Continuing, Kuckertz more specifically details the ancestral feast, explaining the significance of lineage and agnatic kinship and the process from the time when the ancestors demand "food." The two major parts of the ancestral feast are discussed, namely, the ancestral public feast and the ancestral lineage feast. Part One is extensively annotated and includes helpful diagrams. References are appended. Continuing the above theme in Part Two, Kuckertz provides an analysis of the structure of the ancestral feast and the symbolism of the core ritual, showing the developing dynamism and inner logic through which the ritual progresses. The ancestral lineage feast is then analyzed in terms of its two main parts, namely, the informing of the ancestors and the process of the core ritual as an act of contrition, where the afflicted person "admits everything" and engages in ritual dance and songs of contrition before "returning home." In conclusion, the writer discusses the ancestors as a conceptual frame of authority, outlining four terms of reference in which the ancestors are depicted—kinship, the elders, the superhuman, and a superhuman "ultimate" authority. Kuckertz argues that the concept of the ancestors and its importance as symbol and authority can only be fully understood within the specific context or specific homestead where it manifests. Accordingly, traditional ancestor religion is always variable in practice. Diagrams, songs, and footnotes accompany the text and references are appended.

C55 Kuckertz, Heinz (1990). *Creating Order: The Image of the Homestead in Mpondo Social Life*. Johannesburg: Witwatersrand University Press.

Kuckertz's study makes a valuable contribution to social anthropology and the study of religion in South Africa. The book is based on his field research in the late 1970s as a participant observer in the Mthwa chiefdom, Mpondoland and focuses on authority structures and the homestead in the village of Caguba, near Port St. Johns. Because of the discrepancies Kuckertz discovered in the Mthwa social system, as evident in contradictory images of kinship structures reported by individual villagers, Kuckertz concentrates more on individuals and their relationships with one another than on social institutions. His research aims to investigate the validity of the assumption of a "social structure" in the Mthwa chiefdom, finding that their norms and social order are not enshrined in institutions, "but in statements of what is right and in beliefs in what superhuman beings demand and sanction." The author then deals with three institutions, namely, political authority, the family, and ancestor religion. His analysis focuses on social interactions related to those spheres, where the homestead represents the heart of the life of the chiefdom. Chapter Seven, on Mthwa ancestor religion, offers a cogent analysis of the social and religious spheres that overlap in a cosmological system that is rooted in relationship between the living and the dead. The ancestors, says Kuckertz, form the model of authority for Mthwa society. Beliefs and ritual practices associated with death, the agnatic kinship system, and the ancestor-spirits are documented, including examples of speeches and hymns pertaining to thanksgiving, healing, invocation of the ancestors, and contrition. The ancestral feast for the healing of an individual kinswoman or kinsman, where the ancestor-spirit demands food, is a highly complex and symbolic ceremony that is described and analyzed in comprehensive detail. This ritual feast, argues the author, operates at three levels: the individual, the homestead, and the society. These three levels intersect in the homestead. As the point where Mthwa society meets for ritual purposes, the author concludes, the homestead constitutes a symbolic representation of the world. Notes are appended to each chapter and photographs, maps, and diagrams appear throughout the text. A useful bibliography and index are appended to the text.

C56   Lamla, C. Masilo (1981). "The Dead: Prepared to Live in the Spirit World." In Heinz Kuckertz (ed.) *Ancestor Religion in Southern Africa.* Transkei: Lumko Missiological Institute. 14-21.

In this paper Lamla analyzes beliefs and practices associated with life after death, the ancestors, and the spirit world among the twelve Southern Nguni societies of the Transkei. Part One deals with the making of an ancestor in Xhosa-speaking societies through mortuary rituals. Lamla first documents the customary burial of the deceased, emphasizing that the corpse is feared as a source of pollution. However, it is the mortuary rites during the period of mourning that are vitally important for the deceased's passage to the spirit world. The four most important rites are detailed, stressing the significance of the last, *ukubuyisa* (bringing home of the spirit of the deceased), which is held two years or more after the funeral in memory of the deceased. The *ukubuyisa ithongo* ceremony integrates the deceased into his group of ancestors, and is only observed for men, Lamla observes, because only male ancestors are important in these strictly patrilineal societies. *Ukubuyisa* is essential for a homestead head, for it is he who will look after his descendants. Since the shades (or spirits) are believed to take an active interest in the well-being of living descendants, Lamla argues, vague ancestor beliefs are transformed into a vital and socially significant cult. Part Two discusses the spatial geography of the spirit world. The author stresses the value of cattle for the Southern Nguni and the profound religious significance of the cattle byre, beneath which live the ancestors of the homestead. The religious significance of other spirit dwelling places is also described, such as certain heaps of stones and the rivers and ponds where the "river people" dwell. Lamla asserts that the Southern Nguni associate the sky with a "High God" who is regarded as being remote from human beings and therefore is approached only through the mediation of the ancestral spirits. References are appended.

C57   Laubscher, B. J. F. (1937). *Sex, Custom, and Psychopathology: A Study of South African Pagan Natives.* London: George Routledge & Sons.

This ethnological and psychiatric study by a 1930s senior government psychiatrist focuses on the cultural mythology and socioreligious practices of the southeastern Cape Nguni, particularly the Thembu. Laubscher shows that although sociocultural environment and experience shape the psychology of the African, psychopathological conditions are grounded in the "*soma*" or the individual constitution. Laubscher's work is based on his psychiatric work at Queenstown Mental Hospital and fieldwork in Thembuland and Fingoland. To support his hermeneutical purposes, the author essentially applies Western psychiatric models to analyze Thembu mythology, religious beliefs, and ritual practices. Chapters One and Two deal with folklore and mythical beings, such as the "River

People" (*abantubomlambo*) and the *tikoloshe*, and their sexual symbology. Laubscher further analyzes the state of *ukuthwasa*, the period of "psychic abnormality" undergone by neophyte diviners. Chapter Three discusses indigenous doctors, diviners, and sorcerers in relation to healing and witchcraft, affirming that *isanuses* (diviners) and *amagqira* (doctors who also divine) possess telepathic and clairvoyant abilities. A distinction is made between those who work to combat affliction and those who perpetuate witchcraft beliefs among the people, which, according to the author's viewpoint, are rooted in "infantile magical thinking." Chapters Four to Seven offer detailed accounts and interpretations of ritual practices associated with birth and childhood; death and burial rites; and male and female initiation among the Thembu. Thembu marriage customs and rituals are similarly detailed in Chapters Eight and Nine. Chapter Ten examines African conceptions of mental disorder, which, the author contends, are entwined with beliefs associated with witchcraft and *ukuthwasa*. Remaining chapters investigate alleged sexual offenses, suicide, and crime among South African Bantu-speaking societies. Laubscher's text offers valuable insight for study of the history and psychology of indigenous religion in South Africa and early twentieth-century colonial attitudes towards African traditional religion. The author's interpretations, however, are colored by his Western scientific worldview and psychiatric training, leading him to conclude in condescending terms that the African is a "child amidst the complexities of Western civilization." Photographs appear in the text and psychiatric diagnoses and an index are appended.

C58   Laubscher, B. J. F. (1975). *The Pagan Soul*. Cape Town: Timmins.

Laubscher's book studies the psychic and spiritual values that are rooted in the symbolism of Xhosa mythology and ritual. This psychological study is based on fieldwork among Xhosa-speaking people and participation in seances of the "great psychic sensitive" and *isanuse* (diviner), Solomon Daba. In treating the mental disorders of Xhosa-speaking psychiatric patients at Queenstown Hospital, Laubscher observed what he identified as the emergence of ancient remnants of the Xhosa mythical world. Chapter One discusses Xhosa beliefs associated with the life of the spirit after death and the power of ancestral spirits. The role of the ancestral spirits in *ukuthwasa* (the development of mediumship) and in the diviner's clairvoyant techniques of divination is emphasized. The influence of the *abantubomlambo* ("River People") on Xhosa life is also addressed. Chapter Two examines the burial and mourning rites for the head of a kraal. The author stresses the religious character of the sacrificial rites by drawing comparisons with sacrificial practices in ancient Hebrew religion. The *umtendeleko* ceremony, which is performed in times of great trouble, such as drought, is also discussed. Laubscher defines the ceremony as an appeal to the unseen creative power of the Xhosa god, Qamatha, that brings life to nature, comparing the ceremony to Christian holy communion. While Chapter Three offers a detailed analysis of Xhosa male and female initiation rites, Chapter Four addresses the evil creatures of Xhosa myth who invisibly indulge in sexual exploits that break the sexual taboos of Xhosa society. In Chapter Five the author discusses what he calls the "phallic cult" of Xhosa marriage, which emphasizes the male as procreator. The final chapter explores the magical power for evil perpetuated by witchcraft, an evil power that is specifically set in opposition to the power for good practiced by the diviner. Laubscher's work could be defined as a theoretical and comparative study of the spiritual and psychic power that emanates from the ancient symbols, myths, and rituals that are found in many religious traditions, including African traditional religion, ancient Hebrew and Egyptian religions, Hinduism, and Christianity. An index is appended.

C59   Lewis, Jack (1991). "Materialism and Idealism in the Historiography of the Xhosa Cattle-Killing Movement, 1856-1857." *South African Historical Journal*, vol. 25: 244-68.

In this article Lewis attempts to balance Peires' explanation of the Xhosa "Cattle-Killing Movement" in *The Dead Will Arise* with a Marxist materialist perspective that focuses on the historical origins of the religious ideas that appeared in the movement. Lewis indicates that Peires' work, although representing a "pioneering corrective step" in the writing of Xhosa history, stresses the role of ideas—the significance of a "spiritual upheaval," belief in prophecies, and the clash of Xhosa and Christian religious worldviews—as active forces in the production of the Cattle-Killing movement. Thus, according to Lewis, Peires overemphasizes the ideal realm of psychological and cultural influences in a way that isolates it from the social and material relations of production. Rather than religious imagination, Lewis argues, other social relations that structured nineteenth-century Xhosa society, such as gender, age, and kinship, better explain the causes and concepts of the movement. Social change and divisions of class, gender, and age that were generated by the shortage of cattle and land, and exacerbated by lung-sickness, culminated in the dispersal of labor to colonial employment and the erosion of the chiefs' political power. Since neither military action nor diplomatic truce with the colonial forces was viable, the chiefs were confronted with the alternative of inaction. Nongqawuse's prophecies, however, provided another alternative for addressing these complex material realities and, according to Lewis, provided a motive for the chiefs to support the Cattle Killing. They hoped for victory over colonial domination, the return of their power, national unity, and economic renewal. The role of age and gender divisions, the writer concludes, cannot be ignored in analyzing the patterns of opposition to and support for the Xhosa Cattle-Killing movement. The article is extensively annotated.

C60   Maclean, John, ed. (1906). *A Compendium of Kafir Laws and Customs, Including Genealogical Tables of Kafir Chiefs and Various Tribal Census Returns.* Grahamstown: J. Slater (orig. edn. 1858).

Maclean's compendium collects essays from a variety of writers in South Africa during the mid-nineteenth century. Contributions include the Reverend Dugmore on the geography and tribes of Kaffraria, government and legal processes, and marriage customs; Warner on African criminal and civil law and laws associated with Xhosa religious beliefs; Brownlee on criminal law, law of property, the social state, and religious law; and Maclean on chiefs in British Kaffraria and law in relation to land and census returns. The work is a useful indication of the laws and customs ascribed to the Xhosa-speaking peoples of South Africa as observed by the colonial government in the mid-nineteenth century. See the separate entries in this chapter under Charles Brownlee and J. C. Warner.

C61   Malan, Johannes Stephanus (1968). *Die Tradisionele Religie van die Xhosa.* M.A. thesis, Rand Afrikaans University.

Malan's Afrikaans work is a critical departure from colonial and precolonial writing on Xhosa religious beliefs and practices. Contending that Xhosa religion is an integral part of Xhosa life, distinct from other African religions, the author criticizes earlier scholars for imposing a Western framework on their subject matter. The text itself is largely descriptive and covers the geographical area in which Xhosa religion is practiced. Notes are included on ancestors, taboo, magic, prophets, and herbalists. Attention is focused on traditional belief and practice, and only occasionally is discussion given to the effect of Western influences. A bibliography is appended. The text is in Afrikaans.

C62   Manona, C. W. (1981). "The Resurgence of the Ancestor Cult Among Xhosa Christians." In Heinz Kuckertz (ed.) *Ancestor Religion in Southern Africa.* Transkei: Lumko Missiological Institute. 34-39.

Drawing on interviews conducted in Grahamstown and in the village of Burnshill, Ciskei, Manona provides a descriptive account of the revitalization of ancestor rituals among Xhosa-speaking Christians. Examples of ritual practices detailed are as follows: birth rituals (*imbeleko*), in which a goat is slaughtered to introduce the child to the ancestors; rituals of the "necklace" (*intambo*), where a necklace is made from the hairs of the slaughtered animal for healing purposes; "drinking of milk" (*ukudlisa amasi*) for the ritual bonding of husband and wife; formal beer-drink rites that form part of sacrifice to the ancestors; and mortuary rituals in which a beast is slaughtered after the death of a family head. The symbolic significance of the last rite varies, since some people perceive the ritual as a symbol of mourning and others as the traditional symbol of "accompanying." Four brief case studies based on interviews are presented. Reasons for the resurgence of ancestor rituals, Manona argues, are partly rooted in the declining influence of the Church and the end of missionary opposition to indigenous religion and mission control of schools. Rev. Laing in Burnshill, for example, was reported to have burnt initiation houses in the mid-nineteenth century. Another very significant reason, according to the author, has been the growth of Black Consciousness, indicating that ancestor rituals articulate not only religious and symbolic significance, but also a political dimension. Affirmation of blackness, Manona concludes, rejects the colonial assumption that African cultures were inherently inferior to those in Europe before whites came to South Africa. References are appended.

C63   Manson, Andrew. (1991). "An Imaginative Exploration of the World of the Xhosa." *South African Historical Journal*, vol. 25: 240-43.

On the whole, Manson's review of *The Dead Will Arise* by Jeff Peires is a positive appraisal of this major work, which he credits with undoing some of the stereotypes of the past—a reference, no doubt, to the book's central thesis that the Cattle Killing was a "logical and rational response." Manson traces the construction of this argument from the perceived link between the Cattle Killing and the lungsickness of the year before, previous military defeats, and the uncanny coincidences, including the Crimean War and the appearance of the Geyser in the Kei River, that reinforced Xhosa misapprehensions. The villainous roles, especially Sir George Grey, are also documented. However, Manson takes issue with some of Peires' views. He thinks that Peires' analysis of the complexity of the Cattle-Killing movement and related events is so full of contradictions and qualifications as to be confusing, if not altogether unhelpful. At the same time Peires allegedly displays a certain level of uncritical acceptance of conventional wisdom in his interpretation of the Cattle Killing. Vindication of the actions of Xhosa as logical and rational may be useful in refuting past stereotypes, but in the final analysis, it has become a red herring that obscures other important aspects—religious issues, for instance—of the movement and its fatal consequences.

C64   Mayer, Philip (1971a). "Traditional Manhood Initiation in an Industrial City: The African View." In E. J. de Jager (ed.) *Man: Anthropological Essays Presented to O. F. Raum*. Cape Town: Struik. 7-18.

Mayer's anthropological essay contextualizes traditional manhood initiation of Xhosa-speaking youth within the framework of the socialization of youth and the relations between generations. Problems increase between youth and the adults who educate them, argues Mayer, as a more culturally homogeneous and stable society confronts a rapidly changing world. The author draws on his research in the New Brighton township of Port Elizabeth in 1967 and 1970 to explore what the Xhosa thought about "tribal" initiation in a modern urban environment. Noting that the conservative "Red" element is small in the city, Mayer explores why traditional initiation is in fact still regarded as essential for a boy to attain manhood. Xhosa male initiation, therefore, has survived its transition to urban areas, and is still conducted even among Christians and the most fully educated and urbanized members of the population. The process of initiation, often referred to as "bush school," represents a type of education that prepares youth for adulthood on a more profound level of attitudes and values, such as the respect accorded to an adult, than technical and intellectual learning. The essay thus addresses the symbolic significance of the rituals and discusses the people's doubts about the efficacy of the process under urban conditions on the one hand and the reasons for their continuing support of the institution on the other. The author concludes by suggesting that initiation may contribute, to some extent, towards rural African abilities to synthesize their urban experiences in a meaningful way. A bibliography is appended.

C65   Mayer, Philip, with contributions by Iona Mayer (1971b). *Townsmen or Tribesmen: Conservatism and the Process of Urbanization in a South African City.* 2nd edn. Cape Town: Oxford University Press.

Mayer's work draws on research conducted in East London to examine the response of the Xhosa to the process of urbanization. The author develops a sociological explanation for "conservative" and "progressive" attitudes in response to urbanization that are closely linked to the distinction between "Red" people and "School" people. Unlike other urban centers, Mayer argues, East London presents a unique situation of "tribal" unity and relatively little trade union activity, thus allowing idiosyncratic categories to arise. The main sections of the text cover the historical setting and rural background of Xhosa-speaking peoples; resistance to urbanization; the process of urbanization; and the lives of women and children in the migrant situation. Diverse topics are addressed, including race attitudes; kinship, marriage, and child-rearing; wage-earning and recreational activities; friendships and sexual relationships; and religious beliefs and practices. Mayer approaches the issue of religion in terms of both traditional Xhosa cosmology and conversion to Christianity. Chapter Nine, written in collaboration with Iona Mayer, discusses belief in ancestral spirits and witchcraft as a part of Xhosa rural life, examining substitute ritual practices constructed in the urban environment. Chapter Twelve looks at "Red" converts to Christianity, focusing on an analysis of Nicholas Bhengu's Assembly of God church in East London. Appendices, a bibliography, index, and map are provided.

C66   Mayer, Philip (1980). "The Origin and Decline of Two Rural Resistance Ideologies." In Philip Mayer (ed.) *Black Villagers in an Industrial Society*. Cape Town: Oxford University Press. 1-80.

The eight sections of Mayer's chapter present not only a comprehensive account of the salient socioeconomic facets of urban white and rural black contact, but more importantly analyze the diverse ideological responses to a militarily superior and economically dominant white society. Mayer plots both the development of the so-called "Red People"—those who encouraged the renewal of traditional social forms and spurned change—and the so-called "School People"—those who sought social upliftment through education, occupation, and income. He argues that both operate as forms of resistance. Of further significance to the historian of religion are the author's notes on the equally ambivalent responses to Christianity as the religious ideology of an oppressive social elite. Accordingly, Mayer inspects the results of the incorporation of Christian faith into the indigenous religion, a process that led to a double religious allegiance that is freely admitted by School People. By contrast, the conservative Red Xhosa identify the traditional religious discourse as the core of religious ideology and as a poignant means of preserving communal identity. Nevertheless, Mayer refers to the final dissolution of these once rigid traditions owing to rural poverty and proletarianization, yet emphasizes that each has left an important residue in the contemporary black psyche. His work concludes with an incisive examination of Black Consciousness emanating from the townships—a consciousness that embodies a blend of Western material and African cultural values that are deeply rooted in the history of black-white relations. Comprehensive notes are appended.

C67   Mayer, Philip, and Iona Mayer (1970). "Socialization by Peers: The Youth Organization of the Red Xhosa." In Philip Mayer (ed.) *Socialization: The Approach from Social Anthropology*. London: Tavistock. 159-79.

The Mayers' paper draws on field material gathered from rural "Red" (traditionally conservative) Xhosa-speaking people in the then Ciskei and Transkei to analyze the socialization of the young by their peers and near-seniors. The patterns that are identified and discussed are youthful sexual and fighting behavior, the learning of political and judicial techniques, and the integration of a national Xhosa identity transcending that of kinship and community. The authors first chart the stages of age groupings (*intutu; mtshotsho; intlombe*), noting the importance of informal activities in Red youth organization such as parties, dances, and sport. Of great importance in the Xhosa life-cycle is the formal manhood initiation ritual performed between the ages of 18 and 23, where boys reach the stage of *intlombe* and learn about courage and the control of aggression. Since there is no corresponding female initiation rites, girls only move on to *intlombe* through association with their boyfriends. The authors propose that an ideal norm for a certain behavior at a particular stage of life is prescribed by the relevant culture. They therefore define socialization as the process of learning to act in awareness of such cultural norms, a process that is more successfully negotiated by some young people than by others. Using this definition of socialization, the remainder of the paper offers a detailed analysis of each of the behaviors listed above in relation to the organization of Red Xhosa youth. A comment by Max Gluckman on "Gang formation among Xhosa and Samburu" is appended, followed by notes and references.

C68   Mayer, Philip, and Iona Mayer (1990). "A Dangerous Age: From Boy to Young Man in Red Xhosa Youth Organisations." In Paul Spencer (ed.) *Anthropology and the Riddle of the Sphinx: Paradoxes of Change in the Life Course*. London: Routledge. 35-44.

In this chapter the Mayers provide an incisive analysis of the sociopolitical dynamics operating in the rural Xhosa community, with particular regard to youth organizations. Within these communities, youth organizations are viewed as one particular means of socializing youth with regard to, *inter alia*, violence and sexuality. Mayer and Mayer point to the manner in which these self-organizing groups, while meeting at leisure for entertainment, were also transmitting significant ideologies and social skills. This essay specifically focuses on "Red" communities, implying conservative, unschooled, and "pagan" groups as opposed to schooled or missionized ones. The Shixini and the Khalana, in the then Transkei and Ciskei respectively, are used as relevant groups for a case study. The authors provide an informed analysis of the classic "Red" organization, namely, the *Mtshotsho* for boys and the *InHombe* for young men, each also associated with girls and women of the same status. This article is particularly useful in illustrating the deeply entrenched Xhosa notion of boy-man opposition, the latter being defined by self-restraint and dignity and hence fully in the realm of society, while the former is viewed as inconsiderate and uncontrolled and partly in the realm of nature. The implication of such a dialectic and its contemporary significance in terms of the historical colonialist presence is further explored. Notes and references are appended.

C69   McAllister, P. A. (1979). *The Rituals of Labour Migration Among the Gcaleka*. M.A. thesis, Rhodes University.

McAllister's study is concerned with the experience of migrant labor among the Gcaleka, a Xhosa-speaking group in the Willowvale district of Transkei. The author sets out to examine how conservative ("Red") Gcaleka society has adapted to the institution of large-scale oscillating labor migration. This experience, McAllister argues, is largely gained through ritual and symbolic actions associated with a migrant laborer's departure from and return to the community, chiefly the *umsindleko* beer drink. Much of the study is given to an examination of these rituals and their significance for the Gcaleka social and moral framework. McAllister concludes that the rituals of labor migration serve as a cultural device that rigidly separates the realm of work from the morally superior home reality. Accordingly, these rituals enable the community to overcome the threat of migrant labor and facilitate the strengthening of the rural structure. Appendices and references follow the main text.

C70   McAllister, P. A. (1980). "Work, Homestead and the Shades: The Ritual Interpretation of Labour Migration Among the Gcaleka." In Philip Mayer (ed.) *Black Villagers in an Industrial Society.* Cape Town: Oxford University Press. 205-52.

McAllister's study documents how a potentially disruptive process is assimilated into the sacred communal life of the Xhosa-speaking Gcaleka through the acquisition of a ritual dimension. He describes ritual practices against a background of the colonial conquest and economic incorporation of the Xhosa that led to a fundamental reliance on migrant labor to sustain life. Rituals of labor migration, associated with both departure and return, inject such labor with a meaning that allows even the migratory individual to remain a part of the rural value system and social structure of home. The rituals include beer-drinking, invocation of the shades, or ancestral spirits, the ritual preparation of food for the journey, and thanksgiving for a safe return. McAllister relates the rationalization of migrant labor to the meaningful need to "build a homestead," a term that carries with it not only a material sense, but also a social, moral, and religious one too. A further approach employed by McAllister is the application of Van Gennep's schema of rites of passage to migrant labor ritual activity, thus recognizing the change of social status that is attended by rituals that mark the separation, transition, and reincorporation of a migrant worker in relation to the homestead. The author concludes: "A man's rural home and community provide him with status and dignity not obtainable elsewhere, with full human relationships unlike the fragmented and uncertain links in town or mine, and the ancestor cult affords him a sense of continuity, belonging and moral satisfaction." Notes are appended.

C71   McAllister, P. A. (1981). *Umsindleko: A Gcaleka Ritual of Incorporation.* Grahamstown: ISER, Occasional Paper no. 265, Rhodes University.

McAllister's paper is concerned with migrant laborers among the conservative "Red" Gcaleka of the Willowvale district, Transkei, and the ritual and symbolic actions that surround their departure from and return to their homes. McAllister focuses on an examination of the *umsindleko* beer-drink, held shortly after a worker's return home, and defines it as a rite of "incorporation." As such, McAllister argues that rituals linked with labor migration illuminate its meaning to the "Red" Gcaleka by giving labor migration a strong ritual and religious character. He documents the characteristics of Gcaleka beer-drinks, with careful analysis of the extent to which they can be considered religious ritual practice, most notably in terms of relations between kin-group members and their communion with the ancestral shades. Reinforcing this approach, says the author, is the oratory performed at beer-drinks, a form of ritual speech, he argues, which is aimed at securing good fortune by emphasizing that the beer is brewed for the shades. The *umsindleko*, in particular, offers an opportunity for rejoicing and thanksgiving. The author's analysis of *umsindleko* is supported by four specific case studies, indicating that the beer-drink ritual functions to separate work and home environments and to mark the success of the migrant's spell at work. Moreover, McAllister adds, it functions to ensure future success, since the worker is honored, but is also encouraged to produce a "repeat" performance. McAllister concludes the discussion with a summary of the basic *umsindleko* themes and their functions in Gcaleka society. Notes and references are appended.

C72   McAllister, P. A. (1985). "Beasts to Beer Pots—Migrant Labour and Ritual Change in Willowvale District, Transkei." *African Studies*, vol. 44, no. 2: 121-35.

In this paper McAllister analyzes the development of rituals among Xhosa-speaking societies, exploring why some disappear and others persist, and why yet others become radically modified. He therefore focuses on the maintenance and radical change of the *umsindleko* ritual beer-drink of the Gcaleka, which is frequently conducted to welcome home and reincorporate returning migrant laborers. The earlier form of ritual practice for such events—animal sacrifice (*umhlinzeko*)—is described, followed by a description of the currently performed ritual, the beer drink (*umsindleko*). Most of the text is given to a discussion of why one ritual form gave way to another, emphasizing that where *umhlinzeko* is still performed, it has lost its religious significance, while *umsindleko* manifests a definitively religious character. The religious element of the *umhlinzeko* ritual killings for returned migrant workers, therefore, has been transposed to the *umsindleko* beer-drink. McAllister's analysis attempts to relate the changes in form and symbolic meaning of the ritual to changing economic, social, and political circumstances affecting the Gcaleka and other Xhosa-speakers, especially in the light of increasing labor migration and changing homestead structures. The religious nature of the rituals is particularly emphasized and explained. References are appended.

C73   McAllister, P. A. (1986a). "'Releasing the Widow': Xhosa Beer Drink Oratory and Status Change." *African Studies*, vol. 45, no. 2: 171-97.

In this article McAllister argues that in the Sixini administrative area of Willowvale, Transkei, the frequent beer-drinking rituals (or "beer-drinks") in the community are not merely social occasions, but have religious significance that is primarily due to their association with the veneration of ancestors. The "shades" are believed to be present at beer-drinks and to partake of the beer "in spirit." Beer-drinks are held in association with many events, including the return of a migrant worker, the establishment of a new homestead, the promotion of a woman to senior status, and the end of the mourning period for the death of a homestead head or senior person in the community. It is the last that forms the focus of McAllister's analysis, particularly the beer-drink held to "release" (*ukukhula*) a widow (*umhlolakazi*) from mourning the death of her husband. In this type of beer-drink, the oratory accompanying the ritual functions as a collective attempt to transcend mortality. The writer works within the theoretical framework of Van Gennep's assessment of the fundamental issues of pollution, purity, and danger. Ultimately, McAllister argues, these rituals ensure that broken connections at death do not sever or disrupt the crucial ties of interdependence in the homestead essential to survival in an impoverished and hostile socioeconomic and political context. References are appended.

C74   McAllister, P. A. (1986b). "Conservativism as Ideology of Resistance Among Xhosa-Speakers: The Implications for Oral Tradition and Literacy." In Richard Whitaker and Edgard Sienaert (eds.) *Oral Tradition and Literacy: Changing Visions of the World*. Durban: Natal University Oral Documentation and Research Centre. 290-302.

McAllister's paper draws on fieldwork conducted in the Transkei during 1976 and 1977 to analyze the persistence of conservative "Red" Xhosa-speaking communities in that area. The history of militant rural resistance to agricultural "betterment" schemes and migrant labor is traced, showing an explicit "Red" ideology of resistance to white domination and incorporation into the South African political economy. Suggesting that conservatism has been maintained by oral tradition, the writer therefore examines the articulation of an orally constructed worldview in the context of religious ritual. At beer-drinks, animal sacrifices to the ancestors, and rites of passage such as birth, initiation, and death, public oratory and praises play a central role in reinforcing "Red" attitudes and values. McAllister indicates that the traditional worldview is incompatible with formal education and literacy, an opposition inherent in the division between "Red" and "School" people, a division that originated in the hundred years of war, colonial conquest, and education brought by the Christian missions in the nineteenth century. Conversion to Christianity signified "the religion of the book" and an acceptance of Western values, changes that weakened the ability of the Xhosa to resist white domination. Christianity and literacy, McAllister suggests, instigated the separation of religion and ideology from social structure, the weakening of kinship ties, and the growth of individualism. The 1960s and 70s, however, have seen the separation of education from the missions and its connection with higher wages, developments that have steadily reduced the number of "Red" Xhosa communities. Examples of public oratory are included in the text and notes are appended.

C75   McAllister, P. A. (1988). "Inclusion and Exclusion in the Oral Transmission of Ritual Knowledge: A Xhosa Communicative Strategy." In Edgard Sienaert and Nigel Bell (eds.) *Catching Winged Words: Oral Tradition and Education*. Durban: Natal University Oral Documentation and Research Centre. 43-68.

In this paper McAllister draws on extensive primary material to describe Xhosa ancestor rituals, most of which involve the brewing of beer and sacrifice of a beast, followed by the consumption of the beer and meat over three or four days accompanied by formal oratory, song, dance, and praise poetry. The three days of the ancestor ritual are outlined. McAllister indicates that the first day is the most important because communication with the ancestors is initiated. The author focuses on the oratory accompanying the events of the first day, in terms of communicating ritual knowledge and marking each ritual as set apart from ordinary, everyday activities. The speech acts that accompany each stage, argues McAllister, serve to make symbolic statements about social relationships based on kinship, territory, and gender, as well as to reinforce group boundaries, social distance, and degrees of inclusion and exclusion. The rest of the paper is devoted to a functional analysis of selected examples of speech events during the first day, including those accompanying the private meeting of the kin group; the ritual dance; the procession and invocation of the ancestors; the consecration, killing, and tasting of the beast; and the gathering of kin. In conclusion, McAllister summarizes three roles played by ritual oratory: to define relationships and status; to legitimate ritual actions by communicating their nature and "correctness"; and, most significantly, to define relations between the living and the dead and to serve as a medium of communication between those two realms. Verses and diagrams accompany the text and references are appended.

C76   McAllister, P. A. (1991). "Using Ritual to Resist Domination in the Transkei." *African Studies*, vol. 50, no. 1/2: 129-44.

Xhosa-speakers in the Shixini Administrative Area of the Willowvale district, Transkei, use varying forms of ritual and public oratory to perform political functions. McAllister therefore examines the role of Xhosa ritual in the construction, maintenance, and persistence of a conservative ("Red") worldview in Shixini. In a wider political context, Xhosa ritual in Shixini articulates resistance to fuller incorporation into the southern African political economy. In the local political context, ritual formulates meaning and conduct in several areas, for example, migrant labor, widowhood, and male initiation. Ritual is not static, however, but a flexible and dynamic resource produced and reproduced by people to respond to material realities affecting them. McAllister depicts a network of economic relationships between individual homesteads in Shixini that have been relatively unaffected by landlessness and disruptive "betterment" schemes. The people highly value the rural home and community, argues the author, and so migrant labor has been ritualized and rationalized in terms of the need to "build" the homestead in material, social, and religious terms. McAllister therefore carefully analyzes the symbols inherent in the ritual beer-drinks (*umsindleko*) and oratory performed by and for migrant labors on both their departure from and return to the home. The rituals aim to ensure the migrant interprets his experience correctly and controls the benefits he brings back. Defined as a type of rite of passage, McAllister identifies similar themes in other rites of passage. Finally, the author documents recent developments that have put this mode of adaptation in "Red" tradition and lifestyle into serious jeopardy. These developments may call for a different set of ritualized responses to change in Shixini. Notes and a bibliography are appended.

C77   McAllister, P. A. (1993). "Public Oratory in Xhosa Ritual: Tradition and Change." *Ethnology*, vol. 32, no. 3: 291-304.

McAllister explains the importance of establishing a new homestead (*umzi*) among Xhosa-speaking communities in the Transkei, noting changes in the status of the new homestead head and his wife. He argues that the home brings social and economic independence, as well as a certain amount of religious independence. Although the people themselves claim that the formation of a new homestead is rooted in tradition, McAllister points out that it is in fact an innovation that has dramatically changed the structure of the extended family. In this context, the writer focuses on the ritualization of establishing a new homestead and the specific role of public oratory in facilitating, legitimizing, and reinforcing this creation. Although animal sacrifice symbolizes kinship links, beer-drinks are often the preferred ritual because they make explicit statements about relations between neighbors and territorial groups. The core of the paper constitutes a detailed case study of a beer-drink, with careful analysis of the oratory involved. McAllister argues that the Xhosa beer-drinks are dramatic cultural performances that serve to interpret the people's social practice and to provide them with models for future action. In relation to the setting up of an independent homestead, the oratory clearly indicates a self-consciously ritualized process of reflection on the significance of a new home. The choice of a beer-drink, however, reveals an adherence to accepted rules and conventions inherent in this traditional form of communal gathering. Therefore, concludes McAllister, continuity and innovation coexist, as shown in the retention of the beer-drink framework within which the community responds in innovative ways to changed sociopolitical circumstances. Notes and a bibliography are appended.

C78   McLaren, James (1918). "Religious Beliefs and Superstitions of the Xosas: A Study in Philology." *South African Journal of Science*, vol. 16: 418-24.

McLaren's brief paper on the religious beliefs of the Xhosa-speaking peoples of South Africa is based on anthropological information extrapolated from A. Kropf's *Kaffir-English Dictionary* (1899). Adopting the patronizing and pejorative tone of early twentieth-century European rationalism and science, McLaren's text is largely descriptive and devoid of analytical inquiry. The writer first addresses Xhosa beliefs in relation to ancestral spirits, alleging that ideas of a supreme being were "of the vaguest." In his documentation of ritual practices and ancestral veneration, McLaren compares Xhosa sacrifice with that of the Semites. The symbolic power of lightning and the veneration of animals, such as the mantis and the snake, are also discussed. McLaren concludes with a review of Xhosa attitudes towards twins; brief examples of beliefs about diseases and methods of healing; and the association of curses with evil and ill-luck. Since McLaren's sources are extremely limited, no attempt is made to explore and analyze the efficacy and rationality of these beliefs and healing techniques within the paradigm of Xhosa culture and religion.

C79   Mills, Janet J. (1985). "The Possession State Intwaso: An Anthropological Re-appraisal." *South African Journal of Sociology*, vol. 16, no. 1: 9-13.

Intwaso, or *ithwasa*, is a condition experienced among indigenous peoples in South Africa and has been the subject of extensive psychological and psychiatric research over the past fifty years. Drawing on medical anthropological theory, Mills stresses that in order to avoid distorted interpretation of *intwaso*, studies should be contextualized within the micro-structural and macro-structural context of South African society. Criticizing previous studies that have tended to ignore this contextual approach, Mills argues that etiological models and decisions about treatment must be considered. The disease of tuberculosis is used as a control for studying *intwaso*, with special attention to the social contexts that create circumstances in which ancestral possession is the explanation for successive illnesses and afflictions. The writer draws on her fieldwork in the urban black township of Guguletu, Cape Town, where the needs arising from poverty and instability are met by diviner networks and other formal and informal support networks. Findings from case studies of three Guguletu households are presented. Mills proposes that the definition of *intwaso* as an "illness category" limits a wider view of the range of characteristics attributed to the condition. *Intwaso* can be self-perceived and applied to any condition where an individual cannot cope and therefore should not be equated with schizophrenia. To support this argument, Mills points to the fact that despite initial physical and emotional suffering, *intwaso* is also believed to be a gift from the shades to a chosen individual and afflicted persons who improve are then recognized as "truly *intwaso*." Notes and references are appended.

C80   Mills, Janet J. (1987). "Diviners as Social Healers within an Urban Township Context." *South African Journal of Sociology*, vol. 18, no. 1: 7-13.

Mills' paper, the result of research for her M.A. thesis, presents a study of diviner schools or networks in the urban township of Guguletu, Cape Town. Noting that the lives of Guguletu residents are affected by structural constraints, Mills focuses on the role of *amagqira* (diviners) as mediators of social tension in relation to the South African social context, noting their ability to mobilize material support for their social healing practice from many sectors of society. Although diviner schools are considered marginal to the overall social structure, they frequently fulfill the needs of depersonalized and alienated members of a population. The phases of apprenticeship, treatment, and healing in diviner schools are discussed, including a detailed analysis of a cell in a diviner network. For the purposes of the study, Mills uses tuberculosis as a control for the possession state, *intwaso*, showing how an illness is channeled to a particular therapeutic option, depending on the etiological decisions made in the social context of the particular household. The fieldwork was conducted over a period of four years, using a qualitative ethnomethodological approach that takes into account the problems inherent in the translation of meanings from the actor's subjective level of meaning to the observer's analytical level of interpretation. The research project is localized, and although some of the findings can be generalized, Mills stresses that it is the local significance of the research that is of most value. Notes and references are appended.

C81   Morgan, N. (1833). "An Account of the AmaKosae, a Tribe of Caffers Adjoining the Eastern Boundary of the Cape Colony." *South African Quarterly Journal*, 2nd series, vol. 1: 1-12; 33-48; 65-71.

Morgan's article is in three parts. The first focuses on Xhosa history in the Eastern Cape, speculating on a period of conflict with the Khoikhoi in precolonial times, followed by wars with the European colonial forces. The history of

Xhosa chieftanship is documented, as well as the structure of Xhosa society. Brief mention is made of witchcraft trials and punishments. The second part begins with a description of Xhosa villages, huts, and family activities, noting the systems of marriage contracts and the sexual division of labor. Describing the healing practices of Xhosa doctors, Morgan also offers his view of the role of diviners when "bewitching" is suspected. He implies that Xhosa belief in the superhuman is manipulated by the chiefs to acquire the property of wealthy subjects. Burial rites and Xhosa belief in spirits of the dead returning to influence living descendants are also briefly noted. In Part Three the author makes more specific reference to Xhosa religion, stating, however, that "No religion or form of worship exists among them." Nonetheless, Morgan goes on to suggest that the Xhosa have some notion of a supreme being, as well as belief in ancestral spirits and an abundance of "ghost stories." The Xhosa do not worship this supreme being, argues Morgan, but regard him as the dispenser of evil, so that any ill that befalls them is personified and propitiated with sacrificial offerings. Adhering to a theory of religious degeneration, the author claims that other customs, such as sacrificial thanks-offerings to a "Beneficent Deity" at the birth of a child, puberty, and marriage, represent the remains of earlier religious worship and sacrifice to a supreme being. The Xhosa people, explains Morgan, are descendants of people to the east and have lost the religious knowledge they originally possessed.

C82   Mqotsi, Livingstone (1957). *A Study of Ukuthwasa (being a syndrome recognised by the Xhosa as a qualification for being initiated as a doctor)*. M.A. thesis, University of the Witwatersrand.

Mqotsi's thesis studies the phenomenon of *ukuthwasa*, or *ithwasa*, which is recognized in Xhosa society as a qualification for initiation as an *igqira* (doctor). The seventeen chapters set out to explore why belief in *ukuthwasa* flourishes in Xhosa society and what social and psychological functions it serves. Using both psychological theory and cultural anthropology, Mqotsi's data is drawn from fieldwork, genealogical studies, and literature research. *Ukuthwasa*, the author explains, first manifests as sickness (*inkathazo*) but the afflicted person is said to communicate with his or her ancestral spirits as well as to be connected with certain animals that facilitate the "sickness." The social function of *ukuthwasa*, the writer argues, is to help deal with the vagaries of Xhosa life and is closely linked with beliefs in witchcraft, sorcery, and ancestor veneration. It has therefore become institutionalized in Xhosa society to maintain social stability and to protect against evil. The *igqira* therefore holds a professional position of privilege and his or her divination skills must be accorded respect and reverence. Mqotsi contends that *ukuthwasa* is a manifestation of psychological disturbance and emotional instability, although he acknowledges that some doctors undoubtedly possess abilities beyond the parameters of "normal cognition." It is, he continues, a condition of psychic conflict that is ritualized and channeled through the process of initiation. The anxiety and disruption engendered by Westernization has increased the incidence of witchcraft accusations, thus perpetuating the institution of *ukuthwasa* and what the writer terms "mythical thinking." He concludes that as the Xhosa become more integrated into Western institutions and thought, the less they will believe in witchcraft, sorcery, and the "magical powers" of the doctor. Questionnaires, medicinal plants, genealogies, case studies of *ukuthwasa,* a glossary of Xhosa words, references, and bibliography are appended. Photographs and diagrams appear in the text.

C83   Ngxamngxa, A. N. N. (1971). "The Function of Circumcision among the Xhosa-Speaking Tribes in Historical Perspective." In E. J. De Jager (ed.) *Man: Anthropological Essays Presented to O. F. Raum.* Cape Town: Struik. 183-203.

This essay analyzes the meaning and significance of circumcision in the beliefs and practices of Xhosa-speaking people in South Africa. Noting that most studies of the subject have been merely descriptive, Ngxamngxa draws on modern anthropological functionalist theorists to define the concept of function before offering a brief historical overview of Xhosa-speaking societies and the custom of circumcision. The author proceeds to survey the rites and objects involved in the Xhosa circumcision ceremony, covering the preparations, the operation itself, the period of seclusion, and the "coming out" ceremony in which the initiates are joyfully received back into the community. This descriptive part of the article is followed by an analysis of the diverse functions of initiation, including economic, legal, linguistic, educational, political, religious, magical, and entertainment aspects. Particular attention is given to the symbolic significance of the ritual practices, the sacred objects, and the human and ancestral relationships involved. A section is also devoted to explaining the important psychological functions of initiation in the community. The writer concludes by examining the contribution of initiation to the maintenance of society during internal and external conflicts, suggesting that initiation reinforces the structural continuity of kinship and "tribal" structures. References are appended.

C84   O'Connell, M. C. (1982). "Spirit Possession and Role Stress among the Xesibe of Eastern Transkei." *Ethnology,* vol. 21, no. 1: 21-37.

Beginning with reference to I. M. Lewis' theory that spirit possession occurs mainly among marginalized and underprivileged people as a means of gaining recognition, O'Connell aims to redress the lack of data on individual cases of possession in anthropological literature. The paper focuses on the significance of spirit possession (*intwaso* or *ithwaso*) and the ancestors among the Xhosa-speaking Xesibe in the Transkei. Male and female roles in Xesibe society, particularly in the context of marriage, are documented as a point of departure for nine individual case studies of *intwaso* presented. The case-study reports are followed by a discussion of the diviners' school and the therapeutic techniques used in dealing with possession. Noting a comparatively high incidence of *intwaso* among married women, the author rejects Hunter's hypothesis that *intwaso* is a "functional nervous disorder," which implies that women are more inclined to hysteria. Rather than defining *intwaso* as pathological, O'Connell argues that it represents a culturally acceptable adaptive response to stress. The case studies indicate instances of internal stress in terms of individual experience of failure in role performance and it is argued that Xesibe women not only are more exposed to stressful situations than men, but they also have less access to acceptable means of relief. But O'Connell also points to the pressures of external stress inherent in high migration rates, land shortage, and acute poverty in the Transkei and thus also locates *intwaso* and stress in the wider South African context. Further research concerning the therapeutic significance of traditional healers under conditions of oppression is therefore advocated. Tables of data are included in the text and notes and a bibliography are appended.

C85   Olivier, Carel Christiaan (1981). "Die Religie van die Gcaleka." *Miscellanea Anthropologica*, vol. 4, University of South Africa.

Inscribed within the idiom of Afrikaans *volkekunde*, and drawing on the work of anthropologists employed by the Department of Bantu Administration, Olivier's work is of interest to students and readers in the history of religions for its reification of Gcaleka (or Xhosa) religion. Delineating lineage and kinship structure, Olivier extends this interpretation to an exploration of Gcaleka terms for divinity; ancestor veneration; witchcraft (and the role of the diviner or witchdoctor); "magic"; and taboo. Little attempt, however, is made to draw on the work of early travelers in the Eastern Cape. The text is in Afrikaans and a short bibliography is appended.

C86   Oosthuizen, G. C. (1971). "The Interaction between Christianity and Traditional Xhosa Religion." In *The Ciskei—A Bantu Homeland: A General Survey*. Fort Hare: Fort Hare University Press. 108-44.

Oosthuizen's study sets out to investigate to what extent elements of Xhosa traditional religion remain in the religious thought and practices of Xhosa-speaking societies (specifically Xhosa and Mfengu) in the Ciskei. By far the largest percentage of respondents interviewed were women from rural areas, many of whom were household heads. The men interviewed were mostly farmers, laborers, or pensioners. In relation to theological issues, Oosthuizen found that many Christians, including African ministers, consulted diviners and regarded the Christian God to be the same as the traditional God, Qamatha. In assessing the extent of "ancestor worship," the author compares the theology of resurrection with belief in the ancestral spirits. Rituals of animal sacrifice are also described and ethical issues, including sin, guilt, and repentance, are examined. Oosthuizen argues that in traditional African society no act is wrong unless it disrupts the harmony of the community. The importance of initiation among traditional Xhosa cultures is examined. The writer finds that most respondents did not consider it sinful in the Christian context. In terms of marriage, most church members were monogamous, says Oosthuizen, but many members of "nativistic movements" practiced polygamy. Other issues studied include funerals; salvation; afterlife; the Old and New Testaments; the influence of Christianity on life as a whole; magic; witchcraft; ritual prohibitions; symbolic colors; and women's organizations or *manyanos*. Interpreting the study from a missiological perspective, Oosthuizen concludes that Christian influence has not been a strong enough force to solve the problems of modern African life. Although the Church was part of the experience of most of the respondents, the Christian message did not always have significant meaning for them.

C87   Opland, Jeff (1983). *Xhosa Oral Poetry: Aspects of a Black South African Tradition*. Cambridge: Cambridge University Press.

Opland's work is the first detailed study of Xhosa oral tradition to draw on documentary sources and contemporary oral poetry. The writer focuses particularly on the poetry produced by the *imbongi* or court poet. He describes the poet's informal training, diction, improvisation, and the relationship to the chief and the community, arguing that the role of poetry is essentially political. The author then goes on to discuss the genre as essentially eulogistic, comparing it to other traditions of eulogy in Africa and elsewhere. Also examined is the effect of writing on oral traditions. Finally, Opland discusses Xhosa poetry in relation to current theoretical constructs of oral poetry and oral mental process. References and indexes are appended.

C88   Pamla, Charles (1913). *Some Reflections on Native Customs*. Printed for Private Circulation.

This brief pamphlet comprises a reprint of articles that appeared in the *Methodist Churchman*, written by the African Wesleyan Methodist minister, the Reverend Charles Pamla. He addresses the subject of various "Native Customs" among Xhosa-speaking people that, in his view, have retarded Christian progress. Pamla compares the custom of circumcision with the religious custom of the Jews, arguing that for the Africans it has no religious significance at all. He describes it as an unmitigated evil associated with superstitions that only serve to encourage stealing and violence among youths. Dowry, or *lobolo*, is equally criticized as a misinterpretation of Jewish custom, suggesting that it represents another evil that renders women as slaves and as inferior to men. He further admonishes the enormous expenses incurred by unnecessary wedding feasts. The relations between Africans and Christian missions is discussed, emphasizing the efforts to oppose polygamy and the problems it generates in terms of Christian baptism.

C89　　Peires, J. B. (1981). *The House of Phalo: A History of the Xhosa People in the Days of Their Independence.* Johannesburg: Ravan Press.

Drawing on both oral and written sources, Peires' text represents a comprehensive account of Xhosa history until 1850, when Xhosa independence was finally lost. Alternating between narrative and thematic issues, Chapter Five, "Visions and Interpretations," is of most interest for the study of Xhosa religion. The chapter opens with a brief account of possible early influences on religion, indicating that the most important features of Xhosa religious practice were daily domestic rituals associated with ancestor veneration conducted within individual households. Larger-scale communal rites, such as the annual first-fruits ceremony, were the responsibility of the chiefs. Next, the author documents the growing crisis of continuous frontier wars against the might of British colonial forces, showing how religious belief and practice could not be separated from secular life. He argues that the definitive influence of Nxele and Ntsikana was founded not so much on their religious revelations and apparent magical powers as it was on their ability to provide rational solutions in the face of incomprehensible and acute crisis. Briefly describing aspects of Xhosa traditional cosmology and the role of diviners in that context, Peires provides profiles of the war-doctor Nxele and the Christian convert Ntsikana. The chapter undertakes a detailed analysis of the conflict that arose between them. The last section of Chapter Five deals with the response of the Xhosa people to the Christian mission, arguing that it was mainly one of intense resistance tempered by "selective acceptance" of some Christian concepts and rituals. Footnotes referring to each chapter, a useful bibliography of primary and secondary material, and an index are appended to the main text.

C90　　Peires, J. B. (1985). "The Late, Great Plot: The Official Delusion Concerning the Xhosa Cattle-Killing 1856-1857." *History in Africa*, vol. 12: 253-79.

Ever since its happening many interested individuals or groups have sought an explanation for the Xhosa Cattle Killing. One of the official explanations put forward by Sir George Grey was that the Xhosa chiefs organized the Cattle Killing as part of the final onslaught on the Cape colonists. The burden of Peires' article is to refute this theory and to show that Governor Grey and Commissioner Maclean were responsible for this fabrication for political reasons. The article is in four sections. In the first section the author demonstrates from primary sources the absurdity of the "chiefs' plot" hypothesis. The second section is devoted to examining the main advocates of this theory, Grey and Maclean. The last two sections concentrate on showing these two imperialist functionaries actively engaged in constructing their theory in pursuit of the political downfall of the Xhosa chiefs, Mhala and Sarhili. Though not long enough to permit the inclusion of minute detail, the article does sketch the main actors both in the Cape Colony side and among the Xhosa. If oral tradition as a historical source suffers from obvious disabilities of verification, Peires concludes, documentary evidence, for its part, is as vulnerable to the researcher's manipulation.

C91   Peires, J. B. (1986). "Soft Believers and Hard Unbelievers." *Journal of African History*, vol. 27: 443-61.

In this extensively annotated article Peires analyzes the Xhosa Cattle Killing of 1856-1857 in the light of the rift that occurred in almost every Xhosa homestead and chiefdom as a consequence of Nongqawuse's prophetic exhortations to kill cattle and destroy crops. The split occurred between the majority grouping of *amathamba* ("soft" ones, or believers) and the *amagogotya* ("hard" ones, or unbelievers) who constituted a small but significant minority. Peires argues that it was the lungsickness epidemic that first prompted the Cattle Killing, and he further examines how other fundamental factors such as political attitudes towards the Cape Colony, religious beliefs, kinship, age, and gender also contributed to determining individual affiliations. However, says the author, it is an analysis of the Xhosa terms "soft" and "hard" that best illuminates the deeper reasons for the division. At the level of the individual, "soft" denotes one who subordinates his or her own will to that of the community, while "hard" means one who pursues his or her own well-being, even at the expense of the community's integrity. In social terms, the "soft" believers were those who perceived themselves as loyal to the old order of precolonial Xhosa society and put their nation before themselves; the "hard" unbelievers, however, were those who pursued the new opportunities for wealth and status offered by the colonial presence. Peires concludes that the division thus ran far deeper than one of belief and unbelief, arguing that divisive social and class attitudes were implicit in the Xhosa terms that were applied to the two opposing groups. Footnotes accompany the text.

C92   Peires, J. B. (1987). "The Central Beliefs of the Xhosa Cattle-Killing."
Journal of African History, vol. 28: 43-63.

Outlining the story of the prophetess Nongqawuse and the decimation of the
Xhosa through thirteen months of the Cattle Killing in 1856-1857, Peires attempts to clear up misconceived explanations that have been offered for this
tragic event. He argues that the apparently irrational beliefs and practices involved in this moment of history were, in fact, perceived as natural and logical
by the majority of Xhosa people in the 1850s. The writer proposes that the Cattle-Killing movement was not a "pagan reaction" to the intrusion of colonial
forces and the Christian mission, but was initially suggested and subsequently
determined by the lungsickness epidemic of 1854 that had killed 100,000 Xhosa
cattle. Nevertheless, the movement had a distinctively religious character. The
form the movement took rested on concepts that were fundamental to Xhosa
religion, allowing acceptance of ideas such as the belief that the cattle had been
contaminated by witchcraft. Furthermore, religious belief in the resurrection of
the dead was only part of a much wider cosmological perception of the future—
that of the reenactment of creation and the consequent regeneration of the earth.
Lastly, it is argued that Xhosa and Christian religious elements were fused in
the person and heroic leadership of the expected redeemer, Sifuba-Sibanzi, the
broad-chested one. "The central beliefs of the cattle-killing were neither irrational nor atavistic," insists Peires, who poignantly concludes, "Ironically, it
was probably because they were so rational and so appropriate that they were
ultimately so deadly." Footnotes accompany the text.

C93   Peires, J. B. (1989). *The Dead Will Arise: Nongqawuse and the Great
Xhosa Cattle-Killing Movement of 1856-1857*. Johannesburg: Ravan Press.

In addition to providing a history of events from 1850 to the defeat and impris-
onment of Xhosa chiefs in 1858 and 1859, Peires' watershed study of the Xhosa
Cattle Killing examines explanations that have been offered for the movement.
The author definitively rejects imperial arguments suggesting that the killings
were inspired by a "chiefly plot"—that the cattle killings were the result of a
conspiracy by Xhosa chiefs to bring about war with Cape colonists—or that the
killings were caused by a trick played by Sir George Grey to deceive the Xhosa
and bring them to destruction. Instead, Peires argues that the Cattle Killing was
a logical, rational, and perhaps inevitable response by a nation driven to desperation by the colonial predicament of dispossession and disempowerment.
However, the role of Sir George Grey and his administration in encouraging
and then capitalizing on the Cattle Killing is highlighted. A bibliography and
index are appended.

C94   Ralston, Richard D. (1976). "Xhosa Cattle Sacrifice, 1856-57: The Messianic Factor in African Resistance." In David Chanaiwa (ed.) *Profiles of Self Determination*. Northridge: California State University, Northridge. 78-105.

Ralston's theoretical analysis addresses the theological doctrine and messianic-millennial impulses underpinning the Xhosa Cattle Killing in 1856-1857. He aims to dispel pejorative myths about pre-conquest African societies and to develop a fuller understanding of those societies as complex and non-static, as well as of the full range of their resistance to conquest. More specifically, Ralston focuses on the Cattle-Killing movement in relation to the question of whether messianic or millennial movements function as a fundamental component of some African societies, thus providing a predictable basis for resistance to conquest. The writer draws on other theoretical approaches to messianism and resistance, such as those in the work of Ranger and Coleman, in order to analyze three issues: factors that led to the prophecies of Nongqawuse and Mhlakaza; the strength and character of the Cattle-Killing movement; and the significance of the consequences in terms of resistance to colonial conquest. Ralston states that the movement was unquestionably a millennial phenomenon deeply embedded in Xhosa traditional idiom, most particularly in the cosmological context of human relations with the ancestor spirits and those who mediate between them. He argues that the literature emphasizing the role of Christian theology and evangelism in fueling African messianism misses the point. Highlighting the notion that resistance is a function of a people's perception of challenge and the level of impending crisis, the writer stresses the central significance of Xhosa messianism as a vehicle of expression in the face of political oppression and cultural challenge and crisis in South Africa. Notes are appended.

C95   Raum, O. F. and E. J. de Jager (1972). *Transition and Change in a Rural Community: A Survey of Acculturation in the Ciskei, South Africa*. Fort Hare: Fort Hare University Press.

This survey reports the results of fieldwork conducted in 1964 and 1965 to assess the levels of acculturation among Xhosa-speaking peoples in the Ciskei. The authors distinguish between "internal" acculturation between the different traditional cultures, mainly the Xhosa and Mfengu peoples, and "external" acculturation between indigenous Africans and whites. The authors begin by documenting a brief history of the Xhosa-speaking peoples in the region since the eighteenth century. Subsequent chapters examine the types and levels of change in traditional structures of the family, marriage, and the status of women; recreation and education; agricultural practices, the sexual division of labor, and ritual beliefs and practices; and material culture such as dress and furniture. The significance of religious rites is a consistent theme across all these life contexts. The book thus includes analysis of the impact of Christianity, both mission and independent, on traditional religion and how each has appropriated practices of the other. Chapter Ten is specifically devoted to ritual life, starting with an investigation of three rituals, namely, the *ukukhapha* ritual associated with the burial of important persons; the *ukubuyisa* ritual to bring the spirit of the deceased back to the homestead; and the *imbeleko* ritual that is performed after the birth of a child. The extent of the practice of these rituals is measured among Mfengu Christians; Mfengu by residence; Xhosa Christians; and Xhosa Non-Christians. The major part of the chapter deals more extensively with ritual sacrifice and the role of the ancestors in association with several life transitions and activities, including birth; initiation; marriage; death and burial; dedication of the home; healing; and the seasons, rain, and lightning. The chapter concludes by examining the interaction of religious traditions and customs, noting where non-Christians have taken over some Christian rituals, or where Christians have appropriated traditional customs and names. A body of what the authors term "neo-customs" is also identified, customs which are neither traditional nor Western, but are considered "modern" by the people involved. References are appended to the main text.

C96   Scheub, Harold (1975). *The Xhosa Ntsomi*. Oxford: Clarendon Press.

This volume of artistic performances—Xhosa *ntsomi* and Zulu *nganekwane*— was collected by Scheub in the Transkei and Kwazulu from July 1967 to May 1968. The book is based on the author's doctoral dissertation and is divided into two main parts. The first is devoted to analysis of the *ntsomi* (the term used in the remainder of the book for both Xhosa *ntsomi* and Zulu *nganekwane*) as a performing art and covers several essential components. Scheub first discusses the transmission of the *ntsomi* and the apprenticeship of performers, who are almost always women; the materials of composition, that is, the song, chant, or saying that forms the "core-cliché" of the *ntsomi*; and the characters of the narrative, the setting, and the audience. Core-images are developed within the framework of traditional themes, but the artist has complete creative freedom within those bounds and the originality of her performance receives great praise from her audience. Materials that are personal to the performer are also vitally important, such as sound, rhythmic movement, and language. Next, the creative process as a whole is examined. Practice is based on the artist's recall of traditional core-images from her own repertoire. The use of repetition, which constitutes the performance's most explicit structural and aesthetic characteristic, is discussed extensively. *Ntsomi* performances are complex and sophisticated, and the rapport built up between performer and audience is intensely demanding on the artist's creative energy. Moral and philosophical comment form threads of an overall aesthetic whole, but *ntsomi* productions are not intended to be didactic or moralistic. According to Scheub's observation, a great performer's stylistic techniques, brilliant wit, and imagination weave together with philosophical tradition in the performance of *ntsomi*, which remains a dynamic and significant part of Xhosa and Zulu artistic culture. Part Two presents the texts and translations of several *ntsomi* performances. Photographs accompany the text and lists of performances, a bibliography, and an index are appended.

C97   Schweiger, P. Albert (1914). "Der Ritus der Beschneidung unter den AmaKosa und AmaFingo in der Kaffraria, Sudafrika." *Anthropos*, vol. 9: 53-65.

Schweiger writes from the perspective of a missionary who feels that the details of African circumcision rites must be thoroughly understood before any moral judgments can be made concerning them. His information comes from a catechist named Peter Gidimi Saliwa, and as a result of various discussions with others the author feels certain that his data applies not only to the Xhosa but also to the Thembu, Gqika, and Mfengu. Following a series of moral reflections, Schweiger begins his description of the rite by setting the general background. The ceremony is scheduled by the group leader when a number of men between the ages of seventeen and twenty are present in the group. The rite is called *ubukweta*, the initiates are *abakweta,* and the place of initiation is *isikweta*. The preparations for the rite include the gathering of ceremonial dress by the initiates, and the construction of huts on the site which must be a good distance from the village. The various phases of the ceremonies, which last a total of six months, are set forth in detail and the social ramifications of initiation are mentioned. At no point does the author imply that these rites bear religious significance. The text is in German.

C98   Schweiger, P. Albert (1917-1918). "Der Tikolotshe-Glaube und verwandte Anschauungen unter den Kaffern." *Anthropos*, vol. 12/13: 547-57.

In the introduction to his article, Schweiger describes various beliefs throughout Africa concerning small, hairy humans who have tails and possess strange powers. He suggests that practices such as the Niam-Niam's wearing of animal tails as a decoration could have given rise to the mythic tales. He then focuses specifically on variants of the belief in South Africa. The Tikolotshe is described as a small, yellowish, hairy human with a tail that has the ability to make itself invisible. It sometimes lives in the water, has an evil character, plays practical jokes, and is capable of seducing women. It commonly steals its food from the fields by making itself invisible. According to the author the belief is intense and widespread among Bantu peoples. Icanti, a mythical water snake, is a variant of the belief. It too has the power of invisibility and can hypnotize anyone who chances upon it. It often aids sorcerers and can change into the form of a chain, ax, stone or sticks. The author provides several statements by informants who claim to have encountered this creature. He also mentions Qamatha and Thixo, whom he describes as evil spirits that necessitate magical defenses. Schweiger feels that these beliefs are not a matter for amusement or Eurocentric condescension, but rather form the real religion of these people. He gives a thumbnail sketch of the God, uNkulunkulu, showing that he is a remote deity unconnected to the life of the people. In contrast, the author maintains, the fear of spirits and powers pervades all aspects of life. Following a digression on the role of the sacred specialists, such as the *isangoma*, *amagquira*, and *izinyanya*, Schweiger concludes with a discussion of the *umamlambo*, which he describes a root that can be transformed into a magical snake, and the *gqonquo*, which he identifies as a man the size of a hand that eats human beings. The text is in German.

C99   Schweitzer, Robert D. (1977). *Categories of Experience amongst the Xhosa: A Psychological Study.* M.A. thesis, Rhodes University.

Schweitzer's extensive transcultural study of psychological states among Xhosa-speaking people does not assume universal criteria for "mental health" but adopts a cultural relativist position. Categories of experience among the Xhosa are therefore analyzed in terms of their meaning within Xhosa cosmology. In his introductory chapter, Schweitzer clarifies the terms that fall within the parameters of that cosmology. Using an idiographic methodological approach, the author examines the philosophy and practice of a Xhosa diviner (*igqira*), as well as extensive in-depth interviews with his consultees. The study focuses on three categories of experience, namely, *ithwasa*, *phambana*, and *amafufunyana*. Ithwasa is examined in two contexts: first as a crisis in living; and second as a "calling" seen in relation to the communion between the individual concerned and the shades. Schweitzer's case studies of *phambana* identify the distinguishing characteristics of that state, showing that it is predominantly related to custom and witchcraft. Experience of *amafufunyana*, however, is found to be mainly related to disharmonious interpersonal situations within the community. In pursuing an understanding of these states, the author compares Xhosa perceptions of these categories of experience with Western medical nosology. He notes that the universalist position, derived from descriptive psychiatry, has frequently categorized *amagqira* (diviners) as neurotic or even psychotic, a view that is not supported by the findings of his study. In conclusion, Schweitzer discusses the implications of this study for community health services in southern Africa and the positive role that the *igqira* might fulfill in that context. Appendices include details of psychiatric examinations of and interviews with an *igqira* and his consultees, a glossary of Xhosa terms, references, and a bibliography.

C100   Schweitzer, R. D., and M. V. Bührman (1978). "An Existential-phenomenological Interpretation of Thwasa Among the Xhosa." *Psychotherapeia*, vol. 4, no. 5: 15-18.

Noting the confusion arising from attempts to categorize the *ithwasa* state experienced by South African indigenous peoples in a Western medical model, this article attempts to understand the experience within the phenomenological framework of Xhosa cosmology. Drawing on Kruger's definition of *ithwasa* as a "crisis in living" and Bührman's interpretation of it as a "creative illness," Schweitzer and Bührman aim to extend these existential-phenomenological interpretations to an experiential context of disintegration, chaos, and reintegration. First, the authors define their terms, taking care to reformulate pejorative Western translations of the Xhosa diviner (*igqira*) and of the "calling" to the profession and its attendant experience of "sickness" and "disintegration" known as *ithwasa*. A brief account of Xhosa cosmology and an explanation of the relationship between the living and the "shades" (ancestral spirits) is then provided. An individual's experience of *ithwasa*, the authors continue, is believed to have been preceded by disturbance of his or her relationship with the shades, and *ithwasa* is thus deemed essential for the resolution of this conflict. The authors then describe the process of *ithwasa*, offering an ontological interpretation of symbolic processes of chaos and reintegration that are embedded in shared beliefs in the mythology of Xhosa cosmology. It is concluded that this process also takes place at the interpersonal level of the wider community, in which the afflicted person's status and role is changed, thus inducing a renewed and meaningful relationship, a "shared existence" between diviner and community. References are appended.

C101   Segar, Julia (1989). "The Significance of Custom and the Consequences of Powerlessness." In *Fruits of Apartheid: Experiencing "Independence" in a Transkeian Village*. Bellville: Anthropos Publishers. 99-118.

Against the background of the socioeconomic, political, and cultural disruptions of apartheid's "independent homelands" policy, Segar focuses on issues that are foundational to Xhosa religion. She thus presents an important study and interpretation of the meaning and significance of Xhosa customs during the 1980s in the Transkei—their continuity, discontinuity, and revival—with special attention to a changing and dehumanizing political context. Based on her research in the Transkei village of St. Paul's, Segar analyzes diverse factors that have encouraged the continuity of Xhosa male initiation rituals and the revival of female initiation, which appear to serve a humanizing function. Addressing the added resurgence of the more negative elements of ritual murder and witchcraft accusations, Segar argues that they can be explained by the severity of the political context of disempowerment. In conclusion, the author argues that the villagers upheld certain customs because they helped ameliorate anxiety in the particular historical and political milieu of the Transkei. Experiencing few avenues for meaningful self-expression, she argues, the people did not blindly cling to conservative and outmoded customs, but used them within an idiom that represented the emotionally powerful ideas of continuity, identity, and tradition. Chapter references are found in the book's comprehensive bibliography.

C102   Soga, John Henderson (1931). *The Ama-Xosa: Life and Customs*. Lovedale: Lovedale Press; London: Kegan Paul, Trench, Trübner.

Soga's dated work on the Xhosa-speaking societies of South Africa includes an extensive discussion of cultural and religious life. In Chapter Eight, for example, Soga draws comparisons between Jewish and Xhosa sacrificial rites, appropriating a diffusionist theory that accords the "Bantu race" Jewish origins rooted in the Asiatic influences of the Hamites and early Arab colonization of the east coast of Africa. Noting references to sacrificial peace offerings in Leviticus, the author details Xhosa ritual procedures in sacrificing an ox for healing individual affliction. He then argues that Xhosa religion is monotheistic rather than animistic, claiming that worship of the supreme being is conducted through the medium of the ancestral spirits. Other Xhosa rites such as circumcision, purification, lamentations for the dead, and first-fruit ceremonies are also documented, pointing to similarities in Jewish practice. The functions of the diviner as "high priest" in Xhosa religion are discussed in some detail, emphasizing the interpretation of dreams and other important healing techniques. Soga rejects the use of the term "witchdoctor" as a misnomer, arguing that the diviner's sole aim in relation to witchcraft is to expose the evil-doer. Spirit possession and the training of neophyte diviners are addressed in depth, as well as several divination techniques. Chapter Nine turns to other Xhosa beliefs, which Soga defines as "superstitious," such as those relating to various kinds of "water-sprites" and animal spirits. In Chapters Ten to Twelve, the cultural customs and rites associated with marriage, circumcision, and *lobola* (dowry) are further outlined. Soga's work includes sensitive analysis of diverse aspects of Xhosa religion, but his perceptions are underpinned by colonial missionary attitudes that characterize this religion as "imperfect" when compared with a "higher civilization" and with Christian belief and practice. An index is appended.

C103   Soul, Teboho Victor (1974). *A Comparative Study of Rural and Urban Africans on their Attitudes towards Amagqira (Witchdoctors)*. M.A. thesis, University of Fort Hare.

Soul's psychological study compares the levels of belief in the efficacy of the *amagqira* among rural and urbanized Africans, focusing on Xhosa-speakers in the Ciskei. In Chapter One, the writer first defines certain concepts, selecting the terms "traditional doctor," "indigenous doctor," and "traditional psychiatrist" for the *igqira*, rather than the more popular misnomer, "witchdoctor." After detailing aspects of ancestor veneration and associated Xhosa beliefs in relation to illness, witchcraft, and sorcery, Soul argues that Xhosa society stresses group solidarity at the expense of individual freedom. Urban-dwellers, however, still seek to find their place in an alien environment. It is in this changing social context that Soul studies Xhosa attitudes to the *amaqgira*. In Chapter Two he explains the techniques and instruments employed. After discussing the findings of the study in Chapter Three, Soul concludes that the chances of urban Africans suffering from psychological problems are greatly increased as a result of the stress experienced due to the influences of Western culture and technology. In the absence of other alternatives, argues the writer, the majority of black Africans in South Africa resort to indigenous doctors for psychological support. In conclusion, he stresses the need for well organized psychiatric services for black South Africans, but at the same time strongly advocates the official recognition and accreditation of indigenous doctors: "If for centuries they have been identified with healing, the solution of problems and the prevention of harm, it is highly unlikely now that their task will suddenly come to an end." Questionnaires, statistical analyses, and a useful bibliography are appended.

C104   Theal, George McCall (1882). *Kafir Folk-Lore: A Selection from the Traditional Tales Current among the People Living on the Eastern Frontier of the Cape Colony*. Westport, Connecticut: Negro Universities Press.

The folklore of the Xhosa-speaking peoples of the Eastern Cape forms the basis of Theal's volume. The stories, says Theal, express the "imaginative faculties" of the Xhosa and guide the nature of their religious belief, cultural customs, and government structures. Informed by the evolutionist paradigm of nineteenth-century European comparative religionists, Theal interprets the stories as those of "uncivilized peoples" that provide markers of their "stage of progress" in the "human family." Theal's introductory chapter gives a brief outline of the history, social organization, and laws of Xhosa society, followed by a discussion of language, clothing, and military organization. The writer's views of Xhosa physical and psychological traits are likewise included. With regard to religion, Theal emphasizes the centrality of the "unseen world" in Xhosa cosmology and the beliefs and practices surrounding death and the ancestral spirits. Belief in a supreme being, Qamatha, is noted, although ideas among the Xhosa about this distant being are said to be unclear. The role of the ancestors is closer to Xhosa life and, according to Theal, even closer are "a whole host of water sprites and hobgoblins," malevolent or mischievous beings who haunt the mountains, plains, and rivers. Xhosa belief in witchcraft and the powerful position of the diviner are disparaged by the writer, who makes no attempt to analyze their deeper significance for the community. Twenty-one stories drawn from traditional Xhosa folktales, myths, and legends are then presented, followed by a brief collection of proverbs. Theal's explanatory notes relating to each story are appended.

C105   Thelejane, T. S. (1963). "Pondo Rainmaking Ritual: Ukukhonga." *African Studies*, vol. 22: 33-6.

Thelejane's brief, descriptive essay represents a narrative account of rainmaking rituals and the role of the rain diviner in Pondoland. The writer first focuses on the importance of the *khonga* rain ceremony, which was performed in the past by the Mpondo at the graveside of Chief Mhlanga. Thelejane explains the significance of Mpondo genealogy in regard to the *khonga* ceremony and follows this with a description of the ritual process. The exclusion of women from the *khonga* is noted, arguing that the men's ritual enactment constitutes more a "reverent war" than a prayer, showing their displeasure that the ancestors have allowed drought to continue. For example, the army leaders of Pondoland engage in "harsh talk" with the ancestors, and the men wear old, dirty clothes to symbolize the poverty they will soon experience if no rain comes. Ultimately, however, the men carry "sticks of peace" to show that they do not have the power to fight their spiritual superiors. Only when this ceremony fails do they call on the services of the specialist "rain-doctor," who then identifies the misdeeds for which the nation is being punished and mediates appeasement of the ancestors. References are appended.

C106   Thorpe, S. (1984). "Religious Response to Stress: The Xhosa Cattle Killing and the Indian Ghost Dance." *Missionalia*, vol. 12, no. 3: 129-37.

In this article Thorpe draws parallels between the Indian Ghost Dance of mid-eighteenth-century North America and the Xhosa Cattle Killing movement occurring within the same period in southern Africa. She sees both of these movements as indicative of a double breakdown in communication: On the one hand, intercultural communication failed. Not only was there chronic failure to understand the white intruders in each case, but military action, the response of last resort, also proved ineffective. On the other hand, communication with the supernatural broke down. Otherwise, as Thorpe imagines that indigenous people must have thought, the ignominy and pain of foreign domination would not have been permitted. These movements, then, were desperate attempts to regain the attention, certainly not of their adversaries, but of the spiritual world. The author looks for factors within these indigenous cultures that most probably produced the forms of response that she is comparing and contrasting. In both cases the land and the native peoples' relation to it was central to the causes of, as well as responses to, collective stress. Physical displacement on the land led to religious disorientation, since it affected the lines of communication with the ancestors. In the case of the Xhosa peoples, belief in sacrifice provided a basis and a context for the Cattle Killing to take place. Through their failure, these movements became bridges, as it were, not to a glorious millennium, but to a new era with new ways of coping with the stress of domination. Among the Indians of North America, this took the form of the peyote religion, which took on the trappings of a church in the form of the Native American Church. In southern Africa, a new development came in the form of the Independent Churches. Where hope had come neither with military force nor the pacifism of the Ghost Dance and the Cattle Killing, it was now being sought under the aegis of these new religious creations.

C107   Tisani, N. C. (1991). "Peires, Pathbreaker." *South African Historical Journal*, vol. 25: 232-36.

As the title of this article indicates, Tisani acknowledges Peires' groundbreaking contribution not only to analysis of the events of the so-called Cattle Killing, but also to the history of the Xhosa in the 1850s. Added to Peires' incisive research and bold hypotheses are the benefits of learning and using the Xhosa language in relation to both oral and written sources. However, says Tisani, in *The Dead Will Arise* Peires fails to draw upon the insights of psychology to discover that far from being a logical response, the Cattle Killing was an abnormal act of desperation on a collective scale. Once this discovery is made, Tisani argues, other issues gain their proper perspective as examples of the reaching out, be it through religious belief or practice, of a people who find themselves in a situation of dire extremity. Thus the belief in the rising of the dead, for instance, which traditionally would be viewed as witchcraft, must be understood not as the norm, but as a daring product of a puzzling dilemma. In the pursuit of the logic and rationality of the Cattle Killing, Peires misses opportunities to investigate the complexity of the movement. For example, he overlooks the role of young women (barely teenagers in some cases) and of women generally in dispatching the cattle and refraining from agricultural activity. Also, he fails to give an adequate account of the proliferation of a type of visionary that, despite surface similarities, was not exactly a traditional practitioner. These unexamined aspects thus raise the vexed question of the "religious worlds" of all the actors in this tragic drama—an area that Tisani proposes needs further research. One does not necessarily have to identify one of the leading characters, Mhlakaza, as a Christian, as does Peires, in order to realize that Christian ideas were indeed present and influenced the situation. Tisani seems to imply that it is the nature and extent of this influence that needs to be further explored.

C108   Van der Kemp, Johannes Theodorus (1804). "An Account of the Religion, Customs, Population, Government, Language, History, and Natural Productions of Caffraria." *Transactions of the [London] Missionary Society*, vol. 1:
432-507.

As the first London Missionary Society missionary in South Africa, Van der
Kemp's account is of vital importance to historians of comparative religion in
southern Africa. Although the writer notes, therefore, that the Xhosa had no
religion, since religion was to be defined in terms of "reverence to God," he
does outline some of the forms of Xhosa religious belief and practice that appeared remarkable to nineteenth-century missionary sentiment. Included in his
sketch of the religion of the Xhosa, for example, are illustrations of Xhosa divination, witchcraft, sorcery, and exorcism. Of particular note is Van der Kemp's
account of Xhosa god-names, which he suggests originated from translations of
Khoikhoi terms. Also of note is the missionary's account of rituals associated
with cairns and the veneration of an anchor. Van der Kemp believed that the
Xhosa considered the anchor to be invested with power: The anchor had do-
minion over the sea but was able to punish people on the land who attempted to
desacralize it. As such, notes Van der Kemp, the object was treated with respect.
These beliefs and practices, he asserts, exemplified an absence of religion
among the Xhosa.

C109   Warner, J. C. (1906). "Laws and Customs Connected with [the Kafir]
System of Superstition." In John Maclean (ed.) *A Compendium of Kafir Laws
and Customs, Including Genealogical Tables of Kafir Chiefs and Various
Tribal Census Returns*. Grahamstown: J. Slater (orig. edn. Mount Coke:
Wesleyan Mission Press, 1858). 78-112.

Joseph Cox Warner, the mid-nineteenth-century magistrate based at the Tam-
bookie (Thembu) location, rejects earlier missionary claims that the Xhosa have
no religion. Instead, he suggests that a more accurate conclusion is that the
Xhosa adhere to a "system of superstition" or "false religion," which, he trusts,
they will eventually denounce in favor of Christianity. Although the Xhosa have
no notion of a supreme being, according to Warner, they nevertheless put their
trust in other supernatural beings, namely, their ancestral spirits and "a vague
idea of the immortality of the soul." Warner goes on to describe the role of the
Xhosa *isanuse* and *igqira* (diviner and doctor), whom he refers to as "priests"
since they offer sacrifices and officiate at "superstitious rites." The diviner's
initiation process (*ukuthwasa*) and ritual practices are outlined, although they
are described by Warner as "idolatrous" and "satanic." Furthermore, Warner
contends, punishments for "imaginary crimes" such as sorcery are frequently
"cruel and barbarous." The remainder of Warner's report deals with the following themes: the *ukukafula*, a national sacrificial ceremony for strengthening

the army; attitudes, beliefs, and rituals associated with lightning; the *umhlahlo*, or smelling out of witches; preventatives, antidotes, and charms against evil influences; times when women are considered "unclean" and are separated from society (*ukuzila*) and the purification of women after childbirth; *ukuhlonipa*, or the various verbal and active prohibitions imposed on women; circumcision rites; burial and mourning rites for the dead; and the role of rainmakers. Although Warner's descriptions provide useful information for the study of the history of African traditional religion in South Africa, his interpretations are of a derogatory nature and are devoid of analysis of the significance of religious life among Xhosa-speaking societies. Imperialist military action against the Xhosa peoples is justified by Warner as a benevolent measure to liberate them "from the shackles by which they are bound" so that "civilisation and Christianity will no doubt make rapid progress among them."

C110   Wilson, Monica (1951). "Witch Beliefs and Social Structure." *The American Journal of Sociology*, vol. 61, no. 4: 307-13.

In broad terms, Wilson's annotated paper addresses the relation between values and social structure from an anthropological perspective that focuses on witchcraft, which is defined as "the belief in a mystical power innate in certain individuals and exercised by them to harm others." The author proposes that witch beliefs are an expression of the values of a society and that these vary according to the social structure. The analysis is based on the comparison of two African peoples among whom Wilson had conducted extensive fieldwork, namely, the Nyakyusa of Tanganyika and the Pondo of South Africa. In making associations between witch beliefs and the different social structures of these two societies, Wilson finds that obvious differences do exist between their ideas concerning witchcraft, although some overlapping of beliefs can also be found. Wilson details the witchcraft beliefs of each society, the type of person accused, and the kind of behavior thought to excite witch "attacks," reflecting particularly on the possible significance of differences in diet between the two groups. The author's conclusions indicate that the Nyakyusa emphasis on the lust for food as a main incentive to witchcraft is connected to the fact that they live in age-villages, not kinship villages, while the Pondo emphasis on sex in witchcraft is related to their insistence on clan exogamy. Though somewhat dated, Wilson's work remains informative for the study of indigenous religion in South Africa.

C111   Zarwan, John (1976). "The Xhosa Cattle Killings, 1856-57." *Cahiers d'etudes africaine*, vol. 16, no. 3/4: 519-39.

In this analysis of the Xhosa Cattle Killing of 1856-1857 Zarwan points out that it was by no means a unique event and has parallels throughout the world. His interpretation rests on the argument that a people's ethos and worldview are given meaning and expression by symbols. Therefore, if real understanding of the Cattle Killing is to be grasped, an analysis of the symbolism involved in the prophecy and movement as a whole is essential. Although Xhosa contact with whites, and their consequent experiences of military defeat, rapid social change, and deprivation explain the killings to a certain extent, it was the Xhosa's traditional cosmology that underpinned their response to and reaction against that contact. In this context, argues Zarwan, the Xhosa were attempting to regain control of a threatening situation through the supernatural assistance, symbols, and ritual techniques that they had long found effective, such as divination and sacrifice. Furthermore, such millennial impulses, or similar kinds of movements, have been found to be far too common and widespread to be considered abnormal or irrational. The author thus concludes that the Cattle Killing, as a "millennial dream," had its own logic and specific religious dynamic igniting their aim to "meet their ancestors." Zarwan's account of the history of Nongqawuse's prophecy and the Cattle Killing draws particularly on the writings of John Maclean, Charles Brownlee, and A. C. Jordan, while his analysis refers, among others, to the work of Monica Wilson. The text is extensively annotated throughout. An abstract in French is appended.

5 Zulu Religion

During the 1820s, in the midst of massive social disruptions and warfare, a previously obscure clan, the Zulu, emerged to political prominence in southeast Africa. In the historical literature, this period of intense turmoil has been labeled the *mfecane*, the "crushing" of African opposition in the wake of the aggressive state-building of the Zulu chief, Shaka. In conventional accounts, Shaka has appeared as the tyrannical, but legitimate ruler of a new Zulu kingdom. Following the critique advanced by Julian Cobbing, however, historians have begun to reassess conventional accounts of the role of Shaka and the rise of the Zulu kingdom. British propagandists in the 1820s and 1830s had an interest in depicting Shaka as the sole ruler of a region depopulated by African warfare in order to establish diplomatic relations, trade agreements, and treaties, even if they were faked, that ceded vast tracts of land for European settlement. The "myth of the Mfecane," which represented Shaka as a "monster" who had established a kingdom by "crushing" all opposition, disguised European interests in appropriating land and procuring labor in the region. As Cobbing has argued, the forces of European intervention in the region, especially the effects of the slave trade that was based in Delgoa Bay and the demands for land, cattle, and labor coming from the Cape, must be considered as crucial factors in the violent disruptions and dislocations of the period (Cobbing, 1988; for corroboration and criticism, see Eldridge, 1992; Etherington, et al., 1991; Hamilton, 1992).

In the earliest nineteenth-century reports submitted by missionaries, travelers, and traders, the Zulu allegedly had no indigenous religion. By the beginning of the 1850s, however, the Zulu were credited with having a religious system that revolved around the worship of ancestors (see Hexham, 1987). An extensive body of missionary literature on the Zulu provided a basic inventory of that religion. In missionary accounts, uNkulunkulu, whether understood as the Zulu God or original ancestor, assumed a prominent role. Ritual attention to ancestors, who appeared as certain species of snakes, caused some missionaries to conclude that Zulu religion was not only "ancestor worship," but also "serpent worship" (see Gordon, 1880). Other accounts documented Zulu rites of passage and communal rituals of kingship, warfare, and agricultural fertility (Asmus, 1939; Bryant, 1949; Burgess, 1934; L. H. Samuelson, 1912; 1930; R. C. A. Samuelson, 1929; Tyler, 1971). In the most influential nineteenth-century missionary account of Zulu religion, Henry Callaway's *Religious System of the Amazulu* (1868-70), special attention was directed to Zulu practices of divination and healing.

During the twentieth century, anthropological accounts of a Zulu religious system have tested these earlier reports against fieldwork (Krige, 1936; M'Timkulu, 1977). The most thorough and useful overview of Zulu religion, however, was provided by the missionary ethnographer, Axel-Ivar Berglund, who described and analyzed basic elements of Zulu religion—divinities, ancestors, diviners, ritual sacrifice, protection against evil, techniques of healing, and funerary rites—as a system of religious "thought patterns" (Berglund, 1976).

Traditional Zulu thought on the subject of God has been a matter of considerable controversy. Beginning in the mid-1850s, the Anglican Bishop J. W. Colenso and the missionary Henry Callaway engaged in a running argument about the role of a supreme being in Zulu religion. According to Colenso, the Zulu had two divine names—uNkulunkulu and uMvelinqangi—for the same God. Just as ancient Israel knew God under the names Yahweh and Elohim, Colenso argued, the Zulu traditionally had two titles for the same supreme being. By contrast, Callaway tried to prove that the Zulu has no concept of God comparable to the God of the Christian mission. Instead of representing a supreme being, Callaway insisted, uNkulunkulu was understood as the first Zulu ancestor, the "Great-Great-One" who first emerged from the original source of all life (*uhlanga*).

This controversy has persisted in accounts of Zulu religion. Some commentators have followed Colenso in concluding that the Zulu held an indigenous conception of God that was similar to the God of Christian doctrine (Wanger, 1923-1926). Others have argued that the Zulu notion of God, the sky god, or the "Lord of Heaven" was developed under the influence of European Christian missions (Hexham, 1981). A more complex historical analysis of this problem, however, suggests that nineteenth-century Zulu thought about divinity did not form a single system. Rather, it represented an ongoing argument among Zulu-speaking people who were experiencing different degrees of involvement in an expanding colonial context. For those least affected by these changes, uNkulunkulu tended to represent the first ancestor of a specific political grouping. When the political autonomy of a group was destroyed, uNkulunkulu could be reinterpreted as either the original ancestor of all humanity or the supreme being of the world (Etherington, 1987).

In complex and shifting ways, nineteenth-century Zulu religious thought was located in different colonial situations. Traditional resources were mobilized to make sense out of new power relations. In the 1850s, for example, the philologist W. H. I. Bleek recorded a traditional Zulu creation myth. In the beginning, according to this account, uNkulunkulu created human beings, black and white. The creator established basic oppositions—blacks would live on the land, whites would live in the sea; blacks would go naked, whites would wear clothing; blacks would carry spears, whites would use guns—that actually represented oppositions that were situated in the colonial context. Although this myth might have adapted a traditional narrative, it deployed that creation story in the 1850s as a way of making sense out of the violence of colonial conflict (Bleek, 1952: 3-4).

Ritual attention to ancestors, which the missionary A. T. Bryant called the Zulu "cult of the dead" (Bryant, 1917), features prominently in the literature on Zulu religion. In general terms, a distinction appears to be made between the *amadhlozi*, who are ancestors known to the living and belonging to a particular family, and the *amathongo*, a term that embraces both the *amadhlozi* and the general body of ancestors whose names are no longer known. In one respect, ancestors represent a spiritual reality that transcends death. As spiritual beings, humans beings are more than merely physical bodies; they are animated by *umoya* (a vital spiritual force) and develop an *isithunzi* (shadow, personality, or force of character) that can live on after death as an ancestral spirit (Du Toit, 1966; Vilakazi, 1962). The ritual practice of *ukubuyisa*, the rite of bringing the ancestor back home, has persisted as a significant way of affirming this spiritual reality (Nxumalo, 1981). Ongoing relations with ancestors or ancestral spirits depend upon keeping open the lines of communication. The principal medium of communication is animal sacrifice (Heusch, 1985: 38-64; Lambert, 1993). Forms of ritual speech, however, are also crucial in keeping communication links alive between ancestors and the living (Magwaza, 1993).

As the center of domestic religion, the homestead is a sacred site for ritual communication with the ancestors. Certain features of the home, such as the door, the back wall, or the hearth might be especially associated with the presence of ancestors, but the cattle kraal represents the most important ritual space. In addition to rituals of sacrifice, rites of passage, especially ceremonies of marriage, involve rituals that are located in the cattle kraal (Lugg, 1907; Braatvedt, 1927; Reader, 1966). In the literature on Zulu domestic religion, special attention has been given to the role of women. Associated with both birth and death, women have a unique relationship with the danger of pollution and the maintenance of purity (Ngubane, 1976). Operating within a gendered division of labor, women traditionally assumed responsibility for both agriculture and a special agricultural ritual. In honor of Nomkubulwana, the Princess of Heaven, this annual ritual of fertility is performed exclusively by women to guarantee the success of crops. As a reversal of conventional social roles within the patriarchal household, the agricultural ritual asserts the superiority of women within the context of this particular ceremony (Gluckman, 1935; 1963; see Krige, 1969).

In one respect, the traditional Zulu polity was modeled on the pattern of an extended homestead (Kuper, 1993). However, the religion of the polity extended the scope of political relations through royal myth and ritual. Political myth has played an important role in the religion of the polity. Oral traditions about Zulu kings, for example, have been based upon a characteristic Zulu folktale motif of the exile returning to regain his rightful inheritance (Argyle, 1978). During the 1920s, as colonial authorities had largely succeeded in manipulating chiefs and headmen, the mythic aura of sacred legitimacy that marked Zulu kingship made that institution more difficult to control (Marks, 1981). Under conditions of dramatic social change and within the context of complex intercultural relations, political myths of Zulu kingship remained powerful (Gluckman, 1940; 1942; Marks, 1989). In particular, the myth of Shaka—as an heroic African empire builder, as an exemplar of the African freedom struggle, or as precedent for asserting specific ethnic claims—has been subjected to varied interpretations in the twentieth century (Hallencreutz, 1989).

As a symbol of centralized political authority, the king traditionally held the sacred coil, the *inkatha yezwse yakwaZulu*, that represented the unity of the Zulu nation (see Borquin, 1986). Among Zulu political rituals, the first-fruits ceremony has received the most attention. Presided over by king or chief, this *umkosi* ceremony bestowed the ruler's permission for his people to begin eating crops. Besides celebrating the fruits of the harvest, however, this ceremony has involved rites for strengthening the army that display a more obviously political content (Gluckman, 1938; Kück, 1879; Lugg, 1929). Myths, rituals, and other symbols of Zulu royal religion have continued to be reinterpreted and mobilized in changing political situations, demonstrating new ways of reinventing the past in the present to serve interests that are both religious and political (Golan, 1991; Hassim, 1993; Klopper, 1991).

In considering Zulu sacred specialists, scholars have distinguished between the roles of the herbalist (*inyanga*) and the diviner (*isangoma*). However, both can be engaged in diagnosing the cause of illness, usually as the result of either ritual pollution or spirit possession, and in performing techniques of traditional healing (Ngubane, 1977). In the practice of healing, these specialists act not only as medical experts, but also as "moral custodians" of a traditional worldview under the pressures of social change (Ngubane, 1981). Within new urban situations, herbalists and diviners have continued to play significant roles in deploying healing techniques and rituals, in providing spiritual protection from evil, and in aiding people with finding meaning and purpose in their lives. As many commentators have observed, traditional and modern techniques of healing represent medical resources that might effectively be combined (Du Toit, 1971).

In addition to using techniques for healing, however, diviners display remarkable powers of trance, clairvoyance, and the detection of evil influences.

Conversant with the spiritual world, diviners interpret dreams and see into the unknown (Callaway, 1871; Köhler, 1941; Raum, 1987; Schlosser, 1972; 1977). They are particularly skilled in understanding experiences of spirit possession. In general, two types of possession are distinguished: possession by ancestor spirits, the *ukuthwasa* possession, which is often a prelude to initiation as a diviner, and possession by alien spirits that is frequently understood as symptomatic of some psychological pathology (Sibisi, 1975). However, this second type of spirit possession, especially when attained by women, might also be interpreted as an alternative source of spiritual power (Lee, 1969). Diviners assist in rendering these different forms of spirit possession meaningful. While diviners establish special ritual relations with ancestors, another type of ritual expert, "heaven herds," protect people, livestock, and homes from violent storms by establishing a special relationship, not with ancestors, but with uMvelinqangi, the Lord of the Sky (Berglund, 1975). In a variety of specialized roles, therefore, Zulu ritual experts pursue religious disciplines that continue to operate in modern contexts, even, for example, in the ritual preparation and protection of a football team, which might be regarded as representing an alternative form of social allegiance, regimental organization, and warfare in modern, urban society (Scotch, 1970).

D1   Argyle, W. John (1978). "Dingiswayo Discovered: An Interpretation of His Legendary Origins." In John Argyle and Eleanor Preston-Whyte (eds.) *Social System and Tradition in Southern Africa*. Cape Town: Oxford University Press. 1-18.

Argyle's comparative study focuses on legendary accounts of the life of Dingiswayo, taking Eileen Krige's assessment of the traditional account of Dingiswayo's early career as "undisguised fiction" (1936: 7), and her acceptance of other elements of the story as factual, as a point of departure. The essay aims to show that even the elements which Krige accepted as fact were also fiction. Turning to the pursuit of Dingiswayo's true original identity, Argyle reevaluates recent historical perspectives that tend to isolate the rise of the Zulu kingdom from what was occurring in the rest of South Africa. Applying comparative methods, he compares primary material of European colonists (mainly Fynn) relating to Dingiswayo's career with traditional accounts in order to show their legendary nature. The accounts, Argyle insists, correspond closely not only with biblical myth but also, more relevantly, with Zulu folktales that contain the mythological theme of the "exile returning to claim his rightful inheritance." Using his own earlier field research among the Soli people of Zambia to help reconstruct Dingiswayo's original identity, the writer identifies an explanatory theme for "dynastic change." He continues by analyzing different versions of the legend, both African and European, in relation to Dingiswayo's ethnic identity, pointing to implications for the history of the Zulu kingdom that push beyond internal explanation. In conclusion, Argyle essentially advocates the use of anthropological insights to elucidate the historical significance of Dingiswayo, insights that define that significance in the wider field of social and political relationships extending from the Cape to Zululand. Notes and references are appended.

D2 Asmus, Gustav (1939). *Die Zulu: Welt und Weltbild eines büerlichen Negerstammes*. Essen: Essener Verlagsanstalt.

Asmus spent thirty years among the Zulu as a Christian missionary, and the book, published posthumously, is a result of his observations. It covers a broad range of topics, with chapters devoted to the significance of the kraal and its collective society, festivals, family life, and the Zulu art of war. Of particular interest for the study of religion are the chapters treating the divine, ancestors, and the feminine element in Zulu traditional religion. In a chapter entitled "Die Gottheit," Asmus develops the meaning and importance of the general term *uhlanga*, which is the ultimate source of all things. It is from *uhlanga* that the Primal Man, uNkulunkulu, emerges and creates the models for every aspect of Zulu life. In turn, uNkulunkulu "allows" other humans to arise out of *uhlanga* and the Zulu accordingly view him as the dynamic central point around which their existence revolves. The author states that in addition to this demiurgical aspect, God is also seen by the Zulu simply as the primal fact beyond which knowledge does not reach, and is then called by the name uMvelinqangi. The chapter sketches further nuances of this entity's nature and discusses his relationship to the kraal. In the chapter devoted to ancestors, emphasis is placed on the fact that these beings (*amadhlozi*) are not viewed by the Zulu as "spirits" or "ghosts." According to Asmus, the Zulu believe nature and everything in it to be a composite of matter and energy. The deceased form a natural part of this equation. The energy of the ancestors remains a part of the group that is not to be abandoned and that can also be summoned to assist the group. The forms of religion described up to this point conform to the pronounced patriarchal character of Zulu society, but in the chapter on "the feminine element" Asmus turns his attention to the specific and exclusive role of women in the ritual production and preservation of fertility. In this connection he introduces the *inkosasana yaselzulwini* or "heavenly princesses." While describing the various activities and rites associated with them, Asmus asserts that the Zulu do not really envisage the heavenly princesses as divine beings, but rather as a symbolic representation of the collective feminine force of the social group. The text is in German.

D3   Atkins, Keletso E. (1988). "'Kafir Time': Preindustrial Temporal Concepts and Labour Discipline in Nineteenth-Century Colonial Natal." *Journal of
African History*, vol. 29: 229-43.

Atkins' article addresses the history of Natal's colonial "native labor policy" by
moving beyond economic and political factors towards an assessment of the rich
cultural nuances that were inherent in the process of black proletarianization.
Atkins explores the often neglected issue of the preindustrial work ethic of Natal's Zulu-speaking peoples, focusing on their sense of time, or "temporal consciousness." It is argued that one of the main reasons for the mutual
incomprehension between "master" (white settler) and "servant," and thus the
conflict and prejudice that emerged, were rooted in variant perceptions of time
and measurement. Foremost was the Zulu use of a lunar calendar, in contrast to
the settlers' mechanical calendar, and the employers' unwillingness to learn
their workers' language. The article addresses reasons for the gradual change in
Zulu concepts of temporality from preindustrial peasantry to industrialization, a
change augmented by the insistence of missionaries whose cultural chauvinism
only served to perpetuate a contempt for Zulu culture and cosmology. Mission
Christianity was used as a vehicle for conveying Western culture and establishing a "civilizing mission." Henry Callaway, for example, resolved to educate the
Zulu in the values of time, labor, and skill. In conclusion, Atkins suggests that
in order to survive and adjust to a new and threatening environment, Zulu
workers in the early decades of colonial Natal were forced to deviate from their
cultural customs and modify their ideology. Footnotes accompany the text.

D4   Berglund, Axel-Ivar (1975). "Heaven-Herds: A Study in Zulu Symbolism." In M. G. Whisson and M. West (eds.) *Religion and Social Change in
Southern Africa*. Cape Town: David Philip. 34-47.

Berglund introduces his analysis of the symbolism in the work of Zulu heaven-
herds by defining the term "heaven-herds" as "experts on the sky" (*izinyanga
zezulu*)—those men in Zulu society who are believed to have the power to protect people, livestock, homes, and crops from violent storms. Characterized as a
herdsman who "tends the sky," the heaven-herd is always male and does not
have as close a relationship with the shades as does the diviner. Comparing
these two roles, Berglund points out that it appears that any man might become
a heaven-herd, although some type of special relationship with uMvelinqangi,
the "Lord of the Sky," is implied in his apparent immunity from the harmful
power of thunder and lightning. In fact, says Berglund, Zulu heaven-herds of
any repute are few. Drawing on a case study of three renowned heaven-herds in
Zululand, the writer describes the preparation of protective medicines, the ingredients used, and the complex symbolism at work. Seeking to interpret the
symbolic significance and functions of the diverse ingredients, Berglund identi-

fies two main categories: First, those materials and animals chosen by the heaven-herd that represent concepts and symbols closely associated with the ingredients, thus serving to make his practice logical; and second, those ingredients where the required symbols are regarded as far more important than the actual materials chosen. In conclusion, the writer further clarifies symbolic meanings by distinguishing between "antagonistic" and "sympathetic" symbols.

D5   Berglund, Axel-Ivar (1976). *Zulu Thought-Patterns and Symbolism*. London: C. Hurst.

This important anthropological study is based on Berglund's fieldwork during the years 1959 to 1970 and on information gathered from a wide variety of Zulu-speaking informants. In his introduction, the author offers full details of his methods and informants, as well as clear definitions of the terms he uses. Berglund looks at how symbols are translated into the practice of ritual by the people who use them, indicating that those symbols and thought-patterns are logical and intelligent ways of making life in Zulu society a meaningful experience. Insisting that there is more than one way of expressing life and its circumstances, the author emphasizes that it is in no way presupposed that Zulu thought-patterns are inferior to Western rationality and scientific approaches to life. The text is divided into ten chapters that offer a comprehensive survey and analysis of all aspects of Zulu "traditional" thought that undergirds cosmology and religious beliefs and practices. After the introductory chapter, the following topics are covered: divinities; the shades; diviners: servants of the shades; communication with the shades; anger and fertility as expressions of power; resisting evil; medicines; and funerary rites. Each chapter examines the relevant symbols and meanings involved in ritual practice. Berglund's work as a whole makes every effort to interpret those meanings in terms of the Zulu peoples' own interpretations, portraying society as dynamic and fluid. In this regard, Berglund does not ignore the pressures of Western cultural systems, racial discrimination, and Christian missions on Zulu life. A concluding chapter summarizes his findings. Photographs accompany the text and a list of abbreviations, a bibliography, and an index are appended.

D6   Berglund, Axel-Ivar (1989). "Confessions of Guilt and Restoration to Health, Some Illustrative Zulu Examples." In Anita Jacobson-Widding and David Westerlund (eds.) *Culture, Experience and Pluralism: Essays on African Ideas of Illness and Healing*. Uppsala: Acta Universitatis Upsaliensis. Distributed by Almqvist and Wiskell International, Stockholm, Sweden. 109-24.

In this essay Berglund draws on extensive field research to advance the hypothesis that the struggle to establish and maintain life in Zulu society rests on retaining good social relationships in the community. This process, argues the author, implies a condition where "the recognized reality of evil is not allowed to gain the upper hand." Manifestations of the presence of evil, for example, are perceived in experiences of suffering, threat to life, childlessness, and untimely death. Berglund states that traditionally the Zulu did not ascribe to belief in chance or fate and thus there is always someone responsible for any event. In the case of affliction or misfortune, therefore, it is essential first to discover who is at the source of the evil and then, hopefully, to effect a cure. The author focuses on one of many important methods of countering evil, namely, confession. In analyzing the process, Berglund emphasizes that the activity of evil may emerge in small ways but can mature into uncontrollable evil that may be expressed in several ways, such as sorcery and witchcraft. It is in the emergent period, before it becomes uncontrollable, that evil can be deflated and even eradicated. Using specific case studies, Berglund shows how confessions—and sometimes forced confessions—are an institutionalized part of Zulu society. The practice of confession is recognized for its functional role, rather than its detail, and a distinction is made between the functions of "morality-coloured confessions" and those involving "brooding envy." The author describes the ritual process of confessions, where the "speaking out" of the evil (such as envy, suspicion, or jealousy) is central, followed by the necessary expression of goodwill. The vital importance of confessions, argues Berglund, is their holistic intent, that is, the restoration not only of physical health but also the healing of the whole person and the total environment. Extracts from records of confessions are included in the text and references are appended.

D7   Bleek, W. H. I. (1952). *Zulu Legends*. Ed. J. A. Engelbrecht. Pretoria: Van Schaik (orig. edn. 1857).

This small volume of thirty Zulu legends, which relate Zulu traditions and customs, was first published in 1857 and is presented in the original Zulu with Bleek's English translations and explanatory notes. The legends were collected by Bleek in Natal during the summer of 1856 to 1857, and the original manuscript appears as item number 1204 in Bleek's catalog of the Grey Collection. The introduction indicates Bleek's sources and highlights the writing and translation problems he experienced concerning the Zulu language at this early stage of his career in southern Africa. Many of the extracts relate to religious cosmogonic myth and the origin of the creator, uNkulunkulu (the "Great-Great-One"), his acts of creation, and his instructions with regard to daily life and the structure of society. The coming of the "white men" is also accounted for, as well as the invocation of the ancestral spirits and their role in society. Customs and rituals associated with marriage, childbirth, the raising of children, death and burial, witchcraft, and hunting are also included. These are followed by stories of Shaka and his mother. A revised and modernized version of the Zulu text follows the legends and footnotes accompany the text. Extensive explanatory notes by Bleek are appended as is Petermann's map of the Natal colony and its "tribes."

D8   Borquin, S., ed. and trans. (1986). *Paulina Dlamini: Servant of Two Kings*. Compiled by H. Filter. Pietermaritzburg: University of Natal Press.

This collection of papers presents the recollections of Paulina Dlamini, a Zulu woman who spent her adolescent years as a member of King Cetshwayo's household. Dlamini converted to Christianity and her memoirs were recorded by a German missionary, Heinrich Filter. The accounts offer insight into everyday, domestic life in the Zulu royal household before the intrusion of Western influences were felt in traditional Zulu society. Dlamini's narratives often refer to aspects of Zulu religious life and ritual, such as the role of the ancestors in the life of Zulu royalty. The significance of the *inkatha yezwse yakwaZulu*, the "magic coil," is also explained as the symbol of Zulu unity and nationhood. Another account describes the *inkosi ishaya aselwa*, the Feast of the First Fruits, when Dlamini witnessed the king's enthronement according to Zulu custom and the rites performed to strengthen and rejuvenate both the king and the nation. Other occasions documented are a puberty ceremony, the veneration of snakes as representatives of the ancestors, and the invocation of the ancestral spirits through animal sacrifices. Dlamini also tells of her observations of *ufufunyane*, the mental illness believed by the Zulu to be caused by evil spirits, and its treatment by traditional medicine-men. Dlamini's reminiscences, related towards the end of her life, are persistently colored by her Christian concern to free the Zulu from beliefs and customs "which only lead people into darkness." In the final part of the narrative she describes her conversion and mission work in Zululand, pointing out the conflicts within Zulu society between "traditionalists" and Christians. Photographs accompany the text and references are appended.

D9   Braatvedt, H. P. (1927). "Zulu Marriage Customs and Ceremonies." *South African Journal of Science*, vol. 24: 553-65.

The author of this paper, a former assistant magistrate in Empangeni, was the son of a missionary and lived for forty years among the Zulu in Zululand. The customs described by Braatvedt are based on his own observations and explanations from old Zulu informants. Noting that changing Zulu marriage customs in Natal are completely foreign to original Zulu practice, the author documents the procedure of the "real Zulu customs" from the time when the young couple decide to become engaged. Social gatherings and exchanging of gifts between the two families are described, followed by explanation of the complex arrangements for the handing over of cattle for *lobola* and the rituals associated with the procedure at the kraal of the bride's father. This is accompanied by customary forms of singing passed back and forth through the night between the bride's and the bridegroom's parties. Before daybreak, the bride and her attendants leave the hut for a period of seclusion in the bush to prepare for the wedding. The "calling" of the bride and her party follows, with the singing of *isibongo* (praise poems) to the bride's great ancestors. The process of the wedding ritual is extensively detailed, highlighting the praises sung to the *amadhlozi* of the bridegroom's kraal, the slaughtering of the beast for the bride, and the dividing of the meat. Various rituals of exchanging gifts between bride and bridegroom, purification, and respect for the spirits of the kraal are explained. The paper is largely descriptive but is noteworthy for its unbiased and comprehensive account of Zulu marriage customs and rituals.

D10   Bryant, A. T. (1909). "Zulu Medicine and Medicine Men." *Annals, Natal Museum*, vol. 2, no. 1: 1-103.

Bryant's lengthy treatise on Zulu medicine, although at times pejorative and patronizing, examines Zulu scientific and environmental knowledge in the context of European imperialism at the turn of the century. Bryant begins by discussing the person, status, and initiation of the Zulu medicine-man (*inyanga*), and further explains the distinction between doctor and diviner in the Zulu system of healing. Claiming that the Zulu doctor lacks any knowledge of physiology or pathology, the writer argues that Zulu medical practice is founded simply on a knowledge of symptoms. Bryant defines the method as "a fierce frontal attack against each symptom individually, which . . . must often result disastrously." He also perceives the role of "occult" mental forces in the doctor's curative successes. External agents of harm—"malice and magic"—are treated with charms and "counter-magic" as much as with healing medicines. According to Bryant, the doctor's power also resides in his perceived ability to induce physical evils, as well as to eradicate them. After briefly discussing the preparation of medicines and his perception of the "physical and constitutional traits of the native," Bryant provides extensive notes on the treatment of twenty-seven types of diseases ranging from intestinal worms to alcoholism. Appended to the main text is a list of 240 Zulu medicinal plants and their uses, which, Bryant concludes, by no means represents the whole of the Zulu *materia medica*.

D11   Bryant, A. T. (1917). "The Zulu Cult of the Dead." *Man*, vol. 17: 140-45.

Bryant's paper comprises a brief submission about Zulu beliefs and practices surrounding death and dying. Bryant defines a Zulu religious cosmology that includes body and spirit; mind, feelings, and heart; intellect, memory, and understanding; and "a hazily defined something called the *isiTunzi* (shadow, personality), which may originally have been one and the same thing as the *iDlozi* or spirit." Although the soul or spirit survives death and is offered sacrifice, Zulu religion, according to Bryant's Christian worldview, is vague on doctrine concerning immortality of the soul. Most important in Zulu religion as it relates to everyday life, says Bryant, are the departed spirits of the individual's father, grandfather, and other immediate ancestors. Spirit possession and the various techniques of Zulu divination are discussed, particularly in relation to evil. Distinguishing the "spirit-diviner" from ritual specialists or priests and medical doctors or herbalists, Bryant attempts to evaluate the diviner's apparent occult powers of intuition. He challenges popular European skepticism, arguing that "objective" research indicates that, "subjectively," the Zulu practice of divination is genuine—although, frequently, it brings "harmful consequences" to the "Native community." The writer concludes by describing the Zulu kraal, the role of sacred specialists, and the ritual process of communication with the ancestral spirits through animal sacrifice.

D12   Bryant, A. T. (1920). "The Religion of the Zulus." *Native Teachers' Journal*, vol. 1, no. 2: 44–50.

Bryant begins this paper, which was delivered as a lecture, by defining religion "to comprise the whole of man's beliefs and behavior towards spiritual beings." In the case of the Zulu, says Bryant, a dualistic conception of the human being is evident, comprising the body and an immaterial "shadow." After death of the body, the person becomes a "shade" or disembodied spirit (*idlozi*). An ancestral spirit remains on this earth in its own community and may manifest itself in an animal or snake. Bryant explains that the spirit of a family's headman is central to the Zulu religious system and claims that the father of each successive generation becomes that generation's "god." Unkulunkulu, the name adopted by European missionaries for teaching the Zulu about the Christian God, in fact, for the Zulu themselves, refers to the original or great ancestor. According to Bryant, no evidence whatsoever exists that the Zulu have a concept of the Supreme Being, even though Unkulunkulu is also perceived as the creator of the world and humankind. Bryant discusses the "Zulu priesthood," referring to those who officiate at the sacrificial rites of the kraal offered to the ancestral spirits. Zulu veneration of their ancestral spirits, Bryant concedes, indicates that they have a certain kind of belief in immortality or survival of bodily death. The religious and healing practices of spirit-diviners are then discussed. The writer concludes that, by European medical standards, they are usually "individuals of the neurotic type, suffering from some kind of nervous disorder." However, he admits the significance of the diviner's role in Zulu society, their propensity for clairvoyance, and their practice of "prayer" to the spirits. Bryant contends that since the Zulu have no concept of the rewards of heaven or penalties of hell, they adhere only to a limited moral code. Bryant concludes his lecture by emphasizing the value of studying the religion of the Zulu and other "primitive folk" for widening our knowledge of the origins and evolution of "natural religion."

D13   Bryant, A. T. (1949). *The Zulu People As They Were Before The White Man Came*. Pietermaritzburg: Shuter & Shooter (2nd. edn. 1967).

Bryant's comprehensive volume addressing the history and life of the Zulu-speaking peoples draws on information collected during the years 1883 to 1935 when the author worked as a missionary in Zululand. The book deals with Zulu society until around 1900 and the beginnings of migration to urban centers in South Africa. Until such time, says Bryant, "the daily life of the Zulu people had continued practically unaltered (in its fundamental aspects) since the days of Shaka (indeed, since long before his time)." Despite the implication of a static society and a Eurocentric and Christian worldview, Bryant's narrative, which is interspersed throughout with references to Zulu mythology, cosmology, beliefs, and rituals, is particularly valuable in its description of Zulu religion. For example, rites surrounding birth, puberty, marriage, and death, as well as communal rituals associated with the king, the army, and the growth of crops, are interwoven into the relevant chapters. Bryant's interpretations of Zulu religion further draw on the ideas of nineteenth-century European comparative religionists such as Frazer, Lang, and Lubbock. Although he discounts the "erroneous practice" of some contemporary ethnologists who categorized African social and religious systems under the generic term "totemism," Bryant characterizes the Zulu way of life as a multi-faceted order comprising a social system of clan names and social taboos that is supported by a religious system of "ancestor worship." Notes follow each chapter and a bibliography and index are appended to the main text.

D14   Burgess, A. (1934). *Unkulunkulu in Zululand*. Minnesota: Board of Foreign Missions.

Burgess' now dated work offers a comprehensive but anecdotal study of Zulu religion, written by a member of the American Board of Foreign Missions. In Chapter One, Burgess focuses on belief in Unkulunkulu, the "Great-Great One," as central to the origins of Zulu religion. Unkulunkulu is believed to be the creator of the world who, having created human beings, went away and forgot them. As a result, says the author, Unkulunkulu plays no part in the daily religious practices of the Zulu people, "and so they, in like manner, forget God." It is to the ancestral spirits, therefore, that they turn for help and guidance. Burgess explains Zulu belief in the spirit world and thoughts on its location in some detail, noting how the ancestral spirits come into being after death and how they communicate with the living. Chapter Two continues an examination of the ancestral spirits, particularly in relation to aspects of ritual animal sacrifice and to diviners and their practices. Burgess discusses the Zulu kings and the rise of the Zulu nation in Chapter Three. Also included is an overview of the Boer trek into Zululand and the British colonization of Natal. Chapter Four looks at daily life in the Zulu kraal, discussing several cultural customs, such as betrothal and marriage. The practice of polygamy, which the author describes as "heathen," is particularly highlighted. The remaining chapters, Chapters Five to Ten, are devoted to reviewing the history and work of the missionaries who were sent to Natal and Zululand under the auspices of the American Board of Foreign Missions. Burgess particularly focuses on the work of the Norwegian missionary, Hans Schreuder, who arrived in the region in 1844. Photographs appear throughout the text and statistics, a list of missionaries, and a bibliography are appended.

D15   Callaway, Henry (1866-1868). *Izinganekwane, Nensumanansumane, Nezindaba Zabantu (Nursery Tales, Traditions, and Histories of the Zulus).* Volume 1, parts 1-6. Springvale, Natal: John A. Blair; Pietermaritzburg, Natal: Davis & Sons; London: Trübner & Co.

Callaway's introductory preface to this volume of Zulu folklore with English translations explains that the tales were dictated by Zulu informants. He notes that Zulu women, rather than the men, are the depositories of these tales and that for Europeans to gain knowledge of them provides a point of contact with the Zulu people. The tales, argues Callaway, provide clues to the origins of the Zulu, indicating that they are an integral part of humanity. In common with most other peoples, they retain their thoughts and ideas about life in traditional stories. Callaway further expands on his methods of writing and spelling the Zulu language, providing a guide for pronunciation, in the hope that it would be used for teaching English to the Zulu and Zulu to the English. The volume comprises six separate parts, all containing several traditional Zulu tales, cast with dramatic mythological characters who possess magical, but often ambivalent powers. The stories include magical but cunning dwarfs; gigantic cannibals; magical animals who communicate with humans and whose activities symbolize the contest between good and evil; and other natural phenomena, such as the "Magical Tree" and the "Rock of Two-holes," which opens only to those who know the secret code. Part Six concludes with a short collection of Zulu fables and riddles. The collection provides valuable material for comparative mythology and insight into Zulu traditions. Some brief press reviews are appended to Part Six and Callaway provides extensive explanatory footnotes throughout the volume.

D16   Callaway, Henry (1868-1870). *The Religious System of the Amazulu.* Springvale, Natal: A. J. Blair; London: Folklore Society, 1884; Cape Town: Struik, 1970.

This comprehensive work compiled by the nineteenth-century medical doctor and missionary to South Africa, Henry Callaway, is extensively annotated and presented in both Zulu and English. Mostly comprising accounts of Zulu religion written by a Zulu-speaking Christian convert, the text is divided into four parts: "Unkulunkulu; or the Tradition of Creation"; "Amatonga; or Ancestor worship"; "Izinyanga Zokubula; or Divination"; and "Abatakato; or Medical magic and Witchcraft." The volume represents a sensitive account of Zulu traditional religious beliefs and practices, though colored by a nineteenth-century Christian missionary worldview. Frequently, the explanatory footnotes are most illuminating in relation to cultural contact and the effects of the Christian mission on Zulu-speaking converts' own perceptions of their indigenous religion. For example, in reference to a claim made in the first part, concerning Unkulunkulu, that "we [the Zulu] do not possess the truth," Callaway's footnote states: "The reader should note that this is an account derived from an educated, intelligent, Christian native." The work is invaluable for the study of both Zulu religion and the conceptions of European comparative religionists in nineteenth-century South Africa.

D17   Callaway, Henry (1871). "On Divination and Analogous Phenomena among the Natives of Natal." *Journal of the Royal Anthropological Institute,* vol. 1: 163-85.

Henry Callaway's paper, read to the Anthropological Institute in 1871, represents a valuable resource for the study of Zulu religion and the cultural encounter between colonizers and colonized in nineteenth-century Natal. Callaway couches his report on certain "mental phenomena," observed during his mission among the indigenous peoples of Natal, in the metaphysical argument that there exists a spiritual entity in human beings that is distinct from the material organization of the world. These phenomena, Callaway argues, form the basis of Zulu powers of divination. To facilitate explanation of his theories about these complex phenomena, he first analyzes three arguably analogous and more familiar mental phenomena, namely, dreams, sympathy, and presentiment, comparing Zulu and Western experience of these states of consciousness. Then Callaway turns to the phenomena experienced by the "natives of Natal," which he categorizes as follows: "phenomena occurring spontaneously"; "self-mesmerism"; and "the native system of divination." The symptoms of the first are described in detail, indicating that they are at once feared and respected, since they are believed to indicate the disease that precedes the power to divine. The second, self-mesmerism, is described as an inner power that the Zulu are able to activate through intense concentration of the mind in order to become clairvoyant. Finally, Callaway discusses Zulu divination, explaining in intricate detail the different types of diviners, their practices, and their remarkable powers. Callaway concludes by advocating consideration of the possibility that "the soul of man" can look "beyond the sphere of the senses, and even look into futurity, and hold communion with the invisible world of the spirits." Responses to Callaway's paper, both favorable and unfavorable, are appended.

D18   Campbell, Catherine, Gerhard Mare, and Cheryll Walker (1995). "Evidence for an Ethnic Identity in the Histories of Zulu-speaking Durban Township Residents." *Journal of Southern African Studies*, vol. 21, no. 2: 287-301.

This paper reports on a research project exploring the changing social identities of Zulu-speaking workers in Kwazulu Natal, based on an analysis of twenty-four open-ended life-history interviews with residents of a Durban township, Umlazi. Four main issues form the core of the authors' research: evidence for Zulu ethnic consciousness among the interviewees; identifying situations in which Zulu identity becomes salient; how Zulu identity is reinvented in 1990s township life; and the relationship between "everyday" and political features of ethnic consciousness. Aspects pertaining to identities in crisis addressed in the interviews include reference to history and Mangosuthu Buthelezi's construction of a "glorious Zulu past" and its heroes such as Shaka, Cetshwayo, and Dingane. Culturally distinctive symbols and practices are also examined, most particularly, language, customs, and respect in interpersonal relationships and commitment to traditional cultural values. "Traditional customs" such as rites of passage, *lobola*, and the patriarchal gender relations underlying them, are frequently mentioned by interviewees, who mostly imply that these customs were being abandoned or renegotiated to accommodate changing social and material conditions. The authors report that they did not find evidence of a strong ethnic consciousness, except for respondents' commitment to the Zulu language. They further conclude that a gap exists between political mobilization of ethnicity, such as that promoted by Buthelezi, and the use of ethnic identity as a resource for people to understand the conditions of their everyday lives. Further research into the latter is strongly advocated. Footnotes accompany the text and a table of details about respondents is appended.

D19   Carbutt, H. L. (1880). "Some Minor Superstitions and Customs of the Zulus, Connected with Children." *Folk-Lore Journal*, vol. 2, no. 1: 10-15.

This brief article offers Mrs. Hugh Lancaster Carbutt's observations of certain Zulu customs, especially those associated with the protection of children. For example, the writer describes the brief partial burial of new-born infants, and sometimes of children up to six years old, which is said to protect the child against disease. Carbutt further notes another ritual practice to prevent illness, which is performed by young girls and involves the fashioning of reed skirts at the riverside, followed by singing and dancing around neighboring kraals. The enactment of reversed gender roles is also performed at certain times to protect the kraal from sickness. In this case, unmarried girls and women dress in their brothers' clothing and spend a day herding the kraal's cattle. The process of naming children, as well as Zulu custom with regard to deformed children, are also briefly addressed.

D20   Cathrein, V. (1915-1916). "Der Gottesbegriff der Sulus." *Anthropos*, vol. 10/11: 307-22.

Cathrein mentions that Moffat and Fritsch found no belief of a high creator deity among the Zulu. In their view, Unkulunkulu was merely the most ancient and greatest ancestor. More recently Hartland (1901) had taken up these opinions and expanded upon them. Cathrein feels that the issue is of great importance for the history of religions and therefore proposes to subject Hartland's remarks to close scrutiny. Hartland's position is set out. In Unkulunkulu he saw a primal man who somehow made it possible for other humans to come into existence. The vagueness of this mythic structure is illustrated by the various legends that purport to explain primordial events. Hartland shifts to a philological mode of analysis and states that the word Unkulunkulu simply indicates the oldest known ancestor of a clan. Every group has its Unkulunkulu just as every family remembers a great-great-grandfather. He also analyzes the variants *uthlanga* and *umdabuko* in this context. In conclusion Hartland finds no concept of a universal ruling Providence among the Zulu. Cathrein's response to Hartland's analysis is outlined. Cathrein argues that the analysis is too superficial and that etymologies do not necessarily tell us what a word means at a particular point in time. The author points to Hartland's use of the collections made by Callaway, which are said to be indispensable sources. A study of these collections and other sources has led Cathrein to the conclusion that since the beginning of the nineteenth century a shift has occurred in Zulu religion. The remainder of the paper constitutes a discussion of this shift in terms of the following points. First, Unkulunkulu is believed to be the creator god, although the expressions of this belief are unclear and sometimes contradictory. Second, at an earlier time Unkulunkulu was indeed believed to be merely the "first" man. Third, a high Lord of the Heavens stood above Unkulunkulu but was not the object of veneration. Fourth, at some point these two entities were identified, although it is unclear in what fashion this change took place. And fifth, it is impossible to determine the name of this original high deity. The text is in German.

D21   Clegg, Jonathan (1981). "*Ukubuyisa Isidumbu*—Bringing Back the Body: An Examination into the Ideology of Vengeance in the Msinga and Mpofana Rural Locations, 1882-1944." In P. L. Bonner (ed.) *Working Papers in Southern African Studies*, vol. 2. Johannesburg: Ravan Press. 164-98.

Clegg's paper examines the origins and development of the "inter-tribal faction fighting" in the Msinga-Mpofana rural settlement areas of Kwazulu Natal. After explaining traditional Zulu political organization, the author focuses on the 1922 Tembu/Mabaso-Tembu/Majozi conflicts, which were conflicts between small, autonomous groupings that were rooted in the complex interplay between acute land shortage and other historical and cultural factors. For example, argues Clegg, the virtual absence of vertical loyalty to a monarch above the chiefs and the lack of horizontal trans-tribal age regimentation meant that there was no institutional mechanism to bind the territorial and political frameworks together. An exaggerated sense of corporateness emerged, generating territorial feuds that frequently overrode kinship ties. As a result of these stresses, therefore, an ideology of vengeance developed its own momentum, an ideology that was also permeated by ancestor beliefs and expressed through fighting over "bodies." By means of feuding, Msinga men sought to take control over their destinies and the anonymous forces that caused misfortune, doubt, and death, thereby reaffirming their dignity and manhood through confronting death and "bringing back the bodies" of their dead comrades. This notion was embedded in a belief that a man killed in battle could only be installed as an ancestor once he had been avenged. In conclusion, Clegg suggests that the feuding represented the last vestiges of a dream of independence in its assertion of autonomy and in its struggle, against all odds, to maintain control over land. Notes are appended.

D22   Cobbing, Julian (1988). "The Mfecane as Alibi: Thoughts on Dithakong and Mbolompo." *Journal of African History*, vol. 29: 487-519.

Cobbing's article draws on extensive primary material to present a watershed but controversial attack on the Mfecane diaspora thesis, claiming that it rests on dubious historical evidence, despite its almost universal acceptance. He argues that the Mfecane is a still-evolving multiple theme in apartheid and white, liberal historiography in South Africa. The Afrocentrism and Zulucentrism of Mfecane macro-theory are untenable, Cobbing argues, and the implicit notions of "black on black" violence and Zulu expansionism are primarily a convenient apartheid misrepresentation used to justify unequal land division. Cobbing suggests that, among others, missionaries (including Robert Moffat) were responsible for the massacre of Mantatees (Taung) by Griqua forces and their subsequent sale as slaves. Likewise the Fetcani. The writer focuses on the "battles" of Dithakong and Mbolompo to suggest that "disturbances" in the northern Cape were rooted in the Cape Colony's labor and cattle demands, rather than in Zulu expansionism. Missionary reports of cannibalism and human sacrifice might have been valid, Cobbing notes, since deprivation in the northern Cape was manifold. However, Cobbing shows that British reports that colonial forces were acting to counter Zulu invasion has proved to be propaganda. Evidence of white involvement in Shaka's murder is also presented. African societies, he concludes, did not generate the regional violence on their own but were rather transformed over a long period through the activities of external plunderers. Cobbing therefore strongly advocates that the term "Mfecane," and more importantly, the concept, should be abandoned. The article is comprehensively annotated.

D23   Cope, A. T. (1986). "Literacy and the Oral Tradition: the Zulu Evidence." In R. A. Whitaker and E. R. Sienaert (eds.) *Oral Tradition and Literacy: Changing Visions of the World.* Durban: Natal University Oral Documentation Centre. 151-61.

Cope's paper, presented at a conference addressing "changing visions of the world," explores the thesis that a people's "vision of the world" changes as a result of an evolutionary transition from orality to literacy. Deviating from this theory, Cope suggests that changing Zulu-speaking perceptions of reality contingent on this transition have not taken place through an evolutionary development of literacy over several hundred years. Rather, Zulu literacy emerged as a result of rapid domination by a foreign culture and through the influence of European missionaries and educationalists over the last eighty years. Tracing the history of Zulu literature, in fact only fifty years old at the time of writing, Cope argues that Zulu written poetry has ranged from imitation of foreign models, such as Western romantic poetry, to reverberation of the heroic style of the earlier indigenous tradition of oral praise poems, as evident in the work of eminent Zulu poets such as Vilakazi and Dlamini. "Zulu evidence," the writer argues, cannot contribute much to the "change of vision" theory, since literacy is arguably not yet established as a way of life among Zulu-speaking peoples. In conclusion, Cope suggests that the nature of thought expressed in Zulu literature, especially its written poetry, has been shaped by the model a particular poet chooses to adopt, rather than by the degree of literacy in wider Zulu-speaking society. Verses from various Zulu poets appear throughout the text.

D24   Du Toit, Brian M. (1966). "Some Aspects of the Soul-Concept Among the Bantu-Speaking Nguni-Tribes of South Africa." *Anthropological Quarterly*, vol. 33: 134-42.

Du Toit's article presents both a general ontology of the Nguni concepts of soul and spirit and a detailed inspection of the dynamic relationship between the living and the deceased. With elaborate terminology, the writer elucidates the Nguni conception of the human soul, which, it is believed, is able to depart temporarily from the physical body of the living. This dualism ultimately allows for the possibility of the survival of personal identity after death in the spirit world. Thus, death is described as a rite of passage for both the living and the dead. Du Toit stresses the symbiotic relation that is established between the ancestral spirits and their living descendants in which each is dependent upon the other for the maintenance of a comfortable existence. While the ancestors serve in an oracular capacity, assisting the living by providing warnings and messages, the living satisfy the needs of the spiritualized deceased through the regular performance of sacrificial ritual. Du Toit further distinguishes between the spirits of the familial household and those of deceased chiefs and kings, emphasizing that the basic order of the afterworld is merely a continuation of the present. Therefore, the author concludes that the social hierarchy of the mundane world is retained to a greater or lesser degree in the social relations of the spiritual world.

D25   Du Toit, Brian M. (1971). "The Isangoma: An Adaptive Agent Among Urban Zulu." *Anthropological Quarterly*, vol. 44, no. 2: 51-65.

Du Toit's paper focuses on traditional healers in Africa, both those who administer to the body and those who administer to the mind. First, the author briefly reviews some of the literature relating to this topic, before turning to his main concern, namely, to explore why Zulu traditional healers—both the *inyanga* (herbalist) and *isangoma* (diviner)—continue to play such an important role in newly emerging urban complexes. Although in some cases the modern medical doctor and psychiatrist are replacing them, it is to the traditional healers that the Zulu people often turn for help with the problems that they are unable to cope with in a new environment. Referring to the fieldwork that he conducted during 1969 in the urban Zulu-speaking community of KwaMashu, Natal, Du Toit gives examples of such new problems and the healing techniques and rituals used by the *inyanga* and *isangoma* to address them. The author highlights the use of medicines that purify and offer protection against evil, and he emphasizes the high esteem in which the diviner is held for his ability to see into the unknown and to interpret dreams. With reference to emerging urban areas such as KwaMashu, where people are confused and unsettled by new situations, Du Toit argues that no person can completely disassociate himself or herself from his or her cultural values, worldview, and cosmology. The traditional healer and diviner, therefore, help to resolve the contradictions and conflicts that confront urban Zulu-speakers in a way that they can understand. In conclusion, the author advocates that the knowledge of both traditional healers and modern medicine can be usefully combined in southern Africa. References are appended.

D26   Edwards, S. D. (1986). "Attitudes to Disease and Healing in a South African Context." In G. C. Oosthuizen (ed.) *Religion Alive: Studies in the New Movements and Indigenous Churches in Southern Africa*. Johannesburg: Hodder & Stoughton. 90-96.

With a view to investigating how Western and indigenous health systems could be integrated, this essay addresses "traditional" attitudes towards disease and its causes and indigenous methods of healing in South Africa. Drawing on data gathered from research conducted among Zulu-speakers in the township of Esikhawini, Edwards begins by analyzing the distinction between natural and supernatural causes ascribed to various illnesses. In interpreting the holistic approach to disease among the Zulu, the author emphasizes that there is a significant level of agreement between traditional Zulu and Western psychiatric diagnostic systems. For example, the supernatural mystical theory of *umnyama* associated with pollution and contagion fulfills the psychological function of explaining stress linked to major life events such as birth, puberty, and death. Edwards continues by discussing the role of three broad categories of indigenous healers among Zulu-speakers: the traditional doctor (*inyanga*); the diviner (*isangoma*); and faith healer (*umthandazi*). The different diagnostic and healing methods of these three types of healers are compared with the interviewing methods of clinical psychologists. The author's concluding discussion analyzes the present situation with regard to the uses and integration of the two health systems so far, the problems involved, and future research needed. The "communication explosion," urbanization, and sociocultural change, Edwards concludes, generates a sharp increase in specialization and differentiation among all kinds of healing practitioners. Statistical tables and references are appended.

D27   Eldridge, Elizabeth A. (1992). "Sources of Conflict in Southern Africa, c. 1800-30: The Mfecane Reconsidered." *Journal of African History*, vol. 33: 1-35.

In this paper Eldridge begins by noting that the so-called "Mfecane" in 1820s southern Africa has been explained in countless ways by historians, but never adequately. Referring to Julian Cobbing's work that challenges conventional Zulucentric explanations and absolves the Zulu of culpability in the devastating regional conflicts, Eldridge suggests that his research is seriously flawed in its interpretations of evidence. For example, she indicates that the Delgoa slave trade had not developed sufficiently at the time to be implicated as the root cause of political turmoil, as Cobbing claims. Furthermore, although the writer affirms Cobbing's identification of European-sponsored slave-raiding as a major cause of violence on the north-eastern Cape frontier, his accusations of missionary involvement are incorrect. However, Eldridge also finds Jeff Guy's interpretation of the rise of the Zulu kingdom inadequate, since his focus on stock-keeping ignores arable land use and leads to false conclusions about social demographics and political issues of the time. In response, Eldridge argues that the sociopolitical changes and associated demographic turmoil and violence in question arose from a complex interaction between environmental factors and local patterns of economic and political organization. She emphasizes that these historical changes were not only a response to European penetration of the region, but were also caused by increasing competition among indigenous societies in southern Africa for natural resources and trade that had been limited by a series of environmental crises. That competition was transformed into violent struggle. Footnotes accompany the text.

D28   Etherington, Norman (1987). "Missionary Doctors and African Healers in Mid-Victorian South Africa." *South African Historical Journal*, vol. 19: 77-91.

Etherington's article aims to qualify the stereotypical perception of the professional arrogance of European medical missionaries during the colonial period in South Africa, indicating that early encounters between European and African healers were often characterized by a certain degree of mutual understanding. Special reference is made to the work of the missionary Henry Callaway, who left comprehensive records of his medical practice and research among Nguni societies in Natal during the 1850s and 1860s. Callaway was particularly aware that beliefs about healing were an integral part of Nguni religion and, unlike other missionaries, Etherington argues, he did not assume the superiority of European medicine. After briefly describing some of Callaway's Zulu informants, such as Mpengula Mbande, Etherington examines comparative studies of Zulu doctors and diviners and English medical practitioners. While he felt the skills of English surgeons had no rival, Callaway appeared to have great respect for Zulu medicines and divining skills. But the underlying logic of African healing and religion, based on communication with the ancestors, was less easy for the missionary to accept. Callaway adhered to a theory of religious degeneration and the decay of an ancient priesthood in African religion, although he did not agree with other missionaries that the Zulu were atheists. Turning to theoretical interpretation, Etherington then attempts to use Callaway's material, although drawn from a narrow range of informants, to assess the validity of Robin Horton's theory concerning the place of a high god in African religion. Reference to a high god among South African indigenous societies, it is argued, appeared to develop geographically in tandem with the direction of European conquest of frontiers in South Africa from west to east, from the seventeenth to nineteenth centuries. In conclusion, the writer shows how Callaway's tolerance for African religion diminished under the pressure of the Christian mission. After his consecration as Bishop of Kaffraria in 1873, he even condoned war against the Zulu monarchy and the annexation of the Transkei. Footnotes accompany the text.

D29   Etherington, Norman (1991). "The Great Trek in Relation to the Mfecane: A Reassessment." *South African Historical Journal*, vol. 25: 3-21.

Drawing on Julian Cobbing's contentious thesis that the root causes of the Mfecane are to be found not in Shaka's Zululand but in increased slave-trading on the Mozambique coast, Etherington asserts that the other "central event in South African history," the Great Trek, should likewise be reevaluated. It has, Etherington argues, been common practice in apartheid historiography to treat these two central events of South African history, both of which have been retrospectively discovered by nationalists and historians, as isolated and separate occurrences. The paper serves to critique this view and aims to reconstruct three persistent narrative structures in both Great Trek and Mfecane mythography on the Zulu kingdom and the Trekker republics: first, "the onward march of civilization"; second, "the growth of a nation"; and third, "the advance of the capitalist mode of production." Although focusing on reevaluating these narratives in relation to the Trek, which are very differently characterized in Afrikaner and English accounts, Etherington inevitably links his project with Cobbing's revisionist thinking on the Mfecane and the Zulu nation. Here, Etherington points out, the same misconception is identified in repetitive narrative structures, that is, that the Zulu state arose in isolation as a primordial nation that developed only in response to its local environment. Etherington's critique argues that conventional Mfecane theory, as well as Trek mythology, have been manipulated by nationalist historians, such as F. A. van Jaarsveld, to serve the interests of the modern South African apartheid state. Footnotes and maps accompany the text.

D30   Etherington, Norman; Paul Maylam; Johannes du Bruyn; Alan Webster; and Sheila Meintjies (1991). "Colloquium: The 'Mfecane' Aftermath: Towards a New Paradigm." *South African Historical Journal*, vol. 25: 154-76.

The contributors provide annotated reports on a four-day colloquium, held at the University of Witwatersrand, that was devoted to scrutiny of Julian Cobbing's controversial deconstruction and reinterpretation of Mfecane theory. Cobbing deplores conventional Mfecane theory which advances a solely Zulucentric explanation for the devastation and depopulation of the interior and thus ignores the role of imperial agency and the disruptive effects on the Nguni of increased slaving in Mozambique. In "The Aftermath of the Aftermath," Etherington challenges defenders of existing Mfecane theory and critics of Cobbing's theory, and thus supports Cobbing's approach in most instances. However, he agrees with critics who question Cobbing's lack of attention to African oral sources relating to Shaka's reign. He concludes, in opposition to Jeff Peires' assault on Cobbing's intervention, that Cobbing's work has in fact generated enough questions to keep the next generation of historians busy. Paul Maylam's "The Death of the Mfecane?" analyzes the fundamental point extrapolated from Cobbing's critique that if "one throws out Zulucentrism, then the Mfecane goes with it." He essentially applauds Cobbing's persuasive alternative interpretation, but in order to strengthen the case against the Mfecane, Maylam advocates further research in two areas: first, the penetration of predatory colonialism, including slave-raiding around Delgoa Bay in the late eighteenth and early nineteenth centuries, and its consequences; and second, the production of Mfecane theory and the implied charge that all such theory ignores colonialism and serves to legitimate apartheid. Du Bruyn's "Ousting Both the Mfecane and the Anti-Mfecane" finds Cobbing's, and later John Wright's, "anti-Mfecane paradigm" difficult to refute, given the long and unfruitful search for the "as yet elusive causes of the Zulucentric internal revolution." However, Du Bruyn charges that the theory is in danger of being "counter-Mfecane" rather than anti-Mfecane, in that it still uses "Mfecanecentric" language, imagery, and structures. Although Du Bruyn argues that the theory does not represent a completely new paradigm, he acknowledges the profound transformation brought about in the study of nineteenth-century South Africa by the work of Cobbing, Wright, Carolyn Hamilton, and Patrick Harries, particularly in terms of opening up new areas for future research. Webster's contribution, "The Mfecane Paradigm Overthrown," offers a brief summary of the papers presented at the colloquium, mentioning his own focus on new areas of research into the Fingo in nineteenth-century South Africa. The central point of the colloquium—the deconstruction of the term "Mfecane"—is discussed, emphasizing the need for clarity on the definition of the Mfecane and on the reasons why the concept is obsolete. Finally, Meintjies' report, "The Mfecane Colloquium: Impressions," offers a brief account of the status of the Mfecane in South African historiography, noting that this area of inquiry has always represented a contested terrain. Meintjies draws together points for and against Cobbing's debunking of the myths surrounding the Mfecane, concluding that the colloquium had proved more than fruitful in creating exciting opportunities for new research in the field of eighteenth- and nineteenth-centuries South African history.

D31   Fernandez, James W. (1967). *Divinations, Confessions, Testimonies: Zulu Confrontations with the Social Superstructure*. Occasional Paper No. 9. Durban: Institute for Social Research, University of Natal.

Fernandez' address to the Annual Meeting of the Institute for Social Research in 1965 refers to his research on Zulu divination among "traditional" religious cults and Zionist groups in Durban. His analysis draws on the work of American sociologist Erving Goffman, who defines society as the "stage" on which human interaction takes place. But human encounters, according to Goffman's metaphor, are acted out on two different levels of reality—"frontstage" and "backstage." Although Zulu social relations occur naturally on the frontstage, agents of the social superstructure (backstage) can be dangerously intrusive, since they reside in the supernatural realm—for example, witchcraft, the ancestors, and chthonic and pantheonic beings. The diviner, Fernandez argues, plays the empowering and mediating role of providing the information needed to effect a stable relationship between the two realities. The writer focuses on the Zulu *isangoma* (diviner), who is usually female and who communes with the agencies of the dead and of witchcraft to discover the cause of a particular incidence of misfortune. Her ability to construct a bridge between the seen and the unseen is achieved through an arduous process of initiation (*ukuthwasa*) and thus her work is truly regarded as a calling. Having come to terms with her own "backstage" in the spirit realm, a diviner is then able to assist her clients to confront their "backstage." The writer notes that the modern Zulu have not lost their faith in the diviner's powers, whose techniques have not much changed since the nineteenth-century accounts by Henry Callaway. But, remarks Fernandez, changes have occurred among urban Zulu religious cults, particularly in the shift towards "confession," which is closely linked with traditional Zulu notions of purification (*ukuhlanza*) and is found in both traditional and Zionist cults. Fernandez concludes by suggesting that the individualization engendered by the decline of the extended family among urban Zulu is compensated for by membership of such religious cults. Divination and confession serve to support social relations on "frontstage," along with stable and publicly known relations with the superstructure, or "backstage." Footnotes accompany the text.

D32   Gluckman, Max (1935). "Zulu Women in a Hoecultural Society." *Bantu Studies*, vol. 9: 255-71.

In this paper Gluckman assesses the role and subordinate status of women in patriarchal Zulu society, drawing on a case study of a hoecultural ritual associated with the Zulu goddess, Nomkubulwana (Princess of Heaven). Employed to guarantee crop success, the Nomkubulwana ritual is unlike other Zulu hoecultural rituals in that it is performed by women rather than men. In fact, Gluckman notes, during the ceremonies that are performed to honor and appease Nomkubulwana, men are actively suppressed. After providing an informative account of the ritual and of the vividly conceived images of the goddess, the writer identifies the links between the social position of women in Zulu society and the symbolic meaning of the ceremony. The inferior position of women, he notes, is not limited only to the social realm but is also institutionalized in Zulu religion—female ancestors are considered of little importance and the "Zulu pantheon" is almost exclusively male—"thus Nomkubulwana, the goddess, the princess of heaven, is exceptional in the array of male ancestors and virile gods." Addressing aspects of ritual power and its place in Zulu religion in relation to the patriarchal social structure, Gluckman explores the possible significance of this role reversal that gives socially sanctioned superiority to women in the performance of the Nomkubulwana ritual. In conclusion, he offers a proposal as a point of departure for further research—that the ritual perhaps proffers the prospect of psychological gain for Zulu women, thus encouraging them in their prescribed area of labor, namely, hoecultural work.

D33   Gluckman, Max (1938). "Social Aspects of First Fruits Ceremonies Among the South-Eastern Bantu." *Africa*, vol. 11: 25-41.

Gluckman's article briefly describes and then analyzes the central rituals involved in the first-fruit ceremonies of Zulu societies in South Africa. Finding a lack of information on Zulu ritual in the literature, Gluckman also refers to comparative accounts of Swazi, Ngoni, and Matabele rites to assist his analysis. Although the paper arguably falls within the racist lexicon represented by many 1930s cultural anthropologists in southern Africa, Gluckman's analysis pushes beyond a focus on the mystical significance of ritual, found in the work of scholars such as Frazer, to a more comprehensive sociological and functionalist approach. Focusing on the atmosphere produced during the first-fruits ceremony (*umkosi*), the writer aims to discover the significance and functions of the ceremony in the wider social context of Zulu life, rather than to explain only the mystical beliefs held concerning crops and the symbolism of the rituals themselves. For example, the role of the rites performed in terms of preventing waste and maintaining social order are examined, particularly in terms of controlling social behavior and allowing expression of socially approved emotions during a time of celebration. Gluckman concludes by advocating further field research to support the study of the social ramifications of agricultural ceremonies. A bibliography and summary in French are appended.

D34   Gluckman, Max (1940). "Analysis of a Social Situation in Modern Zululand." *Bantu Studies*, vol. 14: 1-30; 147-74.

In this extensively annotated two-part article on the social structure of modern Zululand, Gluckman analyzes black-white relations based on his research in northern Zululand from 1936 to 1938. The first part of the paper addresses the social organization of one area of northern Zululand in relation to the Union of South Africa. Aspects of the South African "reserve system" are outlined. Gluckman then describes particular social situations and events he recorded in northern Zululand, highlighting one such communal event—the opening of a bridge by the Chief Native Commissioner. A colorful array of participants, both

Zulu and European, are portrayed, indicating social positions and actions that represent the complexities of Zulu-European social relationships. Noting that Zulu and Europeans formed separate groups at the bridge, they nevertheless were united in celebrating its opening. It is therefore argued that black-white relationships in the social structure of Zululand show separation and conflict, but also cooperation, expressed through socially defined modes of behavior. Despite conflicts, contradictions, and differences in areas of social action (for example, politics, ecology, and religion), both between and within Zulu and European groups, Gluckman identifies a temporary social equilibrium. But it is the conflicts, he argues, that will lead to future developments and social change in South Africa. In the second part, "Social Change in Zululand," Gluckman analyzes universal processes that operate within social systems to maintain some stability during periods of change. Both fission and fusion, he argues, exist in all social relationships and are inherent in the nature of social structure. Based on this social scientific theory, Gluckman traces the history of the Zulu nation from the fifteenth-century migrations of the Nguni peoples, through to the incursion of Europeans into Zululand. Noting the establishment of several small kingdoms by the early nineteenth century, the author highlights Shaka's military organization that established a centralized system of power residing in the king. Divergent group interests and common allegiance to the king coexisted within "a pyramidal organization from nation, to tribe, to tribal district, to homestead." Black-white relations in Zululand are then analyzed in the context of the advent of British traders, colonial militia, and missionaries to Zululand, as well as the incursion of Boer trekkers. The disintegrative effects of wars and British colonial administration on Zulu political equilibrium are discussed in detail, concluding with the development of a modern Zululand equilibrium based on the integration of Zulus and whites into a single system of oppressive white domination. Revival of old Zulu customs and increasing resistance to white innovations are identified, as well as opposition expressed through the formation of dissident Zulu independent churches. The development of South Africa, and therefore of modern Zululand, Gluckman concludes, is chiefly determined by black-white conflict.

D35　　Gluckman, Max (1942). "Some Processes of Social Change Illustrated from Zululand." *African Studies*, vol. 1: 243-60.

For sociology to become accepted as a scientific discipline, Gluckman argues, social-anthropological studies of particular social systems should move on to the formulation of abstract relations that are divorced from real events. Therefore, Gluckman's largely theoretical paper attempts to formulate abstract processes of social change, using social scientific methods to identify invariable relations between events in changing social systems. Using examples of real historical events drawn from his data on Zulu societies for the purposes of generalization,

Gluckman emphasizes that the processes he constructs cannot fully explain the production of Zululand history. Many types of laws and events, ranging from the physiological to the psychological and sociological, produce the specific types of human behavior that constitute a society's history. The author bases his argument on a distinction between repetitive and changing social systems, as well as on defining a further analytical distinction between "culture" (types of social events representative of a community) and "sociological relations" (abstracted invariable processes by which culture functions). Gluckman develops his theory in further detail under the following headings: "Sociological Movements are Expressed in Culture Terms"; "Social Cleavage and Conflict and Social Inertia"; "The Cultural Expression of Developing Conflicts and Cleavages"; "Social Cleavage and Social Co-operation"; and "The Individual and Social Change in a Society of Heterogeneous Culture-Groups." In his concluding section, Gluckman illustrates the application of these processes with reference to his fieldwork research on social change in Zululand. The paper is extensively annotated.

D36   Gluckman, Max (1963a). *Custom and Conflict in Africa*. Oxford: Basil Blackwell.

This collection of Gluckman's lectures, which were originally aired by the British Broadcasting Corporation in 1953, offers some of his insights into the sociocultural complexities of indigenous African societies. The fourth and fifth papers, "The Logic of Witchcraft" and "The Licence in Ritual," are comparative studies that refer to religious beliefs and practices among the Zulu-speaking peoples of South Africa. In the former, Gluckman critiques nineteenth-century European characterizations of witchcraft belief and the "witch-doctor" as fraudulent. Instead, he explores and analyzes the logic and intellectual coherence of African witchcraft beliefs in their relation to natural events and to human society, as did Evans-Pritchard in his study of the Azande. The paper includes reference to the construction and effects of witchcraft beliefs in various African societies, focusing on his work among the Zulu-speaking people in Natal. Beliefs in magic and witchcraft, Gluckman argues, both resolve and create conflicts of allegiance, but ultimately they only help to distract attention from the real causes of natural misfortune and social conflict. He cautions us to remember that such contradictory principles and conflictual processes found in African societies are just as evident in modern Western society. Any conflictual process in which persons are blamed for misfortunes for which they are not responsible might be regarded as a "witch-hunt." In "The Licence in Ritual" Gluckman looks at religious rituals of role reversal, highlighting the contradictory components of conflict and cohesion: These rites obviously symbolize protest against an established order, but they are also intended to uphold and even strengthen that established order. The rituals therefore represent organized rebellions that are permitted, and even encouraged, because they are valuable for society. The paper focuses on interpreting ceremonies in which women wear men's clothing and carry out activities that are normally denied them. Beginning with Zulu agricultural rites where women and girls acted as men in order to propitiate the goddess, Nomkubulwana, Gluckman found that there were many beliefs and practices that defined Zulu women as ritually ambivalent. Ceremonies that lifted the usual prohibitions, says the author, served to emphasize them. He argues that Zulu women were not feminists seeking to change Zulu society to improve their own status—at most, the rituals were statements of rebellion, but never of revolution. The Zulu ceremonies are then compared with other rituals in Africa, including Kuper's studies of Swazi rituals that insult and reject the king in order to rejuvenate and strengthen him for the arduous duties of kingship. Gluckman concludes by arguing that rituals of rebellion functioned effectively in African societies that had a stable social order and ultimate values (some of them contradictory) that were located on a mystical plane and could not be questioned or doubted.

D37   Gluckman, Max (1963b). "Rituals of Rebellion in South-East Africa." *Order and Rebellion in Tribal Africa*. London: Cohen & West. 110-36.

Drawing on insights found in James Frazer's *The Golden Bough*, particularly in relation to Frazer's interpretations of agricultural ceremonies, Gluckman's influential essay includes extensive use of comparative material and considers the social components of similar ceremonies practiced among African societies in Zululand, Swaziland, and Mozambique. Fundamental to this work is Gluckman's identification and analysis of the links between religious myth, ritual, and the construction and order of society. The essay first focuses on the agricultural ceremonies conducted by Zulu women and girls devoted to the goddess Nomkubulwana, the Princess of Heaven. Analyzing the significance of the "temporary dominant role" of women in these ceremonies, Gluckman addresses their significance in the wider context of ordered gender roles in Zulu society. The writer defines these ceremonies as an example of a traditionally sanctioned and sacred "ritual of rebellion" that paradoxically challenges the established patriarchal order at the same time that it aims to achieve prosperity for that order. The Nomkubulwana ceremonies are then compared with other agricultural ceremonies performed in south-eastern Africa, most particularly drawing on Hilda Kuper's studies of the Swazi *ncwala* ceremony, which is defined by Gluckman as both a typical first-fruits festival and a "ritual of rebellion." Gluckman thus identifies and draws out the complexity of a common theme in which "rituals of rebellion" openly stress social tensions that are ritually expressed through role reversals and, paradoxically, that serve to unify the social structure rather than disrupt it. Citations from Swazi ritual poetry are included in the text.

D38   Golan, Daphna (1991). "Inkatha and its Use of the Zulu Past." *History in Africa*, vol. 18: 113-26.

Golan's paper notes that clashes between supporters of the Inkatha Freedom Party and those of the African National Congress resulted in thousands of deaths between 1985 and 1990, and that the political death toll in the latter year was the highest ever. Golan argues that the Zulu-based Inkatha movement, in its attempt to maintain the divisions of ethnicity afforded it under an apartheid regime, mobilized moments in a perceived historical past and manipulated the symbols of this myth to reinforce political power. Drawing on both the speeches of Inkatha's founder and chief spokesperson, Mangosuthu Gatsha Buthelezi, as well as reviewing the use of the notions of "good citizenship" in Kwazulu schools, Golan gives an account of Inkatha's view of the "Zulu past" and its chauvinist conception of history, a history that ignores neighboring peoples. Indicating how Inkatha blamed white historians for ridiculing Zulu history, Golan offers a careful analysis of how Inkatha forged its own ideology, particularly through the valorization of the person and role of Shaka. The paper is of interest to readers of religion for its account of the making of tradition and myth and its focus on the symbolic resources or cultural capital that are required to inaugurate and maintain such a powerful (and violent) identity. Notes are appended.

D39   Golan, Daphna (1994). *Inventing Shaka: Using History in the Construction of Zulu Nationalism*. London: Lynne Rienner Publishers.

Golan's book provides a cogent analysis and critique of "invented traditions" and their relationship with "imagined communities" in the new South Africa, situated in the context of violent struggles between supporters of the Inkatha Freedom Party and the African National Congress. The work focuses on the battle over myths, symbols, history, and the reconstruction of Zulu history from 1830 until the present. Golan traces the processes by which a history of the Zulu as a "warrior race" was created. The discussion ranges from nineteenth-century colonial perceptions, to early twentieth-century writings of Africans "in search for roots," to 1950s anticolonial historiography, and finally to Inkatha leader Chief Mangosuthu Gatsha Buthelezi's reinvention and manipulation of Zulu history. Central to the reconstruction of Zulu nationalism, argues Golan, has been the formation and manipulation of oral tradition, underpinned by the further manipulation of tensions between young and old and women and men. The author shows how South Africa's internal conflicts over the definition of ethnicity and nationalism are as much contests over personal interests, political control, economic resources, and foreign investments. Powerful influences have been at work, such as the power of "knowledge," money, force, and academic history-making. But the power of people's sense of belonging, acquired through invented traditions, cannot be underestimated. Such invented traditions, concludes Golan, have a strong presence in the communal imagination, even though they have no real existence, and therefore significantly shape people's perception of reality. Notes follow each chapter and an extensive bibliography and index are appended.

D40   Gordon, W. R. (1880). "Izindaba za Mahlozi: Words About Spirits." *Folk-Lore Journal*, vol. 2, no. 6: 100-5.

This brief extract was related to Gordon by the Zulu headman of a large kraal in the Colony of Natal during the late nineteenth century. The account is presented verbatim in Zulu, accompanied by Gordon's English translation. Primarily, it refers to the significance of the *amadhlozi*, or ancestral spirits, who guide the Zulu people. A complex hierarchical structure of the spirit world is implied in the informant's account of the transformation of the spirit into a snake. For example, whereas the spirit of a kraal headman turns into an *imamba*, that of a child, woman, or ordinary man would turn into an *umhlwasi* (a thin, brown whip snake). The vital importance of not harming snakes is explained, but if an *idhlozi* is killed unintentionally, then cattle are slaughtered and the meat offered to propitiate the spirit of the deceased head of the kraal. The informant states definitively that his people know nothing of Utixo or Unyaniso, the God spoken of by white people.

D41   Hall, Martin (1984). "The Myth of the Zulu Homestead: Archaeology and Ethnography." *Africa*, vol. 54, no. 1: 65-79.

Hall uses Late Iron Age archaeological findings to question the validity of what he terms ethnographic stereotypes. A classic example of the latter, he argues, is the Zulu model homestead which has changed little since its description by Bryant. The simple yet persuasive thesis advanced by Hall is that space and time impose variation on any ethnographic model. Tests carried out on Late Iron Age sites in an area that is geographically continuous with Zululand revealed significant differences in architectural forms between the Zulu *umzi* of ethnography (generally found in coastal areas and river valleys) and Late Iron Age homesteads within a more upland distribution. He found, among other things, that the positioning of entrances, enclosures, and byres differed across the two types of homestead. This can only be explained on the basis of the variables of space and time. As perspectives that utilize the ethnographic present in the interests of synchronic analysis, functionalism and structural analysis are here confronted with a serious challenge, for a change in spatial organization inevitably has implications for social structure and function as well as political order and economic arrangements. The danger inherent in ethnographic myths like "the Zulu homestead" is that misleading generalizations can be made on their basis and scholars, including archaeologists, may be tempted to use the myths to fill the gaps in their data. It is salutary that in highlighting this danger, Hall points to none other than his colleague Maggs and himself as having committed this crime in a previous work, a warning to all researchers of the unavoidable pitfalls that litter the ethnographic terrain.

D42   Hallencreutz, Carl (1989). "Tradition and Theology in Mofolo's *Chaka.*" *Journal of Religion in Africa*, vol. 19, no. 1: 71-85.

Generally concerned with the commemoration and appreciation of the Shaka legacy among contemporary African nationalists, Hallencreutz outlines three possible approaches to the employment of the Shaka tradition in a present-day context: as an impressive Zulu empire-builder; as a mythological figure who conveys the inspiration for the African freedom struggle; or, as in the case of the Inkatha movement, as a means of furthering specific ethnic claims. Extensive allusion is made to the heroic image of Shaka in *izibongo* poetry, especially in the work of Mazisi Kunene and Magema Fuze, yet the focal point of the study is the innovative interpretation of Shaka represented by Thomas Mofolo in his book, *Chaka*. Accordingly, Mofolo provides a psychological and theological approach that transcends previous analyses and makes deliberate use of many traditional Sotho and Zulu cosmological and historical episodes in a commentary on the universal human and social quest for ethical soundness.

D43   Hamilton, Carolyn Ann (1992). "'The Character and Objects of Chaka': A Reconsideration of the Making of Shaka as 'Mfecane' Motor." *Journal of African History*, vol. 33: 37-63.

In this paper Hamilton addresses Julian Cobbing's radical and provocative critique of historiography that situates the "Mfecane" as the pivotal concept in nineteenth-century southern African history. While acknowledging the value of his work in challenging assumptions, and the enormous number of new studies and reassessments of history that it has stimulated, Hamilton criticizes Cobbing for misuse of evidence and imprecise periodization. Her paper focuses on a critique of Cobbing's reconstruction of the making of the Shaka myth, identifying a central element of his theory which alleges that "Shaka-the-monster" was a European invention used to cover up illegal land appropriation and labor procurement. "Cobbing's powerful insights and implausible conspiracy theories," Hamilton argues, ultimately fail to address "the full complexity of his primary target, past historical myth-making processes." In response, Hamilton examines in detail various European constructions of Shaka in the 1820s, as well as the many Shakas that were produced by African voices, arguing that both contributed to the Shaka that became central to Mfecane theory. Natal traders of the 1820s, the writer explains, in fact presented Shaka as a "benign patron" and it was only after the Zulu king's death in 1829 that European depictions of Shaka began to include "atrocity" stories. These stories, Hamilton claims, were not entirely invented by whites but also emerged from images of Shaka already prevalent among African societies in southern Africa. The paper is extensively annotated with useful primary and secondary sources.

D44   Hammond-Tooke, W. D. (1977). "Lévi-Strauss in a Garden of Millet: The Structural Analysis of a Zulu Folktale." *Man*, vol. 12, no. 2: 76-86.

In this paper Hammond-Tooke uses Lévi-Strauss' structuralist approach to the study of myth, as well as psychoanalytic theory, in order to unravel a Zulu folktale recorded by Bishop Henry Callaway in his *Nursery Tales, Traditions, and Histories of the Zulus* (1866-1868). The writer introduces the article by stressing Lévi-Strauss' theory that a myth provides the medium for a message that is always in code and always repeated. Relating this to structuralist theory, he reminds us that the essence of that methodology is to focus on all parts of the narrative as a "textual universe" where all elements of the myth are structurally related. A summarized version of Callaway's narrative, related in two episodes and concerning a mythical creature called *Imbulu*, is then presented. Hammond-Tooke's subsequent analysis examines the deeper meaning of the myth by identifying and interpreting the transformational relationship between the two parts of the tale, uniting them into one "textual universe." The role of the characters of the story as mediators who function to effect transitions between life and death, above and below, are particularly noted. It is suggested that the underlying message of the story, represented through the infraction of fundamental taboos, signifies a subliminal attempt to mediate between the strong Freudian drives towards incest and the strict incest prohibitions and exogamy regulations of Zulu culture. While acknowledging that his conclusions are tentative, Hammond-Tooke affirms that an apparently simple "nursery tale" in fact represents a myth of profound meaning that deals with fundamental human and social problems. Notes and references are appended.

D45   Hammond-Tooke (1992). "Twins, Incest and Mediators: The Structure of Four Zulu Folk Tales." *Africa*, vol. 62, no. 2: 203-20.

Hammond-Tooke's paper presents summaries and a psychoanalytic interpretation of four Zulu folktales that were originally recorded by the missionary, Henry Callaway. Suffused with bizarre and unexpected characters and events, the stories tend towards the ridiculous, implying more profound but hidden associations. If uncovered, argues the author, an oversimplified textual analysis can be avoided. Read in sequential narrative form, the four separate tales express successive restatements of the same message, all contextualized within Zulu family structure. Hammond-Tooke thus sets out to extrapolate recurring themes of twinship and incest, suggesting that twins, for the Zulu, are highly ambiguous. Simplistically put, the common theme identified is that "twins become married people" by means of denying kinship. This seems impossible in reality, but in mythopoetic language and through symbolization, such an ambiguity can arguably be resolved. Various recurrent symbols, and their significance in Zulu family culture, are analyzed in terms of their ambiguous connotations. Mediators of the stories, such as monsters and exotic animals and birds, are found to express duality in unity, thus providing an analogy that allows the logically impossible to happen at the level of symbolization. Hammond-Tooke asks: What exactly is the message? The function of myth, according to the structuralist approach of Lévi-Strauss, is to resolve cognitive and emotional paradox—in this case, the problem of the Zulus' entrenched horror of incest and, in contradiction, the arguably widespread desire for it. In Freudian psychoanalytic terms, in other words, the inherently conflictual nature of the universal taboo versus the universal drive is symbolized. The fact that this "problem" is never solved in reality, concludes the author, can only be expected as part of human life. Notes, references, and an abstract in English and French are appended.

D46   Hassim, Shireen (1993). "Family, Motherhood and Zulu Nationalism: The Politics of the Inkatha Women's Brigade." *Feminist Review*, vol. 43: 1-25.

Hassim's extensively researched and cogent feminist analysis of the politics of the Inkatha Women's Brigade identifies the creation of a fundamental discourse permeated by a politically motivated reconstruction of "Zulu tradition." Defining the discourse as one that incorporates conservative, patriarchal, hierarchical, and essentialist nuances, Hassim explores how Inkatha imposed its ideological constructions of gender through appealing to Zulu women's experienced realities of family and motherhood. Fundamental to the process of mobilizing women into Inkatha's political aims was the recreation of Zulu ethnicity, the invention of "tradition" through the creation of a romanticized past, and Inkatha's perceived ability to bridge the "traditional" and "modern" worlds. The socially constructed symbols of motherhood took on heroic proportions, Hassim argues, as Inkatha set about transforming Zulu mothers into "mothers of the nation," entrusted with the essential function of sustaining the forces of change through maintaining the youth of the Zulu nation—a revolutionary nationalist discourse with a paradoxically conservative content. The writer's analysis serves to reveal the underlying tension between the power accorded motherhood by Inkatha's nationalist symbolism, and the reality of powerlessness experienced by women in society. Furthermore, Inkatha's model of the family, with clearly defined gender roles based on the "traditional" patriarchal Zulu family, denies the reality of the many father-absent households headed by women. Hassim concludes by warning that whereas Inkatha offers women centrality in the modern context of the family in Kwazulu Natal, this strategy "may be used to maintain women's subordination rather than remove it." Notes and references are appended.

D47   Heusch, Luc de (1985). "A Calao for the Rainbow, a Black Sheep for the Python, Oxen for the Ancestors (Zulu)." In *Sacrifice in Africa: A Structuralist Approach*. Trans. Linda O'Brien and Alice Morton. Manchester: Manchester University Press. 38-64.

Chapter Three of De Heusch's book *Sacrifice in Africa* focuses on the ritualization of animals in the context of Zulu cosmology. Drawing on Berglund's (1975) work, the author first examines the significance of the sacrificial hunt of certain wild species and the value of the black sheep. Explaining that the hornbill (*calao*), eagle, and python are all considered close to divinity, whether in the form of the Sky Lord or the Rainbow Princess, De Heusch analyzes how they are ritually sacrificed for cosmogonic purposes related to the sky and weather phenomena. Moreover, the python is also the recipient of sacrifice, in the form of the black sheep. Turning to the domestic realm, it is the ox, supreme symbol of economic value and social prestige in Zulu society, that is sacrificed to the ancestors, although sometimes the ox may be replaced by a goat. The sacrificial sequence is related in comprehensive detail, with the help of diagrams, identifying the various instances where sacrifice of an animal generates closeness between the living and the ancestors. The central symbolic significance of the animal's body in the sacrificial procedure is emphasized. Various body parts and fluids, as well as the meat cooked and then consumed by the ancestors, become metaphors for human processes, most particularly sexuality and fertility. Other structural components of sacrificial ritual, such as the significance of speech and silence, good and evil, purification and pollution, are analyzed in relation to sacrifice as a medium of communication between the human and spirit worlds. Chapter bibliographies and an index are appended to the main text.

D48   Hexham, Irving (1981). "Lord of the Sky—King of the Earth: Zulu Traditional Religion and Belief in the Sky God." *Sciences Religieuses/Studies in Religion*, vol. 10: 273-78.

Hexham's paper examines the development of Zulu traditional religion, based on the conviction that African religions do have a history, a conviction, he indicates, that is not altogether evident in African studies by modern historians, theologians, and anthropologists. Central to Hexham's analysis is his argument that there is no evidence of belief in a heavenly deity or sky-god in Zulu religion before the advent of Europeans. Many recent writers—Krige, Schapera, Berglund, Hammond-Tooke, and Mbiti—argue strongly that the "Lord of Heaven" or Zulu sky-god has always been present in Zulu religion, a deity who is greater than the archetypal ancestor and creator, Unkulunkulu. Since these writers have drawn support mainly from Henry Callaway's *The Religious System of the Amazulu*, Hexham undertakes a careful analysis of Callaway's work, as well as of other nineteenth-century primary accounts. In the process, the author finds many statements to support his thesis, statements that were ignored or misinterpreted by later readers of Callaway's text. The last section of the paper aims to understand why modern Zulu society does have such a belief in a sky-god that is cast in traditional terms. Hexham indicates that certain beliefs were "implanted" by European missionaries at a time when the Zulu worldview was entirely bounded by social needs. Zulu society, he argues, met the European challenge with a creative response that drew on its religious traditions to invent a "new" tradition. This new traditional religion further served to give "pagan and Christian Zulu a common heritage which acknowledged the existence of a Supreme Being," thus developing a "civil religion" in Zululand that overcame the divisions created by the Christian mission. Footnotes accompany the text.

D49   Hexham, Irving, ed. (1987). *Texts on Zulu Religion: Traditional Zulu Ideas about God.* New York: Edwin Mellen Press.

Part One of Hexham's volume, "An Overview of Zulu History, Society, and Religion," identifies problems surrounding the study of Zulu history, followed by an informative explanation of the social structure of Zulu society. Hexham provides a brief review of modern literature on Zulu traditional religion and concepts of God, including reference to the work of T. O. Ranger, A-I. Berglund, W. D. Hammond-Tooke, and B. Sundkler. But the core of Hexham's interest, however, is to explore the question of what the Zulu believed about God before the Europeans came to southern Africa, further arguing that no real evidence exists that they believed in a "high" or "sky" god before that time. To this end, Hexham selects texts from key writings on the Zulu people by Europeans during the first fifty years of cultural contact. Each text is introduced with a brief biographical sketch of the writer and the main points presented. Part Two, "Early Accounts of Zulu Religion," comprises texts from Nathanial Isaacs, Allen Gardiner, Francis Owen, and Henry Francis Fynn. Isaacs, for instance, in 1836, says that the Zulu had no religion at all, while Owen, according to the editor, shows the pious and impractical other-worldliness of theologically-educated, early nineteenth-century evangelists. Fynn's writing, however, reveals a lack of missionary bias and provides a detailed account of the practices of Zulu diviners. Part Three, "God in Zulu Oral Tradition," provides accounts by the missionaries John William Colenso and Henry Callaway. Colenso, says Hexham, sought to find a Zulu God which would fit his belief that innate knowledge of the Christian God existed in all people. Part Four, "European Attempts to Understand Zulu Religion and Explain the Zulu Idea of God," includes extracts by Joseph Shooter, Lewis Grout, William Holden, and later work by Callaway. All of these texts, in different ways, represent creative efforts to understand Zulu religion, including healing rituals, ancestor beliefs, and ideas about God. In particular, as Hexham argues, Callaway's later work should dispel the impression that all European missionaries were "religious bigots" who were insensitive to the religion of others. An index, biblical texts, and references are appended.

D50   Jackson, Cecil Gower (1916). "Native Superstition in its Relation to Crime." *Report of the South African Association for the Advancement of Science*, vol. 14: 251-63.

Jackson's early ethnographic study of the Zulu-speaking people of early twentieth-century Zululand and Natal suggests that there is a connection between "superstition" and "crime." Jackson points to belief in "magic" and the fear of witchcraft as the pivotal problems, representing deeply rooted superstitions that European "civilization" has not found easy to eradicate. The crime of ritual killing is the focus of this article. The author examines two forms of sacrifice: the smelling out of a witch or suspected wizard by the Zulu diviner and the subsequent sacrifice of an apparently innocent victim; and ritual murder to acquire body parts for medicines used by the Zulu doctor. Justice Jackson supports his argument by presenting accounts of court cases that were heard by him, concluding that the crimes were committed because of "false superstition." Although Jackson's writing shows the bias and lack of sensitive analysis and empathy towards Zulu beliefs often evident in colonial ethnographic studies in Africa at the turn of the century, he does acknowledge and draw comparisons with the fourteenth- to seventeenth-century history of witch-burning in Britain and Europe. The writer concludes by hoping that native belief in witchcraft, and its attendant crime of human sacrifice, will gradually be removed by the spread of civilization and Christian influence.

D51   Jackson, Cecil Gower (1918). "The Medicine Man in Natal and Zululand." *Report of the South African Association for the Advancement of Science*, vol. 16: 191-204.

Drawing on civil and criminal cases that came before the court, Justice Jackson's paper reviews the status of the medicine healer in the indigenous societies of early twentieth-century Zululand and Natal. Describing the extent to which the healer's practices were regulated by colonial legislation, the writer also looks at his or her status in Zulu society. Medicine men (who may also be women) fall into two categories—those skilled in healing and those who are herbalists—and are quite distinct from diviners (who are mostly women) or "witchdoctors." Diviners, says Jackson, have not been deterred from their occult practices, although such practices constitute a criminal offense. The Zulu medicine man holds a powerful and revered position in society, respected for his psychological and physiological healing skills. But although his knowledge of the properties of plants and herbs may be considerable, his knowledge of pathology, according to the writer, is negligible. Jackson documents a detailed array of indigenous medicines and therapies, and their dangers, as perceived from the unsympathetic stance of European science and medicine. He concludes that some "Natives" who have come under "civilizing influences" show more confidence in European doctors, but most prefer the unskilled ministrations of the indigenous doctor. It is, says Jackson, a problem that must be faced "in the interests of the Natives themselves."

D52   Jenkinson, Thomas B. (1969). *Amazulu: The Zulus, Their Past History, Manners, Customs, and Language*. New York: Negro Universities Press (orig. edn. London: W. H. Allen, 1882).

Jenkinson's text, written on his return to England after six years as a missionary in Natal from 1873 to 1879, provides a descriptive and anecdotal account of colonial Natal and Zululand, as well as his view of the history of the Zulu nation. The first part of the book, "Description of Natal—Manners and Customs," includes notes on Zulu religion. Jenkinson discusses circumcision (stopped among the Zulu by Shaka), initiation, polygamy and dowry, and the feast of the first fruits, interpreting these customs according to a diffusionist theory that historically links indigenous peoples of southern Africa not only to Arabs and Jews, but also to the Irish. The *amathongo*, or shades of the ancestors, are mentioned, indicating a Zulu belief in the transmigration of souls expressed as the deceased spirit's transformation into a snake. The sacredness of a Zulu chief is also discussed, highlighting the rites surrounding the death of royalty. Zulu diviners, says Jenkinson, are the appointed teachers of the people, clearly "a relic of an ancient priesthood." The author describes the diviner's training, divining practices, detection of witches, and relationship with the spirit world. Noting the herbalists' knowledge of poisonous plants, in addition to their healing skills, the author emphasizes the Zulus' "superstitious dread of witchcraft and charms and secret poisoning." Ancestor-worship and animal sacrifice are described as ritual practices performed to avert such evils. Referring to Bishop Callaway's work, Jenkinson adheres to his theory of religious degeneration that characterizes the Zulu as a "degenerated people fallen from a higher state," whose tradition of a Creator, Unkulunkulu, has since become an "unknown God." Footnotes accompany the text.

D53   Klopper, Sandra (1991). "Mobilising Cultural Symbols in Twentieth Century Zululand." In Romaine Hill, Marie Muller, and Martin Trump (eds.) *African Studies Forum*, vol. 1. Pretoria: Human Sciences Research Council. 193-226.

In this paper Klopper analyzes the recreation of myth implicit in the development of Inkatha in the 1970s and 1980s by Mangosuthu Buthelezi, Chief Minister to KwaZulu's King Goodwill Zwelethini. Focusing on Buthelezi's efforts to mobilize an ethnic constituency in rural Zululand, the writer documents the symbols employed in the context of this "politics of culture." Tracing the creation of significant symbols residing in the colors and dress appropriated by Buthelezi for Inkatha, Klopper reveals the emergence of a unique mix of Western military-style uniform, colors of the exiled ANC, and so-called Zulu traditional dress for festive occasions. In the latter, Klopper argues, are far-reaching implications that mask class and religious differences in rural Zululand, embedded in the aim to communicate a common "Zuluness." The writer continues by exploring the significance of Christianity in this production of "Zuluness," highlighting the pressure influencing the Zulu royal family to embrace "civilized" Christian practices. In terms of issues of traditional dress, Klopper touches briefly on the role of Isaiah Shembe's Nazarite Church in reinforcing a Zulu "ethnic consciousness." In this regard, she also refers to King Zwelethini's interest in the recreation of Shakan tradition and myth, again a process expressed through the symbols of dress, many of which (such as leopard-skin head-dresses) were in fact never worn by the Zulu kings of the nineteenth century. In conclusion, Klopper asserts that these transformations and reinventions of so-called traditional dress generated an "ongoing redefinition of social and political relations through appeals to an uncertain, even mythical past." Comprehensive notes and bibliography are appended.

D54   Köhler, M. (1933). *Marriage Customs in Southern Natal*. Ed. and trans. N. J. van Warmelo. Ethnological Publications no. 4. Pretoria: Government Printer.

Based on ten years' experience as a mission doctor at Centocow Mission in Natal, Köhler's study looks at puberty and marriage customs among the Khuze (Zulu) and Bhaca (Cape Nguni) peoples of southern Natal. The text comprises accounts from indigenous informants and Köhler's commentaries. The first chapter covers both male and female puberty rites, while the second describes various aspects of premarital sexual relations among young Zulu and Cape Nguni men and women. Adopting the overtly critical and moralistic viewpoint often found in colonial-mission stereotypes of Africans, Köhler says, for example, that the African "knows of no curbing of his sexual passions, certainly not by any abstract or ethical consideration. This lack of restraint of a religious or moral nature leads to the sexual orgies at the feasts held for the youth of the community." Further chapters address the complex customs associated with betrothal, wedding preliminaries, and the wedding itself. The final chapter on married life in Zulu and Cape Nguni communities identifies associated rules and "taboos" and the customary beliefs and practices surrounding birth of the first child. Appendices document attitudes towards barrenness; abortion, birth control; prostitution, and venereal disease.

D55   Köhler, M. (1941). *The Izangoma Diviners*. Ed. and trans. N. J. van Warmelo. Ethnological Publications No. 9. Pretoria: Government Printer.

The sixty-four brief texts that comprise this government survey were published by the Department of Native Affairs, having been collected by Köhler while practicing as a mission doctor in Natal. The volume provides accounts from Zulu-speaking informants, who include Sikhumbana, an old doctor and *imbongi* (reciter of praises) who converted to Christianity; an old woman who had been an *isangoma* (diviner) and also had converted; a teacher (also a Christian convert); several patients; another *isangoma* (son of Sikhumbana); and a bone-thrower who was not an *isangoma*. The text is presented in the English translation (by Van Warmelo, government ethnologist), followed by the original accounts in Zulu. The introduction contextualizes the role of the diviner in Zulu society, and the beliefs associated with them, emphasizing that diviners were not recognized by the South African government, especially in view of their alleged activity of pointing out sorcerers "who were then killed without mercy." Several of the accounts refer to the calling of the *isangoma* and the subsequent process of training and initiation. The role of the ancestral spirits, dreams, methods of divination, prayers, sorcerers, and the casting of spells are among the many topics covered. Photographs and drawings accompany the text.

D56   Krige, Eileen Jensen (1936). *The Social System of the Zulus*. London: Longmans Green.

Krige's work draws extensively on nineteenth- and early twentieth-century manuscripts and accounts (Bryant; Callaway; Colenso; Lugg; Tyler), as well as on contemporary accounts and personal encounters in Zululand and Natal. The comprehensive overview covers a wide range of topics, including Zulu history; socioeconomic, political, and legal structures; medicine; military organization; mythology; and religion. Ritual practices associated with birth and childhood, puberty, marriage, and death are documented in Chapters Five to Seven, which emphasize the significance of rites of passage in clearly marking the steps of the life-cycle. Chapter Eight is specifically devoted to Zulu religion. Krige notes that religion plays a part in all aspects of Zulu life. Zulu religious conceptions of the creator, Unkulunkulu, "heaven," and Nomkubulwana, the "Princess of Heaven," are introduced. But it is *amathongo*, or ancestral spirits, that are argued to be central to Zulu religious life. Krige describes the form the spirits might take and the dreams, omens, and illnesses through which they communicate to the living. A detailed account and analysis of animal sacrifice, as a means of ritual communication with and propitiation of ancestral spirits, concludes this chapter. The following chapter offers a discussion of Zulu sacred specialists—doctors, herbalists, and diviners—focusing on spirit possession and the training and initiation of the diviner. A bibliography precedes the text, while footnotes and photographs are included throughout. Ten appendices explaining Zulu concepts, names, and activities, in addition to an index, follow the main text.

D57   Krige, Eileen Jensen (1969). "Some Zulu Concepts Important for an Understanding of Fertility and Other Rituals." In *Ethnological and Linguistic Studies in Honour of N. J. van Warmelo*. Pretoria: Government Printer. 13-20.

Krige's point of departure for this essay is that three groups of apparently different Zulu rites, performed by young virgin girls, constitute a closely related ritual complex linked by the singing of fertility songs (*ukubhina*) that are common to all three. Krige therefore sets out to analyze some of the concepts and meanings associated with these rituals to discover how they are connected. The three groups are identified: first, girls' puberty rituals and coming of age rites in readiness for marriage; second, the hoeing of a field for the goddess Inkosazana (the personification of nature) at the beginning of spring; and third, several purificatory rites conducted to "chase out" diseases in people and crops, namely, the mock burial of babies and young children for protection against childhood disease, the ritual crying for the corn to drive away crop disease, and the driving out of pollution thought to be the cause of epidemics. Stressing the importance of examining language in anthropological research, Krige's analysis of the terms used in the above rituals show that all, no matter how different they might appear, are rooted in the importance to Zulu society of the health of the community and the fertility of the women. Both the rain and fertility needed for pasture and crops and women's fertility are incorporated in the domain of Inkosazana and nature, and operate through the same principles of singing fertility songs and driving away evil influences. The "chasing out" ritual and the singing vitalize and generate the beneficent powers of nature. These terms and techniques, concludes Krige, are not limited to the rituals analyzed here, but are used widely in everyday life situations, such as the treatment of sickness and ancestral rites. Footnotes accompany the text.

D58   Kück, H. (1879). "Umkosi Wokwazulu: The Annual Festival of the Zulus." *[South African] Folk-Lore Journal*, vol. 1, no. 4: 134-39.

This brief descriptive article, presented in both Zulu and English, discusses the annual first-fruits festival among the Zulu. Usually celebrated in December, or as soon as the mealies are ripe, the festival represents the King's permission for his people to begin eating their crops. Kück explains that the event is divided into two parts—the "Little Festival" and the "Great Festival." In the first, the drawing of sea water, and its sacred significance in doctoring the King's body, is viewed as vital for strengthening the King's military power. The military theme is continued during the four days of the Great Festival, where the soldiers of the King play the dominant role in performing various rites. The climax of the festival, on the fourth day, is the sacrifice of a bull, after which the King proclaims the law to his people.

D59   Kuper, Adam (1993). "The 'House' and Zulu Political Structure in the Nineteenth Century." *Journal of African History*, vol. 34, no. 3: 293-318.

In this paper Kuper advances an alternative to the widely held view that the rise of Zulu power in the early nineteenth century was the most significant example of a process that transformed clan-based chieftaincies into centralized states in southern Africa. Instead, Kuper argues that the process retained strong continuities with established structures of chieftaincy in the region, to the extent that the Zulu political system was based on a traditional homestead form of organization found among Nguni societies in general. Kuper's spatial analysis shows that the Zulu homestead was divided into two sections, each with its own identity and destiny, a dualistic opposition that was mapped into the layout of both ordinary and royal homesteads, as well as into the organization of regiments. A set pattern of development is revealed, where the homestead and its segments provided both the geographical and structural nodes of the society. Points of segmentation were situated in the "houses" accorded to each major wife and her designated heir. Each of these houses within the homestead in turn represented the relationships formed, through marriage, with outside groups whose leaders aligned themselves with particular political factions within the family. Therefore, Kuper concludes, the political system of the Zulu corresponded with the local traditions of social organization, since the house system provided a model for a polity of much greater range. The author stresses, however, that this system was not static and naturally required innovative developments for its expansion. Nevertheless, the core principles remained constant. Diagrams and extensive footnotes accompany the text.

D60   Lambert, Michael (1993). "Ancient Greek and Zulu Sacrificial Ritual: A Comparative Analysis." *Numen*, vol. 40, no. 3: 293-318.

Lambert's paper attempts a comparative analysis of ancient Greek and Zulu sacrificial ritual in order to test the validity of Burkert's theory of the origins of sacrifice. First, Lambert examines source material to identify the similarities and differences between the two ritual systems. He finds that the Zulu seem to sacrifice exclusively to the ancestors or shades, while the Greeks sacrificed mainly to the gods. On the other hand, the ancient Greeks did not have a fully developed ancestor cult. The realm of the ancestors is clearly delineated in Zulu religion, while the transcendent is vaguely conceived, thus reflecting the Zulu lineage and kinship system. In contrast, both the realm of the dead and that of the transcendent are well defined in ancient Greek religion and stand in opposition to one another. But the lack of an ancestor cult, Lambert argues, reflects the nature of ancient Greek political and cultural systems that cut across boundaries of "tribes." Turning to Burkert's theory that sacrifice originated in the ritualization of the Paleolithic hunt, Lambert carefully documents crucial aspects of the theory that do not seem to be validated by Zulu ritual sacrifice. The author further shows that composite accounts of both Zulu and ancient Greek sacrifice imply misleading emotional responses that might not be evident in individual sacrifices. Lambert concludes that Burkert's theory is neither proved nor disproved, but that the comparative procedure nevertheless indicates that any search for origins, formative antecedents, or global theories of sacrifice is fraught with speculative problems. Extensive notes are appended.

D61   Lawson, E. Thomas (1984). *Religions of Africa: Traditions in Transformation*. San Francisco: Harper & Row.

Lawson's book provides an introductory text on indigenous African religious systems, focusing on a detailed examination of the religious worlds of two African peoples, the Yoruba of Nigeria and the Zulu of South Africa. Chapter Two is devoted to Zulu religious tradition and draws on the work of, *inter alia*, Krige, Berglund, and Sundkler. A brief history of the Zulu is provided until the apartheid creation of Kwazulu, but given the lack of information available on the historical development of their religion, Lawson focuses on Zulu religious life over the last 150 years. Arguing that the Zulu "live and act in a religious world," he describes the structure of the Zulu kraal and the religious roles of the those who act within it. Indicating that political, social, and religious functions are inextricably interwoven, ritual emerges as the pivotal practice of Zulu life. The main role-players in religious activity, says Lawson, are the headman/priest; diviner; herbalist; patient; heaven-herd; supplicant; sorcerer; and witch. The relationship between these religious actors and the ancestors, which is mediated through religious ritual, is fundamental to Zulu life. In addition to examination of the role of the ancestors, Zulu myth and belief associated with a "God of the Sky" and "Princess of the Sky" are also discussed. The chapter offers a comprehensive introduction to Zulu myth and ritual, particularly rites of passage, as well as indigenous medicine, healing techniques, sorcery, and witchcraft. Lawson concludes by acknowledging the flexibility of Zulu religious tradition under the influence of Western culture, Christianity, and industrialization. While Chapter Three conducts a similar analysis of Yoruba religion, the last chapter provides a comparative study of the roles of central individual participants in the two religious traditions. Notes and a reading list are appended.

D62   Lee, S. G. (1969). "Spirit Possession among the Zulu." In J. Beattie and J. Middleton (eds.) *Spirit Mediumship and Society in Africa*. London: Routledge & Kegan Paul. 128-56.

Lee's paper draws on fieldwork and interviews conducted in Natal and Zululand between 1951 and 1957 that were initially researching fits of screaming experienced among Zulu women known as "criers." This paper explores the wider etiology of concepts and practices such as spirit possession, divination, and prophecy among Zulu-speaking peoples in general. Lee argues that spirit possession falls into two distinct categories: first, *ukuthwasa* possession, or possession by the ancestor spirits, which often leads to the initiation of an *isangoma* or sacred specialist; and second, the more recent and diverse manifestations called *amandiki, amandawe, amabutho*, and *izizwe* possession, which, the writer suggests, have been little studied except in Junod's work among the Tsonga. Both kinds of possession were found to be particularly prevalent among Zulu women, accounting in some ways, suggests Lee, for the numerical majority of women in separatist churches such as the Zulu Zionists, who rely on the spiritual power of such ecstatic states. The writer documents causes for increased occurrences of spirit possession, examining how social deprivation and disruption exacerbate claims to possession. He notes an example in this respect consequent to the malaria and influenza epidemics of 1919 to 1920 and 1933 respectively. Primary accounts from the hunter Francis Fynn and the missionary Henry Callaway are also related to identify further reasons for the widespread occurrence of spirit possession and the presence of the ancestors. Lee concludes by arguing that possession states are often induced and manipulated, particularly by women, to mobilize sociopolitical power. A bibliography is appended.

D63   Lugg, H. C. (1907). "Notes on Some Puberty and Other Customs of the Natives of Natal and Zululand." *Man*, vol. 7: 115-19.

Lugg's descriptive article discusses ritual practices associated with puberty, pregnancy, death, and burial among the indigenous peoples of Natal and Zululand. Finding diverse forms of practice among different societies, Lugg focuses on those customs that he perceives to be common to most. Rites of puberty are first described. The author concludes that the reason offered for observing these customs—"these things were done by our forefathers"—is, in his view, unsatisfactory. Next, the customs of burial are discussed in detail, revealing aspects of social hierarchy and the importance of rituals of purification. The process of mourning and human relations with the spirits during the course of the year following the burial of the deceased are also described. Finally, pregnancy and childbirth are briefly mentioned, indicating that a woman's confinement and its management create an exclusively female space in which the woman giving birth is attended only by experienced married women.

D64   Lugg, H. C. (1929). "Agricultural Ceremonies in Natal and Zululand." *Bantu Studies*, vol. 3: 357-83.

As early as 1929, the author reports, the ceremonies he describes in this paper were fast disappearing. In many cases, they reflected the sociopolitical changes that had come with European domination. For example, authentically hereditary chiefs, who were zealous and meticulous in observing these ceremonies, had given way to government-appointed chiefs, who hid their illegitimacy and ignorance by omitting the ceremonies. The article is divided into three sections. After a general description of the ceremonies, rituals of Zulu kings are outlined, followed by accounts of the modified versions given by Chief Langalake Ngcobo and the Amabaso people. Two major annual agricultural ceremonies are identified: the *ukutat amageja* (the taking of the hoes) associated with the planting season and the arrival of the new year; and the *umkosi* (first-fruit) ceremony, which was divided into the "little" *umkosi* and the *umkosi* proper. It is by conducting these ceremonies that the king or chief renders the eating of new crops safe for the whole population and a bounteous harvest is assured. This is achieved by the symbolic purification and strengthening of the society's pillars—the king and his army—in doctorings that are shrouded in secrecy and symbolism. Prayers are offered and the praises of the king's ancestors are recited at the royal burial sites. As the one year draws to a close, old fires are extinguished throughout the land and a new fire, made by friction of sticks, inaugurates the new year as it is introduced to all corners of the polity.

D65   Magwaza, Thenjiwe (1993). *Orality and its Cultural Expressions in some Zulu Traditional Ceremonies*. M.A. thesis, University of Natal.

Magwaza's thesis analyzes the current practice of two Zulu ceremonies, the *umemulo* (for girls reaching marriageable age) and *umabo* (the giving of gifts by the bride's group to her in-laws after the wedding). The author shows that the content of the ceremonies remains largely oral and that they are handed down from generation to generation. Depending as they do on the power of the spoken word and its artistic devices as a means of ritual communication, the author describes how these ceremonies are an integral part of Zulu culture. Furthermore, they provide evidence that Zulu "tradition" has survived the Western influences, advanced urbanization, and industrialization. Since every traditional Zulu ceremony presupposes belief in the ancestors, the ancestors are always informed of the approaching occasion and the speakers also tell the ancestors what is happening throughout the ceremonies. Chapter Two is devoted to the "ancestor cult" and the strong influence the ancestors have on everyday life. Ancestor beliefs and associated ritual practices are described in detail, emphasizing the centrality of oral communication between the descendants and their ancestors. Ancestor manifestations and the ancestral practices associated with marriage are also detailed, explaining the symbolic significance of all the ritual objects and rites involved. In Chapters Three and Four Magwaza provides comprehensive and detailed studies of the oral aspects of the *umemulo* and *umabo* ceremonies respectively, stressing the importance of the social context from which the text arises. A bibliography is appended.

D66   Marks, Shula (1969). "Traditions of the Natal Nguni: A Fresh Look at the Work of A. T. Bryant." In Leonard Thompson (ed.) *African Societies in South Africa*. London: Heineman. 126-44.

This paper offers a preliminary attempt to assess the work of A. T. Bryant, indicating that a complete reclassification of his material would provide a springboard for further research into Nguni and Zulu history. Bryant's work, Marks argues, represents the most important single source of Nguni history before and during the Mfecane, as well as for understanding the structure of the nineteenth-century Zulu state. Identifying the widespread use of the term "Nguni" by current historians who try to avoid the use of the anachronistic term "Zulu" to address the people of the southeastern coast in pre-Mfecane times, Marks' approach is contextualized in a debate concerning the white colonial invention of ethnic and linguistic divisions among the indigenous peoples of southern Africa. Bryant, Marks suggests, would have just cause to lay claim to the invention of the term "Nguni." The central focus of the paper is on Bryant's *Olden Times in Zululand and Natal* and *A History of the Zulu*, aiming to sift through his cumbersome style and consistent intermingling of fact and fantasy, so that the validity of the traditions he records, as well as of the theories he constructs, can be assessed. The numerous and diverse societies studied by Bryant, and their social structures and genealogical complexities, are exhaustively discussed and problematized in the light of scholarship. Current field research, Marks concludes, will provide potential historical and linguistic resources to help confirm or disprove Bryant's hypotheses. The paper is extensively annotated.

D67   Marks, Shula (1978). "Natal, the Zulu Royal Family and the Ideology of Segregation." *Journal of Southern African Studies*, vol. 4, no. 2: 172-94.

Recognizing segregation to be a superstructural reflection of the concrete relations between the dominant and dominated classes, Marks explores Natal's policies of segregation and their bearing on the Zulu royal family in the twentieth century. In the presence of rapid industrialization, segregation policy ultimately served to rationalize bourgeois social relations in the midst of the formation of a massive black proletariat. Thus, by the mid-1920s the government attitude to the Zulu chiefs had altered from one of oppositional paranoia to mutual cooperation in an attempt to maintain a class alliance that linked the Zulu royal family, Natal's African petit bourgeoisie, and Zululand planters. Significant players in this regard were Heaton Nicholls, member of parliament for Zululand, and John Dube, leader of Natal's black bourgeoisie. The threatening intrusion of the Industrial and Commercial Workers' Union (ICU) into Natal is emphasized, showing how it resulted in a renewal of official interest in the Zulu royal family as a bulwark against change and a support for the ideology of segregation. Extensive reference to the traditions of Zulu society, the activities and role of its chiefs, and an emerging "pan-Zulu nationalism," offers valuable resources for the study of traditional African culture and religion in the context of colonial encounters in South Africa in the late nineteenth and early twentieth centuries. The article is extensively annotated from primary and secondary sources.

D68   Marks, Shula (1981). "The Drunken King and the Nature of the State: Aspects of Herrschaft in Early Twentieth Century Zululand." *The Ambiguities of Dependence: State, Nationalism and Class in Early Twentieth-Century Natal*. Johannesburg: Ravan Press. 16-41.

This extensively annotated chapter opens with the dramatic event of Solomon ka Dinuzulu's alleged "premeditated rudeness before a royal guest" at a ceremonial meeting of colonial administrators and African chiefs in July 1930 at Eshowe, the administrative capital of Zululand. The meeting was addressed by the Governor General of South Africa, the Earl of Athlone. Not the first of such episodes, Solomon later offered the excuse that he had been drunk. Whether a true example of in *vino veritas* or not, Solomon arguably used his confrontations with British royalty to boost his own position. The events serve to reveal the subtleties and contradictions inherent in the "many-layered nature of *herrschaft*" in early twentieth-century Zululand and Solomon's ambiguous position as heir to the last independent Zulu king, especially in terms of his relationship with the Natal administration and with his own people. Marks traces the origins of the Zulu kingdom in the nineteenth century up to the annexation of Zululand in 1887, showing that by the twentieth century, Natal's colonial authorities controlled the extraction of surplus in Zululand and Natal through manipulation of the chiefs and headmen. But the established *herrschaft* of the royal house was harder to control, and it was the Zulu king, the colonial administrators felt, who obstructed capitalist expansion in the area. Marks reveals the emergence of an ideology of segregation and domination that rested as much on class, though less overtly, as it did on color. By the 1920s, she concludes, Herzog's policies aimed to refurbish traditionalism, reconsolidate chiefdoms, and increase Solomon's role in uniting the Zulu nation. By these methods, Herzog tried to reinforce government control over African proletarianization and labor in the face of the subversive influences of "bolshevism" that was feared to be at work in labor organizations such as the Industrial and Commercial Workers Union.

D69   Marks, Shula (1989). "Patriotism, Patriarchy, and Purity: Natal and the Politics of Zulu Ethnic Consciousness." In Leroy Vail (ed.) *The Creation of Tribalism in Southern Africa*. London: James Currey; Berkeley and Los Angeles: University of California Press. 215-40.

Marks' insightful essay contributes to the understanding of forces underlying the explosion of violence in Natal in the mid-1980s, which, she argues, reside in the gross social deprivation of Durban's urban locations and informal settlements. The tragic events reveal the apartheid state's manipulation of ethnic politics and conceptual construction of "tribalism," as well as the reactionary influences of conservative African political leadership and "cultural" organizations in Natal that have glorified Zulu ethnic identity. Marks turns to an analysis of the nature and role of cultural ethnicity in the years leading up to Natal's anti-Indian riots of 1949 in order to illuminate the complexities of ethnicity implicit in the more recent violence. Twentieth-century Zulu ethnic consciousness, Marks argues, has been produced by the ideological labor, not only of the white ideologues of South Africa but also of the emerging black intelligentsia, manifest in organizations such as the Zulu Cultural Society formed in 1937. As the pressures of urbanization and proletarianism seemed to erode traditional values, the forces of conservatism focused on the position of African women. White colonial authorities, in particular, were only too ready to cooperate in reinforcing African patriarchal control of Zulu women. The painful ambiguities of cultural contact between Western and African cultures are further identified. The ambiguities of contact are clearly apparent, for instance, in moves to introduce "Bantu Dancing" into the Natal Department of Education's syllabus of 1948. The riots of 1949, like the recent violent eruptions in Natal, were also labeled "tribal." However, concludes Marks, those riots, like the violent conflicts of the 1980s in Natal, were the result of complex forces at work in the process of urbanization, such as social dislocation and intense poverty. Extensive notes are appended.

D70   Mayr, Fr. (1912). "Zulu Proverbs." *Anthropos*, vol. 7: 957-63.

This contribution to early twentieth-century southern African ethnography lists 129 Zulu proverbs—all of them brief and succinct—each accompanied by a literal translation and Mayr's own interpretation. Most revealing, perhaps, is the brief introductory paragraph which includes denigrating conceptions of the Zulu that are typical of European colonial reports at the turn of the century. Mayr depicts a Zulu wisdom, nobility, and pride tainted by savagery and greed, superstitious fears, and a childlike tendency to love those they most fear. The writer does, however, acknowledge the brevity and power of the proverbs.

D71   M'Timkulu, Donald (1977). "Some Aspects of Zulu Religion." In Newell S. Booth (ed.) *African Religion: A Symposium*. New York: NOK Publishers. 13-30.

M'Timkulu's chapter, without bibliography or annotations, provides an introduction to Zulu religious ideas and practices. Fundamental to his approach is a critique of the assumption among sociologists of Africa that the factor of social change is a consequence of the impact of Western culture on African societies. He thus reminds us that, on the contrary, African communities were not static and had an internal cultural dynamic of their own. He identifies two important aspects of social change in Zulu society which produced distinctive concepts within Zulu religion: First, the Zulu were the vanguard of a large migratory movement; and second, the "famous military genius" Shaka effected large-scale nation-building. M'Timkulu links his sociological analysis with the development of religious ideas by focusing on a definition of religion that includes the human creation of the sacred and the question of the individual's place in the universe. The main portion of the paper is devoted to a largely descriptive account of elements of Zulu religion, including the several names for a God or creator in the Zulu language and his role in Zulu life; spirit forces; divination and healing; marriage, family continuity, and the ancestors; and ritual and rites of passage. In addressing the disruptive effects of industrialization and demographic mobility on the family, the writer concludes the paper with a brief account of the development and role of African indigenous churches in this process, with particular emphasis on Shembe's Nazarite church.

D72   Mzolo, Douglas (1978). "Zulu Clan Praises." In John Argyle and Eleanor Preston-Whyte (eds.) *Social System and Tradition in Southern Africa*. Cape Town: Oxford University Press. 206-21.

Mzolo's study of Zulu clan praises sets out to redress the lack of attention to this type of praise poetry by scholars of traditional oral literature among South African Bantu-speaking societies. First, the author explores how Zulu clan identity is still preserved, despite the fact that in recent times members of a clan may be widely dispersed. The clan name, he continues, is usually that of the founder or a particularly famous member, although that name also frequently coincides with the name of some natural phenomenon. Address names (*isithakazelo*), often used as surnames, are also important in Zulu social relations and etiquette. Clan praises address the attributes of a group of individuals within the context of the clan as a collective, and are shared by every member of the clan. Unlike individual praises, which are usually known only by the person involved and the reciter, all clan members are expected to know as many of the clan praises as possible. Furthermore, clan praises do not require a specialist to recite them. It is only individual praises to chiefs that are recited by a specialist (*imbongi*). In relating the performance of clan praises by a professional bard, Mzolo describes how the audience is first prepared and how the recitations of individual praises and clan praises differ. Clan praises, usually performed for smaller audiences, lack the drama of movement and raising of the voice often enacted for individual praises. Stillness and dignity marks clan praising, while the audience reciprocates with respectful silence until the praise-poet is finished. Mzolo then analyzes the social functions of clan praises, showing that they generate a significant cohesive force among members of the clan. Zulu praises also serve to express appreciation and gratitude to a clan member and are often recited at ceremonial occasions, particularly weddings. Most important, the clan praises are performed for ritual purposes, especially for *ukubuyisa*, the bringing home of the spirit of the deceased. The remainder of the article is devoted to literary analysis of the linguistic features and poetic qualities and structure of the praise poems. References are appended.

D73   Neser, L. (1976). *Zulu Ethnography: A Classified Bibliography.* University of Zululand: Kwa Zulu Documentation Centre.

This useful bibliography of literature pertaining to the Zulu-speaking peoples of South Africa comprises twelve chapters that cover historical, cultural, socioeconomic, political, and religious features. Chapter Ten, "Religion, magic and healing," lists material that is particularly relevant for the study of African traditional religion in South Africa.

D74   Ngubane, Harriet (1976). "Some Notions of 'Purity' and 'Impurity' among the Zulu." *Africa*, vol. 46, no. 3: 274-84.

Ngubane's point of departure for this paper is that among the traditional patrilineal Zulu societies of South Africa, women are more often associated with mystical experiences than men. However, she points out, notions of purity and impurity are fundamental in this context. While daughters and sisters are most often associated with positive mystical forces as diviners, women who are wives or mothers are more often associated with negative or polluting mystical energies. In the Zulu language the notion of pollution is expressed by the term *umnyama* ("darkness of the night") and is linked to the marginal state believed to exist between life and death. It is Zulu married women, Ngubane explains, who are associated with birth and death and fulfill the important social role of forming a bridge between "this world" and the "other world" as "mother" of birth and death. When in a polluted state, such as occurs during gestation and childbirth, women are regarded as dangerous because they are marginal and ambiguous. However, by engaging in the correct behavior and ritual, a Zulu woman's procreative capacity is upheld as a benefit to society as a whole. By contrast, the writer points out, the diviner also embodies women's marginality, but in this case, as a point of contact between the two worlds. The diviner therefore occupies a state associated with light and purity. Ngubane's paper offers an informative analysis of the social significance of these two states of pollution and purity in Zulu cosmology, examining the process of stages experienced by women in each category, as well as the associated rituals performed. Notes and references are appended.

D75   Ngubane, Harriet (1977). *Body and Mind in Zulu Medicine: An Ethnography of Health and Disease in Nyuswa-Zulu Thought and Practice*. London: Academic Press.

This comprehensive and lucid analysis of Zulu concepts, beliefs, and practices related to health and disease is contextualized in the family relations and social organization of the Nyuswa-Zulu in the 1960s and 1970s. In Zulu society, the author states, health emerges from a balance between human beings and their environment, an ecological environment that is also fraught with mystical forces and dangers. Ngubane devotes several chapters to beliefs concerning the causes of disease, indicating that certain illnesses are attributed to natural causes, while others are engendered by sorcery, the ancestors, or ritual pollution. Such beliefs serve to articulate the stresses and conflicts within the family system, while ritual symbolism, most notably the color symbolism in medicines, plays a major role in healing and resolving the contradictions inherent in that system. Because of the subordinate position of women in this patriarchal and patrilineal social structure, tensions often arise in relation to rights over the reproductive powers of women. In a chapter on pollution, therefore, Ngubane analyzes the phases of pollution associated with childbirth, as well as those connected with death, where women play the central ritual role. In contrast, the author explains how the female Zulu diviner operates in a state of light and purity in close relationship with the ancestor spirits. In different ways, concludes Ngubane, Zulu women act as a bridge between this world and the other world of the spirits. A final chapter discusses and analyzes the beliefs, illnesses, and healing practices associated with notions of evil spirit possession. In sum, Ngubane portrays a complex and ordered system of ideas and healing practices that have prevailed and sustained the Zulu by providing satisfactory answers to the suffering and stress caused by illness and misfortune. Explanatory notes, a glossary, bibliography, and index are appended.

D76   Ngubane, Harriet (1981). "Aspects of Clinical Practice and Traditional Organization of Indigenous Healers in South Africa." *Social Science and Medicine*, vol. 15, no. 2: 361-65.

In this paper Ngubane draws on her research among the rural Zulu in South Africa to analyze and explain the methods and practices of indigenous healers. She first points to the significant differences in medical practice between Western-trained and traditional healers, particularly in terms of the doctor-patient relationship, documenting details of case-histories, diagnosis, and referral to other practitioners. A further distinction within Zulu indigenous medicine is described, namely, between the *inyanga*, who is usually male and uses African medicines in a non-clairvoyant manner and the *isangoma* (diviner), who is female and uses medicines and clairvoyance in her healing techniques. They both hold in common a view of the patient as a whole person. However, where the *inyanga* treats the patient directly, the *isangoma* is consulted by the afflicted person's family and relies on spiritual insights to identify the patient and to interpret the causes and consequences of his or her suffering. Ngubane pays particular attention to the role of the diviners as moral custodians, examining the networks of *isangoma* that function throughout the Nguni-speaking societies of eastern South Africa, especially among the Zulu. Their role, the writer argues, serves to maintain a meaningful worldview in a society beset by rapid changes and deep contradictions. Indicating that the diviners actively support each other to maintain the highest professional standards and moral conduct, Ngubane concludes that it is ironic that they have not been accepted by Western authorities.

D77   Ngubane, J. B. (1984). "The Role of the Amadhlozi/Amathongo as Seen in the Writings of W. B. Vilakazi." *Religion in Southern Africa*, vol. 5, no. 2: 55-75.

J. B. Ngubane's paper redresses the lack of research on Zulu literature that deals with the role of the *amadhlozi/amathongo* in Zulu religion and cosmology. He therefore discusses the literary works of the Zulu Catholic academic, B. W. Vilakazi (1906-1947), who was the first African to teach at a university for white students and whose Zulu novels and poems express an interweaving of

African and Western cultures. Although Vilakazi did not specifically write about the ancestors and ancestral spirits in his literary works, aspects of the roles of both the *amadhlozi* (those ancestors nearer to the living and belonging to each family) and the *amathongo* (a term that refers to both the *amadhlozi* and the general body of ancestors whose names are no longer known) are evident in his writing. The rest of the article focuses on identifying and examining Vilakazi's conceptions of the *amadhlozi/amathongo* within the framework of Zulu cosmology. Including extracts from Vilakazi's prose and poetry (cited in both Zulu and English), Ngubane addresses six specific points: First, he looks at the ancestors as inspiration for the living, giving them hope and courage for dealing with life in this world. Second, he discusses the notion that the ancestors provide and maintain the beautiful natural objects in the world, a notion that was important to Vilakazi's understanding of Zulu life. Third, he considers how the ancestors reveal themselves and offer guidance through dreams. Fourth, he addresses other ways in which the ancestors reveal themselves to the living in order to provide wisdom and inspiration. Fifth, he observes that the ancestors protect their dependents by ensuring good health and prosperity. Sixth, and finally, he notes how, on the communal level, the ancestors uphold the social and moral order of Zulu society. Reference notes and a bibliography are appended.

D78   Nxumalo, J. A. (1981). "Zulu Christians and Ancestor Cults: A Pastoral Consideration." In Heinz Kuckertz (ed.) *Ancestor Religion in Southern Africa*. Cacadu, Transkei: Lumko Missiological Institute. 65-78.

The focus of Nxumalo's paper is a discussion of the importance of ancestor veneration in the lives of Zulu Christians and Africans in general. Adopting a pastoral point of view, Nxumalo aims to accommodate African values, and in doing so, to enrich the Christian church. Basing his analysis on interviews with Zulu Christians, the writer's point of departure indicates that African traditional religion is not a dead religion dug up from an obsolete African past but is, in fact, very much alive. The ancestors, he asserts, play the central role in this vibrant religion. Nxumalo therefore extensively details the relationship between the ancestors and the living community, describing who the ancestors are and how they appear to the living, as well as the beliefs and ritual practices associated with ancestor veneration. Particular attention is given to *ukubuyisa*, the rite of "bringing back home" and the influence the dead then have on the living, noting from his interviews that levels of belief in the extent of that influence vary considerably. Nxumalo further argues that it is important for the Zulu pastor to consider psychological elements such as the sense of security and community the ancestors provide, and the emotional and feeling level of religious experience that ancestor veneration fulfills. A purely intellectual approach to the mystery of Christian faith will prove inadequate. To bring an appropriate catechism to Zulu Christians, the writer argues, pastors require a sound knowledge of modern social anthropology so that they can appreciate the relationship between the living and the dead in an African family. For Nxumalo, a resolution of the pastoral problem lies in the incorporation of traditional African ancestor veneration under the "Lordship of Christ." References are appended.

D79   Preston-Whyte, E. M. (1987). "Zulu Religion." In Mircea Eliade (ed.) *Encyclopedia of Religion*. New York: Macmillan. 15: 591-95.

Preston-Whyte's brief introductory essay on Zulu religion, informed by the work of anthropologists E. J. Krige and H. Ngubane, focuses on the *amadhlozi* (ancestors). The author contends that the basic concerns of traditional Zulu religion are the pursuit of health, fertility, and harmony between human beings and with nature. The *amadhlozi*, posits Preston-Whyte, are actively propitiated through goat or cattle sacrifice to restore harmony to the community. Whenever illness, misfortune, or any kind of unusual event occurs, the *isangoma* (diviner) is consulted, who then prescribes the requisite reparations to placate the anger of the ancestors. Preston-Whyte continues by identifying and defining the various Zulu deities, in particular, uMvelinqangi, known as the creator god, iNkosi yeZulu, the lord of the sky and heaven, and iNkosazana yeZulu, a female deity closely associated with fertility of crops, cattle, and rain. The natural order, claims the author, impinges closely on human beings who are related to it both physically and psychically. While certain diseases "just happen" as the result of natural causes that can be treated with medicines, others may result from invidious objects that have absorbed improprietous "tracks" (*imikhondo*) in the surrounding atmosphere. Further, certain persons (for example, newborn infants and menstruating women) may temporarily enter a weakened state (*umnyama*), leaving them susceptible to malign influences, sorcery, bad luck, or misfortune. The articles closes with a brief analysis of the phenomenon of "spirit possession" among the Zulu and the role played by the diviner in establishing a cure through rapprochement between the spirit world and humanity. A short section deals with the emergence of African independent churches among Zulu communities that blend Christian and traditional elements.

D80   Raum, O. F. (1973). *The Social Function of Avoidances and Taboos Among the Zulu*. Berlin and New York: Walter de Gruyter.

Raum's comprehensive study makes the semantic distinction between *hlonipha* (avoidance) and *zila* (taboo) in Zulu society, aiming to clarify theoretical complexities concerning ritual prohibitions that are generalized as "taboos" in anthropological literature. *Hlonipha* actions, or deferential avoidance actions, occur in dyadic relations and accentuate the inferior and superior positions in the dyad. This conduct, argues the author, is ritualized in that it is formalized and institutionalized. Raum's detailed analysis indicates that avoidances, expressed in speech, action, and spatial areas, occur in the family, between generations, and in relations with the ancestors. He suggests that sacralization of avoidance is already established at the level of the family, for example, where filial *hlonipha* anticipates the son's attitude towards his deceased father in ancestor veneration. *Zila* behavior, however, focuses on the ritualized conduct of one central actor as part of a group, particularly in the context of diachronic rituals that mark the developmental stages of life. Occupational ritual taboo regimens are also associated with the diviner, weather-maker, hunter, and warrior. The effectiveness of their appeal to the realm of the supernatural, Raum asserts, is contingent on their meticulous observance of the taboos, through which they attain a special psychic or ritual condition. Mystic sanctions, however, always maintain the social and moral order that is rooted in reverence for the ancestors and the creator as founders of that order. In sum, Raum affirms that the important social functions of Zulu adherence to *hlonipha* and *zila* does not imply a type of utilitarian "means-end" conduct, but constitutes symbolic behavior that maintains correct attitudes and well-being in both dyadic and group relations. A list of informants and bibliography are appended.

D81   Raum, O. F. (1987). "A Zulu Diviner Visits a University." *Anthropos*, vol. 82, no. 4/6: 469-87.

Raum's article gives an account of the visits of two Zulu diviners, Laduma Madela and his assistant, Thabethe Muziwezixhwala, to the University of Fort Hare in 1960 and 1963 at the invitation of the Anthropology Department. Laduma gave several lectures on Zulu culture to anthropology students—who were soon joined by theology, philosophy, and science students—covering topics ranging from Zulu creation myths to the role of lightning doctors. Supplementing his talks with his drawings depicting mythological beings and stories, Laduma was also willing to enter into lively debate with the students. Raum's report shows that the students' immediate response to Laduma's teaching and impressive rhetoric was enthusiastic and overwhelmingly positive, although later ideological assessments after the diviners' departure showed a more critical bias. Excursions organized for Laduma and Thabethe to Lovedale Mission Station, a Bushman cave, and the Indian Ocean are also detailed, including their meeting with the Paramount Chief of the Rharhabe. Laduma also consulted the famous Xhosa diviner, Njajula, as well as meeting a well-known European "sensitive," Prof. T. H. Haarhoff. Results of various psychological tests carried out on the two diviners are also recorded, followed by accounts of ideological debate and tension between Laduma and theology students. The article is concluded with Laduma's own report of his visit to Fort Hare. Of particular interest in this descriptive report are the ideological tensions revealed between indigenous and Christian African worldviews. References are appended.

D82   Reader, D. H. (1966). *Zulu Tribe in Transition: The Makhanya of Southern Natal*. Manchester: Manchester University Press.

Reader's anthropological study, originally presented for a doctoral degree, is based on literature research and fourteen months of fieldwork conducted among the Makhanya people of Natal during 1950 to 1951. The book comprises twenty-one chapters divided into four main parts: "The Territorial System"; "The Kinship System"; "The Politico-Judicial System"; and "Social Systematics." Although focusing largely on socioeconomic issues, Reader's work includes reference to Zulu religious belief and ritual. Of particular interest is a comparative study of "pagan" and Christian marriage in Chapters Thirteen and Fourteen. Reader traces the process of Zulu customs and rites from early adolescent "love-relations" through the complex negotiations and preparations for marriage and, finally, the three days of the wedding itself. The symbolic significance of several ritual practices are analyzed, such as ritual dance, speeches, and beer-drinks on the first day; animal sacrifice and integration rites on the second day, reserved for the religious integration of the bride with the ancestors of her new descent group; and further aggregation rites performed on the third day to ensure the bride's acceptance as a functional member of her father-in-law's kin. Chapter Eighteen, describing war and hunting, discusses the ritual purification of the warriors in preparation for battle, as well as the war-doctor's rites for strengthening the warriors. Diagrams, maps, and photographs accompany the text and a glossary, bibliography, and index are appended.

D83   Samuelson, L. H. (1912). *Some Zulu Customs and Folk-lore*. London: Church Printing Company.

In this collection of short stories, Samuelson writes of her experiences of Zulu religion during the years she spent growing up on her father's mission station in Zululand. Although colored by a Christian missionary approach in South Africa at the turn of the century—one that characterized the Zulu people as "heathen" and "backward" and their religion as superstition—Samuelson's stories offer insight into Zulu religious beliefs and practices based on personal observations and experiences. For example, the stories include, among others, a Zulu wedding; a ritual sacrifice to the ancestral spirits; rituals associated with the death of a chief; the rites officiated by the war-doctor before battle; the detection of "wizards" by the diviner, under the instruction of the *amadhlozi* (ancestral spirits); the activities of the Zulu king's rain-doctors; and the annual prayers for crops, when young girls go out into the hills for a day to fast and pray to Nomkubulwana (the Heavenly Princess) for a good harvest. Another very brief story tells of an instance when Samuelson, as a child, tried to kill a snake—"an accursed creature"—only to be stopped by several Zulu men who claimed the snake to be the spirit of their chief's dead father. The author's account illustrates the oppositional character of Christian and Zulu systems of belief that were both rooted in their respective religious mythologies and situated in colonial encounters.

D84   Samuelson, L. H. (1930). *Zululand: Its Traditions, Legends, Customs, and Folk-lore*. Natal: Mariannhill Mission Press.

This volume combines new narrative accounts of Zulu stories (in Part One) with Samuelson's previous collection (1912), which is presented in Part Two. The first part, "Zululand, Its Traditions, Legends and Customs," includes Zulu folktales, as well as customs associated with religious beliefs and rituals. For example, the burial and mourning rites for Zulu kings are described with reference to the death of King Mpande in 1872. Samuelson also documents beliefs concerning the spirit world and the training of diviners, both men and women, although their practices are characterized by the author as "tricks and impostures." In "Spirits of various ranks," she argues that the Zulu classify their spirits to correspond with social rank among the living, referring to the ranking of different types of "spirit-snakes." The collection as a whole offers insight into Zulu myth and oral tradition, but is primarily of interest as an illustration of Christian missionary perspectives on African traditional religion in Zululand during the late nineteenth and early twentieth centuries. Photographs and drawings accompany the text.

D85   Samuelson, R. C. A. (1929). *Long, Long Ago*. Durban: Knox.

Samuelson's memoirs of childhood and youth on his father's Natal mission station in the latter half of the nineteenth century contain anecdotal stories of events and travels, ranging from family picnics to European opinions about the Bambatha rebellion. Accounts of Zulu religion, and colonial missionary attitudes towards it, appear mostly in the numerous appendices. For example, burial and mourning rites are discussed in some detail, describing ceremonies such as *ukubuyisa*, where the spirit of the deceased is invited to return to the family. Samuelson's invective against Zulu "witchdoctors" portrays figures of murderous intent "possessed of greatest cunning and hypocrisy." Responsible for death and suffering among their people, he continues, the diviner plays on their superstitions and fear of witchcraft. Another piece, taken from his father's papers, gives an account of Nomkubulwana, the "Goddess of Heaven," and the young Zulu girls' annual festival, where the goddess is petitioned for the fertility of the year's crops. Other customary religious rites are briefly documented, such as boys' circumcision rituals and puberty rites for girls. In terms of religious worship, the Great, Great One (Unkulunkulu) is mentioned, although, says the author, the Zulu are most influenced by the ancestor spirits, who are thought to be the origin of all that befalls them, good or bad. Written at a time when ethnologists sought for the origins of South African indigenous peoples, Samuelson offers his own contributions to diffusionist theory. Not only were the Zulu descendants of the Ethiopians under Moses, but they also had contact with Romans and were used as gladiators in Rome. Also, claims the author, Zulu ancestors clearly had contact with Greeks and Jews. Photographs accompany the text.

D86   Sayce, R. V. (1926). "Lightning Charms from Natal." *Man*, vol. 26, no. 41: 69-70.

This brief contribution to the study of indigenous religion in Natal in the 1920s describes the use of ritual objects for protection against lightning. Before the first storms of spring, Sayce reports, the people call on the *"Umgoma"* (translated as "witch doctor" by the writer) to perform the necessary ritual to protect their huts from the destructive power of lightning. Wooden pegs treated with special medicines are driven into the ground at intervals around the hut. But of central importance is the "lightning stone," a stone peg that is placed just outside the hut at the foot of the right door-post. This stone, usually of dolerite, is most often obtained from a hill-top where lightning has struck and fractured the rock. A charm made of special ingredients is placed in the hole before inserting the peg to prevent the stone from being dislodged by lightning. Once the stone peg is in place, it, too, is dressed with protective medicines. Recompensed with some money and an ox, the *"Umgoma"* returns each year to reapply medicines to the pegs. Sayce's information was gathered from a "native servant" and interpreted by two colonial officers.

D87   Schlosser, Katesa, ed. (1972). *Zauberei im Zululand: Manuskripte des Blitzzauberers Laduma Madela*. Kiel: Kommissionsverlag Schmidt and Klaunig.

The introductory section of the book provides a biographical sketch of Madela, a prophetic figure living in Cezaberg who claimed to have been receiving visions and hearing voices from the creator God uMvelinqangi since 1950. The fundamental categories that structure the book are introduced and elaborated. Essentially these are constituted by the roles of the *inyanga* (healer), the *isangoma* (prophet, soothsayer), and the *abathakathi* (practitioners of black magic). The remainder of the massive volume consists of Madela's teachings, interpretations, and narratives which develop and illustrate how these technicians of the sacred function within Zulu society. Two main theological themes emerge in Madela's interest in the origin of death and the forms of immortality. The text is in German.

D88   Schlosser, Katesa ed. (1977). *Die Bantubibel des Blitzzauberers Laduma Madela*. Kiel: Kommissionsverlag Schmidt & Klaunig.

The volume is a "Bantu Bible," asserts Laduma Madela, who composed the text after being instructed to do so by the creator God, uMvelinqangi. An introductory section describes the elaborate visions of the God that were experienced by Madela, along with his own interpretation of those epiphanies. According to Madela the God commanded him to compose a Bible that would call Zulus back to their own traditions, yet still serve as a "brother" to the Christian Bible. The text itself forms an elaborate creation myth that describes the origin and nature of the "five worlds" and their inhabitants. The figure of Sibi, uMvelinqangi's evil brother, is introduced, and certain analogues to the Christian Satan are brought in to clarify the nature of this evil deity. The volume is illustrated by photographs of Madela and contains a number of his own drawings. The text is in German.

D89   Scotch, Norman A. (1970). "Magic, Sorcery, and Football among Urban Zulu: A Case of Reinterpretation under Acculturation." In John Middleton (ed.) *Black Africa: Its Peoples and Their Cultures Today*. London: Macmillan. 248-52.

In this brief essay Scotch follows Gluckman's theory that African witchcraft beliefs may expand and change in the process of acculturation, frequently persisting as a causal explanation for the inexplicable in relation to disease, conflict, and misfortune. Focusing on his recent research among Zulu-speakers in Durban, the author discusses one such innovative application of magic and sorcery in the context of urban Zulu men's enthusiasm for football. Each football team usually employs an *inyanga* (Zulu doctor) to strengthen the team through ritual and magic, as well as to forestall any sorcery that might be directed against them from a rival team's *inyanga*. Success or failure of a team, it seems, often depends more on the skills of the *inyanga* than those of the players. Although much importance is placed by a team on acquiring "star players," the supernatural is enlisted through ritual and ceremony for many occasions. For example, the propitiatory slaughter of a goat is often performed, and players are doctored with various medicines by the *inyanga* during the "camping out" or seclusion of the team the night before a match. Doctoring rituals and the formation of the team as it enters the field, argues the author, reveal a strong parallel to the Zulu military preparations and formations of Shaka's time. Consistent victories by a particular team are almost always explained with reference to magic—if it is not the practices of an *inyanga*, then it is believed to be the "magic" of injections used by European doctors. Most significantly, Scotch concludes, the use of sorcery and warfare rituals in the context of the sport illustrates the adaptation of old ways of expressing aggression and conflict in the modern conflictual and anomic situation of African urban life in South Africa. References in the essay refer to the bibliography appended to the main text.

D90   Shooter, Joseph (1857). *The Kafirs of Natal and the Zulu Country.* London: E. Stanford.

The eleven chapters of this volume by British missionary, Joseph Shooter, represent four years of study of the Zulu people in the mid-nineteenth century. The work draws heavily on the anecdotal writings of Francis Fynn and covers domestic, political, legal, social, and religious institutions in Zulu society, as well as arts and crafts and the military. In reference to domestic life (Chapter Three), Shooter includes a description of marriage ceremonies, while discussion of social institutions (Chapter Seven) covers burial and death rites. Chapter Six, under the heading "Superstitions," is devoted to Shooter's observations on Zulu religion. Although he begins with discussion of Unkulunkulu, the creator, and Zulu cosmogonic mythology, the author continues by claiming that the Zulu ascribe great power to the ancestral spirits, elevating them to the rank of deities who are worshipped along with Unkulunkulu. Status in the spirit world reflects that which was held in life, where the departed spirit of a chief, for instance, cares for the tribe and that of a father cares for his family. Sacrifices offered to the ancestors are detailed in three categories: sacrifices for averting evil; sacrifices to procure a blessing; and sacrifices to offer thanks. "Seers and prophets" or "witchdoctors" (diviners), who include both men and women, are largely characterized as clever impostors who hold power and influence according to their perceived close relationship with the spirits. Shooter offers accounts of their divining activities in pointing out evil-doers, as well as the process of initiation, where the neophyte diviner manifests an array of exotic symptoms. In addition, the author refers at length to past Xhosa prophets and the Xhosa Cattle Killing. Appendices refer to missionary operations in Natal, a list of tribes, and the Zulu orthography. Illustrations appear in the text.

D91   Sibisi, H. (1975). "The Place of Spirit Possession in Zulu Cosmology." In M. G. Whisson and M. West (eds.) *Religion and Social Change in Southern Africa.* Cape Town: David Philip. 48-57.

Sibisi's anthropological paper explores the phenomenon of spirit possession among the Nguni-speaking peoples of South Africa. First the author explains the concept of spirit in Zulu cosmology, particularly in relation to the passage of the spirit from the "world below" to "this world" during birth. Sibisi points to the spiritual and social significance of gender in Zulu society, indicating how married women are associated with both birth and death and are therefore considered marginal. Traditional spirit possession of the diviner (*isangoma*) is discussed, emphasizing that the majority of Zulu diviners are women. These women are known to be particularly close to the spirits and thus fulfill the essential social role of forming a bridge between the spirit and human worlds. Moving to an analysis of the notion of evil, the author discusses the new types of spirit possession (*indiki* and *ufufunyane*), and medicines used to treat them, that accompanied the onset of industrialization at the turn of the century in Natal and Zululand. In her conclusion, Sibisi argues that "the notion of evil-spirit possession among the Zulu is used as an idiom to handle the escalating incidence of psychoneurosis" that is frequently associated with the acute stress involved in adapting to life in colonial and postcolonial industrial society. Recognizing the need to ensure the continuity of Zulu society, the author insists, the diviners and "ethno-doctors" use prophylactic measures "taken at a mystical level of treatment to reassure people that their young are protected." The paper is annotated.

D92   Tyler, Josiah (1971). *Forty Years Among the Zulu*. Cape Town: Struik (orig. edn. Boston and Chicago: Congregational Sunday-School & Publishing Co., 1891).

Reverend Tyler's book is based on his life as a missionary in South Africa from 1849 to 1889. The numerous chapters that comprise this volume include several that relate to Zulu religious belief and practice. Chapter Eleven, for instance, is devoted to "Spirit Worship" offering Tyler's view of Zulu veneration of their ancestors. He notes that the Zulu believe in the survival of the spirit (*umoya*) after death, and that spirits, both good and evil, often manifest on earth in the form of a snake. Arguing that the Zulu in fact worship the ancestral spirits, Tyler describes propitiatory animal sacrifices that are offered to the spirits in the face of events such as illness or misfortune. The author also addresses the role of diviners, claiming that "they work powerfully on the superstitions of their countrymen"—superstitions, he continues, that are legion among the Zulu people. Chapter Twelve covers his observations concerning these "superstitions." The next chapter addresses the subject of polygamy, portraying the "evil practice" as the greatest barrier to Christianity. Zulu wedding ceremonies, funerals, and death rites are also discussed. Much of the text describes difficulties facing the Christian missions and Tyler's account of the evangelization and education of the Zulu. Illustrations are included in the text and an index is appended.

D93   Van Rensburg, K. A. J. (1973). "Acculturation and the Zulu Concept of God." *Missionalia*, vol. 1, no. 3: 142-46.

In order to ascertain the influence of the "traditional" Zulu concept of God in the process of acculturation, it is necessary to define what that concept of God is, suggests Van Rensburg. His short essay, outlining typical Zulu terms for divine beings such as uMvelinqangi and uNkulunkulu, is of note, however, more for its theoretical bias that reproduces the stereotype of an unchanging traditionalism than it is for an historical account of changes in meaning that occurred as a result of modernism and urbanization. Defining Zulu culture as less complex than Western culture and the Zulu concept of God as vague, Van Rensburg contends that studies of traditional Zulu religion show that the divine beings represented in Zulu cosmology have very little influence on daily life in the context of modernization and urbanization. He further concludes that because the traditional concept of God is overly anthropomorphic, making the distinction between God and "man" too faint, it cannot be incorporated into the Christian faith in which the line between divinity and humanity is clearly drawn. Little space is given to early traveler or missionary accounts of terms for a high god in African religion, and the material is drawn primarily from the work of *volkekunderists* and white South African missiologists. Footnotes accompany the text.

D94   Vilakazi, Absolom (1962). "Religious Aspects of the Social Order." *Zulu Transformations: A Study of the Dynamics of Change*. Pietermaritzburg: University of Natal Press. 87-107.

This annotated chapter of Vilakazi's study of the effects of social change in Zulu-speaking societies focuses on indigenous religious systems, as well as on the effects of Christianity on those systems. First, the author notes that the Christian teachings of God's omnipotence has affected even the "traditionalist" ideas about uNkulunkulu or uMvelinqangi, the creator of the world. But fundamental to traditional Zulu religion, says Vilakazi, is the distinction made between the following three human components: *inyama*, the physical body that decomposes after death; *umoya*, the vital force that keeps the human being alive; and *isithunzi*, "a shadow," meaning the personality or force of character that, according to Zulu thought, lives on after death as an ancestral spirit. Discussing the role of the ancestral spirits, the author emphasizes the great distance that exists between uNkulunkulu or uMvelinqangi and humanity. Vilakazi argues that the idea of the ancestors as mediators between humans and the creator is relatively undeveloped in Zulu thought and, in fact, he defines the human relationship with the ancestral spirits as "worship." The pivotal part played by the ancestral spirits in everyday practice of traditional Zulu religion and the central significance of the husband's ancestors are stressed, indicating a system of religious thought that is founded on closely knit agnatic kinship bonds. The rest of the chapter looks at the functions of the church as a symbol of integration, status, and social control, analyzing emerging class distinctions and conflictual leadership struggles between "traditionalists" and a new educated Christian elite.

D95   Wanger, W. (1923-26). "The Zulu Notion of God According to the Traditional Zulu God-Names." *Anthropos*, vol. 18/19: 656-87; vol. 20: 558-78; vol. 21: 351-85.

Rev. Wanger's specialist philological treatise, in three extensive parts, addresses the question of whether the Zulu-speaking peoples have "any notion of the true God," basing his arguments on a study of their "traditional God-names" and religious traditions. Therefore, Wanger implies a distinction between the "true God" of European Christianity and African religious conceptions of God. However, he introduces his study with an incisive critique of early scientists and missionaries who came to south-eastern Africa and identified the indigenous peoples as, among other things, barbarous savages, heathens, and superstitious fetish-worshippers who could not possibly have any notion of the true God—citing the one exception of Colenso, whose more empathetic and sensitive approach to the Zulu was well known. The problems of communication arising from a lack of understanding of African rules of social etiquette, and most significantly, from a lack of linguistic and philological training among Europeans, are also considered. The remainder of the first part of the paper is devoted to an exhaustive analysis of written works concerning Zulu religion and god-names by several missionaries and scholars, including Colenso, J. L. Döhne, Callaway, A. T. Bryant, W. Schneider, Andrew Lang, and W. Schmidt. The second part continues with an analysis of works by C. Meinhof, V. Cathrein, and Sir Harry H. Johnston. Underpinning Wanger's approach is the problematic of the pronunciations and interpretations of the Zulu god-name Unkulunkulu, particularly with regard to Zulu conceptions of the ancestors and arguments that the name, differently pronounced, can refer to either the "most ancient" or the first man or woman. For example, suggests Wanger, "*kulu*" could mean either "old" or "great." Arguments are made for the coexistence of both a knowledge of the true God, Unkulunkulu, and a concept of the first ancestor, *unkulunkulu*, which formed the basis of Zulu "ancestor-worship" and "paganism." The third and concluding part of Wanger's thesis specifically addresses what the Zulu-speaking peoples themselves have to say about the problem of god-names. The writer draws on information tendered to both Colenso and Callaway, including the telling of ancient Zulu cosmogonic myths that imply diverse interpretations of Unkulunkulu, followed by explanations of several further Zulu god-names. Wanger concludes that Zulu tradition shows knowledge of the "true God" to a far greater extent than had previously been acknowledged. Furthermore, he argues that cultural contact and the influence of Christian missions has not invalidated research on indigenous religion in Africa—ancient Zulu tradition and myths of origin have remained unchanged, even if presented in modern form.

D96   Werner, Alice (1921). "Some Notes on Zulu Religious Ideas." *Folk-Lore*, vol. 32: 28-44.

Werner's article is devoted to a close examination of papers left by Henry Callaway that were written after the publication of his major text, *The Religious System of the Amazulu*. First, Werner deals with Callaway's notes on divine and quasi-divine names, most specifically Unkulunkulu. Names found to be used among the Xhosa-speaking peoples, such as Umdali, Utixo, and Qamatha, are also addressed in some detail. For example, Werner notes Callaway's argument that Utixo was the praise-name given to an ancient hero after victory in battle. Circumstances where prayers and rituals are offered to these various divine beings and the question of the confusion between a "high god" and "first ancestor" are also found in Callaway's notes. Second, Callaway's accounts of the initiation of doctors and diviners, their various levels of expertise, and their healing techniques are discussed and explained. A final section examines Callaway's research on the rules of *hlonipha* (the avoidance of names), both in speech and action, within the Zulu family system. In this regard, relations of respect between men and women, children and parents and parents-in-law, and grandchildren and grandparents, are suffused with complex customs and regulations concerning the utterance of names. The consequences of and atonement for the breaking of *hlonipha* are included in this account. Footnotes accompany the text.

6 Sotho-Tswana Religion

In the aftermath of the South African War, the British War Office compiled a report on the beliefs, customs, and society of Sotho-Tswana-speaking people in the Transvaal. That report paid special attention to religion, detailing traditional Sotho-Tswana beliefs and practices with respect to totems and taboos, ancestors and witchcraft, marriage and burial, and other aspects of African religious life. Although the War Office insisted that the Sotho-Tswana could not be regarded as monotheists, since "no trace can be discovered among the ancient traditions of belief in any one universal supreme being corresponding to God," it nevertheless found that religion performed an important function in their social order. According to the War Office, African religious traditions maintained the "tribal" cohesion of small-scale African political groupings. The War Office identified its own practical interest in keeping African "tribal" units intact. If they disintegrated, the War Office warned, "a general fusion of hitherto antagonistic tribes would then be possible, and this would constitute a far greater danger to the white community than is to be apprehended from any of the present tribes" (Massie, 1905: 121). As a military strategy, therefore, the British War Office recommended measures to recognize and preserve the distinctive religious traditions of Sotho-Tswana communities in southern Africa.

Certainly, this military strategy was at odds with the religious objectives of Christian missionaries in the region, such as the Reverend J. A. Winter, who insisted that the Sotho-Tswana had no religion, and, as a result, were nothing more than deluded, lazy, morally corrupt, beer-drinking heathens (Winter, 1915). Throughout the nineteenth century, Christian missionaries had consistently denied the existence of any Sotho-Tswana religion. The Sotho-Tswana might have had "superstitions," but they had no religion. In the early decades of the twentieth century, however, the missionary slander repeated by the Rev. Winter was for the most part replaced by vigorous attempts to document in detail the traditional religious beliefs and practices of the Sotho-Tswana.

Although archaeologists have argued that the basic distinction between Sotho and Tswana can be traced back to different settlement patterns over the past five hundred years (Maggs, 1976), a diversity of Sotho-Tswana political groupings took shape during the nineteenth century under the pressures of intercultural contact, advancing colonialism, emerging capitalism, and, in certain cases, the influence of Christian missions (see Burman, 1981; Eldridge, 1993; Legassick, 1969; Lye, 1969; 1971; Lye and Murray, 1980). In the scholarly literature, these political groupings have been organized into different constellations—Southern Sotho, Northern Sotho, Pedi, and Tswana. These basic divisions are also reflected in the literature on Sotho-Tswana traditional religion.

As a result, we find summary overviews of African traditional religion among the Southern Sotho who lived in colonial Basutoland and independent Lesotho, from the early missionary reports (Casalis, 1861; Ellenberger, 1912) to the more recent anthropological and historical accounts (Ashton, 1952; Dutton, 1923; Sheddick, 1953). By contrast, the literature on Northern Sotho religion is almost exclusively anthropological, exemplified by classic studies of the beliefs and practices of Sotho-speaking people in the Transvaal, the Lovedu (Krige, 1932; 1954; Krige and Krige, 1943; 1954) and the Kgaga (Hammond-Tooke, 1981). Receiving special attention in the anthropological literature, the Pedi polity of the Transvaal has been documented by one book-length monograph that pays particular attention to religion (Mönnig, 1967), but it has also been the subject of specific research on initiation ritual (Pitje, 1950; Roberts and Winter, 1916); on rainmaking ritual (Eiselen, 1928); on fire ritual (Eiselen, 1929); on witchcraft accusations (Sansom, 1972); on beliefs in God (Mogoba, 1981); and even, again by the Reverend J. A. Winter, on the persistence of an alleged Pedi "phallus cult" (Winter, 1913). Finally, the religion of Tswana-speaking communities has been thoroughly inventoried (Alverson, 1978; Brown, 1926; Molema, 1920; Pauw, 1955; Willoughby, 1928; 1932).

The general character of these overviews and inventories of Sotho-Tswana religion can be suggested by the work of the missionary, ethnographer, and comparative religionist, W. C. Willoughby. Arriving in 1893, Willoughby represented the London Missionary Society among the Tswana until he left for the United States in 1919 to become Professor of African Missions at the Kennedy School of Missions at Hartford Theological Seminary in Connecticut. Although Willoughby published reports on Tswana totemism and initiation while he was in southern Africa (Willoughby, 1905; 1909), his comprehensive volumes—*The Soul of the Bantu* (1928) and *Nature Worship and Taboo* (1932)—gave the broadest and most detailed picture of African traditional religion. As summarized in these two books, Tswana religion encompassed beliefs and practices in relation to ancestor spirits. It posited an underworld that was inhabited by spirits of the dead and modeled after the familiar pattern of the human community of the living. The Tswana achieved communication with the ancestors through dreams, spirit possession, and techniques of divination; they propitiated the ancestors through sacrifice, libations, prayers, and praises. The natural world provided points of entry—sacred stones, caves, fountains, trees, and celestial phenomena—through which ancestral spirits intervened. The social world was organized by taboos governing diet, gender relations, sexuality, and death, that were enforced by ancestral sanctions. In all these respects, Sotho-Tswana religion could be represented as religious, spiritual, or ritual relations with ancestors.

The precise role of God in Sotho-Tswana religion has been a controversial question. During the nineteenth century, European Christian missionaries appropriated a Sotho-Tswana term—Morimo, Molimo, or Modimo—to designate the Supreme Being of Christianity. Although some commentators have argued that Modimo emerged as the God of African traditionalists through an innovative adaptation of Christian missionary ideas (Sheddick, 1953), it is extremely difficult to disentangle the strands of Christian and traditional discourse about Modimo. S. M. Molema suggested that the Sotho-Tswana held hazy and vague ideas about God that nevertheless revealed sparks of a "higher faith" such as the faith found in Christianity or Islam (Molema, 1920). By contrast, Gabriel Setiloane insisted that Sotho-Tswana religion disclosed a God that was bigger, deeper, and more profound than the God of Christianity. As numinous power or vital force, Modimo is a supra-personal identity—the supreme "It"—that can only be described in terms of a "negative theology" as an invisible, intangible, unknown, and unspoken mystery (Setiloane, 1973; 1976; see Nürnberger, 1975).

The ancestors (*badimo*) have certainly played a prominent role in Sotho-Tswana religion. Although the anthropologists E. J. Krige and J. D. Krige referred to Lovedu ancestors as "gods" and as divine beings addressed through prayer (Krige and Krige, 1943; Krige, 1954), the *badimo* have most often been interpreted as intermediaries between humans and the spiritual world (Mogoba, 1981) or as the "living dead" that maintain ongoing relations with the living and thereby make up the broader human community (Setiloane, 1976). That human community is anchored in the home, homestead, or settlement.

In Sotho-Tswana religion of the home, religious practices are dedicated to strengthening the spiritual aspect (*siriti*) of the person that is most evident in the quality of interpersonal relations (Mönnig, 1967). The spiritual harmony of the home is established at the intersection of a symbolism of sacred space and a symbolism of "coolness" and "heat." In the spatial symbolism of Sotho-Tswana domestic religion, the settlement (*motse*), which is spiritually strengthened through ongoing ritual relations with ancestors, is distinguished from the wild, unpredictable, and potentially dangerous region of the bush (*naga*) (Comaroff, 1981). But the life of the homestead is also structured through an elaborate symbolism of "coolness" and "heat." In simple terms, rain, good health, and social harmony are "cool"; blood, birth, abortion, menstruation, and contact with death are "hot" and must be dealt with through rituals designed to reduce "heat" and produce "coolness" (Schapera, 1979; Verryn, 1981). At the same time, however, certain forms of heat, such as fermentation, gestation, and transformation in rites of passage marking birth, initiation into adulthood, marriage, and death, are positive (Bosko, 1981). The religion of the home, therefore, requires a sensitivity to the spiritual temperature of human action.

Cattle and beer are the primary ritual media used in ancestral rituals of the home. In the "bovine mystique" of Sotho-Tswana religion, cattle are maintained for symbolic, religious, and social reasons (Ferguson, 1985; Comaroff and Comaroff, 1990). Rituals may be performed to strengthen cattle and to protect the cattle kraal from the evil influences of witches or sorcerers (Schapera, 1930). Specially brewed beer has a sacred significance as the ritual food of the ancestors. In many cases, beer offerings have been the preferred method of communicating with the *badimo* (Krige, 1932).

Among traditional rites of passage, Sotho-Tswana initiation and marriage have received special attention in the literature (see Schapera, 1930). Tswana initiation required two separate, but coordinated ritual sequences, the *bogwera* for boys and the *bojale* for girls (Roberts and Winter, 1916; Willoughby, 1909). In both cases, initiation represented not only a ritual transition but also a program of education (Pitje, 1950). Although different gender roles were reinforced during these rites of initiation, religion arguably provided a significant avenue of independence for women (Kinsman, 1983).

Rather than a single event, traditional marriage is an extended process. The stages of that process involve negotiations between families, the transfer of gifts, a period in which the couple resides with the wife's family, the establishment of a household with the husband's family, and the presentation of the traditional bridewealth (*bogadi* or *bohali*) by the husband to the wife's family (John Comaroff, 1980; Jean and John Comaroff, 1981; Kuper, 1975; Matthews, 1940; Murray, 1976; 1977; Schapera, 1957; 1971). As elsewhere in southern Africa, the Sotho-Tswana practice of paying bridewealth was vigorously attacked by Christian missionaries. "Only by renouncing the heathen concept of *bogadi*," one missionary declared in the 1930s, "is it possible to build up a vigorous Christian Church among the Natives of South Africa" (Jennings, 1933). That practice, however, formed an integral part of a ritual process that linked entire families in relations of exchange. As such, it has been central to the religious life of the home.

Literature on religion and society in the traditional Sotho-Tswana polity has emphasized mechanisms for maintaining social order. In the earlier literature, Sotho-Tswana "totemism"—the supposed "worship" of sacred animal emblems—was identified as a religious mechanism for maintaining the social bonds of different "tribes" (Lekgothoane, 1938; Lestrade, 1928; Willoughby, 1905). By the 1930s, however, with the publication of Isaac Schapera's classic *Handbook of Tswana Law and Customs* (1938), focus shifted from "totemism" to the role of African traditional or customary law in maintaining social order (Comaroff and Roberts, 1981; Roberts, 1972; 1985). In Schapera's account, religion permeated the legal system, since chiefly ceremonies, initiation, divination, rainmaking, and other religious practices were governed by traditional law. More than a system of rules, however, law was designed to be interpreted and applied through a participatory politics that depended upon the deliberations of a council of advisors (*lekgotla*) and open debate within a public assembly (*pitso*) (John Comaroff, 1975). Although the authority of a chief could be reinforced by religion (see Morton, 1985; Price, 1879; Schapera, 1965; 1967), it also depended upon a politics of consensus.

The most important religious ritual of the traditional polity was rainmaking. Under the authority of a chief, a sacred specialist in rain ritual (*moroka wa pula*) assumed responsibility for the ceremony. Traditional Tswana practice distinguished between an annual rainmaking ceremony and special rain rites—the "land-cleansing," "field-sprinkling," and "cloud-summoning" rites—that could be performed during the year (Schapera, 1971). As described in the 1920s, the annual Pedi rainmaking ceremony required the participation of young girls over a two-day period in collecting water in a sacred rain pot, singing traditional rain songs, and sprinkling the consecrated water on cultivated fields (Eiselen, 1928). A similar rainmaking ceremony has been documented for Tswana-speaking BaKgatla (Schapera, 1930) and BaKwena, BaHurutshe, and BaTlokwa religious practice (Feddema, 1966). Although Lovedu tradition attributed a distinctive role to the Rain Queen (Mujaji), who assumed royal responsibility for rain and fertility (Krige and Krige, 1943), all rainmaking ritual had a political character that linked agricultural fertility with the well-being of the polity.

In addition to ritual experts in rainmaking, Sotho-Tswana sacred specialists—*ngakas*—can be divided into four basic types (Setiloane, 1976). First, *selaodi* cast and interpret sets of divining bones, stones, or wooden blocks (Eiselen, 1932; Junod, 1925; Laydevant, 1933; Roberts, 1914; 1915; 1917). Second, *senoga* "smell out" sorcerers and witches (*baloi*), those evil agents who use natural materials or supernatural power to effect harm to persons or property (Krige and Krige, 1954; Niehaus, 1993; Sansom, 1972; Schapera, 1934; 1970). Third, *lethugela* treat conditions of spirit possession, sometimes using tobacco smoke to symbolize the "head-clearing" power of the ancestors (Murray, 1975). Finally, *dingaka tse dinaka*, or "horned doctors," prepare medicines for protecting a homestead (Laydevant, 1932; Watt and Brandwijk, 1927; Watt and Van Warmelo, 1930). Much of this ritual effort is directed towards healing, but it is a healing practice in which health is broadly defined as a condition of harmony. That condition of health has a definite social character. As J. H. Booyens has observed, the Tswana term for health (*boitekanelo*, from *go lekana*, "to be equal") depends upon social relations being in balance (Booyens, 1985). Accordingly, Sotho-Tswana religious concepts of illness and healing are necessarily related to changes in the social order (Jean Comaroff, 1980).

Analysis of change in traditional Sotho-Tswana religion during the twentieth century has generally been based on a distinction between public and private religious practices. As Isaac Schapera observed in the 1930s, colonial agencies and missions restricted or outlawed the public rituals of marriage, male and female initiation, and the practices of the *ngaka* in rainmaking, first-fruits ceremonies, and rites for strengthening the army. However, more private forms of traditional religion continued in the domestic rituals of ancestor veneration, in private consultations with sacred specialists, and in the use of traditional healers instead of Western medical practitioners (Schapera, 1935; 1969). By the 1970s, however, Schapera found that among the Tswana-speaking Kgatla even the private or domestic practices of ancestor veneration had "virtually disappeared." According to Schapera, attention to ancestors only survived in the professionalized practices of sacred specialists. In popular belief, he suggested, the ancestors had lost their power (Schapera, 1971). In these terms, therefore, Isaac Schapera outlined a process of historical change during the twentieth century in which traditional Sotho-Tswana religion became increasingly privatized until it was only found in the private practice of professionals.

However, this analysis of religious change might overlook profound forms of persistence in the public efficacy of traditional Sotho-Tswana religion. For example, as Jean and John Comaroff have suggested, an operative conceptual distinction in Sotho-Tswana discourse between productive work, which builds up the life of a homestead, and wage labor might very well continue the religious commitment to maintaining the ancestral sacred space of the home in traditional religion (Comaroff and Comaroff, 1985). At the same time, the ancestors might be invoked in public for protection against enemies. Within the context of the homeland politics of Lebowa, for example, witchcraft accusation could be a salient political strategy in public battles over power and position. As Isak Niehaus has shown, chiefs, comrades, youth organizers, and members of the legislative assembly sought to identify and punish witches as a way of gaining political legitimacy (Niehaus, 1993). In complex ways, therefore, public effects of Sotho-Tswana traditional religion may persist in the midst of change.

E1   Alverson, Hoyt (1978). *Mind in the Heart of Darkness: Value and Self-Identity among the Tswana of Southern Africa*. New Haven: Yale University Press.

Drawing on detailed field-notes, Alverson's wide-ranging work examines correspondences between the content of conscious self-identity and the institutions of colonial society among Tswana-speakers of the South African-Botswana borderland. He argues, based on a phenomenological reading of sociocultural and political domination in a society that is characterized, he suggests, by Conrad's metaphor of colonial oppression, that Tswana self-identity is not merely the predictable sum of a series of accumulated behavioral patterns and acquiescences to colonial rule. Rather, Tswana values are constructions, or "objects of belief," that emerge in processes of resistance to social forces. In asserting this position in Chapter One, Alverson argues that self-identity is premised upon the individual's ability to construct meaning within the context of specific material constraints, among them "the scars of bondage" indicative of colonial incorporation. In Chapter Two, entitled "Social and Historical Background of the Tswana," those social forces and cultural conditions, historical and contemporary, are outlined. Brief notes on Tswana beliefs and practices associated with the sacred are included: God is autonomous but immanent; belief in ancestors is universal; and while evil is committed, sometimes by sorcery, bodily disease and social disorder can be dealt with effectively by traditional medicinal or sacred specialists. Analyzing aspects of the adaptation of Tswana belief and practice consequent on incorporation into colonial political economies in Chapter Three, including changes in agricultural rites due to migrant and mine-labor in the Kweneng and Gaborone regions, the writer proceeds to review in Chapters Five through Eight the significance that the Tswana give to their own social world and the colonial institutions within which they are circumscribed. With extensive use of interviews and the deployment of a wide range of analytical tools, Alverson reinforces his argument in the concluding chapter by suggesting that colonialism does not succeed entirely in radically altering consciousness: While the Tswana incorporate elements of modernity into their self-identity, change is as much the result of the meanings that are invested in altered material conditions as it is the result of meanings that institutions of colonialism seek to impose. The book is indexed and contains a bibliography of secondary materials.

E2   Ashton, Edmond H. (1937). "Notes on the Political and Judicial Organization of the Tawana." *Bantu Studies*, vol. 11, no. 2: 67-83.

Written in response to Isaac Schapera's request for information toward the publication of his *Handbook of Tswana Law and Custom* (1938), Ashton's preparatory paper describing the origins of Tswana customary law provides a somewhat more detailed account of Pedi political administration during the period of British colonial rule than the "notes" of the article's title suggests. Indeed, in drawing on materials collected by M. Mocuminyane, the Assistant District Commissioner of Ngamiland highlights several salient events in the history of the Tawana Reserve of north-west Bechuanaland (present-day Botswana) prior to examining administrative innovations he argues were associated with the advent of colonial rule in the predominantly Tswana-speaking region during the last decades of the nineteenth century. Among those innovations he lists as indicative of the "weak and diffused," but "undisputed" political organization of the Reserve following protection granted by the Crown to chiefs Moremi and Sekgoma in 1894, are non-royal district administrators (*kgamelo*) and four categories of courtly councilors responsible for judicial administration: the *basekotso*, *basimane*, *dikgosana*, and *badintlha*. Ashton's paper outlines reasons for the emergence of these styles of administration, many of them based on stratified or hierarchical forms of British colonial administration. Foremost, he argues, the various administrative positions the chiefs inaugurated were enrolled to ensure chiefly rule during a period of enforced social decentralization and displacement. Of interest to historians of religion insofar as it documents reasons for political reconstruction in the context of societal change, Ashton's remarks remain pertinent primarily because of his precarious position as the enforcer of a colonial system that occasioned religious innovation. The paper is annotated but no bibliography is appended.

E3   Ashton, Edmond H. (1938). "Political Organization of the Southern Sotho." *Bantu Studies*, vol. 12: 287-320.

Social anthropologist and colonial agent Edmond Ashton provides in this paper a brief structuralist account of the political organization of the Southern Sotho. The writer argues that the period of the so-called *difaqane* restructured traditional Basuto politics and augured the change from tribal economy to nation-state. Based on data gathered during fieldwork in the years 1934 and 1935, and drawing on the missionary accounts of Ellenberger and MacGregor, Ashton first produces a rough chronology of Basuto history up to the formation of the Protectorate in the 1920s. Thereafter, he discusses the pre-*difaqane* period and the tribal economy and political organization with which it is associated. The tribe (*lichaba*), claims Ashton, was a "close-knit" unit under the protection of a single chiefly authority, the *morend*. Large-scale disruption of land ownership associated with the *difaqane*, however, resulted in the formation of new political units that attempted to manage aspects of social displacement and dispossession that the *morend* was incapable of undertaking. In this regard, argues Ashton, the political authority of the chief and the social cohesion of the tribe under his jurisdiction was undermined, and the nation-state was born. Presided over by the paramount chief, the nation-state was administered by local authorities in various districts, wards, and villages that nonetheless shared a common language, culture, and political affiliation. Ashton identifies a number of structures associated with the decentralized control of the paramount's authority, among them the Basutoland Council (subsequently, the National Council), numerous public councils (*pitsos*), and village councils presided over by local headmen. The writer concludes that these sub-chiefs and councilors remained loyal to the paramount chief even in the face of the political emasculation that was suffered during the period of British administration. The paper is annotated.

E4   Ashton, Edmond H. (1939). *An Ethnographical Survey of the Ba-Sotho (Southern Sotho)*. Ph.D. thesis: University of Cape Town.

Ashton's thesis furnishes a comprehensive descriptive inventory of Southern Sotho culture based on two periods of fieldwork among the Sesotho-speaking Tlokwa (considered by the writer to provide the "best preserved" examples of "original" Sotho culture). The study combines a structural-functionalist and biographical approach to describe in sixteen chapters central moments in Sotho life-cycles and rites of passage. It begins with a brief historical background describing aspects of family, village, clan, and national structure. Notes on birth, puberty, and marriage rites, including a discussion of polygyny, divorce, and widowhood appear in the next chapter. Subsequent analysis is then directed toward rituals associated with agriculture, animal husbandry, and social routinization. This is followed with an overview of Sotho legal procedures. In Chapters Fifteen and Sixteen, "Old Age and Death," and "Medicine, Magic, and Sorcery," Ashton then analyzes Sotho religious belief, claiming that human beings are considered to be constituted of a corporeal body (*mele*) and spirit (*siriti*). The ancestors (*badimo*), he asserts, are not malevolent beings, but have some influence pertaining to the success of crops and harvesting. The work is annotated and a bibliography is included.

E5   Ashton, Edmond H. (1943). *Medicine, Magic, and Sorcery Among the Southern Sotho. Communications from the School of African Studies*, no. 10. Cape Town: University of Cape Town.

Ashton provides a largely descriptive account of Sotho belief and medicinal practice, magic, and sorcery during the first half of the twentieth century. The writer argues that in the face of missionary education and economic change, aspects of Sotho culture remained practically unshaken. Emphasis is placed on distinguishing between practitioners of magic—doctors; diviners; sorcerers; and witches. Similarly, the techniques of Sotho magic, divination, and doctoring are described in detail. Ashton also elaborates on how the Sotho integrated aspects of ritual and myth and how there was consequently no distinction between the practices of healing and so-called magic. In so doing, the writer provides a rationale for what he argues has been the relative lack of missionary success in attempting to gain converts in Lesotho.

E6   Ashton, Edmond H. (1952). *The Basuto*. London: Oxford University Press.

Ashton's comprehensive ethnographic study of the Sotho is based upon fieldwork performed in 1934 at Phamong in the south of Lesotho and, from 1935 to

1936, at the bastion of Southern Sotho culture in Batloka. Information was volunteered by friends and only rarely paid for. The study comprises sixteen chapters, beginning with an historical introduction and social background that delineates Sotho history and classifies the social and political structures of the nation, and several families, villages, and clans. Further chapters describe life-cycle events, including conception, birth and childhood, education and marriage, and death. In the chapter on "Religious Beliefs of the Sotho," Ashton focuses on the relationship between the living and the ancestor spirits (*balimo*) whom, he argues, were formerly considered responsible for illness and misfortune. However, encounters with Christian missionaries caused a shift toward belief in a supreme being, Molimo (Modimo), with the result that the ancestors were then only consulted and propitiated (usually by sacrificing an animal) when maladies (including sterility) occurred. Indeed, asserts Ashton, the presence of Christian missionaries caused a certain amount of confusion between erstwhile beliefs concerning the spirit leaving the body at death and Christian concepts pertaining to heaven and hell. Further chapters enumerate aspects of Sotho agriculture, land tenure, and animal husbandry. The study concludes with a description of political and judicial structures and procedures among the Sotho. Appendices, plates, a glossary, and figures listing paramount chiefs and headmen are included in what remains a comprehensive albeit dated description.

E7   Beyer, G. (1919). "Suto Astronomy." *South African Journal of Science*, vol. 16: 206-10.

Beyer argues that the Sotho "possess a more or less limited knowledge" of astronomy. Any inquiry into how these "primitive peoples" perceived the celestial world, he contends, might nonetheless reveal data critical to an analysis of their position in the hierarchy of human progress. To this end, the missionary compares aspects of astronomical "ignorance" among various "tribes" in southern Africa. Notes on Sesotho names and myths associated with the sun (*le-laka*), moon (*ngwedi*), and several stellar constellations (*di-naledi*) are included. Beyer asserts in this regard that the various phases of the moon were associated with specific calendrical and agricultural rites. For example, when a child was two months old, he or she was "shown" to the moon in a ritual known as *mokuruetjo*. Also, when the moon was full, a light beer was brewed. And when the "horns" of the moon pointed upwards, an aspect considered by the Sotho to be a bad omen, plowing was suspended. Although the phases of stars and planets were not considered as important as lunar events, brief notes are included on rituals and myths associated with various planets and stars, such as Venus (*se-falabogogo*, the "crust-scrapings" supper star), Canopus (*se-thlako sa naka*, the "shield" star), and Pleiades (*selemela*, the "plowing" constellation). The paper is not annotated.

E8   Beyer, G. (1926). "Religiöse Anschauungen und Bräuche der südafrikanischen Bantuneger." *Mission und Pfarramt*, vol. 19, no. 1: 4-9.

In this brief paper Beyer describes beliefs and rituals associated with hunting and the preparatory purification rites required by Tswana-speaking Matlale "witchdoctors" during periods of war. He notes that dogs were sometimes eaten prior to a hunt to ensure success. Also, he observes that the head of an animal killed during a hunt was sometimes presented to the chief in the belief that the head contained an essence or "soul" of powerful political influence. Following Price (1879) and Willoughby (1923), the author further recalls what appears to be elements of the *dipheku* rite—the ritual sacrifice of a black ox prior to war. Beyer notes that weapons were consecrated with the blood of the animal. Brief notes on cannibalism, "magic," and belief in a high god, Kchove, and a creator god, Choveane, are also included. The paper is briefly annotated and the text is in German.

E9   Booyens, J. H. (1985). "Aetiology as Social Comment on Life amongst Tswana-Speaking Urbanites." *African Studies*, vol. 44, no. 2: 137-57.

In this paper, Booyens advances a line of research into African understandings of the origin of illness that is in contrast to the persistent identification of "personalistic" forces as the progenitors of illness and misfortune and in opposition to the general view that ancestors (*badimo*) or sorcerers (*baloi*) are the initiators of disorder and disease among African peoples. Instead, the author examines the etiology of "natural" illnesses (*tlholego*) among Tswana-speaking respondents in the urban areas of the western Transvaal. In this regard, the writer focuses upon states of "pollution" and sickness that are deemed to be motivated independently of ancestral affliction. These natural illnesses, including "hotness" (*bollo*), leprosy, stomach problems, polio, coryza, tuberculosis, mumps, and strokes are thus not caused by any external agents but, rather, are the result of disharmonious relations between men and women generally, or, during a woman's menses, because of inappropriate sexual relations. Importantly, Booyens argues that natural illnesses are viewed as being of greater danger to the well-being of others than are illnesses occasioned by sorcery or the displeasure of the ancestors. However, in terms consistent with Ngubane's view that "equilibrium" between people, the environment, and mystical forces among Zulu-speakers is an essential ingredient for the continuity of moral order, the writer concludes that the maintenance of health, or *boitekanelo* (from *go lekana*, "to be equal") among Tswana-speakers can be secured if social relations remain "balanced." The paper is rich in detail, drawing on the verbatim responses of a number of participants. A list of references useful for comparative analysis in the field of medical anthropology in southern Africa is also appended.

E10   Bosko, D. (1981). "Why Basuto Wear Blankets." *African Studies*, vol. 40, no. 1: 23-32.

In search for a convincing explanation of the Sotho's apparent preoccupation with blankets, Bosko looks beyond mere utilitarian values to examine the links between symbolic significations and domestic signs. He suggests that there is almost no limit to the symbolic references associated with blankets among the Sotho, with the controlling metaphors embedded in the thermal capacity of the cloth. Not only is the heat that the blanket generates homogeneous with the heat of fermentation and gestation (both life-giving or transforming processes), but it is also associated with periods of major transition, including the rites of passage relating to birth, initiation, marriage, and death. The article traces a hermeneutical link between biological procreation and social reproduction, both of which processes are symbolically mediated by the blanket as vagina and womb: It is a sheath for the life-giving penis and the gestating embryo; or a covering for grain to aid fermentation during ancestral beer rites. The key metaphors are "making" or "creating," an act that calls for the heat of transformation. The blanket symbolizes this heat, and the Basuto wear the cloth, even in the scorching sun, suggests Bosko, to celebrate life and its fecundity.

E11   Breutz, Paul-Lenert (1969). "Sotho-Tswana Celestial Concepts." In *Ethnological and Linguistic Studies in Honour of N. J. van Warmelo*. Pretoria: Government Printers. 199-210.

Comprised of four sections, namely "Sky," "Sun," "Moon," and "Stars," Breutz's paper gives examples of central "mythological ideas" among various Sotho-Tswana-speaking communities. Primarily, however, he attempts to introduce a discussion about parallels between these core ideas and other African mythologies. In the first section, for example, Breutz notes that unlike other African communities, the Sotho-Tswana appear to have little interest in a sky god. Rather, the Sotho believe that the sky is made of stone, a belief that apparently originated with the Venda, suggests Breutz. In the following section the writer relates Sotho myths concerned with the sun. For example, he notes that the Northern Sotho believe that the sun is "masculine" because of its merciless cruelty. The Tswana belief that the sun is the "eye of God" is then compared by Breutz to the Egyptian concept of "the eye of Horus" and the Malay expression "*mata hari* (eye of the sky)." In the following section the writer describes Sotho myths associated with a man in the moon. Etymological parallels between the Sotho word for moon (*kgadi*, or *ngwedi*) and words for lunar events in East and Central African languages are enumerated. The waxing and waning of the moon is subsequently compared to cycles of fertility, menstruation, rainfall, and the death of a chief. In the final section, "Stars," Breutz traces Sotho beliefs about celestial constellations, including the Southern Cross, Pleiades, and

Orion's Belt. The article is premised upon the belief that "mythological ideas are not limited to individual cultures, but extend in diffusionist ways across a wide spectrum." Consequently, parallels with other African cultures are frequently entertained.

E12   Brown, J. Tom (1921). "Circumcision Rites of the Becwana Tribes." *Journal of the Royal Anthropological Institute*, vol. 51: 419-27.

Brown's description of circumcision rituals among Tswana-speaking peoples in the Bechuanaland Protectorate begins with an account of the difficulties the writer experienced in obtaining historical information about the origins of a number of local chiefdoms. He is unsure whether this is due to the nature of Tswana oral tradition, or whether the Tswana did not wish to divulge these matters to outsiders. The writer's review of challenges encountered in attempting to overcome his informer's reticence and secure information related to more "esoteric" topics, including inquiries concerning the meaning and practice of circumcision, is even more pronounced. One informant assured him that these rites simply could not be interpreted. After surmising that circumcision rites were originally religious in nature, Brown nonetheless proceeds (in the absence of any coherent evidence) to describe with great lucidity the "abominable" rites. He distinguishes between rituals for males and females and attempts to indicate the age at which adolescent Tswana-speakers were initiated. The "celebrants," he suggests, were nominated in a special ceremony and various warnings and taboos leading up to the rite were enumerated during the period of puberty. Drawing on papers forwarded by W. C. Willoughby and Noel Roberts, Brown describes the painful nature of the circumcision operation and discusses the medical problems attendant upon it. The "ordeal of chastisement" that he suggests follows the operation is examined, and other central ritual activities, such as the "songs of the salt," are described. What Brown interprets as the obscene nature of the songs leads him to take exception to those that claim transmission of moral norms as a major function of puberty rites. He consequently assumes that there is a lack of ethical content prescribed for the duration of such rituals. The analysis closes with the writer stressing that the importance assigned to the conservation of traditional customs appears ironically to take the place of moral teaching during the rites. The paper is not annotated and no bibliography is included.

E13   Brown, J. Tom (1926). *Among the Bantu Nomads: A Record of Forty Years Spent among the Bechuana*. London: Seeley, Service.

Asserting in the preface that the Bechuana did not generally withstand the pressures of colonial advancement or missionary influence, anthropologist A. R.

Radcliffe-Brown praises Brown for his attempt to record the changing beliefs and rites of the Tswana-speaking peoples of the Bechuanaland Protectorate. Having lived in this region from 1885 until 1924, he argues, Brown's "competence to speak on these matters is guaranteed." The writer's account of Tswana belief in the *badimo* (ancestors), *medimo*, or "demi-gods," and Modimo (supreme being); his description of the role of the *dingaka*, or "priest-doctor," and *baloi* (witch); and his sketch of rituals associated with initiation (*bogwera* and *bojale*), divination, and healing is indeed broad and detailed. The book begins with an account of the "totemic" structure of Tswana social organization and kinship systems, wherein the writer relates that the BaMangwato, for example, were known as the BaPhuti, or people of the duiker (*phuti*). Similarly, the BaRolong had as their totem the kudu (*tholo*); the BaHarutshe the hartebeest (*kgama*), eland (*phohu*), and baboon (*chwene*); and the BaKwena the crocodile, or *kwena*. Chapters describing other aspects of Tswana kinship, family life, and marriage, law, and custom are included. However, it is Brown's detailed accounts of Tswana belief in the *badimo* (Chapter Seven), *medimo* (Chapter Eight), and Modimo (Chapter Nine), as well as his account of "priestcraft," religious ceremonies, including the "sacrifice of atonement," and myths, folklore, and proverbs in Chapters Fifteen through Nineteen that is perhaps of most interest to historians of religion in southern Africa. Analyzed in a peculiarly Christian idiom, and articulated in a theoretical paradigm indicative of late nineteenth-century comparative anthropology, Brown's work remains an important, if dated contribution, to Tswana ethnography. The book is not annotated and no index and bibliography are included.

E14   Burman, Sandra B. (1981). *Chiefdom, Politics and Alien Laws: Basutoland Under Cape Rule 1871-1884*. London: Macmillan.

Burman investigates Cape magisterial rule in colonial Basutoland following the death of Moshoeshoe in the "explosive" years between 1871 and 1884. In this regard, she focuses on both the efforts of Cape administrators attempting to effect rapid social and political transformation in Basutoland, and Sotho resistance to these "civilizing" aims. Deploying a social-legal line of analysis and discourse, the writer draws on primary resources, including the official records of British and Cape administrations, Cape and Basutoland newspapers, and missionary reports and periodicals. Beginning with a brief overview of the creation of Basutoland under Moshoeshoe, Burman elaborates on the "conflicting values" that were obviously apparent between the "Christian" intentions of colonial government agents and Sotho traditionalists. Issues such as polygyny, initiation practices, and ancestor veneration are highlighted as aspects of conflict in the convergence of Cape colonial administration and Sotho customary law. In the following chapters, entitled "The Cape Administration" and "Neutralizing the Chiefs," Burman analyzes bureaucratic difficulties encountered by "efficient" colonial administrators, who frequently faced resistance to their policies. Foremost among these was the unpopular "Governor's Code," implemented in 1871, which limited the Sotho chief's authority and instigated tax revolts. In the closing chapters, Burman describes in detail the open revolts of the so-called Moorosi rebels. These revolts, suggests the writer, culminated in the Basutoland Rebellion and, in 1881, in the War of the Guns, both of which precipitated the discontinuation of colonial administration and the return of Basutoland to traditional rule. Burman's annotated study includes several maps, a series of plates, and an extensive bibliography.

E15   Casalis, Eugène (1861). *The Basutos, or Twenty-Three Years in South Africa*. London: James Nisbet.

The pioneering French Protestant missionary Eugène Casalis presents in this formative work an impressionistic study of Sotho custom and belief. Beginning with an introductory chapter on the classification of southern African tribes, the writer distinguishes between the "Hottentot," "Bushmen," "Caffre," and Sotho-Tswana speaking "Bechuana," of whom the Sotho form a part. Drawing on diffusionist and comparative theories and frames of reference, he posits, for instance, that the Hottentot legend of the "great basket" can be "traced up to the ark," and that these people apparently "sprung from a man called Noh (Noah)." Part One of the work, entitled "Journeys of Exploration—Labours," describes Casalis' journey to the west of the Maluti Mountains and his missionary activity in that region. Written in a somewhat journalistic style, personal experience is pronounced as Christian polemic. Part Two, "Manners and Customs of the Basutos," enumerates aspect of social and political structure and domestic life. In the chapters on "Notions upon the Origin of Things—Religious Ideas," and "Amulets—Superstitious Practices," Casalis furnishes detailed materials for the student of comparative religion. The writer claims, for example, that the Sotho belief in a "world of spirits" in the "bowels of the earth," in a place called "*mosima* (the abyss)," is analogous to the Hebrew *sheol* and the Teutonic *hell*. Indeed, Casalis generally attempts to evaluate Sotho belief and practice in terms of Semitic or European standards; if no parallel is to be found, *sui generis* belief is labeled "superstition." Therefore, Sotho practice associated with the rubbing of dust on the forehead prior to entering a new territory is considered by Casalis to be ridiculous. Not withstanding this bias, the writer describes in detail aspects of Sotho initiation, rainmaking, purification rites and sacrifices, and beliefs in Molimo (the "sky-god") and the *balimo* (ancestors). A series of fifty-one proverbs are outlined to illustrate the character of Sotho morals, and a map of southern Africa showing various mission stations extant in the early 1860s is appended.

E16   Comaroff, Jean (1980). "Healing and the Cultural Order: The Case of the Barolong boo Ratshidi of Southern Africa." *American Ethnologist*, vol. 7: 637-57.

Within the context of marked cultural change, Comaroff uses experiences of illness and healing among the Tswana-speaking Barolong boo Ratshidi of the Botswana-South Africa borderland as a lens through which to clarify broader theoretical issues in the dialectic between cultural order (Tswana social and cosmic order) and subjective experience (socially configured illness). In this sense, she debunks the continuing reification of an African worldview perceived as timeless and unchanging, asserting that specific interpretations of affliction and the metaphors of causality that define them are constantly shifting in the context of altered sociopolitical patterns and conditions. Consequently, her sophisticated examination of indigenous perceptions of bodily health and social disorder among the Tshidi suggests that affliction is structurally configured in a manner that is derivative of an implicit symbolic scheme. Moreover, once the sociopolitical condition or cosmological scheme is altered, she suggests, the categories used to define affliction or health are correspondingly reconfigured. The paper begins with a brief introduction to literature related to healing in Africa in general, and to interpretations of illness and affliction in the Tshidi social order specifically. Here the writer highlights both Robin Horton's study of healing in African traditional thought, and Isaac Schapera's studies of Tswana social organization. Comaroff argues in this section that Tshidi social structures are predicated on a series of potentially conflicting organizational principles comprising a hierarchized chiefdom and an essentially polygamous social order. She notes that since healing is fundamentally concerned with the reconstruction of physical, social, or spiritual order, it cannot be examined without recourse to an analysis of the wider sociocultural system from within which it emerges. In the second part of the paper the writer turns to an analysis of indigenous Tshidi strategies of nosology, or the classification of disease. These strategies include etiologies of ill-health or affliction (*botlhoko*) associated with sorcery, or caused as a consequence of the polluting by-products of a careless breach of sexual taboo resulting in a type of disruptive "heat" known as *bothitho*. Both ill-health and affliction, argues, Comaroff, require recourse to the specialist healer, or *ngaka*. But both, she suggests, can only be interpreted or evaluated by focusing on the afflicted person's perception of illness and his or her relationship with the environment. In short, "there is no objective knowledge of illness which is of relevance when set apart from its subjective experience." Drawing on a number of case studies in the last section of the paper, the writer concludes by identifying indigenous perceptions of order and disorder in terms of the therapeutic logic of Tshidi cosmology. The paper is annotated and a bibliography is included.

E17   Comaroff, Jean (1981). "Healing and Cultural Transformation: The Case of the Tswana of Southern Africa." *Social Science and Medicine*, vol. 15, no. 2: 367-78.

Fearing that current theoretical trends might render medical anthropology parochial in relation to mainstream anthropological research—insofar as these trends appear to promote the quest for "closure" in the study of African systems of healing—Comaroff contends that "medical systems" can neither be viewed as natural or discrete elements in an empirical domain, nor as isolated aspects of an ahistorical social process. Rather, the study of healing requires that models of analysis that further the examination of sociocultural forms, and permit an inquiry into the dynamic interaction between these forms and sociohistorical and political processes, are developed. The case of the Barolong boo Ratshidi of the South African-Botswana borderland is consequently employed to suggest how a focus on healing systems might usefully engage in and contribute to the study of wider processes of sociopolitical change while simultaneously confusing the static, "Procrustean" dichotomy between structure and history. Indeed, Comaroff argues that the interrelationship between healing systems and particular sociocultural processes is the key to understanding healing and social innovation, not as an inevitable evolutionary movement between these static poles, but as a dynamic expression of the dialectic between systems of meaning and politico-economic influences. Her analysis begins with an inquiry into the social value of symbolic healing among the Tshidi. She notes that while healing everywhere is concerned with a "culturally specific" attempt to intervene in disorder, both affliction and the evolution of therapeutic systems among the Tshidi can only be analyzed with recourse to information concerning the relationship between individual experience and the spatial and symbolic structure of sociocultural conditions. Identifying basic symbolic oppositions between the sacred and profane—between the domain of everyday political activity in the urban order of the settlement (*motse*), for example, and the wildness of peripheral and undisciplined life in the bush (*naga*)—is thus central to understanding both social order and bodily disease or disorder. In these terms, the writer uses illness and healing as a lens to clarify broader theoretical issues in the dialectic between cultural order and the subjective experiences of socially configured illness. The paper, rich in descriptive detail and sophisticated in its theoretical analysis, is annotated and a bibliography is appended.

E18   Comaroff, Jean, and John L. Comaroff (1981). "The Management of Marriage in a Tswana Chiefdom." In E. J. Krige and J. L. Comaroff (eds.) *Essays on African Marriage in Southern Africa*. Cape Town: Juta. 29-49.

Drawing on extensive fieldwork notes taken while working among the Barolong boo Ratshidi of the South Africa-Botswana borderland, anthropologists Jean and

John Comaroff carefully analyze how flexible Tshidi definitions of marriage, although representing a conceptual framework for ordering complex forms of social interaction, do not determine behavior or transform the content of social ties. They argue, by way of contrast to Kuper's earlier (1975) work, therefore, that marriage cannot be defined or interpreted in terms of any jural analysis, the transfer of conjugal rights, or static social privileges. Rather, marriage among the Tshidi is marked by, and must be interpreted within the context of, a profound definitional flexibility, or "negotiability," that often operates as a political resource for building careers or overcoming rivals. The paper is divided into four sections. The first section reviews a range of frequently cited anthropological accounts of marriage in southern African societies, among them Kuper's (1975) analysis of Tswana marriage rites; Roberts' (1977) review of Kgatla marital concepts; and Schapera's landmark (1940) study of married life among Tswana-speakers in the Bechuanaland Protectorate. The second and third sections then establish a structural framework within which to define the meaning of marriage. Detailed notes are included on various interpersonal arrangements—concubinage (*bonyatsi*), "living together" (*ba dula mmogo*), and the official negotiations that confirm forms of union as marriage (*nyato*). However, the central findings of the paper emerge in the fourth section, where ethnographic analysis is focused upon the politics of Tshidi marriage. Here, the Comaroffs highlight aspects of the "resource potential" of marriage, describing how marriages in Tshidi society are "managed." In these terms, the writers assert that definitional flexibility is utilized to secure or further the professional status or power of participants. The paper is annotated and a bibliography is included.

E19   Comaroff, Jean, and John L. Comaroff (1990). "Goodly Beasts and Beastly Goods: Cattle and Commodities in a South African Context." *American Ethnologist*, vol. 17: 195-216.

In this paper anthropologists Jean and John Comaroff note how in the nineteenth century the Tswana viewed cattle as "commodities." In this sense, cattle were closely associated with processes of production and strategies of exchange; they were, the writers argue, "prime media for the creation and representation of value in a material economy of persons and a social economy of things." In the context of expanding colonial control in the Bechuanaland Protectorate, however, livestock were also implicated in an ideological and material contest over meaning and power. Consequently, cattle functioned simultaneously as icons of "traditional" order and as powerful symbolic weapons in the Tswana's resistance to modernity. The various meanings and values that were associated with cattle in colonial Bechuanaland—ranging from seeing cattle as "goodly beasts" to seeing cattle as "beastly goods"—thus provide significant materials, suggest the Comaroffs, for an interpretation of the function of commodities in pre-capitalist non-European social contexts. Rich in descriptive detail and sophisticated in its analytical approach, the paper presents many useful resources for the historian of religion interested in the myths, rituals, and symbols of Sotho-Tswana religion.

E20   Comaroff, John L. (1974). "Chiefship in a South African Homeland: A Case Study of the Tshidi Chiefdom of Bophuthatswana." *Journal of Southern African Studies*, vol. 1: 36-51.

Examining the contemporary condition of traditional government and politics among Tswana-speakers in southern Africa, Comaroff reconsiders Schapera's earlier (1938) analysis of the role of the chief in traditional Tswana societies. He argues that the case of Tshidi chiefship in Bophuthatswana aptly illustrates processes of transformation that have occurred in the strategies of Tswana rule in the region. Particularly, however, the writer asserts that an examination of the transformation of Tshidi politics can yield insights into the contrasting perspectives of Tswana and Bantu Administration and Development policies regarding local-level government in Bophuthatswana. The paper begins, however, with an overview of some well-documented features of traditional Tswana government. Included is a discussion of the chief, who, as executive head, presided over the highest court and wielded exclusive authority over indigenous coercive and administrative agencies. Central to the writer's argument is an overview of Schapera's account of procedural "discontinuities" and disputes related to the election of a new chief or regent. Comaroff argues that these disparities were not unusual or anomalous. Rather, constant competitive processes relating to the legitimacy of successors lay at the heart of Tswana politics. In this regard, the legitimacy of the ruler was not always guaranteed by birth. Frequently, chiefship was related to the office-holder's ability to "perform" in a way that might manipulate authority and satisfy the preconceptions of his subjects. Comaroff's detailed accounts of ritual performance provide historians of religion with compelling resources for an analysis of the role of ritual in contemporary Tshidi politics. In the concluding section of the paper, "The Structure of the Homeland Government," the writer also contrasts this performative and "processional" view of Tshidi politics with the perceptions of Tswana government and succession promoted by apartheid administrators and homeland leaders in the Republic of Bophuthatswana. Comaroff argues in this respect that homeland policies and tribal authorities, in particular the elected *lekgotla* (chiefly council) system of administration, promoted an interpretation of Tswana politics that emphasized permanent and unchanging features of Tswana chiefship. Consequently, he argues in conclusion, the council effectively closed off the usual channels of competition for power and ignored the more complex dynamics of Tswana chiefly rule. The paper is annotated and draws on extensive use of the writer's field-notes.

E21   Comaroff, John L. (1975a). "Rules and Rulers: Political Processes in a Tswana Chiefdom." *Man*, vol. 13, no. 1: 1-20.

In this paper, anthropologist John Comaroff scrutinizes political and administrative processes associated with the Tswana-speaking Barolong boo Ratshidi. Drawing on Max Gluckman's (1963) account of the nature of political order and "rebellion" in African administrative systems, he argues that traditional Tswana polity is governed by a persistent manipulation of political power. Competition for chiefship, however, is not the sole ingredient of conflict, suggests the writer. Indeed, political rivalry, governed by indigenous "rule-sets," reflects a continuous process, of which succession to office is only one of a series of potential outcomes. Under these conditions, Comaroff re-examines genealogical manipulation and political history among the Barolong. In the first half of the paper, prescriptive rules associated with accession to office are reviewed. Most rules, suggests the writer, are derived from agnatic ranking principles, usually premised upon the principal notion of primogeniture: the eldest son of the principal wife of a chief (*kgosi*) is his rightful and legitimate heir. However, Comaroff asserts that the Tshidi view legitimacy to be a negotiable value. Indeed, chiefly authority emerges at the confluence of legitimate hereditary claims to power and the incumbent's ability to perform as a ruler. Thus, although power is not allocated by popular consent, participatory politics, and in particular the evaluation of chiefly performance by the council of advisors (*lekgotla*) and his public assembly (*pitso*), represent important media through which rules governing election are contested. In order to examine how this repertoire was expressed in competition over chiefship in one Tswana-speaking community, Comaroff turns in the second half of the paper to a description of Tshidi royal genealogy between the years 1911 and 1919. In this respect, he recalls the strategies used for struggle and the "resources" deployed to legitimate the rise to power of the Barolong chief Montshiwa, his sons Besele and Badirile, and their successors Lekoko, Joshua, Bakolopang, and Lotlamoreng. The paper is annotated and includes a bibliography.

E22   Comaroff, John L. (1975b). "Talking Politics: Oratory and Authority in a Tswana Chiefdom." In Maurice Bloch (ed.) *Political Language and Oratory in Traditional Societies*. London and New York: Academic Press. 141-61.

In an examination of the power relations inherent in political negotiation, Comaroff analyzes aspects of Tshidi oratory, describing the juxtaposition of respectively courteous and insulting remarks employed by Tswana-speaking rhetoricians to contest chiefly authority. He argues that these dual styles of ritual speech are not arbitrarily deployed, however. Ritualized statements in the *lekgotla* (council of headmen) or *pitso* (public assembly), for example, are mobilized in a logic that reflects the processual and negotiated nature of chiefly authority. Indeed, Tshidi orators repeatedly make remarks about the chief, suggests Comaroff, in order to compile a set of criteria against which the legitimacy of the chiefly office might be indexed and encoded. Without these rhetorical criteria, evaluation has no referent; with them, argues the writer, listeners at the *kgotla*, or chief's meeting place, can be compelled to enter into debate and to evaluate the inherently negotiable position of authority. Thus, the use of a formal code, the code of ritualized authority concerning chiefship, "should be understood as the means by which public speakers translate their evaluations into the currency of political debate." Comaroff suggests, furthermore, that this interpretation of the "formal-evaluative" relationship between oratory and political processes among the Tshidi explains variations in the freedom of speech. The range of oratorical references uttered is dependent on the power relations present. In this sense, he concludes, freedom of speech appears an apposite phrase since it is as much political freedom as it is linguistic autonomy that is at issue. The paper, which draws on the experiences of an extensive period of fieldwork among the Barolong boo Ratshidi of the South African-Botswana borderland is annotated and of particular interest to historians of comparative religion in the region insofar as it recalls Robert Moffat's (1842) account of Tswana political oratory.

E23   Comaroff, John L. (1980). "Bridewealth and the Control of Ambiguity in a Tswana Chiefdom." In John L. Comaroff (ed.) *The Meaning of Marriage Payments*. London and New York: Academic Press. 161-96.

Contrasting with Kuper's (1975) "jural approach" to the study of marriage, an approach premised on the opinion that the meaning of marriage is best interpreted as a "bundle of rights," or a "contractual" agreement, Comaroff asserts that marriage among the Tswana-speaking Tshidi is not necessarily signaled by the transfer of conjugal rights, or by the accumulation of static social privileges. Rather, marriage among the Tshidi is marked by and must be interpreted within the context of a profound definitional flexibility. Indeed, ambiguities surrounding the creation and categorization of heterosexual alliances among the Tshidi, from conjugality (*nyato*) to concubinage (*bonyatsi*) and casual liaisons (*ba dula mmogo*), demand that marriage be seen as a non-linear, "negotiable" set of complex dialectical processes. Bridewealth, or *bogadi*, the writer asserts, is an integral aspect of that dialectical process. However, many other ritual procedures are elements constitutive of this fluid rite of passage: negotiation (*patlo*) between kin; the transfer of gifts (*mokwele*); co-residence, ideally beginning uxorilocally, followed by the establishment of a permanent patrivirilocal household in which the couple assume conventional conjugal roles; the presentation of *bogadi*; and public recognition are all central aspects of what is conventionally termed "marriage." While *bogadi*, argues the writer, is the only non-negotiable component of the conjugal process, the presentation of *mokwele* may constitute the right of sexual access, although even the presentation of these gifts are frequently omitted. The paper, which draws on Comaroff's extensive periods of fieldwork among the Barolong boo Ratshidi in the early 1970s, is annotated and contains a bibliography of definitive secondary works relating to the study of marriage and marital rites in southern African societies. In this regard, it provides a mandatory resource for comparative analysis. To cite one example: In arguing in the introduction to this book that the Tswana-speaking Kgatla provide their daughters with a dowry of arable land, called the *serotwana*, Comaroff contests Radcliffe-Brown's earlier (1950) assertion that dowry in Africa is absent.

E24   Comaroff, John L. (1982). "Class and Culture in a Peasant Economy: The Transformation of Land Tenure in Barolong." In Richard P. Werbner (ed.) *Land Reform in the Making: Tradition, Public Policy and Ideology in Botswana*. London: Rex Collins. 85-116.

Making the point that historical processes are configured by a dialectical and occasionally contradictory relationship between internal structures and external political forces, Comaroff examines aspects of rural economy and sociocultural order among the Barolong boo Ratshidi of Botswana. In this sense, he examines how "traditional," or "historically prior" sociocultural structures managed to shape or were absorbed within new systems of relations. Particularly, the writer focuses on how the Tribal Land Act of 1968, although attempting to perpetuate "customary" tenure arrangements, ironically failed to halt political and economic polarization consonant with the emergence of a decentralized chiefdom, a new ward administration system, and a burgeoning commercial and peasant capitalist economy. In spite of its intentions, therefore, the Act failed to secure customary land-tenure practices. As a result, personal rights to land were no longer guaranteed by virtue of citizenship. Rather, land was acquired and protected by constant individual effort. The paper, which draws on several secondary materials, is annotated and a bibliography is included.

E25   Comaroff, John L., and Jean Comaroff (1987). "The Madman and the Migrant: Work and Labor in the Historical Consciousness of a South African People." *American Ethnologist*, vol. 14: 191-209.

In what the writers term an "excursion into the poetics of history," anthropologists John and Jean Comaroff examine the nature of historical consciousness, and its relation to culture, among the Tswana-speaking Tshidi-Barolong of South Africa. On the basis of an interpretation of imagery used by two informants—a "madman" and a former migrant laborer—they suggest that general questions regarding the connection between consciousness, culture, and representation can be clarified. In particular, they assert that contrasting rhetorical concepts of work and labor, one associated with *setswana* (Tswana ways) and the other with *sekgoa* (European ways), can be seen as major tropes through which the Tshidi construct their past. These particular rhetorical forms, the writers contest, are widely deployed in situations of rapid social change. The paper begins by describing the metaphors of "affliction" used by the madman (whose "crazy" religion was created in a mental institution in Mafikeng) and the migrant laborer (whose experiences of mine-labor are expressed through the idioms of industrial death). The detailed description of the madman's religion is of particular note to historians of religion. In the following sections of the paper the writers proceed to examine in detail how, in everyday acts of resistance, in visual imagery or verbal metaphor, the afflictions of the madman and the migrant laborer succeed in authentically articulating the historical experiences of Tshidi alienation and displacement. It is hardly surprising, they suggest, that historical consciousness and affliction should be evaluated in terms of these contrasting images of fulfilling work and dehumanizing, destructive labor: missionaries, government agents, and colonial administrators sought to induce the Tswana into a market economy from the time of colonial rule. Indeed, any resistance to the condition of servanthood or slavery was interpreted as an example of ill-discipline or, as Silus M. Molema bluntly put it, the "laziness of the Kafir." The sophisticated and illuminating analysis of language, labor, and the semiotics of historical consciousness that the Comaroffs illustrate draws on a wide range of primary and secondary materials, including the writings of Samuel Broadbent, Emil Holub, David Livingstone, Robert Moffat, W. C. Willoughby, and John Campbell, as well as Michel Foucault, Raymond Firth, Raymond Williams, Paul Friedrich, and Marshall Sahlins. The paper is extensively annotated and a bibliography of reference material is appended.

E26   Comaroff, John L., and Simon A. Roberts (1981). *Rules and Processes: The Cultural Logic of Dispute in an African Context*. Chicago: University of Chicago Press.

Combining refined theoretical reflection with rich ethnographic description, Comaroff and Roberts develop a complex analytical model that profoundly challenges orthodox explanation in the study of legal anthropology. Focusing on the form and content of political and judicial discourse among Tswana-speakers in the South African-Botswana borderland, the writers thus outline a theory of political structure and dispute procedure that explores the dialectical relationship between sociocultural order and individual experience. In this regard, they employ an extensive array of theoretical apparatus to examine vernacular court (*kgotla*) records and question why the Tshidi and Kgatla in particular conceived of their world as paradoxically rule-governed but open to pragmatic manipulation. They conclude, by way of contrast to structuralist paradigms established in the writings of Gluckman (1955), and functionalist theoretical readings in the work of Malinowski (1926)—as reinforced in Schapera's recapitulation (1938)—that judicial systems and legal institutions are not clearly circumscribed, mechanical, rule-centered structures. Rather, "traditional" dispute resolution procedures among the Tswana are inherently enigmatic, intensely competitive, and highly individualistic. Essential reading for anthropologists, the book contains valuable material foundational to the history of religion in southern Africa. Particularly noteworthy are the writers' comments on ritual and belief associated with marriage and bride-price (*bogadi*).

E27   Coplan, David B. (1987). "Eloquent Knowledge: Lesotho Migrants' Songs and the Anthropology of Experience." *American Ethnologist*, vol. 14: 413-33.

Geographically circumscribed almost entirely by South Africa, Lesotho has become, consequently, dependent on labor exports to its neighbor for economic survival. Coplan's study aims to assess internal, culturally reflexive accounts of the experience of labor migration by drawing on a document of oral tradition (*sefela*). As part of an architecture of humanization, he suggests, *sefela* helps maintain an integrated, positive self-identity amid strategies of social displacement, fragmentation, and dehumanization inherent in the migrant labor system. Advanced by both men and women, *sefela* also enables persons to create a system of persistent autonomy, that is, to constitute an identity built on the inalienable redefinition—through performance—of human agency in the context of a life tied to labor in the political economy of South Africa. An extended bibliography is included.

E28   Coplan, David B. (1994). *In the Time of the Cannibals: The Word Music of South Africa's Basotho Migrants*. Chicago: Chicago University Press.

Drawing on his earlier analyses of how the Sesotho language functioned as a prime mechanism of cultural self-identification among the Basotho, anthropologist David Coplan creatively examines elements of symbol, myth, and tradition contained in the musical literature and oral poetry of Lesotho's migrant laborers. Included in his wide-ranging and imaginative analysis are notes on the historical conditions, political dynamics, and social and religious forces represented in the language and performance of this ethnoaesthetic tradition. Of particular interest to historians of religion in the region, however, are the writer's notes on *lobola* (bridewealth), the *magadi* rituals associated with female initiation (especially *bale*), exorcism and spiritual healing, and sacrificial feasts. While the work draws primarily on ethnographic inquiry and fieldwork studies among migrant laborers, Coplan also draws on a vast body of historical travel writing and anthropological analysis, including the works of Alverson, Arbousset, Burchell, Casalis, Comaroff, Jacottet, Jones, and Murray. The work is rigorously annotated and an extensive bibliography and useful index are appended.

E29   Crisp, William (1896). *The Bechuana of South Africa.* London: Society for Promoting Christian Knowledge.

Crisp identifies in this tract several aspects of Tswana belief, ritual practice, and symbolic iconography considered to betray the Egyptian or North African origin of this southern African "tribe." The work begins, however, with a brief historical account wherein the writer suggests that alongside Hamitic influences, the Tswana were "tinged with Israelitish" effects. In this regard, Crisp notes that the "dispersion of many South African tribes" was in some way contiguous with the "final disruption of Israel." Following short chapters on the "Bechuana Village," "The Food of the Bechuana," and "Their Laws and Language," proverbs, fables, and idioms indicative of the patriarchal and polygamous social structure of the Tswana are described. However, it is in Chapter Nine, "Religious Ideas," that the writer contributes most fruitfully to nineteenth-century debate and the comparative study of religion in the region. In that chapter, Crisp recalls that the Tswana did "not inherit a systematized religion, with definite objects of worship." However, the Tswana acknowledged the presence of "a Supreme Being." That Being, asserts Crisp, was called Molimo, a term that referred to a "capricious" if perhaps "impersonal" being. Aspects of Tswana religion are tabulated, among them the practices of ancestor-worship, propitiatory sacrifice, medicinal healing, divination, rainmaking, witchcraft, and "infant-killings." In Chapters Ten and Eleven, aspects associated with the introduction and influence of Christianity in Bechuanaland in the years following 1815 are described. Notably, Crisp argues that a long-standing belief in polygyny prevented "national conversion." The tract is not annotated and no bibliography is included.

E30   Dennis, Caroline (1978). "The Role of Dingaka tsa Setswana from the Nineteenth Century to the Present." *Botswana Notes and Records*, vol. 10: 53-66.

Written against the backdrop of increasing interest in non-Western methods of healing, Dennis outlines in this paper several traditional healing techniques common to Tswana societies. She notes that illness, disease, death, and social disorder among the Tswana was often perceived to be the result of ancestral displeasure. Thus, the *badimo* (ancestors) were deemed to be the arbiters of justice and the guardians of morality. Following a brief discussion of the various categories of healers (*dingaka*) and sorcerers (*baloi*)—both day sorcerers (*baloi ba motshegare*) and night (*baloi ba bosigo*)—the writer documents events relating to the selection and training of doctors; divination by way of throwing bones (*go thela bola*); rituals of healing and cleansing; the procurement of medicinal herbs for the treatment of infection; and rainmaking. She cites nineteenth-century travelers, among others, Mackenzie, Moffat, Chapman, and Holub, to suggest that for the most part missionaries and traditional healers worked side by side. The paper concludes with an analysis of reasons for the declining status of traditional healers during the period of Protectorate administration. A bibliography citing official publications and archival manuscripts of the Bechuanaland Protectorate, including a 1908 paper, "Suggested Measures for the Suppression of Witchcraft," are included.

E31   Dornan, S. S. (1928). "Rainmaking in South Africa." *Bantu Studies*, vol. 3, no. 2: 185-95.

Drawing on information supplied to him by the missionary D. F. Ellenberger and a so-called "witch-doctor" named Monyani, Dornan describes in detail different rainmaking ceremonies conducted in Tswana and Sotho-speaking societies, highlighting in particular the importance of the rainmaker, or *moroka wa pula*. Among those ceremonies the writer relates are procedures associated with the rainmaker's art of prognostication. Rituals associated with the consumption of a part of the gall bladder and of the "smelling out" of wizards are described. However, rites of sacrifice conducted by the chief and his subjects, contingent upon the failure of the rainmaker's art, arc also disclosed. For example, Dornan notes that oxen, baboons, and antelopes were frequently slaughtered to secure rain in times of drought. Not infrequently, he notes, humans were sacrificed. Indeed, human sacrifices were "the fountain head from which all other sacrifices for rain came." However, when humans could not be found, or when human sacrifices were outlawed, grass images of human beings were frequently burnt or thrown into rivers as offerings to the ancestral spirits. Following a detailed ethnographic account of rainmaking and human sacrificial rites in what was Northern Rhodesia, Dornan concludes by questioning why, "amongst those who have a fairly high conception of religion," including the Tswana, human sacrifices for rain persisted, whereas "among the Bantu whom we consider lowest in their religious conceptions," the ritual slaughter of humans never prevailed. The paper is not annotated and no reference materials are cited.

E32   Dornan, S. S. (1933). "Some Beliefs and Ceremonies Connected with thc Birth and Death of Twins Among the South African Natives." *South African Journal of Science*, vol. 29: 690-700.

Dornan's broad-ranging analysis of beliefs associated with twin-births in South Africa begins with a comparative overview of attitudes related to general reproductive "spectacles," or unusual births, in different cultures. The writer asserts that among the ancient Greeks and Romans, the Indians of Peru, the Iroquois of America, and the Hebrews of Canaan, twins are considered to be semi-divine. By contrast, among more "primitive" peoples, which the author identifies as the indigenous inhabitants of Australasia, Asia, and Africa, among them the Aryans of India and the Tswana-speaking people of South Africa, twins are deemed demonic, unnatural, or the monstrous portends of evil. The general inventory outlined in the first half of the paper is then followed by a more detailed account of specific rituals and beliefs related to twin-births among San, Khoikhoi, and Sotho-Tswana-speaking "natives." Dornan's sketch of Ovambo practices dealing with burial rites, purification rituals, and scarification techniques are also included. The author notes that among the Tswana, twin-birth burials and mourning rites sometimes continued for a period of six months or more, during which time the mother was isolated for fear that her "miscarriage" would result in drought. Importantly, however, Dornan suggests that not all South African "tribes" viewed twin-birth as unfortunate. The more "sophisticated" advanced "tribes," like the Xhosa and Zulu, he asserts, historically considered twin-births to signify good fortune. The writer maintains, however, that in southern Africa generally, twins are viewed as signs of social disorder and consequences of the displeasure of ancestors. In this sense, he concludes, the "ancient" and "primitive" rationale for the destruction of twins is "religious" or "magical," rather than economic.

E33   Dutton, E. A. T. (1923). *The Basuto of Basutoland*. London: Jonathan Cape.

Major Dutton, a resident with the British forces in Basutoland in the first decades of the 1900s, presents in this brief but popular monograph a sympathetic overview of Sotho history and custom. The study, replete with more than forty plates and maps of the Thaba Bosigo region, begins with a short description of the physical environment of Basutoland. Reasons for the presence of Bushman hunter-gatherers in the region are enumerated. An incomplete account of historical origins (hindered by the absence of complete records) is then followed by notes on the formation of the Sotho nation under Moshoeshoe immediately after the upheavals of the *difaqane*. Brief chapters further deal with the "People," "Their Life," and "Family Structures." Although little attention is specifically directed towards documenting religious beliefs and practices, the author, in a concluding chapter on "Superstition," displaces common Christian biases to acknowledge that Sotho belief, although initiated from "uncommon" assumptions, is no less logical than the tenets of Western European reason. The concluding chapter presents two Sotho folktales. The monograph ends with appendices delineating demographic and ethnographic statistics, as well as a short bibliography.

E34   Edgar, Robert. (1987). *Prophets With Honour: A Documentary History of Lekhotla la Bafo*. Johannesburg: Ravan Press.

Drawing on materials contained in archival sources, speeches, petitions, and published newspaper articles, Edgar provides a scholarly history of the Basutho resistance movement, Lekhotla la Bafo (Council of Commoners). Locating his document of the movement within the context of colonial British rule and concomitant economic and political exploitation in Basutoland—from 1868, when the British first administered the colony, through 1875, when the Cape Colony first established a national *pitso* (council), to the period of increased local resistance from 1923 to 1962, when the call for a united front in Basutoland was first made by the Lekhotla la Bafo—the writer contends that the movement was at the forefront of the defense of Sotho chieftainship. Focusing on the biographies of two leading figures in the movement, Josiel and Maphutseng Lefela, issues such as white trader exploitation, prohibitive British government trader licensing policies, and European circumvention of land ownership laws (prohibiting non-Sotho from acquiring land in the region) are highlighted. So too is the Lekhotla la Bafo's criticism of the National Council, appointed by the British to act as custodians of Sotho culture and conservative chieftainship. In this light, Edgar classifies the movement as a "self-help scheme" designed to preserve Sotho political, economic, and cultural institutions in the wake of exploitative and manipulative British colonial policy. A series of Lekhotla documents, presented in chronological order, are included, among them articles written for the Sesotho newspaper *Naledi* and the communist-informed journal *Umsebenzi* (formerly, *The South African Worker*). Other documents include letters to D. F. Malan and the United Nations Organization. The book, which is indexed, concludes with nineteen Lekhotla la Bafo songs (in Sesotho and English) that encapsulate the movement's basic beliefs and practices. An extensive list of notes is also appended, and the book is illustrated with a series of photographs.

E35   Eiselen, Werner M. (1928a). *Nuwe Tekste van Volkekundige Beland met Vertaling en Verklaarende Aantekenings*. Kaapstad: Nationale Pers.

In continuing the work of his predecessors Beyer, Hoffman, and Jacottet, Eiselen presents in this paper primary ethnographic materials from several Pedi, Lovedu, and Sotho orators and informants. The author provides the texts in the vernacular and gives a rough rendering of their contents in Afrikaans in the second half of the paper. The study is divided into five sections, beginning with material supplied by the informant Serote. The texts defy simple classification, but represent a mix of vague historical, legendary, and mythic material. In the piece entitled "Uit die Ou Dae (From the Old Days)," for example, the informant describes the "dark days" of the *difaqane*, but gives only scanty details.

Subsequent informants, among them Makuse, Magavi, and Mahlangu provide similarly brief stories concerned with burial, circumcision schools, female puberty rites, and prophecy. While authorial comment remains limited, Eiselen's presence is indisputable in the rendering of Sotho concepts into disparaging Afrikaans terms. In this regard, the choice of censorious subject headings is remarkable.

E36   Eiselen, Werner M. (1928b). "Die Eintlike Reendiens van die BaPedi." *South African Journal of Science*, vol. 25: 387-92.

Eiselen's paper describes aspects of the Pedi rain rite, originally conducted by Sotho-Tswana-speaking Pedi communities to secure good harvests during times of scarcity. The *volkekunderist* and ethnographer notes that while the ritual was initially prescribed for the beginning of the agricultural season, or for the commencement of plowing, the predominance of Christian converts in the Sekhukhuniland region of the north-eastern Transvaal beginning in the 1880s led to the abandonment of the procedure, except during times of drought. However, the rite remained largely unchanged prior to that time: Directed by the chief and his assistant rainmaker, the *moroka wa pula*, the ritual commenced with the selection of suitable girls, all virgins who had not yet had their first menstruation. The girls were then instructed to empty the contents of a ritual "rain pot" into a sacred enclosure around the rain hut, a ritual space referred to as the *ngwako wa pula*. The following morning, suggests Eiselen, the girls gathered in the *kgotla*, removed all European garments and ornaments, and refrained from consuming food or liquid before repeating the previous day's ritual, this time, however, sprinkling doctored water on the cultivated fields while singing traditional rain songs. The paper then enumerates the ritual procedures and taboos that are adhered to by young males during the course of the entire ritual process. Eiselen concludes by providing what he regards as an appropriate framework for the academic interpretation of the rites: They are forms of "*toergeloof* (sorcery)," he insists, that are comparable with the magical rites of the Amerindians and Sinhalese. The paper, written in Afrikaans, is briefly annotated but no bibliography is appended.

E37   Eiselen, Werner M. (1929). "The Sacred Fire of the Bapedi of the Transvaal." *South African Journal of Science*, vol. 26: 547-52.

Observers have noted that among some peoples fire is not prized for its utilitarian value alone but also for the mystical or magical powers with which it is associated. This article investigates the origin and development of what the author calls "fire worship" among the Pedi. However, Eiselen's explanatory theory assumes an evolutionary schema whereby veneration of fire is found in a primary sense among hunter-gatherers and only derivatively as a survival from earlier times among pastoralists or hoe-farmers, such as the Bapedi. In this regard, the Pedi are considered to provide evidence of what is termed the tribal or clan fire, a form of fire worship that possesses features both from hunter and pastoralist fire worship. Within this framework, the author sees the fire of the boys' initiation camp as an element of earlier hunter-gatherer fire rites. Similarly, the fire of the first-fruit festival is considered to lend legitimacy to obvious links with pastoralist fire veneration. In this context, initiations associated with the clan fire, in the introduction of the chief's principal wife into the capital, for example, is viewed as an occasion warranting the extinguishing and rekindling of the eternal fire of the realm. The article draws to a close on a speculative note about the probability that fire rites had their origin in obligations dictated by the civilizational process but eventuated in religious sentiment which, like all religious belief, endured even after the conditions that initially called them into being disappeared. A short bibliography, largely formed from German texts, is included.

E38   Eiselen, Werner M. (1932). "The Art of Divination as Practiced by the BaMasemola." *African Studies*, vol. 6: 1-29; 253-63.

Eiselen's article, though incomplete by the author's own admission, seeks to contribute to what was in the first decades of the twentieth century a thinly documented area of research: the "art" of divination. Based on the testimony of Tumise Maledimo, a diviner from the Northern Sotho-speaking Masemola community in the Middleburg district of the Transvaal, much of the article is devoted to a description of divining apparatus, that is, to the bones or wooden chips used in divination. Four major bones are identified: *more o moxolo*; *selumi*; *makxadi*; and *selumi se sethsadi*. Thereafter, forty-two minor "totemic" bones are categorized. Processes of divination are then outlined. In essence, the procedures are dependent on the skillful recognition and manipulation of so-called "male" and "female" principles contained in the pieces and considered to be reflections of the cosmic order. An elaborate analysis of the gender symbolism implicit in the art are included. Briefly, the writer argues that the symbolism of diversity, as expressed in the divining pieces, is a representation of various clans, natural phenomena, and even "unknown quantities," like strangers. When the bones are thrown to initiate the diagnostic process, their position in relation to the thrower as well as to each other provides clues for reading the individual and social text. In a system where interdependence and cooperation is greatly valued, therefore, the bones are not taken for granted; praises are sung to humor and respect them and to unlock the secrets of their hidden messages. Fittingly, two-thirds of the article consists of Sesotho praise-songs associated with the forty-one discrete formulas used in the interpretation of the divining bones.

E39   Eldridge, Elizabeth A. (1993). *A South African Kingdom: The Pursuit of Security in Nineteenth-Century Lesotho*. Cambridge: Cambridge University Press.

Eldridge's sophisticated historical reconstruction of nineteenth-century Lesotho analyzes changing sociopolitical and economic conditions among the Sotho subsequent to what the writer terms a pre-capitalist period of political autonomy. Details of Sotho responses to environmental and political challenges are, however, highlighted within a methodological framework that eschews both Bundy's "dependency theory" (which recognizes European encounter as the primary dynamic for change in African communities) and broader Marxist analyses that have focused on the interstices between precolonial societies and capitalist economies. By contrast, Eldridge adopts a complex, multifarious methodological infrastructure that analyzes the relationships between trade and settlement trends, political and gendered relations, local patterns of production and exchange, and the interactions between human agency and environmental geography. Drawing on interviews, missionary publications and correspondence, newspaper articles, periodical literature, and official publications from Cape and Basutoland colonial archives, she argues that the Sotho initially achieved security in the wake of colonial intrusion by successfully managing change and pursuing adaptive political strategies. The study, comprising fourteen chapters, an appendix, maps, illustrations, and tables, begins with an attempted reconstruction of settlement and trade patterns in Lesotho prior to 1830. The author contends that the dissemination of metal goods prior to that date substantiates claims that the Sotho were linked by a loose but extensive trading network from at least the period of the Iron Age. Indeed, surplus production for exchange predated European encounter by many years. Eldridge then examines the demographic and political setting of Basutoland subsequent to the *difaqane* in the 1820s. In Chapter Six, "Food and Politics: Feasts and Famines," she argues that the Sotho advanced a workable economic strategy during frequent periods of war and famine. The following chapter highlights gendered relations in nineteenth-century Lesotho. Here the author adeptly argues that women played a central role in Sotho economies insofar as they were valued for their reproductive and labor power, and for their roles as agents of social cohesion. The closing chapters of the study discuss the rise of regional European markets, colonial imposition, and the failure of local economies in contending with the widespread emergence of migrant labor.

E40   Ellenberger, D. Fred. (1912). *History of the Basuto, Ancient and Modern*. Trans. J. C. Macgregor. London: Caxton.

Ellenberger's standard historiography, a reflection of the concerns of the Paris Evangelical Missionary Society with which he was associated, provides a detailed account of Sotho oral history to the year 1833. The monograph is divided into two historically discrete sections, the "Ancient History of the Basuto," and the "Lifaqane Wars." In the first section, the writer attempts to reconstruct in fourteen chapters the origin of the Sotho-speaking peoples of southern Africa. Ellenberger traces Sotho origins to the "first man," Mopeli (or Tlake), whose descendent, Napo, appears at the beginning of both BaFokeng and BaKwena genealogies. In succeeding chapters the writer delineates the alignments of later Sotho-speaking tribes to these earliest Sotho communities. In the second section, which documents in twenty-seven chapters events associated with the *difaqane*, Ellenberger describes invasions by the Mantatisi, Matabele, and Zulu beginning in the year 1822. The section concludes with a chapter on the arrival in Thaba Bosiu of the first missionaries, among them Ellenberger. Concerning religion, the author draws on the works of Casalis, Moffat, and Rolland to claim that the Sotho "idea of God" became so "obliterated," and their religious tradition so "dim," that there was "nothing of religion among the people beyond a lively fear of bad spirits." However, consonant with developing nineteenth-century "scientific" discourse in the comparative study of religion, the missionary nevertheless illustrates aspects of Sotho totemism and witchcraft that did appear consistent with other "savage systems." As such, Sotho rainmaking rites are described in detail. The study concludes with a series of appendices describing the religion, superstition, social, civil, and political life, laws, and customs of the "ancient Basuto."

E41   Exton, H. (1870). "The Bojale: A Bechuana Ceremonial and Some Affinities of Native Customs." *Cape Monthly Magazine*, (n.s.) vol. 1: 281-89.

Remarking on the coincidences of similar religious practices among diffuse peoples, Exton confirms in the first half of this paper on female initiation rites among the Tswana that nineteenth-century diffusionist assertions legitimate his findings concerning possible and generic evolutionary patterns of descent. He argues, in this regard, that parallel religious beliefs and customs, including the prevalence of widespread flood narratives, suggest that the "barbarians" of Africa and the races of Europe and the Americas could have originated in a common Asian ancestry. Burial rites; calendrical calculations based on numerology; procedures for the "purchase" of wives (*bogadi*); and circumcision rites in Bechuanaland were consequently not only similar to rituals and beliefs in other parts of the world (including India, Tibet, Mongolia, Japan, and even Mexico), but were examples of Asian religious practices from which disparate religious experiences evolved. However, the paper is primarily concerned with highlighting the prevalence of circumcision rituals (male *bogwera* and female *bojale* rites) among the Tswana. Endorsing Livingstone's "Arabian" etiology, Exton asserts in the second half of the essay that male circumcision rituals were continuous with Muslim roots rather than Asian or Jewish origins. His description of the "Spartan" *bojale* rites, by contrast, relies perhaps on a more Greco-Roman epitome. The "mysterious" new moon *bojale* rites he witnesses in the Ngwaketse town of Kanye in 1869 were, notwithstanding, also analogous with the puberty rituals of the Egyptians described by Diodorus Siculus. Of interest to historians of comparative religion in southern Africa for its wide-ranging use of reflexive analogy, Exton's work remains of only passing importance for interpreters of the meaning, function, and structure of *bojale*.

E42   Fairclough, T. L. (1904-1905). "Notes on the Basuto, their History, Country, etc." *Journal of the African Society*, vol. 4, no. 13: 194-205.

In this brief record of Sotho history, of interest to readers of comparative religion primarily for its discussion of male and female initiation rites, Fairclough dispels all claims concerning the premodern etiology of Sotho societies in southern Africa as "myth." He suggests, instead, that the Sotho emerged in what became known as Lesotho in the seventeenth century. Having argued this fact, his review of Sotho records begins in 1814 with the death of the paramount Mohlomi. Details of Moshoeshoe's genealogy are then provided. Also, anecdotes relating to Moshoeshoe's "sarcastic" presentation of cattle to Mzilikazi's warriors, following the latter's unsuccessful attempt at invading Thaba Bosiu, and the Sotho's propensity for human flesh, are enumerated. In this regard, claims Fairclough, cannibalism became an "acquired taste" with the Mayiane clan, who were deprived of their lands and cattle during the *difaqane*. "From eating the flesh of their enemies killed in battle, as a means of subsistence, it was an easy step," claims the author, "to the confirmed habit" of anthropophagy. The writer's central concern, however, appears to be related to initiation schools and rites. Perhaps because "little or nothing is known as to what is taught in these schools," which is "just as well," suggests Fairclough, there is also little or nothing that the writer reveals that is either new or true in his account of these rites.

E43   Feddema, J. P. (1966). "Tswana Ritual Concerning Rain." *African Studies*, vol. 25, no. 3: 181-95.

Supplementing Eiselen's (1928) account of rain rituals among the Pedi in the northern Transvaal, and comparing his notes with Schapera's (1930) analysis of BaKgatla rainmaking rites in the Bechuanaland Protectorate, Feddema highlights aspects of the "first rains" (*tseola*, or *sephai*) rites prevalent among the BaKwena, BaHurutshe, and BaTlokwa. Consulting the communications of missionaries, government agents, and Tswana-speaking informants, his paper outlines the role of the *moroka wa pula* (rainmaker) in rituals associated with the invocation of the chief's ancestors; the use of fire rituals in the *kgotla*, or community meeting-place; and instructions for the use of the so-called "rain pot" in the rain enclosure, or *sogatlwana sa pula*. Confirming Dornan's (1928) earlier observations, and referring to Willoughby's (1923) account of the sacrifice of a black ox by the BaNgwato in the 1860s, Feddema also describes Tswana preparations for the infrequent sacrifice of humans during periods of national peril or extremity. The importance of sacrifices to a rain "god" known as Thobega, as well as to his assistant, Motsidi—both of whom were said to be resident in the sacred western Transvaal mountain called Tswenyane—are recounted. So too are aspects associated with preparatory rites of purification. Feddema notes that prior to the rain ritual proper the fields were ritually purified by young girls in a rite known as the *go thlapisa lefatshe*. Following a brief account of taboos associated with rain, or occurrences associated with the prevalence of drought, including "*dibela*" or "harmful medicines" related to abortion, miscarriage, or adultery, the writer analyzes reasons for the disappearance or modification of rainmaking rites. Among the reasons he identifies include contact with Europeans and Christian cooperation with traditional Tswana-speaking chiefs. The paper is briefly annotated and a bibliography is appended.

E44   Ferguson, James (1985). "The Bovine Mystique: Power, Property and Livestock in Rural Lesotho." *Man* (n.s.) vol. 20: 647-74.

Ferguson's paper proposes a rethinking of common or "utilitarian," "dualist" theoretical interpretations regarding livestock-keeping in Lesotho. Adopting the "new historicist" approach favored by anthropologist Colin Murray, the writer argues that "cultural rules" define and "valorize" livestock as a special category of property. In this sense, power relations, centered on the hierarchical associations between men and women, seniors and juniors, and patrons and clients serve to reinforce the contested nature of what Ferguson calls a "bovine mystique." In turn, that "mystique" establishes social, political, and economic interests within the ruling group that confirm the writer's opinion that livestock are maintained for religious, social, and symbolic reasons not necessarily commensurate with their economic or commodity value alone. He presents as evidence for this opinion oral interviews that patently debunk crude utilitarian models, but insists that the dual economy theory is only a beginning; social, political, and economic conditions structuring livestock-keeping must be accommodated. Following his evidence for these assertions, Ferguson locates the debate within the household, community, and migrant labor systems, focusing on power relations and socioeconomic realities that have organized livestock-keeping in Lesotho. He contends that the "one-way barrier" that prevents livestock from being transferred into cash serves to reinforce the interests of those in power. For example, within the household and wider community, the "bovine mystique" enables an absent migrant laborer to support his wife, child, and other dependents, in turn ensuring a more fruitful future. The paper is annotated.

E45   Franz, G. H. (1931). "Some Customs of the Transvaal Basuto." *Bantu Studies*, vol. 5: 241-46.

Subtitled "The Customs and Religious Observances of the Native People," this short article comprises several translations of Sesotho texts relating primarily to agricultural and political ritual. No mention is made of either the method of collection or the informants who contributed to the work. The article focuses almost entirely on the agricultural year of the Sotho and the seasonal cycle of activities that are organized around it. Sotho life is depicted as a "pendulum" that swings back and forth between ceremonies of jubilation and thanksgiving following a rainy season and supplications for rain in the event of drought. Details of divining and redressive rituals that are performed at various intervals during the agricultural year are outlined and descriptions of the key actors involved are provided. In this regard, the author develops brief notes on the officiating functions performed by the chief and his use of pubescent youths in rituals. The specific medicines used in the various ceremonies are also identified. The article closes with a supplementary explanation of several Sesotho terms.

E46   Griffith, Charles (1877-1878). "Some Observations on Witchcraft in Basutoland." *Transactions of the [South African] Philosophical Society*, vol. 1, no. 2: 87-92.

In this brief paper, read before the South African Philosophical Society by J. X. Merriman, Griffith discusses the institution of witchcraft among the Sotho. Informed by racist discourse consonant with late nineteenth-century diatribe, the writer, a British government agent in Basutoland, maintains that the witchdoctor—"a blood-stained fetish worshipper"—is the "great foe of civilization and good government." Moreover, the "terrorism" of witchcraft, a product of "calibanesque intellect," Griffith asserts, is intimately connected with ancestor veneration, which he insists is "itself a branch of Animism." Of more interest to the history of the comparative study of religion than Griffith's sweeping denunciations of Sotho religion, perhaps, is his distinction between three types of witches: Day doctors (*bongaka*); night witches (*baloi*); and rainmakers. Doctors, he contends, aim to cure the sick or find witches by deploying divinatory objects (including bones, or *ditaola*). *Baloi*, by contrast, "run around naked at night." They ride on horses and are accompanied by monkeys who spill their blood on unsuspecting victims. The rain-doctors (*ngaka ea pula*) are mischievous but politically important persons in periods of drought. "Happily," confides the author, "the missionaries have . . . the reputation of being the best rain-doctors." In conclusion, Griffith maintains that the "world-wide error" of witchcraft "fetishism" is one of the "dark facts" of nature that neither civilization nor education can subdue.

E47   Hammond-Tooke, W. D. (1981). *Boundaries and Belief: The Structure of a Sotho Worldview*. Johannesburg: Witwatersrand University Press.

Informed by the structuralist methodological concerns of Claude Lévi-Strauss, and drawing on the diffusionist predilections of French missionary-ethnographer Henri-Alexandre Junod, Hammond-Tooke examines in this work aspects of Sotho cosmology among the Kgaga of the Lowveld. His analysis of their conceptual or symbolic worldview suggests that the Kgaga postulate the presence of "super-empirical" intelligences that can alter events pertaining to social realities. Their "quadripartite causative theory," in direct opposition to impersonal Western worldviews, Hammond-Tooke contends, consists of a sky god (Kutshane), ancestors (*badimo*), witches, and sorcerers, all of which inform aspects of social structure. Hammond-Tooke suggests, for example, that belief in ancestors provides a potent sanction against breaches of communally-oriented kinship patterns and a charter for the performance of life-cycle rites. The study is divided into five chapters, beginning with an outline of Kgaga social organization in which are included notes on chieftaincy, marriage, and kinship. Chapter Two, entitled "The Threshold of Understanding Kgaga Initiation," analyzes in detail four initiation rituals: *bodika* (circumcision) rituals for boys, *bojale* rites for girls, and *bogwera* or "friendship" rites for boys and for girls. These rituals, asserts Hammond-Tooke, introduce to young Kgaga men and women central elements of the moral and cognitive universe of Sotho society. In Chapter Three, the writer examines beliefs and practices associated with the supreme being, Kutshane, ancestor cults, and witchcraft. This is followed by a discussion in Chapter Four of ritual pollution in terms of Trevor Verryn's conceptual schema pertaining to the symbolism of "heat" and "coolness" in Sotho-Tswana religion. The concluding chapter enumerates several comparisons with Pedi, Tsonga, and Zulu social organization. The work is richly annotated and maps and a bibliography are included.

E48   Harries, C. L. (1929). *The Laws and Customs of the Bapedi and Cognate Tribes of the Transvaal*. Johannesburg: Hortors.

Written in an attempt to solve the "Native Question" in southern Africa, Major Harries draws on a wealth of expert experience, notably as Pass Officer, Native Sub-Commissioner, and Magistrate, to "correctly advise native clients in matters regarding their domestic and tribal affairs." His "indulgences" are divided into eight chapters. The first enumerates aspects of customary law associated with courtship, marriage, polygamy, impotency, infidelity, incest, desertion, divorce, and the delivery of *lenyalo* (*lobolo*). The second and third examine inheritance laws and land and agricultural distribution; the fourth, native circumcision (*bodikane* and *bogwera*) schools; and the fifth, "inter-tribal customs" associated with warfare and *dingaka* legislation. The final three chapters then describe customary laws dealing with murder, incest, rape, seduction, abduction, concealment of birth, treason, assault, the installation of chiefs and, in Chapter Eight, "Native Superstition," laws regarding the practices of the *ngaka* (doctor), *moneshapula* (rainmaker), and *baloi* (sorcerers). The work includes a glossary and facsimile of the Native Administration Act no. 38 of 1927.

E49   Hoffmann, C. (1928). "Sotho texte aus dem Holzbusch-Gebirge in Transvaal: Part I: Ehenfrau, Mutter und Kind; Der Ackerbau." *Zeitschrift für Eingeborenen Sprachen*, vol. 18, no. 4: 241-72.

In the first of five articles on the religious beliefs and practices of the Northern Sotho, Hoffmann examines several agricultural rites and first-fruit ceremonies predominant among the Letsoalo of the Transvaal. Extended notes on rainmaking rituals, including rain hunts, are provided, as are Hoffmann's records of rituals of taboos associated with death and illness. The paper is annotated. The text is in German.

E50   Hoffmann, C. (1929). "Sotho texte aus dem Holzbusch-Gebirge in Transvaal: Part II: Gottesglaube und Ahnenverehrung bei den Basutho; Propheten und Zauberdoktoren; und Religiöse Vorstellungen und Gebote." *Zeitschrift für Eingeborenen Sprachen*, vol. 19, no. 4: 268-308.

In the most wide-ranging of the writer's recollections of the religion of the Northern Sotho, Hoffmann describes beliefs associated with ritual impurity and deity veneration among the Letsoalo. Primarily, he recalls that masturbation, menstruation, adultery, birth, illness, and death were all considered ritually polluting. However, notes on the rites for doctoring agricultural lands and cattle, the use of animal entrails and stellar constellations in divination and prophecy, and belief in a number of deities, among them Hotlo, Hodi, and Hubeane, or Lebepe, are also described. The paper is annotated. The text is in German

E51   Hoffmann, C. (1931). "Sotho texte aus dem Holzbusch-Gebirge in Transvaal: Part III: Toteme und Verbote." *Zeitschrift für Eingeborenen Sprachen*, vol. 21, no. 2: 98-122.

Following his earlier overview of overtly religious aspects of Northern Sotho society, Hoffmann examines in this paper examples of totemism and taboo. First, he enumerates the various Sotho-speaking societies and their respective totems (*seano*). For example, he recalls that the BaTlokwa had as their totem the leopard; that the BoLubedu followed the impala and porcupine; the Dikgale, the hyena; the Hananoa, the crocodile; and the Masemola, the lion. Second,

Hoffmann describes in detail taboos associated with diet, initiation, and death and burial, including abortion. Of particular interest is the writer's overview of Northern Sotho taboos associated with women. Analytical notes on reasons why women were excluded from several social events due to conditions of ritual impurity or "pollution," including menstruation and post-natal seclusion, are included. The paper, in German, is annotated.

E52   Hoffmann, C. (1932a). "Sotho texte aus dem Holzbusch-Gebirge in Transvaal: Part IV: Naturgeiste und Zauberkräfte." *Zeitschrift für Eingeborenen Sprachen*, vol. 22, no. 3: 161-79.

In this very brief paper Hoffmann provides notes on ancestor veneration, divination, and "animism," or the worship of spirits believed to inhabit natural phenomena, like stones and trees. He suggests that the Northern Sotho of the Transvaal were acquainted with techniques that required diviners to read "omens" indicated by celestial constellations, the cosmic patterns of comets and meteorites, and lunar phases. The text is in German.

E53   Hoffmann, C. (1932b). "Sotho texte aus dem Holzbusch-Gebirge in Transvaal: Part V: Die Seele (Geist) im Tode und nach dem Tode." *Zeitschrift für Eingeborenen Sprachen*, vol. 23, no. 1: 59-75.

In the final paper in a series of articles on the religious beliefs and practices of the Northern Sotho, Hoffmann describes several rituals associated with post-mortem experience among the Transvaal Letsoalo. While the writer repeats facets of Sotho religion previously examined, among them "animist" inclinations, informative materials relating to dreams and divination are recorded. For example, Hoffmann recounts the experiences of Sotho-speaking wizards (*baloi*), among them a man called Sereke, who said that he returned from the land of ancestral spirits following an extended period of "dreaming." Brief notes on the practice of procuring special protective medicines from human flesh, especially the flesh of aliens killed in war, are also included. The paper, in German, is briefly annotated.

E54   Hunt, D. R. (1931). "An Account of the BaPedi." *Bantu Studies*, vol. 5, no. 4: 275-326.

Hunt's professedly historical account of the Tswana-speaking Pedi people of the northern Transvaal draws on the writer's experiences as Native Commissioner of Sekhukhuniland in the 1920s. He asserts that the Pedi, who originated from a small BaKgatla community living at Mapogole, near the source of the Vaal

River, took their name from an iron-making clan, the Vhambedzi, whom they encountered in what is now the Steelpoort River region of the northern Transvaal. Adopting the totem of the porcupine, or *noko*, in the 1650s, the Pedi, argues Hunt, began to subjugate the local Baroka peoples—"a degenerate offshoot of the BaRonga"—and, by the 1880s, had incorporated a number of Swazi and Ndebele clans under their rule. The paper, which is divided into eight short chapters, proceeds to delineate events in Pedi history, further illustrating the writer's diffusionist interest in the genealogy of Tswana-speaking communities in the northern Transvaal. In Chapter Three, Chief Sekwati's defense of the Pedi stronghold at Phiring is narrated, as is his successful defeat of Hendrik Potgieter's Boer commandos in 1852 and his entering into a treaty between the Pedi and the Lydenburg Republic in 1857. Chapters Four through Eight highlight events in Chief Sekhukhuni I's reign, from the time of Sekwati's death in 1861 to Sekhukhuni's own death in 1882. Notes on the influence of missionaries among the Pedi are also narrated from the date of the Berlin Missionary Society's initial mission, in 1860, to 1929, when the Roman Catholic Church inaugurated its first mission at Morgenzon. The paper is not annotated, although genealogical tables listing Pedi chiefs are appended.

E55   Jacottet, Eugene (1908). *The Treasury of Basutho Lore*. London: Kegan Paul.

Jacottet, who was a Paris Evangelical Missionary Society agent at Mount Moria, presents a selection of forty-three folktales in Sesotho with English translations. The tales are divided into three categories: First, "marvellous tales," in which incidents belonging to the "fabulous world" are enumerated; second, "animal tales"; and third, "moral and household tales." In his brief introduction, Jacottet charts the history of published works dealing with Bantu folklore, acknowledging his indebtedness to the missionaries Arbousset and Casalis. He considers the folktales these missionaries collected to be ancient because they contain little or no substance related to European encounter (unlike later Ronga and Angolan folklore). The volume professes to be the first installment of further publications intended to present additional material pertaining to Sesotho folklore. Detailed footnotes suggesting similarities, parallels, and derivations from adjacent southern and central African communities are provided.

E56   Jennings, A. E. (1933). *Bogadi: A Study of the Marriage Laws and Customs of the Bechuana Tribes of South Africa*. Tiger Kloof, Kuruman: London Missionary Society.

Drawing on intelligence supplied by local informants, among them several "native" Christians, European traders, and Tswana traditionalists, including

Reverend Andrew Kgasa (a BaNgwaketse Marriage Officer); Morolon Monnakanye (a deacon at the London Missionary Society church in Kuruman); and Sekgoma, the BaMangwato chief, Jennings questions the justification for allowing the practice of *bogadi* or "bride-price" transactions in the Bechuanaland Protectorate. He concludes that, under the pressures of colonial control, migrant labor, the collapse of chiefly authority, and the dissolution of traditional "tribal" administration, the retention of *bogadi* is unwarranted. However, his conclusion is premised upon a number of more wide-ranging arguments. First, that polyandry and bride-price rites in many lands (including Tibet) have disappeared. Second, that *bogadi* contracts imply not only that a woman's reproductive rights are purchased, but that a child's life is traded. *Bogadi*, in this sense, is a form of slavery. Third, however, Jennings' principal objection to this "unconscionable" transaction appears to be conditioned by personal religious conviction. "Only by renouncing the heathen concept of *bogadi*," he asserts, "is it possible to build up a vigorous Christian Church among the Natives of South Africa." While at one time *bogadi* might have enhanced the value of a child's life, compensated for the cost of bringing up a child, or made marriage subject to the jurisdiction of the chief, thus securing social order, aspects such as the loaning of wives to friends and the contractual arrangements that make marriage a form of "sexual slavery," suggests the writer, endorse opinions that *bogadi* is an "uncivilised" and "unchristian" practice. The monograph is not annotated.

E57   Jones, G. I. (1951). *Basutoland Medicine Murder: A Report on the Recent Outbreak of Diretlo Murders in Basutoland*. Command Paper no. 8209. London: His Majesty's Stationary Office.

In a paper presented to the British parliament on behalf of the Secretary of State for Commonwealth Relations and the High Commissioner for Basutoland, the Bechuanaland Protectorate, and Swaziland, Cambridge University anthropology lecturer G. I. Jones provides an outline of the nature and significance of ritual or "medicine murders" in Basutoland. Included is a general survey of Sotho public opinion, an in-depth investigation of Sotho attitudes to ritual "medicine killings" in Butha Butha, Maketeng, and Mokhotlong, and a detailed analysis of criminal records connected with *diretlo* (ritual medicine) "murder." The paper is divided into eight chapters. In the first, Jones provides background notes on historical relations, sociopolitical activity, and economic structure in Basutoland. In the second, he reviews several paradigmatic legal cases dealing with *diretlo* murders in Basutoland in the 1940s. He notes that because of internecine warfare in the region in the early nineteenth century the flesh of tribal enemies killed in battle was often used by sacred specialists or *dingaka* to produce *lenaka*, or "protection medicine." Parts of the bodies of victims were also used to promote the fertility of crops or increase the prestige of powerful political figures. Following Marwick (1940), he notes in Chapters Three and Four,

"Heathen Institutions," and "European Influences," that the Sotho considered such practices to have been imported from the Zulu or as a result of "evil white" influences. In this regard, the writer proposes that Basuto Pioneer soldiers who were exposed to the dangers of battle in the Second World War, and who found that ritual sacrifices for *diretlo* actually "worked," were responsible for perpetuating such practices in twentieth-century Basutoland. Thus, the procurement of human "medicines," he suggests, was thought by many to be a "regrettable" but "necessary" practice. In part, asserts Jones, positive attitudes to *diretlo* were also a consequence of more general and widespread beliefs in "witchcraft" and "sorcery." Chapters Five through Eight report case studies that associate *diretlo* sacrifices with chieftainship, native administration, and judicial reform. The final chapter is of particular interest, insofar as Jones raises issues related to colonial and police collusion in matters of "ritual" murder—a view, he asserts, not as "unreasonable" as it might sound. The report is annotated with reference to secondary ethnographic evidence and includes a summary of cases and lists of murders believed to be associated with *diretlo* "murder."

E58   Jones, G. I. (1966). "Chiefly Succession in Basutoland." In Jack Goody (ed.) *Succession to High Office*. Cambridge: Cambridge University Press. 57-81.

Drawing on information supplied in tables documenting genealogical succession in the line of Moshoeshoe, Letsie I, Lerotholi, and Letsie II, Jones examines the procedural structures utilized by paramount and ward chiefs to facilitate succession in Lesotho in the years 1868 to 1920. In this regard, the writer argues that "agnatic succession" enabled chiefs to ensure lawful and consensual rule while developing a decentralized government based on an essentially nepotistic system. Furthermore, the establishment of councils and judicial systems of rule based on agnatic patronage, implemented upon a paramount's death, ensured the stable transition of power at a time of possible political instability. Jones mentions that the Sotho custom of allowing the eldest son of the senior (first) wife to succeed the chief allowed the incumbent ruler to "build up" the heir, endow him with authority and power, and generally construct legitimacy. The brief article is annotated and an appendix furnishing detailed genealogies of the Makhaula and Molapo wards is included.

E59   Kinsman, Margaret (1983). "Beasts of Burden: The Subordination of Southern Tswana Women, 1800-1840." *Journal of Southern African Studies*, vol. 10: 39-54.

Kinsman's paper examines reasons why women were condemned to a subordinate position in Tswana societies. Pointing out that these societies were distinctly patriarchal, she notes that scholarship has nonetheless avoided gender-sensitive issues in African history. While they have analyzed the social upheavals experienced by African societies during the nineteenth century, they have failed to explore reasons for the social conditioning of subordinance among women. In these terms, her paper seeks to redress an historical lacuna by examining the social structures that served to restrain Southern Tswana women in the years between 1800 and 1840. Starting from the theoretical position proposed by social analysts E. P. Thompson and Pierre Bourdieu, Kinsman first describes the socioeconomic organization of Tswana society, analyzing enterprises associated with family-based economic activities. The gendered economic roles enacted by women in society are highlighted. Primarily, argues Kinsman, these roles consisted of cultivating the land, gathering wild foods (*veldkos*), and fabricating family utensils. While essentially manual laborers, women were also placed in positions of dependency, since men owned the land and other critical resources. Kinsman describes this situation in great detail. Of particular significance to readers of Tswana religion, however, is her analysis of how religious activity was the one outlet that allowed women to articulate independent ideas and actions. The role of women in the preparation of rainmaking rites, and in dancing in rain ceremonies, she suggests, provided women with an arena within which to express personal opinion. Consequently, the predominance of female prophets or "oracles" in Sotho-Tswana societies, she suggests, ought not be thought of as unusual. In some respects, however, Kinsman also notes that religious rituals served to inhibit the independence of women. Indeed, certain religious ideas that were inculcated during female initiation (*bojale*) reinforced positions of submissiveness. The paper is annotated and a bibliography is appended.

E60   Kooijman, Kunnie F. M. (1978). *Social and Economic Change in a Tswana Village*. Leiden: African Study Centre.

Drawing on historical records, oral tradition, and case studies accumulated during two years of fieldwork among a Tswana-speaking BaKgatla community in the South African-Botswana borderland, anthropologist Kunnie Kooijman analyzes the processes of social change indicative of colonial conquest and imperial displacement. Her analysis of one village, Bokaa, suggests that with the breakdown of traditional leadership roles under colonial rule, a significant rise in "individualism" in contemporary BaKgatla society occurred. In economic activities, she argues, this social phenomenon became apparent in the breakdown of kinship structures. Similarly, settlement patterns were altered as a result of increasing individualism. Whereas the village was traditionally viewed as the focus of economic and social activity, many BaKgatla communities began from the 1950s to live semi-permanently on agricultural land or in migrant labor settlements in South Africa. The thesis, divided into seven chapters, begins with an account of early BaKgatla history, moving in Chapters Two and Three to an overview of the changing role of BaKgatla chieftainship and economic organization from the 1890s. In Chapters Four through Six the writer then analyzes changing patterns of political organization in Bechuanaland during the latter half of the twentieth century. Aspects of change that the author examines include the "totemic" nature of lineage patterns in Chapter Four; betrothal and *bogadi* (bridewealth) rites in Chapter Five; and the shifting symbolisms associated with cattle and agricultural wealth in Chapter Six. The last chapter highlights the more subtle changes in social values that occurred in BaKgatla societies as a consequence of the general movement from "communalism" to individualism in social relations. The study is annotated and a bibliography is included.

E61   Krige, Eileen Jensen (1932). "The Social Significance of Beer Among the Balobedu." *Bantu Studies*, vol. 6: 343-57.

In an examination of four different varieties of beer made from sorghum, or "*mpoho*" (*byaloa, mapoto, kapea, and kekoakoa*), anthropologist Eileen Krige analyzes the multivalent social, economic, and religious significance of beer among the Balobedu (Lovedu) of the Drakensberg region of the north-eastern Transvaal. Her paper begins, however, with a brief overview of the uses of marula beers. These beers, she notes, exerted only a marginal influence in society because of their seasonal availability. The paper then turns to analyze the significance of *mpoho*. Primarily, Krige suggests, the most important value of the beer was associated with nutrition. But *mpoho* was also an acceptable form of payment in transactions concerned with exchanges for the procurement of traditional medicines or for offering tribute to local headmen (*legota*). The section of the paper entitled "Social and Ritual Value of Beer," however, contains the central thesis of the argument. Here, Krige delineates the use of beer as a reconciliatory agent or as a consummating signal in Northern Sotho sexual relations. In "the old days," when a bride was required to be a virgin, notes the writer, a "virginity calabash" was brewed to celebrate required purity; if a bride was deemed impure by the inspecting woman, the calabash would receive a ritual piercing and the erstwhile bride sent home. In this sense, Krige notes, beer drinking and brewing was intimately tied to rites of passage. In the final section, an assessment of the relationship between beer and "religious life" is undertaken. For example, the writer examines the sacred character of *mpoho*, considered as "the food of the gods." Krige contends that beer offerings were in many cases the preferred method of propitiating the ancestors. The *komana* (agricultural) rituals, which Krige maintains are the most important rites in the religious life of the Sotho-speaking Lovedu, all entail the presentation of beer to the ancestors in pleas for the blessings of rain or good harvests. The paper is annotated.

E62   Krige, Eileen Jensen (1954). "A Lovedu Prayer—The Light it Throws on the Ancestor Cult." *African Studies*, vol. 33: 91-97.

Krige gives a brief but positive and sympathetic portrayal of the ancestor cult as practiced by the Northern Sotho Lovedu. Based on research conducted in several South African urban areas, the author documents reasons for the continued resilience of ancestor cults. Analyzing the Lovedu Prayer, she suggests, can help to highlight the central ideas that have sustained the ancestor cult in the face of change. Thus, the Khilovedu text of the prayer is given and an English translation is included. Thereafter, an analysis of the content of component phrases is provided. Essentially, Krige notes how the prayer describes practices associated with the queen's attempt to forestall or overcome drought by offering beer or meat to her ancestors. In this regard, she concludes that the relationship between the queen and the ancestors (whom the author refers to as "gods") is one indicative of human warmth but parental authority. However, even this authority operates within a cosmic and moral order that reminds the queen of her status as arbiter between humans and ancestors. Krige concludes that it is the stabilizing effect of this morally-grounded relationship, and the sense of security it engenders, that defies the eroding forces of time and keeps the ancestor cult not only alive but relevant to an ever-changing environment.

E63   Krige, Eileen Jensen, and J. D. Krige (1943). *The Realm of the Rain Queen*. Oxford: Oxford University Press.

Comprising an anthropological account of the life of a Sotho-speaking community in the north-eastern Transvaal, this landmark study of the Lovedu "Rain Queen" is based upon personal observation and the accounts of informants obtained during fieldwork conducted in the Drakensberg from 1936 to 1938. The title of the work refers to the rain cult of the queen, Mujaji, who was reputed to have the ability to transform clouds and induce precipitation. However, while the work focuses on the role of the rain queen, several of the seventeen chapters cover topics ranging from Lovedu agricultural practices to the social and symbolic structures of Lovedu rites. In the chapter entitled "Fertility and the Drum Cult," for example, an essentially structural-functionalist analysis of the ritual use of a "sacred drum" in procuring rain is provided. Referring to the structure of Sotho religion in a later chapter, "The Role of the Ancestors," the Kriges argue that the Lovedu neither worshipped "nature spirits" nor "hero gods." Rather, their "gods" were "ancestors." The ancestors, the writers suggest, were responsible for crop fertility, healing, and the protection of the community from harm. Numerous rituals are described in detail, including the *thugula* (earth) ceremony, during which beer was brewed and a cow sacrificed to propitiate ancestors. In the chapter specifically concerned with the "rain cult," the Kriges claim that the powers of the queen were not absolute; the queen was assisted by rain-doctors and could control rain only in agreement with her ancestors. Moreover, certain occurrences, including abortion, miscarriage, or being struck by lightning could weaken the queen's "rain charms." Such eventualities could be corrected, the authors note, by the burial of the deceased in a wet place so that the negative abundance of "heat" generated by impurity might be overcome. In the event of drought, usually believed to be caused by "wrong burial," or when "rain taboos" were broken, various measures, including the propitiation of gifts and the performance of dances, were thus utilized to induce pity and compassion in the rain queen. The concluding chapters analyze Lovedu attitudes to beer, sex, and the pressures of Western Christian conquest. The comprehensive study includes maps, illustrations, and an index.

E64   Krige, Eileen Jensen, and J. D. Krige (1954). "The Lobedu of the Transvaal." In Daryll Forde (ed.) *African Worlds*. London: Oxford University Press. 55-82.

Interpreting aspects of the structure of Lovedu society, social anthropologists Krige and Krige claim that natural order among Sotho-speakers in the northeastern Transvaal region of South Africa is premised upon the assumption that "cosmic forces" are controllable events. Hence, they identify four methods whereby the Lovedu control natural phenomena: First, *vunaga*, is the skilled use of impersonal power believed to be inherently concentrated in persons and objects. The authors claim that *vunaga* is a "medico-magical" practice performed by an expert doctor (*ngaka*) and applied in the interests of health and well-being. Second, suggest the authors, *dithugula* is deployed to indirectly influence the ancestors; the ancestors may cause harm and sickness to descendants who neglect them and are therefore propitiated to ensure good crops, fertility, good fortune, and success. Here, the use of objects once in the possession of, or in close contact with ancestors (beads, animals, or clothing), are employed. Third, the divine queen may be approached to secure the regularity of seasonal change; her death, by contrast, might mark the onset of drought, famine, or the breakdown of social order. Fourth, and finally, cosmic forces can be controlled or manipulated to promote abundance and rain by using a "sacred drum" during the designated *digoma* (drum) ritual. Prior to the authors' examination of these four techniques, however, the article briefly describes the subsistence economies and patrilineal social structures of Lovedu society. Thereafter, "Myths of Origin" are discussed; Khuzwane, a distant creator god; Modimo, a god equated with "conditional destiny"; and myths representing accounts of the origin of political order are mentioned. In the section entitled "Conception of the Natural Order," the authors then examine the etiology of evil in Lovedu society. They suggest that evil is symbolically represented by "heat" or "burning" (*leswa*). Indeed, heat is perceived to denote a disturbance caused by negative events such as abortions and miscarriages. "Cooling" medicines, such as the burying of dead fetuses in wet soil, by contrast, are considered effective mechanisms for realigning social imbalance. In a concluding section entitled "Witchcraft and Sorcery," the authors distinguish between "day witches" (sorcerers), and night witches. The (day) sorcerer utilizes "natural, known powers of medicine for anti-social ends," while the (night) witch utilizes evil powers beyond ordinary understanding. The article, while providing little discussion of the material conditions that gave rise to Lovedu belief and rituals (aside from a brief mention of Western Christian economic and political encroachment), highlights aspects of primary importance to historians of religion in the region. The paper is sparsely annotated.

E65   Kropf, A. (1879). "The Gods of The Basuto." *[South African] Folk-Lore Journal*, vol. 1, no. 2: 32-33.

In this report Kropf extracts entries from the diaries of a Berlin Missionary Society agent stationed among Malaboch's peoples at Blaauberg in the Transvaal. He reports that, in "explaining the articles of our belief," the missionary, a man called Stech, discovered that the Northern Sotho knew of twelve different gods. "At the head of these stands Ralabepa, the Father of all might and power, to be feared for his revenge, and power of fire." Also, notes Kropf, the Sotho believed in a god of water, Ramachosoa; a god of stone, Ramaepa; a forest god, called Sedatyane; a vengeful snake-god, called Toona; and a god of dance, called Lotiloe. Finally, asserts Kropf, the Sotho believed in several celestial bodies, foremost among them a comet known as Modututsa. The report is not annotated.

E66   Kuper, Adam (1975a). "Preferential Marriage and Polygyny Among the Tswana." In M. Fortes and S. Patterson (eds.) *Studies in African Social Anthropology*. London, New York, and San Francisco: Academic Press. 121-34.

In general support of Schapera's argument that marriage strategies among Tswana-speakers must be interpreted in terms of social organization and political function, Kuper analyzes reasons for the decline of preferential close-kin marriages in what was the Bechuanaland Protectorate. Accepting Schapera's thesis, the writer argues that the distinctive predilection for lineal-kin marriages among Tswana nobles, in particular, declined as a consequence of a general weakening of polygamous relations and political disorder. In this regard, Kuper asserts that the incentive to marry among close kin decreases as chiefs and their advisors attempt to make marriage as politically advantageous as possible. Drawing extensively on Schapera's account, however, he confirms that agnatic marriages have remained an important aspect of Tswana social organization: Close-kin alliances counterbalance the divisive tendencies of the ward system while reinforcing the accumulation of economic power by fostering the retention of bridewealth (*bogadi*). The paper contains a short bibliography citing secondary resources.

E67   Kuper, Adam (1975b). "The Social Structure of the Sotho-Speaking Peoples of Southern Africa." *Africa*, vol. 45, no. 1: 67-81 and no. 2: 139-49.

In this paper Kuper examines aspects of tribal organization and chiefdom administration to assess the relationship between political arrangements and marriage preferences among the Sotho-speaking peoples of southern Africa. The paper is divided into two parts. In the first part, Kuper notes that the Southern Sotho have a relatively decentralized political economy divided according to chiefdoms. Each chiefdom, he notes, is in turn divided into wards, often ruled over by brothers, brothers' sons, or the sons of chiefs. All chiefs are linked in competition through marriage with other close agnates. By way of contrast, the writer outlines in the second part of the paper interesting Lovedu and Pedi departures from these "paradigmatic" Southern Sotho structures—structures present in Tswana, Southern Sotho, and Kgalagadi societies. In this regard, he notes that Lovedu women, unlike their Southern Sotho counterparts, play an important role in family affairs and public administration, often holding positions of office. Indeed, four out of five recent Lovedu rulers were women. Consequently, argues Kuper, linked brother-sister ties are predominant in Lovedu society, as are corresponding relations between agnates and the father's sister. This relationship, he notes, is reflected in kinship terminology, which tends to underline the "relatively greater status of women on Lobedu society." The paper, which concludes that "political analysis" rather than "cultural examination" is of benefit to the study of social systems, is annotated and a bibliography citing the works of, among others, Ashton (1937), Casalis (1861), Gluckman (1950), Lévi-Strauss (1966), and Schapera (1938; 1940; 1957) is included.

E68   Lagden, Godfrey (1909). *The Basutos: The Mountaineers and Their Country, Being a Narrative of Events Relating to the Tribe from its Formation Early in the Nineteenth Century to the Present Day.* 2 vols. London: Hutchinson.

Lagden's overview of important events in the history of the Sotho covers the period from the time that several Tswana-speaking "tribes" first emerged in the region north of the Vaal River in the early eighteenth century, until the area now known as Lesotho was granted "Responsible Government" in 1907. Of interest to historians for its account of the rise of Moshoeshoe, his entanglement with British colonial policy-makers and Boer secessionists, among them Harry Smith, Henry Pottinger, George Grey, Philip Wodehouse, and the Orange Free State president, John Brand, as well as for an account of Sotho relations with

French Protestant missionaries prior to the advent of the South African War in 1899, Lagden's work is also of interest for readers of comparative religion. In this regard, the writer's brief notes on witch-killings, anti-witchcraft legislation, and the prohibition of traditional beer-brewing rites are informative. An index is appended to the second volume.

E69   Laydevant, F. (1932). "Religious or Sacred Plants of Basutoland." *Bantu Studies*, vol. 6: 65-69.

Laydevant explores in this paper the uses of medicinal plants in Sotho ritual. He begins by noting the considerable influence of plant medicines in "magical customs" among "primitive" peoples, including the Druids, Gauls, Persians, (among them the "Hashishim" sect), and Dionysian orgiastic circles. Notes on the use of mistletoe, hashish (Indian hemp, or *dagga*), mushrooms (*amanita phalloides*), and grapes in several rituals are discussed. While Laydevant points out that *dagga* is not smoked among the Sotho, he does suggest that an intoxicating "porridgy" substance containing an intoxicating plant called *buphane toxicaria* (*leshoma*) was given to young boys during initiation ceremonies. He notes that the substance had an hallucinogenic, anesthetic, and intoxicating effect and that it was mixed with several ingredients, including the flesh of enemies killed in war. The potion, asserts the writer, was said to "make men" of the initiates. Brief notes on the preparation of several mind-altering substances are then outlined. Notes on the production of preparations for the remedy of mental illnesses, among them hysteria, are also included. The paper concludes with a brief discussion of the uses of corn in the brewing of sorghum beers. Throughout his examination, however, Laydevant betrays an essentially Christian bias against what are perceived to be superstitious, primitive, and non-scientific practices.

E70   Laydevant, F. (1933). "The Praises of the Divining Bone Among the Basuto." *Bantu Studies*, vol. 7: 341-73.

The French missionary François Laydevant presents in this paper a compilation of forty-one Sotho praise songs based upon the Sesotho version (with English translations) of Mapetla, entitled "*Liphoofolo, linonyana, litaola le lithoko tsa tsona.*" The brief introductory passage contends that insofar as there are no fixed forms, the oral transmission of praise songs allows "witch-doctors" the freedom of artistic expression in the composition of new praises. A short list of the divining bones that form the focus of praise songs in this paper is then provided. They include the "Big One" or the "Male"; the "Female"; the male "*phalafala*"; and the female "*phalafala.*" A list of the full set of bones (*litoala*) is completed with the addition of various smaller skeletal pieces, among them those from the anteater, the springbok, sheep, goat, monkey, and steenbok. The writer highlights aspects associated with the positioning of bones and their requisite praise songs. Explanations are provided by informants. Each song has a title appended and a combination of letters that act as a key to understanding the meaning of positions associated with divining bones. The article thus provides valuable primary material and brief explanations of Sotho custom and practice.

E71   Legassick, Martin (1969). "The Sotho-Tswana People Before 1800." In Leonard Thompson (ed.) *African Societies in Southern Africa*. London: Heineman. 86-125.

Legassick sets out in this paper to investigate historical, social, and cultural factors and processes that contributed to the formation of the Sotho-Tswana. He contends that previous analytical approaches to the study of Sotho-Tswana societies have suffered from flawed methodological speculation. In particular, Legassick highlights the failures of difussionist and evolutionary assumptions in historical and anthropological debate. Against this background the author proposes a methodological point of entry based on an analysis of multiple small-scale migrations in what later became the Botswana-South African borderland. In this respect, the author provides extensive observations on cattle-rich, client-recruiting, and iron-working lineage clusters in the region. The central point of his analysis, however, is not so much the fact that small-scale population migrations occurred, but that they resulted in the distribution of generally discrete cultural and linguistic traits. Consequently, the analysis of migration and clustering patterns, Legassick asserts, might contribute to the recovery of a datable common cultural pool that could be used as an historical baseline for measuring the emergence of later cultural distinctions. In this respect, the writer suggests that a "base-date" of around 1500 is feasible. The essay is supported by detailed annotation.

E72   Lekgothoane, S. K. (1938). "Praises of Animals in Northern Sotho." *Bantu Studies*, vol. 12, no. 3: 189-213.

In this brief paper, the writer, a composer of several original *direto* or praise-songs, translates a series of about twenty vernacular praises originally recited by the Dikxala of the Pietersburg district in the northern Transvaal. Of primary interest to Tswana orthographers, the work remains useful for students of African religion in the region for its disclosure of local *direto* related to the *tau* (lion); *nkew* (leopard); *phiri* (hyena); *thsweng* (baboon); *tlou* (elephant); *kwena* (crocodile); *kolobe* (wild boar); *noko* (porcupine); *phuti* (duiker); and *noxa* (snake).

E73   Lestrade, G. P. (1926). "Some Notes on the Bogadi System of the Ba-Hurutshe." *South African Journal of Science*, vol. 23: 937-42.

Lestrade's largely descriptive article provides a "representative" account of the laws governing marriage, including *bogadi*, or "brideprice," among the BaHurutshe of the western Transvaal, British Bechuanaland, and the Orange Free State. An account of the information-gathering process is followed by detailed descriptions of the practice of *bogadi* in terms of the three pivotal steps that are followed in consultations between the families of the bride and groom. Practices associated with these steps, according to the author, include the transfer of cattle from one family to another, the purchase of a woman's reproductive rights, and the acquisition of her productive power. The article offers details of this system in a manner that seems calculated to elaborate the writer's opinion that *bogadi* is a form of economic transaction complete with social and legal safeguards.

E74   Lestrade, G. P. (1928). "Some Notes on the Political Organization of the BeChwana." *South African Journal of Science*, vol. 25: 427-32.

Lestrade provides in this paper a descriptive account of the political infrastructure and social organization of the Tswana-speaking BaHurutshe "tribes" of the western Transvaal. Defining a tribe in the first part of the paper as a political unit owing allegiance to a chief (*kgosi*), he notes that "ethnic" similarities among BaHurutshe clans that claim to be descended from the same semi-mythical hero, Mohurutshe, and whose *seboko* (totem) is the baboon (*tswene*), do not, however, necessarily constitute any form of political homogeneity. The BaGanawa in the Blaauwberg, for example, although "ethnically" of BaHurutshe origin, are organized independently of the BaHurutshe of the Marico district of the western Transvaal. Thus, although a "tribe" could be considered an essentially homogeneous and localized ethnic community, Lestrade asserts, the term "tribe" should be defined more accurately in terms of political allegiance. In the case of Tswana-speaking tribes, however, the social order of political allegiances are distinctive: Unlike other Bantu-speaking communities in southern Africa, the Tswana are administered along androcratic, democratic, and gerontocratic lines. In these terms, all Tswana women are deemed incapable of political administration, while all initiated men are considered eligible for election to positions of authority in the tribal *lekgotla* (council), including the office of *kgosana* (ward chief), or headman (*mogolwane*). Moreover, in the context of localized political administration in the *lekgotalana* (ward councils), the *kgosi*, or chief, suggests Lestrade in the final part of the paper, must function as an interpreter and executive of the general will of the tribe, rather than as an independent despot. The article, which provides brief comparative notes on forms of political administration and organization among Venda- and Sotho-speaking peoples in the region, is not annotated and no bibliography is included.

E75   Lye, William F., and Colin Murray (1980). *Transformations on the Highveld: The Tswana and Southern Sotho*. Cape Town: David Philip.

Asserting that the most significant social boundaries in southern Africa are linguistic, rather than ethnic, Murray begins his wide-ranging analysis of the historical origins and changing sociopolitical conditions of the Sotho-Tswana by exposing in Chapter One the role played by Afrikaner *volkekunderists* in supporting "separate development" policy. He argues that, in reifying the concept of culture, German-trained ethnologists in South Africa, among them Prime Minister Hendrik Verwoerd's close friend, the social theorist W. M. Eiselen, reinforced apartheid programs and disempowered African polities. The formation of "independent" homelands, among them Bophuthatswana and QwaQwa, consequently contributed to both the disappearance of political, economic, kinship, and ritual relations, and the perpetuation of an "idealized" traditional "culture" that served to legitimate segregationist policy. The problems in defining the Tswana and Sotho established in this preamble to the work are picked up by Lye in Chapters Two through Five. In this section of the book the writer highlights central facets of the historical emergence of Sotho-speaking societies in the region. Notes on the *difaqane* and its aftermath, and on the role played by chiefs Sebetwane, Sekonyele, and Moshoeshoe in the reconstruction of several Sotho states are included. In Chapter Five an overview of Sotho-Tswana responses to colonial rule is provided, and in Chapter Seven an account of the changing kinship structures and marriage contracts common to the Sotho-Tswana are sketched. Of particular note to historians of religion is Colin Murray's overview of ritual practice and belief in Chapter Eight. Brief notes on rainmaking rites, the ancestors (*badimo*), and "affliction" as a consequence of *baloi* (witchcraft) are incorporated. The writers thus provide an impressive introductory analysis that also contains a useful bibliography and index.

E76   Mabille, H. E. (1905). "The Basutos of Basutholand." *Addresses and Papers of the British and South African Associations for the Advancement of Science*, vol. 3: 158-94.

In an expansive overview of several aspects of Sotho society and social structure, Mabille illustrates distinctive elements of myth, ritual, and belief associated with the inhabitants of Basutoland. The paper is divided into ten sections. The first delineates facets of demography; the second, historical origins; the third, language; the fourth, industry, agriculture, and pastoral life; and the fifth, customs. Noting that it is impossible to describe every custom and every law, Mabille nonetheless makes a valiant attempt to reduce the myths and rituals associated with marriage, circumcision, war dances and ceremonies, witchcraft, sorcery, divination, rain- and hail-making, and healing and inoculation to a sufficiently "unoffensive" state. The sixth section of the paper, "Religious

Ideas," outlines what "might be more justly termed superstitious ideas, as the Basuto has no religion." In this regard, Mabille points out that the word Modimo ("God") comes from the same root as the word "*ledimo*" (cannibal). Notes on sacrifice, burial, and folklore are included in the chapter. The four final sections of the paper describe elements of government, chieftainship, and land tenure. The writer concludes that the "whole question of the Basutos" can be summed up in terms of another, unanswered, conundrum: "Who is right or wrong in his conception of what they ought to be, the philanthropist who believes that they can be raised to a high standard of civilization and become more and more useful members of the community at large, or the unscrupulous money-maker or politician, who provided he attains his object, does not hesitate to defend the policy of might is right."

E77   MacGregor, J. C. (1905). *Basuto Traditions*. Cape Town: Argus Printing & Publishing Company.

The British Commissioner of the Leribe district in Basutoland presents in this work a brief ethnographic record of oral historical traditions from thirteen so-called Sotho "tribes." Concentrating on the period prior to written historical reports, the writer delineates epoch-making events in "tribal" history. The work is divided into fourteen chapters, and includes an outline of Moshoeshoe's early career. Names of chiefs, migratory patterns and regions of settlement, as well as notes on significant wars are included. However, the work contains little that relates directly to the religious traditions of the Sotho.

E78   Maggs, Timothy M. (1976). "Iron-Age Patterns and Sotho History in the Southern Highveld." *World Archaeology*, vol. 7, no. 3: 318-32.

Archaeologist Tim Maggs investigates in this abbreviated version of a subsequent book the history of Iron Age settlements in the southern Highveld, an area closely approximating what is today known as the Free State. Identifying three types of "settlement units" during the five centuries prior to the *difaqane* and the advent of Christian missionaries in the region in the 1820s, Maggs locates the oldest type (Type N) in the north-east corner of the Highveld. He contends that radiocarbon dating suggests that nascent Iron Age settlements existed on the tops or slopes of mountains in this region during the fourteenth or fifteenth centuries. A second type (Type V), he suggests, dates from the sixteenth or seventeenth century. That type introduced a new "corbelled stone" architectural style. A third discrete type (Type Z), which dates from roughly the same period, inaugurated a distinctively "ceramic style." The writer then correlates archaeological, oral historical, and ethnographic evidence to assert that the Sotho-speaking Koena, Fokeng, and Tlokoa peoples were inhabitants of the region during the earliest settlement period. Foremost, therefore, his paper suggests that the dichotomy between Sotho and Tswana-speaking communities might be traced back to the five-hundred-year separation of settlement patterns that are associated with types N and Z. In this regard, claims Maggs, the distinctions between Sotho and Tswana "are more significant than it is generally considered." Two diagrams showing the distribution of Iron Age and types N, V, and Z settlement patterns, as well as their Sotho and Tswana equivalents, are included.

E79   Manyeli, Thomas Lesaoana (1992). *Religious Symbols of the Basotho.* Mazenod, Lesotho: Catholic Centre.

First presented for the degree of Master of Arts at the University of Ottawa, Manyeli's thesis is reproduced here to help missionaries in Lesotho "eliminate bad elements" and "supply missing characters" in the religion of the Basotho. He notes that if missionaries worked with "the law and principle of analogy," images, archetypes, symbols, and rites taken from Sotho mythology could "be given a Christian interpretation and as a result rendered useful in Christian rites." The preamble aside, Manyeli nonetheless provides an incisive, if somewhat partial account of the polyvalent "grammar" of symbols present in Sotho myth and ritual. For example, in Chapter Two, "Myth," and Chapter Three, "Notions of Divinity," he draws on the ethnographic research of Casalis and Laydevant to examine myths associated with the "archetypal" figures of Molimo ("God") and the *badimo* (ancestors). In this regard, he recalls that these archetypes were found in the myths of many pagan peoples, from Athens to Alexandria. Although Sotho myths were associated with Christ-like figures or, in the case of the so-called *Kholumo-lumo* myth, with "satanic" monster-gods, this did not imply that Sotho myths were inspired by Jewish or Christian contact, as claimed by Laydevant. Rather, the myths proved that god-like, ancestral, and evil archetypes or symbols were present in all religions. Consequently, following an overview of Sotho sacrificial and purification rituals in Chapter Four, and initiation rites for boys (especially the preparatory *malingoana* rites) and girls (especially the *marallo* and *motanyane* rites) in Chapter Five, Manyeli enumerates several of the most important Sotho symbols. Among those reviewed include the horn (power and confidence); water (purification); night (transition); and the moon (life and death). In the final chapters notes on the possibility of adapting "sacramental" rites and foundational myths is assessed. For example, Manyeli questions whether or not baptism could replace traditional water purification and initiation rites; or whether Sotho myths of divinity and death, and creation and punishment could be supplanted by overtly Christian traditions. The book is annotated and a bibliography citing several of the more obscure French and Swiss missionary reporters in nineteenth-century Lesotho is included.

E80   Martin, Minnie (1903). *Basutoland: Its Legends*. London: Nicolas.

Martin, the spouse of a British government official operative in Basutoland from 1892, provides in this impressionistic autobiographical sketch a brief document of Sotho legend and custom. Assisted by her ability to speak Sesotho, and drawing on knowledge accumulated during frequent investigative field-trips, her work nonetheless reinforces nineteenth-century imperialist discourse denigrating Sotho custom as "superstition." For example, the writer castigates missionary activity for being too lenient and recommends that the British remain in the region in order to bring the native "up to" Christian standards. The book begins with a brief outline of Sotho history from the time of Moshoeshoe. Thereafter, brief notes on the geography of the region and the appearance and character of Sotho settlements and agricultural practices are discussed. In Chapter Five, Martin reviews the allegedly widespread phenomenon of "Basuto cannibalism," recalling the story of an old woman's narrow escape from the hands of flesh-hungry natives in the north of Basutoland. Ridiculing and dramatizing customs of Southern Sotho "cannibals," Martin goes on to describe "some sort of belief in the transmigration of souls," claiming that the "spirits of ancestors" revisited the Sotho in the form of snakes, dogs, and baboons. In Chapter Eight, notes on Sotho rainmaking records are enumerated, although Martin suggests that the *ngaka* (diviner) essentially played upon the "credulity of his victims with the solemnity of the seer of old." Thereafter, Martin examines the case of the "Thokolosi" (the "poisoner" or "evil one"), a creature who "is not much bigger than a baboon but without a tail." The remaining chapters document several Sotho legends, among them stories such as "How Khosi became a Wife," "Morongoe and the Snake," and "The Village Maidens and the Cannibal." Of value primarily as a document of colonial representations, the work contains no bibliography or annotations.

E81   Martin, Minnie (1904). "Folk-Lore of the Basuto." *Folk-Lore*, vol. 15: 244-263.

In an alarming narrative of close encounters with Sotho-speaking cannibals—men who had eaten the flesh of white women's hearts—Martin identifies for her readers the distinguishing marks of anthropophagists supposedly inhabiting several regions of Lesotho. Thereafter, drawing on her experiences as the wife of a British government official, she enumerates some Sotho beliefs associated with the "transmigration of souls." In this regard, Martin recalls that many Sesotho-speakers believed that *medimo* ("spirits") were resident in the wet noses of certain types of cattle. Brief notes on beliefs endorsing the efficacy of human "flesh-charms," divination, prognostication, and the ritual labor of a "medicine man" (*ngaka*) are included. So too are several "quaint" customs associated with marriage and the birth of a first child. The report concludes with a description of Sotho burial rites. Included are aspects concerned with the positioning of graves, correct observances for the sacrifice and ritual consumption of cattle, and post-mortem taboos. The paper is not annotated and no bibliography or reference material is appended.

E82   Massie, R. H. (1905). *The Native Tribes of the Transvaal, Prepared for the General Staff of the War Office*. London: His Majesty's Stationary Office.

With its subtitle suggesting the author's strategic intentions, Massie's *Native Tribes* provides an illuminating account of the interrelationship between ethnology, colonial administration, and comparative religion in nineteenth-century South Africa. The book is divided into eleven chapters, the first seven of which provide brief notes on the historical origins and geographical dispersion of the BaRolong, BaHarutshe, BaKwena, BaKgatla, and BaTlaung. Chapter Eight, "Administration," and Chapter Nine, "Native Wars," describe aspects of internecine aggression and Sotho and Tswana land-tenure and taxation systems. In Chapter Ten, "Bantu Ethics and Society," Massie follows his analysis of customary law and government highlighting customs associated with marriage (especially polygyny and *lobolo*), death and burial, weaponry, and dress. An extended overview of religious beliefs, inclusive of a discussion of *seano* (totems), taboo, witchcraft, and *badimo* (ancestors) is provided. Massie notes that "no trace can be discovered among the ancient traditions [of the Sotho-Tswana] of belief in any one universal supreme being corresponding to God." Consequently, any ideas on this subject are "traceable to missionary influence." The book concludes with a chapter on language and orthography, and includes appendices listing traditional chiefly strongholds and native missions. An index and a list of cited works (predominantly Native Affairs Commissioner's Reports and Blue Books) are also provided.

E83   Matthews, Z. K. (1940). "Marriage Customs Among the Barolong." *Africa*, vol. 13: 1-23.

Matthews' article describes marriage customs associated with the inhabitants of the area adjoining present-day Botswana and the Republic of South Africa. He notes that although discrete tribal identities such as the Ratlou, Tshidi, Seleka, and Rapulana were present in the region, these peoples all shared, by dint of history, language, and culture, a collective identity known as the BaRolong. Although BaRolong social structures were clearly altered under the pressures associated with colonial expansion, marriage institutions, suggests Matthews, remained exceptionally resistant to these changes, as confirmed by the persistence of *bogadi* (giving of cattle by the groom to the bride's father). This resilience, he argues, can be traced back to the fact that marriage functioned in

BaRolong society as a guarantee of political status and prestige or as a symbolic affirmation of the possibility of self-perpetuation. Attention is drawn to the inherently social nature of marriage among the BaRolong. Brief notes on grounds for the prohibition of marriage are also included. As a general rule, Matthews asserts, marriage and sexual relations were prohibited between a parent and a child and between siblings. Preferred spouses or sexual partners were the daughters of the mother's brother (*malome*), although other first cousin marriages were also considered desirable. The institution of marriage was not confirmed as a consequence of a single rite of passage, however. Marriage was a consequence of a long process, marked at various points by the exchange of gifts and culminating in the gift of *bogadi*. The paper is only briefly annotated.

E84   Meeuwsen, J. P. (1879). "Customs and Superstitions Among the Betshuana." *[South African] Folk-Lore Journal*, vol. 1, no. 2: 33-34.

In her brief report, Meeuwsen provides a description of some Tswana rainmaking rites. Primarily, her paper describes how, in times of drought, the Tswana would set off on a special hunting expedition in order to sacrifice a specific type of animal. Alternatively, she notes, the *ngaka* would sacrifice an ox in the belief that the smoke from the sacrificial fire would gather into dark rain clouds. If the sacrifice was only partly successful, she suggests, an arrow doctored with special medicines would be shot into the sky. Following her brief description of the rite associated with this practice, Meeuwsen provides a short account of the sorcerer's art, particularly as regards the prevention of illness. Medicines to halt the spread of contagious diseases were said to have been placed on stones at the entrance of villages, for example. The paper concludes with a short paragraph on the "wonderful" treatment of women widowers: Prior to her return to the village a widow would have to smear herself with cow dung. The short report is not annotated.

E85   Mogoba, Stanley M. (1981). "The Erosion of the Bapedi Religious World. A Study of the Impact of Christianity and Western Life on Bapedi Religion." In Heinz Kuckertz (ed.) *Ancestor Religion in Southern Africa*. Cacadu, Transkei: Lumko Missiological Institute. 52-64.

In this contribution to a broader collection of essays on ancestral religion in southern Africa, Mogoba analyzes the extent to which Christianity eroded traditional Pedi belief and religious practice. Focusing on the geographical region of Sekhukhuniland, he notes how "Pedi theology" placed God at the apex of an hierarchically ordered cosmology consisting of ancestors, the living, and nature. Other features of Pedi "theology," he asserts, included beliefs and practices associated with death and "judgement." Special care is taken to portray the ancestors as intermediaries and not objects of worship. With this "theological" premise outlined, the author proceeds to document patterns of change in Pedi religion. Aspects that have informed the emergence of a distinctively Pedi theology, in particular socioeconomic change and colonial and missionary expansion, are enumerated. Out of the maelstrom of urbanization, labor migration, and Christianity, therefore, an innovative form of Pedi religion emerged. For Mogoba, innovation implies an inevitable "mixing up" of traditional and Christian practice. Though obviously perturbed by this "syncretic" mixing, Mogoba is emphatic that any quest for a pure faith (be it Pedi or Christian) is misplaced romanticism. The article concludes with an appendix of interviews with informants and a brief list of references.

E86 Molema, Silas Modiri (1920). *The Bantu, Past and Present: An Ethnographical and Historical Study of the Native Races of South Africa*. Edinburgh: Green & Son.

Molema's "portrayal of the life of the Bantu," drawing on a wide range of writers, among them the works of Robert Moffat and F. Max Müller, is dedicated to describing for the "governing races" of Europe's "scientists" the "primitive" conditions and "arbitrary customs" of the "backward races" of Africa. His work, written at the conclusion of the 1914-18 War, in which African soldiers participated on the side of Britain, begins with an overview or "revelation" of the "Antiquity of Man in Africa." He notes that the Khoikhoi and San were some of the most primitive races known to humanity: The San are "stunted," "fear ghosts," speak a rude, guttural language akin to Coptic and, in fact, appear to be descendants of the pygmies described by Herodotus; the Khoi, who believe in a supreme being, called Gounza Ticquva—"an undefined sort of deity"—are "imaginative" participants in lunar worship. The author proceeds in the second part of the work to describe historical, linguistic, and religious beliefs and practices associated with aspects of various southern African "ethnic groups," among them the Tswana (BaLala, BaThlaping, BaRolong, BaKwena, BaNgwato, and BaNgwaketse), Sotho, Xhosa, Zulu, Tsonga, and Swazi. Chapter Eight, "Religious Beliefs," is of particular interest to historians of Tswana religion: Drawing on the definitions of religion provided by F. Max Müller, William James, and James Frazer, Molema asserts that the Tswana, unlike the San, were a religious people, although their religion was a form of "primitive and unevolved" paganism. Arguing that the ancestor spirits constituted their deity and shaped their destinies to greater or lesser degrees of malevolence, the author emphasizes that "magic" was at the very foundation of their religion. Magic is defined as the art or science of controlling natural and supernatural forces, performed by sacred specialists commonly known as magicians, witch-doctors, or medicine men. In relegating Tswana practice to pagan superstition and magic, Molema refers to rituals associated with doctoring armies, diagnosing sickness, and "smelling out" witches as forms of divination. The Tswana's hazy and vague idea of God, concludes Molema, reveals sparks of a "higher faith." A bibliography and chronological chart precede the main text and an index is appended.

E87   Mönnig, H. O. (1967). *The Pedi*. Pretoria: Van Schaik.

Mönnig's monograph of this central Transvaal people provides a comprehensive survey of Pedi history, religion, rites of passage, and social, economic, judicial, and political organization. The work begins with a detailed history and geographical overview of the region that the Pedi inhabit—a region bounded by the Oliphants River in the north and the Steelspoort River in the east. Notes on origins and settlement patterns are delineated. In the second chapter, entitled "Religion," Mönnig claims that Pedi religion is both individual and communal. Belief in a creator god called Modimo, who is perceived as a distant figurehead, is almost universal. The writer deals at length with the Pedi conception of human life in which a person consists of a body (*mmele*), soul (*moya*), and spirit (*siriti*). Mönnig contends that the Pedi are primarily concerned with strengthening their *siriti* by deploying "magical" practices, "love potions," and amulets. Principles and practices associated with ancestor spirits (*badimo*) are outlined. The following chapter, entitled "Rites of Passage," covers such topics as birth and name-giving, the initiation of the youth, and institutions of polygamous Pedi marriage and burial. The concluding chapters are primarily concerned with economic life and social and political organization. Notes on kinship, chieftainship, tribal law, and taxation are included. Several plates accompany the text and tables and maps supplement the work. An index is also included.

E88   Morton, R. F. (1985). "Linchwe I and the Kgatla Campaign in the South African War, 1899-1902." *Journal of African History*, vol. 26: 169-91.

In a revisionist historical reading of the role of Africans in the South African War (1899-1902), Morton shows how Tswana-speaking BaKgatla ba ga Kgafela regiments in the Bechuanaland Protectorate and western Transvaal initiated military action and pursued political goals independent of British administration or Boer rule. Indeed, he argues forcefully that the war created autonomous economic and political opportunities for the Kgatla leader, Linchwe I (1874-1924). Fighting alongside Protectorate forces, the chief could carry out British military strategies in the Saulspoort area that simultaneously afforded opportunities for him to secure allegiances from Kgatla communities previously resistant to his rule. Morton argues, therefore, that Linchwe's allegiance to the British was motivated, primarily, by an internal political agenda: The British defeat of Boer forces helped Linchwe regain control of recalcitrant BaKgatla communities in the Transvaal. With the redistribution of BaKgatla wealth consequent on the termination of hostilities, in part due to a devastating rinderpest epidemic in the Transvaal in 1897, as well as to the reduction of colonial interference by British administrators in Bechuanaland who were thankful for Kgatla support, Linchwe's economic and political position was strengthened. While the paper makes only passing reference to the role of religion in protecting the Kgatla's powerful position in the region—notably, in relation to the sustenance of Linchwe's mythic status—Morton's analysis illuminates an intriguing historical situation, one that lends critical detail to the complex conditions of change experienced by Tswana chiefdoms in the late nineteenth century. The paper is rigorously annotated and draws on primary materials from Native Commissioner Reports and government archives.

E89   Murray, Colin (1975). "Sex, Smoking and the Shades: A Sotho Symbolic Idiom." In Michael G. Whisson and Martin West (eds.) *Religion and Social Change in South Africa*. Cape Town: David Philip. 58-77.

In a tribute to Monica Hunter's ground-breaking work, Murray applies the anthropologist's methodological procedure of pushing interpretation beyond personal exegesis to reexamine the social phenomenon of smoking among the Sotho. Tracing symbolic associations within a broad semantic field, the writer documents how in Sotho custom an old woman would take a young boy's penis in her hand and, putting her other hand to her nose, "smoke the child," commenting simultaneously that the tobacco (*kwae*) was strong. According to the Sotho, the action was a statement about the boy's coming maturity and his responsibility to use his penis to create life. Beyond the associations between tobacco and male organs in everyday conversation, asserts Murray, lies a more formal institution, one in which tobacco symbolizes sexual relations. Two contexts are especially telling in this respect. One is marriage, where the slaughtering of a sheep (called *kwae*) for a bride in her new home marks the official commencement of sexual relations. The other is spirit possession, in which *kwae* is taken by men to invoke the head-clearing power of the ancestors in divination, or is given to possessed women to tame the spirits. In the case of marriage, as in the practice of "smoking a child," *kwae* may be viewed as an idiom for the ancestors' responsibility for and control over physical and social reproduction.

E90   Murray, Colin (1976). "Marital Strategy in Lesotho: The Redistribution on Migrant Earnings." *African Studies*, vol. 35: 99-121.

Murray's analysis of marriage and marriage payments in Lesotho provides a wealth of statistical data, including notes on stock prices and sales and migrant labor wages, to argue that bridewealth payments constituted an integral part of the "household" structure. Initially, the writer establishes reasons for changes in traditional stock-oriented bridewealth payment schemes, proposing that cash became the predominant medium of exchange when workers were integrated into the migrant labor system. Thereafter, he examines to what extent marriage can be conceived of as an "evolving process" rather than a clearly defined social event or rite of passage. The study concludes with seven case studies that examine forms of bride-price. The studies constitute the preliminary empirical data from which later publications are planned.

E91   Murray, Colin (1977). "High Bridewealth, Migrant Labour, and the Position of Women in Lesotho." *Journal of African Law*, vol. 21: 79-96.

Social anthropologist Colin Murray investigates in this paper the persistence of high bridewealth prices in Lesotho. Based on fieldwork conducted in the Leribe district between the years 1972 and 1974, the writer adopts Isaac Schapera's methodological approach to analyze the changing political, economic, and social conditions influencing Sotho bridewealth. He argues that the transition of Lesotho's economy from "granary to labour reserve," and the alteration of the balance of authority between senior and junior generations, was an important feature in the maintenance of high bridewealth prices in the region. He claims that large *bohali* (bridewealth) prices nevertheless redistributed the wealth of junior generation migrant laborers among older rural dwellers. Furthermore, he suggests that women who assumed managerial roles in the household in the absence of their husbands and brothers were also able to manipulate *bohali* prices to establish and maintain claims on male labor. The article begins, therefore, with an analysis of the sociopolitical and economic changes that occurred in Lesotho during the second quarter of the nineteenth century. Murray identifies the rapid accumulation of cattle by Moshoeshoe and his chiefs in the post-*difaqane* period, as well as the rise of the dominant *koena* aristocracy's exploitation of cattle, as formative influences on the initially high price of *bohali*. Thereafter, the writer investigates the changing social and jural configurations associated with household "development and dissolution" in the twentieth century that then contributed to rural householder dependency on migrant laborers. The article contains an appendix outlining socioeconomic profiles in three Sotho households.

E92   Murray, Colin (1980). "Sotho Fertility Symbolism." *African Studies*, vol. 39, no. 2: 65-76.

In this brief article Murray examines the structural and symbolic context of Sotho fertility rites. Utilizing Monica Wilson's argument that Sotho-Tswana cosmology posits a connection between the natural world and social order, he examines Sotho attempts to manipulate the forces that govern human fertility. However, Murray's short study, based primarily upon fieldwork conducted in Lesotho between 1972 and 1974, also analyzes the forms of various fertility rites in order to highlight common themes in the relationship between natural fecundity and human reproduction. The writer's detailed descriptive consideration of fertility rituals first highlights the symbolic features associated with fecundity in Sesotho. Here, the writer gives an account of how diviners instructed pre-adolescent girls in the ways to draw water from a spring. This account is followed by a description of how the diviner directed women in the art of obtaining a stick used for stirring *lesokoana* porridge. Further notes on the diviner's administration of rites deployed in gathering slime from a black-water serpent are provided. Thereafter, the writer discusses associations between water and human fertility, claiming that the womb in Sotho society contains a metaphorical relationship to both water and fecundity. Detailed notes are then enumerated describing taboos associated with eating, particularly those related to the prohibition of eggs and sheep's intestines for adolescent girls. Eating eggs, claims the writer, was thought to make pubescent girls "hot," or impure. In this regard, eggs preempted untimely sexual desire. Brief notes on ophidian symbolisms are also related. One such narrative pertains to the story of MaMetsi (Mother of Water), in which the seer of the Hlakoana clan utilized the snake Monyohe in order to secure the health of a sick child.

E93   Niehaus, Isak A. (1993). "Witch-Hunting and Political Legitimacy: Continuity and Change in Green Valley, Lebowa, 1930-1991." *Africa*, vol. 63, no. 4: 498-30.

Drawing on an archive of press reports and a number of scholarly writings from the last six decades, among them the works of Krige (1947), Willis (1968), and Sansom (1972), the article investigates the involvement of chiefs, comrades, youth organizers, and Legislative Assembly members in witch-hunting in the courts of Lebowa, then an independent Bantustan or African "homeland" in the north-east region of the Transvaal. In arguing against common notions in anthropological literature that suggest that witch-killings are a consequence of attempts to intimidate opponents or mystify exploitation, the author asserts that the link between witch-hunting and political action in southern Africa is the result of a far more complex relationship. He argues that witch-killings can be seen as creative attempts to eliminate evil and avoid future occurrences of misfortune. However, through time, chiefs and comrades, for example, found it politically convenient to identify and punish witches (*baloi*) in Lebowa in their efforts to obtain legitimacy and to assert political power among Tswana-speaking villagers in the region. The paper is divided into six sections. The first undertakes a review of anthropological analysis in which the writer provides a critique of Harris' (1974) "scapegoat" theory and Marwick's (1965) "political expediency" paradigm. He suggests that most theories lack cogent or satisfactorily complex reflection. The second section introduces the historical circumstances of the political, social, and linguistic "bricolage" that characterized the Green Valley and Bushbuckridge regions of Lebowa. He notes that an elaborate system of beliefs and practices drawn from Tswana, Sotho, Nguni, and Tsonga traditions were prevalent in the area in the 1980s. In the following sections an analysis of the role of chiefs in the conviction of ritual murderers (*maemae*) and witchcraft-killings in the *kgoro* courts from 1930 to 1956 is undertaken. Thereafter the writer contrasts reasons for witch-hunting among comrades and youth organizations in the region from 1986 to 1990. The paper ends with a case study of a 1991 Christmas witch-hunt when, after the death of nine residents of Green Valley, political organizations coordinated numerous witch-killings that, the author suggests, exploited popular perceptions that the government supported witches to gain wider political power. The political potential of witch-killings, Niehaus argues, remains a result of multiple and diverse meanings associated with witches. The paper is annotated and a bibliography is included.

E94   Nürnburger, Klaus (1975). "The Sotho Notion of the Supreme Being and the Impact of Christian Proclamation." *Journal of Religion in Africa*, vol. 8, no. 3: 174-200.

In an essentially theologically oriented paper presented at the biennial conference of the African Studies Association of the United Kingdom, Nürnberger attempts to establish attributes associated with the Sotho supreme being, Modimo. In this regard, the theologian analyzes transformations and developments pertaining to the changing notion of divinity that occurred in Basutoland in the wake of Christian colonial and missionary expansion. The paper begins by postulating the "religious context" within which Sotho notions of divinity must be viewed. The writer identifies a "dynamistic conception of reality," a highly institutionalized social framework, and the social status and kinship structure of Sotho society as the definitive life-force, or "*weltanschauung*," of the Sotho. In the second section of the paper, entitled "Modimo—The Power Beyond," the writer delineates the purported attributes of the Supreme Being. He claims that Modimo "does not speak," so that, consequently, there is no evidence of revelation in the form of dreams, oracles, or prophecies. Thereafter, Nürnberger asserts that Modimo does not act in the sense of the Hebrew God of history. Nor is Modimo to be confused with the God of the Deists. Rather, suggests the writer, "Modimo denotes a comprehensive universe of power which is always potentially present." Modimo is, he claims, best conceptualized as "Fate" or "Fortune." In the following section, "The Impact of the Christian Proclamation," Nürnberger discusses the Sotho adoption of Jesus, claiming that the Son of God was reinterpreted as the "prime ancestor." Modimo, he concludes, was then distinguished by four basic characteristics: as source of experiential reality; as giver of the law; as merciful father instituting the means of redemption through the "suffering self-exposure" of Christ; and as the personal source and channel of the life force of a new community.

E95   Pauw, B. A. (1955). *Social and Religious Institutions of the Tlhaping of the Taung Reserve*. Ph.D. thesis, University of Cape Town.

Pauw's now dated account of the Tswana-speaking peoples of the Phuduhut-swana chiefdom, later published as *Religion in a Tswana Chiefdom* (1960), draws on the writer's experiences as a missionary and anthropologist in Taung Reserve to highlight aspects of Tlhaping social structure and changing patterns of Tswana religious life in the mid-1950s. Following a brief introductory history of the chiefdom, and an account in Chapter Two of the social organization and ethnic, territorial, and political administration of the Tlhaping, the writer outlines in Chapter Three aspects of "pagan" ritual and belief indicative of the changing shape of Tswana religion. He suggests that although Christian missionaries were active in the region from at least the 1820s, remnants of "pagan worship" and practice remain prevalent. For example, Pauw asserts that the Tlhaping continue to venerate a supreme being called Modimo, a name that was adopted by missionaries to designate the Christian God. The "dominant cult" of the Tlhaping, however, concerns the veneration and ritual propitiation of ancestors, called *badimo*. Extensive and detailed notes on the use of ritual medicines (*ditlhare*) and treatments employed by the sacred specialist, the *ngaka*, are included, as are descriptions of sorcery and the role the sorcerer (*baloi*), and the *pulanyana* or rain rituals, regarded as the work of the *moroka wa pula*, or rain-maker. The chapter recalls examples of initiation and rites of passage, among them taboos associated with birth and puberty. However, the thesis is predominantly concerned with tabulating the effects of indigenous involvement in African initiated or separatist churches in the region. Pauw notes in this regard, in Chapters Four through Eight, that the presence of a number of Christian missions in Taung occasioned new forms of ritual for healing and purification and alternative techniques of prayer for rain. The thesis, which draws on the writings of Willoughby (1928; 1932), Schapera (1938; 1940), and Wilson (1952), is extensively annotated. A bibliography and appendices are included, among them notes on churches and church affiliation in the Reserve.

E96   Pauw, B. A. (1990). "Widows and Ritual Danger in Sotho and Tswana Communities." *African Studies*, vol. 49, no. 2: 75-99.

Drawing on ethnographic fieldwork studies and the writings of several social anthropologists, including Mönnig, Hammond-Tooke, and Schapera, Pauw examines the symbolic structure of ritual "pollution," "dirt," and danger of contagion (*mokgoma*) among the Tswana-speaking Mashabela peoples of Phokwane. In particular, the writer analyzes aspects of purity and danger associated with the status of widowhood. The paper is divided into five sections. In the first, a brief description of political and social structure in Phokwane is provided. In the second, entitled "Rituals for Widows," extended notes on rituals of purification required of wives following the death of a husband are enumerated. Washing (*go hlapa*) rites necessary to ameliorate the perceived status of uncleanness are described, as are the myths associated with illness, social disharmony, or disease should a widow not fulfill the requirements necessary to depreciate her defiling and dangerous powers, called *tshuma*. An essentially structural-functionalist account of prohibitions is included, wherein Pauw describes rituals of inversion associated with dietary and dress codes. In the third and fourth sections the writer provides comparative information regarding widow taboos and symbolisms of danger and dirt among the Tsonga and Venda, before highlighting in the final section features of continuity and change associated with the phenomenon in Lesotho and Botswana. The paper is annotated and a bibliography is included.

E97   Pitje, G. M. (1950). "Traditional Systems of Male Education Among the Pedi and Cognate Tribes." *African Studies*, vol. 9, no. 2: 53-76.

In what Pitje considers to be the first serious attempt at a coherent and comprehensive analysis of pedagogical procedures and initiation rites among Tswana-speaking male adolescents in Sekhukhuniland, the writer analyzes how attendance at preparatory and initiation schools conferred on Pedi youth the status of manhood. However, the writer further describes how, by contrast, non-attendance could confirm the role of perpetual social and political minor. Consequently, he suggests that initiation extended to the youth the privileges and responsibilities of adulthood, including the "franchise," but that failure to attain the status of adulthood consequent on the completion of initiation could result not merely in political emasculation among the living, but elimination from the community of the dead. In these terms, a rich descriptive account of initiation rites and religious practices associated with Pedi society is provided. However, the paper serves also to situate descriptive detail and insightful analysis within an historical context of shifting colonial interests in the chiefdoms that constituted what was later known as Sekhukhuniland. In this regard, the paper begins with a brief account of changing features in Pedi social structure and administration in the "native reserves" of Groblersdal, Pietersburg, and Lydenburg. Among the most salient features of that social structure, the writer asserts, was the view that women were considered to be perpetual minors. However, because older women, or *bakxolo*, were also considered to be repositories of knowledge in matters relating to religion and ritual, women were entrusted with the education and socialization of infant males. Consequently, it is the pedagogical role of women in educating infant and pubescent boys that constitutes the major part of Pitje's subsequent analysis. The paper, part of a thesis in social anthropology presented to the University of South Africa in 1948, is annotated. No bibliography is appended.

E98   Price, Roger (1879). "The Ceremony of Dipheku." *[South African] Folk-Lore Journal*, vol. 1, no. 2: 35-36.

In this brief report, the London Missionary Society agent Roger Price provides notes on the annual BaMangwato *dipheku* ritual. A "yearly sacrifice" performed for the protection of a town from pestilence or war, the ritual comprised the sacrifice of a black ox. The animal, he reports, was brought into the village, whereupon its eyelids were sewn together. In this state, the beast wandered freely for three days. Thereafter, it was sacrificed and cooked under the direction of a doctor (*ngaka*) and the chief. Its blood was then daubed on a pole situated in the chief's *kgotla*, and on the poles that guarded the entrances and exits to the village. Price supposes that the ritual was performed so that the sight of doctored poles would make enemies "*nyera marapo* (have the marrow oozed from their bones)." The paper is not annotated.

E99   Rey, Charles F. (1988). *Monarch of All I Survey: Bechuanaland Diaries, 1929-1937*. Eds. Neil Parsons and Michael Crowder. Gaborone: Botswana Society.

In 1930 Charles Rey assumed duties as Resident Commissioner of the Bechuanaland Protectorate. He stayed in Gaborone for eight years. During this period the Commissioner frequently clashed with the young Tswana-speaking Regent of the region, the BaMangwato chief Tshekedi Khama. Their contest culminated when the Royal Navy was brought to the Kalahari to crush a fictitious "native rising" that Rey supposed Khama had instigated. In editing the commissioner's journals, however, Parsons and Crowder do more than relate the historical details of the illustrious colonels' career. Rather, their reading of Rey's seminal contribution to political order in the Bechuanaland Protectorate serves to highlight facets of contested colonial rule in what is now Botswana. Outlining Rey's accumulatively paternalistic racism, patriotic nationalism, and apparently contradictory admiration for Afrikaner anti-British self-rule prior to the South African War, the editors illustrate, for example, how imperial policies often collapsed under the sophisticated manipulation of chiefly authority in Botswana. While many of the diary entries, dating from 1929 to 1937, are concerned with aspects of colonial administration (of particular note is Rey's concern for the coronation visit in 1934), brief records of the beliefs and practices of the BaTawana, BaMangwato, BaNgwaketse, and BaKgatla are included. In this regard, Rey's remarks about the politicization of *bogwera* (circumcision) rites is informative, as are his accounts of the sorcery trials when Tshekedi Khama's estranged wife was accused of witchcraft. The book is extensively annotated and an index is appended.

E100 Roberts, Noel (1914). "A Few Notes on To Kolo, a System of Divination Practiced by the Superior Natives of Malaboch's Tribe in the Northern Transvaal." *South African Journal of Science*, vol. 11: 367-70.

In this brief essay, Roberts discusses astragalomancy, or the art of divination, as practiced in Malaboch's Tswana-speaking chiefdom in the Blaauwberg region of the northern Transvaal. Primarily, asserts Roberts, only the chief and the so-called witchdoctor, or *ngaka*, are able to "throw" and "read" the five tablets (enumerated as the *lekholo lekhuamen*; *chuadima*; *selumi*; *lengwana*; and *chweni*). As opposed to its practice in what Roberts calls "less superior tribes," divination remains the prerogative of the elite among the Northern Tswana. The paper is not annotated, although a number of sketches demonstrating how the diviner operates are included.

E101 Roberts, Noel (1915). "The Bagananoa or Ma-Laboch: Notes on their Early History, Customs, and Creed." *South African Journal of Science*, vol. 12: 241-56.

Relying on information extracted from Chief Kgalushi Malaboch, and drawing on evidence accumulated by Berlin missionary, government administrator, and ethnographer C. A. T. Winter, Roberts highlights several aspects of religious belief and practice among Tswana-speaking people of the northern Transvaal. In particular, the writer outlines aspects of the *siboko*, or "totemic structure" of Tswana society. Following Stow, he argues in the first part of the paper that the Bagananoa, who are descendants of the BaHurutshe, were known by their clan totem *puthi*, the duiker or small gazelle. However, the writer suggests that the *kwena*, or crocodile, was also treated with extreme respect by the Bagananoa. A Sub-Native Affairs Commissioner in the Blaauwberg region reported to the writer that the totem, depicted in iconographic form, was actually worshipped as a deity by Malaboch's men. More generally, however, Roberts describes in the first half of the paper how clan totems were employed in the art of divination, or astragalomancy. By contrast, in the second half of the paper an analysis of male initiation rites indicative of Tswana ritual is undertaken. Included is a graphic and detailed description of the art of the surgeon (*mpakana oa banna*). Peculiarly, the writer notes that an essential aspect of the initiation procedure was the revelation and veneration of the painted crocodile described earlier. Photographic plates depicting the "hideous" creature are included. In the appendices, Tswana customs related to the *kuena* are compared to the myths and rites of the ancient Egyptians (in the Seth and Horus cycle in the *Book of the Dead*). The comparisons, among them a detailed analysis of ophidian symbolism in Egypt and South Africa, are drawn in part from the writings of Frazer and Churchward. They are validated, according to the writer, insofar as "rude intaglio" marks on rocks near Metseng provide epigraphic evidence of "extraordinary similarities" among the religions of "uncivilized man."

E102   Roberts, Noel (1917). "Bantu Methods of Divination: A Comparative Study." *South African Journal of Science*, vol. 14: 397-408.

Defining divination as the acquisition of knowledge by occult means, Reverend Roberts distinguishes between two techniques of "magical" prognostication: first, supernormal perception, whereby the diviner relies on dreams and visions; and second, artificial aid, including bones and sticks, that a sacred specialist "reads" in order to obtain esoteric knowledge. Both techniques, he argues, express for the African "savage" what science ("systematized knowledge founded on the records of observation") represents for the European "savant." In Robert's view, therefore, as long as magical predictions are based on observable relationships, the *ngaka's* divining art is also a science and its conclusions legitimate. However, at the point where observable phenomena are discredited, predilections based on supernormal perception or artificial aids become fallacious. The "totemic" rules prescribed for choosing the diviners' objects, for example, argues Roberts, represents nothing more than a form of artistic "pretense." Following a brief overview of the prevalence of totemism in southern Africa—defined as a "generic system of classification found in primitive societies"—the writer refers to the works of James Frazer, W. F. Barrett, and Andrew Lang to describe in detail aspects of astragalomancy among Bantu-speaking peoples in the region. Detailed descriptions are provided and a general comparison is outlined between the Bantu and Egyptian deployments of oracle bones and diviners' bowls (*dikomana*) and sacred drums. The paper is illustrated with photographic plates but, although briefly annotated, it includes no bibliography.

E103   Roberts, Noel, and C. A. T. Winter (1916). "The Kgoma, or Initiation Rites of the Bapedi of Sekukuniland." *South African Journal of Science*, vol. 13: 561-78.

In his introductory remarks on initiation rituals among the Pedi of the northern Transvaal, Roberts outlines the unique theoretical and ethnographic value of evidence collected by the Berlin missionary and government agent C. A. T.

Winter. Winter's chief informants, he notes, were all relatives of paramount chiefs or "native witch-doctors." The paper, initially based on the reports of a chief *rabadia* (circumcision-lodge master) among the Bagananoa, is nonetheless largely descriptive. It begins with Winter's account of the timing and structure of the *Kgoma* or native initiation school. The writer proposes that the preparatory rites performed at these schools should be analyzed according to two discrete parts: first, a three-month private *bodika* ceremony, during which time the *tipane* (cutter) performs the circumcision rite; and second, the *bogwera* proper. During the first part, the *bodika*, Winter notes that a number of "psalms" are chanted by the initiates (the *madikane*), among them the *Mankikana* (Traitor), *Goegoane* (Little Frogs), *Magopheng* (Aloes), and *Tsaoi* (Salt) songs. A detailed description of the *phiri* (ashes) ceremony associated with the singing of the *Tsaoi* song is then outlined. This is followed by a graphic account of ritual practices associated with the construction of a symbolic "cone" used during the demarcation of initiates into regiments (*moruto*). The entire procedure, including the period of isolation, concludes the writer, might justifiably be considered an essentially "magical rite." Therefore, citing the work of the anthropologist James Frazer, Winter views Pedi initiatory ceremonies, including male circumcision rites, as marking the transition into adulthood and as exemplary of the universal "language" of rites of passage among the world's religions. The paper is briefly annotated.

E104   Roberts, Simon A. (1972). *Tswana Family Law*. London: Sweet & Maxwell.

Drawing on materials collected while he was acting as Customary Law Advisor to the Botswana Government, Roberts provides a detailed account of family law among the Tswana-speaking "tribes" of what was the Bechuanaland Protectorate. His work, which relies on the written records of customary chiefs' courts and community *lekgotla* (councils), and includes consideration of almost one hundred case studies from 1926 to 1968, identifies predominant practices and rulings concerning the law of persons, the family, marriage and divorce, property, and succession. Organized into nine major chapters, with each chapter corresponding to one of the major "tribes" in Botswana, specific issues related to adultery, *bogadi* (bride-price), and settlement procedures for matrimonial disputes are incorporated. Included among the groups investigated are the BaKgatla, BaMalete, BaTlokwa, BaKwena, BaHurutshe, BaNgwaketse, BaRolong, BaNgwato, and BaTawana. In addition to focusing on family law, the book provides a brief historical overview of the territorial organization, government, and kinship groupings of the Tswana-speaking peoples of Botswana. Rigorously annotated from primary resources, the text includes appendices relating to Tswana Law Panels and customary law court records. An index and a brief bibliography are also included.

E105 Roberts, Simon A. (1985). "The Tswana Polity and Tswana Law and Custom Revisited." *Journal of Southern African Studies*, vol. 12, no. 1: 75-87.

Roberts acknowledges that recent theoretical readings of postcolonial social order in African societies, in the works of Hobsbawm and Ranger (1983), for example, have served to highlight aspects of organizational discontinuity and agency, rather than more sentimental discussions of indigenous survival. The notion that "customary law," or "traditional African law," might even be an "invention" supportive of the project of colonial rule, suggests Roberts, has also helped to shift the focus of examination away from the treatment of African societies as helpless prisoners of larger colonial forces. However, while the notion of "invention" has rendered problematic the links between contemporary forms of administration and the precolonial past, the writer argues, to postulate that customary law is an entirely new construction is somewhat unsophisticated. In the Tswana context, he suggests, many instances of social and political continuity exist. For example, while the missionaries of the Dutch Reformed Church initially opposed the transfer of bridewealth (*bogadi*) by Christian Kgatla, they eventually had to accept these customary legal (*mekgwa le melao*) transactions, incorporating them into local Christian marriage rites. In a careful examination of customary law and traditional polity among the Tswana-speaking Kgatla of the South African-Botswana borderland, Roberts reconsiders the relationship between political order, colonial rule, and traditional administration. In the first part of the paper a careful analysis of precolonial Tswana polity is undertaken. Drawing on Isaac Schapera's foundational work (1938; 1952; 1966), the writer includes notes on the role of the *kgosi* (ruler) and his advisors, or *banna ba lekgotla* (men of the court). The analysis is followed in the second part of the paper by an overview of the extent to which Kgatla law and custom might be conceived of as an entirely innovative construction. Roberts' interpretation in this section of the importance of Schapera's *Handbook of Tswana Law and Custom* (1938) is particularly illuminating. The anthropologist, he suggests, was used as an authoritative reference point for Tswana customary law in such a way that he was "played back to some degree into Tswana culture." The paper, which draws almost exclusively on secondary material, is annotated.

E106 Sansom, Basil (1972). "When Witches Are Not Named." In Max Gluckman (ed.) *The Allocation of Responsibility*. Manchester: Manchester University Press. 193-226.

Concentrating almost entirely on the Pedi peoples of the Megwang chiefdom, Sansom poses a pivotal question in witchcraft studies: Why is the possibility of witchcraft accusation a virtually rejected alternative in the reconstruction of disharmonious relationships among the Pedi? In resolving this issue, the article recognizes witchcraft accusation to be a serious remodification of social relations. Such an accusation would inject a marked ambiguity into the social tissue while also contributing to the degradation of social status. The author thus inspects aspects of local censorship—ideological and institutional—that discouraged accusation. In this regard, notes Sansom, the idiosyncratic nature of the chiefdom, particularly its volatile social structure, was thought to reinforce awareness that witch accusation was a highly hazardous exercise. A list of the range of viable alternatives used to seek out the sources of personal misfortune is then provided. Thus, a significant section of the paper seeks to highlight the importance of the *ngaka* or divining "doctor." Since the diviner operated in secret, recourse to his secluded "art" was deemed a viable alternative to public spectacle. Consequently, the paper documents the relationship between client and doctor. Sansom considers the relationship to be one of "secrecy" insofar as secrecy was viewed as a necessary safeguard against witchcraft accusations in public.

E107   Schapera, Isaac (1930a). "Some Ethnographical Texts in SeKgatla." *Bantu Studies*, vol. 4, no. 2: 73-93.

Schapera's annotated translations of a number of SeKgatla texts provides the reader with a first-hand account of several ceremonies associated with birth, marriage, and death among the Tswana-speaking BaKgatla ba Kgafela of the Bechuanaland Protectorate. In the first translation, the writer notes, for example, that after a woman gives birth to her first child, both mother and child begin a period of ritual seclusion that lasts for two months. Schapera's informant, Manyalo (Hendrik Molefi), further suggests that a sheep or calf is killed by the father following the period of seclusion so that an animal skin can be fashioned and used to carry the child. In the second translation Schapera's informant provides information regarding marriage rites, and in particular rituals associated with *bogadi*. In the third, post-mortem rites concerned with the preparation of unsalted *mosokoana* porridge, the slaughter of the *mogaga* beast, and the consumption of unrefined beer, called "dirt," are described. In this section, the informant describes customs observed by members of the deceased's family. These include ritual prescriptions concerning the mother's brother, or *malome*, who is required to wear the deceased's clothing, and, in the case of the burial of royalty, prescriptions governing the protection of graves from the work of wizards (*baloi*). In the last translation, Schapera documents rituals associated with *magoane* initiation (the incorporation of boys into the "tribal" regiment, or *mophato*). These include the ritual procedures associated with circumcision (*bogwera*). However, as the writer notes, the observance of these rituals and procedures had been discontinued, since the last regiment to pass through the traditional *bogwera* ceremony was in 1901. The paper contains a number of brief annotations and orthographic notes. No bibliography is included.

E108   Schapera, Isaac (1930b). "Some Notes on Cattle Magic and Medicines of the Bechuanaland BaKxatla." *South African Journal of Science*, vol. 27: 557-61.

Schapera contends that everyday activities among the BaKgatla of the Bechuanaland Protectorate, as with other "primitive" peoples, were accompanied by a variety of magical rites that were regarded as indispensable for propitiating ancestors and securing prosperity. In a series of brief reports, he describes some of the more common of the rituals and beliefs associated with the "doctoring" of cattle (*xo alafa dikxomo*) in this Tswana-speaking chiefdom. Notes on the art of the *ngaka* (sacred specialist or doctor) are cataloged, among them his or her preparation of either protective or devastating herbal prescriptions, including *tsithlo* and *thoxadimo*. Schapera describes how the black *tsithlo* powder, for example, was used in the construction of the kraal as a precautionary defense against the evil spells of *baloi* (wizards). By contrast, he notes that the red *thoxadimo* remedy was deployed as a potent "medicine" to inflict disease or disorder among the cattle of an opponent. An index of similar remedies and prescriptions is enumerated, among them *morero, mpherefere, mmilo, moloxa,* and *mosetha.* For the most part, suggests Schapera, these medicines were all used to promote fecundity. While the writer is essentially concerned with describing the rites and practices of the *ngaka*, the paper concludes with several accounts of beliefs associated with the protection of cattle. Foremost, these beliefs concerned restrictions placed upon menstruating or pregnant women, whom the BaKgatla considered had the propensity to "pollute" cattle by entering the kraal during periods of "doctoring." The paper, which provides a taxonomy for most of the medicines mentioned, has no notes or bibliography.

E109   Schapera, Isaac (1930c). "The Little Rain (Pulanyana) Ceremony." *Bantu Studies*, vol. 4, no. 4: 211-16.

Inspired by Eiselen's earlier account of Pedi rainmaking rituals, Schapera provides a detailed description of an annual *pulanyana* or rain ceremony conducted by Tswana-speaking Kgatla communities to secure good harvests in the Bechuanaland Protectorate. He notes that while the ritual was initially prescribed for the beginning of the agricultural season, or for the commencement of plowing, the predominance of Christian converts in the region in the 1920s led to the abandonment of the procedure, except during times of extreme drought. Aside from these changed conditions, asserts the writer, the *pulanyana* ritual remained remarkably similar to Pedi rain rites: Directed by the chief and his assistant rainmaker, the *moroka wa pula*, the rite commenced with the selection of suitable girls, all virgins who had not yet had their first menses. The girls were then instructed to empty the contents of a ritual "rain pot," the *sethsaxa sa pula*, into a sacred enclosure, called the *xotlwana sa pula*. The following morning, suggests Schapera, the girls gathered in the *kgotla*, removed all European garments and ornaments, and refrained from consuming food or liquid before repeating the previous day's ritual, this time sprinkling doctored water on the cultivated fields while singing traditional rain songs. Examples of a number of these song are provided. The paper enumerates the ritual procedures and taboos adhered to by young males (*basimane*) during the rite. Schapera concludes by describing briefly Chief Lentswe's sacrifice of an ox at the grave of his father, Chief Kxamanyane, prior to a rainmaking rite in the Saulspoort region of the western Transvaal. The paper is briefly annotated but no bibliography is appended.

E110   Schapera, Isaac (1932a). "A Native Lion Hunt in the Kalahari Desert." *Man*, vol. 32: 278-82.

Documenting the status of a "degenerate" BaKgatla chiefdom in the Kalahari, Schapera highlights elements of Tswana taboo (*moila*), ritual, magic, and myth observed while participating in a lion hunt near the town of Molepolole. The writer notes, for example, that it was taboo for European women to accompany their male counterparts because the Tswana trackers feared that their presence would jeopardize the success of the kill. One of the trackers, a *ngaka* ("magician"), prepared a ritual solution known as *tsithlo*, into which weapons were placed and with which the spoor of the lion was "doctored." Brief notes on purification rites associated with the termination of hunting procedures are included, among them the MaSarwa's use of a lion's penis and testicles to produce forms of *tsithlo*. Schapera's brief description ends with examples of BaKgatla victory songs. The essay is not annotated. However, several photographic plates accompany the text.

E111   Schapera, Isaac (1932b). "Kxatla Riddles and Their Significance." *Bantu Studies*, vol. 6, no. 3: 215-32.

Based upon material collected in the course of several trips to the Bechuanaland Protectorate during the years 1929 to 1931, Schapera provides examples of a number of BaKgatla riddles (*dithabalakane*). Noting that the riddle is essentially a form of "entertainment" widely distributed among the Bantu-speaking peoples of southern Africa, the writer outlines structural and stylistic continuities between the riddles of the Tswana and those of the Sotho, Xhosa, Venda, and Tsonga. In this regard, the work relies on the writings of Norton and Velaphe, Godfrey, Lestrade, and Junod. The paper consists of approximately one hundred and thirty examples, divided into eight sections, namely, natural phenomena; the vegetable world; the animal world (insects and domestic animals); crops and other foods; the human body; utensils and other objects; and the white man's culture. As an example of the fluid aesthetic of Tswana orality, and the use of language to accommodate or resist colonial conquest and displacement, the paper is of interest to historians of religion in southern Africa.

E112   Schapera, Isaac (1933). "Premarital Pregnancy and Native Opinion: A Note on Social Change." *Africa*, vol. 6: 59-89.

Consistent with Bronislaw Malinowski's emphasis on the wide-spread predominance of "principles of legitimacy" in African systems of marriage and kinship, Schapera examines the attitudes of indigenous South African "tribes" to premarital sex and pregnancy. More specifically, the writer focuses on changing attitudes to premarital pregnancy among the Tswana-speaking BaKgatla of the Bechuanaland Protectorate. The paper begins, however, with an overview of the relationship between marriage and the right to bear children among Thonga-, Xhosa-, and Zulu-speaking South Africans. Drawing on the ethnographic surveys of Junod (1927), Duggan-Cronin (1931), and Eiselen (1928), brief notes on *lobolo* and *bogadi* are included. Primarily, Schapera seeks to highlight the profound distinctions that exist between institutionalized or sanctioned premarital sex among the Thonga and Xhosa, including the *gangisa* customs of the Thonga and the *hlobonga* practices of the Xhosa, and the restrictions placed upon unmarried women in Tswana-speaking societies. In this regard, the writer asserts that among the Kgatla, bride-price was often reduced if a women was thought to have participated in premarital sexual acts or, particularly, if it was discovered that she had borne a child. More recently, and under the pressures of European influence, traditional restrictions have been modified, suggests the writer. Specifically, the predominance of Christian missions in Bechuanaland caused traditional initiation and puberty rites (*bogwera* and *bojale*) that restricted premarital sexual encounters to restructure and redefine premarital prohibitions and regulations. To cite one example, Schapera suggests that Christian restrictions on polygyny reduced possibilities for marriage. Similarly, missionary censure of so-called "mocking songs" and *mantlwane* (role-play) rituals, during which time young couples acted out intimate sexual relations usually restricted to married life, increased the possibilities of premarital pregnancy while restricting objections to sanction. The paper contains brief notes on abortion, concubinage, and customary law.

E113   Schapera, Isaac (1934). "Oral Sorcery Among the Natives of Bechuanaland." In E. E. Evans-Pritchard, Raymond Firth, Bronislaw Malinowski, and Isaac Schapera (eds.) *Essays Presented to C. G. Seligman*. London: Routledge. 293-305.

Drawing on Evans-Pritchard's landmark analysis of Zande sorcery, Schapera identifies several structural elements and functional aspects of oral sorcery among the Tswana-speaking BaKgatla of the Bechuanaland Protectorate. He asserts that whereas the Venda and Thonga, for example, have identified two discrete classes of magician—the "wizard" who willingly inflicts disorder by means of magic (*madambi*), and the sorcerer (*baloi*) who unconsciously acts as a nocturnal spirit to bewitch (*u loya*) the innocent—Tswana-speakers have generally collapsed these categories. According to Schapera, therefore, nothing exists in the BaKgatla classification of magic that might correspond with the physiological condition of the sorcerer in Venda society. Consequently, the BaKgatla believe that all *baloi* act consciously, obtaining their medicines (*dithlare*) from the *ngaka* (professional magicians) so as to inflict deliberate disorder or disease. Particularly, the paper illustrates two techniques that the *baloi* utilize in order to "bewitch." First, suggests Schapera, the *baloi* employ rituals and medicines to "doctor" the enemy, a practice known as the "bewitching of medicines" (*baloi ba dithlare*). In this method, rites that transcend particular social taboos are undertaken. For example, the blood from a victim's *seano* (totem animal) might be used to secure ill-health or death. Second, suggests the writer, the sorcerer might deploy spells or oral forms of sorcery, a practice known as the "bewitching of the mouth" (*baloi ba molomo*). This technique is in turn divided into two forms: cursing (*go hutsu*), and *kgaba*, or evil intention. Examples and case studies of both are enumerated. Schapera recalls that in all cases of sorcery, the ritual washing of the body is required. In some cases, ritual sacrifices to the *badimo* are also considered beneficial. The paper, which is rich in descriptive detail, and borrows from the writings of Henri-Alexandre Junod, W. C. Willoughby, and H. A. Stayt, is essential reading for both students of comparative religion and historians of sorcery in southern Africa.

E114   Schapera, Isaac (1935). "The Social Structure of the Tswana World." *Bantu Studies*, vol. 9: 203-24.

Drawing on examples from Tswana-speaking communities, anthropologist Isaac Schapera examines aspects of the complex social organization of Kgatla and Ngwato political structures in what was the Bechuanaland Protectorate. He argues that, in general, certain features of the Tswana "tribal system" differ substantially from social and organizational patterns prevalent in other Bantu societies. For example, while the household presents a more or less stable social organism, reflecting the same characteristics among the Tswana as it does among other societies in southern Africa—although multiple wives of a polygamous marriage are ranked somewhat differently—the combination of households into larger social units presents a considerable departure from the sociological organization of other Bantu peoples and, therefore, poses a problem for comparative analysis. Included in his overview of the distinctive and hierarchical levels of Tswana society is an analysis of how the "wards" of the *dikgo-*

sana (patrilineal relatives) and *bathlanka* (commoners of long-established social networks) are structured. In describing the importance of marital relations, political associations, and ancestral ties, the paper is perhaps of only limited interest to historians of religion. However, brief notes on totemic affiliation, including descriptions of the *kwena* (crocodile); *moyo* (heart); *tlou* (elephant); *phuti* (duiker); *nare* (buffalo); *kgabo* (ape); *sebata* (lion); *kubu* (hippopotamus); and *kolobe* (boar) are indicative of the role of religion in distinguishing patrilineal non-exogamous groups in Tswana society. The paper is annotated.

E115   Schapera, Isaac (1937). "The Contributions of Western Civilization to Modern Kxatla Culture." *Transactions of the Royal Society of South Africa*, vol. 24: 221-52.

Following a brief account of the historical origins and social structure of the Kxatla (BaKgatla) of the Bechuanaland Protectorate, Schapera examines the effects of European encounter on Tswana culture. He notes that the BaKgatla were forced to move from the Rustenburg region of the western Transvaal in the 1840s due to the expansion of Boer nation-builders in that area. And that, from 1864, missionaries began to establish a number of stations surrounding the subsequent Kgatla capital at Mochudi in what is today Botswana. One consequence of the mission, argues Schapera, was the introduction of European educational facilities and medical services. These colonial agencies began to restrict traditional rites associated with *bogadi* (bride-price), initiation and puberty (*bogwera* and *bojale*) rituals, and, particularly, the practices of sacred specialists, including magicians (*dingaka*) and sorcerers (*baloi*) accused of witchcraft. While some European practices and beliefs were initially accepted, the replacement in 1885 of traditional social structures with alternative forms of colonial administration was vehemently opposed. Therefore, although the use of alternative agricultural technologies and Christian beliefs were often adopted, (the Kgatla chief Lentswe converted to Christianity in 1892), for the most part indirect rule and its consequences (among them the emergence of labor migration) were frequently rejected or resisted. The predominance of ancestral veneration, the consultation of magicians for the purposes of ensuring rain, and the use of traditional healers rather than Western medical doctors, for example, was thus not easily abandoned. The paper, which includes brief notes on the modification of marriage rites, is annotated.

E116   Schapera, Isaac (1938). *A Handbook of Tswana Law and Customs*. Oxford: Oxford University Press.

Schapera's widely-read survey of Tswana customary law, introduced by the former Resident Commissioner of Bechuanaland, Sir Charles Rey, is a landmark study of "tribal" and family law among the Kgatla and Ngwato constituencies of what was the Bechuanaland Protectorate. In fact, as Simon Roberts (1985) has observed, the survey was used by Tswana-speaking authorities and jurists as the primary legal resource in the *lekgotla*, or traditional legislative council, and as such was "played back" into Tswana jurisprudence in the "absence" of indigenous knowledge. Describing in detail issues related to "tribal constitutional law," including chieftainship and chiefly prerogatives; the order of succession; ceremonies to be conducted at the installation of regents; and customs associated with citizenship and male (*bogwera*) and female (*bojale*) initiation, the encyclopedic account also highlights issues related to family law, marriage, and polygamy. Included are extensive notes on betrothal ceremonies, incorporating bride-price (*bogadi*), sexual relations, sterility and impotence, divorce, and remarriage of widowers; kinship obligations; the laws of property, in which Schapera outlines aspects of jurisprudence concerned with land tenure, demarcation, and property inheritance; and laws of contract associated with barter and sale, cattle-herding, labor, and the employment of magicians (*dingaka*). As an ethnographic index of Tswana belief and ritual practice, Schapera's unprecedented account catalogs a whole range of issues, among them abortion, adultery, beer-drinking, bestiality, burial, capital punishment, concubinage, divination, incest, infanticide, homicide, homosexuality, rainmaking, rape, sodomy, sorcery, taboo, torture, totemism, and witchcraft. The book is indexed and genealogical tables of Tswana royal families and regiments (*mephato*) are included.

E117   Schapera, Isaac (1940). "The Political Organisation of the Ngwato in Bechuanaland Protectorate." In M. Fortes and E. E. Evans-Pritchard (eds.) *African Political Systems*. London: Oxford University Press. 56-82.

Contributing to Evans-Pritchard's comparative analysis of political systems, Schapera concurs that kinship, lineage, territorial organization, and political authority, if "stripped of their cultural idiom and reduced to functional terms," conceal structural similarities. Highlighting the context of colonial rule that constrained the independence of traditional political systems in what was the Bechuanaland Protectorate, however, Schapera's essay punctuates the need to contextualize any structural-functionalist analysis within the confines of historical circumstance. In this regard, his account of the political organization of the Tswana-speaking Ngwato chiefdom in Bechuanaland focuses on how territorial constitution altered under colonial administration following the advent of British rule in 1885. The paper is divided into four sections. In the first, Schapera outlines aspects of the ethnic composition and historical predominance of the Ngwato. Included is a brief overview of the political consequences of Chief Kgama III's (1837-1923) conversion to Christianity. Notes on the *motse* (ward) system, the *kgotla* (council), and the *kgosana* (headman) are incorporated. In the second section, "The Administrative System," the writer describes how centralized administrative hierarchies implicit to traditional Ngwato government were modified under the pressures of European control. In 1927, when "witchcraft" became a statutory offense, for example, the chief's power was curtailed insofar as the trial of alleged sorcerers was removed from his jurisdiction and handed over to the District Commissioner—an occurrence vociferously challenged in an essay in 1936 by Seretse Khama's successor, Tshekedi. From 1934, however, when the Native Tribunals Proclamation Act was instituted, matters dealing with treason, sedition, murder, culpable homicide, rape, assault, and conspiracy against the chief were also removed from the jurisdiction of the tribal courts. In the final two sections, "The Powers and Authority of the Chief" and "The Rights and Responsibilities of Chieftainship," Schapera concludes by suggesting that chieftainship under indirect rule was far removed from the system of political administration promised Kgama by the British Secretary of State in London. The paper is briefly annotated.

E118   Schapera, Isaac (1943). *Native Land Tenure in the Bechuanaland* Protectorate. Alice: The Lovedale Press.

In a detailed descriptive account of tribal customary law among the Tswana, undertaken for the Bechuanaland Protectorate, and informed by commissioners' reports and the correspondence of a number of chiefs, including Batheon II, Schapera highlights changing practices related to land tenure in the Tswana-speaking Ngwato, Tawana, Kwena, Ngwaketse, and Kgatla chiefdoms. However, the monograph, divided into fifteen chapters, includes a wide range of apparently independent issues, among them rituals and myths relating to animal husbandry, grazing rights, and game protection, as well as beer-brewing legislation, labor migration, and seasonal taboos. Schapera's brief comments on rainmaking rituals and myths associated with totemism (*seano*) are of particular significance. For the most part, his comments on these particular issues are drawn from W. C. Willoughby's (1928) standard description. The work is briefly annotated and an index is included.

E119   Schapera, Isaac (1950). "Kinship and Marriage among the Tswana." In A. R. Radcliffe-Brown and Daryll Forde (eds.) *African Systems of Kinship and Marriage*. London: Oxford University Press. 140-65.

In this article Schapera compares the rules and customs governing marriage among nine Tswana "tribes" with a view to determining why the Tswana-speaking residents of the South African-Botswana borderland adhered to fewer social restrictions concerning marriage than any other southern Bantu peoples. To this end, the article examines the social structure of kinship organization in the household, family-group, and ward (*motse*). In the first section of the paper, several categories of relational restrictions are identified. With a few "irregular" exceptions, notes Schapera, marriage was taboo between parents and their offspring, as well as between siblings, including half-brothers and sisters. Ideally, therefore, a young man would marry the daughter of his mother's brother (*molume*). Among other advantages, it was held that alliances between the male and the *molume's* daughter cemented political and diplomatic relations. However, while the article includes detailed analysis and several tables, it contains little of immediate relevance to the study of comparative religion in southern Africa.

E120   Schapera, Isaac (1952). *The Ethnic Composition of the Tswana Tribes*. London School of Economics Monographs on Social Anthropology, no. 11. London: London School of Economics.

Following an historical overview and an analysis of "tribal" expansion in the Bechuanaland Protectorate, anthropologist Isaac Schapera establishes an index of discrete Tswana-speaking ethnic identities in what is today Botswana. His catalog, comprising notes on the Tshidi-Rolong, Ngwaketse, Kwena, Ngwato, Tawana, Khurutshe, Seleka-Rolong, Kgatla, Tlokwa, and Malete chiefdoms first enumerates statistical documentation from the 1946 census returns. Notes on ward (*motse*) subdivisions are included, as are records pertaining to class affiliation and division. In this regard, Schapera identifies three separate classes common to most chiefdoms: *dikgosana* (nobles, or "little chiefs" descended from the ruling line); *batlhanka* (commoners, or "servants"), also termed *basimane ba kgosi* (foreigners absorbed into the "tribe" and made retainers of the chief); and *bafaladi* (aliens, or refugees). While the paper is perhaps of only passing interest to readers of comparative religion, the writer's detailed description of the processes of historical succession, as well as his account of totemic structure is informative. Among the *seano* (totems) Schapera lists are the *tshwena* (baboon) of the Hurutshe; the *thol* (kudu) of the Tlhaping; the crocodile of the Kwena; the duiker of the Ngwato; and the elephant of the Kgwatlheng. The monograph is briefly annotated and draws on Ellenberger's *History of the Basuto* (1912) and Van Warmelo's landmark *Preliminary Survey of the Bantu Tribes* (1935).

E121   Schapera, Isaac (1953). *The Tswana*. London: Kegan Paul (rev. edn. 1991).

Long regarded a watershed in the history of African ethnography, Schapera's monograph provides a comprehensive analysis of Tswana language, economy, social organization, government, and religion. Leaving aside aspects of nomenclature, demography, wage-labor and land tenure, kinship, customary law, and judicial processes, the chapter on religion, entitled "Religion and Magic," contains ample material for historians of religion in southern Africa. For example, in the section of the chapter called "traditional cults," Schapera cites Mackenzie (1871), Brown (1926), and Willoughby (1928; 1932) to relate several myths associated with the Tswana high god Modimo, the demi-gods Lôôwe, Tintibane, Matsieng, and Thobega, and the dominant ancestral dead, the *badimo*. Similarly, ritual procedures associated with the doctoring of armies (*go foko marumo*) and tribal boundaries (*go bapola lefatshe*), the consecration of the capital (*go thaya motse*), the initiation of boys and girls into age-regiments (*bogwera* and *bojale*), and, above all, the making of rain (*go fetlha pula*) are all itemized. The section is followed with a brief account of "modern survivals" of Tswana custom: Schapera asserts that "the old religious beliefs and practices are seldom encountered." Likewise, "all the great ceremonies formerly conducted by the chief have been widely abandoned." In the following section of the paper, entitled "Magicians and Magic," Schapera maintains that although the "religious system" was disappearing, certain magical practices, among them protective *ditlhare* (medicine) rites performed by "doctors" (*ngaka*) remained almost universally popular. A "morphology" of magic divided according to the dual categories of medicinal magic and spells is outlined. The analysis then turns to a brief description of divination (*go laola*). Notes on "bone-throwing" (the "reading" of *thlabane* tablets) and "omens" are included. The chapter ends with an examination of *baloi* or sorcery. The 1991 revised edition leaves Schapera's text largely unchanged but features a preface by John L. Comaroff and an updated bibliography.

E122   Schapera, Isaac (1957). "Marriage of Near Kin Among the Tswana." *Africa*, vol. 27, no. 2: 139-59.

Having noted briefly in a previously published (1950) paper that near kin marriage among nobles was prevalent in Tswana societies, Schapera examines the genealogical lines of nine ruling chiefdoms to assess more accurately the changing conditions of close-kin marriages among the descendants of chiefs. Particularly, the paper analyzes the chiefly lineages of the Kwena (Motswasele II, 1807-1822); Ngwato (Sekgoma I, 1834-1875); Tawana (Tawana, 1795-1820); Ngwaketse (Makaba II, 1790-1824); Tshidi-Rolong (Montshiwa, 1815-1849); Kgafela-Kgatla (Kgamanyane, 1853-1874); Tlokwa (Matlapeng, 1835-1880); and Malete (Mokgosi II, 1830-1886). Beginning with the premise that these chiefly lineages prefer first cousin marriages, the article goes on to elaborate various patterns and permutations of relationship and marriage among Tswana-speakers generally. Detailed statistics are tabled to indicate type, degree, and frequency of kin and polygynous close-kin marriage. Broadly stated, Schapera concludes that nobles married near-kin relations more frequently than they did commoners, and that nobles tended to marry within the agnatic line, with first cousins. By contrast, commoners showed a preference for cross-cousin marriage. In addition, polygyny increased among upper classes. In part, suggests the writer, both the predominance of close-kin and polygynous marriage among nobles was a consequence of attempts to cement social status. More generally, however, Schapera asserts that the Tswana practice of close-kin marriage is an anomaly; their immediate neighbors, the Nguni, are strictly exogamous. The paper is annotated and includes several tables.

E123   Schapera, Isaac (1963). "Kinship and Politics in Tswana History." *Journal of the Royal Anthropological Institute*, vol. 93: 159-73.

Defending structural-functionalist anthropological analysis from the critique of ahistoricism, Schapera attempts to show how localized comparative history can add to the understanding of kinship systems. More precisely, he undertakes to reveal how a comparison of the political histories of several Tswana chiefdoms reveals common and recurrent forms of civil conflict, dictated to by the nature of kinship patterns, that help to explain the contrasting and contradictory roles of agnatic or maternal kin structures. The paper begins with a brief historical and demographic overview of eight principle Tswana chiefdoms, namely the Kgatla, Kwena, Malete, Ngwaketse, Ngwato, Rolong, Tawana, and Tlokwa. In that overview Schapera identifies three features of primary concern: First, that the Tswana are divided into patrilineal descent groups, notably lineages and totemic clans, that are not exogamous. Second, that each chiefdom, or "tribe," is ruled over by an hereditary chief, his advisers, and a formal council of ward-heads. And third, that a considerable proportion of people live in the chief's settlement. Unlike the Zulu and other Nguni peoples, therefore, the Tswana uncharacteristically discouraged localized dynastic administration. In the following section of the paper, however, Schapera contends that conflict between chiefs and their near relatives was not infrequent. Among the eight chiefdoms under consideration, for example, 107 internal disputes, aside from "inter-tribal" wars with British administrators, occurred in Bechuanaland during a period of seven decades from 1850. Although altercations also originated as a consequence of separatist church movements, dissonance arose primarily as a result of dynastic dispute following the establishment of the Protectorate in 1885. Ironically, one immediate corollary of British administration was the disappearance of civil war. In examining a number of case histories involving dynastic disputes, Schapera concludes in the last two sections of the paper that prior to the imposition of colonial administration, Christian tradition, and the relaxation of polygynous marital relations, those disputes often resulted in civil war. British intervention, however, resulted in fewer conflicts, which, instead of involving close agnates, were negotiated by such relatives as first cousins or uncles and nephews. Nonetheless, the writer asserts, accusations of witchcraft or sorcery (*baloi*), for example, remained symptomatic of latent tensions in Tswana social relations. The paper is only briefly annotated, but a bibliography of cited materials is included.

E124   Schapera, Isaac (1965). *Praise Poems of Tswana Chiefs*. Oxford: Oxford University Press.

Drawing on two years of fieldwork among the Tswana-speaking Kgatla of what was the Bechuanaland Protectorate, and employing materials gathered from shorter periods of residence among the Ngwato, Kwena, and Ngwaketse during the years 1929 to 1943, Schapera's account of Tswana praise poetry provides an in-depth analysis of the work of the *mmoki* (praise-poet) and his *maboko* (praises). In an extensive introduction, Schapera analyzes the function of the praise poem in Tswana society and provides detailed notes on thematic interest, structure, stylistic peculiarity, and cultural setting. He recalls that while praise-poems were generally composed in honor of chiefs, headmen, and famous warriors, many poems were dedicated to natural phenomena, notably cattle, crops, trees, and even inanimate objects, including divining bones, schools, railway trains, and bicycles! In the first chapter, praise-poems dedicated to Kgatla chiefs, among them Masellane, Kgwefane, Molefe, Mmakgatso, Pheto, Senwelo, Motlotle, Pilane, Kgamanyane, Lentswe, Ramono, Isang, and Molefi Kgafela are narrated. In Chapter Two, poems recalling the prowess of a number of Kwena chiefs, including Motswaselel I, Seitlhamo, Legwale, Tshosa, Moruakgomo, Kgakge, Sechele, and Sebele are documented. The third chapter recalls praise-poems dedicated to the Ngwaketse chiefs Makaba II, Sebego, Segotshane, Gaseitsiwe, Batheon I and II, and Seepapitso. The last chapter identifies a number of Ngwato chiefs who were the recipients of praise. They include Kgama Mathiba, Kgari Kgama, Sekgoma Kgari, Kgama Sekgoma (Khama), Sekgoma Kgama, and Tshekedi Khama. While most accounts were recorded by Schapera, portions of Kgatla and Ngwato praise-poems previously recorded by Norton (1922), Leseyane (1941), and Seboni (1947) are included. Of special interest is the writer's brief overview of nineteenth-century travel literature identifying examples of praise-poetry. Included are the recollections of Moffat (1842), Smith (1834-1836), Livingstone (1857), Casalis (1859), and Chapman (1868).

E125   Schapera, Isaac (1967). *Government and Politics in Tribal Societies*. New York: Shocken Books.

Based on a series of Josiah Mason lectures delivered at the University of Birmingham entitled "Politics and Law in Primitive Society," Schapera examines in this book aspects of "tribal" government and political organization in the

Bechuanaland Protectorate. Divided into six chapters, the broad-ranging work provides a structural-functionalist analysis of several aspects of chiefly administration and judicial function. Included is a consideration of Khoisan political organization, and kinship, military, labor, and legislative structures implicit to Sotho-Tswana jurisprudence and social order. While brief notes on the function of sacred specialists are incorporated, including comments on the role of sorcerers (*baloi*) and the rituals associated with magicians (*dingaka*) and rainmaking rites, the book is essentially an account of chiefly rule and administration. Of particular interest to historians of religion, however, are Schapera's comments on the mythic origins, rituals of installation, death and burial rites of chiefs, and occasions of suicide among nobles. The Venda's regard of the chief as a semi-divine being, who in abjuring all contact with women and performing a solitary ritual dance (*u pembela*) confers upon himself the status of a god (*Mudzimu*), is also noteworthy. The book is carefully annotated and an extensive bibliography and index are included.

E126   Schapera, Isaac (1969). "Some Aspects of Kgatla Magic." In *Ethnological and Linguistic Studies in Honour of N. J. van Warmelo*. Pretoria: Government Printers. 157-68.

Schapera's largely descriptive article is based on data gathered over a period of thirty years. An introduction carefully explaining SeTswana terms flows into a meticulous enumeration of types of magic. These are listed as personal, social, economic, and communal, but cover the whole spectrum of social experience. To illustrate the workings of medicine magic in the different categories identified, the author introduces several case studies, including one that examines techniques used to doctor cattle. The second half of the paper documents how public rituals, among them rainmaking rites and war-doctoring rituals performed for chiefs, suffered visible decline with the advent of Christianity. By contrast, private rites continued almost unaffected. Schapera recalls in this context that while some rites could be performed by individuals for private use, the more complex the ritual the more the services of a professional *ngaka* (doctor) were called for. Schapera stresses the fact that doctors of all categories were products of extended training. Apprenticeship could also consist of mystical experiences, among them the revelation of new medicines in dreams.

E127   Schapera, Isaac (1970a). "Sorcery and Witchcraft in Bechuanaland." In Max Marwick (ed.) *Witchcraft and Sorcery*. Harmondsworth: Penguin. 108-20.

In 1889 the Kwena chief Sechele killed five men suspected of being witches; that between the years 1910 and 1916 the Ngwaketse chief Seepapitso put to death twenty-six suspected witches; and that in 1927 the Kwena chief Sebele II accused his maternal uncle Kebohula of having tried to bewitch him by burying a "doctored" hoe in the royal *kgotla* or council place. Beginning with these instances, Schapera examines aspects of witchcraft or "sorcery" in the Bechuanaland Protectorate. In part, the analysis is located in the context of colonial legislation—the 1934 Native Tribunals Proclamation that removed from the jurisdiction of tribal courts all statutory offenses, including witch-accusations and killings, and the revised 1943 Proclamation that granted to the Ngwato, Ngwaketse, and Kgatla chiefs permission to deal with cases of witchcraft. But the analysis is framed by attention to local cultural constructions of law and order. Schapera notes that the Tswana identify only one distinct form of "magician" who is associated with what is commonly called witchcraft. Whereas Evans-Pritchard, for example, observes the distinction between evil agents who act intentionally and those who act unintentionally because they suffer from an hereditary pathological condition, Schapera argues that the Tswana see all witches as intentional evil agents who deliberately attempt to inflict harm. As such, they are identified as sorcerers or *baloi*. Divided into two groups—the *baloi ba bosigo* or (female) night sorcerers, and the *baloi ba motshegare* or (male) day sorcerers—these evil agents are responsible, he suggests, for malicious practices performed for reasons of greed, vengeance, or envy. They are responsible for the iniquitous and their abilities extend to the magical: They can walk through walls; they can travel on the backs of hyenas that the Kgatla say they fashion out of porridge; and they can bewitch a victim by merely fixing them with a stare. More often, however, the *baloi* are said to obtain sacred medicines (*ditlare*) that, when fed (*go jesa*) to the victim, secure their infection or capitulation (*go neelela*). The wide-ranging and detailed descriptive account includes many examples of how the *baloi* perform their ritual work, as well as how sorcerers have sought protection from the medicines deployed by adversaries. Brief notes on reasons for wanting to secure the services of a *baloi* are also included (to punish the person responsible for social disorder that was deemed attributable to ancestral infliction, or *kgaba*, for example). The chapter is not annotated and no bibliography is included.

E128   Schapera, Isaac (1970b). *Tribal Innovators: Tswana Chiefs and Social Change, 1795-1940*. London: The Athlone Press; New York: Humanities Press.

In a completely revised version of an earlier monograph, *Tribal Legislation Among the Tswana of the Bechuanaland Protectorate* (1943), Schapera highlights the role of the Tswana chief as an agent of social change in what came to be Botswana. He describes, in this regard, legislative processes inaugurated in the area by the various chiefs of five Tswana-speaking groups, including the Kgatla, Ngwato, Ngwaketse, Tawana, and Kwena. He further suggests how tribal administration, government, economy, religion, and social relations were adapted under the jurisdiction of the chief in the context of increased colonial expansion and missionary pressure. An extensive array of resources, among them government reports, unpublished archives, and the manuscripts of the Ngwaketse chiefs Batheon I and Seepapitso, as well as missionary correspondence and the published writings of W. C. Willoughby and E. Sidney Hartland, are employed in the monograph. Schapera thus provides an incisive account of social transformation and religious change from 1795, when Pheto II was crowned Kgatla chief, to 1940, by which time Kgama I was made ruler of the Ngwato. While extensive notes on tribal administration, land tenure, labor migration, and the emergence of colonial forms of legal control are included, it is Schapera's rich detail regarding the changing role of religion among Tswana-speakers in the region that is most impressive. Included in the writer's analysis, for example, are accounts of changing attitudes and legislation concerning circumcision rites, magic, marriage, polygamy, and rainmaking. Chapter Six, entitled "Religion and Magic," describes in detail the changes that transpired in Tswana belief and practice when London Missionary Society, Hermannsburg Lutheran, and Dutch Reformed Church agents were invited to settle among the Tlhaping (from 1817), Ngwaketse (from 1848), Ngwato (1857), and Kwena (1866). Schapera notes, for example, that with the baptism of Sechele I in 1848, and the conversion to Christianity in 1881 of the Tawana chief Moremi II, traditional religious practice was continually undermined. Sabbath laws were introduced, "separatist" movements were resisted, rainmaking and first-fruits ceremonies were abandoned, and initiation rituals and the "doctoring" of armies were outlawed. The work, which contains an extensive bibliography and index, is essential reading for any student interested in the changing role and meaning of religion among the Tswana.

E129   Schapera, Isaac (1971a). *Married Life in an African Tribe*. Harmondsworth: Penguin.

In this book Schapera describes changing beliefs and practices associated with marriage and family life among the Kgatla of the Bechuanaland Protectorate. The writer argues that, following the advent of Christian missions, colonial administrative control, and "Western civilization" in the region, traditional values among these Tswana-speaking people were threatened. For example, traditional rites associated with betrothal, including the payment of gifts of cattle, called *bogadi*, were undermined by Christian and Western marriage rites and customs. These particular transformations are documented in the first two chapters of the work. However, the adaptation of African custom and the consequent employment of Western rites remains a persistent theme throughout Schapera's account. For example, in Chapters Four and Five the changing status of African customary law and traditional values associated with the role of women in Kgatla economies is reviewed. In Chapter Six sexual relations and taboos associated with periods of "hotness," including menstruation, are outlined in the context of prohibitions related to the advent of Western Christian models of monogamous marriage. Similarly, in Chapter Nine, changing beliefs and practices associated with the responsibilities of parenthood and the rites of initiation into adulthood are examined. The wide-ranging and rich descriptive detail of Schapera's observations traverse these and many other related issues, among them traditional and changing prescriptions regarding divorce and separation, and observances associated with mourning and the rites of burial and death. Of particular interest to historians of religion in this regard are the writer's observations regarding changing attitudes to the "worship of the dead." Schapera suggests that while ancestor veneration was "the outstanding feature of Kgatla religion," it had "virtually disappeared," or was practiced only by "magicians" when preparing their medicines or performing important ceremonies. The work is indexed but no bibliography or annotations are included.

E130   Schapera, Isaac (1971b). *The Rainmaking Rites of Tswana Tribes*. Leiden: Afrika-Studiecentrum; Cambridge: African Studies Centre.

Schapera's monograph provides a detailed descriptive account of beliefs and rituals associated with rainmaking among the Tswana-speaking BaKgatla of south-eastern Botswana. His account, which draws on fieldwork conducted in the region during the years 1929 to 1942, begins with a brief narrative in Chapter One of a rainmaking ceremony that was performed at the enthronement in 1929 of the Kgatla chief Molefi: The writer notes that the rite, attended by more than ten thousand members of the Kgatla "tribe," was originally held to mark a harvest thanksgiving. Because the date coincided with the anniversary of the Kgatla's migration from their former home in the Transvaal, however, it also commemorated "a national patriotic day." Therefore, Schapera suggests, rainmaking rites among the Tswana were not only employed to ensure rain, but were mobilized to engender patriotic support for Tswana nationalism. In the following five chapters the writer provides evidence to support this observation, beginning in Chapter Two with a more general account of the role of the chief in the politics of rainmaking. Notes on the ritual significance of "rain medicines," among them a type of snake, called *kwanyape*, are included. In Chapter Three a detailed account of these medicines, and of the equipment of the professional rainmaker or *ngaka*, is then provided. Thereafter, the writer documents in Chapters Four and Five rainmaking rituals associated with "Annual Rainmaking Ceremonies" and "Special Rain Rites," among them the "land-cleansing," "field-sprinkling," and "cloud-summoning" rites. Notes on special rites requiring human sacrifice during the "rain hunt" are also appended. Many of these "special rites," suggests Schapera, were abandoned following chief Lentswe's conversion to Christianity. The final chapter documents rainmaking rites consistent with the practice of Tswana-speaking peoples from the Khurutshe, Kwena, Ngwaketse, and Ngwato "tribes." The work is annotated and includes photographic plates and a bibliography useful for comparative analysis, citing, for example, the works of Dornan (1928), Feddema (1966), and Willoughby (1932).

E131   Schapera, Isaac (1978). "Some Kgatla Theories of Procreation." In John Argyle and Eleanor Preston-Whyte (eds.) *Social Systems and Traditions in Southern Africa: Essays in Honour of Eileen Krige*. Cape Town: Oxford University Press. 165-82.

Obtaining the opinions of a number of "witchdoctors" (*dingaka*), among them Natale Morema and Rapedi Letsebe, Schapera draws on an extensive period of fieldwork to outline several topics concerned with conception, barrenness, and contraception among the Tswana-speaking Kgatla of the Bechuanaland Protectorate. He notes in the first section of the paper that while the Kgatla once informed their children that conception occurred following the visit of an elderly woman to a "bearded snake" who resides in a pool of water, adults believed that conception rightly occurred following copulation and the mixture of a man's semen (*maree*) with a woman's menstrual blood (*mosese*). Brief notes on *thobalo* (sexual intercourse) among children are also included. The writer notes that pre-pubescent girls were referred to as *basimane* (boys) because they had not yet menstruated. In the second section, relating to barrenness (*boopa*), Schapera enumerates several rites associated with ensuring a woman's fertility. A description of the *ngaka's* performance of *gokopanye madi* rites (the ritual "cutting" of the female *mons pubis*) is also given, as are brief explanations of the possible causes of barrenness, which might include, suggests Schapera, the presence of sorcery (*baloi*). Medicines prescribed for barrenness are tabulated, among them the roots of the *mothata* and *monokana* plants as well as, occasionally, the fluid from the womb of a goat. In the final section, traditional techniques for preventing conception, including *coitus interuptus* (*gontshetsa madi kwantle*) and the use of purgatives, are enumerated. The paper is not annotated and is of only passing interest to historians of religion in southern Africa.

E132   Schapera, Isaac (1979). "Kgatla Notions of Ritual Impurity." *African Studies*, vol. 38: 3-15.

Originally intended to form part of a revised edition for his account of married life among the Tswana, Schapera draws on information supplied by several *dingaka* (doctors), among them Rakgomo Segale, Rapedi Letsebe, and Natale Macheng, to reexamine aspects of ritual impurity among the Tswana-speaking Kgatla of the Bechuanaland Protectorate. Particularly, the writer identifies how "hot blood" (*madi abollo*), including menstrual and post-natal blood, signified a state of ritual pollution among the Tswana. In this regard, he notes that only pre-pubescent or virgin girls and sexually inactive boys, because they were classed as "cool" (*tsidifala*), could perform rainmaking, annual national purification (*gotlhapisa lefatshe*), and war-doctoring rites. Following a series of examples of people thought to be "hot" (*obollo*), including women who had recently aborted, miscarried, or been widowed (*baswagadi*), Schapera enumerates the precautionary rituals undertaken or taboos observed to nullify or avoid resulting suffering or misfortune. For example, a menstruating woman was forbidden to wash below the breasts, and her clothing was to be buried lest other women used them to bewitch her. Similarly, all "hot" people had to refrain from entering the hut of either a new mother (*motsetse*) or a sick person (*molwetse*) unless "doctored" with the *mogato* or *mogaga* bulb. Schapera's use of a wide range of case studies in the latter half of the paper makes his account of particular interest to historians of religion in southern Africa. The paper is briefly annotated and includes a short bibliography.

E133   Sechefo, Justinus (n.d). *Customs and Superstitions in Basutoland.* Mazenod Lesotho: Catholic Centre.

In this cursory and somewhat disjointed index, the Sotho-speaking Catholic convert Justinus Sechefo adopts essentially censorious Christian interpretive categories to denigrate aspects of Sotho custom and belief. Notes on rites associated with death and burial, witchcraft, sorcery, and ancestor veneration are inserted throughout forty-nine chapters, beginning with a description of requisite mortuary procedures, among them embalming, the cutting of hair, and the distribution of the deceased's clothing. In the concluding chapters, the writer recounts Sotho "superstitions" concerned with witchcraft and sorcery. Here, he asserts that the witch is considered by all Sotho-speakers to be the cause of social disharmony and sickness. What the study lacks in coherent interpretive analysis is perhaps made up for in its range of anecdotal detail and descriptive reconstruction.

E134   Sechefo, Justinus (n.d). *Material Clothing of the Basuto.* Mazenod, Lesotho: Catholic Centre.

Sechefo, a Catholic convert and secretary to the late Sotho Paramount Chief Lerotholi, provides in this work a detailed inventory of traditional clothing worn by the Sotho. Vernacular terms and a brief description of each article is given. Items include the *tseha* (men's loin dress), *kobo* (skin blanket), *khaebana* (hat), *mose* (ox-skin petticoat), and *lefeha* (short frontal lappets). Procedures associated with tailoring, beginning with the stabbing of the animal, as well as techniques required for subsequent pegging, scraping, fraying, and refining skins are reviewed. The author's Catholic Christian convictions come to the forefront, however, insofar as these processes, and the apparel in general, are denigrated as primitive or inferior to Western styles of dress.

E135   Sechefo, Justinus (n.d.). *The Twelve Lunar Months Among the Basuto.* Mazenod, Lesotho: Catholic Centre.

In this brief paper Sechefo shows that the Sotho calendar, although calculated according to the waxing and waning of the moon, the birth-time of animals, the growth of plants, and the movement of stars, remains roughly commensurate with the adopted Christian calendar of the West. One important distinction, however, is that the advent of a new year is considered to come about in the month of August. The booklet, divided into twelve chapters, highlights several "ludicrous" and "comical" stories associated with each month. Praise songs, agricultural practices, such as planting and harvesting crops, and botanical developments are mentioned. The study contains explicitly condescending Christian polemic designed to denigrate indigenous Sotho culture and reinforce an impression of the seriousness of the writer's recent conversion to Catholicism.

E136   Sekhukhune, Phatudi D. (1990). "Social Meaning in North Sotho Ritual Symbolism." *South African Journal of Ethnology*, vol. 13, no. 1: 30-32.

Following Wilson (1954), Turner (1961; 1967), Leach (1966), and Bloch (1974), Sekhukhune asserts that ritual symbols in African societies functioned as sociolinguistic phenomena. Capable of communicating as a linguistic code, ritual symbols conveyed meanings that were nonetheless culture-specific. In the *lepheko* ritual, for example, Sekhukhune notes that a stick placed across the front door of a Northern Sotho house served to signify restricted entry following the birth of a child, the onset of infection, or death. The *lepheko* stick thus signaled impurity and danger. In a more dramatic description of Sotho semiotics, Sekhukhune notes how a stick was used to signify ritual disgrace in some societies: A burning piece of wood was inserted into the anus of a dead bachelor in order to encourage young Sotho men to marry. The paper contains a short bibliography of secondary works.

E137   Sekhukhune, Phatudi D. (1993). "Symbolism of Food and Drink: A Survey on Rituals and Other Forms of Ceremonial Interaction." *South African Journal of Ethnology*, vol. 16, no. 1: 64-68.

In this paper Sekhukhune examines the structure and function of food and drink symbolism in Northern Sotho ritual. In the section entitled "Toward a Theory of

Ritual Interpretation," Sekhukhune draws on several folklorists and anthropologists, among them Malinowski (1935), Krige (1943), Turner (1967), and Firth (1973), to analyze foodstuffs in terms of a five-fold structural-functionalist taxonomy of ritual symbolism. First, he argues, food functioned as a form of currency in "transactional symbolisms." Second, food was present as a "sacrificial symbol" in Sotho ritual. Third, food and drink were central to "ceremonial symbolisms," in the go *neśa pula* (rainmaking), go *phekola ngwaga* (prediction), and go *loma ngwaga* (first-fruit) rituals. Fourth, foodstuffs predominated in "communal symbolisms" associated with go *phapha hlogo ya moswe* (the presentation of the bride), and *magadi* or *lobola* rites. And fifth, food functioned in "restrictive" or taboo symbolisms, particularly during times of bereavement. The writer points out that, as with the Hindus, food and drink in Northern Sotho societies was regulated according to "culture-specific beliefs, values, norms, customs and traditions." Moreover, in the ritual setting of Sotho ceremonies, food and drink functioned as economies of rank and status. The paper is particularly noteworthy for its attempt to compare food symbolisms in Sotho ritual with mortuary rites in Hindu societies.

E138   Setiloane, Gabriel (1973). "Modimo: God Among the Sotho-Tswana." *Journal of Theology for Southern Africa*, vol. 4, no. 4: 6-17.

Setiloane's brief article provides a critical analysis of the attributes and praisenames of the Sotho-Tswana God, Modimo. The writer enumerates and evaluates Christian missionary interpretations of the name Modimo, asserting that Modimo is essentially a supra-personal identity. His article begins, however, by distinguishing between the *badimo* (ancestors or the "living dead") and Modimo, contending that while the former participate in numerous divine activities, the Sotho-Tswana only experience what Tempels referred to as *force vitale,* or what Otto called the *mysterium tremendum et fascinans,* in relation to Modimo. Setiloane claims, in these terms, that although unspoken mystery is the primary feature of Modimo, various epithets are nevertheless used to describe "It." The writer proceeds in the second half of the paper to analyze and evaluate sixteen attributes and praise names. For example, Setiloane examines claims that Modimo is invisible, intangible, and unknown, suggesting that although Modimo manifests in physical phenomena such as lightning and thunder, these are "no more than manifestations and not Modimo Itself." Further attributes of Modimo are analyzed, among them the terms "supreme," "one," "midwife," and "sky." However, continuing his line of argument, the writer suspects that the epithet "Modimo is *Lesedi* (Light)" to be of recent vintage, an example of Christian missionary influence. The article thus attempts to correct certain Christian misunderstandings, such as the claims by Robert Moffat and Eugène Casalis that the Sotho-Tswana were generally "ignorant" about the presence of a high god. The paper is briefly annotated.

E139   Setiloane, Gabriel (1976). *The Image of God Among the Sotho-Tswana.*
Rotterdam: A. A. Balkema.

Based on detailed ethnographic observation, critical historical analysis, and
research among the papers of Robert Moffat, Eugène Casalis, and the archives
of the London, Paris Evangelical, and Wesleyan Methodist missionary societies,
Setiloane combines a synchronic examination of "traditional" Sotho-Tswana
society with a less reified historical analysis of the successes of nineteenth-
century Christian missionary encounters to analyze aspects of Sotho-Tswana
religion. Asserting that life among Sotho-Tswana-speakers is essentially of a
religious nature, Setiloane recalls, along with W. C. Willoughby (1928), that
"religion so pervades the life of the people that it regulates their doing and governs their leisure to an extent that it is hard for Europeans to understand." However, the intent of the work is not merely to document aspects of an innately
religious life among traditional Tswana-speakers. Rather, Setiloane sets out to
bridge an historical lacuna in Tswana ethnography by highlighting the development of an emergent Sotho-Tswana theology and ecclesiology subsequent to
the advent of missionaries in the Transvaal and Lesotho, or what the writer
identifies as Sotho-Tswana land, beginning in the early nineteenth century. As
such, the writer evaluates to what extent missionaries like Archbell, Broadbent,
Edward, Evans, Hamilton, Hodgson, Jenkins, Lemue, Read, and Rolland shaped
the Sotho-Tswana notion of divinity and to what degree notions of sacrality are
inherent in Sotho-Tswana tradition. Following his analysis of the nature and
scope of Sotho-Tswana social relations in Chapter Two, Setiloane introduces in
Chapter Three the central concept of b*otho* or humanity. He argues forcefully
that among Sotho-Tswana-speakers the meaning of true humanity is contingent
on initiation (*bogwera*) into the wider community. However, the natural guardians of social harmony and religious order, he asserts, are the *badimo*, or ancestors. Extensive notes on the role and meaning of *badimo*, the Tswana high-god
Modimo, and the work of *baloi* (sorcerers) and *ngaka* (sacred specialists, or
healers) in Chapters Four through Six are provided. Here, Setiloane distinguishes between four types of *ngaka*: *selaodi*, who use the *ditaola* (sets of divining stones) to interpret social events; *senoga*, who "smell out" enemies or
evil; *lethugela*, who diagnose attempts to deploy sorcery and treat spirit possession; and *dingaka tse dinaka*, or "horned doctors," who produce potions used
for the protection of the homestead. In the second half of the work, details of
early missionary attitudes to Sotho-Tswana concepts of divinity are enumerated.
The last section then provides a case study of how four generations of Tswana-
speakers responded to the impact of Christian missionaries following social and
political destabilization in the wake of the *difaqane* in the years between 1822
and 1840. Consequently, an examination of contemporary "syncretism" and the
enrollment of Christianity in traditional belief and practice is outlined. Appendices reproducing Moshoeshoe's 1854 ban on alcohol; lists of Tswana names for
Modimo; and biographical sketches of selected missionaries employed in nine-

teenth-century Sotho-Tswana land are included. The text is annotated and a bibliography but no index is appended.

E140   Sheddick, V. G. J. (1953). *The Southern Sotho*. London: International African Institute.

Sheddick's survey provides an overview of the physical demography and economy of Basutoland as well as an account of the social, political, and religious life of its peoples. In this regard, the monograph draws on the French missionary accounts of Casalis, Jacottet, and Laydevant, the subsequent anthropological studies of E. H. Ashton, and various official reports from the Cape archives in an attempt to reconstruct Southern Sotho history. The brief preliminary chapters focus on demographic detail and topography and include information relating to climate, population size, and agriculture. Thereafter, Sheddick examines aspects of social organization and economy. Marriage and kinship systems are described in detail. A subsequent chapter on "Religious Beliefs and Cults" describes how Sotho belief in a supreme being named Modimo emerged as an innovative adaptation from Christian missionary ideas prevalent in the region in the first half of the nineteenth century. Sheddick argues in this regard that ancestor veneration was the central feature of religious life among the Southern Sotho until the advent of Christian missionaries. He argues that ancestors "do not operate collectively." Rather, the ancestor of each kin group is deemed responsible for misfortune or benefit. In the second half of the chapter Sheddick also identifies diviners as important facets of Southern Sotho religion. Three types of diviners are distinguished: first, the "seer" (*sehoho*) who diagnoses illness and foretells the future; second, the "bone-thrower" (*selaodi*) who acquires his skills of prognostication as the result of a rigorous apprenticeship; and third, the "ventriloquist" (*ngaka ea baloetse*), thought by Sheddick to have originated among the Transvaal Pedi. Notes on female sorcerers and witches are included in the chapter. A useful bibliography is included and a map of Basutoland appended.

E141   Southall, Aidan (1987). "Tswana Religion." In Mircea Eliade (ed.) *The Encyclopaedia of Religion*. New York: Macmillan. 16: 75-77.

In this brief overview, Southall draws on Setiloane's (1976) inventory of Sotho-Tswana religion to describe salient features of Tswana religion in southern Africa. Included in his overview are notes on the importance of Modimo, the *badimo* (ancestor spirits), *seriti* (human personality), and *baloi* (sorcery). Southall asserts that distinctions among the intangible and all-pervasive divinity, Modimo, the ancestral *badimo*, and human beings should be viewed as distinctions of degree rather than distinctions of kind. In these terms, the *badimo* act as intermediaries between humans and the supreme being insofar as they preserve social harmony and order. The Tswana conception of *seriti* reflects in turn the Tswana's concern for communal propriety. The article concludes with a discussion of the functions of *dingaka* (doctors or sacred specialists). Southall contends that Tswana view human suffering as largely caused by ancestral displeasure or as a consequence of the evil action of *baloi*, of whom two kinds are enumerated: the "night" or "heart" *baloi* and the "day" or "mouth" *baloi*. The article is briefly annotated.

E142   Speight, W. L. (1935). "Human Sacrifice in South Africa." *The Nongqai*, vol. 26: 152; 164.

This article, published in the journal of the Lesotho Mounted Police, recalls the inability of European rulers to banish from Lesotho so-called "ritual murders," "mutilations for *muti*," and the killing of twins. It documents the continued use of ritual murder to procure rain, and the inability of the courts to abolish this practice, particularly in Lesotho, Natal, and the Transvaal district of Louis Trichardt.

E143   Spiegel, A. D. (1991). "Polygyny as Myth: Towards Understanding Extramarital Relationships in Lesotho." *African Studies*, vol. 50, no. 2: 145-66.

Employing a methodological framework that is consistent with "folk model" analysis, Spiegel examines in this paper the apparently widespread phenomenon of extramarital relations among the Sotho. He argues that traditional (male) explanations that often referred to the expression "*bonyatsi*" (the abstract form of *nyatsi*—paramour) interpreted "infidelity" in terms of its relation to the demise of polygyny in contemporary Sotho society. Indeed, he asserts that the male's inability to procure bridewealth for more than one wife, and the preclusion of sexual activity with the wife during her period of weaning, was employed by male Sotho to explain and justify the practice of infidelity. A further Sotho justification, Spiegel notes, was a belief among men that *bonyatsi* was merely the extension of a nineteenth-century practice allowing a chief's poorer political "clients" access to junior wives. Sotho men thus considered their economic deprivation as a "right of access" to women. In this regard, some Sotho men cited Chief Moshoeshoe's practice of making junior wives available to visiting dignitaries with whom he desired to establish favorable relations. That practice, some Sotho men claim, cemented *bonyatsi* as a legitimate social institution among the Sotho. Spiegel consequently asserts that Sotho men justified *bonyatsi* in terms of an earlier traditional social charter, and explained its present practice in terms of an apparent verisimilitude with the past. The paper is annotated.

E144   Van Staaten, M. C. (1948). "Muti Made from Human Flesh." *The Nongqai*, vol. 39: 146-49.

A member of the Basutoland Mounted Police, Lieutenant Van Staaten's narrative account of three "ritual murders" in Lesotho during the 1940s provides an arresting account of the role of so-called "strong medicines" in Sotho ritual. Evidence of Chief Mahlomola's use of human "*muti*" in securing the continuation of his authority is established: a young woman's legs and left arm were dismembered and her blood collected in order that what the writer terms "the balance of favour" would be turned in the direction of the chief. Further evidence is accumulated by Van Staaten from court proceedings at the Basutoland High Court. An analysis of the role of the "witch-doctor" is outlined and details regarding murderous ceremonies are described. The article concludes with a proclamation that "thirty natives were sentenced to death on charges of ritual murder during the year 1947." Although moralistic and pedagogic in tone, the paper provides useful primary evidence of the ritual sacrifice of humans in extraordinary circumstances in Lesotho.

E145   Verryn, Trevor (1981). "Coolness and Heat among the Sotho Peoples." *Religion in Southern Africa*, vol. 2: 11-38.

Verryn presents ethnographic data dealing with concepts of "coolness" and "heat" among the Sotho-Tswana. Utilizing materials published in the writings of Pauw, Mönnig, Krige, and Schapera, he posits that the conceptual categories of "heat" and "dirt" represent things that are "out of place, dangerous and offensive." By contrast, "coolness" and "purity" symbolize what is "good, normal, and desirable" in society. In this regard, rain, health, and social harmony are exemplary of "coolness," while blood, funerals, birth, abortion, and menstruation are indicative of "heat" and "dirt." The article begins with an elucidation of data concerning "coolness" and "heat." Thereafter, a list of cooling antidotes related to situations in which a person might become defiled is provided. Thus, for instance, the turtle (a "very cool" animal) is considered by the Sotho to be useful for producing medicine to cure bleeding. Verryn identifies four special concepts involving heat. First, *dibeela*, or "astonishing objects," are believed to provoke drought, desolate the country, or despoil the clouds. A special hunt, organized by the chief and diviners, is initiated to look for anything astonishing "where it has no right to be." Second, *ditshila*, or "dirt," is associated with anomalous objects, including twins, malformed children, children born with teeth, children born feet first, and miscarried fetuses. The treatment for *ditshila*, suggests Verryn, consists of "cooling" off the dead by burial in wet soil. Third, *makhuma* is a form of evil contracted by direct contact with impure *dibeela*. For example, a child who drinks milk from a woman who has aborted and whose breasts are not purified, will contract *makhuma*. Fourth, and finally, suggests

Verryn, *dikgaba* occurs when junior kinsmen behave incorrectly towards seniors, causing illness and even drought. In the closing sections, the writer discusses taboos associated with death and remedies used to alleviate maleficent influences. He contends, however, that *sepe*—violations of the natural and social order considered by ancestors as punishable acts—is best translated as "sin." Verryn concludes his article by noting the logic of a symbolism based on coolness and heat in a region where drought is a common and threatening phenomenon.

E146   Watt, J. M., and M. G. Brandwijk (1927). "Suto Medicines." *Bantu Studies*, vol. 3, no. 1: 73-100; vol. 3, no. 2: 155-78; and vol. 3, no. 3: 297-319.

Watt and Bradwijk, both lecturers in the Department of Pharmacology at the University of the Witwatersrand, provide in a series of articles a list of seventy-two important Sotho medicines. In this regard, they present "a precise analysis" of medicines and establish a recognizable taxonomy that includes botanical, family, and common names in English, Afrikaans, SeSotho, and Xhosa. Examples of "native uses" are also appended and details of chemical composition and pharmacological action are listed.

E147   Watt, J. M., and N. J. van Warmelo (1930). "The Medicines and Practices of a Sotho Doctor." *Bantu Studies*, vol. 4: 47-63.

The pharmacologist Watt and the ethnologist Van Warmelo present in this paper an inventory of divination bones, medicines, and surgical instruments employed in Sotho divining and healing practices. Based upon a series of interviews with the Ndebele diviner Monkwe Mojapelo, the writers list eighteen different types of divining bones, forty-two medicines used in the treatment of patients, and a further fifteen medicines used for purposes other than for the treatment of the sick. The article concludes with a short list of the diviner's surgical instrumentation and brief explanations of purpose. Four plates, representing Mojapelo's bones and medicines, incorporating a baboon's paw, are included.

E148   Willoughby, W. C. (1905). "Notes on the Totemism of the Becwana." *Addresses and Papers of the British and South African Associations for the Advancement of Science*, vol. 3: 295-314.

In a wide-ranging analysis and detailed descriptive account, Willoughby examines in this paper the relationship between myth, ritual, and totemic belief among the Tswana of the Transvaal, Bechuanaland Protectorate, and Orange

River regions of southern Africa. Conversant with European scholarship in the field of comparative religion, in the works of F. Max Müller and James Frazer, he argues that while all Tswana-speakers conform to taboos associated with totemism, their totems, including the duiker, elephant, wild-boar, and crocodile, "had practically no influence upon their great rites and everyday customs." By contrast, because the sacrifice of cattle remained prevalent in their rituals and beliefs allied to rainmaking, the protection of crops and peoples against ill-fortune, and rites of passage associated with circumcision, marriage, and death, he concludes that in the past cattle were possibly pan-Tswana religious totems. By extension, therefore, the present totems of the Tswana are possibly modern accretions. The paper begins with a brief overview of Tswana history and clan structure. Willoughby notes that although the term "Tswana" lacks scientific precision, it essentially serves to refer to a diverse linguistic community divided according to four central "stocks," namely the BaTlhaping, BaRolong, BaHurut-she, and BaKgalagadi. In turn, each "stock," and their "sub-stocks," among them the BaMangwato, BaNgwaketsi, and BaKwena, is delineated according to a tribal totem (*sereto*, or *seano*). For example, the BaRolong are known by the "hammer" totem; the BaHurutshe by the eland or hartebeest; the BaKgalagadi by the elephant; and the BaKwena by the crocodile. Extended attention is focused on taboos associated with the killing or eating of totems, especially among the BaKwena. Following his assertion that myths governing the relationship between these totems and tribal practices are essentially of a non-religious character, and that these totems almost never play a part in so-called "sacrificial meals," Willoughby analyzes why it is that cattle are so prevalent in Tswana ritual. In this regard, he develops Max Müller's etymological inquiry into the Sanskrit root of the term "*go*" to suggest that cattle were the original Tswana totems. Detailed descriptions of myths and rituals associated with the sacrifice of oxen for the founding and protection of a new *kgotla* in the *dipheku* rite, along with *bogadi* rites, mortuary rituals, and war proceedings, are included. Information is also obtained from several informants concerning Sekhoma's use of cattle in rainmaking rites. The paper contains an extensive analysis of beliefs and rituals originally associated with several plant and tree totems, particularly with regard *bojale* and other female initiation rites. Although not annotated, the paper remains an invaluable primary resource for historians of comparative religion and ethnology in the region.

E149   Willoughby, W. C. (1909). "Notes on the Initiation Ceremonies of the Becwana." *Journal of the Royal Anthropological Institute*, vol. 39: 228-45.

Highlighting the need for an adequately trained philologist of Bantu languages, Willoughby, the South African correspondent of the Royal Anthropological Institute and later Professor of Missions in the African Department of the Kennedy School of Missions, Hartford Seminary, reports in this article on two forms of Tswana initiation: initiation rites for boys (*bogwera*) and rituals of initiation for girls (*bojale*). He argues that while the significance of the rituals are generally unknown among participants and practitioners alike—so that "the method of direct interrogation concerning them will generally defeat its own ends"—anthropologists can "throw upon it the light of other lands and other epochs in the history of the evolution of man." Employing the tools of comparative analysis consistent with evolutionary theory, therefore, the writer briefly identifies a number of central elements in Tswana circumcision rituals. However, the paper is predominantly descriptive and, given the resistance of Tswana women to divulge "tribal secrets," restricted to a report of male *bogwera* rites. The writer recalls that these rituals take place during the new *Tlhakole* (February) moon; that the "neophytes" are divided according to regiments; and that during March the boys are circumcised. Willoughby points out that the Tswana word for foreskin is the same as that for mouth (*molomo*). The paper highlights further details indicative of *bogwera*, including prescriptions associated with certain foods and the necessity of rites of purification: The writer cites one informant to suggest that there were as many washings in the *bogwera* as there were "among the Jews of whom we read in the Bible." The paper concludes with an inventory of Tswana songs, called "Songs of the Law," that are intoned by initiates during the period of *bogwera*. The paper is not annotated and no bibliography is included.

E150   Willoughby, W. C. (1928). *The Soul of the Bantu: A Sympathetic Study of the Magico-Religious Practices and Beliefs of the Bantu Tribes of Africa.* London: Student Christian Movement.

In this, the first of three planned volumes on the nature and classification of "Bantu" religion, Willoughby contributes to the comparative study of religions by examining aspects of ancestor veneration among the Tswana. In order that "he who regards the religious ideas . . . as the incoherent babblings of disordered fancy" might not miss whatever value they contain, his "sympathetic" study begins with an introductory overview of the relation between mission Christianity and Bantu religion. In this regard, Willoughby argues that insight into "heathen" religion would be helpful for church growth. In Chapter One, "Ancestor-Spirits," notes on the origins of ancestral veneration are provided. The writer highlights in this chapter the difficulties he experienced in obtaining information pertaining to the soul and afterlife because of "native reticence." He concludes, however, that the Bantu, with "no bent to philosophic investigation and no craving for logical consistency," all believe that death is not the end of life and that an underworld exists. Unlike the Hades of the Greeks and the Sheol of the Hebrews, the Bantu-speaking peoples of southern Africa believe that this underworld is inhabited by the spirits of the dead and modeled after the pattern of the tribe. In Chapter Two, Willoughby proceeds to document how ancestors communicate with the living. Notes on dream "revelation," possession, and divination are included. Chapters Three and Four recall occasions for and modes of ancestral veneration. Among the "modes" of communication examined are sacrifice, libation, prayer and praise; the construction of shrines, altars, chapels, temples, and ancestral stones; and the consecration of domestic animals to the gods. The final chapter, "Ancestor-Worship and Christianity," affords readers a review of how far Willoughby sees the religious ethics, rites, and symbols of the Bantu to be "preparatory" to the reception of Christianity. Conversant with nineteenth-century ethnography and the developing disciplines of comparative religion, the book contains a wealth of material foundational to the study of religion among the Tswana. An index and bibliography are included.

E151   Willoughby, W. C. (1932). *Nature-Worship and Taboo*. Hartford, Conn.: Hartford Seminary Press.

In his preparatory remarks to the second of three planned works on "Bantu" religion, Willoughby argues that while the theory that the worship of heavenly bodies was the beginning of religion had been abandoned, an examination of Tswana rituals and beliefs associated with the worship of personified natural phenomena provided new evidence for its antithesis. In this regard, he proposes to inspect elements of "pagan" belief and ritual in order to evaluate the extent to which these "oddments in the medley of Bantu social practices, veiled by the cobwebs of antiquity," were cognate with some of the earliest "trappings of nature-worship." After studying aspects of ancestor veneration in *The Soul of the Bantu*, therefore, Willoughby asks whether there were also nature-spirits to whom the Bantu (primarily the Tswana-speaking BaMangwato) paid homage. The work is divided into two discrete sections, the first entitled "Nature-Worship," and the second, "Taboo." Brief notes on Tswana belief in marine "spirits," and spirit inhabitants of stones and cairns, caves, fountains, trees, the earth, sky, sun, stars, moon, clouds, lightning, and rainbows are included. Comparing these convictions with examples of Tsonga, Sotho, and Khoikhoi rites, in the works of Casalis, Junod, and Haddon, Willoughby then cites the Alexandrian geographer Strabo and the anthropologist James Frazer to confirm that all peoples of the earth revered natural objects. However, the Tswana not only propitiated or adorned these objects, but their attitudes to the numinousness of nature was also a consequence of their belief that the spirits of the underworld "had entered earth by way of these portals." In the second section, "Taboo," the writer relates that magic and animism, "the attribution of living souls to animals and objects," were also distinctive features of Bantu religion. Examining the various taboos associated with dietary prescriptions, menstruation, cohabitation, pregnancy, childbirth, death, contact with the supernatural, and numerology, among other occurrences, he concludes that, "if religion is the recognition of supernatural powers and of man's duty to obey them, then taboos, however unreasonable from our standpoint, contain the germ of religion." The book is thoroughly indexed and annotated.

E152   Winter, Johannes August (1913). "The Phallus Cult Among the Bantu, Particularly the Bapedi of the Eastern Transvaal." *South African Journal of Science*, vol. 10: 131-36.

Following his translation of Martinus Sebusane's narrative describing *koma*, or male circumcision rites, Winter erects an argument that briefly traces comparative links between Pedi ritual, Egyptian mythology, and Old Testament "phallic cults." Primarily, his paper relates events imperative to the "mysteries" of Pedi circumcision. First, Winter describes the initiatory stage of *"go balla"*—"to go out." Taboos associated with clothing and the consumption of certain foods are enumerated. Second, notes on the choice of circumcision masters are retold. Winter describes techniques used to circumcise the *praepatium* "in the same way as described in Genesis 17." Third, the writer recalls that hymns and songs in praise of manliness and female "parts exceedingly indecent" were chanted. He concludes by noting that the secret "half cult half custom" of circumcision, along with prescriptions for fasting and the recitation of indecent and "immoral" lessons, provided the "heathen baptism" that was the backbone of the Sotho-Tswana way of life.

E153   Winter, Johannes August (1915). "The Mental and Moral Capabilities of the Natives, Especially of Sekhukhuniland (Eastern Transvaal)." *South African Journal of Science*, vol. 11: 371-83.

Winter's paper is essentially a caustic denunciation of myths and rituals associated with traditional African religion. Citing his experience as a missionary in Botshabelo, the writer describes the religion of the Tswana as superstition. In these terms, the Tswana-speaking residents of Sekhukhuniland in the northeastern Transvaal, he argues, should not be considered as "fetish-adorers," but rather as deluded, lazy, polygamous, morally corrupt, beer-drinking heathens. Because of his love of the "native," however, Winter questions what can be done "to prevent them from going under like the Red Indians in America?"

E154   Wylie, Diana (1990). *A Little God: The Twilight of Patriarchy in a Southern African Chiefdom*. Johannesburg: University of the Witwatersrand Press; Hanover and London: Wesleyan University Press.

Asserting that colonial narratives and legalistic examinations of Tswana custom and politics have ignored the complexities of Ngwato history, Wylie draws on an extensive period of fieldwork in Tshekedi Khama's chiefdom in the years immediately prior to Botswana's independence to analyze the relationship between power and wealth within this Tswana chiefdom. In this regard, her wide-ranging work narrates the story of Tshekedi Khama's rule and asks to what degree a coexistent indigenous administration and an imperial system of overrule affected changes in political organization; to what extent capitalism altered political ideas and practices; and to what level popular beliefs and rituals, particularly those associated with patriarchy, were transformed under the pressures of "modernity." Traversing numerous topics, from agricultural methods to regimental labor and labor migration; from beer brewing to divorce proceedings, patriarchal patronage, and female inheritance; and from theories of conversion to drought, dynastic rivalry, rainmaking, and *mafisa* (or cattle loans), the changing face of the Ngwato regency prior to 1966 is narrated. Wylie argues most importantly, and persuasively, however, that the Ngwato regent, like the leaders of many southern African polities, was not a "little god" presiding over a fixed political identity. Rather, the regent was responsible for attempting to manage periods of rapid transition and colonial incorporation by resorting to sometimes paradoxical practices. Many, like Tshekedi's contemporary, the Swazi king Sobhuza, attempted to revive lapsed ceremonies and customs, including the *ncwala* (national harvest rite), in order that a sense of "tribal" identity might be resuscitated. Others, like Khama, resorted to legalistic political strategies that, suggests the writer, eventually led to the emergence of the independent state of Botswana. The book, which is divided into five chapters documenting central events that led to the breakup of the chiefdom (among them Seretse Khama's marriage to his English fiancée, Ruth Williams) contains extensive notes, a bibliography, and index.

7   Swazi Religion

Emerging from a combination of Nguni and Sotho-Tswana groups during the nineteenth century, Swazi political identity was solidified through a royal ideology that placed the king and his mother at the apex of society (Kuper, 1950). In the literature on Swazi religion, the myths and rituals of sacred kingship have received the greatest academic attention. Since it was revived by King Sobhuza II in the 1920s, the annual Swazi royal ritual—the *ncwala*—has become a privileged test case for developing anthropological theories of religion and politics. Certainly, other aspects of Swazi traditional religion have been noted. Beliefs in a remote creator God (Mvelincanti or Mvelamqandi) have been recorded. Sacrificial rituals for ancestral spirits (*emadloti*), rites of passage, and the practices of diviners have been documented (Kasenene, 1993; Kuper, 1947; 1986; Marwick, 1940). However, Swazi political religion, as exemplified by rainmaking ritual, by the annual *umhlanga* ceremony or Reed Dance that celebrates female virtue and agricultural fertility, and by the first-fruits ceremony of the *ncwala* that celebrates the sacred power of the king, has definitely been the focus of research.

Gaining special access to the Swazi court, the anthropologist Hilda (Beemer) Kuper produced a distinctive record of observation and analysis during half a century of research on Swazi traditional religion. Drawing upon her fieldwork in 1935, Kuper was able to point out the inaccuracies of a recent report on Swazi rainmaking ritual (Schoeman, 1935). Neither the reporter nor his informants could possibly have observed the rainmaking ceremony, Kuper noted, because it was restricted to the king, his mother, and only three members of the court (Beemer, 1935).

In a series of publications, Kuper described and analyzed the supreme Swazi royal ritual, the *ncwala*, in ways that were sensitive to both its symbolic structure and its history. The *ncwala* has been performed annually since 1921, when King Sobhuza II revived the ceremony after a lapse of twenty five years, as a six-day ritual demonstration of the sacred power vested in Swazi kingship. In the *ncwala*, the king appears as the mediator between the spirit world and his subjects. Through dramatic animal symbolism and symbolic performances, the ceremony reinforces what Kuper identified as two sets of differences: It reinforces the different gender roles ascribed to males and females and it reinforces the class distinction between royalty, especially the king and the queen mother, and the common people. These symbolic structures, however, have been subject to historical change. As Kuper proposed, the nineteenth-century ceremony was essentially a ritual of Swazi unity. From the 1920s, however, the *ncwala* became a symbol for a distinctive political identity—a Swazi nation—that has been asserted as being entirely separate from other political groupings or allegiances in southern Africa (Kuper, 1947; 1972; 1973; 1978).

These effects, however, are derived from a ceremony that features ritual songs, speeches, and insults that are directed against the king. How can the sacred power of the king be reinforced by a ceremony that requires such acts of denigration? This question has been central to the anthropological analysis of Swazi royal religion. Five different answers, each based on a different theoretical framework, have been offered to account for the ritual disrespect that is apparently shown to the king during the *ncwala* ceremony.

First, a functional explanation was provided by Max Gluckman to account for the *ncwala* as a "ritual of rebellion" that provides a religious "safety valve" for the harmless release of social aggression, tension, and conflict. By allowing for the open expression of antagonism against the king, the annual ritual actually diffuses social tensions and thereby unifies the social order (Gluckman, 1954; 1963).

Second, a psychological explanation was advanced by T. O. Beidelman by arguing that the *ncwala* has to be interpreted in terms of the indigenous Swazi worldview. According to Beidelman, the psychological meaning and significance of the ceremony can only be appreciated by taking into consideration Swazi assumptions about the dangers of defilement and the need for purification. From this perspective, the *ncwala* is an annual ritual of purification for the king that also serves to purify Swazi society (Beidelman, 1966).

Third, a sociolinguistic explanation was proposed by Andrew Apter to account for the disrespect shown to the king during the *ncwala* as an example of what the anthropologist A. R. Radcliffe-Brown called a "joking relationship." In relations between a mother's brother and a sister's son, for example, satire, ridicule, and verbal abuse are required but not taken literally. A "joking relationship," according to Radcliffe-Brown, fuses the "pretense of hostility and real friendliness." According to Apter, the Swazi *ncwala* incorporates such practices of "permitted disrespect" that reinforce real relations of loyalty to the king (Apter, 1983).

Fourth, a structural analysis was advanced by Luc de Heusch to conclude that the king is symbolically rejected and killed during the *ncwala* so he can be symbolically reborn with restored purity and renewed power. The ritual sacrifice of the black ox, which according to De Heusch is slaughtered as a substitute for the king, achieves the purification and empowerment of his sacred royal identity (De Heusch, 1985).

Fifth, a strategic analysis was formulated by historian of religions Bruce Lincoln to highlight the ways in which the ritual creates not only bonds of affinity, but also effects of estrangement. In Lincoln's analysis, the *ncwala* reinforces the sacred power of the king precisely by protecting him from witches, enemies, and other strangers. In its historical context, Lincoln argued, those strangers would have included the British colonial administration. Therefore, the *ncwala* worked to establish strategic relations among the Swazi and against the British (Lincoln, 1987).

A concern with historical context and social change has been evident in other discussions of Swazi traditional religion. For example, the colonial era dramatically affected the practice of Swazi sacred specialists through legislation that identified both healers and diviners as practitioners of witchcraft. As a result, traditional specialists who were responsible for protecting people against the evil effects of witchcraft were drawn into colonial courts as witches (Booth, 1992). However, for all the disruptions of traditional religious practice, persistence can be observed. As the North American visitor James Hall learned, Swazi *sangomas* preserved traditional religious knowledge and practices of healing, divination, and protection from evil influences. However, he also learned that some were willing to initiate him into that tradition (Hall, 1994). As in other forms of African traditional religion, Swazi tradition manages persistence through change.

F1   Apter, Andrew (1983). "In Dispraise of the King: Rituals 'Against' Rebellion in South-East Africa." *Man*, vol. 18: 521-34.

Apter attempts to resolve the tension in interpretation between Gluckman's (1963) and Beidelman's (1966) accounts of the *ncwala* ritual by using sociolinguistic theory. While Gluckman's interpretation of the *ncwala* rests on his theory of rituals of rebellion and the functional implications of conflict, Beidelman's approach seeks to interpret the psychological meaning of the ritual as a process of purification. Both, however, develop their divergent theories by analyzing the *simemo* songs that seem to insult and blaspheme the Swazi king. Relying on Radcliffe-Brown's notion of "permitted disrespect," Apter tries to show how the *simemo* songs used "against" the king actually function to support him. Focusing on the structure of the songs—what the author calls "dispraises" as opposed to "praises"—Apter interprets them as a "species of joking relation-ship." Whereas praises are used to validate the authority and status of the king when he is absent, the "joking" of dispraise represents permitted and ritualized "familiarity," used to purify and revitalize the king's person on special ritual occasions when he is present among his people. As speech acts, dispraise serves to mobilize the people's loyalties to their king, especially prior to battle, while praises, on the other hand, oblige the king himself to maintain the values and responsibilities inherent in his position. Notes and references are appended.

F2   Beemer, Hilda (1935). "The Swazi Rain Ceremony: Critical Comments on P. J. Schoeman's Article." *Bantu Studies*, vol. 9: 273-80.

In response to P. J. Schoeman's account of the Swazi rain ceremony, Hilda (Beemer) Kuper claims that his article is erroneous and misleading because it is based on unreliable sources. Since the *Indlovukazi* (the queen mother), her son (the king), and three other members of the community are the only people who witness the full rites, the writer notes, Schoeman's informants could not have provided first-hand knowledgeable accounts. Kuper lists and reinterprets several of Schoeman's incorrect points, the central one being that it is the *Indlovukazi* who is the main actor in the rain ceremony. Schoeman's emphasis on the king's medicines and his presence as essential for the efficacy of the "rain magic" is criticized, pointing to a misinterpretation of Swazi political organization. In addition, Kuper indicates that Schoeman's account is incomplete and that his theoretical hypotheses are superficial. His focus on "magical powers," Kuper argues, ignores the vital significance of the Swazi's practical knowledge of their natural environment and their organized economic system of which the ritual is part. Most important are Kuper's comments on the potential value of anthropo-logical theory, which, she asserts, requires full descriptive analysis based on data gathered from qualified informants and independent investigators in the field—information that should then be verified by members of the society stud-ied. Kuper calls for integrity and authenticity in the discipline of anthropology, and above all, respect for the people among whom the researcher is working.

F3   Beidelman, T. O. (1966). "Swazi Royal Ritual." *Africa*, vol. 36: 373-405.

Drawing on Kuper's ethnographic accounts of the Swazi, Beidelman's article presents a reinterpretation of the annual royal rites of the Swazi nation, focusing on the central rites of the *ncwala*. Beidelman presents a critique of Max Gluck-man's (1963) "rituals of rebellion" thesis, challenging his emphasis on conflict and aggression that interprets the rites as institutionalized expression of rebel-lion against the king's authority. Instead, Beidelman insists that the *ncwala* can be understood mainly in terms of psychological and physiological (rather than functional) rituals of purification that symbolize the separation of the king from various social groups within the nation. This ensures that the king is free and fit "to assume the heavy supernatural powers of his office as king-priest of the nation." To substantiate this reinterpretation, Beidelman first reconstructs Swazi cosmology, stressing the importance of exploring the symbolic vocabulary and cultural perspective of the people involved. He then discusses the *ncwala* ritual, detailing how it conforms to his analysis of Swazi cosmology and how it relates to Swazi social structure and kingship. In the process of his analysis, Beidelman points to questionable aspects of Gluckman's thesis. In conclusion, the problems inherent in the sociological and psychological study of ritual are addressed. Here Beidelman refers particularly to the works of Durkheim, Lévi-Strauss, and Turner. Notes accompany the text, and a bibliography and summary in French are appended.

F4   Booth, Alan R. (1983). *Swaziland: Tradition and Change in a Southern African Kingdom*. Boulder, Colorado: Westview Press; Hampshire, England: Gower.

In this volume Booth assesses the past hundred years of Swaziland's history, drawing on what is known as "underdevelopment theory" in relation to Africa's colonial period. The author looks at the needs and aspirations of the Swazi people and the decisive leadership that has been evident during this period of the nation's history. The second chapter is devoted to Swaziland's sociocultural system within which religious belief and ritual practice play a central part. Swazi society places great value on traditionalism that is maintained through a conservative political hierarchy headed by a dual monarchy—the king and the queen mother—who together embody all power. Although the *umhlanga* (reed dance) ceremony is an important celebration in honor of the queen mother and feminine virtue and beauty, the center of Swazi power resides in the king and is reenacted and reproduced through religious ritual. It is therefore the annual *ncwala* ceremony that serves to revitalize the king. Booth details the procedure of the three-week festival, explaining the symbolic significance of the sacred rites involved, followed by an analysis of traditional Swazi religion that revolves around the ancestral veneration. Whereas the king appeals to his ancestors on behalf of his people in communal matters, the head of each family officiates at domestic rites offered to the ancestors for events such as birth, marriage, and death. The important role of ritual specialists—both medicine men and diviners—is discussed as are matters associated with evil and the diviner's task of "smelling out" and neutralizing witches. The latter practice has been outlawed, but by all accounts, according to Booth, its occult practice has increased "among a people haunted by feelings of helplessness and inadequacy in a complex and threatening world." Booth concludes his discussion of Swazi traditional religion by documenting the challenge of Christianity in the twentieth century, noting the burgeoning popularity of the "separatist" Zionist denominations. Chapter notes are appended to the main text.

F5   Booth, Alan R. (1992). "European Courts Protect Women and Witches: Colonial Law Courts as Redistributors of Power in Swaziland." *Journal of Southern African Studies*, vol. 18, no. 2: 253-75.

Booth's article begins by noting that the imposition of colonial law in Swaziland by the British administration in 1907 led to a reallocation of power among various elements and groupings of traditional Swazi citizenry. The writer argues that the main beneficiaries of this shift in power were young, educated women who resorted to the colonial courts for protection against the discriminatory justice of traditional chiefs' courts in matters of physical and sexual abuse and enforced marriage. Among the greatest losers, notes Booth, were those individuals who practiced forms of ritual specialization, principally healers and diviners, both of whom were looked upon indiscriminately by the colonial authorities as practitioners of witchcraft, thus representing a threat to civilized practices and to colonial jurisdiction. To the degree that many sacred specialists were female, argues Booth, the access of Swazi women to this means of independence and upward mobility in a sexually exploitative society was blocked. Likewise chiefs whose overall powers had been severely truncated by the imposition of colonial courts suffered a further diminution of power. Drawing on archival material and recent theoretical work on witchcraft and colonial administration, Booth's paper is of interest to readers in religious studies concerned with changing patterns of ritual activity in the context of expanding mercantilism and colonial control. Extensive footnotes accompany the text.

F6   Cook, P. A. W. (1930). "The Inqwala Ceremony of the Swazis." *Bantu Studies*, vol. 4: 205-10.

Drawing on fieldwork conducted in the Zombode district of Swaziland, Cook's brief descriptive article outlines the events and rituals of the six-day *ncwala* ceremony (feast of the first fruits). None of the new season's products, the writer notes, can be eaten by any member of the community before this ceremony is performed. First, Cook identifies the historical origin of the ceremony and then details the preparatory ritual pilgrimage to the sea to fetch sea-water that is essential for the doctor's preparation of medicines used in the ceremony. After this, the two-day "small *ncwala*" (*inqwala lencane*) takes place, where the king goes into his *intlambelo* (hut) with the dying moon and emerges with the new moon, accompanied by ritual singing and dancing. The remainder of the article describes each part of the six-day "big *ncwala*" (*inqwala elikulu*) in order of occurrence, including the collection, cooking, and ritual application of herbs; the *ncwala* dance; the *cunga* ceremony, comprising the chief's symbolic eating of pumpkin; the *ukutila*, or period of the king's seclusion with his wife; and the final day, when the bones of the black bull and the remains of the pumpkin are burned to symbolize the end of *ukutila* and the freedom to dance in the new year.

F7   Cook, P. A. W. (1931). "History and Izibongo of the Swazi Chiefs." *Bantu Studies*, vol. 5: 181-201.

The material for this paper, the result of meetings with elders of the Swazi nation under the Paramount Chief, Sobhuza, was collected during Cook's visit to Swaziland in 1929. A brief outline of the history of the Swazi people is provided, with a genealogical list of Swazi kings. Another section is devoted to a discussion of *izibongo*, the poems composed and recited in praise of a chief. Cook emphasizes the historical, literary, and philosophical significance of these praise-poems, since their form is permanent and they tell of the most important events in the lives of the chiefs. The paper includes the *izibongo* for six Swazi chiefs, accompanied by line for line English translation, thus providing a valuable primary source for the study of Swazi culture.

F8   Dumbrell, H. J. E. (1952). "Pyre Burning in Swaziland." *African Studies*, vol. 11, no. 4: 190-91.

Dumbrell's short paper presents reports, gathered from both colonial administrators and Swazi informants, which indicate that at some point in their history certain groups of Swazi burned their dead. The accounts point to the possibility that cremation had been an early practice among the Maseko and Simelane groups. Certain ritual practices and symbolic sites are documented, such as damming part of a river-bed as a site for building the funeral pyre, and burning the wood of the *isihlangu*, a particular type of thorn tree. The paper is extremely brief and does not include critical analysis. However, the editor adds a footnote claiming that Cook's evidence of Swazi cremation supports "other evidence" for Indian influence on Swazi culture.

F9   Evans, Jeremy (1993). "'Where Can We Get a Beast Without Hair?' Medicine Murder in Swaziland from 1970 to 1988." *African Studies*, vol. 52, no. 1: 27-42.

Evans' analysis of the phenomenon of "medicine murder" in Swaziland begins by examining the tenuousness of Marwick's (1940) study, which was based on inadequate court records of murder trials. Later scholars, most notably A. R. Booth, H. Kuper, H. Ngubane, and A. B. van Fossen, have noted the apparently high rate of medicine murders in the 1970s and early 1980s. The relevance of social dynamics within a community, and the stresses of political disruption, industrialization, and urbanization during that period, are all identified as significant factors by these writers. Evans bases his own approach on a careful analysis of fifty-eight transcripts of court cases concerning medicine murders from 1970 to 1988, and his discussion and conclusions follow extracts from nine of those transcripts. Several motives are examined, including financial gain, the strengthening of chiefs, and the enhancement of sociopolitical status. However, Evans finds that the alleged role of "ambition" is overgeneralized and is not necessarily a major factor, arguing that murders occur most often in response to socioeconomic pressures and to prevent misfortune. In conclusion, the author advocates a multifaceted approach to the study of fluctuating incidences of Swazi medicine murders, cautioning against generalized theoretical statements about these killings that fail to consider important details contained in court records. Since the transcripts clearly show there is no single cause of the increase in Swazi medicine murders in the 1970s, Evans concludes that both historical and modern pressures of social change deserve careful attention. Notes and references are appended.

F10   Gluckman, Max (1963). "Rituals of Rebellion in South-East Africa." *Order and Rebellion in Tribal Africa*. London: Cohen & West. 110-36.

Drawing on the insights found in Frazer's *The Golden Bough*, particularly in relation to his interpretations of agricultural ceremonies, Gluckman's watershed essay includes extensive use of comparative material and considers the social components of similar ceremonies in African societies in Zululand, Swaziland, and Mozambique. Fundamental to this work is Gluckman's identification and analysis of the links among religious myth, ritual, and the construction of order in society. The essay first focuses on the agricultural ceremonies conducted by Zulu women and girls devoted to the goddess Nomkubulwana, the Princess of Heaven. Analyzing the significance of the "temporary dominant role" of women in the Nomkubulwana ceremonies, Gluckman addresses their significance in the wider context of ordered gender roles in Zulu society. The writer defines these ceremonies as examples of traditionally sanctioned "rituals of rebellion." Such rituals, he suggests, paradoxically challenge the established patriarchal order while simultaneously achieving prosperity for that order. The Nomkubulwana ceremonies are then compared with other domestic ceremonies practiced in south-east Africa, most particularly drawing on Hilda Kuper's studies of the Swazi *ncwala* ceremony, which is defined as a typical first-fruits ceremony. The writer identifies and draws out the complexity of a common theme in which these rites openly stress social tensions that are ritually expressed through role reversals and, paradoxically, serve to unify the social structure rather than disrupt it. Citations from Swazi ritual poetry are included in the text.

F11   Hall, James (1994). *Sangoma: My Odyssey into the Spirit World of Africa*. New York: G. P. Putnam's Sons.

James Hall, a Midwestern American Catholic, writes in this autobiographical work an account of two years he spent in Swaziland during which he undertook a spiritual journey or *kutfwasa* training in the arts of the *sangoma* (diviner). In fascinating detail, Hall describes for the reader his calling and his experiences of physical, psychic, and spiritual struggle until his graduation. His initiation into psychic powers and traditional healing skills, such as the reading of divination bones and the collection and preparation of medicinal herbs, form the core of the narrative. The text is conversational and anecdotal, but nevertheless offers insights into ritual experience and healing and divination practices among the Swazi. Photographs accompany the text.

F12   Heusch, Luc de (1985). "The King on the Sacrificial Stage (Swazi-Rwanda)." *Sacrifice in Africa*. Trans. Linda O'Brien and Alice Morton. Manchester: Manchester University Press. 98-124.

In *Sacrifice in Africa*, De Heusch develops a structuralist analysis of ritual sacrifice in African religion, a problem that he notes has been neglected in the field of religious anthropology. Chapter Five presents a comparative study of the symbolic structure of sacred kingship in Swaziland and Rwanda. First, the author discusses how the Swazi king regularly assumes his ritual function in the annual *ncwala* rite, as the principal participant in a "great cosmological game." De Heusch analyzes the ambiguous meanings of the diverse and complex symbolic acts carried out during the *ncwala*, focusing specifically on the ritual sacrifice of a black ox. Its color links the ox to death and sorcery, symbolizing the violence, danger, and pollution of the Swazi people which is concentrated in the person of the king. Since the black ox is slaughtered in place of the king in order to drive out the "blackness" in him, the author argues that the *ncwala* represents a great ritual of purification performed to restore "whiteness" or beneficence in the sacred person of the Swazi king. De Heusch then discusses Rwanda rituals of sacred kingship, where the body of the king is identified with the wider physical territory of the kingdom. Ritual sacrifices of expulsion are also analyzed, stressing the symbolic significance of one of the sacrificial victims, a black bull found among a herd of white cows. The author conducts an extensive analysis of the similarities and differences evident between Swazi and Rwanda royal sacrificial rituals, indicating that they essentially represent the same symbolic system of sacred kingship, where "whiteness" and "darkness" connote the same principles in both contexts. A bibliography and index are appended to the main text.

F13   Kasenene, Peter (1993). *Religion in Swaziland*. Braamfontein, South Africa: Skotaville.

Kasenene's phenomenological and comparative study of religion in Swaziland discusses the beliefs and practices of Swazi traditional religion, Christianity, Islam, and the Baha'i faith in that country. A comprehensive chapter is devoted to traditional religion, pointing to a corporate religiosity that embraces the whole of life, where the religious and the secular are inextricably interwoven. Swazi religious mythology speaks of an ultimate reality or creator, known as Mvelincanti—"he who was there from the beginning." However, says the author, Mvelincanti is too remote to be relevant in Swazi everyday life and so it is the ancestral spirits (*emadloti*) who guide and protect the living. Evil spirits are also believed to exist, which cause suffering, sickness, and death. Kasenene describes the significant role the ancestors play and the ways in which they reveal themselves to the living. Ritual performance, the most important religious practice in Swazi religion, always involves the participation of the ancestors. The author describes rites of passage—those rituals performed at the level of the family, associated with birth, initiation, marriage, and death—in some detail. A section on national rituals includes the *ncwala* ceremony that celebrates kingship and the *umhlanga* (reed dance) fertility ceremony. Under "magical rituals," Kasenene discusses sorcery, witchcraft, divination and the activities of diviners, and sacred sites. In conclusion, the author assesses the impact of Swazi traditional religion on society in terms of social relations, politics, and economic welfare. Once more, the role of the ancestors is stressed—through them, argues Kasenene, both the family and the nation are united. References are appended.

F14   Kuper, Hilda (1947). *An African Aristocracy: Rank Among the Swazi*. London; New York; Toronto: Oxford University Press.

Kuper's anthropological study examines Swazi culture in the context of rank and social status within the traditional milieu. Swazi religion forms a recurrent theme in several of the topics covered in sixteen chapters. Chapter Six, "Ritualization of the King," shows that Swazi ritual depends on a person's status in the political hierarchy and that by ritualizing the crises of life, the individual is protected from misfortune. The Swazi king, as symbol of the nation, is therefore treated with unique rites for each stage of his life, setting him apart from ordinary subjects. In Chapter Eleven, "Individual Variability and Ritual," Kuper turns to the topic of ritual specialists, who are condemned and categorized as "magicians" by European scientific standards, but who are revered as representatives of law and knowledge by the Swazi. Swazi thought, argues the author, acknowledges the tremendous diversity of human qualities and psychological types, and it is the ritual specialist (*inyanga*) who diverges most from the ideal and yet follows a stereotyped pattern. She therefore details the process of becoming a ritual specialist, including the phenomenon of spirit possession, emphasizing that it is the diviner (*isangoma*) who is most esteemed. Chapter Twelve, "Death as an Index of Rank," shows how Swazi burial rites reflect social status. The power of the dead and transition into the realm of the ancestral spirits is discussed. Kuper explores how social hierarchy and authority among the ancestors is respected just as it is among the living. Chapter Thirteen, "The Drama of Kingship," then provides a comprehensive and insightful analysis of the complex ritualized stages of the annual *ncwala* ceremony that serves to unite the people and strengthen the king. The royal ceremony, concludes Kuper, is a dramatization of historically developed rank—a "play of kingship." Appendices include royal genealogies, Swazi clans, geographical diagrams, a bibliography, and index.

F15   Kuper, Hilda (1950). "Kinship Among the Swazi." In A. R. Radcliffe-Brown and Daryll Forde (eds.) *African Systems of Kinship and Marriage*. London; New York; Toronto: Oxford University Press. 86-110.

In this essay Kuper defines the Swazi people as an amalgamation of Nguni and Sotho clans that were subordinated within a centralized military and political system by Nguni conquerors in the late eighteenth century. The Swazi king and his mother, characterized as symbolic parents of the people, constructed a fictional kinship through which their supreme authority was expressed. In the field of religion, therefore, the rulers appeal to their royal ancestors on behalf of the whole nation, just as the head of each homestead appeals to his ancestors on behalf of his dependents. In the essay, however, Kuper focuses on the domestic domain of Swazi kinship. First, Kuper defines and describes the clan, the family unit, and the homestead, noting that in the homestead hierarchy Swazi religion gives greater power to males than to females. It is men who officiate as family priests for domestic ritual, although both men and women become ancestral spirits after death. The role and influences of the ancestral spirits remain a recurrent theme in the following discussion of basic behavior patterns in the family structure with regard to husband and wife, parent and child, and sibling relationships. Kuper then addresses extended kinship and affinal ties, referring to various taboos that are observed within these systems. The essay is concluded with a brief look at the importance of rank by birth in Swazi kinship. In this matter, the selection of a main heir is determined by the rank of the mothers, a preference shown for women that is particularly important in relation to the ruling clan, especially the sisters and daughters of the king. Footnotes and diagrams accompany the text.

F16   Kuper, Hilda (1972a). "The Language of Sites in the Politics of Space." *American Anthropologist*, vol. 74: 411-25.

In this article Kuper seeks to interpret the concept of "space" based on fieldwork done in Swaziland in 1966, focusing on the significance attached to particular sites as "special pieces of space" in relation to political change. She reviews anthropological approaches to the concept of space (especially those of Durkheim and Mauss, Radcliffe-Brown and Evans-Pritchard, Gluckman, Lévi-Strauss, Malinowski, Hall, Eliade, and Burke) in order to forge a new perspective on the relationship between space and political events. These insights are then applied to three case studies of special sites in Swaziland, employing her "language of sites" theory to interpret a politics of space. The case studies highlight the symbolic significance and tensions involved in constructions of the precolonial space of the *sibaya* (a large open-air arena) and the colonial space of the "Office" in the traditional Swazi capital of Lobamba. While the first space, as an enclosure for cattle, was thought of as a central religious and economic space in the Swazi community, it was also the site of important national and royal rituals. The "Office," on the other hand, symbolized the Swazi's position as a subjugated nation under colonial rule. Kuper concludes by arguing that the desegregation of Swaziland's colonial society was perceived by the colonized as more than simply the removal of discriminatory legislation. Rather, it meant the production of a new sense of orientation in space. Kuper demonstrates how a new "politics of space" in Swaziland required the reallocation of social and physical space that led not only to the redistribution of land and other resources, but also to the creation of new sites of Swazi national identity. This process of spatial reorientation, Kuper concludes, points to a politics of space that is commonly found at the end of periods of colonial domination. Notes and references are appended.

F17   Kuper, Hilda (1972b). "A Royal Ritual in a Changing Political Context." *Cahiers d'Etudes Africaine*, vol. 12, no. 42: 593-615.

The central ideology underpinning the *ncwala* ritual is the unique power vested in hereditary Swazi kingship. Kuper's annotated article examines how and why this ritual persisted, arguing that it served as a resource for political leadership from precolonial times to Swaziland's independence. The writer explains how the role of the king as mediator between the spiritual world and that of his subjects was disrupted by Western influence and colonial officials who separated secular and spiritual authority. The continuity of Swazi concepts of kingship were therefore maintained through the *ncwala*. However, Kuper stresses that Swazi culture is dynamic and fluid and despite the "uniquely unalterable core" of the *ncwala* ritual as a symbolic constant, the ritual has mediated the expression of changing political meanings. She therefore looks at the significance of the *ncwala* during three different eras: the precolonial period; the stages of colonial rule; and the inception of Swaziland as a self-governing, independent kingdom. In short, a ritual that united a nation in precolonial times became a symbol of political and cultural differentiation in the colonial period. Thereafter, Kuper asserts, it was manipulated as a strategic symbol for inspiring independent Swazi nationalism. Pointing to the link between myth, ritual, and political power, Kuper concludes by predicting that as long as the myth of Swazi kingship retains power over the people, it will continue to be ritualized through the royal ceremony of the *ncwala*. Nevertheless, she also identifies the trend of political expediency in a modern nation where a "priest-king" still influences secular appointments, arguing that some Swazi continue to participate in the ritual mainly to avoid exclusion from political office. A bibliography is appended.

F18   Kuper, Hilda (1973). "Costume and Cosmology: The Animal Symbolism of the Ncwala." *Man* (n.s.), vol. 8: 613-30.

In this essay Kuper draws on social anthropological theories that address the relationships among animal symbolism, social organization, and the internal logic of conceptual systems. She focuses on animal symbolism in the wider paradigm of the political system of a whole nation, as portrayed in the ritual costumes of the *ncwala*, the central annual national ritual of Swazi kingship. The essay aims to show how animal symbols (among many others) articulate a complex cosmology that includes the natural and social realms, as well as the way animals are incorporated into the Swazi social world. A section is devoted to describing the costumes, and their symbolic significance, showing that different types of costume are worn on different parts of the body according to the person's social status. Swazi informants' interpretations of animal symbolism are detailed prior to Kuper's theoretical analysis of the structure of the Swazi cosmos that is revealed through the animals chosen for ritual costumes. For example, she highlights two main sets of social differentiation implicit in the *ncwala* costumes: first, differences between male and female; and second, differences between the special status of the king and queen mother in relation to their people. A theme of conceptual differentiation is also revealed, where certain animal species represent a range of cosmic powers. The diversity of the king's costume identifies him with these diverse powers, stressing his position as mediator between Swazi society and the cosmos and his transcendence of the boundary between the social and the natural worlds. Correlations between social hierarchies of the animal and human worlds are drawn, although their complexity, contradictions, and fluidity are acknowledged. The *ncwala* is a ritual of national rejuvenation, Kuper concludes, serving to maintain the Swazi nation's contact with the forces that are believed to sustain kingship. Notes and references are appended.

F19   Kuper, Hilda (1978a). "The Monarchy and the Military in Swaziland."
In John Argyle and Eleanor Preston-White (eds.) *Social System and Tradition
in Southern Africa.* Cape Town: Oxford University Press. 222-39.

Against the background of Swaziland's international recognition in 1968 as an
independent kingdom, Kuper's article examines the relationship between the
authority of a monarchy and the organization of force at various stages of the
reign of Sobhuza II. Kuper bases her study on an historical perspective of Swazi
culture, since Sobhuza frequently referred to the traditions and customs of an
idealized Swazi past (most particularly the *libutfo* or age-class system) for the
purpose of planning the nation's future. The functional role of the age-class
system is analyzed in the context of Swazi military history in the eighteenth and
nineteenth centuries, until the installation of Sobhuza II as Swazi king in 1922.
Emphasizing Sobhuza's consistent efforts to retain cultural identity and promote national unity, Kuper describes his attempts to integrate the regimental
system into Swazi education, with the aim of bridging the gap between West-
ern-oriented pupils and those trained in the disciplines of *libutfo*. Kuper shows
that this cultural tension underpinned wider economic and political developments in Swaziland until Sobhuza's highly symbolic repeal of the 1968 constitution in 1972. The king's birthday celebrations of July 1973 further served to
symbolize the notion of a king who was inspired by the ideals of the best in
"traditional African monarchy" and was "the 'mouthpiece' of the majority of
the people." Kuper concludes by contending that Sobhuza was indeed successful
in securing the monarchy and its legitimacy by the use of its own traditional
defenses, thus avoiding the violence and *coup d'etats* that have characterized
other postcolonial African territories. Notes and references are appended.

F20   Kuper, Hilda (1978b). *Sobhuza II: Ngwenyama and King of Swaziland.*
London: Duckworth.

Kuper's volume offers a comprehensive and sensitive biography of Sobhuza II,
King of Swaziland, which the author herself describes as "the history not only
of an outstanding man but of the culture with which he has deliberately identified himself." Commissioned by the Swazi government to write the official biography of King Sobhuza II, Kuper's work is based on her friendship with the
king and several periods of time spent in Swaziland since 1934. According to
the author, Sobhuza II used Swazi traditional culture as a springboard for planning the nation's future. Therefore, traditional Swazi religious thought and
practice is an underlying theme throughout the biography. Since the life of the
Swazi king symbolizes the life of the Swazi nation, each stage of his life from
birth onwards is ritualized in a way that enhances the development of kingship.
For example, Chapter Five describes and explains the ceremonial rituals that
celebrated Sobhuza's attainment of manhood in 1919; his subsequent mar-

riages; and his investment with full authority as king in 1921. At this time, Sobhuza became Ngwenyama (Lion) and the first *ncwala* ceremony for twenty-one years, the drama of full kingship, was celebrated. This *ncwala*—"a new production of an ancient and sacred script"—has been reenacted every year since 1921. The sacred rites of the six-day ceremony are described in detail, indicating the important role of sacred specialists and the ancestors in a process that symbolizes the strengthening of kingship and the purification of the nation. Photographs accompany the text; a bibliography and index are appended.

F21   Kuper, Hilda (1986). *The Swazi: A South African Kingdom*. 2nd. edn. New York: Holt, Rinehart & Winston.

In this study Kuper examines the cultural changes that have taken place in Swazi life from 1934 to 1983. The book is based on anthropological data collected at different periods during those years. The author's work comprises eleven chapters divided into two main parts, and her analysis rests on the structural-functionalist approach in anthropological theory. Most valuable for the study of traditional Swazi religion is Chapter Five, "The Supernatural." First, Kuper examines the Swazi notion of the world of the ancestral spirits, which reflects the world of the living. Family relationships and individual status, she suggests, are continued and projected into this world after death. This ancestral "cult," the foundation of Swazi religion, is set within a kinship framework that is extended to the nation through the person of the king, whose ancestors are the most powerful in the spirit world. Kuper discusses the rituals associated with the ancestral spirits in relation to illness, death, the propitiation of the ancestors, and the forces of nature. Next, she analyzes the significance of the specialists in ritual—the medicine men and diviners—who are revered as the possessors of esoteric knowledge. The training and initiation of the diviner and divination techniques are given particular attention. The Swazi notion of witchcraft, and ways of dealing with it, are also documented, as are the challenges posed by Christianity to traditional Swazi religion. The final portion of the chapter details the annual ritual of kingship, the *ncwala*. Kuper sensitively analyzes the complexity and rich symbolism of the rites involved, pointing to the ambivalence of the Swazi king's position and the final resolution of the rite and its dramatization of the triumph and sanctity of kingship. Photographs accompany the text and a glossary, bibliography, and index are appended.

F22   Kuper, Hilda (1987). "Swazi Religion." In Mircea Eliade (ed.) *The Encyclopedia of Religion*. New York: Macmillan. 14: 189-92.

Kuper's concise entry in the *Encyclopedia of Religion* discusses the salient features of Swazi religious belief and practice, beginning with a brief outline of

Swazi political history and social organization. Turning to the Swazi conception of reality, Kuper argues that no rigid division between the natural and the supernatural is perceived and thus the universe is thought to be "alive with powers" (*emandla*). The author further contends that a diversified hierarchy of powers constitutes the Swazi symbolic system: Mvelamqandi ("who appeared first") is the power "above," one who is unapproachable, unpredictable, and of no specific sex. The ancestors (*emadloti*), claims Kuper, represent the means through which the Swazi confront ideas of morality and mortality. The *emadloti* may be responsible for illness and misfortune as a form of punishment, but they do not inflict cruelty or death. Upon death, the Swazi believe that the spirit, after a short period of aimless wandering, is ritually "brought back" to the family circle, thereafter becoming part of the realm of the ancestors. The role of diviners is then briefly analyzed, suggesting that their main function is to reveal the cause of illness and misfortune and to prescribe the requisite cure—for example, ritual sacrifice, purification, or medicines. Kuper concludes with a brief description of the *ncwala* ritual, a national ceremonial ritual performed at the year-end liminal period, pointing out the multivalent symbolic significations it represents.

F23   Levin, Richard (1991). "Swaziland's Tinkhundla and the Myth of Swazi Tradition." *Journal of Contemporary African History*, vol. 10, no. 2: 1-23.

Levin's study of Swazi myth is underpinned by the theory that human mythical thought portrays reality through analogy, a type of thinking that draws consistently on symbols and images of nature to explain the world and its changes. Arguing that the power of myth relies on great orators and communicators, Levin indicates that it was King Sobhuza II's mythical thinking and vision that invented and reconstructed Swazi "tradition," thus mobilizing forces during the decolonization of Swaziland. The central aim of the paper is to examine one facet of the "traditional" Swazi state, the *tinkhundla*, or local authority structures that were formally legislated under the Establishment of Parliament Act of 1978. First, the writer briefly outlines the events leading to the suspension of the constitution and the closure of parliament, which cleared the way for a complete reconstruction of both traditional ideology and the state. Sobhuza, the writer contends, manipulated the propagation of tradition to maintain royal hegemony and to portray the "Swazi way of life" as superior to the Western lifestyle introduced by colonialism. Levin then analyzes the role of the *tinkhundla* in the development of the Swazi state, identifying their repressive ideological potential and revealing the mixture of repression, poverty, and underdevelopment that was the reality of daily life for most Swazi people. Turning to the post-Sobhuza II era, the writer examines the surfacing of popular pressure against the *tinkhundla* and King Mswati III's subsequent review of the system. He reveals an emerging crisis in relation to Swazi "tradition," where the myth of such a tradition began to crack in favor of mass support for democratic reform. Notes are appended.

F24   Lincoln, Bruce (1987). "Ritual, Rebellion, Resistance: Once More The Swazi Ncwala." *Man*, vol. 22: 132-56.

Lincoln offers an important contribution to ritual theory and interpretation in this classic anthropological case study, which serves to show how sociopolitical and sentimental dimensions of ritual combine to create either affinity or estrangement. The article reconsiders the *ncwala* ritual, an annual revitalization of Swazi society, polity, and natural environment, drawing on Hilda Kuper's reports on her fieldwork of 1934 to 1936. The *ncwala* ritual process itself is summarized, emphasizing the ritual power of the Swazi king and the role of the ritual assistants (*tinsila*) in protecting the king against witchcraft. Particular attention is given to the *ncwala* during the reign of Sobhuza II. Lincoln analyzes the political significance of the rites performed by the king. Reviewing the limitations of previous studies of ritual, particularly Gluckman's "rituals of rebellion" theory, Lincoln's central argument moves beyond structuralist approaches, proposing that careful attention must be paid to the historical context of any given ritual performance. Lincoln therefore reinterprets the *ncwala* ritual in the context of the British colonial period, portraying the ceremony as a powerful instrument of resistance to British domination whereby the solidarity of the Swazi nation was reaffirmed and those who threatened it were ritually expelled. Discussing the broader implications of this interpretation for ritual theory, Lincoln argues that ritual actors strategically construct, deconstruct, and reconstruct society. Verses from ritual songs and explanatory diagrams accompany the text. Notes and references are appended.

F25   Macmillan, Hugh (1989). "A Nation Divided? The Swazi in Swaziland and the Transvaal, 1865-1986." In Leroy Vail (ed.) *The Creation of Tribalism in Southern Africa*. London: James Currey; Berkeley and Los Angeles: University of California Press. 289-323.

Macmillan's essay examines the changing relationship between the Swazi in Swaziland and those in the Transvaal during the period between 1865, when the border was drawn between them, and 1986. Referring to the precolonial creation of a single Swazi identity and the consolidation of political power, Macmillan traces changing patterns of ethnic consciousness and material conditions in the two parts of the divided nation, noting the symbolic role of religious ritual and Swazi kingship in the political process. Although the Swazi elite in Swaziland did not assert many claims on the Transvaal during colonial rule, Macmillan shows that from 1910 to 1970 an emerging cultural nationalism and increasing ethnic mobilization eventually led to the consolidation of political power in Swaziland and claims to power in the eastern Transvaal. He suggests, however, that the renewal of ethnic awareness among South African Swazi can be traced more directly to the efforts of their chiefs in the 1920s, rather than to the pressures of the Native Administration Act of 1927, which introduced a state policy of "retribalization" in South Africa. It was only in the 1950s that the state took notice of the Swazi "retribalization," he argues, when straightforward segregationist policy shifted to the more devious encouragement of "specific ethnic formulations of political awareness." The author concludes that the attempt to "reunite" the Swazi in the 1980s was doomed to failure, since it was opposed by a burgeoning exclusionist cultural nationalism after independence in Swaziland on the one hand, and competing ethnicities in South Africa and a broad-based South African nationalism on the other. Footnotes are appended referring to extensive primary and secondary material.

F26   Marwick, Brian Allan (1940). *The Swazi: An Ethnographic Account of the Natives of the Swaziland Protectorate*. Cambridge: Cambridge University Press.

Marwick's work is based on fieldwork conducted in 1934 and on nine years as a government official in Swaziland. The author emphasizes the resilience of Swazi culture in the face of European influence, a resilience that is woven into the people's daily lives and upheld by their own institutions. A pivotal part of culture is the Swazi traditional religion, which Marwick addresses at length in Chapter Five, "Religion and Magic." The chapter begins with a detailed account of the ritual procedure of the six-day *ncwala* (first-fruits ceremony), drawing heavily on P. A .W. Cook's (1930) work. Thereafter, Marwick examines "ritual murders"—killings connected with fertilizing crops and killings carried out for the purpose of procuring medicine—a topic of vital importance, in the author's view. Lengthy court records are presented to prove the pervasiveness of this practice in Swazi society, although, paradoxically, Marwick finds evidence to suggest that ritual killing was a foreign practice that had recently been imported into Swaziland. Discussions are devoted to rainmaking ceremonies, rites associated with death and burial, and Swazi conceptions of divinity, including a supreme being (Mkhulumnqande) and a female deity, known as Nomkubulwana, who is accorded offerings for the removal of sickness. The chapter is completed with an extensive discussion of "ancestor worship," "magic and witchcraft," and "disease and healing." The role of the ancestral spirits within the Swazi kinship system is addressed. Other topics include the forms of sorcery, witchcraft, and spirits; the role of diviners; and the techniques and medicines for healing disease. Footnotes and photographs accompany the text and a glossary, index, and map are appended.

F27   Schoeman, P. J. (1935). "The Swazi Rain Ceremony." *Bantu Studies*, vol. 9: 169-75.

Schoeman draws on government agents and anthropologists (*volkekunderists*) in an attempt to outline the myths and rituals associated with the Swazi rain ceremony and associated cosmogonic myths. Identifying the rain ceremony as one of the two most important rituals in Swazi community life—the other being the *ncwala* ceremony—Schoeman particularly investigates reasons why women play an important role in this ceremony, considering the patrilineal-patrilocal structure of Swazi society. According to Schoeman, it is the king's mother (*Ndlovukati* or "royal mother") and the king who play the pivotal roles on which the success of the ritual rests. The main part of the brief article outlines the procedures of the ritual, followed by short descriptions of Swazi beliefs and practices relating to rituals that fail because they bring either no rain or too much rain. Schoeman's selective use of "misinformants" is criticized by Hilda (Beemer) Kuper in a rejoinder to this article (see Beemer, 1935).

F28   Temple, H. C. (1926). "Witchcraft or Worship?" *The Nongqai*, vol. 17, no. 5: 342; 356.

This article, written by a sergeant in the Swaziland police force, notes the continued practice of necromancy, witch-finding, human sacrifice, and *muti*-killings among the Swazi, making a comparison with the earlier witchcraft beliefs and witch-hunts in Europe. Referring to court cases witnessed, Temple describes the fear people still have of the "doctors"—whether herbalists, medicine-men, or diviners—and the powers they are believed to possess. The writer details two cases of human sacrifice, both of which were alleged to have been performed for doctoring crops. Temple suggests that these sacrifices, particularly when involving medicines manufactured from human genitals, have their origin in the phallic worship performed by the Phoenicians who are believed to have come to Africa for gold and whose fortress-temple ruins are found in Zimbabwe. He concludes that "Bantu" religions may have originated in this contact with Phoenicians who supposedly practiced sidereal and phallic worship.

F29   Twala, Regina G. (1952). "Umhlanga (Reed) Ceremony of the Swazi Maidens." *African Studies*, vol. 11, no. 3: 93-104.

Twala's descriptive article addresses the significance of the *umhlanga* (reed dance) ceremony in Swazi society, drawing on the verbatim reports of a participant in the July 1950 ceremony. First, she explains the structure of the Swazi kraal and the uses of reeds in the royal kraals. In preparation for the dance, as Twala notes, the cutting of the reeds is performed, followed by the organization of the young girls into various groupings (according to age and physical development). The maiden's march, undertaken by the girls before the ceremony, was led in 1950 by a daughter of King Sobhuza II. Twala describes the types of hairstyles and costumes made for the girls, who are dressed before the ceremony by their mothers. In Swazi society, the author notes, different types of dress provide an important means of social control for young girls, distinguishing who is a child, a maiden, a marriageable woman, a bride, or a wife. A description of the *umhlanga* dance forms the core of the article. The author includes examples of the songs sung by the young girls. Twala explains how the ceremony constitutes a means of imparting discipline, character, and sex education to Swazi girls, a process in which the queen mother and other royal consorts play central roles. In conclusion, the ways in which the custom of *ukuhlonipha* (avoidance) is observed during the ceremony is discussed, for example, in the young girl's avoidance of the ancestral spirit hut, the kraal, her in-laws, the shadow of royal persons, and sacred places. Footnotes accompany the text.

F30   Vail, Leroy, and Landeg White (1991). "Swazi Royal Praises: The Invention of Tradition." In *Power and the Praise Poem: Southern African Voices in History*. Charlottesville: University Press of Virginia; London: James Currey. 154-97.

Vail and White begin this essay by tracing the history of Swazi "traditional songs" (*tibongo*) composed and sung in praise of monarchies from the late eighteenth century. The authors set out to analyze how the twentieth-century surge of academic interest in Swazi history and customs on the part of white anthropologists (for example, Winifred Hoernlé, Isaac Schapera, P. J. Schoeman, and Hilda Kuper) related to the reconstruction of Swazi "traditions" that were practiced to strengthen the legitimacy of the royal house of King Sobhuza II. Interest in the *ncwala* ceremony and its accompanying *tibongi* are particularly examined, referring to the academic debate concerning whether the *ncwala* was in fact closely connected with the agricultural cycle, or was more definitively aimed to strengthen kingship. Use of the *ncwala* ritual became central to Sobhuza's own official version of history, which, the authors argue, became reflected in much of the modern literature about Swaziland's history. In the later part of Sobhuza's reign, the *tibongo*, widely propagated through Swaziland's media and education system, became "the poetic history of the Swazi kingdom according to the royal house." Vail and White conclude that whereas oral poetry and song in southern Africa most frequently function as mechanisms for dialogue between those who exercise power and their subjects, Swazi *tibongo* became increasingly redefined as a monologue in the service of the Swazi state. The *tibongo*, recreated as explicit praises to Sobhuza, were broadcast to the nation as "traditional" songs in support of the "traditional" monarchy. Examples of *tibongo* are analyzed throughout the text and notes are appended.

8   Tsonga Religion

As a separate and distinct African tradition, Tsonga traditional religion emerges from a remarkable history of nineteenth-century missionary intervention and twentieth-century ethnic formation. Appearing under different designations in the literature, including Ronga, Thonga, and Shangaan, a Tsonga identity was distilled from Zulu- and Swazi-speaking clans who in the early nineteenth century occupied large parts of Mozambique and the eastern Transvaal (Harries, 1989). People in the region spoke different languages and dialects; they formed different political allegiances; and they observed different religious traditions. When they entered this region, however, Swiss Protestant missionaries, most notably the missionaries Henri Berthoud and Henri-Alexandre Junod, identified and documented Tsonga language and culture (Harries, 1981). As historian Patrick Harries has shown, the work of these missionaries reveals the historical production of linguistic borders and "ethnic divisions" that did not exist before the second half of the nineteenth century (Harries, 1987). By the twentieth century, a Tsonga-Shangaan ethnic identity had been consolidated (Harries, 1989).

In this process of linguistic, cultural, and ethnic definition, a standardized version of Tsonga traditional religion entered the academic literature. The missionary-ethnographer Henri-Alexandre Junod was instrumental in representing Tsonga religion as a separate and distinct tradition in southern Africa. In conversation with recent developments in the European academic disciplines of social anthropology, comparative philology, folklore studies, and comparative religion, Junod produced an extensive body of literature on the cultural life of the Tsonga (Harries, 1981; 1993). Junod's research on the Tsonga was widely accepted in Europe as an authoritative account of the language, culture, and religion of an African community. As a result, the Tsonga emerged as a classic case study of African traditional religion.

Junod's major work, his two-volume *Life of a South African Tribe*, which originally appeared in 1912, devoted most of its second volume on "Mental Life" to a survey and analysis of Tsonga traditional religion. Although he displayed a missionary bias and evolutionary assumptions, Junod's account in this text was certainly a comprehensive and detailed survey of traditional religious life (Junod, 1924). In other publications, Junod documented Tsonga oral traditions (1897; 1898); ancestral ritual (1905); taboos and avoidances (1910); sacrifice (1911); and religious responses to illness and misfortune (1918). All of this research made Henri-Alexandre Junod one of the leading international authorities on African traditional religion in southern Africa. He was regularly cited by European scholars, from James Frazer to A. R. Radcliffe-Brown (1952), as an authoritative source. Outside of Junod's body of work, however, very little interest has been shown in Tsonga traditional religion.

G1   Berthoud, Henri (1930-1931). "Thonga-Marchen au Transvaal" and "Weitere Thonga-Marchen." *Zeitschrift für Eingeborenen Sprachen*, vol. 20, no. 4: 241-55; vol. 21, no. 1: 54-74; vol. 21. no. 2: 122-58; vol. 21. no. 4: 310-19; vol. 22. no. 1: 114-20.

In a series of brief articles on the myths and folklore of the Transvaal Thonga, the Swiss missionary-ethnographer Henri Berthoud describes several beliefs and rituals associated with important rites of passage, among them birth and the naming of children, initiation and puberty, marriage, and death. Notes on kinship and marriage, addressing polygyny, *lobola*, and divorce, are also included. However, most narratives relate events in the lives of Thonga cultural heroes, foremost among them the figure of Nwampfundla, the Hare. The papers are not annotated and no bibliography is included. In part this is due to Berthoud's indebtedness to Thonga-speaking informants, among them Yozefa, Murandiwane, and Mandlati.

G2   Bill, Mary C. (1994). "Refusal to Eat and Drink: A Metaphor for Safe Sex in Tsonga Folktales." *African Languages and Cultures*, vol. 7: 49-77.

Inspired by the writings of the French Africanist ethnolinguist Geneviève Calame-Griaule, Bill examines in this paper aspects of Tsonga, Ronga, and Tshwa folklore to reveal aspects of the sociocultural world of Tsonga-speakers in the Transvaal and Mozambique. In particular, her readings of several unpublished folktales recorded in Gazankulu in 1982 suggest that folk narratives disclose long-standing motifs associated with dietary prohibitions and sexual purity. The paper is annotated and contains a bibliography that refers readers to several collections of Tsonga folklore, among them those of missionary ethnographers Henri Berthoud and Henri-Alexandre Junod.

G3   Bishop, Herbert L. (1922a). "A Selection of SiRonga Folklore." *Report of the South African Association for the Advancement of Science*, vol. 24: 383-400.

Bishop's collection of six Tsonga folktales documents examples of myths associated with a cultural hero called Nwampfundla (The Hare). Narrated by Samuel Mabika, an elder of the Ronga peoples of coastal Mozambique, the stories focus on the "*dramatis persona*" of Nwampfundla, describing his wisdom, ingenuity, and mischievousness. Adventures with the lion, leopard, buck, and elephant are narrated in detail in successive chapters. The cycle of stories, asserts Bishop, differs considerably from those recorded by Henri-Alexandre Junod in his *Life of a South African Tribe*. As such, they provide resources for comparative analysis.

G4   Bishop, Herbert L. (1922b). "A Selection of SiRonga Proverbs." *Report of the South African Association for the Advancement of Science*, vol. 24: 401-15.

In the early 1920s, Herbert Bishop, a missionary working in the coastal regions of Mozambique, collected ninety-four proverbs extant among the Ronga. The proverbs, collated with the assistance of J. T. Chembeni and T. D. Mabika, provide the basis for Bishop's paper, which the author considers to be a useful corrective to the relatively sparse attention given to proverbs in Junod's seminal work. However, an examination of the translations, suggests the missionary, fails to reveal any "close parallels" with European parables. The text is in Tsonga and English.

G5   Cipriani, Lidio (1929). "The Anthropological Investigation of the Ba-Tonga of Northern Rhodesia." *South African Journal of Science*, vol. 26: 541-46.

The Florentine writer and ethnographer Lidio Cipriani recalls in this paper that he was drawn to the study of the Thonga of northern Rhodesia because the customs, physical appearance, religion, and language of these peoples represented the most "primitive" and "ideal type" of southern African Bantu. Insofar as it describes the author's techniques of human measurement, principally the "zoological method," the paper provides useful materials for the critical historian of comparative religion in the region. Extended notes are included on the exacting procedures required of ethnographers wishing to evaluate aspects of "racial structure," "hybridization," and "intermingling." Thus, the "Mongolian" character of a Thonga woman's breasts, Cipriani asserts, "offers useful material for exact anthropological investigation." Inscribed in a peculiarly late nineteenth-century scientific diffusionist idiom, the paper is not annotated and no bibliography is appended. A brief note in the appendix relates that Thonga language and culture should remain of interest to Italian anthropologists.

G6   Clerc, André (1938). "Marriage Laws of the Ronga." Trans. Helene Borel. *African Studies*, vol. 12: 75-104.

In an extensive article on the myths, rituals, and traditions associated with marriage among the Ronga, Clerc examines in detail several aspects pertaining to matrimonial jurisprudence. In Section One, entitled the "Capacity to Contract Marriage," he notes that the Ronga seldom choose whom they marry. Rather, family councils gather to debate the respective benefits or shortcomings of prospective partners. In Section Two, "Physical Development," he notes that a Ronga man must have reached puberty and a woman must have menstruated prior to the drawing up of marriage contracts. Brief notes are also included on "prohibitions on marriage," included among them notes on the illegibility of matrimony between the descendants of the father and mother. Section Three, "Betrothal," outlines ritual procedures required of the "first contact" and subsequent *sigila* (capital money or cattle) contracts. In Section Four, "Marriage," Clerc describes aspects pertaining to the payment of *lobola*, the nuptial procession, and the marriage feast. Thereafter, in Section Five and Section Six, entitled "Nullity" and "Dissolution," rules concerning grounds for divorce are tabulated. Clerc mentions several cases, including death, sterility of the wife, adultery, and ill-treatment by the husband. Lastly, Section Nine describes procedures for choosing levirate substitutes following the death of a husband. That section also examines in detail the payment of *lobola*. The paper is not annotated and no bibliography is included.

G7   Harries, Patrick (1981). "The Anthropologist as Historian and Liberal: H-A. Junod and the Thonga." *Journal of Southern African Studies*, vol. 8. no. 1: 37-50.

Drawn to the field of African anthropology by the politician, historian, and friend of Sir James Frazer, James Bryce, Henri-Alexandre Junod became one of the foremost South African archivists and interpreters of Thonga language, culture, and religion. However, because of his attraction to the work of R. R.

Marrett, E. Sidney Hartland, and W. C. Willoughby, his evolutionary and diffusionist theories concerning the origin of the Thonga were severely criticized.
Radcliffe-Brown, for example, viewed Junod's assertion that polygamy and endogamous preferential marriages were the remnants of a former matriarchal
stage to be "pseudo-historical" inventions. Likewise, the functionalist viewed
Junod's contention that the incorporation of the flesh of dead enemies in
Thonga war medicines was constituent of a residual anthropophagous phase, to
be fallacious. In an incisive review of these criticisms, and of Junod's intellectual heritage more generally, historian Patrick Harries provides a wide-ranging
analysis of Junod's contribution to Thonga historiography and the emergence of
Thonga ethnicity in southern Africa. He notes, for example, that while evolutionism influenced Junod's speculative history of the Thonga, that theoretical
impulse also served to support the anthropologist's argument that the Thonga
were in a state of social and religious stagnation. In this regard, Harries argues
that Junod was perhaps trapped within the limitations of his age: He was be-
queathed an intellectual system that demanded a series of categorizations and
discrete classifications that in reality did not exist. Junod's description of
Thonga religion is a case in point: The anthropologist's claim that Thonga ancestral veneration was typical of an early form of religious practice is viewed by
Harries to be a consequence of an evolutionary bias in anthropological studies.
However, Harries concludes that Junod was not merely captive to a nineteenth-
century intellectual impulse. Rather, his evolutionary and diffusionist theories
served the interests of South African ideologues of ethnicity who were concerned with perpetuating tribal divisions in the latter half of the twentieth century. The paper is annotated.

G8   Harries, Patrick (1987). "The Roots of Ethnicity: Discourse and the
Politics of Language Construction in South-East Africa." *African Affairs*, vol.
346: 25-52.

In an analysis of the linguistic constructions present and codified in written
Tsonga, Harries argues that African language "was a product of nineteenth-
century discourse"—in particular, missionary debate—"rather than a reflection
of local reality." The writer further contends that "linguistic borders" were established according to relatively subjective social and political criteria. Consequently, the "ethnic divisions" that were extrapolated from colonial discourses
and European codes did not exist, even in a conceptual form, before the latter
half of the nineteenth century. In pursuing this argument, Harries draws on an
extensive array of Swiss missionary correspondence, including the letters of
Paul and Henri Berthoud and Henri-Alexandre Junod. In the opening sections,
"Discovering the Subject" and "Defining the Language of the Other," the writer
describes the efforts of Ernst Creux and the Berthoud brothers to establish a
linguistic taxonomy for the "*pot-pourri*" of "Gwamba" and "Tsonga" refugees

who resided in the greater Spelonken coastal region of Mozambique. Henri Berthoud's progress in systematizing the grammar of written Gwamba and in producing various pedagogical texts and biblical translations is emphasized. Harries proceeds, in the section entitled "Language Classification and the Discourse of Modernization," to delineate the linguistic classifications that transpired in Henri Berthoud and Henri-Alexandre Junod's late nineteenth-century evolutionist and Cartesian thought. He suggests, in the concluding sections, "Language and Structures of Power" and "Adapting Borders: The Emergence of the Ronga," that the Swiss missionaries played a crucial political role in constructing and manipulating a "linguistic monopoly" in the coastal regions of Mozambique. That monopoly, and the concomitant standardization of the Tsonga language, he asserts, provided missionaries with a number of concrete advantages, foremost among them the possibility of gaining more African converts and of teaching Africans to think in the "systematic" and "rational" manner assumed to be "characteristic" of European discourse. The paper is richly annotated from primary resources. It provides important resources for readers in the history of comparative religion in southern Africa insofar as it examines African "traditional" religion and missionary contributions to an abiding ethnicity that more often than not characterized interpretation.

G9   Harries, Patrick (1989). "Exclusion, Classification and Internal Colonialism: The Emergence of Ethnicity Among the Tsonga-Speakers of South Africa." In Leroy Vail (ed.) *The Creation of Tribalism in Southern Africa.* London: James Currey; Berkeley: University of California Press. 82-117.

In this wide-ranging essay, historian Patrick Harries draws on the writings of sociologist Harold Wolpe to analyze the formation of ethnicity among Tsonga-speaking peoples of the northern and eastern Transvaal. He argues that the notion of an ethnic Tsonga identity was invented in colonial strategies of religious classification and exclusion, first by nineteenth-century Protestant missionaries and anthropologists, foremost among them Henri-Alexandre Junod, and second by apartheid policy-makers in the 1950s and 1960s, including government ethnologist and segregationist N. J. van Warmelo. The paper is divided into eight sections. In the first, "The Migrations of Tsonga-speakers," the writer asserts that the people who were later to be defined as the Tsonga were essentially comprised of a number of Zulu and Swazi-speaking clans who in the early nineteenth century occupied large parts of Mozambique and an area south of the Sabi River in the eastern Transvaal. Ecological disaster and civil war, notably the Gaza uprisings in the late 1850s, subsequently forced refugees to migrate to the region, and it is from the diverse linguistic and political allegiances that were formed as a consequence of these events, suggests Harries, that later historians premised their arguments for a so-called Tsonga "tribalism." In truth, however, Harries suggests that the notion of an ethnically "pure" Tsonga identity is a misnomer. Based primarily on an arbitrary linguistic classification, the term "Tsonga" was employed in the late nineteenth century to describe a diverse population who spoke numerous and varied dialects. In the following sections, including "Missionaries and the Definition of the Tsonga Tribe," the "African Mode of Production," and "Africans and the Land," Harries employs extensive use of archival materials, including the letters of the influential Swiss missionary Henri Berthoud, who arrived in the region in the late nineteenth century, to further his argument that the Tsonga were in a sense the product of missionary discourse and social and political exigencies. In the final two sections of the essay, namely, "The Consolidation of a Tsonga-Shangaan Ethnic Awareness" and the "Role of the Apartheid System," Harries concludes by arguing that whereas the bantustan land policies of the National Party were well-served by the continuing invention of this ethnic Tsonga identity, the breakdown of chiefly power, the imposition of capitalist labor economies, and increasing territorial dispossession undermined a Tsonga "tribalism" that earlier had provided chiefs with at least some degree of power. The paper is richly annotated and utilizes the writings of Portuguese, German, and French missionaries, many of whose works were published in local journals, among them the *Berlin Missionsberichte*.

G10   Harries, Patrick (1993). "Through the Eyes of the Beholder: H-A. Junod and the Notion of the Primitive." *Social Dynamics*, vol. 19, no. 1: 1-10.

In an essay that examines Henri-Alexandre Junod's contribution to South African ethnography, historian Patrick Harries describes how the Swiss missionary-anthropologist constructed an image of Africa that successfully replaced long-standing metaphors of "darkness" and "irrationality" with a more "scientific, universal system of signification." Particularly, he notes how the ethnographer, who was regarded by such luminaries as Frazer, Malinowski, Schapera, Evans-Pritchard, Gluckman, Lévi-Bruhl, and Mauss as "magisterial," tamed the continent's otherness by viewing African art, culture, and religion as representative of a "primitive" stage in human experience. Drawing on Junod's published ethnographies and letters, among them James Frazer's correspondence with Junod contained in the Wren Library, Trinity College, Cambridge, the paper thus situates Junod's work firmly within a late nineteenth-century European evolutionist conversation. Junod's ethnographic account of the Thonga was emblematic of that academic discourse. In this sense, Harries outlines the central moments of Junod's analysis of the Thonga as a "primitive, childish race," "an inferior race" of "weak character," that was "comparable to a child who has hardly entered into conscious life." Set against the background of Junod's experiences in the northern Transvaal, and his alarm at the presence of the rival Methodist missionary, millenarian, and one-time African migrant worker and Thonga linguist, Robert Mashaba, Harries' work provides an insightful entry into the world of nineteenth-century ethnography, Thonga religion, and the developing competitive science of comparative religion.

G11   Harris, Marvin (1959). "Labour Migration Among the Mozambique Thonga: Cultural and Political Factors." *Africa*, vol. 29: 50-65.

Noting that Thonga migrant laborers played a strategic and significant role in the economic development of South Africa, Harris examines in this paper the historical and cultural factors that prompted workers to enter wage-labor markets in the Transvaal in the late nineteenth century. In the first part of his paper, historical events are documented. Harris notes, for example, that the defeat of Gugunhana in 1895 precipitated the first of many trade agreements between the Republic of South Africa and Mozambique, foremost among them the Transvaal-Mozambique Convention of 1897. In the second section of the paper, cultural factors influencing labor migration are documented. In this regard, Harris examines Junod's accounts of Thonga social stratification, clan (*shibonga*) organization, and traditional patterns of the division of labor. He asserts briefly that witchcraft, among other reasons, contributed to the dissolution of social structures and prompted in part the move toward labor migration. The paper is annotated and a short bibliography is included.

G12   Heusch, Luc de (1985). "The Thonga's Goat." In *Sacrifice in Africa: A Structuralist Approach*. Trans. Linda O'Brien and Alice Morton. Manchester: Manchester University Press. 65-97.

De Heusch asserts that whereas the ox or goat represents the index of value *par excellence* in most southern African agrarian societies, the Thonga of the eastern Transvaal and Mozambique almost never use the goat in socioeconomic or political life, either as a substitution for *lobola*, or as a mark of aristocratic status or rank. Rather, the goat constitutes the primary sacrificial reserve for the most important ritual acts. Of particular interest to ethnographers and historians of religion, therefore, the Thonga's use of the goat provides researchers with a provocative problem: Why did the Thonga, unlike the Mpondo, for example, fail to convert goats into the currency of matrimonial exchanges regulated by *lobola* but employ them in sacrificial acts? Drawing on the writings of the ethnographer Henri-Alexandre Junod (1910; 1927), De Heusch begins by examining the structural environment of the Thonga village. He notes that an ancestral altar and cooking pot (*gandjelo*) was invariably situated to the right of the main entrance of the men's meeting place, where it was used in rituals of offering (*mhamba*) or sacrifice. Thereafter, an analysis of the different contexts in which *mhamba* offerings occurred is provided, among them occasions of extreme distress where "negative offerings" were made. Here, the so-called bitter "offering of charcoal" is discussed. A brief analysis of how the sacrifice was used to divert social disorder or the destructive powers of ancestors is included. In the field of "positive offerings," De Heusch analyzes blood sacrifices in which the goat is deployed, particularly in association with the rites of mourning and marriage. Following his reading of the relationship between ancestors and sacrifice in the section entitled "The Locus of Ancestors," the writer examines the symbolic role of the goat in private offerings, matrimonial alliances, or "battles," and mourning in the three months following a person's death. Brief notes on the relationship between goat sacrifices and exorcism are also included.

G13   Jaques, Alexander A. (1929). "Terms of Kinship and Corresponding Patterns of Behavior Among the Thonga." *Bantu Studies*, vol. 3, no. 4: 327-48.

In examining the classificatory schemas and principle behavioral patterns implicit to Thonga kinship "systems," the French missionary Alexander Jaques delineates several rule-governing relations among the inhabitants of the eastern Transvaal and Mozambique. In this regard, the writer describes behavioral patterns in relation to *lobola*; daughters-in-law; fathers; mothers; brothers and sisters; paternal aunts; grandchildren, uterine nephews, nieces, and cousins; grandparents, maternal uncles, their wives, and brothers; and sisters-in-law. He concludes that the Thonga kinship "system" is far more fluid than the patterns of kin relations indicative of European society.

G14   Junod, Henri-Alexandre (1897a). *Les chants et les contes des Ba-Ronga de la baie de Delagoa*. Lausanne: George Bridel.

In one of the first book-length ethnographic accounts of the Thonga-speaking peoples of southern Africa, the Swiss missionary-anthropologist Henri-Alexandre Junod narrates aspects of myth, ritual, and religious belief indicative of this apparently "child-like" and "irrational race." Divided into two sections, the first dealing primarily with "Songs" and the second with "Myths," Junod examines both the place of music and the value of myth in Thonga life. In the first section, "Songs," information relating to the use of musical instruments and systems of notation are described. Several songs associated with love and marriage, mourning and sorrow, and exorcism, hunting, and war are tabulated. In the second section, "Myths," Junod examines the place of myth and folklore in Thonga society. In the first chapter of this section, he assesses the diverse genres of mythic tradition found among the Thonga and attempts to evaluate the philosophical value of these folktales and myths against the index of European science. Essentially, the myths serve to reinforce his assertion that the Thonga represent a linguistically distinct and culturally discrete race of "primitive" disposition. The following chapter relates several "Animal Myths." Among the animals presented in the narratives are the Hare (Nwampfundla), Frog, Swallow, Chicken, and Chameleon. The next chapter, a collection of tales dealing with ogres and demons, includes several narratives relating to the trickster figure Nyandzoumoula and the ancestor-gods Ngoumba-ngoumba, Nouamoubia, and Namachouke. The next two chapters then disclose myths pertaining to morality. In Chapter Five, however, several myths attributed by Junod to "foreign" influences are narrated. In this regard, the writer notes that several Thonga myths can be traced to Muslim, Hindu, or Catholic Christian influence. The book, written in French, is illustrated with several photographic plates and line drawings. However, the work is not annotated and no bibliography is included.

G15   Junod, Henri-Alexandre (1897b). "L'art divinatoire, ou, la science des osselets chez les Ronga de la baie de Delagoa." *Bulletin de la Société Neuchateloise de Geographie*, vol. 9: 57-83.

Essentially an index of French translations for Sironga terms pertaining to divination, this brief paper recalls the Swiss ethnographer-missionary's discussions with a Ronga diviner of the Ribombo region of Mozambique. The diviner, named "Spoon" by his European employers, provided Junod with a list of the names of some twenty-seven of these divining objects, most of which are bones. Included among the Sironga names for the bones identified are the *ngoloabe ya nhoba ntchoune* (signifying the male ancestor), *ngoloabe ya nhoba mpoele* (female ancestor), *foutcho* (village), *makanyi* (medicine), and *mangoulwe*, which, Junod notes, corresponds to evil. In the second section a discussion of the manner in which the bones are "thrown" (*tinhlolo*) and interpreted is followed by several line-drawings depicting methods of assessment. The writer asserts that the "system" of divination can perhaps be regarded as the "edifice of Ronga paganism." The essay, in French, contains neither annotations nor bibliographic notes.

G16   Junod, Henri-Alexandre (1898). "Les Ba-Ronga: Etude ethnographique sur les indigenes de la baie de Delagoa." *Bulletin de la Société Neuchateloise de Geographie*, vol. 10: 5-500.

In what remains perhaps the most wide-ranging and detailed descriptive account of the Ronga—an account proclaimed by anthropologist Bronislaw Malinowski as "magisterial"—the Swiss missionary-ethnographer Henri-Alexander Junod outlines in this work several aspects of the religious beliefs and rituals, myths, folklore, and customs of the Sironga-speaking peoples of the northern Transvaal and Mozambique. Divided into six sections, the work begins with two chapters on the "Life-Cycle" of the Ronga. Notes on rituals and beliefs associated with birth and the naming of children are included, as are details concerning youth, puberty, marriage, and death rites. In these chapters, Junod draws attention to the disappearance of circumcision rites and the persistence of several initiation ceremonies for pubescent men and women among the Ronga. In Section Two, "Family Life," details concerned with kinship, marriage prohibitions and polygyny, *lobola*, and divorce precede the author's account of village life, particularly with regard gendered divisions of labor. Section Three, "National Life," outlines aspects of chiefly authority and "tribal law." Of interest to historians of religion is the chapter in this section describing warfare: Junod notes that war was an essentially religious rite, a way of displaying the efficiency of protective medicines, charms, and chants. Prior to his analysis of religion proper in Section Six, however, agricultural and industrial life and artistic abilities are enumerated. The function of Ronga proverbs, myths, and folktales are discussed and translations from the Sironga are provided. In Section Six, "Religious Life and Superstition," however, the structure and system of overtly religious Ronga rites and beliefs are analyzed. Extended and detailed records about ancestral cults, notions of the soul, sacrifice, sorcery, and divination are incorporated. Throughout, Junod asserts that the rituals and beliefs associated with these "superstitions" indicate that the Ronga remain in a "retarded," "primitive" psychological state. In this regard, their "childish" beliefs correspond, he suggests, to a "stagnant," animistic stage in the development toward higher, monotheistic religions. The book contains an exhaustive table of contents.

G17   Junod, Henri-Alexandre (1905). "The Ba-Thonga of the Transvaal." *Report of the South African Association for the Advancement of Science*, vol. 3: 222-62.

Junod's essay on the history, language, and religion of the Tsonga of the Transvaal begins with his argument for the use of the term "Thonga." The writer suggests that that term should be used in preference to other designations, including "Tsonga," "Magwamba," "Shangaan," or even "Knobneusen." However, within the perimeters of that designation Junod lists six substantially different groups of Thonga peoples, each associated with a different linguistic and geographical "boundary." These boundaries, he suggests, logically infer variant physical, ethnic, and religious characteristics. However, the religion of the Thonga, according to Junod, might generally be regarded as a "superstitious" form of animism and ancestor worship. That superstitious religion, he argues, is also inferior to the "pure doctrines" of Christian "monotheism." The paper is divided into three sections comprising the "History of the Ba-Thonga"; the "Language and Literature of the Thonga"; and the "Morality and Religion of the Thonga Tribe." In the first, the writer delineates the complex patterns of migration that, initiated by internecine conflict and war with their Zulu rivals, forced the Thonga from the coastal regions of Natal and Mozambique into the eastern Transvaal in the period 1835-1900. In the second, Junod distinguishes Thonga language from the Sotho and Zulu, contrasting Thonga grammatical constructions and phonetic discontinuities to prove ethnic independence. These discontinuities, he argues, provide the foundation for an examination of distinctive Thongan physical and intellectual characteristics, including ear-piercing, artistic temperament, imaginative orientation, "moral sensitivity," and a "lively conscience." The essay concludes with an examination of Thonga "systems" of divination and an account of "witchcraft" practices, ancestor veneration, and sacrifice. These practices, asserts the writer, provide evidence for the "dark side of the morality of the natives" and the "diseases" of their "enchantment" with gods. In this respect, Junod reflects the Christian evolutionary bias of nineteenth-century anthropology in southern Africa.

G18   Junod, Henri-Alexandre (1907). "The Best Means of Preserving the Traditions and Customs of Various South African Native Races." *South African Association for the Advancement of Science Report*, vol. 4: 141-59.

In a paper presented before the Anthropological Section of the South African Association for the Advancement of Science, Junod rearticulates Haddon's earlier argument for forming a South African Anthropology Society. The necessity, he asserts, becomes all the more critical in the light of a rapid dissolution of African custom and the transformation of African "tribal life." In this sense, while the progress of Christianity, Western science, and European political administration is both inevitable and desirable, he argues, it requires that special care be taken to record for posterity the "primitive" and "childish" pagan practices of African animists prior to their disappearance. Several techniques are proposed as adjuncts to the formation of the Society, foremost among them a renewed endeavor to publish ethnographic studies pertaining to African history, anthropology, folklore, language, and religion. This last category, notes Junod, poses acute problems and will require careful and intelligent handling, insofar as a confusing "trace of monotheism or pantheism" is prevalent in the religions of southern African peoples. A second technique the writer proposes, however, requires that native commissions be established and missionaries and "educated natives" be trained in the practical methods of ethnology. To this end, Junod suggests that mission societies be contacted and the earlier ethnographies of Bleek and Theal be consulted. The paper is not annotated.

G19   Junod, Henri-Alexandre (1910). "The Sacrifice of Reconciliation Amongst the Ba-Ronga." *South African Journal of Science*, vol. 7: 179-82.

Almost universally, the implicit relationship that exists between religion and morality in the Christian tradition, asserts Junod, remains largely absent in African belief and ritual. Bantu "animism"—inclusive of gods, spirits, and ancestors—he argues, "has very little to do with morality." By contrast, however, among the Ronga of the Delgoa Bay region, and the Thonga and Shangaan of the northern Transvaal and Matabeleland, "some traces of an organic union between religion and morality exist." Indeed, as Junod develops this argument, the Ronga word *hahla* (sacrifice) was often used by one of his Tsonga informants, Mboza, to signify a promise rather than the ritual observances of ancestral ritual. Nevertheless, Junod concludes in this brief paper that was delivered before the Anthropological Section of the South African Association for the Advancement of Science, "we cannot expect amongst these animist tribes anything like the spiritual morality of a theistic religion." In part, he asserts, the "absence" of a religiously-inspired morality can be demonstrated by the fact that the spiritual jurisprudence and moral guidance represented by the authority of the ancestors did not extend beyond the boundaries of their own direct descendants.

G20   Junod, Henri-Alexandre (1918). "Native Customs in Relation to Small-Pox Amongst the Ba-Ronga." *South African Journal of Science*, vol. 16: 694-702.

Drawing on empirical evidence that documents and describes the changing religious rites of the Tsonga, Junod gives a brief but comprehensive analysis of how Ronga rituals dealt with a smallpox epidemic that occurred in the southeastern Transvaal in 1918. The Protestant missionary and anthropologist accounts for these rituals within a broadly Christian framework of interpretation. For example, Junod proposes that the "initial proclamation" and the "taboos of the marginal period," which he documents in Chapter One—events during which the Tsonga are described as abstaining from meats and salts and sex—are reflections of a "Christian" concern with sin and confession. These prescriptive taboos, suggests Junod, prevented states of "defilement" that arose as a consequence of smallpox. In Chapter Two, the "Way of Proceeding to the Inoculation," Junod recounts that divinatory bones were "thrown" by the sacred specialists of the Tsonga in order to select reliable nephews of the chiefs to fetch serum from neighboring clans. In the central chapter of the thesis, the "Religious Act," the writer describes rituals and prayers of confession offered by the ill to the *mabutise*, a "questioner," Junod asserts, who is thought to personify the smallpox virus. That impersonator, argues Junod, is entrusted to "sniff out" elements of witchcraft (*baloyi*) in the community. The writer concludes that the presence of the *mabutise* proves that the Tsonga have a "rudimentary" "moral conscience." Although the writer betrays a definite Christian bias in framing his interpretation, the paper nevertheless provides an important account of how "native medical art" adjusted to changing patterns of physical and social affliction.

G21   Junod, Henri-Alexandre (1924). *The Life of a South African Tribe*. 2 vols. London: Macmillan (orig. edn. 1912).

In this two-volume monograph, the Swiss Protestant missionary and anthropologist Henri-Alexandre Junod undertakes a comprehensive and systematic analysis of the "Tsonga tribe." Drawing on James Frazer's method of analysis, and employing the questions Frazer developed for ethnographic study, the writer illustrates the "immense complexity" of Tsonga society and religion. The monograph is divided into six sections and is prefaced by an account of the myths of origin and "ancient migrations" of the Tsonga. Volume One, Part One, "The Life of the Individual," describes the various stages of life from birth to death and includes an analysis of circumcision rites, marriage ceremonies, and *lobola* (bridewealth) customs. In Part Two, "The Life of the Family and the Village," topics concerned with "blood relationships" and kinship are analyzed. The third part, concluding Volume One, is titled "National Life." It investigates the structures of the "Court and Tribunal," "Army," and "Chieftainship." Volume Two, subtitled "Mental Life," details the "Agricultural and Industrial Life" of the Tsonga. Customs relating to fishing and folktales relating to "animal wisdom" and "morality" are included. The volume focuses more directly on the "Religious Life and Superstitions" of Tsonga tradition. Junod classifies these superstitions as "ritualistic," "unphilosophical," "non-moral," and "animistic." The writer further asserts that Tsonga religion can be considered to embrace divination, possession, and witchcraft. Although comprehensive and rich in descriptive detail, the work suffers from a particular Christian evolutionary bias that considers African religion inherently inferior to European Protestant belief and practice.

G22   Junod, Henri-Philippe (1934). *Henri-Alexandre Junod: Missionaire et savant, 1863-1934*. Lausanne: Mission suisse dans l'Afrique du sud.

In a biographical tribute to his father on the anniversary of the publication of *Life of a South African Tribe*, Henri-Philippe Junod recalls events in the life and extracts from the writings of the ground-breaking Swiss missionary and Ronga ethnographer. The essay begins, in Section One (1863-1903), with a brief account of Junod's birth in 1863, his infancy and youth in Switzerland, and his theological training in Berlin. Included in the section is a narrative description of Junod's marriage in 1889 and his journey to Mozambique as a missionary in the same year. Extracts from letters and journals serve to convey Junod's initial response to the Tsonga inhabitants of the region of Delgoa Bay, where the Swiss missionary and educationalist Paul Berthoud had established a mission. An account of Junod's publication in 1897 of *Les chants et les contes des Baronga* is also provided. In Section Two, "Ministry" (1903-1920), and Section Three, "Synthesis" (1921-1934), detailed descriptions of Junod's life at the Rikatla mission station are sustained and several responses from European ethnographers to the publication his *Life of a South African Tribe* (1912) are incorporated. Throughout the work, the author recalls his father's love of the Tsonga and their art and folklore, which he regarded as exemplary of a "stagnant" or "primitive" stage in the universal human language of culture and religion. In this regard, brief extracts from Junod's writings on Tsonga magic and divination are included. The essay, written in French, contains several photographic plates, notably one portraying Junod's acolyte, the Tsonga missionary Calvin Mapope in Geneva in 1925.

G23   Junod, Henri-Philippe, with Alexander A. Jaques (1935). *Vutlhari Bya Vatsonga-Machangana, or The Wisdom of the Tsonga-Shangaan People.* Cleveland: Central Mission Press.

Drawing on the records of Jaques, Ribeiro, and Rita-Ferreira, Henri-Philippe Junod compiled in the 1930s more than 1600 proverbs of the Tsonga-speaking people of the north-eastern Transvaal. Best known for his work on penal reforms in the South African prison system, Junod divided this expansive published account of Tsonga proverbial wisdom into three parts. In the first, the writer describes "Proverbs Connected with Animal Folklore," in which he suggests that the animals, including animals listed under the subclassifications "Dangerous Animals" and "Domestic Animals," are in some respects anthropomorphized creations. In the second, "Ways and Habits of People," Junod elucidates various aspects of the "social and spiritual life" of the Tsonga-Shangaan of the Transvaal and Mozambique. The third section includes examples of Tsonga riddles. Although primarily interested in description, the writer does attempt to explain the "hidden meaning" of obscure and apparently "simple expressions." The text, he suggests, throws light on "the minds and the ways of thinking of the Tonga people." Those ways of thinking, he argues, convey a moral and philosophical dexterity that should serve to displace European misconceptions about a "primitive" and so-called "superstitious" people.

G24   Mathumba, Isaac (1988). *Some Aspects of the Tsonga Proverb.* M.A. thesis, University of South Africa.

In an examination of the linguistic structure and social function of Tsonga proverbs, Mathumba provides in this thesis brief notes on the contribution made by nineteenth-century scholars to Tsonga ethnography. However, his analysis of the literary form is of interest not only to readers of African languages, but also to anthropologists and historians of religion. In particular, Chapter One evaluates Henri-Alexandre Junod's contribution to the study of Tsonga culture and language and the "invention" of what he considered to be an ethnically distinct and "primitive" people. Also of note is Mathumba's brief review of H. A. Bishop's (1922) study of Sironga proverbs. In Chapter Four, "Proverbs as a Mirror of the Tsonga People's Philosophy of Life," the writer's observations concerning marriage, sexual life, polygyny, the role of women in Tsonga society, neighborliness, tribal courts, and death and mourning serve to delineate further several aspects of Tsonga religious belief and ritual. Bibliographic notes citing contemporary collections of Tsonga proverbs are included, as is an alphabetical list of more than two hundred proverbs cited by the author in the text.

G25 Radcliffe-Brown, A. R. (1952). "The Mother's Brother in South Africa." In *Structure and Function in Primitive Society*. London: Cohen & West. 15-31.

In an important contribution to kinship studies in southern Africa, anthropologist A. R. Radcliffe-Brown reexamines Henri-Alexandre Junod's thesis that the mother's brother (*malume*)-sister's son (uterine nephew) relationship in Thonga societies presupposes primitive matriarchal patterns of social organization. Problematizing the terms patriarchal and matriarchal, and defining for readers the terms patrilocal and matrilocal, the writer consequently invokes a comparative analysis of Herero, Nama, Zulu, Pedi, and even Polynesian kinship systems to assert that so-called matrilineal relations among the Thonga are perhaps best understood as derivative of more general, patrilineal patterns of behavior consistent with the biological relationship between mother and child. Citing as his evidence of this finding the essentially patrilineal rituals and myths associated with ancestor veneration among the Thonga, Radcliffe-Brown mentions several rituals of marriage payment, among them rites concerned with *lobola* and *ditsoa* (the cattle received by a girl upon her marriage and later given to her mother's brother). The paper is not annotated.

9 Venda Religion

Like other African traditions, the traditional religion of Venda-speaking people in the northeastern Transvaal and southern Zimbabwe was summarized in early missionary reports as a "long succession of fear and superstition" (Gottschling, 1905) or as a "reign of superstition" (Wessen, 1908). As missionaries adopted terms of analysis from the academic disciplines of anthropology and comparative religion, they could achieve a similar effect by dismissing Venda traditional religion as a "combination of animism and totemism" (Macdonald, 1933). By the 1930s, however, anthropologists had settled on a standard inventory of Venda religion that included the following elements: a creator God (Raluvhimba or Raluvimbi); a rain deity (Mwali); ritual sacrifices for ancestors (*medzinu*); male and female initiation; and the specialized practices of the healer (*nyanga*) and the diviner (*sangoma*) (Stayt, 1931a; Van Warmelo, 1932; see Roumeguère-Eberhardt, 1963).

Henri-Alexandre Junod thought that two religions could be distinguished in Venda tradition: a monotheistic cult based on worship of the creator God, and an ancestor cult based on sacrifices to ancestral spirits (Junod, 1920). In subsequent research, the role of the "High God" has given rise to speculations about the dynamics of intercultural contact and exchange in the history of Venda traditional religion (Schutte, 1978). However, the literature on divinity, ancestors, and ritual in Venda tradition is extremely limited.

Largely through the efforts of the anthropologist John Blacking, female initiation has been the most thoroughly documented aspect of Venda traditional religion. Although male initiation, with its ritual of circumcision and instruction in the circumcision lodge, received some early attention in the literature (Bullock, 1926; Wheelwright, 1905), female initiation has been the more recent focus of research. Based on fieldwork conducted in the 1950s and 1960s,

Blacking was able to identify three stages in the transition of a girl into the status of an adult woman in traditional Venda society.

First, the puberty school (*vhusha*) marks the beginning of that process by introducing girls to the secret knowledge and wisdom associated with adulthood. In the puberty school, a girl is placed under the care of an elder woman who serves as a ritual guide, or, in Blacking's terms, as a "fictitious mother," in leading the girl through the initiation and teaching her the laws (*milayo*) of the community (Blacking, 1959). Second, the intermediary initiation school (*tshikanda*) advances the transition into adulthood by further instructing girls in the social hierarchy and historical legacy of Venda tradition. On the last day of the intermediary school, a historical drama is enacted that demonstrates the submission of the early hunters of the region and the division between the ruling class and commoners. As Blacking has suggested, this ritual drama celebrates and reinforces the social interests of the ruling families in Venda society (Blacking, 1969). Third, the premarital school (*domba*) marks the final passage into adulthood by marking a young woman's preparation for marriage. The *domba* includes special rites, dramas, and songs. The "Great Domba Dance" symbolizes the mystical process of sexual union, conception, gestation, and childbirth (Blacking, 1969a; see Nettleton, 1992). The entire process, therefore, marked out a woman's knowledge, position, and power in Venda traditional religion (Blacking, 1964).

The idealized image of religious tradition, stable hierarchy, and social order found in this account of female initiation is certainly in tension with the intense social conflicts that animate accusations of witchcraft and ritual killing. As recent research has shown, these aspects of a traditional symbolism of evil have been mobilized as "political weapons" under conditions of extreme uncertainty and social instability (Mihalik and Cassim, 1993; Minnaar, Offringa, and Payze, 1992).

H1   Beuster, C. L. (1879). "Das Volk der Vavenda." *Zeitschrift für Geschichte Erdkunde [Berlin]*, vol. 14: 236-40.

Beuster's paper represents what is probably the first account of the religion of the Venda-speaking peoples of the northern Transvaal. The author's brief inventory of Venda beliefs and rituals is consequently of considerable importance to historians of comparative religion in southern Africa. That inventory lists Ralowimba as the Venda creator god who, Beuster notes, lived in a sacred grove known as *motsindule*. He also notes that ancestor veneration was the primary article of Venda religion. As such, sacrificial rituals were prominent in religious activities. The paper, which provides a short account of the history, migration, and wars of the Venda, including an account of conflicts with a neighboring polity known as the *Knobneusen* (knob-nosed), also describes rites pertaining to death and burial. Beuster notes, for example, that death was often a consequence of witchcraft. The paper is not annotated.

H2   Beuster, C. L., and Max Bartels (1896). "Die Koma- und Busche-Gebrauche der Bawenda in Nord Transvaal." *Zeitschrift für Ethnologie*, vol. 28: 35-36.

In a very brief description of puberty rites among the Venda of the Blaauuwberg region of the northern Transvaal, Beuster and Bartels comment on the distinctive wooden figurines, called "*matono*," that were used in female *domba* or premarital "initiation" rituals. The paper, which draws on the eye-witness accounts of several informants resident at the Berlin mission station near Molokong, also describes what is perhaps one of the earliest illustrations of the role of the crocodile, or *ngwenya*, in Venda myth and ritual.

H3   Blacking, John (1959). "Fictitious Kinship Amongst Girls of the Venda of the Northern Transvaal." *Man*, vol. 59, no. 243: 155-58.

Blacking's analysis of the emergence of a regime of "fictitious kinship" among school-going Venda girls in the 1950s investigates ostensible connections between kinship rites established in formal schools and the values inscribed at traditional *vhusha* or puberty schools. Drawing on field research and the published accounts of Stayt and Van Warmelo, the writer suggests in the initial section, entitled "Traditional Puberty Schools for Girls," that pubescent girls attending the *vhusha* ceremonies were designated an unrelated, fictitious mother, or "*mme wa u tamba*," by the senior woman president. The "mother's" task, according to Blacking, was to shepherd the "child" through the period of initiation, teaching her the laws of the community or *milayo*. In the second section, entitled "At Modern Primary and Secondary Schools," Blacking describes a similar institution among school-going girls. These girls, he notes, adopted during periods of play an older "mother" who then acted as a guide and matchmaker. Blacking's analysis of kinship continuities present at the school, outlined in the third section of the paper, suggests that these "school kinship games" were not really an extension of traditional features extant in the *vhusha*. Rather, the games were a form of "social craze" brought on by the alienation and social displacement experienced by Venda girls at European-styled schools. Therefore, argues the writer, "the chief factor that distinguished the whole complex of the school from traditional relationships established at the *vhusha*, was the matter of individual choice." The article thus provides an incisive account of how Venda ritual traditions are creatively adapted in changing social contexts. The paper is annotated.

H4   Blacking, John (1961). "The Social Value of Venda Riddles." *African Studies*, vol. 20, no. 1: 1-31.

Blacking analyzes the "social value" of riddles among the Venda of the northern Transvaal. He argues that riddles are important not only as exercises in intellectual skill but also as "assets" that accord fuller privileges in Venda life. The analysis, based on two years of fieldwork between 1956 and 1958, is promoted with the presentation of a pilot project in which the writer records the results of twenty-five participants and their varying abilities in responding to traditional riddles. Based on the results of the project, Blacking asserts that riddles were perhaps "the most significant and powerful" elements of Venda tradition and that "knowledge of words" in Venda society conferred a "magical power." Therefore, knowledge of riddles was not educational, in the sense that it developed powers of logic or reason. Rather, knowledge of riddles was "mechanical," in the sense that it conferred social power. The article is divided into seven sections, beginning with an analysis of the "Proper Occasions for Asking Riddles" and the "Form of the Riddle Contest." In the sections entitled "Knowledge of Riddles a Social Asset," and the "Educational Value of Venda Riddles," Blacking discusses how "great honor" and social acceptance are conferred upon youths proficient at riddles. He also asserts that Venda riddles serve as an introduction to the *milayo*—the formulaic laws—associated with Venda rites of passage. The study concludes with an examination of the meaning of more than three hundred Venda riddles, including a number drawn from the writings of Henri Philippe Junod. These riddles are classified according to Isaac Schapera's taxonomy, and include riddles associated with "Natural Phenomena," the "Animal World," "Clothing and the Human Body," and "European Culture." The compilation and interpretation provides a useful antidote to earlier anthropological and missionary assertions that the Venda were either "primitive" or "superstitious." Instead, by analyzing the edification by puzzlement that is afforded by riddles, this essay opens fruitful avenues for thinking through Venda religion.

H5   Blacking, John (1964). *Black Background: The Childhood of a South African Girl*. New York: Abelard Schuman.

Blacking's account of the early life of a Venda woman provides an anthropological perspective on persons occupying that space "midway between the worlds of the peasant and industrial economies." In his lengthy introduction, the writer describes Venda cultural practices and rituals associated with birth, puberty, marriage, and child-bearing. He outlines family structures and the material and social environment of Venda society and discusses the adaptation of Venda culture in the context of an expanding Western industrial ideal in South Africa. Blacking argues that educated Venda people tried to disassociate themselves from traditional culture in an attempt to adapt to and assimilate Western influences and open educational and economic opportunities. In the autobiography that follows, Dora Thizwilondi Magidi (a pseudonym for the informant-author) describes the rich Venda heritage in which she grew up, demonstrating the ultimate cultural ambivalence into which she emerged in South Africa in the 1950s. The account is a warm personal description of events, rituals, and religious practices, and concludes with Dora passing standard six at the age of seventeen. Included are sixteen pages of photographs. A select bibliography is appended.

H6   Blacking, John (1969a). "Songs, Dances, Mimes, and Symbolism of Venda Girl's Initiation Schools." *African Studies*, vol. 28: 3-35; 69-118; 149-99; and 215-66.

Blacking's detailed record, collected during two years of fieldwork in the Sibasa district of the northern Transvaal from 1958, provides an incisive analysis of *vhusha*, *tshikanda*, and *domba* initiation schools among the Venda. Drawing on the writings of government ethnologist N. J. van Warmelo, the four-part paper begins with an examination of the "social reasons" that encouraged Venda women to attend initiation schools. The writer notes that the *milayo* ("laws" or instructions) taught at the schools informed girls about etiquette and correct standards of social and sexual behavior. In this regard, the schools conferred on the girls the social status of adulthood. A detailed analysis of sixty-one songs performed by the young women during the three stages of *vhusha* is provided. In the second part of the paper, entitled "Milayo," Blacking reviews the procedures whereby Venda women acquired the esoteric knowledge and wisdom associated with the status of adulthood. The meanings of the various actions and symbolic objects employed in these initiation rituals are explained and observations concerning the role of the four initiation masters during *domba* are outlined. In the third part of the article, entitled "Domba," Blacking argues that initiation was essentially a preparation for marriage insofar as it encouraged "institutionalized motherhood" and the continued support of women in tribal economies. The writer classifies the ritual sequence of the *domba* into three basic stages, namely, *dzingoma* (special rites); *matano* (mimes or shows); and *nyimbo dza mitambo* (recreational songs). Detailed descriptions of each stage in the ritual process are provided. In the final part, entitled "The Great Domba Song," Blacking argues that the *domba* "dance" was intended to symbolize the mystical processes of sexual communion, conception, the growth of the fetus, and childbirth. An English translation of the song, comprising 460 lines, is given. The paper, while not overtly comparative, is rich in descriptive detail. Numerous photographic plates provide visual images to support an insightful account of the structure and function of female initiation rituals in Venda traditional religion.

H7   Blacking, John (1969b). "Initiation and the Balance of Power: The Tshikanda Girl's Initiation of the Venda of the Northern Transvaal." In *Ethnological and Linguistic Studies in Honour of N. J. van Warmelo*. Pretoria: Government Printer. 21-38.

In this paper, Blacking again elucidates the sociological significance of the Venda "intermediary initiation schools" called *tshikanda*. Drawing on the empirical findings of the anthropologist Hugh Stayt and government ethnologist N. J. van Warmelo, as well as on his own fieldwork in the Thengwe district of the northern Transvaal in the 1950s and 1960s, the writer argues that the *tshikanda* effectively entrenched the interests of ruling families among the Venda. He notes, for example, that the timing of *tshikanda* during the harvest season ensured that the chief of the ruling family secured cheap labor. The essay begins with an introduction that distinguishes between three initiatory schools—the *vhusha* or puberty school; the *tshikanda* or intermediary initiation school; and the *domba* or premarital school. In Section One, Blacking analyzes how *vhusha* and *domba* schools were "nationalized" by ruling clans who arrived in the northern Transvaal in the nineteenth century, bringing with them a more comprehensive social system. The ensuing appropriation of the rites of the commoner clans, asserts Blacking, thus simultaneously affirmed the cultural interests of the commoners while sustaining the power of the ruling clans. In the central sections, which relate "The Drama of Thovela and Tshishonge" and the "Interpretation of the Story of Thovela and Tshishonge," the writer discusses the political overtones of a drama that was performed on the final day of the *tshikanda*, arguing that the play represented a lesson in political history—a dramatization of the submission of the early hunters of Vendaland and the division between commoner and ruling clans. The essay contains ten plates detailing the drama and dances of *tshikanda* and an appendix of the songs and dances associated with the initiation school.

H8   Blacking, John (1978). "Uses of Kinship Idiom in Friendships at Some Venda and Zulu Schools." In John Argyle and Eleanor Preston-Whyte (eds.) *Social Systems and Traditions in Southern Africa: Essays in Honour of Eileen Krige*. Cape Town: Oxford University Press. 101-17.

Drawing on his knowledge of fictive kinship patterns practiced both at traditional puberty schools and at modern primary and secondary schools in Natal and the northern Transvaal, Blacking describes "mother-child" and "husband-wife" games developed by Zulu and Venda girls in the 1940s and 1950s. He notes that these games, many of which included role-plays invoking a play-mother, or *mme wa u tamba*, and play-child, *inwana wa u tamba*, were used in traditional *domba* (puberty) rites to expand and solidify social relations, "bring girls into a family," and provide a safe, affectionate arena in which to explore responsibilities associated with marriage and sexual relations. The paper, which is not annotated, thus provides resources for a comparative analysis of kinship systems and puberty rituals predominating in Zulu and Venda society.

H9   Blacking, John (1985). "Movement, Dance, Music, and the Venda Girls' Initiation-Cycle." In Paul Spencer (ed.) *Society and the Dance*. Cambridge: Cambridge University Press. 64-91.

In another paper drawing on materials gathered during a two-year period of fieldwork in 1956 and 1957, Blacking analyzes elements of Venda dance. In particular, he examines to what extent dance and music are non-verbal, liberating expressions of collective cultural identity. Following the work of Lévi-Strauss (1963), he concludes that Venda initiation dance is an essentially sensuous and symbolic, or embodied cultural code. Contributing to theoretical readings pertaining to the anthropology of the body, therefore, the essay outlines this basic premise, but is developed by way of analogy to the discursive *mudras* (signals) of Indian Bharata Natya Sastra and the expressive *hsiu* (sleeve gestures) of Chinese classical dance. In the third part of the essay, "Dance and Music in Venda Society," detailed notes on the structure and function of initiation performances among the Venda of the Sibasa district of the northern Transvaal and southern Zimbabwe are provided. Blacking notes that each performance is guided by a manager (*nduna*), musical director (*malagwane*), and choreographer (*maluselo*), and that dances are classified as either *ngoma* (literally "drum," and hence sacred rite), or *mitambo* (game, or play). Principally, the *ngoma* dances included *tshikona*, performed at the installation of rulers, at the commemoration of ancestors, or at the first-fruit sacrifices; *vhusha*, *tshikanda*, and *domba*, the three-part initiation dances performed by girls between puberty and marriage; *sungwi*, a modern initiation school dance organized by ritual specialists; and *ngoma dza midzumu* or possession dances. The *mitambo*, or "play" dances, included female *tshigombela* and both-sex *tshikanganga* reed dances, and *dhzombo*, or *ad hoc* moonlight dances. The format and style of each is described and diagrammatic sketches are included. In the fourth part, "Vhusha, Tshikanda, and Domba," an analysis of the function of female initiation dances is advanced. Blacking suggests that during these dances, pubescent girls "learnt the laws" (*uguda milayo*) of childbirth, marriage, and motherhood. The physical "language" of individual dancers, he asserts, represented the climax of a corporate symbolic rebirth. The essay ends with some brief comments on the future of *domba* dances. In this regard, the writer notes that while participation increased during the nineteenth century, supposedly as a symbolic statement of Venda resistance to colonial rule and missionary intolerance, its sacral appeal diminished with the advent of urbanization. Consequently, the enactment of the *domba* became a barometer, not of political authority or ritual ability, but of economic viability as the performance of the traditional Venda ritual was marketed as a tourist attraction. The paper is briefly annotated and includes a short bibliography.

H10   Blacking, John (1990). "Growing Old Gracefully: Physical, Social, and Spiritual Transformations in Venda Society, 1956-1966." In Paul Spencer (ed.) *Anthropology and the Riddle of the Sphinx: Paradoxes of Change in the Life Course*. London: Routledge. 121-30.

Blacking provides in this paper a comprehensive analysis of the Venda conceptualization of the human life-cycle. In this sense, he focuses on complex patterns of kinship found in Venda society in relation to individual, physical, social, and spiritual development. The article is consequently concerned with aging and the methodological problems of analyzing data years after collection. A discussion of problems related to the aging of the author and the effects of life experience on his anthropological analysis is thus followed by an ethnographic survey of how, among the Venda, physical and spiritual growth are inexorably linked. The data is interpreted chiefly in relation to a set of ideas about life, aging, and death that are invoked both to explain particular actions and events and as part of a general speculation about the coherence of a worldview which many Venda people share.

H11   Blacking, John (1992). "The Body as a Source of Cosmological Exploration and Personal Experimentation in Venda Tradition." In Joan Maw and John Picton (eds.) *Conception of the Body/Self in Africa*. Wien: Veroffentlichungen der Institue fur Afrikanistik und Agyptologie der Universitat Wien. 87-95.

In an examination of the relationship between social construction and private, embodied experience, Blacking draws on the work of Maurice Merleau-Ponty (1962) and Mary Douglas (1973) to analyze how riddles, songs, and proverbs functioned in Venda initiation schools to relate parts of the body to natural and cultural experience. In this regard, he notes how initiation rites, dances of spirit possession, and the *milayo* (laws, instruction, or wisdom) of the Venda deployed the body in techniques of alteration and change that equated parts of the body with features of the home and countryside. Thus, the vagina was a "path," the fetus a "drum," and semen the "ashes of a fire." Several pairs of relationships predominant in Venda proverbs and rites of passage prevalent in the *vhusha* and *tshikanda* initiation dances and songs are included in the analysis, among them the metaphorical relationship between a girls' breasts and ostrich eggs; pubic hair and cut grass; a pregnant woman and a closed doorway; and a young boys' penis and the hinge-pin of a door. In these terms, suggests Blacking, the conceptualization of the body in Venda proverbs and riddles functioned as an aid to self-discovery and identity. In conclusion, the writer notes that the creative use of the body in Christian mythology ironically made that religion an attractive alternative to traditional religionists insofar as it provided a safe outlet for resistance to racist classifications of the Venda body as barbaric. The paper is not annotated but a short bibliography is included.

H12   Bullock, Charles (1926). "Notes on the BaVenda." *Southern Rhodesian Native Affairs Department Annual*, vol. 4: 62-66.

In a short note on the religious rites of the Venda-speaking peoples residing in the southwestern districts of Rhodesia, Native Commissioner Charles Bullock provides an incisive account of Venda circumcision rituals. He argues that these rituals acted as initiatory acts that helped participants relinquish a "care-free" and innocent boyhood in order to effect a "rebirth" into adulthood. The procedure of the rite is sketched by the author, beginning with the *mashuwuru* (uninitiated) being dragged before the fire of the elders. Detailed notes on the initiates' circumcision and subsequent instruction in circumcision lodges are provided. Subsequent renaming rituals and the procedures associated with the acquisition of new forms of clothing are described. The narrative nonetheless betrays the writer's bias insofar as he views Venda rites as "barbaric."

H13   Dicke, B. H. (1926). "The BaVenda Sacred Object." *South African Journal of Science*, vol. 26: 935-36.

Drawing attention to the frequency with which phallic-shaped, hollow copper ingots have appeared in the region of Messina, Dicke examines the possibility that Venda-speaking people in the far northern Transvaal produced them as sacred objects for religious or sacrificial purposes. He cites as the sole evidence of this possibility the now extinct Venda practice of keeping similarly-shaped insect-eating plants as sacred objects. The paper is illustrated.

H14   Du Plessis, H. (1945). "Die Territoriale Organisasie van die Venda." *African Studies*, vol. 4: 122-27.

In a brief examination of the political organization and social structure of Venda societies, Du Plessis describes mechanisms used to configure, inaugurate, and administer several regional polities, among them districts (*mivhundu*) and sub-districts (*zwisi*). Illustrations of the gendered spatial organization of Venda *mudi*, the smallest political units of administration, are included. In this regard, Du Plessis draws attention to the distinction in Venda society between married women's huts (*tshitanga*) and married men's quarters (*nndu*). The paper, which draws largely on Stayt's foundational (1931) description of Venda society, contains several annotations reflecting the author's indebtedness to informants in the Soutspansberg region of the northern Transvaal.

H15   Eberhardt, Jacqueline (1955). "Quelques aspects du marriage chez les Venda." *Journal de la Société Africainistes*, vol. 25: 77-88.

In this paper, anthropologist Jacqueline Eberhardt analyzes social structure and patterns of descent among Venda-speakers in the northern Transvaal. In particular, her paper examines apparently contradictory accounts of the place of the *malume* (mother's brother) and *makhulu* (maternal or paternal grandparent) in Venda and Tsonga society as reflected in the writings of Van Warmelo (1931), Stayt (1931), and Junod (1927). The paper, in French, is briefly annotated.

H16   Eberhardt, Jacqueline (1958). "The Mythical Python Among the Venda and Fulani: A Comparative Note." *Archiv für Volkekunde*, vol. 13: 15-24.

In a comparative analysis of ophidian symbolism among the Venda of the northern Transvaal and the Fulani of Sudan, Eberhardt examines information gathered from Venda-speaking informants in the Soutspansberg region during the years 1951 to 1958. However, the writer also revisits the works of Stayt and Van Warmelo to evaluate the validity of ethnographic surveys describing the position of snakes, and pythons in particular, in the myths, rituals, and taboos of these peoples. By way of contrast to Stayt and Van Warmelo, Eberhardt notes, for example, that the python played a prominent role in female fertility or *domba* rites among the Venda. Indeed, the *domba* dance was called the *"Tharu ya Mabidhigami"* or "Uncoiling Python Dance." In this regard, the python's association with female fertility is highlighted, an association that was reinforced, suggests the writer, insofar as the python's skin was important to subsequent *tshikanda* rites. The skin was in fact worn around a sterile woman's loins in order to encourage fecundity. Several myths invoking the python are retold and symbolic associations discussed. Eberhardt notes that the python was often to be found in myths of origin and in symbols that were associated with "coolness." The paper, which concludes with a brief overview of similarities between Venda and Fulani religion, is briefly annotated.

H17   Frobenius, Leo (1938). "Die Waremba, Träger einer fossilen Kultur." *Zeitschrift für Ethnologie*, vol. 70, no. 3/5: 159-75.

Originally appearing in 1929, Frobenius' paper on the "judische" (Jewish) Lemba of the northern Transvaal region of Messina provides the reader of comparative religion in southern Africa with a wealth of information regarding the beliefs and practices of these Venda-speaking peoples. The paper is divided into seven sections. In the first two sections, the writer provides information relating to the early history of the Lemba in the region north of the Limpopo River. Notes on migration patterns are also included. In section three, *"Korper und Geist,"* aspects indicative of a presumed "Semitic" psychological make-up are enumerated. The logic of the writer's assertions in this regard is extended in the following section, which outlines several dietary prohibitions distinctive of the Lemba and thought to be indicative of their "Jewish" origins. Notes on ritual prescriptions for the slaughter of animals are included. Sections five and six describe Lemba beliefs and rituals pertaining to marriage and sexuality. Taboos reflecting prohibitions on premarital pregnancy, adultery, and marriage between aliens are described. Detailed notes on male initiation and circumcision are also included. The last section contains notes on burial practices and beliefs related to a form of "phallic" worship associated with a sacred object known as the *muschuku*. This illustrated paper, in German, contains no bibliography.

H18   Gottschling, E. (1905). "The Bawenda: A Sketch of their History and Customs." *Report of the South African Association for the Advancement of Science*, vol. 3: 195-221; 365-72.

In this report before the Association, the German missionary E. Gottschling provides a descriptive overview and cursory analysis of the history and customs of the Venda. Drawing on the foundational research of fellow missionaries and anthropologists, the writer posits that the Venda, situated between the Limpopo and Levuvu rivers of the northeastern Transvaal, originated in the Great Lake regions of Eastern-Central Africa. He considers the "heathen" descendants of these peoples to have acceded to a "long succession of fear and superstition." Haunted by their "gods and the ghosts of their ancestors," the Venda were influenced by "all manner of hobgoblins." Remarkable, perhaps, for its European evolutionary bias, the paper is divided into fourteen short sketches, the first of which provides a brief historical outline. In that outline, Gottschling traces the eighteenth-century migrations of the Venda and their great King, Thoho ea Ndou (Elephant Head). Thereafter, the writer recounts numerous internecine wars among the Venda and the powerful Zulu polities they encountered while fleeing the Ndebele of Mzilikazi. In the following chapters, entitled "Venda Personality and Character," and "Venda Habits of Life," Gottschling describes purported physical and psychological characteristics presumed to be indicative of the Venda. Facts concerning eating, sleeping, and clothing are enumerated, as are the writer's observation of rites of passage associated with puberty, marriage, and death. A brief delineation of the structures of national life, including an overview of "tribal constitution and administration," is followed by an account of the religious customs of the Venda. In that account, Gottschling identifies Kosana as the Venda creator god; Ralowimba as the rewarder of good and punisher of evil; and Thovela as a Venda mediator between these gods and the realm of humanity. Nine categories of "witch-doctor" are also described before a brief sketch of the "cult" of ancestors is outlined. The paper concludes with a cursory glance at Venda "proverbs" and, interestingly, a discussion of Venda attitudes to German missionary activity. A statistical resume of the "results" of mission work in the Transvaal is provided.

H19   Huffman, Thomas N., and Eswino O. M. Hanisch (1987). "Settlement Hierarchies in the Northern Transvaal: The Zimbabwe Ruins and Venda History." *Bantu Studies*, vol. 46: 79-116.

Alert to widespread historical relations between the Venda and Shona, archaeologists Huffman and Hanisch examine in this paper connections between Venda settlement patterns and the formation of the Zimbabwe ruins. In this regard, their paper recalls aspects of Venda history and migration, particularly consequent on the dissolution of Singo consolidation during the reign of Thoho ea Ndou and the foundation of the Venda paramount's capital at Dzala in the northern Transvaal. They argue that the history of Venda migration supports an early etiology in the region of the ruins. Moreover, the Venda term for their place of origin, Vhukalanga, translates as Zimbabwe. The paper, which is essentially of interest to archaeologists, contains only brief notes on Venda religion.

H20   Jaques, A. A. (1931). "Notes on the Lemba of the Transvaal." *Anthropos*, vol. 26: 245-51.

In this brief paper, the missionary-ethnographer A. A. Jaques draws attention and provides additions to Junod's earlier (1908) account of the historical origins and religious practices of the Lemba of the Soutspansberg, Pietersburg, and Potgietersrus regions of the northern Transvaal. He notes that although the Lemba "succeeded in preserving their tribal individuality in the past," they rapidly lost the original character of their language and religion. The paper is divided into several short sections delineated under the headings "Physical Characteristics," "Clothing," "Beliefs and Customs," "Crafts and Industries," and "Religion and Religious Ceremonies." In the section on physique, the writer notes that the Lemba had "typically Jewish noses." Brief notes on dietary regulations relating to *sindza* or *sindja* (slaughter) rituals and "oriental" or "rabbinic" taboos associated with the left hand are also included, as are analyses of marriage rites and prohibitions, burial techniques, and lunar observances. In the section on religion and religious beliefs, however, the writer contests Junod's assertion that the Lemba were once Muslims. A strong predilection for "ancestrology" precluded such an assertion. The authors notes on orthography suggest, however, that the Lemba could once have been influenced by Arabic or Hebrew languages and that, by extension, these southern African Bantu peoples could be traced to some form of Semitic origin. The paper is not annotated.

H21   Junod, Henri-Alexandre (1908). "The Balemba of the Zoutspansberg (Transvaal)." *Folk Lore*, vol. 19: 276-87.

In this foundational paper, the French missionary-ethnographer Henri-Alexandre Junod examines aspects of the history and religious practice of the Venda-speaking Lemba of the northeastern Transvaal. Of primary interest to historians of comparative religion in southern Africa for its writer's diffusionist proposal—that the Lemba were originally in contact with Muslims or Jews in North Africa—the paper begins with a brief overview of Lemba migration. Notes on ceramic production and metallurgy are provided in support of an immigrant thesis. Following several examples of Lemba medicinal practices in the middle-part of the paper, the writer pursues the diffusionist theory of Lemba etiology to argue that dietary prohibitions, including abstinence from pork, as well as several prescriptions and procedures required for the ritual slaughter of animals, were model examples of earlier Muslim or Jewish contact. Initiation rites, the practice of shaving during particular lunar transitions, and, especially, methods of circumcision are cited to reinforce that argument. Indeed, Junod asserts that the Lemba were the first South African "tribe" to practice male circumcision and that they subsequently introduced this practice to the Venda and several Nguni African communities in the region. The oral testimony of a Venda initiate called Makhata is cited to endorse this assertion. The paper concludes with a comparison between Venda and Lemba initiation rites.

H22   Junod, Henri-Alexandre (1920). "Some Features of the Religion of the BaVenda." *South African Association for the Advancement of Science*, vol. 17: 207-20.

Junod's account of the most salient features of Venda religion is based on evidence gathered by the writer from informants living in the Soutspansberg region of the northern Transvaal. In an interpretation of responses to a questionnaire disseminated among these respondents, the writer distinguishes between two forms of Venda religion: namely, a "vague monotheistic" cult concerning the worship of a creator God, called Raluvimbi, and an "ancestor worship" cult incorporating numerous rituals applicable to overcoming misfortune. The writer further claims that Venda religion contains elements of "totemism," citing as evidence a number of Venda taboos associated with the killing of animals, among them "totem animals." The paper comprises three sections. In the first,

Junod distinguishes some of the primary characteristics of the creator God Raluvimbi. He recounts several myths relating to the deity, notably the story of Raluvimbi's power as a rainmaker. In the second section, the writer proceeds to review several rituals related to overcoming agricultural misfortune, including the rituals of grain and animal sacrifice and a distinctive Venda rite that Junod identifies as "the possession of the assegai." Junod concludes his outline of Venda religion with an examination of the totemic character of Venda ritual and belief.

H23   Lestrade, G. P. (1927). "Some Notes on the Ethnic History of the BaVenda and their Rhodesian Affinities." *South African Journal of Science*, vol. 24: 486-95.

In a brief paper read before the South African Association for the Advancement of Science, government ethnologist G. P. Lestrade reviews various theories concerning the origin of the Venda "tribe." Drawing on the oral testimony of the Native Commissioner for Spelonken, E. T. Stubbs, and employing the logic of assertions made earlier by German missionary-anthropologists working in the region, among them E. Gottschling, Lestrade suggests that the Venda originated from the Great Lakes region of Eastern-Central Africa. From that region, he argues, the ancestral Venda migrated through the Karanga region, north of the Limpopo River, and thereafter "wandered" southward to their present position in the northeastern Transvaal. The review begins with a detailed account of oral traditions regarding Venda migration. Thereafter a critique of German missionary arguments for Congolese etiology is conducted. The "logic" of Lestrade's own thesis is then outlined. The study is valuable, perhaps, insofar as it attempts to synthesize primary empirical data, oral history, and popular nineteenth-century diffusionist theories regarding the origin of South African religions and peoples.

H24   Lestrade, G. P. (1930a). "The Political Organization of the Venda-Speaking Tribes." *Africa: Journal of the International Institute of African Languages and Culture*, vol. 3: 306-22. Reprint in N. J. van Warmelo (ed.) *Contributions to Venda History, Religion, and Tribal Rituals*. Ethnological Publications, nol. 3. Pretoria: Government Printer, 1932. i-xxviii.

In this paper, government ethnologist G. P. Lestrade provides an analysis of the political organization of the Venda-speaking peoples of the northeastern Transvaal. His argument, based on information obtained from members of the Mphaphuli and Madzivhandila "tribes," suggests that there are three levels of political organization extant among these peoples: namely, the household (*mudi*) or extended household (*midi*); the district (*kavhelo*), comprising a number of households; and the tribe (*lushaka*), made up of a number of districts under the political authority of the chief (*khosi*). In these terms, suggests Lestrade, the Venda are not unlike other southern African "tribes." However, two basic characteristics are cited to distinguish the Venda from the Sotho-Tswana and other African groups. First, the Venda recognize in the chief the purveyor of "absolute authority." For example, the chief acts not only as a political leader but also as a "high priest" in order to protect the village against evil and to ensure the invincibility of his soldiers before battle. Second, in contrast to the Sotho-Tswana, Venda women hold a relatively advanced position in sociopolitical structures. For example, women in Venda society may succeed to the role of "headman" (*mukoma*) of the household or "headman" (*nduna)* of the village or district. The paper is annotated.

H25   Lestrade, G. P. (1930b). "The Mala System of the Venda Speaking Tribes." *Bantu Studies*, vol. 4: 193-204.

In a largely descriptive account of *mala* customary law and practice among Venda-speaking peoples in the northeastern Transvaal, government ethnologist G. P. Lestrade highlights "distinctive features" of this "system" of bridewealth. He argues, therefore, that a number of differences are prominent when Sotho *bogadi* rites, Zulu, Xhosa, and Tsonga *lobola* rituals, and Venda *mala* ceremonies are compared. The paper begins, however, with a consideration of the selection processes associated with Venda *mala* rituals before recounting details concerning the announcement of bride-prices (*thakha*). A comprehensive document of legal practices necessitated by the betrayal of marriage contracts is also included. The writer notes that male impotence, female infertility, or ill-treatment of either partner may constitute grounds for withholding *thakha*. However, little evidence to support the writer's claim concerning the distinctiveness of these peculiarly Venda rites is suggested. Rather, the paper serves to reinforce Lestrade's appeal that ethnologists should insist on distinguishing between discrete ethnic or "tribal" constituencies among the peoples of southern Africa.

H26   Lestrade, G. P. (1947). "Some Venda Folk Tales." *Communications from the School of African Studies* (n.s.), vol. 6: 16-35.

Lestrade's translation of seventeen Venda folktales from the northeastern Transvaal draws on work by N. J. van Warmelo and the Venda-speaking mission-school teacher W. M. D. Pophi. The topics of the tales are extremely diverse, ranging from "The Man Who Died for his Wife" to "The Veranda-Pole which Changed and Became a Woman." Technical notes concerned with lexicography are appended.

H27   Liesegang, Gerhard (1977). "New Light on Venda Traditions: Mahu-mane's Account of 1730." *History in Africa: A Journal of Method*, vol. 4: 163-81.

Citing the written testimony of several Dutch travelers who had visited the region of Delgoa Bay, and drawing on the oral testimony of the Venda-speaking historian who was known as Mahumane, Liesegang reexamines aspects of eighteenth-century Venda history in Mozambique and in the northern Transvaal region between the Limpopo and the Ngwenya (Crocodile) rivers. The paper is divided into four sections. In the first section, "The Venda and their Historical Traditions," the writer cites several German missionaries in the Louis Trichart region, among them Wilhelm Grundler (1897), to argue that the Venda did not have a unified kingdom in the late nineteenth century. In the second section, "The Dutch at Delgoa Bay," the writer outlines the scope of Dutch knowledge of the peoples of this region. Thereafter, in the section entitled "The Report of Mahumane," extracts of the written testimony from a Venda-speaking subject of Chief Mpfumo is extracted from colonial papers housed in the Cape Town Archives Library (C442, *Inkomende Brieven, 1729-1730*). In several extracts, comments relating to witchcraft and to the production of gold among the Venda and Lemba are included. The paper is annotated and a bibliography is appended.

H28   Loubser, Jannie H. N. (1989). "Archaeology and Early Venda History." In J. Deacon (ed.) *South African Archaeological Society Goodwin Series*, vol. 6: 54-61.

In an evaluation of competing and contradictory hypotheses relating to the prehistoric origins of the Venda-speaking people in the northern Transvaal, archaeologist Jannie Loubser examines the settlement patterns and ceramic evidence that can be used in support of what several scholars have called the "local origination" thesis. In this regard, the author refutes claims that the Venda of the Soutspansberg region originated in prehistoric central Africa. Rather, he argues that an independent Venda identity developed in the region in the sixteenth century subsequent to the merging of Shona and Sotho-speaking communities. Evidence for the relatively recent development of that identity, he proposes, is to be found not only in material testament, but also in linguistic structure (Gottschling, 1905; Van Warmelo, 1956) and vocabulary (Lestrade, 1932); in oral history and traditions (Schapera, 1952); and in the practices of religious custom and ritual (Beuster, 1879; Blacking 1969). Primarily, however, the paper examines archaeological evidence for the development and subsequent fragmentation of the Singo state and the emergence of the Venda as a discrete ethnic identity in South Africa. The paper is annotated and a short bibliography is included.

H29   Loubser, Jannie H. N. (1990). "Oral Traditions, Archaeology, and the History of the Venda Mitupo." *African Studies*, vol. 49. 2: 13-42.

In an attempt to determine whether extant traditions concerning the supposed homogeneity or political concord of Venda ethnicity can be supported, Loubser examines Venda *mitupo* (totemic group) traditions in the context of myths of origin, language, custom, and ritual. He concludes that whereas Venda rulers and "traditionalists," among them E. Mudau (1940), M. F. Mamadi (1940), and V. N. Ralushai (1977), have been correct about the dating of settlement in the Soutspansberg region of the northern Transvaal, a closer examination of changing burial practices reveals inaccuracies regarding Venda origins, the development of the Venda language, and the achievements of predecessors. The paper, which focuses primarily on material relating to the archaeology and history of the dominant Singo *mitupo*, contains an extensive bibliography.

H30   Macdonald, David (1933). "Vendaland." *The Blythswood Review—A South African Journal of Religious, Social and Educational Work*, vol. 10, no. 110: 12-13; no. 111: 28; no. 112: 28-29.

Macdonald's collection of articles on the Venda of the northern Transvaal comprises three brief sketches that provide passing details concerning Venda custom, religious belief, and ritual. However, the sketches are of interest to historians of comparative religion in southern Africa primarily insofar as they reflect an analytical bias consistent with nineteenth-century comparative analysis rather than for any ethnographic validity they review. In this regard, the work betrays an overtly Christian imperative: Macdonald, a priest in the region who was "familiar with the physical and moral characteristics" of the Venda, views traditional practices associated with Venda ancestor veneration to be exemplary of a "combination of animism and totemism." The three articles are divided into twelve chapters, the first of which provides details concerning the topography of the northern Transvaal region and the physical characteristics of its inhabitants. In the last article, which asks whether the Venda have any idea of God, the writer suggests that while this might be the case Venda perceptions of the divine are principally "superstitious" and "primitive." The benefits of British rule, Macdonald concludes, could help in reversing these primitive superstitions.

H31   Mihalik, Janos, and Yusuf Cassim (1993). "Ritual Murder and Witchcraft: A Political Weapon?" *South African Law Journal*, vol. 110, no. 1: 127-40.

Citing several newspaper accounts and government commissions, legal academics Mihalik and Cassim examine to what extent ritual killings in the "independent homeland" of Venda were a response to changing political structures and expressive of popular resistance to bantustan policy. At the nexus of legal history, witchcraft studies, and ritual theory, the paper thus serves to examine the reasons for human sacrifice, or murder, predominating in times of social disharmony and political disorder. The paper begins with a brief account of the emergence of Venda as a South African bantustan in the 1950s and traces events that led to the occurrence of a *coup d'etat* in the region in 1988. The findings of the Le Roux Commission of Inquiry into causes of "unrest" and increased "ritual murders" in Venda during 1988 and 1989 are tabulated. While several examples of witch killings and human sacrifice for bodily parts, or "*muti*," are documented, the paper does not essentially offer any analytical reading of the evidence. Rather, the authors seek to draw attention to legal problems related to the adjudication of cases concerning ritual sacrifice in southern Africa. In this regard, it forms a useful adjunct to Ralushai's recently published *Interim Report of the Commission of Inquiry into Witchcraft Violence and Ritual Murder in the Northern Province* (1996). The paper is briefly annotated.

H32   Minnaar, A. de V., D. Offringa, and C. Payze (1992). *To Live in Fear: Witchburning and Medicine Murder in Venda*. Pretoria: Human Sciences Research Council.

Against the backdrop of widespread witch killings in Venda in the late 1980s, Minnaar, Offringa, and Payze examine beliefs and customs that may have contributed to an increase in incidents of human sacrifice, or ritual murder, in the region. The book begins, in Chapter One, with a short history of the origins of the Venda in Zimbabwe, Mozambique, and the Soutspansberg area of the northern Transvaal. That history draws on the published writings of Huffman and Hanisch, Lestrade, and Van Warmelo. Included are brief notes from the travel diaries of Coenrad Buys and Joao Albasini, who were two of the first European travelers to meet the Venda in the early nineteenth century. Allusions are also made to the works of Berlin missionaries who arrived in the region in the 1870s. In Chapter Two, "Traditional Beliefs and Customs," the writers cite Van Rooy (1978) to describe the Venda worldview, which they suggest reflects ritual practices based on ancestral veneration and beliefs in a "limited cosmic good." Notes on the role of the *nyanga* (healer), *mungone* (diviner), and *muloi* (witch or sorcerer) are included, and aspects associated with social and political structure, patterns of descent, and judicial procedures applicable to property transference are addressed. Proceeding to provide an overview of South African laws prohibiting witchcraft, in particular the Witchcraft Suppression Act no. 3 of 1957, the authors in Chapter Three, "Witchcraft and Supernatural Belief," define the meaning of witchcraft and "ritual murder." They assert that ritual murder can be interpreted as the "killing of innocent victims in order to obtain certain body parts," which are called in Venda *mushonga* or "medicine." The following chapters, "The Burning of Witches" and "Witchcraft and Politics," provide a summary of information obtained from more than twenty informants, as well as from several legal cases, to arrive at a general explanation for the occurrence of more than one hundred and sixty cases of accusations of witchcraft or witch killings in Venda during the period between 1989 and 1991. The authors assert that jealousy, economic deprivation, and political instability were all contributing causes. The book is thoroughly annotated and includes several appendices, notably a copy of the Witchcraft Suppression Act, a list of informants, and a bibliography that contains references to numerous newspaper articles.

H33　Mphelo, Manassah N. (1936). "The Balemba of the Northern Transvaal." *Native Teachers Journal*, vol. 16, no. 1: 35-44.

Manassah Mphelo, a Venda-speaking Lemba and lecturer at Adams College, provides in this paper a comprehensive overview of the historical origins, beliefs, customs, religious practices, and social structure of the Lemba of the northern Transvaal. His paper is divided into ten sections, the first of which draws on Junod's (1908) account of a Lemba myth of origin to suggest that the Bakhalaka, or Lemba, originated in Zimbabwe. Indeed, the terms by which the Lemba are known, among them the Munyani or Mukhalaka, refer to that geographic province. The second section follows with notes describing the language of these "wandering Jews." Mphelo suggests that many of the distinctive features of Lemba language have been lost and that most Lemba now speak Venda. Subsequent to his notes on physical characteristics and clothing in sections three and four—in which he cites Jaques' (1931) comments that the Lemba presented "typically Jewish features"—the writer provides brief notes on the structure of the Lemba family and clan. The sixth section, "Education," follows. Here, Mphelo describes in detail the distinctively "Semitic" features of Lemba puberty rites and circumcision rituals. Notes on the totemic nature of worship and the educational function of myth are included. It is in the sections on "Belief and Custom" and "Religion and Religious Ceremonies" that the writer specifically addresses aspects of ritual and belief. Of particular interest to historians of religion are the writer's comments on the distinctive dietary prohibitions present among the Lemba. He notes that animals were never eaten unless they were *shidya*, a term, he suggests, that is equivalent to *kosher*. Indeed, Mphelo suggests that because the Lemba refused to eat pork flesh, adhered to exogamous patterns of marriage, and shaved their hair at the new moon, research into whether the Lemba were once in contact with the Muslims of North Africa, or in fact, "whether all the Bantu people came from Asia," might be fruitful. In the section on religious ceremonies, however, several distinctively African features of Lemba religion are enumerated. These aspects of African religion include, suggests Mphelo, belief in a supreme being, Mudzimu, and ancestral prayers, known as *malombo*. The paper concludes with the writer's plea that the Lemba be given land in order to sustain their characteristic customs and religious way of life. In this appeal, the author attempts to promote an independent ethnic identity, supported by a traditional religion, that might secure greater socioeconomic and political power for the Lemba in southern Africa.

H34   Nettleton, Anitra (1989). "The Crocodile Does not Leave the Pool: Venda Court Art." In A. Nettleton and D. Hammond-Tooke (eds.) *African Art in Southern Africa: From Tradition to Township*. Johannesburg: A. D. Donker. 67-81.

In an analysis of the role of religious symbolism in Venda art and ritual, Nettleton examines aspects of the "visual language" of royal court objects among the Venda of the Soutspansberg region of the northern Transvaal. In particular, she examines how the symbols of the python (*mabidhigami*) and crocodile (*ngwenya*) were deployed in various rituals and associated with several myths of fertility, kingship, divination, and healing. Consequently, brief notes on the use of wood carvings in female *domba* and male *thondo* initiation rituals, ancestral sacrificial practices performed by the king's sister-in-law (*makhazi*), and chiefly installation and burial rites are included. Notably, the writer describes aspects associated with the production of wooden *matono* figurines and drums used in the *domba* ritual. Ophidian symbolism is then discussed. In this regard, Nettleton views the python as a central symbol in Venda art insofar as it predominates in myths and rituals of fertility, ancestral mediation and divination, and healing. Likewise, artistic forms associated with the crocodile are described. Extensive comments on the relationship between the crocodile and the suitability of the chief are included. The writer notes, for example, that at the installation of a new ruler, small pebbles believed to have originated in the stomach of a sacred crocodile were consumed by the designate. Moreover, sacrifices to a sacred crocodile at Tshidadwane were viewed by some Venda-speakers, she asserts, to be essential to the well-being of the state. The paper, which is illustrated, contains a short bibliography.

H35   Nettleton, Anitra (1992). "Ethnic and Gender Identities in Venda Domba Statues." *African Studies*, vol. 51. no. 2: 203-30.

Nettleton argues that sculptures are used as didactic tools in female initiation rites among the Venda of the northern Transvaal. Beginning with the puberty rites of the *vhusha* ceremony, and culminating in the premarital *domba* schools, she asserts, clay and wood figurines are deployed to reinforce sayings, laws, or customs (called *milayo*) that are consistent with traditional codes of conduct or Venda cosmology. Consequently, the statues reflect and rearticulate the proper position or status of women in Venda society and have served to contribute to the maintenance of an exclusive Venda identity. The paper begins with a brief analysis of the position and identity of the Venda as an independent ethnic group in southern Africa. Nettleton notes that several linguistic and cultural characteristics have been identified in order to separate the Venda from Shona-speakers to the north, North Sotho-speakers to the west and south, and Tsonga-speakers to the east of the Soutspansberg region where they are predominant. Citing among others Weelwright (1905) and Harries (1989), she notes that eighteenth-century internecine warfare, German missionaries, Boer republics, and more recently apartheid ideologues all contributed to the preservation of this identity. The analysis subsequently turns to a comparative analysis of the structure and function of puberty rites among the North Sotho and Venda. Brief notes on North Sotho male initiation (*bodika* and *bogwera*) and female puberty (*bojale*, or *byale*) rites are included. Thereafter, a detailed description of the preliminary *vhusha* and subsequent, premarital *tshikanda* and *domba* rites is provided. The writer relies primarily on Gottschling's (1905) report and the subsequent writings of anthropologist and ethnomusicologist John Blacking (1969a; 1969b). Information obtained from interviews with several Venda-speaking informants is also included. The description then shifts towards an analysis of social structure and the general position of Venda women in an essentially patrilineal and patriarchal society. The writer mentions, however, that women assumed important ritual roles: Women conducted ancestral sacrifices and women rainmakers were known to have held positions of political power in the towns of Piphidi and Mianzwi. The author's wide-ranging and incisive account, containing several photographic plates, notes, and a bibliography thus analyzes the most salient features of *domba* and, while focusing on the use of figurines in initiation rites, serves as an instructive introduction to the place of religion in Venda society.

H36   Schloemann, Fr. (1894). "Die Malepa in Transvaal." *Zeitschrift für Ethnologie*, vol. 26: 64-70.

Drawing on his experiences as a missionary on the Molokong mission station in the Blaauuwberg region of the northern Transvaal, Schloemann provides in this paper brief notes on the beliefs and practices of the Venda-speaking Lemba. Following an overview of the early history and migration of the Lemba from north of the Limpopo River, the writer describes several practices associated with initiation and puberty rites for girls and boys. Particularly, he notes that both men and women were "circumcised" at puberty—a practice, he proposes, that was adopted from the North Sotho. These apparently "Semitic" rites, he suggests, were later mediated by Muslim influence. Indeed, Lemba beliefs associated with lunar rites, in particular the Lemba practice of shaving the hair upon sighting of the new moon, he notes, were indicative of a possible Muslim influence. The paper, which is not annotated, concludes with a brief account of the "barbarous" practice of "twin killings" allegedly performed by Lemba and other African communities.

H37   Schutte, A. G. (1978). "Mwali in Venda: Some Observations on the Significance of the High God in Venda History." *Journal of Religion in Africa*, vol. 9: 109-22.

Inspired by Ranger's (1967) research on the cult of Mwari among the Shona in Zimbabwe, Schutte examines in this paper aspects of myth and ritual connecting this fertility deity with the Venda rain deity Mwali. In this regard, his paper explores the evidence of oral testimony to suggest that the Zimbabwean Shona and northern Transvaal Venda and Lemba were in some way historically connected. Particularly, the paper draws attention to the so-called *ngoma-lungundu* myth—a Venda myth of origin containing elements that some interpreters have viewed as distinctively Semitic in origin. Thus, the Venda drum that plays a significant role in the narrative is viewed by interpreters as a sort of Israelite "ark of the covenant." Following his review of oral testimony, the writer proceeds to examine in the next section ethnographic evidence, predominantly in Stayt's (1931) account of the Venda, but also in the archival materials of several Native Commissioners in the Transvaal in the 1890s, to suggest that Mwali should be identified with the Venda creator deity Raluvimbi. Information supplied by several Venda informants confirms this association, Schutte suggests. Indeed, according to the author, while Mwali was undeniably an ancestor-king among the Shona, his position as an agricultural or rain deity among the Venda is difficult to dispute in the face of a widespread belief that the deity had visited the Venda in the 1920s during periods of harvest. The paper is briefly annotated.

H38   Stayt, Hugh A. (1931a). *The Bavenda*. London: Oxford University Press.

Stayt's foundational but largely descriptive monograph of Venda society is based on research that was conducted by two "fully initiated" translators who worked for the anthropologist among the Venda of the northeastern Transvaal and southern Rhodesia for three years in the 1920s. Drawing on their findings and on the published accounts of several German and Swiss missionary-anthropologists, among them Beuster, Gottschling, Junod, and Wessman, the study systematically documents almost all aspects of Venda personal, social, and religious life. Undertaking this comprehensive anthropological study, Stayt composed twenty-five chapters that cover issues related to Venda history, agriculture and settlement patterns, food, industry, psychological development, religious beliefs and rituals, social structure, folklore, music, and culture. In the chapter that is devoted to religion, Stayt provides a detailed overview of Venda mythology that includes an account of Raluvhimba, the high god; Mwali, the rainmaker; and important figures in the spirit world, among them the ancestors or *medzinu*. Aside from an assertion that these figures developed from animistic origins and were related to sacred places, little analysis is provided. However, in the chapter on medicine and magic, which describes the role of the *nyanga* (medicine healer) and *sangoma* (diviner), Stayt shows the connections between religious belief, ritual, and health in Venda society. Photographs and illustrations accompany the text and two appendices and a brief bibliography are included.

H39   Stayt, Hugh A. (1931b). "Notes on the Balemba." *Journal of the Royal Anthropological Institute*, vol. 61: 231-38.

Supporting the findings of several earlier reports, among them those of the Berlin missionary Schloemann (1894) and the Swiss missionary-ethnographer Henri-Alexandre Junod (1908), Stayt draws attention to the possible Semitic or Muslim features of Lemba religion predominant in the northern Transvaal. He notes, for example, that the people known by the names Lemba, Mwenya, Remba, Malepa, or Bahere were called by the Boer farmers of the region "*Slamsche*" (Muslim) Africans. In an attempt to legitimate claims that the Lemba represent a distinctive religious and cultural identity, however, the writer enumerates aspects of their supposedly "Armenoid" appearance. Historical events and aspects associated with social organization are recounted. Stayt notes that although endogamous Lemba society was not composed of "totemic sibs," the elephant, or *ndou* was generally considered the totem of the group. Following an account of social structure and kinship, however, detailed notes on new moon rituals redolent of Muslim rites are enumerated. So too are Lemba practices associated with "Semitic" circumcision rituals. Stayt tentatively argues that the Lemba were the first southern African "tribe" to introduce the rite in the region. Mortuary rituals and procedures for burial are similarly ascribed to a Semitic origin. Likewise, prohibitions on certain foodstuffs, particularly pork, and prayers ending with the pronouncement "Amen" are attributable to earlier Muslim contacts. In these terms, Stayt asserts that there can be "little doubt that the BaLemba are the descendants of some of the early Muhammedan [sic] traders who settled between the twelfth and the sixteenth century." The dominant Lemba family known as the Hadzi, he argues, is further evidence of an earlier Muslim origin, since the word *hadzi* is supposedly cognate with the Arabic term *hadji*. The paper is briefly annotated and illustrated with several photographic plates.

H40   Thompson, Louis C. (1942). "The Balemba of Southern Rhodesia." *Southern Rhodesian Native Affairs Department Annual*, vol. 19: 76-86.

In a brief description of the geographical location, historical origins, and allegedly "degenerate" religious beliefs and rituals of the Lemba of the northern Transvaal and southern Rhodesia, Thompson highlights features presumed to be distinctive of Semitic or Arabic origin. Notably, the writer recalls that the Lemba, like the "*Slaamzyn* (Muslim)" Africans or Falashas, the "Black Jews of Abyssinia," believed the year to have started only after a new moon had been observed. Similarly, the Lemba "priesthood" was an hereditary class of persons, signaling, the writer asserts, the superior intellect of these Bantu peoples and their obvious etiology in the ancient Near East. Brief notes on the "sacred groves" of the Lemba and their rituals and taboos associated with birth, marriage, and death are included. The paper ends with an account of Lemba industries, most notably their involvement in the mining and smelting of gold and copper. The paper is annotated and cites the only references made to the Lemba in the early nineteenth century—Thomas Baines' *The Gold Regions of South Africa* and Andrew Anderson's *Twenty-Five Years in a Wagon in the Gold Regions of Africa*.

H41   Van der Waal, C. S. (1979). "Woonwyse van die Venda." *South African Journal of Ethnology*, vol. 2: 11-27.

Van der Waal's paper describes traditional and contemporary settlement patterns of Venda people. After a brief introductory history of the Venda, and an account of social organization, the author discusses the criteria that determine choice of site. An exposition of four types of settlement follows: the village, the chief's village, the kraal, and the grid pattern with individual stands. Examples with maps and illustrations accompany the text. In conclusion, Van der Waal argues that growth, continuity, and movement are important characteristics that continually affect the composition and location of settlements. Included are photographs of Venda settlements. A useful condensed bibliography is appended. The text is in Afrikaans.

H42   Van Rooy, J. A. (1978). *The Traditional World View of Black People in Southern Africa*. Potchefstroom: Instituut vir die Bevordering van Calvinisme.

Van Rooy argues that African traditional beliefs and practices as a whole constitute a logically integrated worldview. The pamphlet focuses on Venda cosmology as a model for identifying themes that are consistent among the peoples of southern Africa. First, Venda cosmology is interpreted as a "hierarchy of forces" that influence one another and can be manipulated by magical techniques. That cosmic hierarchy, says the author, is reflected in African social relations and the importance of seniority and status in African society. The place of humans is "somewhere below the spirits and above the animals and plants," offering humankind a sense of security as part of a cosmic unity. Venda ideas about God are addressed, locating God at the top of the hierarchy as the creator and "parent" of humanity. Van Rooy identifies three further themes in relation to the Venda: first, "the idea of limited good"; second, "the priority of interpersonal relations" in Venda society and African societies in general; and third, "spirits and magic," focusing on the influence of the ancestor spirits on everyday life in Venda society. Fear of witchcraft is also discussed. Van Rooy claims that belief in the magical power of supernatural forces results in "less incentive to hard work in Venda society." Aspects of the Venda worldview that reflect the above themes are then discussed, including issues concerning property, reciprocity, spirit possession, fatalism, protective magic and sorcery, and the roles of sacred specialists, the spirits, and the chief. Van Rooy concludes by affirming that the African worldview is a religious one that can only be evaluated against the "Gospel of Jesus Christ as norm." His paper thus elucidates a Calvinistic religious commitment, with its corresponding work ethic, as much as it does an African religious worldview. He concludes: "Africans will have to learn that resources and wealth cannot be increased by magical means, but rather by skill and hard work, and that corruption and nepotism, acceptable as they may be from a traditional African point of view, are destructive to the community as a whole." Footnotes accompany the text.

H43   Van Warmelo, N. J. (1931). "Volksgebruike van die Venda." *South African Railways and Harbours Magazine*, vol. 25: 998-1000.

Van Warmelo's paper provides a brief, popular description of puberty rites and initiation practices associated with male *thondo* and female *domba* initiatory schools among the Venda of the northeastern Transvaal. The writer and foremost government ethnologist notes that while the *thondo* provide young Venda-speaking males with instruction in the art of warfare (*krygskuns*), and the *domba* instruct Venda girls about their sexuality, both serve to reinforce Venda social norms associated with the security and longevity of society: the former emphasizes the necessity of conscription, while the latter supports the importance of pregnancy during marriage. The article begins with a brief discussion of male initiatory rites associated with the *thondo* before outlining in detail *domba* rituals performed by women initiates in order to secure the appraisal of ancestors. The writer concludes that *thondo* rituals have become almost entirely obsolete due to the impact of modern Western industrialization and the subsequent inappropriateness of traditional African forms of warfare. The text is in Afrikaans.

H44   Van Warmelo, N. J. (1932). *Contributions Towards Venda History, Religion and Tribal Ritual*. Department of Native Affairs, Ethnological Publications, nol. 3. Pretoria: Government Printers.

In this monograph, government ethnologist N. J. van Warmelo provides an extended overview of several aspects of the historical origins and religious beliefs and rituals of the Venda of the northern Transvaal. Particularly, the writer examines the structure and function of puberty (*vhusha*) rites and premarital (*domba*) initiation schools for girls; puberty (*vhutuka*) and circumcision (*murundu*) rites for boys; chiefly burial and installment rites; sacrificial and divination practices; and beer-drinking and related cultural and religious practices among the Venda. In the sense that the paper draws on the testimony of several Venda-speaking informants, the work is an invaluable contribution to South African ethnology and the study of Venda religion. Puberty rites, in particular, are described in considerable detail, as are sacrificial rituals associated with the royal *thevhula*; annual healing or *swondo*; agricultural *mafula*; and ancestral *mapfumo* or *malembe* rites. Photographs accompany the text and an index is appended.

H45   Van Warmelo, N. J., ed. (1940) *The Copper Miners of Musina and the Early History of the Soutspansberg*. Department of Native Affairs, Ethnological Publications, no. 8. Pretoria: Government Printer.

Drawing on the expertise of several informants and vernacular historians, government ethnologist N. J. van Warmelo collects in this volume several articles outlining events foundational to the origin of the Venda in the Soutspansberg region of the northern Transvaal. Included in the collection is Dzivhani's essay, "The Chiefs of Venda," and Motenda's paper on "The History of the Western Venda and of the Lemba." Also represented are Mudau's "The Dau of Tshakhuma" and Mamadi's "The History of the Sebola (Tshivhula)" and "The Copper Miners of Musina [and Tshumbe]." Several vernacular essays in Sotho and Venda are incorporated in the collection, which is illustrated with a number of photographic plates, primarily depicting "Lemba types." An index of proper names is also included.

H46   Van Warmelo, N. J., and W. M. D. Phophi (1948). *Venda Law*. 5 vols. Department of Native Affairs, Ethnological Publications, no. 23. Pretoria: Government Printer.

In their parallel English-Venda account of the customary laws of the Venda-speaking peoples of the northern Transvaal, Van Warmelo and Phophi provide detailed notes on several aspects of Venda jurisprudence, ranging from African customary laws of marriage, to inheritance and property rights. In the first volume, "Betrothal, Thakha, and Weddings," the writers describe beliefs and ritual practices associated with desirable and prohibited marriages; *thaka* (brideprice); *luambiso* and *misho* (betrothal gifts); and bridal taboos and "inspection" rites. Detailed notes on issues ranging from same-sex marriages and premarital initiation rites (*domba*) for girls are included. In the second volume, "Married Life," aspects associated with the life, duties, and rites of *muselwa* (newly married wives) and the obligations and conjugal rights of husbands are discussed. Duties and rites accorded to various categories of cohabiting couples and nuptial associations are delineated. Such categories, suggest the writers, are frequently determined by the origin of bride-price. In Volume Three, "Divorce," detailed descriptions of causes for divorce, among them witchcraft, wife-beating, and neglect, are followed by several chapters describing invalid grounds for the termination of nuptial agreements. Issues discussed in this regard include adultery, habitual insolence, barrenness, desertion without cause, and presumption of death. Notes on the use of special medicines to "doctor" barrenness or defer desertion are incorporated. So too are issues relating to the costs of litigation and the custodianship of children. These issues are expanded in Volumes Four and Five, which are entitled "Inheritance" and "Property," through further discussions of personal law. Each volume contains an extensive index that acts as an easy reference guide for readers of African customary law and the religious beliefs and rituals of the Venda. Several volumes are illustrated with photographic plates.

H47   Weelwright, C. A. (1905). "Native Circumcision Lodges." *South African Journal of Science*, vol. 3: 294-99. Reprint *Journal of the Royal Anthropological Institute*, vol. 35: 251-55.

Weelwright's description of male initiation and circumcision rites among the Venda of the Soutspansberg district of the northeastern Transvaal is based on a short period of field research conducted by the author in 1904. The writer argues that circumcision rites have their origin among a "family of peoples" known as the Lemba, who purportedly migrated from the Congo valley in the early nineteenth century. Weelwright further claims that "hereditary circumcision priests," usually members of the Lemba clan, appear to have influenced the Venda in a number of other "Semitic" practices, among them dietary regulations associated with the eating of pork or the consumption of animals not slaughtered in accordance with particular ritual procedures. He asserts that although "debauchery and licentiousness" persist, the fact that some Semitic practices prevail suggests that an element of religiosity can also be found among the Venda. The essay is accompanied by plates illustrating the "circumcision kits" used by initiates and the circumcision lodges constructed for the duration of the rites.

H48   Wessman, R. (1908). *The BaVenda of the Spelonken—A Contribution Toward the Psychology and Folklore of African Peoples*. London: The African World Ltd.

Wessman's "collection of BaVenda cameos" draws on the writer's experience of Venda politics and religious life while working as a missionary in the Spelonken region of the far northern Transvaal. His observations are informed by a European Christian polemic, and consist predominantly of Venda "fables" that appear, he suggests, to "caricature" Christian belief. However many of Wessman's comments provide resources instructive for an evaluation of impulses specific to the development of a kind of comparative religion in the region in the late nineteenth century. The book is divided into twenty-seven chapters, the first of which outlines fundamental aspects of Venda society and politics. Chapters on the "Venda System of Rule" and "Venda Family Life" are included, as are chapters on "The Reign of Superstition," "Religion and Rites," and "Demonology and Medicine Men." The study is accompanied by photographs and maps, and an appendix providing details of an interview between a Venda chief and Leo Weinthal of the *Pretoria Press* is included.

Index

About the Authors

DAVID CHIDESTER is Professor of Comparative Religion and Director of the Institute for Comparative Religion in Southern Africa at the University of Cape Town. His recent books include *Savage Systems: Colonialism and Comparative Religion in Southern Africa* (1996); *Religions of South Africa* (1992); and *Shots in the Streets: Violence and Religion in South Africa* (1991).

CHIREVO KWENDA is Lecturer in Religious Studies and Associate Director of the Institute for Comparative Religion in Southern Africa at the University of Cape Town. His dissertation (1993) was entitled *True Colors: A Critical Assessment of Victor Turner's Study of Ndembu Religion.* He is coauthor of *African Religion and Culture Alive* (forthcoming, 1997).

ROBERT PETTY is Research Associate at the Institute for Comparative Religion in Southern Africa at the University of Cape Town. His dissertation was on the fragments of Numenius.

JUDY TOBLER is Research Manager for the Institute for Comparative Religion in Southern Africa at the University of Cape Town. She completed her doctoral research in Religious Studies in 1997 with the dissertation, *Gendered Signs of the Sacred: Contested Images of Mother in Feminism, Psychoanalysis, and Hindu Myth*, at the University of Cape Town.

DARREL WRATTEN is Lecturer in Religious Studies and Associate Director of the Institute for Comparative Religion in Southern Africa at the University of Cape Town. His dissertation (1995) was entitled *Buddhism in South Africa: From Textual Imagination to Contextual Innovation.*

Chidester, Tobler, and Wratten are coauthors of *Christianity in South Africa: An Annotated Bibliography* and *Islam, Hinduism, and Judaism in South Africa: An Annotated Bibliography* (both Greenwood, 1997).

ISBN 0-313-30474-2

EAN

9 780313 304743

90000>

HARDCOVER BAR CODE